MANAGING PEOPLE AT WORK

Managing
People
at Work

READINGS IN PERSONNEL

Second Edition
Dale S. Beach

Professor, School of Management

Rensselaer Polytechnic Institute

Macmillan Publishing Co., Inc.
New York
Collier Macmillan Publishers
London

Macmillan Publishing Co., Inc.
866 Third Avenue, New York, New York
10022

Collier-Macmillan Canada, Ltd.

Library of Congress Cataloging in Publication Data:

Beach, Dale S   comp.
    Managing people at work.

    Includes bibliographical references.
        1. Personnel management—Addresses, essays, lectures.
    2. Industrial relations—Addresses, essays, lectures.
    I. Title.
    HF5549.B325   1975   658'.3'008   74-10453
    ISBN 0-02-307021-8

Printing: 1 2 3 4 5 6 7 8   Year: 5 6 7 8 9 0

PREFACE

The professor who wishes to have his students delve into the rich literature contained in journals, conference proceedings, monographs, and research reports faces a formidable task because of the difficulty of obtaining adequate numbers of copies. The practicing manager also faces a sizeable problem in trying to keep abreast of significant developments in his field. This book of readings has been prepared to help answer these problems. It has been created by careful review of many hundreds of articles that have appeared within the past few years. From them, selections judged to have outstanding value have been made. Among the criteria for selection have been depth of inquiry, quality of thought and expression, originality, and diversity of viewpoint. Some have been chosen because they synthesize and summarize recent important research studies. Others have been chosen because of their emphasis upon philosophical, ethical, and value issues. Certain of the articles challenge conventional points of view. All the selections in this book deal with important issues that must be faced by executives and administrators who are involved in managing people at work. The majority of the articles have been written by university scholars and researchers; a substantial share have been written by personnel and behavioral researchers in industry and by management practitioners and consultants.

Managing People at Work: Readings in Personnel, Second Edition, is intended for use as a supplementary textbook in college and university courses, both undergraduate and graduate, in personnel management, human resources management, organizational behavior, and industrial relations. It can also be utilized by executives and administrators to enable them to keep current with the best thinking in this field.

A great deal has happened in this growing field in recent years. This second edition retains twenty-three articles from the first edition that are of enduring value. Many of these have come to be regarded as classics. Because of space limitations some excellent works appearing in the first edition had to be dropped for articles that cover new and important matters. Entirely new to this second edition are twenty-one selections that have been included to fairly represent contemporary developments in human resources management. Principal new topics covered in this edition are the "Work in America" theme (i.e., worker satisfaction versus alienation), equal employment opportunity and government affirmative action efforts, the learning and motivational concepts of B. F. Skinner which have recently been introduced into industry, transactional analysis, organization development, new developments in participative management, administrative justice on the job, recent concepts in employee incentives and management compensation, the Occupational Safety and Health Act, the spectacular growth in collective bargaining in the public sector, and human resource valuation.

Covering the principal issues in personnel management and human resources management, the readings in this book are grouped into ten main parts. The introduction to each part gives a brief overview of the subject area and discusses the nature of each article. Discussion questions for classroom use or for testing are given at the conclusion of each article.

Part I, "Perspectives on Managing People at Work," brings out key propositions pertaining to man and his work and important trends in organizational life for the future. Part II provides a critical examination of the personnel profession, examines the varying degrees of influence exerted by practitioners in their organizations, and identifies forces for change and growth over the next twenty-five years. Part III, "Employee Satisfaction and Alienation," focuses upon the "Work in America" theme, which holds that a significant portion of modern industrialized workers are deeply dissatisfied with their work roles and conditions of employment.

Part IV, "Employment and Development of People," is divided into sections devoted to employment policies and selection, equal employment opportunity and the disadvantaged, performance appraisal, training and development, and organization development. Part V, also divided into sections, covers systems of management, motivation, leadership and supervision, morale–attitude studies, participative management, communication, administrative justice, and value systems in organizational life. These processes constitute the heart of management–employee interaction.

Part VI looks at financial compensation from the standpoint of innovative policies for the operation of employee wage incentives, the structure and content of executive compensation systems, and important research findings concerning management compensation.

The major new Federal effort in occupational safety and health is discussed in Part VII. This part also includes an article that provides important insights into mental health in industry. Part VIII compares and contrasts collective bargaining in the public and private sectors. Initiatives contributing to peaceful resolution of labor–management conflict are also examined.

Part IX describes significant work that has been done in developing a comprehensive predictive framework for explaining organizational performance based upon an analysis of causal and intervening variables. Part X provides fresh insights into the matter of moral education for the business manager.

I wish to express my sincere appreciation to the authors whose works are here reprinted and to the publishers for granting permission to use these articles. Specific acknowledgment of the authors and publishers is given on the first page of each paper. I wish to thank Colonel Edward C. Kennedy of the United States Air Force for assistance in reviewing and analyzing selections for the first edition of this book. I am grateful to Mrs. Anita Baillargeon for typing and preparing the material for the first edition and to Mrs. Ruth Ashley for comparable work on this second edition.

Dale S. Beach

CONTENTS

B. Equal Employment Opportunity and the Disadvantaged

C. Performance Appraisal

D. Training and Development

E. Organization Development

PART V

Motivation and Management of People   **217**

A. Systems of Management

B. Motivation

PART VI

Financial Compensation

PART VII

Health and Safety

PART VIII

Collective Bargaining

PART IX

Building and Assessing Organizations

PART X

Ethics in Management

MANAGING PEOPLE AT WORK

PART I

Perspectives on Managing People at Work

Organizations are essentially human systems. Students and managers concerned with the functioning of these human systems must have knowledge of how management policies and programs affect both the viability of the enterprise and the lives of the participants. The articles in Part I deal with important issues of human resource management and changing human requirements for organizations of the future.

In "Man and His Work," Eli Ginzberg elucidates findings and conclusions based upon nearly twenty years of research in the field of human resources. He discusses the centrality of work in human life and states that human resources are the key to economic development. His message has important implications for public and private manpower policy. Of special pertinence for the personnel policy makers in the private organization are his conclusions regarding personnel selection, career systems, professional employees, staffing of research facilities, personnel assessment, and training.

The systems of personnel management and of organization that executives devise must accurately reflect the changing problems confronting the organization. Warren Bennis in "Organizations of the Future" analyzes changes occurring in modern large-scale organizations, primarily in a human or people context, and predicts the end of bureaucracy. Bennis sees integration, distribution of power, collaboration, adaptation, and revitalization as the principal human problems of the next twenty-five years.

1

1.

Man and His Work

ELI GINZBERG

The modern world faces many problems arising from man's industrial and technological development: unemployment; the obsolescence of skills; lack of work opportunities for the aged, young people, and minority groups; individuals' difficulties in adjusting to rapid change; the necessity of improving personnel practices; and the uncertain future of underdeveloped areas, to name but a few. All of these relate to the efficient use of resources in modern society, particularly human resources.

Except for the war years between 1942 and 1946, my associates at Columbia and I have been engaged in research investigations in the conservation and utilization of human resources since 1939. We have worked from the start as an interdisciplinary team. Our studies could never have been planned, and certainly not executed, by any one person. Though we have neither sole nor even primary claims to the findings that follow, they represent the highlights of what we have learned.

Our point of departure and the focus of our interest have been the centrality of work in human life. We believe that the best way to understand the behavior of human beings–the behavior of groups— is to start from a consideration of how work regulates the life of the individual, the operating units in the economy, and the total society. I have grouped our finding under these three rubrics: work from the point of view of society at large; work from the point of view of the employer; and work from the point of view of the individual. These are somewhat arbitrary distinctions but they do provide a framework for discussion.

The first proposition is a simple one: human resources are the key to economic development. This is a very old proposition which stems from Adam Smith's *The Wealth of Nations*. Our group has long believed that Smith had a deeper understanding of the inner workings of a dynamic economy than any of his followers. Our own adaptation of his premise is this: how people think about work, and what they consider to be important goals in life, will determine whether their country will develop or not. The notion that material resources are the key to development is fallacious. Brazil has tremendous

© 1962 by The Regents of the University of California. Reprinted from *California Management Review*, Vol. 5, No. 2 (Winter 1962) pp. 21–28, by permission of The Regents and the author.

Eli Ginzberg is Director, Conservation of Human Resources and Hepburn Professor of Economics, Columbia University.

material resources. Israel has very poor resources. The difference in the level of these two economies is largely a reflection of the differences in quality of the human resources of the two countries.

The kind of an economy a country develops depends in considerable measure on the kind of economy it wants. For example, people can decide to sit and fish. For a very long time, the French did just that. But more recently they decided that they wanted refrigerators and automobiles, and their economy has undergone a major transformation. Incidentally, this is largely due in my opinion to the export of American values. We are Americanizing the world. The key element in this proposition is that the values, attitudes, and general orientation of the people of a country determine its economic development.

The next point in my catena is the scourge of unemployment. Our work at Columbia began in the late 1930's with studies of people who had been unemployed for a long time. One study dealt with unemployment in South Wales, a region where people had been out of work for so long that they had forgotten the meaning of time; no day of the week was distinguished from any other.[1] Unemployment is a scourge because it destroys the adults, and prevents their children from growing up properly. A country must have a national policy aimed at preventing and alleviating unemployment.

Third Finding

The third finding in this category of work as it relates to the society concerns the major transformation of the role of work in contemporary life. This is the first time in the history of the world that the masses have options, somewhat similar to those previously known only by

the wealthy, about the kind of life they want to lead. They can decide whether they want to throw the major part of their efforts and energies into the job or into activities unconnected with the job. For the first time the mass of the population has enough free time and enough money to make such options meaningful. When I first went to California years ago, billboards urged us to "Work and Play." Now they suggest that we "Stay and Play"; soon they may simply command us to "Play!" This suggests the nature of the transformation.

The fourth finding can be subsumed under a heading called the reach of democracy. The notion that democracy relates solely to the political arena is an incorrect one. The values that people hold, the objectives that they seek, the motives to which they respond, penetrate all aspects of their lives. My children are constantly telling me that my decisions "aren't fair." Such complaints seem to have particular attraction for children brought up in a democracy. Children in an autocratic society are unlikely to challenge their parents on points of fairness. Likewise, the major thrust of trade unionism must be seen not from the viewpoint of wages and hours but in terms of control of work in the shop. This reflects the determination of workers in a democracy to control their own lives as much as possible and to reduce to a minimum the authority of others over them. This is the nub of the issue; it helps to explain the reach of democracy into the industrial arena.

Dynamic American Economy

The fifth point has to do with the moving escalator. The dynamic American economy makes it possible even for people who are standing still to get ahead.

[1] Eli Ginzberg, *Grass on the Slag Heaps: The Story of the Welsh Miners* (New York: Harper, 1942).

All one has to do is to step on the escalator. Many people who do not want to work very hard can still enjoy a substantial gain in real income. Time alone will push them ahead.

The next point relates to the family, which, having long been the consumption unit, is now becoming the employment unit. With 30 million women working for wages at some time during the course of a year, the question of whether a man will change his job depends increasingly on whether his wife must also change her job. The issue is no longer the optimization of a man's income and career opportunities but of the family's. This first showed up in the armed services. Married women officers would remain in the service only if their assignments could be dovetailed with their husbands'.

This proposition can be broadened to include considerations affecting the education of one's children. Several years ago I discovered that one of the big advantages that California had over the East in procuring technical personnel was its superior public education system. Many scientists and engineers, who generally are greatly interested in the education of their youngsters, have moved to the West not only because of the weather but because of the schools.

Next, I believe that work as a mechanism of social adjustment has not been properly appreciated. Much pathology in our society reflects interferences with people's opportunities to work. If you lock people in mental institutions . . . or men and women in prison . . . or young adults in schools, you almost insure their deterioration. Human beings require an opportunity for expression through work, which is the best tie between themselves and reality. We have failed to use work properly as an instrument of therapy and rehabilitation.

Now I want to look at work from the viewpoint of the employer. The first proposition is that performance must be con-sidered as multifaceted. How people perform depends on (1) their capacities and limitations, (2) management policy, and (3) the pressures and opportunities in the larger society. The performance of an individual cannot be measured without reference to the kinds of policies governing his work and to the pressures in the society that are exerted upon him. Meaningful understanding of performance requires a multifaceted approach.

Our second theory concerns the adjustment potential. This represents a more sophisticated approach to performance than those which lay stress on emotional adjustment alone. The adjustment potential was developed because human beings are usually able to meet the demands that are made of them. This is particularly true if they are part of an organization and if their future depends on their meeting certain demands. A second element implicit in the concept of the adjustment potential is the availability of a wide range of jobs, so that an individual is able to choose one within his limits. One of the advantages of an intricate economy is the wide difference between the demands made on a doorman and those made on a president.

Adjustment Potential

Such elasticity helps the individual to adjust, for he can determine his own level of aspiration and performance. Moreover, most human beings have strengths that compensate for their weaknesses. We tend to focus on people's weaknesses and forget their strengths. The adjustment potential takes into account the individual's compulsion to perform, the variations in the levels of aspirations, and the existence of compensatory mechanisms.

The third theorem is the vulnerability of selection. Most personnel divisions would like to solve their personnel problems through selection, because they believe that then they would have no further problems. But it does not work out that simply. Selection always has logistical implications. One can never select better people than exist in the pool from which they are drawn. Industry, for example, wants creative scientists but the pool contains Ph.D.'s. The two are by no means synonymous. Moreover, there are serious limitations to assessment. All one knows about a Ph.D. is that he has gone through school and was able to give his professors the answers they wanted. There are no diagnostic tools for discerning the drive, self-confidence, and special qualities that will make one man creative and not the other.

Simplify Procedures

The question of costs must also be weighed. We contend that large corporations should simplify their selection procedures. They should ignore the upper 5 per cent of a graduating class because most of these men will probably not be happy in a large corporation, and they should ignore the lower 15 per cent of the class because they may not have the capacity to work effectively. The personnel officers should concentrate on those in the middle, paying special attention to those who say that they would like to work for a particular company.

The next principle is called deviation tolerance. In recent years in this country we have misapplied psychiatric concepts in personnel work. We have used clinical categories such as misfit, unfit, unbalanced, unstable, without really understanding the terms. There is no direct link possible between the categories of mental illness and work adjustment.

Moreover, people's emotional states vary. Our study, *The Ineffective Soldier*,[2] revealed that many severely disturbed

Army people stabilized very quickly once they got out of the service. The only importance of emotional deviation derives from the extremes, and there one does not need subtle theories. There are, of course, seriously disturbed people who cannot fit into any normal work group. But most people are only a little disturbed and only at times, and they can fit into most work groups.

Compulsivity of Power

The fifth point has to do with the compulsivity of power. In a society organized around power some people spend a great deal of energy playing the game of power. Large organizations, profit and nonprofit alike, are characterized by constant struggles of people to gain more power. The major skill of the successful contestants often is not technical or intellectual; it is political, and their advancement depends primarily on how well they manipulate people. Some years ago the Chairman of the board of one of America's great public utilities commented that he could see very little difference between his company and Tammany Hall. Part of the continuing shortage of good scientific and technical personnel is an outgrowth of the way in which power and rewards are distributed. If in addition to being a good chemist or physicist an individual is interested in power, he moves very quickly away from the laboratory into the administrative hierarchy. He is not pulled away; he wants to move into the arena where the payoff is. In the United States we do not like to face the reality of power and its influence on behavior. But it is essential that we do, if we ever expect to understand our society.

The sixth proposition is called the eval-

2 Eli Ginzberg, James K. Anderson, et. al., *The Ineffective Soldier: Lessons for Management and the Nation* (3 volumes: *The Lost Divisions, Breakdown and Recovery*, and *Patterns of Performance*; New York: Columbia University Press, 1959).

uation trap. Most work is performed by groups, not by individuals; hence it is very hard to assess individuals. Moreover, supervisors assess the supervised, and this results in serious contamination of the evaluation procedures, for those who do the ratings are the potential or actual competitors of those whom they rate. The more able the subordinate, the more likely that the evaluation will be faulty.

The seventh point deals with the accelerated obsolescence of skill. Promotions in large organizations depend primarily on years of service. A man becomes a vice president or president of a large organization in his late forties or early fifties. In a rapidly advancing scientific and technological society men get close to the top when they are already obsolete. At least it is likely that their knowledge of the science and technology on which the company's future depends will be out of date. Recently, at least one large American corporation has perceived this danger, and has taken steps to retrain its senior technical personnel who hold important managerial positions.

The eighth proposition is the creativity dilemma. The genius of American industry was the development of the mass production of standardized goods, based for the most part on simple line organization. However, we are now entering a period in which the production of ideas is essential for our further progress. The success of many companies will depend less on the operation of the plant and more on the efficiency of its research and development laboratory. The problem here is that we have an antiquated system of management. New, flexible rules and procedures must be introduced for the management of professional people. Professionals cannot be treated in the same manner as hourly employees.

Career Development

We come now to work from the viewpoint of the individual. This includes a consideration of the individual's preparation for work. Our first contention is that occupational choice is a process resolvable only by compromise and in its later stages is more or less irreversible.[3] We have found that the process of occupational decision-making starts in the preschool period and remains largely subconscious until around the age of eleven. At this point it intrudes on the individual's consciousness, where it remains for many years while he explores his interests, capacities, values, and reality. Toward the end of adolescence—about eighteen to twenty—the decisions that are made become increasingly irreversible. It is too late for a senior in medical school to decide that he really wanted to be a lawyer.

In our current research on talent and performance we have discerned important differences in career patterns. There are those whose career development appears to progress without handicap, while others encounter serious impediments. Some of the differences may lie in different values held by people: some are willing to work for seven days a week, while others prefer to go fishing on their days off. Some of the differences may reflect external circumstances: one young man may have been deferred during the Korean War, while another is set back two years. It will be some time before we have classified and evaluated the complexities that we have uncovered in the process of career development.

Illiteracy

The third proposition is one of fact; it relates to the pervasiveness of illiteracy in

[3] Eli Ginzberg, Sol W. Ginsberg, Sidney Axelrad, and John L. Herma, *Occupational Choice: An Approach to a General Theory* (New York: Columbia University Press, 1951).

American society. Earlier studies disclosed that one out of every nine young men screened for military service in World War II was either totally illiterate or borderline illiterate, which meant that the could be trained only as a duty soldier. This is not "ancient history," however; the Commissioner of Motor Vehicles of North Carolina recently discovered that about 20 per cent of the applicants for drivers' licenses were illiterate. They were unable to fill in simple blanks. And this situation is not peculiar to North Carolina. Inadequate education is a particular characteristic of older workers, whose employability frequently is hindered more by lack of education than by consideration of age.

A fourth proposition is the infantilization of youth. We have elongated the school system to a ridiculous extreme. While I have a positive view toward education in general, I believe that many youngsters are forced to remain in school beyond the point of diminishing returns. I submit that by the age of fifteen, or the latest sixteen, many boys, possibly one out of every three or four, have learned all that they are able to learn from books, at least at this point of their lives. They may be able to learn more at a later stage. But at this age these youngsters need the opportunity to work; they need close relations with adults; they need to learn by doing and to earn some money.

These remarks also have pertinence for girls. One-fourth of all the girls in the United States are married by the age of eighteen; half of them are married before they are twenty-one. Since many stay in school until they are twenty or twenty-two, many marry before they have acquired much adult experience. I submit that this lack of experience may be related to the lack of permanence of many first marriages.

The next proposition is the inequality of equality. This doctrine relates to disadvantaged groups. If these groups are presented with the same opportunities as the more advantaged, they will continue to lag behind them in accomplishment. What they need are extra services, special help, so that they can truly achieve an approximate equality with the more favored sectors of society.

Next is the desirability of a second chance. Adolescence is a period fraught with disturbance. It is impossible to communicate effectively with adolescents. It is not possible to influence them directly. Many young people will inevitably make decisions which they will later find to have been wrong. In a rich society like ours, it is important that they have a second chance. It is important to keep avenues open to them.

The Sequence of Careers

The seventh proposition relates to sequential careers. To cite an unusual example: in Iran by the time a young person reaches fifteen he must be ready to start on a second career. The very young children who weave rugs lose their nimbleness by the time they are adolescents and must look for a second career. In the United States we have always had some experience with sequential careers, especially for those in professional sports. An athlete slows down by thirty, thirty-five, or forty at the latest. The necessity to shift from one major area of activity to another will probably become much more prevalent. Consider the instance of married women. By their middle thirties, they have finished having children and their youngest child is in school. They have many years stretching ahead of them— one-quarter of all the women in the United States will live to be at least eighty-five.

More and more groups will have sequential careers. Recently the Air Force has recognized that its requirements for pilots will drop over time. Hence it is writing contracts for pilots to cover a ten-year tour of duty. The lesson here for large corporations is to restudy their personnel policies to see whether they might not be able to encourage some people to leave earlier than they otherwise would—while they still have time to get in somewhere else.

The eighth point stipulates that only a small minority is work-oriented. Only a small proportion of any work group is really interested in working very hard. I submit that the world's work is always carried by a small minority. Management should seek to discover the work-oriented individuals. It is very difficult to force people to work, and this enhances the importance of locating those who like to. One way to do this is to allow more scope for self-determination.

My final point is that success is different from satisfaction. Success relates to the objective world; satisfaction, to the way in which a man feels about his work. An interesting characteristic of affluent societies which presents a problem is the large number of options open to people. The more successful a man is, the more chance he has to become dissatisfied, because of the many options that he sees but cannot exercise. Possibly it was arranged that there be some balance between poor and rich. The poor are frustrated by lack of options; the rich, by an excess of opportunities.

Let me point out very briefly some of the more important implications of these propositions for public and private policy. In the arena of public policy the importance of a continuing high level of employment is the major implication. With a high level of employment, many problems can be solved; without it most problems become intractable. The most important single domestic challenge is to increase the number of jobs available. Even the number of mental patients is sensitive to the employment index: in good times, marginal people find it possible to keep jobs. The problems set out above relating to youth, minority groups, older people, cannot be solved unless employment is at a high level.

Essential Investment

Next, in a world characterized by rapid advances in science and technology substantial and sustained investment in human resources is essential. There is much waste of the nation's scientific and technical personnel, stemming directly from the fact that the skills of many trained people have been permitted to obsolesce because employers would not invest in their future development.

Third, we need to experiment with work as an instrument for social adjustment. We need work-study programs for the nonintellectual youth, for mental hospital patients, for inmates of prisons, for older persons. We need new patterns of employment for workers too old to obtain jobs through regular competitive channels but too young to retire. We have demonstrated very little social imagination to date and it has been an expensive lack; we put people on the relief rolls but we are unwilling to secure them jobs.

Next, we need new designs for the more effective guidance, education, and employment of the "mature woman." This is the woman in her early or middle thirties whose family responsibilities are beginning to lighten and who sooner or later may be interested in entering or re-entering the labor force. Again, we are doing very little that is imaginative.

The fifth point is the tremendous need for improved articulation between the school system and the education and training provided by the armed services, industry, and other adult education units.

The above are five areas for consideration from the point of view of public policy. Now let me suggest five in the domain of business management. The first stresses the need to shift attention from selection to assignment. I indicated earlier my conviction that selection is a weak reed on which to lean. Much more attention should be devoted to improving assignment and evaluation techniques. Moreover, indoctrination programs have become overelaborate. Some companies force a young man to spend a year or more before he is permitted to get to work. My recommendation is to let him learn by working.

Re-examine the System

The second suggestion stresses the need to re-examine the career system. Thirty years ago the petroleum companies and some other large companies established career systems. At that time this was a progressive move. They said to the young man, "You come with us and attend to business, and your future will be secure." They established elaborate systems of deferred benefits, including liberal pension schemes. But this is the wrong tack for companies operating in the economy of the 1960's and 1970's. It should be made easier, not more difficult, to separate people who no longer are productive. A company will always, without even trying, accumulate people who have begun to lose energy and initiative. The problem is to separate people who have become liabilities because they block others from efficient performance. Recently, a junior college in California had the imagination to find good jobs for youngsters who were doing badly in their studies. Industry can learn from this example. It, too, should make special efforts to move people on just as fast as it discovers that it cannot use them effectively.

Special Problems

The third recommendation centers on the need to alter policies and procedures developed for hourly employees to meet the special problems presented by scientific and technical personnel. Many problems must be reconsidered: freedom to work, hours of work, freedom to publish, freedom to study. People who work with their minds cannot be controlled. They must control themselves. At best they can be encouraged. The incentive system must be reappraised and reordered, if necessary.

Even the ponderous Army recognized this in 1946 when it provided that a senior medical officer who remained in his speciality could go to the top of the Medical Corps and become a major general without having to assume administrative duties. I know of no industrial corporation where the top scientist is recompensed at a rate that even approaches that of the chief executive officer. There is great need for basing remuneration on contribution, not on title.

The fourth point has to do with the urgent necessity for more experimentation with the restructuring of research and development. I do not think that every large American company can hope to build up and maintain a first-rate research and development effort. They can maintain development laboratories, but there just is not enough talent available for twenty or thirty, not to mention fifty or one hundred, concerns in an industry to attract, on a full-time basis, the order of talent required to solve the more difficult scientific and technological problems that they face. We need radical new departures in the employment of scientists. Here we may be able to pick up a clue or two from the Germans, the Dutch, even the Italians, who have long been forced to economize in the use of scarce resources.

The fifth suggestion relates to the adjustments implicit in the transformation of work and the need for corresponding changes in personnel policies and procedures. For example, further studies are needed in such areas as assessing plant location in relation to the places where well-trained people prefer to live; better identification of the work-oriented person; introducing more self-selection for the work-oriented; deeper understanding of the reasons why workers seek greater control over their work.

In conclusion, let me say that our group at Columbia fully appreciates that we do not have mastery over all the propositions that have emerged from our research. Nor do we claim that all these findings are unique to our work. But we believe that they are important, and we appreciate that we were able to contribute to their formulation only because of a constructive environment that facilitated cooperation between the university, business, and government. The extent to which we as a people succeed in advancing knowledge of human resources and applying it will depend on the strengthening of such co-operative efforts. Basic and applied research must progress hand in hand.

QUESTIONS

1. Discuss the full implications of the author's statement that the way people think about work and what they consider to be important goals in life will determine whether their country will develop or not. Relate this concept to the United States and to other nations.

2. What forces shape the attitudes and values of a people in regard to work, economic progress, and achievement?

3. Discuss the following points raised by Eli Ginzberg in relation to work from the perspective of the employer:
   a. Selection policies
   b. Power
   c. Evaluation trap

4. Do you feel that people's career decisions tend to become irreversible as they reach their early twenties?

5. What are the implications of Ginzberg's findings and proposals from the standpoint of national policy? From the standpoint of an individual large company?

6. In what ways should professionals be treated differently from hourly employees?

2.

Organizations of the Future

WARREN BENNIS

Recently, I predicted that in the next 25 to 50 years we will participate in the end of bureaucracy as we know it and the rise of new social systems better suited to 20th Century demands of industrialization.[1] This forecast was based on the evolutionary principle that every age develops an organizational form appropriate to its genius and that the prevailing form of pyramidal-hierarchical organization, known by sociologists as "bureaucracy" and most businessmen as "that damn bureaucracy," was out of joint with contemporary realities.

I realize now that my prediction is already a distinct reality so that prediction is foreshadowed by practice.

I should like to make clear that by "bureaucracy" I mean the typical organizational structure that coordinates the business of most every human organization we know of: industry, government, university, R&D labs, military, religious, voluntary, and so forth.

Bureaucracy, as I refer to it here, is a useful social invention, perfected during the Industrial Revolution to organize and direct the activities of the business firm. Max Weber, the German sociologist who developed the theory of bureaucracy around the turn of the century, once described bureaucracy as a social machine.

The bureaucratic "machine model" was developed as a reaction against the personal subjugation, nepotism, cruelty, and capricious and subjective judgments that often passed for managerial practices during the early days of the Industrial Revolution. Bureaucracy emerged out of the need for more predictability, order, and precision. It was an organization ideally suited to the values and the demands of Victorian Empire. And just as bureaucracy emerged as a creative response to a radically new age, so today new organizational shapes and forms are surfacing before our eyes.

I shall try first to show why the conditions of our modern industrialized world will bring about the decline of bureaucracy and force a reconsideration of new organizational structures. Then, I will

Reprinted by permission from *Personnel Administration*, Vol. 30, No. 5, September–October 1967 issue. Copyright 1967, Society for Personnel Administration, 485–87 National Press Bldg., 14th and F. Streets, N.W., Washington, D.C. 20004.

Warren Bennis is President, University of Cincinnati.

[1] "The Decline of Bureaucracy and Organization of the Future." Invited address presented to the Division of Industrial and Business Psychology at the American Psychological Association meeting, Los Angeles, Calif., Sept. 5, 1964.

suggest a rough model of the organization of the future. Finally, I shall set forth the new tasks and challenges for the training and development manager.

Why Is Bureaucracy Vulnerable?

There are at least four relevant threats to bureaucracy. The first is a human, basically psychological one, which I shall return to later on, while the other three spring from extraordinary changes in our environment. The latter three are (1) rapid and unexpected change, (2) growth in size where volume of organization's traditional activities is not enough to sustain growth, and (3) complexity of modern technology where integration of activities and persons of very diverse, highly specialized competence is required.[2]

It might be useful to examine the extent to which these conditions exist *right now*.

Rapid and Unexpected Change. It may be enough simply to cite the knowledge and population explosion. More revealing, however, are the statistics that demonstrate these events:

• Our productivity per man hour now doubles almost every 20 years rather than every 40 years, which was true before World War II.
• The federal government alone spent 16 billion in R&D activities in 1965 and will spend 35 billion by 1980.
• The time lag between a technical discovery and recognition of its commercial uses was 30 years before World War I, 16 years between the wars, and only 9 years since World War II.
• In 1946 only 30 cities in the world had populations of more than one million. Today there are 80. In 1930 there were 40 people for each square mile of the earth's land surface. Today, there are 63. By the year 2000, there are expected to be 142.

Growth in Size. Not only have more organizations grown larger, but they have become more complex and more international. Firms like Standard Oil of New Jersey (with 57 foreign affiliates), Socony Mobil, National Cash Register, Singer, Burroughs, and Colgate-Palmolive derive more than half their income or earnings from foreign sales. A long list of others, such as Eastman Kodak, Pfizer, Caterpillar Tractor, International Harvester, Corn Products, and Minnesota Mining and Manufacturing make from 30 to 60 per cent of their sales abroad.[3] General Motors' sales are not only nine times those of Volkswagen, they are also bigger than the gross national product of The Netherlands and well over those of a hundred other countries. If we have seen the sun set on the British Empire, it will be a long time before it sets on the empires of General Motors, ITT, Royal Dutch/Shell and Unilever.

Today's activities require persons of very diverse, highly specialized competence. Numerous dramatic examples can be drawn from studies of labor markets and job mobility. At some point during the past decade, the U.S. became the first nation in the world ever to employ more people in *service occupations* than in the production of tangible goods. Examples of this trend are:

• In the field of education, the *increase* in employment between 1950 and 1960 was greater than the total number employed in the steel, copper, and aluminum industries.
• In the field of health, the *increase* in employment between 1950 and 1960 was greater than the total number employed

---

[2] A. H. Rubenstein and C. Haberstroh, *Some Theories of Organization* (Revised Edition). Irwin-Dorsey, Homewood, Ill., 1966.

[3] Richard J. Barber, "American Business Goes Global." *The New Republic.* April 30, 1966, 14–18.

in automobile manufacturing in either year.

• In financial firms, the *increase* in employment between 1950 and 1960 was greater than total employment in mining in 1960.[4]

Rapid change, hurried growth, and increase in specialists: with these three logistical conditions we should expect bureaucracy to decline.

CHANGE IN MANAGERIAL BEHAVIOR

Earlier I mentioned a fourth factor which seemed to follow along with the others, though its exact magnitude, nature, and antecedents appear more obscure and shadowy due to the relative difficulty of assigning numbers to it. This factor stems from the personal observation that over the past decade there has been a fundamental change in the basic philosophy that underlies managerial behavior. The change in philosophy is reflected most of all in:

• A new concept of *Man*, based on increased knowledge of his complex and shifting needs, which replaces an oversimplified, innocent push-button idea of man.
• A new concept of *power*, based on collaboration and reason, which replaces a model of power based on coercion and threat.
• A new concept of *organization values,* based on humanistic-democratic ideals, which replaces the depersonalized mechanistic value system of bureaucracy.

These transformations of Man, power, and values have gained wide intellectual acceptance in management quarters. They have caused a terrific amount of rethinking on the part of many organizations. They have been used as a basis for policy formulation by many large-scale organiza-

tions. This philosophy is clearly not compatible with bureaucratic practices.

The primary cause of this shift in management philosophy stems not from the bookshelf but from the manager himself. Many of the behavioral scientists, like McGregor or Likert, have clarified and articulated—even legitimized—what managers have only half registered to themselves. I am convinced that the success of McGregor's *The Human Side of Enterprise* was based on a rare empathy for a vast audience of managers who were wistful for an alternative to a mechanistic conception of authority. It foresaw a vivid utopia of more authentic human relationships than most organizational practices allow. Furthermore, I suspect that the desire for relationships has little to do with a profit motive *per se*, though it is often rationalized as doing so.[5] The real push for these changes stems from some powerful needs, not only to humanize the organization, but to use the organization as a crucible of personal growth and development, for self-realization.[6]

Core Organization Problems

As a result of these changes affecting organizations of the future, new problems and tasks are emerging. They fall, I believe, into five major categories, which I visualize as the core tasks confronting organizations of the future.

1. *Integration* encompasses the entire range of issues having to do with the incentives, rewards, and motivation of the individual and how the organization succeeds or fails in adjusting to these needs. In other words, it is the ratio between individual needs and organizational demands that creates the transaction most satisfactory to both. The problem of *in-*

[4] Victor R. Fuchs, "The First Service Economy." *The Public Interest.* Winter 1966, 7–17.

[5] Chris Argyris, *Interpersonal Competence and Organizational Effectiveness.* Homewood, Ill.: Irwin-Dorsey, 1962.

[6] *The Varieties of Religious Experience.* The Modern Library, Random House, N. Y., 1902, 475–476.

tegration grows out of our "consensual society," where personal attachments play a great part, where the individual is appreciated, in which there is concern for his well-being, not just in a veterinary-hygiene sense, but as a moral, integrated personality.

2. The problem of *social influence* is essentially the problem of power and how power is distributed. It is a complex issue and alive with controversy, partly because of an ethical component and partly because studies of leadership and power distribution can be interpreted in many ways, and almost always in ways which coincide with one's biases (including a cultural leaning toward democracy).

The problem of power has to be seriously reconsidered because of dramatic situational changes that make the possibility of one-man rule or the "Great Man" not necessarily "bad" but impractical. I am referring to changes in the role of top management. Peter Drucker, over 12 years ago, listed 41 major responsibilities of the chief executive and declared that "90 percent of the trouble we are having with the chief executive's job is rooted in our superstition of the one-man chief." [7] The broadening product base of industry, impact of new technology, the scope of international operations, make one-man control quaint, if not obsolete.

MANAGING CONFLICT

3. The problem of *collaboration* grows out of the very same social processes of conflict and stereotyping, and centrifugal forces that divide nations and communities. They also employ furtive, often fruitless, always crippling mechanisms of conflict resolution: avoidance or suppression, annihilation of the weaker party by

the stronger, sterile compromises, and unstable collusions and coalitions. Particularly as organizations become more complex they fragment and divide, building tribal patterns and symbolic codes which often work to exclude others (secrets and noxious jargon, for example) and on occasion to exploit differences for inward (and always fragile) harmony. Some large organizations, in fact, can be understood only through an analysis of their cabals, cliques, and satellites, where a venture into adjacent spheres of interest is taken under cover of darkness and fear of ambush. Dysfunctional intergroup conflict is so easily stimulated, that one wonders if it is rooted in our archaic heritage when man struggled, with an imperfect symbolic code and early consciousness, for his territory. Robert R. Blake in his experiments has shown how simple it is to induce conflict, how difficult to arrest it. [8] Take two groups of people who have never been together before, and give them a task that will be judged by an impartial jury. In less than one hour, each group devolves into a tightly-knit band with all the symptoms of an "in-group." They regard their product as a "masterwork" and the other group's as "commonplace," at best. "Other" becomes "enemy;" "We are good; they are bad. We are right; they are wrong." [9]

Jaap Rabbie, conducting experiments on the antecedents of intergroup conflict at the University of Utrecht, has been amazed by the ease with which conflict and stereotype develop. [10] He brings into the experimental room two groups and distributes green name tags and green pens to one group and refers to it as the "green group." He distributes red pens and red name tags to the other group and

---

[7] D. Ron Daniel, "Team at the Top." *Harvard Business Review*, March–April 1965, 74–82.
[8] Robert R. Blake, Herbert A. Shepard and Jane S. Mouton, *Managing Intergroup Conflict in Industry*, Gulf Publishing, Houston, Texas, 1964.
[9] Carl Rogers, "Dealing with Psychological Tensions," *Journal of Applied Behavioral Sciences*, Jan.–Feb.–March 1965, 6–24.
[10] Personal communication, Jan. 1966.

refers to it as the "red group." The groups do not compete; they do not even interact. They are in sight of each other for only minutes while they silently complete a questionnaire. Only 10 minutes is needed to activate defensiveness and fear.

In a recent essay on animal behavior, Erikson develops the idea of "pseudo-species." [11] Pseudo-species act as if they were separate species created at the beginning of time by supernatural intent. He argues:

Man has evolved (by whatever kind of evolution and for whatever adaptive reasons) in pseudo-species, i.e., tribes, clans, classes, etc. Thus, each develops not only a *distinct sense of identity* but also a conviction of harboring *the* human identity, fortified against other pseudo-species by prejudices which mark them as extraspecific and inimical to "genuine" human endeavor. Paradoxically, however, newly born man is (to use Ernst Mayr's term) a generalist creature who could be made to fit into any number of pseudo-species and must, therefore, become "specialized" during a prolonged childhood. . . .

Modern organizations abound with pseudo-species, bands of specialists held together by the illusion of a unique identity and with a tendency to view other pseudo-species with suspicion and mistrust. Ways must be discovered to produce generalists and diplomats, and we must find more effective means of managing inevitable conflict. This is not to say that conflict is always avoidable and dysfunctional. Some types of conflict may lead to productive and creative ends.

4. The problem of *adaptation* is caused by our turbulent environment. The pyramidal structure of bureaucracy, where power was concentrated at the top, seemed perfect to "run a railroad." And undoubtedly for the routinized tasks of the nineteenth and early twentieth centuries, bureaucracy was and still is an eminently suitable social arrangement. However, rather than a placid and predictable environment, what predominates today is a dynamic and uncertain one in which there is a deepening interdependence among the economic and other facets of society.

5. Finally, the problem of *revitalization*. As Alfred North Whitehead says

The art of free society consists first in the maintenance of the symbolic code, and secondly, in the fearlessness of revision. . . . Those societies which cannot combine reverence to their symbols with freedom of revision must ultimately decay. . . .

Growth and decay emerge as the penultimate conditions of contemporary society. Organizations, as well as societies, must be concerned with those social structures that engender buoyancy, resilience, and a "fearlessness of revision."

I introduce the term "revitalization" to embrace all the social mechanisms that stagnate and regenerate and with the process of this cycle. The elements of revitalization are:

• An ability to learn from experience and to codify, store, and retrieve the relevant knowledge.
• An ability to "learn how to learn," that is, to develop methodologies for improving the learning process.
• An ability to acquire and use feedback mechanisms on performance, to develop a "process orientation," in short, to be self-analytical.
• An ability to direct one's own destiny.

These qualitities have a good deal in common with what John Gardner calls "self-renewal." For the organization, it means conscious attention to its own evolution. Without a planned methodology and explicit direction, the enterprise will not realize its potential.

Integration, distribution of power, collaboration, adaptation, and revitalization are the major human problems of the next

---

[11] Erik Erikson, "Ontgeny of Ritualization." Paper presented to the Royal Society in June 1965.

25 years. How organizations cope with and manage these tasks will undoubtedly determine the viability and growth of the enterprise. [See Table, p. 23.]

Organizations of the Future [12]

Against this background I should like to set forth some of the conditions that will determine organizational life in the next two or three decades:

1. *The Environment.* Rapid technological change and diversification will lead to interpenetration of the government with business.

Partnerships between government and business will be typical. It will be a truly mixed economy. Because of the immensity and expense of the projects, there will be fewer identical units competing for the same buyers and sellers. Organizations will become more interdependent.

The four main features of the environment are:

• Interdependence rather than competition.
• Turbulence and uncertainty rather than readiness and certainty.
• Large-scale rather than small-scale enterprises.
• Complex and multi-national rather than simple national enterprises.

2. *Population Characteristics.* The most distinctive characteristic of our society is, and will become even more so, education. Within 15 years, two-thirds of our population living in metropolitan areas will have attended college. Adult education is growing even faster, probably because of the rate of professional obsolescence. The Killian report showed that the average engineer required further education only 10 years after gaining his degree. It will become almost routine for the experienced physician, engineer, and executive to go back to school for advanced training every two or three years. Some 50 universities, in addition to a dozen large corporations, offer advanced management courses to successful men in the middle and upper ranks of business. Before World War II, only two such programs existed, both new, both struggling to get students.

All of this education is not just "nice," it is necessary. As Secretary of Labor Wirtz recently pointed out, computers can do the work of most high school graduates—cheaper and more effectively. Fifty years ago education was regarded as "nonwork" and intellectuals on the payroll were considered "overhead." Today the survival of the firm *depends* on the effective exploitation of brain power.

One other characteristic of the population which will aid our understanding of organizations of the future is increasing job mobility. The ease of transportation, coupled with the needs of a dynamic environment, change drastically the idea of "owning" a job—or "having roots." Already 20 percent of our population change their mailing address at least once a year.

3. *Work Values.* The increased level of education and mobility will change the values we hold about work. People will be more intellectually committed to their *professional* careers and will probably require more involvement, participation and autonomy.

Also, people will be more "other-directed," taking cues for their norms and values from their immediate environment rather than tradition. We will tend to rely more heavily on temporary social arrangements.[13] We will tend to have relationships rather than relatives.

4. *Tasks and Goals.* The tasks of the

---

[12] Adapted from my earlier paper, "Beyond Bureaucracy," *Trans-Action*, July–August 1965.

[13] "On Temporary Systems." In M. B. Miles (ed.), *Innovation in Education*, Bureau of Publications, Teachers College, Columbia University, N. Y., 1964, 437–490.

organization will be more technical, complicated, and unprogrammed. They will rely on intellect instead of muscle. And they will be too complicated for one person to comprehend, to say nothing of control. Essentially, they will call for the collaboration of specialists in a project or a team-form of organization.

There will be a complication of goals. Business will increasingly concern itself with its adaptive or innovative-creative capacity. In addition, meta-goals will have to be articulated; that is, supra-goals which shape and provide the foundation for the goal structure. For example, one meta-goal might be a system for detecting new and changing goals; another could be a system for deciding priorities among goals.

Finally, more conflict and contradiction can be expected from diverse standards of organizational effectiveness. One reason for this is that professionals tend to identify more with the goals of their profession than with those of their immediate employer. University professors can be used as a case in point. Within the University, there may be a conflict between teaching and research. Often, more of a professor's income derives from outside sources, such as foundations and consultant work. They tend not to be good "company men" because they divide their loyalty between their professional values and organizational goals.

ORGANIC—ADAPTIVE STRUCTURE

5. *Organization.* The social structure of organizations of the future will have some unique characteristics. They key word will be "temporary"; there will be adaptive, rapidly changing *temporary systems.* These will be "task forces" organized around problems-to-be-solved by groups of relative strangers who represent a diverse set of professional skills. The groups will be arranged on an organic rather than mechanical model; they will evolve in response to a problem rather than to programmed role expectations. The "executive" thus becomes a coordinator or "linking pin" between various task forces. He must be a man who can speak the diverse languages of research, with skills to relay information and to mediate between groups. People will be evaluated not vertically according to rank and status, but flexibly and functionally according to skill and professional training. Organizational charts will consist of project groups rather than functional groups. This trend is already visible today in the aerospace and construction industries, as well as many professional and consulting firms.

Adaptive, problem-solving, temporary systems of diverse specialists, linked together by coordinating and task evaluating specialists in an organic flux—this is the organizational form that will gradually replace bureaucracy as we know it. As no catchy phrase comes to mind, I call this an organic-adaptive structure.

6. *Motivation.* The organic-adaptive structure should increase motivation, and thereby effectiveness, because it enhances satisfactions intrinsic to the task. There is a harmony between the educated individual's need for meaningful, satisfactory, and creative tasks and a flexible organizational structure.

There will, however, also be reduced commitment to work groups, for these groups, as I have already mentioned, will be transient structures. I would predict that in the organic-adaptive system, people will learn to develop quick and intense relationships on the job, and learn to bear the loss of more enduring work relationships. Because of the added ambiguity of roles, time will have to be spent on continual rediscovery of the appropriate organizational mix.

AMERICANS PREPARED

The American experience of frontier neighbors, after all, prepares us for this, so I don't view "temporary systems" as such a grand departure. These "brief encounters" need not be more superficial than long and chronic ones. I have seen too many people, some occupying adjacent offices for many years, who have never really experienced or encountered each other. They look at each other with the same vacant stares as people do on buses and subways, and perhaps they are passengers waiting for their exit.

Europeans typically find this aspect of American life frustrating. One German expatriate told me of his disenchantment with "friendly Americans." At his first party in this country, he met a particularly sympathetic fellow and the two of them fell into a warm conversation which went on for several hours. Finally, they had to leave to return to their homes, but like soul-mates, they couldn't part. They went down into the city street and walked round and round on this cold winter night, teeth chattering and arms bound. Finally, both stiff with cold, the American hailed a cab and went off with a wave. The European was stunned. He didn't know his new "friend's" name. He never saw or heard from him again. "That's your American friendship," he told me.

That *is* American friendship: intense, spontaneous, total involvement, unpredictable in length, impossible to control. They are happenings, simultaneously "on" and transitory and then "off" and then new lights and new happenings.

A Swiss woman in Max Frisch's *I'm Not Stiller* sums it up this way: "Apparently all these frank and easy-going people did not expect anything else from a human relationship. There was no need for this friendly relationship to go on growing." [14]

Training Requirements For Organizations of the Future

How can we best plan for the organizational developments I forecast? And how can training and development directors influence and direct this destiny? One

thing is clear: There will be a dramatically new role for the manager of training and development. Let us look at some of the new requirements.

1. *Training for Change.* The remarkable aspect of our generation is its commitment to change, in thought and action. Can training and development managers develop an educational process which:

• Helps us to identify with the adaptive process without fear of losing our identity?
• Increases our tolerance for ambiguity without fear of losing intellectual mastery?
• Increases our ability to collaborate without fear of losing individuality?
• Develops a willingness to participate in our own social evolution while recognizing implacable forces?

Putting it differently, it seems to me that *we should be trained in an attitude toward inquiry and novelty rather than the particular content of a job;* training for change means developing "learning men."

2. *Systems Counseling.* It seems to me that management (and personnel departments) have failed to come to grips with the reality of *social systems.* It is embarrasing to state this after decades of research have been making the same point. We have proved that productivity can be modified by group norms, that training effects fade out and deteriorate if training goals are not compatible with the goals of the social system, that group cohesiveness is a powerful motivator, that intergroup conflict is a major problem facing modern organization, that individuals take many of their cues from their primary work groups, that identification with the work group turns out to be the only stable predictor of productivity, and so on. Yet this evidence is so frequently ignored that I can only infer that there is something naturally preferable (almost an involuntary reflex) in locating the sources of all problems in the individual and diagnosing

[14] Penguin Books, Harmondsworth, Middlesex. 1961, p. 244.

situations as functions of faulty individuals rather than as symptoms of malfunctioning social systems.

If this reflex is not arrested, it can have serious repercussions. In these new organizations, where roles will be constantly changing and certainly ambiguous, where changes in one sub-system will clearly affect other sub-systems, where diverse and multi-national activities have to be coordinated and integrated, where individuals engage simultaneously in multiple roles and group memberships (and role conflict is endemic), a systems viewpoint must be developed. Just as it is no longer possible to make any enduring change in a "problem child" without treating the entire family, it will not be possible to influence individual behavior without working with his particular sub-system. This means that our training and development managers of the future must perform the functions of *systems counselors*.

3. *Changing Motivations*. The rate at which professional-technical-managerial types join organizations is higher than for any other employment category. While it isn't fully clear what motivates them, two important factors emerge.

The first is a strong urge to "make it" professionally, to be respected by professional colleagues. Loyalty to an organization may increase if it encourages professional growth. Thus, the "good place to work" will resemble a supergraduate school, abounding with mature, senior colleagues, where the employee will work not only to satisfy organizational demands but, perhaps primarily, those of his profession.

The other factor involves the quest for self-realization, for personal growth which may not be task-related. That remark, I am well aware, questions four centuries of encrusted Protestant Ethic. And I feel uncertain as to how (or even *if*) these needs can be met by an organization. However, we must hope for social inventions to satisfy these new desires. Training needs to take more responsibility for attitudes about continuing education so that it is not considered a "retread" or a "repair factory" but a natural and inescapable aspect of work. The idea that education has a terminal point and that adults have somehow "finished" is old-fashioned. A "drop-out" should be redefined to mean anyone who *hasn't returned* to school.

However the problem of professional and personal growth is resolved, it is clear that many of our older forms of incentive, based on lower echelons of the need hierarchy, will have to be reconstituted.

4. *Socialization for Adults*. In addition to continuing education, we have to face the problem of continuing socialization, or the institutional influences which society provides to create good citizens. Put simply, it means training in values, attitudes, ethics, and morals. We allot these responsibilities typically to the family, to church, to schools. We incorrectly assume that socialization stops when the individual comes of age. Most certainly, we are afraid of socialization for adults, as if it implies the dangers of a delayed childhood disease, like whooping cough.

Or to be more precise, we frown not on socialization, but on conscious and responsible control of it. In fact, our organizations are magnificent, if undeliberate, vehicles of socialization. They teach values, inculcate ethics, create norms, dictate right and wrong, influence attitudes necessary for success and all the rest. The men who succeed tend to be well socialized and the men who don't, are not: "Yeah, Jones was a marvelous worker, but he never fit in around here." And most universities grant tenure where their norms and values are most accepted, although this is rarely stated.

Taking conscious responsibility for the socialization process will become imperative in tomorrow's organization. And finding men with the right technical capability will not be nearly as difficult as finding men with the right set of values and attitudes. Of course, consciously guiding this process is a trying business, alive with problems, not the least being the ethical one: Do we have the right to shape attitudes and values? We really do not have a choice. Can we avoid it? How bosses lead and train subordinates, how individuals are treated, what and who gets rewarded, the subtle cues transmitted and learned without seeming recognition, occur spontaneously. What we can choose are the mechanisms of socialization—how coercive we are, how much individual freedom we give, how we transmit values. What will be impermissible is a denial to recognize that we find some values more desirable and to accept responsibility for consciously and openly communicating them.

5. *Developing Problem-solving Teams.* One of the most difficult and important challenges for the training and development manager will be the task of promoting conditions for effective collaboration or building synergetic teams. Synergy is where individuals actually contribute more and perform better as a result of a collaborative and supportive environment. They play "over their heads," so to speak. The challenge I am referring to is the building of synergetic teams.

Of course, the job isn't an easy one. An easy way out is to adopt the "zero synergy" strategy. This means that the organization attempts to hire the best individuals it can and then permits them to "cultivate their own gardens." This is a strategy of isolation that can be observed in almost every university organization.

(Until universities take a serious look at their strategy of zero synergy, there is little hope that they will solve their vexing problems. The Berkeley protests were symptomatic of at least four self-contained, uncommunicating social systems [students, faculty, administration, trustees] without the trust, empathy, interaction [to say nothing of a tradition] to develop meaningful collaboration. To make matters even more difficult, if possible, academic types may, by nature [and endorsed by tradition] see themselves as "loners" and divergent to the majority. They all want to be independent together, so to speak. Academic narcissism goes a long way on the lecture platform but may be positively disruptive for developing a community.)

Another approach has the same effect but appears different. It is the pseudo-democratic style, in which a phony harmony and conflict-avoidance persists.

In addition to our lack of background and experience in building synergy (and our strong cultural biases against group efforts), teams take time to develop. They are like other highly complicated organisms and, just as we wouldn't expect a newborn to talk, we shouldn't expect a new team to work effectively from the start. Teams require trust and commitment and these ingredients require a period of gestation.

Expensive and time-consuming as it is, building synergetic and collaborative frameworks will become essential. The problems that confront us are too complex and diversified for one man or one discipline. They require a blending of skills, slants, and disciplines for their solution and only effective problem-solving *teams* will be able to get on with the job.

6. *Developing Supra-organizational Goals and Commitments.* The President of ABC (the fictitious name of a manufacturing company) was often quoted as saying:

The trouble with ABC is that nobody aside from me ever gives one damn about the over-all goals of this place. They're all seeing the world through the lenses of their departmental biases. What we need around here are people who wear the ABC hat, not the engineering hat or the sales hat or the production hat.

After he was heard muttering this rather typical president's dirge, a small group of individuals, who thought they could wear the ABC hat, formed a group they called the ABC HATS. They came from *various* departments and hierarchical levels and represented a microcosm of the entire organization. The ABC HATS group has continued to meet over the past few years and has played a central role in influencing top policy.

It seems to me that training and development managers could affect the development of their organizations if they would encourage the formation of HATS groups. What worries me about the organization of the future, of specialized professionals and an international executive staff, is that their professional and regional outlook brings along with it only a relative truth and a distortion of reality. This type of organization is extremely vulnerable to the hardening of pseudo-species and a compartmentalized approach to problems.

Training and development can be helpful in a number of ways:

• They can identify and support those individuals who are "linking pins," individuals who have a facility for psychological and intellectual affinity with a number of diverse languages and cultures. These individuals will become the developers of problem-solving teams.
• They can perform the HATS function, which is another way of saying that training and development managers should be managers who keep over-all goals in mind and modulate the professional biases which are intrinsic to the specialists' work.
• They can work at the interface of the pseudo-species in order to create more inter-group understanding and interface articulation.

Today, we see each of the intellectual disciplines burrowing deeper into its own narrow sphere of interest. (Specialism, by definition, implies a peculiar slant, a segmented vision. A cloak and suit manufacturer went to Rome and managed to get an audience with His Holiness. Upon his return a friend asked him, "What did the

Pope look like?" The tailor answered, "A 41 Regular.") Yet, the most interesting problems turn up at the intersection between disciplines and it may take an outsider to identify these. Even more often, the separate disciplines go their crazy-quilt way and rely more and more on internal standards of evidence and competence. They dismiss the outsider as an amateur with a contemptuous shrug. The problem with intellectual effort today (and I include my own field of organizational psychology) is that no one is developing the grand synthesis.

Organizations, too, require "philosophers," individuals who provide articulation between seemingly inimical interests, who break down the pseudo-species, and who transcend vested interests, regional ties, and professional biases in arriving at the solution to problems.

To summarize, I have suggested that the training and development director of the future has in store at least six new and different functions: (1) training for change, (2) systems counseling, (3) developing new incentives, (4) socializing adults, (5) building collaborative, problem-solving teams, and (6) developing supra-organizational goals and commitments. Undoubtedly there are others and some that cannot be anticipated. It is clear that they signify a fundamentally different role for personnel management from "putting out fires" and narrow maintenance functions. If training and development is to realize its true promise, its role and its image must change from maintenance to innovation.

I have seen this new role develop in a number of organizations, not easily or overnight, but pretty much in the way I have described it here. It might be useful to review briefly the conditions present in the cases I know about:

The personnel manager or some subsystem within personnel (it might be called "employee relations" or "industrial

Human Problems Confronting Contemporary Organizations

PROBLEM	BUREAUCRATIC SOLUTIONS	NEW 20TH CENTURY CONDITIONS
Integration The problem of how to integrate individual needs and organizational goals.	No solution because of no problem. Individual vastly oversimplified, regarded as passive instrument. Tension between "personality" and role disregarded.	Emergence of human sciences and understanding of man's complexity. Rising aspirations. Humanistic-democratic ethos.
Social Influence The problem of the distribution of power and sources of power and authority.	An explicit reliance on legal-rational power, but an implicit usage of coercive power. In any case, a confused, ambiguous shifting complex of competence, coercion, and legal code.	Separation of management from ownership. Rise of trade unions and general education. Negative and unintended effects of authoritarian rule.
Collaboration The problem of producing mechanisms for the control of conflict.	The "rule of hierarchy" to resolve conflicts between ranks and the "rule of coordination" to resolve conflict between horizontal groups. "Loyalty."	Specialization and professionalization and increased need for interdependence. Leadership too complex for one-man rule or omniscience.
Adaptation The problem of responding appropriately to changes induced by the environment.	Environment stable, simple, and predictable; tasks routine. Adapting to change occurs in haphazard and adventitious ways. Unanticipated consequences abound.	External environment of firm more "turbulent," less predictable. Unprecedented rate of technological change.
"Revitalization" The problem of growth and decay.	Underlying assumption that the future will be certain and basically similar, if not more so, to the past.	Rapid changes in technologies, tasks, manpower, raw materials, norms and values of society, goals of enterprise and society all make constant attention to the process of revision imperative.

relations" or "career development") took an *active, innovative* role with respect to organizational goals and forcibly took responsibility for organizational growth and development.

Secondly, this group shifted its emphasis away from personnel functions *per se* (like compensation and selection) and toward organizational problems, like developing effective patterns of collaboration, or fostering an innovative atmosphere or reducing inter-group conflict, or organizational goal-setting and long-run planning.

Thirdly, this group developed a close working relationship to various sub-systems in the organization, an organic, task-oriented relationship, not the frequently observed mechanical "line-staff" relationship.

Fourthly, they were viewed as full-fledged members of the management team, instead of the "head-shrinkers" or the "headquarters group." This was the hardest to establish in all cases, but turned out to be the most important. In fact, in one case, the man responsible for spearheading the organizational development effort has recently taken an important line job. The reverse happens, too. Line management participates in so-called personnel activities, almost as if they are an adjunct to staff. Distinctions between line and staff blur in this context and an organic linkage develops, often serving as a prototype of a collaborative, problem-solving team.

One single factor stands out in retrospect over all others. There was always the conviction and the ability to make the training and development department the leading edge, the catalyst for organizational change and adaptability. Rather than performing the more traditional role, these groups became centers for innovation and organizational revitalization, and their leaders emerged as change-agents, the new managers of tomorrow's organizations.

I should now add another point in conclusion. It emerges from the previous points. They describe a far more autonomous, organizationally influential, self-directed role than trainers have been given or have asked for in the past.

If the training group is to be concerned with adult socialization, for example, it would be myopically irresponsible if not worse for them to define socialization in terms of momentary needs of the organization. Rather, they must take at least some of the responsibility for enunciating the goals and conditions of the enterprise. In a way, their systems counseling function is "organizational socialization." If they take responsibility for socializing both the members as people and the organization as a human system, then they must have values and standards which are somehow prior and outside both.

In fact, the emerging role I outline implies that the roles of the top management and training director become more interchangeable than ever before.

QUESTIONS

1. What is a bureaucracy?
2. What changes in managerial behavior does the author see happening?
3. What are the major human problems of organizations for the next twenty-five years?
4. The author asserts that management must take positive responsibility for the "socialization of adults" in the organization. What are the implications of this?
5. How does the role of the corporate training and development director of the future compare with the role of the typical training director of today?
6. What is meant by an organic-adaptive organization structure?

PART II

The Personnel Function

Although it is true that human resource management problems pervade an entire organization, in practically all establishments, except the very smallest, there is a designated department specifically charged with the responsibility for planning, organizing, initiating, and controlling personnel programs. This organizational unit is commonly called the personnel department. Oftentimes it may bear the name industrial relations or employee relations unit.

In studying the personnel field we must take cognizance of the content of the personnel functions and be aware of emerging trends and changes. We must also be concerned with personnel as a professional field of work and of its achievements and shortcomings.

Lawrence A. Appley, a close friend of the personnel field, speaks frankly and convincingly of the need for the profession to lift its horizons. He asserts that the personnel profession has not lived up to its opportunities and challenges, and offers guidelines for objectives he feels personnel executives ought to pursue.

Dale Yoder, a pioneering scholar in the personnel–industrial relations field, describes three distinct kinds or levels of roles in this field as they exist in work organizations. He further identifies major forces causing change in the personnel–industrial relations area and makes a number of predictions for the future.

3.

Management Is Personnel Administration

LAWRENCE A. APPLEY

The personnel profession has not lived up to its opportunities and its challenges, in my opinion, and if some radical changes are not made in the attitudes and practices of most of the members of the personnel profession, it may disappear as such.

Most of the major staff activities and management functions have broadened in scope and risen in stature. Some incumbents grew with these changes; others remained as they were. Office management broadened into management systems and administrative services. Accounting broadened into controlling and from there to financial vice-presidencies. Packaging engineers became packaging managers, and insurance buyers became risk managers. Marketers became vice-presidents for distribution.

Some personnel executives became vice-presidents for corporate development, but there were and are those who were, are, and will remain bookkeepers, buyers, personnel directors, and so forth. Their common denominator is paper shuffling; their criterion is how many times and to how many different documents a person can sign his name. These are the members of the chairborne division of the paragraph troopers.

A Double Orientation

At a personnel conference of the American Management Association in Philadelphia in 1937, Thomas G. Spates, vice-president for personnel of General Foods Corporation, made the keynote address, and in that address he said, "Management *is* personnel administration." A good manager is a good personnel administrator. A good personnel administrator is a good manager. In other words, a competent line executive must be personnel-minded and a competent personnel executive must be management-minded. However, my experience in the last 20 years

Reprinted by permission of the publisher from *Personnel*, March–April 1969 issue. © 1969 by the American Management Association, Inc.

Lawrence A. Appley is former Chairman of the Board and Chief Executive Officer of the American Management Association.

has given me the distinct impression that line executives have been increasing their personnel-mindedness much more rapidly than personnel executives have been increasing their management-mindedness.

Forty years ago, personnel executives were pleading for other executives to give their recognition and approval to formal personnel programs. All that was asked of a president was that he "drop in for five minutes" or "open a meeting with a brief statement" or "enter a few favorable sentences in a report or a speech." Twenty years ago, company officers were asked to participate in personnel programs for varied periods of time. Today, people in similar positions are leaders in the advancement of that which the personnel executive once promoted, and many of them are beckoning to personnel executives to catch up.

"Interest Begets Interest"

It is perfectly right that the general executive or the manager of an area of specialization should become a leader in good human relations practices. It is a credit to the personnel profession that the general manager has increased his sophistication in personnel matters. The question now arises, however, whether today's personnel executive is showing the way toward greater sophistication and is challenging general management to higher and higher levels of personnel administration.

The great pioneers in personnel administration used to tell us that if we wanted other executives to become interested in the work of the personnel department, then the personnel department should become interested in the work of other executives. This was another way of stating the old psychological principle that "interest begets interest." To be of the greatest service to other activities in the business, the personnel executive has to acquaint himself with marketing, manufacturing, financing, engineering, et cetera.

An able personnel executive is not just a personnel expert; he is a management expert. This means that he knows the nature of management and how it functions. It means that he has a record of attainment in management, even if it does not extend beyond the administration of his own department. It means that he understands the basic processes of management and knows that personnel techniques are management techniques.

Management Basics

The first basic function of management is *long-range planning* This is the foundation of corporate development, and the personnel executive should be the leading proponent of it and expert in it.

Manager manpower planning goes hand in hand with *long-range planning.* It requires the use of appraisal systems, executive inventories, and replacement tables. It is a prime personnel technique and an essential management tool, and, in fact, there is no more effective top management control over the affairs of the business.

Organization designing and building is a matter of great concern to every executive, and particularly to top management. Promotion of it and expertise in it should emanate from the personnel department.

The development of *managerial standards of performance* ranks high among desirable management practices, and, here again, the leadership should come from the personnel executive.

Progress reviews are systems for determining "people" performance as compared with standards. This, too, is a management and a personnel technique.

Performance improvement is another term for education, training, and individual development. This field is the very essence of supervisory responsibility, and the personnel department probably has had the leadership in it as much as in any other.

Incentives and rewards have to be appropriate, adequate, and timely if they are to be a motivating influence in the attracting, holding, and performance of competent people. Wage and salary administration and the development of nonfinancial incentives have always been identified as major interests of a personnel department.

The Right-Hand Man

This analysis is not to say that the personnel executive should run the business. The chief executive officer runs the business. He runs it by long-range planning, manpower planning, organization building, establishing standards of performance, setting up a system of progress reviews, finding ways for improving performance, and providing appropriate rewards. But he needs help and consultation from a vice-president for corporate development who is the staff officer for long-range planning, manpower planning, personnel administration, and labor relations. He isn't going to turn to such a person for help and consultation, however, unless that person has understanding and expertness in these areas, as well as top management stature and poise.

If he is to gain such a position within an organization, the personnel executive must free himself from the nuts and bolts of personnel manuals and procedures, and see to it that his department does not have the image of a bottleneck in progress. This means that once a new personnel activity of program has been adopted and established, it should be placed in other departments for purposes of administration.

I fail to see any reason why pension and insurance plans, medical benefits, employment, payroll, cafeteria management, safety rules and inspection, and other matters of this kind should be considered as appropriately within the domain of a personnel department. They are matters of concern to a personnel executive, of course, but they do not have to be administered by his people for him to maintain influence on them.

Education and training, yes— this is the basic program of personnel administration. Through it the influence of the personnel activity is extended, because it is the very backbone of staff work in the area of corporate development.

The Wrong Yardsticks

Too many personnel executives have thought that their prestige and influence were to be measured by the number of people within their departments and the number of personnel actions that needed their approval. This has been a sad mistake. The work of a personnel department should be measured only in terms of the quality of personnel activities and the effectiveness of their administration by other line and staff departments. Since management *is* personnel administration, it is the job of the personnel executive to help the chief executive officer see that this is done well, rather than do it himself.

The great value of management techniques lies in the process of applying them. No value is to be found in the technique itself, or in the meticulousness of the resulting paper work. No position description has value, as such. Its value stems from the fact that in order to write it a supervisor has to sit down with one of his people for the purpose of clarifying responsibility and authority. No standard of performance has any value in itself. The value is to be found in the process of developing it.

Therefore, personnel executives are interested in getting managers and supervisors to use these techniques, but the minute the personnel department uses them *for* the manager or supervisor, the processes of good management have deteriorated into an exercise. When personnel practice has no impact upon people performance, it is nothing more than maladministration and wastefulness.

The Concerns That Count

My plea to members of the industrial relations, or personnel, profession is that we give adequate attention to and be continuing students of these considerations:

1. *The extent to which the organization of which we are a part is professionally managed and how it may be made more so.*

A professionally managed business is managed by professionals who act like professionals. Over the next twenty years, *only* professionally managed businesses will survive after they have reached that point in entrepreneurial experience and continued growth where the chief executive has to take off his tin hat and his overalls and move from the shop into the front office.

Personnel executives must be deeply immersed in this concept. They must be guided by a driving motivation to see that all managers around them understand the significance of such a development and how to take advantage of it at the earliest possible time.

2. *The long-range future of the organization and the adequacy of the scientific processes utilized to determine it.*

The time is past when any executive concerned with institutional growth and personal development could question the practicability of long-range planning. The company that practices scientific long-range planning sees current difficulty as purely temporary, because management sights are set far beyond. Because of the growth of professional management and long-range planning as an integral part of it, I think it is safe to say that none of us will ever see a deep depression in this country such as we experienced in the early 1930's.

To the personnel executive, long-range planning should be second nature. Through it the future is as clear to him as the present, and he understands the soundness of short-term losses for long-term gains. This awareness is an absolute requirement for growth and progress.

3. *The caliber and quality of the manager manpower and reserves available within the organization, how they are related to the long-range corporate planning, and how adequate they are to support it.*

Scientific manager manpower planning is not new; most good techniques are old and tested by the time they come into general use. Now, however, manager manpower planning stands on the threshold of dramatic utilization, comparable to that of corporate long-range planning. Indeed, the two are interdependent; many corporate long-range plans have failed because of inadequate management talent to implement them.

The personnel executive must become skilled in the most reliable and productive techniques of management manpower development. This is no longer a luxury; it is a requisite, at the very heart of any sound human relations effort. The basic function of a chief executive officer today is to develop managers, and the greatest assistance the personnel administrator can give to his chief executive is leadership in the administration of a program designed to develop these managers.

4. *Improvement of the relationship of business—the segment of society within which we work—to other segments and activities, such as religion, education, government, and organized labor.*

The top management of free enterprises has two major responsibilities, to manage those enterprises successfully and to protect the right to manage them successfully. The latter involves the impact of the enterprise upon the community, and business and industrial managements must be far more active in exercising leadership in the community. The executive has a responsibility to the community not because he is a businessman, but because of leadership capabilities that have made him an executive and that he should now make available to the community in which he lives and works.

As our society has grown from the small village to the massive urban community, high specialization has developed in the various segments of our society. Clergymen, educators, government representatives, labor leaders, editors and publishers have developed cocoons of their special interests. They have their own vocabularies, their own professional societies, and their own technical publications, all of which tend to isolate them, so that their communication with others is breaking down. There must be aggressive action by business and industrial managements to bring leadership groups together for the purpose of common dialogue and increased understanding, and the personnel executive should be a leader in this endeavor.

5. *The parts our institutions play in fulfilling our responsibilities to the young and future leaders of the nation by making our facilities, capabilities, and knowledge available to high school and college students.*

The young people on university and college campuses throughout the world have recognized that our educational institutions and systems are outmoded. They are not preparing our young people for leadership. They are not preparing them to survive in the world in which they live and have any significant impact on it. Industry and business have not scratched the surface of the contribution they should be making of their abilities, facilities, and potential on university and college campuses. They have much to offer, and our young people want it. Personnel

executives must foster programs that bring their top management people and the college community together.

6. *The basic philosophy, the management creed, the code of ethics, the character of the institutions of which we are a part.*

If there is anything a personnel executive should be into up to his ears, it is the nonfinancial incentives present within an organization. When an individual stays with the company instead of going somewhere else for more money, or when he leaves to go somewhere else for less money, the determining factors have to be other than financial. Many of these factors lie in the climate within which people work.

Climate is a reflection of the basic philosophy practiced by management, from chief executive to first-line supervisor. This philosophy is a kind of control over management practice. It needs study, clarification, and dissemination, and here again the personnel man has a key role to take.

A Broader Involvement

If personnel executives of the future turn their study, their minds, and their activities in these directions, leaving the administration of routine and established personnel procedures to others and letting other people exercise line authority, there is great hope for the future. If they do not do this, there is grave doubt as to the future of personnel administration, either as a profession or as a specific staff activity. In other words, personnel executives must be continuing students of good management—the nature of it, the processes of it, and the character it takes. This study makes them expert in the problem areas of their fellow executives, and keeps them involved in the matters that are of prime importance to others on the team.

The pioneers of personnel administration had a relatively simple job of hiring, training, insuring, protecting, and pensioning people. If a comparison were made, one would be overwhelmed by the impact since that time of increased government regulation, social legislation, organized labor activity, community pressures, and standards of excellence. It is a much bigger job today; it is a much harder job today; it is a much more important job today. Personnel executives, like all other executives, must so organize their activities that day-by-day operations are handled by day-by-day administrators, and executives are left free for much broader and more significant functions.

QUESTIONS

1. According to the author, in what ways has the personnel profession failed to live up to its opportunities and challenges?
2. Explain the meaning of "Management *Is* Personnel Administration." Is management essentially a human process or a technical process? Discuss.
3. Lawrence Appley identifies several areas in which the personnel executive should be expert and play a leading role. Give and discuss these. Would you add other functions?
4. What factors determine the stature of a profession?

4.

Personnel Administration

DALE YODER

To be in character and in tune with the original goals of IRRA, a forecast should report the findings of some sort of "futures" or Delphi study. That research would begin by developing a schema for identifying the major questions about and clues to likely changes. It would submit and resubmit appropriate questions to members of a knowledgeable panel, allowing them to compare their responses and revise their opinions until significant consensus and clearcut divisions emerged.[1] Such a study could have great value, particularly for those with career interests in the field and for professional associations and universities.

The editors' request for this chapter did not mention a grant for such a study. In the absence of volunteer sponsors or obviously easy touches, the chapter had to be cut back to a semblance of stage one in such a future study. The objective here will be to suggest relevant areas of inquiry and pertinent questions

and thus to set the stage for a real futures study of personnel administration.

To discover such questions, attention has to be focused on what is and has been happening in the personnel field. We need to consider (a) the current role of and assignment to personnel workers and departments, with emphasis on identifiable dimensions; (b) notable changes and trends in these assignments during the past quarter century; (c) what appear to have been the proximate or immediate sources of pressure for these changes; and (d) a first approximation of the likely pattern of similarly influential forces and their impact on the next twenty-five years.

The Personnel Image and Role

Personnel management or administration has developed a fairly distinct and widely recognized role and image. The common job titles—manager, director,

Reprinted from *The Next Twenty-Five Years of Industrial Relations*, Madison, Wisconsin: Industrial Relations Research Association, 1973, by permission of the publisher and author.

Dale Yoder is Professor and Director, Bureau of Business Services and Research, California State University, Long Beach.

[1] See David M. Kiefer, "The Futures Business," C&EN (ACS Publications, 1155 16th St., N.W., Washington, D.C. 20036), August 11, 1969, pp. 62–75; Alan R. Fusfeld and Richard N. Foster, "The Delphi Technique: Survey and Comment," *Business Horizons*, Vol. 14, No. 3, June, 1971, pp. 63–74; Burt Nanus and Harvey M. Adelman, "Profiles of the Future: Work and Leisure, 1980," *ibid.*, Vol. 14, No. 4, August, 1971, pp. 5–10.

administrator, technician, specialist, consultant, counselor and others—have achieved recognition and acceptance. The term "personnel administration" is a generic designation, roughly comparable to manpower or human resources management and frequently regarded as synonymous with "industrial relations," which is the second most popular title for those in charge of personnel programs.

Personnel administration is recognized as a sub-set and specialized division in the broad occupational classification of managers. Personnel and industrial relations people (hereafter described as PAIR or PAIRers) are concerned with the inevitable management problems inherent in the employment of people. Within the larger category of managers, PAIRers hold assigned responsibilities for managing the *human* resources of working organizations—as distinguished from their material or financial and other resources. PAIR practitioners work for, with, and in management in solving its "people management" problems.

Functional Scope, Range. No simple occupational outline could describe everything PAIRers do. Many current programs developed like Topsy; as assistants to and helpers in management, personnel workers have been firefighters, assigned to whatever "people" problems appeared to deserve top priorities and timely attention. From the top management viewpoint, such critical problems have varied from time to time; at one point, for example, attention to the discovery and selection of help may seem most urgent, at another the prevention of, or negotiation with, unions.[2] In another firm or agency, training—job, supervisor, or manager—may

have a high priority; in others wage and salary administration or improving administrative style.[3]

Individual firm and agency assignments may represent many or few of these functional or activity areas. Within these areas, some PAIR practitioners have narrowed their interests and specialized their competence—for example, in recruiting, testing, negotiating or counseling. For convenience in subsequent discussion, these specialists are identified as PIRTs, i.e. personnel or industrial relations technicians.

Other working organizations have sought to integrate and coordinate their assigned functional programs by creating PAIR departments, with a director or manager of these personnel services. Such service managers or administrators represent a second somewhat distinctive type of PAIR practitioner, herein designated as PIRMs.

Many organizations with comparatively broad ranges of functional areas have visualized their needs in the management of people as requiring still further integration and coordination. At the same time, they have been impressed with the necessity for overall consistency and compatibility of policies and programs within total management, in which personnel management is recognized as a central and pervasive concern. Such organizations have created a PIREX (personnel and industrial relations executive) job; the incumbent is expected not only to coordinate PAIR services but also to represent them in top management decision-making. The PIREX is essentially a director and leader of all PAIR services. He is also a generalist in management,

[2] For much more on historic changes, see Cyril C. Ling, *The Management of Personnel Relations.* Homewood, Illinois: Richard D. Irwin, Inc., 1965.

[3] For details see the many textbooks in this field; see also George Ritzer and Harrison Trice, *An Occupation in Conflict,* Ithaca, N.Y.: New York State School of Industrial and Labor Relations, 1969; for a broader international perspective on the variety of assignments, see Clerk Kerr, John T. Dunlop, Frederick H. Harbison, and Charles A. Meyers, *Industrialism and Industrial Man,* Cambridge, Mass.: Harvard University Press, 1960.

capable of relating such areas as staffing or training or personnel research to management problems in finance, accounting, marketing, environmental protection, or other general management concerns.[4]

The present total, inclusive functional or activity dimension of PAIR can be suggested by such a snapshot as is illustrated in Table 1. The classification is admittedly arbitrary, designed to facilitate our central problem of forecasting. Probably the most important comment is a reminder that the mix of PAIR programs in individual firms and agencies may be as broad as the entire table or as narrow as one or two of its subdivisions.

Responsibility/Authority. A second dimension of PAIR measures the depth of

TABLE 1   Principal Function/Activity Areas in PAIR

1. STAFFING
   Screening, interviewing, recruitment, testing, personnel records
   Job analysis, job description, staffing tables
   Promotion, transfer, job enlargement, etc.

2. PERSONNEL MAINTENANCE
   Counseling, personnel appraisals, inventories, turnover control
   Health services and accident prevention
   Employee benefits and services, etc.

3. LABOR RELATIONS
   Group relationships with organized or unorganized employees
   Negotiation, contract administration, grievances, arbitration
   Third-party involvement, mutual aid pacts, etc.

4. TRAINING/DEVELOPMENT
   Job training, supervisor and foreman training, manager and executive development, pre-employment and special purpose training, retraining, etc.

5. COMPENSATION
   Wage and salary surveys, incentive pay plans, profit sharing, stock ownership, financial and non-financial rewards, job enrichment, wage and salary controls, etc.

6. EMPLOYMENT COMMUNICATIONS
   House organ, employee handbook, rumor control, listening
   Attitude, morale and expectations surveys, feedback analysis, etc.

7. ORGANIZATION
   Structural design, planning and evaluation, innovation
   Utilization of formal and informal, reducing conflict
   Overcoming resistance to organizational change, etc.

8. ADMINISTRATION
   Explanation and interpretation of options—authoritative, consultative, participative, self-management styles
   Assistance in change, etc.

9. PERSONNEL POLICY AND PLANNING
   Defining organizational goals, policy guidelines and strategies
   Identifying, translating, and complying with public manpower policy
   Forecasting manpower needs, selecting optional courses, etc.

10. REVIEW, AUDIT, RESEARCH
   Program reporting and recording; evaluation of policies and programs
   Theory testing, innovation, experimentation
   Cost/benefit studies, etc.

---

[4] See Thomas L. Wood, "The Personnel Staff: What Functions Does It Perform?," *Personnel Journal*, Vol. 46, No. 10, November, 1967, pp. 643ff.; William L. Grey, "The Modern Role of the Industrial Relations Manager," *Personnel*, Vol. 46, No. 4, July–August, 1969, pp. 70–73; Dale Yoder, "ASPA and the Three PAIRs," *The Personnel Administrator*, Vol. 14, No. 2, March–April, 1969, pp. 39–42.

managerial authority granted its practitioners. The range in this regard is from very shallow, sharply defined and restricted delegations, at the minimal extreme, to very heavy allocations of responsibility, with similarly broad grants of power, authority and discretion, at the maximum. Put another way, this range is from narrowly defined, specific "program" authority to broad, organization-wide influence in policy determination.

At the lower extreme, all major and minor policy decisions about "people management" are made by line managers; they also decide which personnel services and programs are required to implement such policy. PAIR is assigned responsibility for specified tasks, and authority is restricted to decisions essential to the performance of these delegated duties. In such practice most PAIRers are PIRTs (they exercise what may be called "consultant" authority). They are responsible only for technical effectiveness and authorized only to make technical decisions—for example, to choose tests for selection, to define passing and cutting scores, to specify textbooks and other training materials, or to settle individual grievances arising under a negotiated agreement.

PIRMs exercise somewhat heavier delegations of authority than the PIRTs; they are authorized not only to coordinate a variety of personnel services, but also to advise line managers on appropriate policies and the selection of programs. They may make decisions with respect to priorities among specified programs, how resources shall be apportioned among them, how their performance and contribution shall be evaluated, and how program needs shall be interpreted and communicated to top management. In this arrangement, although PAIRers exercise authority deeper than that of

program consultants, personnel management remains essentially the provision of coordinated services as ordered for implementing general policy decisions made by line management.

In some working organizations, PAIR exercises much greater power. In that pattern, PAIR's leader is an accredited member of the executive group. He holds responsibility for recommending personnel policies as well as for directing a variety of PAIR programs. Basic decisions—for example, whether or not to experiment with new organizational forms or with modified administrative styles, whether to buy or train, to recognize a union, to restructure jobs, to offer a "cafeteria" compensation program—all involve policy questions for which PAIR supplies analysis, explanations, interpretations and recommendations.

In addition, PAIR's leader exerts a direct influence on all other top management decisions. At this extreme, the PIREX is essentially a line manager both in directing PAIR crew members and in sharing top management responsibility for policy. The weight of his authority is comparable to that of a production, marketing or finance manager. In many large firms, this level of responsibility/authority is defined in the PAIR leader's title; he is the corporate PAIR vice-president.[5]

In summary, a current snapshot of the personnel field would highlight (1) the wide horizontal range of PAIR programs, (2) the similarly broad differences in the level or depth of authority delegated to PAIR practitioners, and (3) wide firm-to-firm variations in both program-mix and in delegated power.

A Quarter-Century of Change

The preceding section has sought to identify major dimensions with which to

---

[5] See Dale Yoder, "Personnel Ratios in American Firms and Agencies, 1970," *Occasional Paper No. 2*, Bureau of Business Research, California State University, Long Beach, 1971, p. 4.

measure the current "state of the art" in PAIR. Our design or schema contemplates further steps in which, (a) recent trends in PAIR are related to these dimensions; (b) major sources of pressure behind these changes are suggested; and (c) these and similar forces for change are evaluated in terms of their implications as seeds and sprouts likely to generate further change in the quarter century ahead.

Proliferation of Programs. The most obvious change in PAIR during the past twenty-five years is in its scope or range. More managements have encountered—or recognized—more "people management" problems. They have developed more functional programs and services. The activity dimension has broadened.

Most early personnel programs emphasized staffing, together wth paternalistic efforts to help needy employees solve personal problems. PWs—personnel workers —were preliminary screening interviewers ("at the gate") and nonprofessional counselors in a variety of "welfare" activities such as mutual benefit plans, legal aid, and debt control. After World War I, venturesome managements expanded the staffing assignment to include recruiting, testing, and recordkeeping; other firms added collective bargaining, grievance handling, and sometimes impressive curriculum in job and supervisor training.[6]

World War II encouraged additional assignments to PAIR. Wartime managers discovered the potential payoff in realistic job descriptions and standardized job titles; PAIR contributed expertise in using the D.O.T. The war spotlighted problems in the compensation area; PAIR offered competence in wage surveys, cost-of-living adjustments, the correction of inter- and intra-plant inequities, job evaluation, and bonus and incentive pay plans.

In the 1940s, '50s and '60s other areas listed in Table 1 became common assign-

ments to PAIR. Special knowledge and skill in job analysis and description gave PAIRers an inside track for organizational planning and modification. Managerial concern about employee morale, commitment, and contribution suggested attitude surveys and innovations in financial and non-financial rewards. PAIR experience in training led to PAIR programs in manager development and on to PAIR experiments with differing management styles—hard *v* soft management and consultive and participative patterns.

Firms that anticipated serious problems of future recruitment and retention tried simple forms of manpower planning; some of them recognized the need for planning both policy and programs. Some PAIR departments were expected to forecast future manpower requirements and to evaluate "buy or make" strategies for meeting expected needs. Meanwhile, as PAIR assignments expanded, PAIR's cost-effectiveness inevitably became a matter of growing concern. PAIR managers were asked to review and audit their activities—to demonstrate cost/benefit payoffs.

Timing and program-mix. The dating of various new programs cannot be precise. Some of them represented new assignments in old program areas; others were distinctly new. Meanwhle, details of the kaleidescopic change are somewhat obscure, largely because the mix of individual firm programs was constantly changing. More firms assigned more program areas to PAIR. This trend was countered, however, by a parallel tendency to spin off some earlier personnel programs, placing responsibility for them outside the formal PAIR department. Many firms, for example, set up a separate unit to provide labor relations services; others followed that pattern in training. Others spun off wage and salary administration and organization planning.

Changing Delegation. Modifications in

---

[6] See Cyril C. Ling, *op. cit.*

the authority/power dimension of PAIR during the years since World War II have been extensive, but the pattern is complex. Total managerial responsibility and authority delegated to PAIR practitioners probably increased, in part because more PAIRers were employed and they were, in total, assigned a growing range of functions. At the same time, however, this general trend was complicated by increased specialization within PAIR, so that growing numbers of PIRTs became concerned almost exclusively with "program" authority within one or more of the functional areas.

Total PAIR "voting power" has grown; today's PAIR practitioners are more numerous than they were at the beginning of the post-war period. Much of that expansion, however, is balanced by the growing labor force; PAIR's rate of growth is in part a reflection of increased employment. That conclusion is supported by an actual reduction, in the last decade, in *personnel ratios*—the numbers of professional/technical personnel workers per hundred employees in the same working organizations. Specialist PAIR services have apparently been spread more widely and thinly in many firms, and this development has been paralleled by increased numbers of independent PAIR consultants—temporary help. Most of the latter are program oriented—not generalists in policy.[7]

PAIR As Staff. Delegations of authority to PAIR practitioners have reflected the fact that many of them see themselves as "staff" to and for management and prefer to keep it that way. They see their role as one of providing specialized, technical-professional advice to line managers, together with similarly specialized knowledge and skill in directing programs in such areas as are selected by line managers. They offer services to line managers in implementing policies established by line managers. Decisions with respect to the organization's goals and guidelines of intended courses to be followed are, in this view, the sole province of the line. These advocates of "staffism" prefer to minimize their managerial responsibility and authority. They propose to get most of their satisfactions out of planning and directing programs. To a degree, they view themselves as semi-independent consultants, on retainer to line managers as clients.

This development of professional-technical specialization in PAIR is a major change in the authority dimension of PAIR. From one viewpoint, these PIRTs have achieved greater authority and influence, but in smaller spheres. Far-out examples could include yesterday's sensitivity trainers or today's organization developers, or test or interview validators.

PIREX PAIRers. In sharp contrast to this "staff specialist" movement in the field, a growing number of personnelers has elected to move in the opposite direction. These PIREXes have been assigned and have accepted much broader and deeper authority. They are distinctly "policy"—rather than "program"—oriented. Their popularity to some degree reflects changes in top management perspectives, in which executives have concluded that policy with respect to the employment of people cannot be separated from the total of management policy. Neither can sound general policy ignore policy in people management. Policy in personnel management, in this view, has to be a major consideration in all top-level management decisions—for example in mergers, or organizational

---

[7] See Roberta J. Nelson, George W. England and Dale Yoder, "Personnel Ratios, 1960: An Analytical Look," *Personnel*, Vol. 37, No. 6, November–December, 1960, pp. 18–28; see also "Personnel Ratios in American Firms and Agencies, 1970," *op. cit.*

change, or product mix, or distribution. "People management" is viewed as a central component in all management.

In implementing this viewpoint, organizations have required some of their PAIR people to accept generalist manager authority. They have expanded PAIR responsibility from the program level to include policy and the integration of personnel policy in the total of management policy. They have changed the role and status of PAIR from one of providing services *for* general management to one in which PAIR participates *in* and as a recognized part of general management.

One evidence of this change is the growing proportion of firms reporting that their PAIR departments are represented by vice-presidents. These top PAIRers are recognized as full members of the executive team. In an even larger segment of the field, a transitional process is evident; the head of PAIR—a PIRM—not only coordinates services for managers but also counsels with top executives in major decisions and plans.

These complex authority developments in PAIR have exerted a divisive influence in the field. PAIR's professional associations have encountered difficulties in finding common ground in the goals and concerns of members. Problems and subjects of interest to PIRTs may not turn on PIREXes. Some PIRMs may be somewhat mystified about their identities and roles and natural allies.

Generators of Change in PAIR

To suggest the most critical question about what is likely to happen to PAIR in the future, we need to identify the forces and pressures that appear to have been most influential in past change and to appraise the impacts of the same or similar variables in the years ahead. We may start by recognizing that PAIR is in no sense a closed system. Further, it

is a subset within management, which is also subject to inputs and impacts from its broader environment. Change in PAIR, therefore, has presumably been occasioned and shaped by pressures from both within and outside management.

Identifying these sources of change has to be essentially a difficult sleuthing process. To come up with a widely acceptable rationale would probably require the discerning insight and perception of Sherlock Holmes. Attempting to evaluate the relative influence and impact of significant inputs is somewhat like selecting characters for top billing in a prisoner performance of Robin Hood. The process, from here on, has to be largely judgmental and discretionary. Resulting interpretations can be questioned and doubted; they can be suspected and defended; they cannot be conclusively demonstrated.

It seems proper to insist, however, that only proximate causes or inputs should be listed here. The search for and appraisal of causal variables cannot trace these clues all the way to ultimates. Some PAIR developments, for example, appear to reflect changing public policy and legislation, which may, in turn, express changing citizen value systems or philosophies, which might reflect a rising tide of nationalism, traceable in large measure to population explosions. Such backtracking explanation seems definitely beyond any special expertise of this author or of readers.

Other PAIR developments might be followed back to the generation gap in incomes or in perspectives in work and welfare. Still others probably express, to some degree, the impact of new management theory, itself a special case of new behavioral science theory with reference to needs, dissatisfiers and expectancy, with the latter at least partially attributable to the generosity of the Ford Foundation and the cooperation of the Internal Revenue Service.

With full awareness of such built-in limitations, Table 2 directs attention to some of the intermediate, proximate sources of change in PAIR. The variables listed at the left appear to have significantly influenced changes in the major dimensions of PAIR. Column II suggests their prospective influence as compared with the past.

The table is not esoteric, complex or obscure; it reflects no special intuition or mystic insight; it needs little supplementary explanation here.

Crucial Questions Re Future Change

A preliminary question, inevitably suggested by Table 2, has to consider the hazard that additional important variables—within or outside the management system—may have been overlooked in reviewing past experience. A preliminary question in our Delphi inquiries, therefore, would ask what additional factors—not included in Table 2—are likely to be significant change generators affecting the future scope and depth of PAIR.

War, not specifically mentioned in the table, could become such a source; past "big" wars have had powerful impacts on manpower management. World-wide peace could generate changes. Reduced international tensions and expended world trade—particularly if they encouraged international mobility in manpower—could be influential. A trend toward zero population growth could exert a delayed impact on labor market supplies and hence on working relationships. Drastic changes in the distribution of income, or in popular value systems and attitudes toward work would create a whole new ballgame for PAIR. The influence of the so-called world-wide "youth movement" could supplement and modify factors listed in Table 2.

Such factors, and others like them, would presumably be suggested in the first go-around of responses in a futures study. Those mentioned in the table could be helpful in suggesting other such change generators.

A variety of questions in the "PAIR futures" study must be concerned with changes in and attributable to such historically significant inputs as are suggested by Table 2. Column II can serve as a starting point for such inquiries. Most of the predictions in Column II represent extrapolations of current trends and assumptions of similar impacts on the twin dimensions of program scope and depth of authority. Several of them point toward an overall increase in the range of PAIR programs. For example, PAIR may have to provide expertise with respect to the management of people in mergers and in multi-national operations. PAIRers may have to lead in improving the ethical practices of managers and in advancing their professional qualifications.

Some of the same developments suggest expansion within one or more of the current functional areas. A futures study should evaluate, for example, the likelihood the PAIRers will be asked to give more attention to experimental changes in organizational structures, to short-term temporary organizational forms; and to new administrative or leadership patterns and styles. Attention would be directed to employee expectations with respect to leadership, rewards systems, and public responsibility and to pre-employment training and life-long retraining and refresher training; to work-related health problems and hazards and new forms of "unions" and new collective bargaining practices. Questions would inquire about job-redesign and restructuring; non-financial rewards; employment communications; micro manpower planning; and to cost/benefit analyses, theory-testing research, and systematic review and audit.

At the same time, several possible implications with respect to developments in the authority/responsibility dimension of PAIR have been suggested in Column II of the table. In general, strictly staff

TABLE 2   Changing PAIR—Proximate Sources of Change

I Input Variables, 1945–1972	II Prospective Influence, 1972–1997	I Input Variables, 1945–1972	II Prospective Influence, 1972–1997
1. WORKING ORGANIZATIONS (Public and Private)		**4. MANAGERS**	
Size, growing number of employees	Continued, multinationals	Increased sophistication	Continued
Technologies, new and changing	Continued	Higher formal educational attainment	Continued
Stuctures—innovation, complexity, temporary	Increased	More formal education—radio, television	Continued
White v. blue collar ratio, rising	Continued	Retraining, continuing education	Increased, life-long learning
Manning-staffing—temporary help	Continued	Philosophy, values	Continued
2. PUBLIC MANPOWER POLICY		Expectations of manager capabilities	Increased
Extending range, coverage	Continued	Expectations of work satisfactions	Increased
Manpower planning (macro and required micro)	More	Freedom of expression, criticism	Increased
Equal employment opportunity	Continued	Declining acceptance of obligation to work	Increased
Occupational health	Continued	**5. GENERAL MANAGERS, EXECUTIVES**	
Manpower development, MDTA	Continued	Trend toward professionalization	Continued
Collective bargaining in public service, growth	Continued	Mobility and independence	Increasing
Improved productivity, pressure for	Continued	Career education; theory, policy, ethics	Increasing, revised accrediting
Controlled inflation, pressure	Continued	Specialization: technical, procedural	Doubtful
3. UNIONS		Professional associations	Increasing
Growth of white collar	Continued	**6. PAIR PRACTITIONERS**	
Expansion in the public sector	Continued	Trend toward professionalization	Increasing
New forms of unions, new titles, tactics	Increased	Staff specialization	Doubtful
Changing alliances, mergers	Continued	Career educational preparation	Increasing
Improved capabilities of representatives	Continued	Professional associations	Increasing
Improved public relations programs	Increased	Qualification as generalist manager	Increasing

41

status for PAIR seems likely to face rough going. Expectations of both line managers and of managees seem likely to regard the staff role as a cop-out. Those who provide technical-professional services in testing, for example, are already under pressure to accept added responsibility for policy in other selection programs, and, at the same time, to guarantee the validity of their procedures and their assurance of equal employment opportunities.

Demands for the acceptance of policy responsibility have already appeared in the health and accident prevention area and, indeed, rather generally across the range of PAIR activities. Increased sophistication on the part of both line managers and managees makes very clear the fact that programs are selected to implement policy. Technically effective programs will be socially acceptable only if the underlying policy is also acceptable. The message is clear; more critical concern must be directed at policy guidelines. Managers will increasingly recognize their need for specialized competence in personnel *policies*—intentions—for example in decisions about whether and why to train, or test, or restructure jobs, or bargain collectively, rather than simply in technical adequacy in specific programs.

The result may well be more radical change in the policy/responsibility continuum than in the program range or mix. Top management strategic planning and decision-making has to be based on a broad, management-wide, perspective; programs must reflect that range of concern. Policy guidelines for staffing, training, collective bargaining and other PAIR activity areas must harmonize with the totality of management strategies, including those in finance, marketing, buying—the whole process, from procuring to peddling, so that the total measures up to public as well as managee expectations.

To meet this requirement, the total of executive capabilities must include broad understanding of manpower management problems and of optional solutions in both policy and program areas. This means that PAIR's specialized capabilities must be effectively represented in the executive suite. At the same time, however, it means that the PAIR executive who provides that representation must be qualified to recognize and comprehend the totality of management problems; he must be able to relate financial problems to training, and marketing problems to organization, and public relations problems to compensation, staffing and labor relations. In short, PAIR's representative in top management must be a generalist in management as well as a fully-accredited PAIRer.

These developments may tend to force PAIRers to accept ever broader responsibilities—both for what they do in the programs they direct and for what top management does in establishing the guidelines they thus implement. Individual PAIR practitioners in all activity areas are likely to need added expertise in policy to parallel their specialized competence in programs. Specialist PIRTs will have to become more knowledgeable and critical in policy areas if they are to avoid charges of unethical behavior and malpractice. PAIRers who lead and direct PAIR activities will tend to become PIREXes—managers qualified as generalists with special capability in the PAIR field as a whole. Educational preparation for careers in PAIR will have to be tailored to meet these new requirements.

In this view, the days of the PIRT as a full-time PAIR crew member in most firms may be numbered. The program specialist may become even more of a consultant; only in that capacity can he avoid heavier responsibility for organizational policy and the exercise of similarly greater authority. PIRMs, in turn, will either become qualified as manager generalists or released to "on call," "when, as, and if needed" consultant relationships. Only the largest working organizations—able to afford permanent consultant services—are likely to maintain a larger PAIR "staff" division.

The impact of such changes will be reflected in collegiate educational programs and in PAIR's professional associations.

Both can be expected to recognize the need for much wider capabilities and persistent concern for policy.

It is inevitable that such a forecast as this raises many controversial issues. They are precisely the questions that should define the research design in any acceptable futures study. Both the need for such a study and the promise of significant payoffs should be obvious.

QUESTIONS

1. Show how the scope and influence of the personnel–industrial relations function in various enterprises may range from a technician role to a top executive policy-influencing role. What accounts for these sharply differing roles?
2. The author points to two somewhat contradictory trends. One is toward greater technical expertise in very narrow personnel functions whereas the other is toward a generalist, top management, policy orientation. Can these two trends be reconciled, or are they mutually exclusive?
3. In addition to the many proximate sources of change affecting the personnel and industrial relations field given by Dr. Yoder, add other forces that you think are operative.
4. In modern complex organizations there has been a distinct trend away from the older line–staff dichotomy wherein line departments held all the power and staff units held a distinctly subordinate advisory role. How do you see this affecting the personnel–industrial relations field?

PART III

Employee Satisfaction and Alienation

In the purely materialistic aspects of their jobs, American working people have made great progress over the past half century in terms of higher real wages; better protection against the risks of illness, old age, and unemployment; and more time off the job per year through longer vacations and more holidays. But when one examines the quality of working life there is serious question as to whether progress has been made. Both in the factory and office, jobs have been narrowed and atomized in scope. Many jobs are of very short cycle and require only surface attention. The work pace in many plants is fast and the pressure for production is relentless. There are still countless industrial jobs that are dirty, noisy, and dangerous.

A generation or two ago working men and women were glad just to be employed regularly at reasonable wages. Nowadays a better educated work force expects more from employment. They expect job satisfaction, opportunities for social interaction, and many expect opportunities for promotion to better jobs.

The first selection in this Part, "Work in America," is taken from the report of the same name prepared by a Special Task Force to the U.S. Secretary of Health, Education, and Welfare. It examines the functions of work in contemporary society, attitudes and expectations of working people, the nature of alienation and its causes, and the special problems of blue-collar workers, white-collar workers, and young workers.

Whereas research investigators, university professors, and some industrial executives propose job enrichment, self-managed work groups, challenging job assignments, and better leadership as solutions to worker alienation, trade union

45

leaders tend to be wary of management-initiated programs to improve the attitudes and satisfactions of working people. In his article, "Job Satisfaction: A Union Response," William W. Winpisinger, an official of the machinists union (the International Association of Machinists and Aerospace Workers), asserts that worker discontents can best be corrected by traditional union actions to obtain higher wages, shorter hours, better benefits, and better physical conditions of work.

5.

Work in America

1. Introduction

Homo Faber

It is both humbling and true that scientists are unable, in the final analysis, to distinguish all the characteristics of humans from those of other animals. But many social scientists will agree that among those activities most peculiar to humans, work probably defines man with the greatest certainty. To the archaeologist digging under the equatorial sun for remains of the earliest man, the nearby presence of primitive tools is his surest sign that the skull fragment he finds is that of a human ancestor, and not that of an ape.

Why is man a worker? First of all, of course, man works to sustain physical life —to provide food, clothing, and shelter. But clearly work is central to our lives for other reasons as well. According to Freud, work provides us with a sense of reality; to Elton Mayo, work is a bind to community; to Marx, its function is primarily economic. Theologians are interested in work's moral dimensions; sociologists see it as a determinant of status, and some contemporary critics say that it is simply the best way of filling up a lot of time. To

the ancient Greeks, who had slaves to do it, work was a curse. The Hebrews saw work as punishment. The early Christians found work for profit offensive, but by the time of St. Thomas Aquinas, work was being praised as a natural right and a duty—a source of grace along with learning and contemplation. During the Reformation, work became the only way of serving God. Luther pronounced that conscientious performance of one's labor was man's highest duty. Later interpretations of Calvinistic doctrine gave religious sanction to worldly wealth and achievement. This belief, when wedded to Social Darwinism and laissez-faire liberalism, became the foundation for what we call the Protestant ethic. Marx, however, took the concept of work and put it in an even more central position in life: freed from capitalist exploitation, work would become a joy as workers improved the material environment around them.[1]

Clearly, work responds to something profound and basic in human nature. Therefore, much depends on how we define work, what we conceive work to be, what we want work to be, and whether we successfully uncover its meaning and purpose. Our conceptions (and misconceptions) of ourselves, the wisdom with

This article contains Chapter 1, Introduction, and part of Chapter 2, Problems of American Workers, from *Work in America—Report of a Special Task Force to the Secretary of Health, Education, and Welfare.* Cambridge, Mass.: The MIT Press, 1973. Prepared under the auspices of the W. E. Upjohn Institute for Employment Research. The report was written by a team under the chairmanship of James O'Toole.

[1] Wilensky, Harold, "Work As a Social Problem" in Howard S. Becker, ed., *Social Problems: A Modern Approach*, New York; John Wiley & Sons, 1966.

which public policy is formulated on a range of issues, and the rationality with which private and public resources are allocated are influenced greatly by the degree to which we penetrate the complex nature of work.

Because work, as this report illustrates, plays a pervasive and powerful role in the psychological, social, and economic aspects of our lives, it has been called a basic or central institution. As such, it influences, and is influenced by, other basic institutions—family, community (particularly as a political entity), and schools—as well as peripheral institutions. Work, then, provides one institutional perspective—but a broad one—from which to view these interrelationships that affect ourselves and our society.

Toward a Definition of Work

We measure that which we can measure, and this often means that a rich and complex phenomenon is reduced to one dimension, which then becomes prominent and eclipses the other dimensions. This is particularly true of "work," which is often defined as "paid employment." The definition conforms with one readily measurable aspect of work but utterly ignores its profound personal and social aspects and often leads to a distorted view of society.

Using housework as an example, we can see the absurdity of defining work as "paid employment." A housewife, according to this definition, does not work. But if a husband must replace her services— with a housekeeper, cook, baby sitter— these replacements become workers, and the husband has added to the Gross National Product the many thousands of dollars the replacements are paid. It is, therefore, an inconsistency of our definition of work that leads us to say that a woman who cares for her own children is not working, but if she takes a job look-

ing after the children of others, she is working.

Viewing work in terms of pay alone has also produced a synonymity of "pay" and "worth," so that higher-paid individuals are thought by many to have greater personal worth than those receiving less pay. At the bottom of this scale, a person without pay becomes "worthless." The confusion of pay with worth is a result of historical events and traditions apparently rooted in the distinction between "noble" and "ignoble" tasks.[2] History might have been otherwise and garbage men, for example, in recognition of their contribution to health, might have been accorded monetary rewards similar to those received by physicians. Certainly, it takes little reflection to conclude that, except in crude economic terms, no one is worth nothing, nor is anyone worth a hundred times more than another merely because he is paid a hundred times as much.

We can come closer to a multi-dimensional definition of work if we define it as "an activity that produces something of value for other people." This definition broadens the scope of what we call work and places it within a social context. It also implies that there is a purpose to work. We know that the housewife is *really* working, whether she is paid or not; she is being productive for other people. Substituting the children a woman cares for does not change the nature of her work, only the "others" for whom she is productive. And voluntary tasks are certainly work, although they are not remunerated. Some people at various stages of their lives may be productive only for themselves, a possible definition of leisure.

The Functions of Work

The economic purposes of work are obvious and require little comment. Work

2 Veblen, Thorstein, *The Theory of the Leisure Class*, Modern Library, 1934.

is the means by which we provide the goods and services needed and desired by ourselves and our society. Through the economic rewards of work, we obtain immediate gratification of transient wants, physical assets for enduring satisfactions, and liquid assets for deferrable gratifications. For most of the history of mankind, and for a large part of humanity today, the economic meaning of work is paramount.

Work also serves a number of other social purposes. The workplace has always been a place to meet people, converse, and form friendships. In traditional societies, where children are wont to follow in their parents' footsteps, the assumption of responsibility by the children for one task and then another prepares them for their economic and social roles as adults. Finally, the type of work performed has always conferred a social status on the worker and the worker's family. In industrial America, the father's occupation has been the major determinant of status, which in turn has determined the family's class standing, where they lived, where the children went to school, and with whom the family associated—in short, the life style and life chances of all the family members. (The emerging new role of women in our society may cause class standing to be co-determined by the husband's *and* wife's occupations.)

The economic and societal importance of work has dominated thought about its meaning, and justifiably so: a function of work for any *society* is to produce and distribute goods and services, to transform "raw nature" into that which serves our needs and desires. Far less attention has been paid to the *personal* meaning of work, yet it is clear from recent research that work plays a crucial and perhaps unparalleled psychological role in the formation of self-esteem, identity, and a sense of order.

Work contributes to self-esteem in two ways. The first is that, through the inescapable awareness of one's efficacy and competence in dealing with the objects of work, a person acquires a sense of mastery over both himself and his environment.[3] The second derives from the view, stated earlier, that an individual is working when he is engaging in activities that produce something valued by other people. That is, the job tells the worker day in and day out that he has something to offer. Not to have a job is not to have something that is valued by one's fellow human beings. Alternatively, to be working is to have evidence that one is needed by others. One of these components of self-esteem (mastery) is, therefore, internally derived through the presence or absence of challenge in work. The other component (how others value one's contributions) is externally derived. The person with high self-esteem may be defined as one who has a high estimate of his value and finds that the social estimate agrees.

The workplace generally, then, is one of the major foci of personal evaluation. It is where one finds out whether he is "making the grade"; it is where one's esteem is constantly on the line, and where every effort will be made to avoid reduction in self-evaluation and its attending sense of failure.[4] If an individual cannot live up to the expectations he has of himself, and if his personal goals are not reasonably obtainable, then his self-esteem, and with it his relations with others, are likely to be impaired.

Doing well or poorly, being a success or failure at work, is all too easily transformed into a measure of being a valuable or worthless human being, as Erich Fromm writes:

Since modern man experiences himself both as the seller and as the commodity to be sold on the market, his self-esteem depends

[3] Levinson, Harry, "Various Approaches to Understanding Man at Work," *Archives of Environmental Health,* Vol. 22, May 1971.

[4] Kahn, Harry and J. R. P. French in *Social Issues,* July 1962.

on conditions beyond his control. If he is successful, he is valuable; if he is not, he is worthless.[5]

When it is said that work should be "meaningful," what is meant is that it should contribute to self-esteem, to the sense of fulfillment through the mastering of one's self and one's environment, and to the sense that one is valued by society. The fundamental question the individual worker asks is "What am I doing that *really* matters?"[6]

When work becomes merely automatic behavior, instead of being *homo faber*, the worker is *animal laborens*. Among workers who describe themselves as "just laborers," self-esteem is so deflated that the distinction between the human as worker and animal as laborer is blurred.[7] The relationship between work and self-esteem is well summarized by Elliot Jaques:

working for a living is one of the basic activities in a man's life. By forcing him to come to grips with his environment, with his livelihood at stake, it confronts him with the actuality of his personal capacity—to exercise judgment, to achieve concrete and specific results. It gives him a continuous account of his correspondence between outside reality and the inner perception of that reality, as well as an account of the accuracy of his appraisal of himself. . . . In short, a man's work does not satisfy his material needs alone. In a very deep sense, it gives him a measure of his sanity.[8]

Work is a powerful force in shaping a person's sense of identity. We find that most, if not all, working people tend to describe themselves in terms of the work groups or organizations to which they belong.[9] The question, "Who are you?" often solicits an organizationally related response, such as "I work for IBM," or "I'm a Stanford professor." Occupational role is unusually a part of this response for all classes: "I'm a steelworker," or "I'm a lawyer." In short: "People tend to 'become what they do.'"[10]

Several highly significant effects result from work-related identification: welfare recipients become "nobodies"; the retired suffer a crucial loss of identity; and people in low-status jobs either cannot find anything in their work from which to derive an identity or they reject the identity forced on them.[11] Even those who voluntarily leave an organization for self-employment experience difficulties with identity—compounded by the confusion of others—as the following quote from an article entitled "Striking Out on Your Own," illustrates

No less dramatic . . . are those questions of identity which present themselves to the self-employed. These identity crises and situations usually come packaged in little episodes which occur when others find that they have encountered a bona fide weirdo without a boss. . . . You are stopped by a traffic policeman to be given a ticket and he asks the name of your employer and you say that you work for yourself. Next he asks, "Come on, where do you work? Are you employed or not?" You say, "Self-employed." . . . He, among others you meet, knows that self-employment is a tired euphemism for being out of work. . . . You become extremely nervous about meeting new people because of the ever-present question, "Who are you with?" When your answer fails to attach you to a recognized organization . . . both parties

---

[5] Fromm, Erich, *The Revolution of Hope*, New York: Bantam Books, 1971.

[6] Coles, Robert, "On the Meaning of Work," *The Atlantic*, October, 1971.

[7] Seligman, Ben, "On Work, Alienation, and Leisure," *The American Journal of Economics and Sociology*, Vol. 23, No. 4, 1965.

[8] Jaques, Elliott, *Equitable Payment*, New York: John Wiley & Sons, 1961.

[9] McPartland, T. S. and Cummings, J. H., "Self-conception, Social Class and Mental Health," *Human Organization*, Vol. 17, 1958.

[10] Kahn and French, *op. cit.*

[11] Wilensky, *op. cit.*

to the conversation often become embarrassed by your obscurity.[12]

Basic to all work appears to be the human desire to impose order, or structure, on the world. The opposite of work is not leisure or free time; it is being victimized by some kind of disorder which, at its extreme, is chaos. It means being unable to plan or to predict. And it is precisely in the relation between the desire for order and its achievement that work provides the sense of mastery so important to self-esteem. The closer one's piece of the world conforms with one's structural plans, the greater the satisfaction of work. And it follows that one of the greatest sources of dissatisfaction in work results from the inability to make one's own sense of order prevail—the assembly line is the best (or worst) example of an imposed, and, for most workers, unacceptable structure.

These observations have been verified a number of times in investigations of mass and protracted unemployment. Loss of work during the Depression was found to produce chronic disorganization in the lives of parents and children, as documented in several studies of the 1930's.[13] Cynicism, loss of self-confidence, resentment, and hostility toward the Federal Government, helplessness, and isolation are all experienced during such difficult periods.[14] According to Charles Winick,

Inasmuch as work has such a profound role in establishing a person's life space, emotional tone, family situation, object relations,

and where and how he will live, either the absence of work or participation in marginal work often makes it likely that he will develop a pervasive *atonie*.[15]

Atonie is a condition of deracination —a feeling of rootlessness, lifelessness, and dissociation—a word which in the original Greek meant a string that does not vibrate, that has lost its vitality.

Besides lending vitality to existence, work helps establish the regularity of life, its basic rhythms and cyclical patterns of day, week, month, and year.[16] Without work, time patterns become confused. One recalls the drifting in T. S. Eliot's "The Wasteland":

What shall I do. . . . What shall we do tomorrow?
What shall we ever do?

When duration of unemployment has been prolonged, unemployed workers progress from optimism through pessimism to fatalism. Attitudes toward the future and toward the community and home deteriorate.[17] Children of long-term unemployed and marginally employed workers uniformly show poorer school grades.[18] And, despite the popular notion that unemployed people fill their "free" time with intensified sexual activities, the fact is that undermined egos of former breadwinners lead to diminished libidos.[19] "There are so many unconscious and group needs that work meets," Winick writes, "that unemployment may lead not only to generalized anxiety, but to free-floating hostility, somatic symptoms and

[12] Dickson, Paul, "Striking Out on Your Own," *Washington Monthly*, August 1971.

[13] Ginzberg, Eli, *Grass on the Slag Heaps*, New York: Harper, 1942 and Bakke, E. W., *The Unemployed Worker*, New Haven: Yale University Press, 1940.

[14] Bakke, *Ibid.*

[15] Winick, Charles, "Atonie: The Psychology of the Unemployed and the Marginal Worker," in George Fish, ed., *The Frontiers of Management Psychology*, New York: Harper and Row, 1964.

[16] Frankel, E., "Studies in Biographical Psychology," *Character and Personality*, Vol. 5, 1963.

[17] Winick, *op. cit.*

[18] *Ibid.*

[19] Ginzberg, Eli, "Work: The Eye of the Hurricane," *Humanitas*, Vol. VII, No. 2, Fall 1971.

the unconscious selection of some serious illnesses." [20]

Many of the studies revealing the disorganizing effects of unemployment during the Depression have found echoes in recent "ghetto ethnographies." Such studies as Liebow's *Tally's Corner* show these effects to be as much a function of unemployment and marginal employment *per se* as of economic catastrophe. This is so because to be denied work is to be denied far more than the things that paid work buys; it is to be denied the ability to define and respect one's self.

It is illusory to believe that if people were given sufficient funds most of them would stop working and become useless idlers. A recent economic analysis shows that as people increase their earnings and acquire wealth they do not tend to decrease the time and energy that they invest in work.[21] In another study, when a cross-section of Americans were asked if they would continue working even if they inherited enough to live comfortably without working, 80% said they would keep on working (even though only 9% said they would do so because they enjoyed the work they were doing).[22] Some people may not want to take specific jobs—primarily because of the effects on their self-esteem—but working, "engaging in activities that produce things valued by other people," is a necessity of life for most people.

Some of the most compelling evidence about the centrality of the functions of work in life comes from the recent efforts of women to fill what some interpret as a void in their lives with the sense of identity derived from work. As some social critics have noted, the desire for all that work brings to the individual is at the foundation of the women's liberation movement.

There is also considerable evidence that work has the same meaning among the poor and among welfare recipients that it has for middle-class and employed individuals:

—A recent study for the Labor Department on the work orientations of welfare recipients found that "the poor of both races and sexes identify their self-esteem with work to the same extent as nonpoor persons do." The study found that although people on welfare are as committed to the work ethic as middle-class people, their attitudes differ in that they are not confident that they can succeed on a job. After experiencing failure, they are more likely to accept the dependence on welfare.[23]

—A recent study in South Carolina of 513 underprivileged workers found that the poor did not differ markedly from the middle class in the kind of satisfactions that they derived from work.[24]

—The Office of Economic Opportunity has sponsored a three-year study to assess the validity of the assumption that the working poor would stop working if they were guaranteed an annual income. *Preliminary* findings have shown little slackening in work effort among those urban families receiving a guaranteed income. In fact, hourly earnings appear to be higher for those in the experiment than for those in a control group. Although it is too early to assess the results of the experiment, there are signs that withdrawal from work effort is not as extensive as some had feared.[25]

In this regard, it must be realized that

[20] Winick, *op. cit.*

[21] Morgan, James N., Survey Research Center.

[22] Morse, Nancy C. and Weiss, Robert S., "The Function and Meaning of Work and the Job," *American Sociological Review*, Vol. 20, April 1955.

[23] Goodwin, Leonard, "A Study of Work Orientations of Welfare Recipients."

[24] Champagne, Joseph E. and Donald King, "Job Satisfaction Factors Among Underprivileged Workers," 1967.

[25] Watts, Harold, "New Jersey Experiment: Notes for Discussion," 1972.

although *work* is central to the lives of most people, there is a small minority for whom a *job* is purely a means to a livelihood. To them a job is an activity that they would gladly forgo if a more acceptable option for putting bread on their table were available. What little evidence there is on this point indicates that for most such individuals the kinds of jobs that they see open to them do little to provide the sense of self-esteem, identity, or mastery that are the requisites for satisfying work. These individuals turn to other activities (music, hobbies, sports, crime) and other institutions (family, church, community) to find the psychological rewards that they do not find in their jobs. In effect, these activities, for these people, become their real work. This unusual phenomenon helps to explain the small amount of job withdrawal that occurs among welfare recipients. For example, welfare mothers may choose the personally fulfilling work of raising their children to the alternative of a low-level, unchallenging job—the only kind available to them.

The Change in Attitudes Toward Work

Although social scientists have long disputed the precise contribution of the Protestant ethic to the genesis of capitalism, they generally agree that thrift, hard work, and a capacity for deferring gratification historically were traits widely distributed among Americans. Moreover, as part of the legitimacy of the economic system, individual members of our society were to be credited or blamed for their own circumstances, according to the degree of their prosperity.

But the ethic, or what has passed for it, appears to be under attack. Some futurists tell us that automation will make work unnecessary for most people, and that we may as well ignore work and look to other

matters, such as "creative leisure." More immediately, our attention is drawn to these alleged signs of work's obsolescence:

• The growth in the number of communes.
• Numerous adolescents panhandling in such meccas as Georgetown, North Beach, and the Sunset Strip.
• Various enterprises shifting to 4-day workweeks.
• Welfare caseloads increasing.
• Retirement occurring at ever earlier ages.

All of these are relatively benign signs; more malignant signs are found in reduced productivity and in the doubling of mandays per year lost from work through strikes. In some industries there apparently is a rise in absenteeism, sabotage, and turnover rates.[26]

Ironically, many of these symptoms have increased despite the general improvements in physical conditions and monetary rewards for work. In comparison with the dreary lot of most workers during the industrial revolution and, indeed, until quite recently, the workplace today is an Elysian field. Sweatshop conditions have all but disappeared. The extreme dangers of work appear to have declined in most industries. Women and children are seldom engaged in backbreaking drudgery. Arbitrary wage cuts and dismissals are relatively rare, and enlightened laws, personnel policies, and labor unions protect the worker in a variety of ways.

Quantitatively, the lives of workers away from work similarly have improved. Real income, standard of living, health status, and life expectancy have all risen markedly. Among most classes of workers, homes and cars are owned in abundance, and bank accounts continually grow. For those without work, there is social security, unemployment compensation, workman's compensation, and an

---

[26] Walton, Richard, "Work Alienation and the Need for Major Innovation," 1972 (Commissioned paper).

income floor will very likely be established under welfare compensation. On the average, then, no workers have ever been as materially well-off as American workers are today. What, then, is wrong?

Social scientists are suggesting that the root of the problem is to be found in the changing needs, aspirations, and values of workers. For example, Abraham Maslow has suggested that the needs of human beings are hierarchical and, as each level is filled, the subsequent level becomes salient.[27] This order of needs is

1. Physiological requirements (food, habitat, etc.).
2. Safety and security.
3. Companionship and affection.
4. Self-esteem and the esteem of others.
5. Self-actualization (being able to realize one's potential to the full).

It may be argued that the very success of industry and organized labor in meeting the basic needs of workers has unintentionally spurred demands for esteemable and fulfilling jobs.

Frederick Herzberg suggests an alternative way of looking at the needs of workers—in terms of intrinsic and extrinsic factors.[28] Under this rubric, job satisfaction and dissatisfaction are not opposites but two separate dimensions. Extrinsic factors, such as inadequate pay, incompetent supervision, or dirty working conditions may lead to dissatisfaction, which may be reduced in turn by such "hygienic" measures as higher pay and "human relations" training for foremen. But such actions will not make workers satisfied. Satisfaction depends on the provision of intrinsic factors, such as achievement, accomplishment, responsibility, and

challenging work. Satisfaction, then, is a function of the content of work; dissatisfaction, of the environment of work. Increases in productivity have been found to correlate in certain industries and occupations with increases in satisfaction, but not with decreases in dissatisfaction. Hence, hygienic improvements may make work tolerable, but will not necessarily raise motivation or productivity. The latter depends on making jobs more interesting and important.

A recent survey, which lends some support for this emphasis on job content, was undertaken by the Survey Research Center, University of Michigan, with support from the Department of Labor. This unique and monumental study, to which we often refer in this report, is based on a representative sample of 1,533 American workers at all occupational levels. When these workers were asked how important they regarded some 25 aspects of work, they ranked in order of importance:

1. Interesting work.
2. Enough help and equipment to get the job done.
3. Enough information to get the job done.
4. Enough authority to get the job done.
5. Good pay.
6. Opportunity to develop special abilities.
7. Job security.
8. Seeing the results of one's work.

What the workers want most, as more than 100 studies in the past 20 years show, is to become masters of their immediate environments and to feel that their work and they themselves are important—the twin ingredients of self-esteem.[29] Workers recognize that some of

[27] Maslow, Abraham, *Motivation and Personality*, New York: Harper and Row, 1954.

[28] Herzberg, Frederick, *Work and the Nature of Man*, Cleveland: World Publishing Company, 1966.

[29] Kahn, Robert L., "The Meaning of Work: Interpretations and Proposals for Measurement," in A. A. Campbell and P. E. Converse, eds., *The Human Meaning of Social Change*, New York: Basic Books, 1972.

the dirty jobs can be transformed only into the merely tolerable, but the most oppressive features of work are felt to be avoidable: constant supervision and coercion, lack of variety, monotony, meaningless tasks, and isolation. An increasing number of workers want more autonomy in tackling their tasks, greater opportunity for increasing their skills, rewards that are directly connected to the intrinsic aspects of work, and greater participation in the design of work and the formulation of their tasks.

Who Is Dissatisfied?

When we cite the growing problem in the country of job dissatisfaction using the criteria laid out above, are we talking about 5% or 50% of the workers in the country? It is clear that classically alienating jobs (such as on the assembly line) that allow the worker no control over the conditions of work and that seriously affect his mental and physical functioning off the job probably comprise less than 2% of the jobs in America.[30] But a growing number of white-collar jobs have much in common with the jobs of autoworkers and steelworkers. Indeed, discontent with the intrinsic factors of work has spread even to those with managerial status. It is, however, almost as difficult to measure these feelings of discontent about work as it is to measure such other basic feelings as pride, love, or hate. Most of the leading experts on work in America have expressed disappointment over the unsophisticated techniques commonly used to measure work dissatisfaction.

The Gallup poll, for example, asks only "Is your work satisfying?" It is not surprising that they get from 80% to 90%

positive responses (but even this crude measure shows a steady decrease in satisfaction over the last decade). When a similar question was asked of auto and assembly-line workers, 60% reported that their jobs were "interesting." Does this mean that such high percentages of blue-collar workers *are really satisfied* with their jobs? Most researchers say no. Since a substantial portion of blue-collar workers (1) report being satisfied with their jobs *but also indicate they wish to change them* and (2) report they would continue working even if they didn't have to *but only to fill time*, then this can only mean that these workers accept the necessity of work but expect little satisfaction from their specific jobs.[31]

Those workers who report that they are "satisfied" are really saying that they are not "dissatisfied" in Herzbergian terms— i.e., their pay and security are satisfactory, but this does not necessarily mean that their work is intrinsically rewarding. This distinction is illustrated by an interview sociologist George Strauss held with a blue-collar worker on a routine job. This worker told Strauss, in a rather offhand way, "I got a pretty good job." "What makes it such a good job?" Strauss responded. The worker answered:

Don't get me wrong. I didn't say it is a *good* job. It's an O.K. job—about as good a job as a guy like me might expect. The foreman leaves me alone and it pays well. But I would never call it a good job. It doesn't amount to much, but it's not bad.[32]

Robert Kahn suggests that the direct question of satisfaction strikes too closely to one's self-esteem to be answered simply:

For most workers it is a choice between no work connection (usually with severe attend-

[30] Based upon an analysis of the Bureau of Labor Statistics for the number of "operatives" and other job categories likely to have "assembly-line" features.
[31] Kahn, *op. cit.*
[32] Strauss, George, "Is There a Blue Collar Revolt Against Work?", 1972 (Commissioned paper).

TABLE 1. Percentages in Occupational Groups Who Would Choose Similar Work Again

PROFESSIONAL AND LOWER WHITE-COLLAR OCCUPATIONS	%	WORKING-CLASS OCCUPATIONS	%
Urban university professors	93	Skilled printers	52
Mathematicians	91	Paper workers	42
Physicists	89	Skilled autoworkers	41
Biologists	89	Skilled steelworkers	41
Chemists	86	Textile workers	31
Firm lawyers	85	*Blue-collar workers, cross section*	*24*
Lawyers	83	Unskilled steelworkers	21
Journalists (Washington correspondents)	82	Unskilled autoworkers	16
Church university professors	77		
Solo lawyers	75		
White-collar workers, cross section	*43*		

ant economic penalties and a conspicuous lack of meaningful alternative activities) and a work connection which is burdened with negative qualities (routine, compulsory scheduling, dependency, etc.). In these circumstances, the individual has no difficulty with the choice; he chooses work, pronounces himself moderately satisfied, and tells us more only if the questions become more searching. Then we learn that he can order jobs clearly in terms of their status or desirability, wants his son to be employed differently from himself, and, if given a choice, would seek a different occupation.[33]

More sophisticated measures of job satisfaction designed to probe the specific components of a job offer great contradictions to simple "Are you satisfied?" surveys. When it asked about specific working conditions, the Michigan survey found that great numbers of "satisfied" workers had major dissatisfactions with such factors as the quality of supervision and the chance to grow on a job. A 1970–71 survey of white, male, blue-collar workers found that less than one-half claimed that they were satisfied with their

jobs most of the time. The proportion of positive responses varied according to the amount of variety, autonomy, and meaningful responsibility their jobs provided.[34]

Over the last two decades, one of the most reliable single indicators of job dissatisfaction has been the response to the question: "What type of work would you try to get into if you could start all over again?" Most significantly, of a cross section of white-collar workers (including professionals), only 43% would voluntarily choose the same work that they were doing, and only 24% of a cross section of blue-collar workers would choose the same kind of work if given another chance (see Table 1).[35] This question, some researchers feel, is a particularly sensitive indicator because it causes respondents to take into account the intrinsic factors of the job and the very personal question of self-esteem. Those in jobs found to be least satisfying on other measures seldom would choose their present occupation again.

Another fairly accurate measure of job

[33] Kahn, *op. cit.*

[34] Sheppard, Harold and Neal Herrick, *Where Have All the Robots Gone?*, New York: The Free Press, 1972.

[35] Kahn, Robert L., "The Work Module: A Proposal for the Humanization of Work," 1972 (Commissioned paper).

satisfaction is to ask the worker the question: "What would you do with the extra two hours if you had a 26-hour day?" Two out of three college professors and one out of four lawyers say they would use the extra time in a work-related activity. Strikingly, only one out of twenty nonprofessional workers would make use of the extra time in work activity.[36]

We are able, then, to differentiate between those jobs that are satisfying and those that are dissatisfying to the people who hold them. The prestige of an occupation is often an accurate predictor of the level of satisfaction found in a job (while the ranking of occupations by prestige does not correspond exactly with either salary or the amount of education needed to perform well on the job).[37] Moreover, prestige ranking of jobs is nearly identical with the ranking of jobs according to who would choose the same work again. Evidently, people know what work is satisfying and what work is not, even if they are unable to articulate the characteristics of each.

We also find that the jobs people find most satisfying contain most or all of the factors cited previously that workers find important in their jobs. The dissatisfying jobs contain only some or none of these factors. . . .

Demographic factors also play a part in the difference between satisfaction and dissatisfaction in the workplace. Young workers and blacks were found to be the most dissatisfied segments of the population in the University of Michigan Survey of Working Conditions. But even dissatisfaction among these groups was often found to correlate with specific kinds of jobs and job situations. For example, highly trained women in low-level jobs were often extremely dissatisfied, but women and men with the same training in the same jobs were equally satisfied.

Sources of Dissatisfaction

Based on what we know about the attitudes of workers toward their jobs, we can identify the following two factors as being major sources of job dissatisfaction: the anachronism of Taylorism and diminishing opportunities to be one's own boss.

The Anachronism of Taylorism. Frederick Winslow Taylor, father of time and motion studies and author of *Principles of Scientific Management*, propagated a view of efficiency which, until recently, was markedly successful—so long as "success" was measured in terms of unit costs and output. Under his tutelage, work tasks were greatly simplified, fragmented, compartmentalized, and placed under continuous supervision. The worker's rewards depended on doing as he was told and increasing his output. Taylor's advice resulted in major, sometimes spectacular, increases in productivity.

Several events have occurred to make Taylorism anachronistic. Primarily, the workforce has changed considerably since his principles were instituted in the first quarter of this century. From a workforce with an average educational attainment of less than junior high school, containing a large contingent of immigrants of rural and peasant origin and resigned to cyclical unemployment, the workforce is now largely native-born, with more than a high school education on the average, and affluence-minded. And, traditional values that depended on authoritarian assertion alone for their survival have been challenged.

Simplified tasks for those who are not simple-minded, close supervision by those

[36] Wilensky, *op. cit.*

[37] Rossi, Peter, "The Prestige Standing of Occupations: Characteristics and Consequences," 1972 (Commissioned paper).

whose legitimacy rests only on a hierarchical structure, and jobs that have nothing but money to offer in an affluent age are simply rejected. For many of the new workers, the monotony of work and scale of organization and their inability to control the pace and style of work are cause for a resentment which they, unlike older workers, do not repress.

Attempts to reduce the harmful effects of Taylorism over the last two generations have not got at the nub of the problem. For example, the "human relations" school attempts to offset Taylor's primacy of the machine with "tender, loving care" for workers.[38] This school (which has many adherents in personnel offices today) ignores the technological and production factors involved in a business. This approach concentrates on the enterprise as a social system—the workers are to be treated better, but their jobs remain the same. Neither the satisfaction of workers nor their productivity is likely to improve greatly from the human relations approach. Alternatives to Taylorism, therefore, must arise from the assumption that it is insufficient to adjust either people to technology or technology to people. It is necessary to consider both the social needs of the workers and the task to be performed.[39] This viewpoint challenges much of what passes as efficiency in our industrial society.

Many industrial engineers feel that gains in productivity will come about mainly through the introduction of new technology. They feel that tapping the latent productivity of workers is a relatively unimportant part of the whole question of productivity. This is the attitude that was behind the construction of the General Motors auto plant in Lordstown, Ohio, the newest and most "efficient" auto plant in America. Early in 1972, workers there went out on strike over the pace of the line and the robot-like tasks that they were asked to perform. This event highlights the role of the human element in productivity: What does the employer gain by having a "perfectly efficient" assembly-line if his workers are out on strike because of the oppressive and dehumanized experience of working on the "perfect" line? As the costs of absenteeism, wildcat strikes, turnover, and industrial sabotage become an increasingly significant part of the cost of doing business, it is becoming clear that the current concept of industrial efficiency conveniently but mistakenly ignores the social half of the equation.

It should be noted that Taylorism and a misplaced conception of efficiency is not restricted to assembly-lines or, for that matter, to the manufacturing sector of the economy. The service sector is not exempt. For example, in the medical care industry, the phenomenal growth in employment over the past decade or so has occurred largely in lower-level occupations. This growth has been accompanied by an attempt to increase the efficiency of the upper-level occupations through the delegation of tasks down the ladder of skills. This undoubtedly results in a greater efficiency in the utilization of manpower, but it rigidifies tasks, reduces the range of skills utilized by most of the occupations, increases routinization, and opens the door to job dissatisfaction for a new generation of highly educated workers.

As we have seen, satisfying jobs are most often those that incorporate factors found in high-status jobs—autonomy, working on a "whole" problem, participation in decision making. But as Ivar Berg and others have noted, as a result of countless public and private policies and

38 Elton Mayo's work is an example of this school's thought.
39 Davis, Louis and Eric Trist, "Improving the Quality of Working Life," 1972 (Commissioned paper).

decisions that determine our occupational structure, growth in occupational opportunities has occurred largely in middle and lower levels. The automation revolution that was to increase the demand for skilled workers (while decreasing the need for humans to do the worst jobs of society) has not occurred. What we *have* been able to do is to create such jobs as teacher aides, medical technicians, and computer keypunch operators—not jobs with "professional" characteristics. Undoubtedly, these jobs have opened opportunities for many who would otherwise have had no chance to advance beyond much lower-skilled positions. But it is illusory to believe that technology is opening new high-level jobs that are replacing low-level jobs. Most new jobs offer little in the way of "career" mobility—lab technicians do not advance along a path and become doctors.

This problem of a fairly static occupational structure presents society with a formidable barrier to providing greater job satisfaction to those below the pinnacle of the job pyramid. Without a technological revolution there is little hope of flattening out this structure in order to give more workers higher-status jobs. It then becomes crucial to infuse middle- and lower-level jobs with professional characteristics, particularly if we plan to continue offering higher and higher degrees of education to young people on the assumption that their increased expectations can be met by the world of work.

Diminishing Opportunities to Be One's Own Boss. Our economic, political, and cultural system has fostered the notion of independence and autonomy, a part of which is the belief that a hardworking person, even if he has little capital, can always make a go of it in business for himself. Or, to put it another way, if things get too bad in a dependent work situation, it has been felt that the individual could always strike out on his own.

This element of the American Dream is rapidly becoming myth, and disappearing with it is the possibility of realizing the character traits of independence and autonomy by going into business for oneself. The trend of the past 70 years or more, and particularly in recent years, has been a decrease in small independent enterprises and self-employment, and an increase in the domination of large corporations and government in the workforce. In the middle of the 19th century, less than half of all employed people were wage and salary workers.[40] By 1950 it was 80%, and by 1970, 90%. Self-employed persons dropped from 18% in 1950 to 9% in 1970. Individual proprietorships in service trades declined from 81% to 78% in only five years—from 1958 to 1963. From 1960 to 1970, government workers increased from 12% of the civilian labor force to more than 15%. Out of 3,534,000 industrial units employing 70% of the civilian labor force, 2% of the units accounted for 50.6% of the employees, and more than 27% of the employed were accounted for in 0.3% of the units.

Among a class of occupations notable for their autonomy—managers, officials, and proprietors (excluding farms)—self-employment fell from 50% in 1950 to 37% in 1960. On the farms, wage and salary workers increased as a percentage of all farm workers from 61% in 1950 to 80% in 1960. Even among authors, self-employment dropped from 62% to 38% in this period, while self-employed photographers declined from 41% to 34%. Although the percentage of self-employed lawyers has remained almost constant, in 1967 nearly half reported working in firms having 8 to 50 or more lawyers, suggesting some limitation on their autonomy and independence.

---

[40] All figures in this section are from Maccoby, Michael and Katherine A. Terzi, "Work and the American Character," 1972 (Commissioned paper).

As these data attest, the trend is toward large corporations and bureaucracies which typically organize work in such a way as to minimize the independence of the workers and maximize control and predictability for the organization. Characterologically, the hierarchical organization requires workers to follow orders, which calls for submissive traits, while the selection of managers calls for authoritarian and controlling traits. With the shift from manufacturing to services— employment has gone from about 50–50 in 1950 to 62–38 in favor of services in 1970—the tyranny of the machine is perhaps being replaced by the tyranny of the bureaucracy.

Yet, the more democratic and self-affirmative an individual is, the less he will stand for boring, dehumanized, and authoritarian work. Under such conditions, the workers either protest or give in, at some cost to their psychological well-being. Anger that does not erupt may be frozen into schizoid depressed characters who escape into general alienation, drugs, and fantasies. More typically, dissatisfying working environments result in the condition known as alienation.

Alienation exists when workers are unable to control their immediate work processes, to develop a sense of purpose and function which connects their jobs to the over-all organization of production, to belong to integrated industrial communities, and when they fail to become involved in the activity of work as a mode of personal self-expression.[41]

Social scientists identify four ingredients of alienation: (1) powerlessness (regarding ownership of the enterprise, general management policies, employment conditions and the immediate work process), (2) meaninglessness (with respect to the character of the product worked on

as well as the scope of the product or the production process), (3) isolation (the social aspect of work), and (4) self-estrangement ("depersonalized detachment," including boredom, which can lead to "absence of personal growth").[42] As thus broken down, alienation is inherent in pyramidal, bureaucratic management patterns and in advanced, Taylorized technology, which divides and subdivides work into minute, monotonous elements. The result of alienation is often the withdrawal of the worker from community or political activity or the displacement of his frustrations through participation in radical social or political movements.[43]

It seems fair to conclude that the combination of the changing social character of American workers, declining opportunities to establish independence through self-employment, and an anachronistic organization of work can create an explosive and pathogenic mix.

What Can Be Done— A "Social Efficiency" Model

One of the main burdens of this report will be to verify that work, health, welfare, family stability, education, and other matters of major concern do not reside in discrete compartments, but rather that we live in a closed system—"spaceship earth" to use Kenneth Boulding's phrase. These spheres of action are mutually influential, but one may be more dominant than the others. The empirical evidence and theoretical formulations presented in this report strongly suggest that, from the point of view of national policy, work plays a dominant role. This means that "trade-offs" might be made between work and these other concerns: i.e., the more that

[41] Blauner, Robert, *Alienation and Freedom: The Factory Worker and His Industry*, Chicago: University of Chicago Press, 1964.

[42] *Ibid.*

[43] See Chapter 2, Problems of American Workers, for a discussion of this phenomenon.

is done about work along the lines advocated in this report, the less that might have to be done about, say, medical care or public assistance or certain social programs for the aged.

It would be well to note, however, that acting on the trade-off potential will probably require a marked shift in perspective, particularly with regard to the lodgement of responsibility. If work is to become a lever for action, the responsibilities of employers, for example, would have to be greatly changed; they would no longer be considered as essentially producers of goods and services, but as actors who affect, and who in turn are affected by, the major institutions in society.

This shift in perspective may be highlighted through a contrast of industrial efficiency with "social efficiency." Other coinages would do equally well to illuminate the differences—for example, Willis Harman's "humanistic capitalism." [44] The contrast is between the narrow interest of producing goods and services and the broader interest of relating that production to other social concerns.

"Industrial efficiency" is here defined in its usual economic sense: the goal of an enterprise is to obtain the maximum output at a given level of costs (or a given level of output at a minimum cost). In optimizing costs and outputs, all substitutions ("trade-offs") are internal to the operation of the enterprise. Labor and capital—including intellectual, managerial, and the accumulation of skills, as well as physical capital—are substituted for one another to achieve efficiency for the firm, without regard to external effects.

"Social efficiency" draws on the economic notion of "externalities," which recognizes that the production of goods or services by a firm may result in costs or benefits that occur in society and which are not accounted for in the internal audit of any firm or all firms together. If the externalities are "diseconomies," the firm may be industrially efficient but socially inefficient. If the externalities result in social "economies," the firm may not be industrially efficient even though it is socially efficient. The social efficiency concept includes a variety of noneconomic social costs, such as the costs of social and political alienation. In the area of pollution control the concept has been used by the Federal Government in its attempts to have the industries responsible for pollution internalize some of the costs of cleaning the environment. The allocation of such social costs is a complex matter. In many cases, communities or societies choose to bear these costs in order that the industry may be able to continue to provide a valued service. But the need for sensitivity to the interrelations between social and industrial efficiency is increasingly being recognized by businessmen. A few far-sighted leaders even see that one depends on the other, and that businesses can sustain their long-run profitability by defraying many of the social as well as economic costs they incur.[45]

Some business leaders recognize that their firms capitalize on free or public goods and that it is their responsibility to replenish the public storehouse when they partake of its largesse. J. Irwin Miller of the Cummins Corporation says that "Every business is the beneficiary of services such as schools and government, and of enriching elements such as art and religion, which it did not pay for and without which it could not exist." [46] Other businessmen, such as Sidney Harman,

[44] Harman, Willis, "Key Choices of the Next Two Decades," address before the "White House Conference on the Industrial World Ahead," February 1972.
[45] Gooding, Judson, "The Fraying White Collar," *Fortune*, December 1970.
[46] *Ibid.*

President of Jervis Corporation, and Alfred J. Marrow, Chairman of the Board of the Harwood Companies, have expressed concern over the attitude of industry toward human capital. Harman writes

In addressing the question of the employer's obligations to society, to stockholders and workers, [the businessman] must see them as intricately interrelated. One cannot, in effect, serve society at all if he does not serve its people. One cannot serve shareholders effectively if he does not act to make business itself an agent for human growth and fulfillment. For, unless the businessman-employer . . . recognizes this as a minimal obligation, he will in the long run (and more likely in the short term) participate in the destruction of the very instrument from which stockholders draw nourishment.[47]

Harman goes on to say that "work satisfaction—which is to say the attainment of a sense of purposefulness in his or her work, the achievement of a sense of personal worth and dignity—should be seen as a fundamental right of employees, and therefore a fundamental obligation of employers." Furthermore, "the consistent implementations of this view throughout the business community is the most reliable assurance of the preservation and constructive development of the free enterprise system." [48]

Extension of Corporate Responsibility

While there is growing evidence that a sense of corporate responsibility for the larger efficiency of society is emerging, there are a large number of areas in which the responsibility could be increased or lodged for the first time. Occupational health and safety is a prime example.

In 1969 workmen's compensation, covering 84.5 percent of the labor force, paid out a total of $2.5 billion—$1.5 billion for disability, $875 million for medical benefits, and $185 million for survivors benefits.[49] The $3.2 billion in insurance premiums paid by employers represents some "internalization" of the social disadvantages of hazardous employment but only a small portion and, obviously, not enough.

The inadequacy is to be found not only in the need for the recently enacted special legislation and funding for black lung disease—an example of a failure of industry to internalize costs—nor only in the small amount of compensation relative to earning capacity but also in the increasing injury-frequency rate, the rising average days of disability per case, and the increasing severity rate, which has been the lot of a majority of occupations. In 1968 a total of 14,311 people died in industrial accidents, about the same as the number of American fatalities in Vietnam that year.[50]

In the same year, 90,000 workers suffered *permanent impairment* from industrial accidents, and a total of 2,100,000 suffered total but temporary disability. . . . In 1969, [exposures to industrial pollutants in the workplace] caused one million new cases of occupational disease. Among the casualties were 3,600 dead and over 800,000 cases of burns, lung and eye damage, dermatitis, and brain damage.[51]

If the social diseconomies of hazardous employment were fully internalized by industry, one would expect the injury and disease rates to decline, on the assumption that it would be worthwhile to reduce the contribution of this factor to industrial inefficiency. It is not obvious how

---

[47] Harman, Sidney, "Responsibilities of Businessmen," 1972 (Contributed paper).
[48] *Ibid.*
[49] U. S. Bureau of the Census, *Statistical Abstract of the United States: 1971.*
[50] Sexton, Patricia Cayo and Brendan Sexton, *Blue Collars and Hard Hats: The Working Class and the Future of American Politics,* New York: Random House, 1972.
[51] *Ibid.*

much industry should spend (either through legal enforcement of standards or out of a sense of responsibility) to reduce occupational hazards, but we cannot ignore the point that the failure to protect workers results in deaths, ruined lives, medical costs, public assistance, and other costs borne by individuals and society, not by industry.

We need only translate this social efficiency model to the less obvious problem that is a prime topic of this report—the effects of large-scale, bureaucratic and assembly-line forms of work organization on the mental and physical well-being of workers.

Occasionally, a news story will report that a worker has gone berserk as a result of the conditions of his work and has killed a co-worker. Recently, a jury refused to convict an employee who killed two foremen and another worker in an auto plant on the grounds of temporary insanity, when testimony pointed up inhumane working conditions.[52] One may also read that an assembly-line worker in an automobile plant finds it necessary to consume large quantities of whiskey at lunch to face the relentless assembly-line in the afternoon. To what extent have modern production methods spawned alcoholism and violence? And to what extent would the revitalization of planning and decision making among employees lead to greater mental and physical well-being?

The redesign of work, as this report spells out in detail, *can* lower such business costs as absenteeism, tardiness, turnover, labor disputes, sabotage, and poor quality, all of which is to the advantage of employers and consumers. The evidence suggests that meeting the higher needs of workers can, perhaps, increase productivity from 5% to 40%, the latter figure including the "latent" productivity of workers that is currently untapped.[53] Indeed, the potential gains in productivity are so impressive, it is very likely that the redesign of jobs must be accompanied by an equivalent effort to create jobs, if the commitment of all concerned—particularly labor unions—is to be obtained.

Our final instance of the difference between industrial and social efficiency pertains to the unemployed person, who, in the existing accounting system, is an "inefficient resource." Whether it is because of changes in demand or in production methods, it is not efficient to retain an employee whose marginal product is of less value than his earnings and the capital costs supporting his work.

In humanistic and social terms, however, no one is "inefficient," and modern societies, recognizing this, find it worthwhile to provide some assistance when one is unemployed. But the assistance is generally very little, and the mental and physical suffering from unemployment quite large. The social efficiency model would assert that there are always jobs that need to be done in society, that the costs of unemployment are too high to be tolerated, and it is for people that employment exists, not the other way around.

For society, the main benefits from an increase in both the quantity and quality of jobs will be in avoiding some of the very large costs now incurred by the present way we do business. These costs are not fully tallied in the annual reports of our corporations and bureaucracies; they are the costs of such job-related pathologies as political alienation, violent aggression against others, alcoholism and drug abuse, mental depression, an assortment of physical illnesses, inadequate performance in schools, and a larger number of welfare families than there need be. These costs are borne by the citizen and by society; they must be included in

---

[52] *Time* (Law Section), June 2, 1971.
[53] Walton, *op. cit.*

any systematic accounting of the costs and benefits of work in America. A precedent for this has been established in environmental policy; the precedent needs to be extended to social policy.

2. Problems of American Workers

No one model can serve as representative of the problems of "the American worker." There are many workers, and the problems of the workplace impinge on different categories of workers in many different ways. In this chapter some of the demographic complexities of an inadequate quantity or quality of jobs are explored from the perspectives of the following groups: blue-collar and white-collar workers and managers, and young, minority groups, female and elderly workers.

Blue-Collar Blues

The "blue-collar blues" is probably one of the most misunderstood social phenomena of our time. Sam Zagoria, the director of the Labor-Management Relations Service, offers an explanation for the blues that transcends "hard-hat" or political stereotypes:

I suspect that much of the current voter unhappiness "with things as they are" is directed not only to the political decisions and domestic tensions about which candidates and office-holders are speaking, but also to the dreary way in which many people spend their working days. . . .[1]

Work problems spill over from the factory into other activities of life: one frustrated assembly-line worker will displace his job-generated aggression on family, neighbors, and strangers, while a fellow worker comes home so fatigued

from his day's work that all he can do is collapse and watch television. The difference in reactions may only be a function of their ages, as this Studs Terkel interview with a steelworker illustrates:

You're at the tavern. About an hour or so?
Yeah. When I was single, I used to go into hillbilly bars, get in a lot of brawls. . . .
Why did you get in those brawls?
Just to explode. I just wanted to explode. . . .
You play with the kids . . . ?
When I come home, know what I do for the first 20 minutes? Fake it. I put on a smile. I don't feel like it. I got a kid three-and-a-half years old. Sometimes she says, Daddy, where've you been? And I say, work. I could've told her I'd been in Disneyland. What's work to a three-year-old? I feel bad, I can't take it out on the kid. Kids are born innocent of everything but birth. You don't take it out on the wife either. This is why you go to the tavern. You want to release it there rather than do it at home. What does an actor do when he's got a bad movie? I got a bad movie every day.[2]

A study in British Columbia concluded that a restrictive and narrow work environment "is a burden not easily dropped at the mill gates." For example, workers who had socially isolated jobs tended to be unable to integrate into community life.[3] Other studies show that leisure cannot fully compensate for a dissatisfying work situation.[4]

There is now convincing evidence that some blue-collar workers are carrying their work frustrations home and displacing them in extremist social and political movements or in hostility toward the government. For other workers apathy is the reaction to the same set of social circumstances. The symptoms of the blue-collar blues are part of the popular sociology in America. The middlemass, the hard-hats, the silent majority, the forgotten Amer-

---

[1] Letter to the *Washington Post* in 1972.
[2] Terkel, Studs, "A Steelworker Speaks," *Dissent*, Winter 1972.
[3] *Occupational Mental Health*, Vol. 1, No. 2, Winter 1971.
[4] Meissner, Martin, "The Long Arm of the Job: A Study of Work and Leisure," *Industrial Relations*, Vol. 10, October 1971.

icans, the Archie Bunkers as they have been variously called are characterized as alienated from their society, aggressive against people unlike themselves, distrusting of others, and harboring an inadequate sense of personal or political efficacy. Yet, contrary to popular opinion, Stanley E. Seashore and Thad J. Barnowe found that the blues are not confined to any one cohort—sex, age, income status, collar color, or any combination of these traits.[5] Rather, the blues are associated with the possessor's conditions of life at work. But adequate and equitable pay, reasonable security, safety, comfort, and convenience on the job do not insure the worker against the blues. The potent factors that impinge on the worker's values, according to Seashore and Barnowe, are those that concern his self-respect, a chance to perform well in his work, a chance for personal achievement and growth in competence, and a chance to contribute something personal and unique to his work.

Further evidence that political and social attitudes and behavior are related to work experiences and expectations comes from a recent study of blue-collar union members by Harold Sheppard.[6] He found that where aspirations relating to work are not realized, it is not uncommon to find a degree of bitterness and alienation among workers that is reflected in a reduced sense of political efficacy. These "alienated" workers tend to participate less in elections and, when they do vote, tend to cast their ballots for extremist or "protest" candidates. These dissatisfied workers are far more likely than satisfied workers to believe that the lot of the average person has been getting worse. They are more authoritarian in their views (they tend to prefer strong leaders to democratically developed laws). The key

variable in this study, as in the previously cited study, appears to be the nature of the tasks performed by the workers. For example, those workers with jobs that measure high on variety, autonomy, and use of skills were found to be low on measures of political and personal alienation.

An earlier study of 1,156 employed men revealed that the best independent predictors of work alienation are (1) a work situation and hierarchical organization that provide little discretion in pace and schedule, (2) a career that has been blocked and chaotic, and (3) a stage in the life cycle that puts the "squeeze" on the worker (large numbers of dependent children and low amounts of savings).[7]

These findings offer hope for positive action. Had it been, as most have felt, that the blues *were* strongly linked with such attributes as age, sex, class, collar color, race, or educational achievement, there would have been little opportunity for effective action to moderate the destructive elements of the blues. But fortunately, working conditions are far easier to change than demographic factors.

Furthermore, it appears that conditions in the workplace cannot be ignored when considering the requisite conditions for a politically healthy citizenry. As Robert Dahl states, if workers were to

discover that participation in the affairs of the enterprise . . . contributed to their own sense of competence and helped them to control an important part of their daily lives, then lassitude and indifference toward participation might change into interest and concern.[8]

The blue-collar blues, undoubtedly, have more than one well-spring of discontent. The economic squeeze, an inequitable tax system (for example, the propor-

---

[5] Seashore, Stanley E. and Barnowe, J. Thad, "Demographic and Job Factors Associated with the 'Blue-Collar Blues,'" mimeographed, 1972.

[6] Sheppard and Herrick, *op. cit.*

[7] Wilensky, *op. cit.*

[8] Dahl, Robert, *After the Revolution?* New Haven: Yale University Press, 1970.

tion of earned income paid in social security and sales taxes is higher for blue-collar workers than for workers in higher income groups), the erosion of neighborhoods, and the decline in municipal services are real and tangible blue-collar grievances. But genuine alleviation of the blues is unlikely without changes in the quality of working life for middle-Americans. To accomplish these changes we must first identify clearly the *special* problems of workers. One of these work-related problems appears to be that the blue-collar worker sees his mobility and his children's mobility blocked.

Worker Mobility. Many blue-collar workers do not believe that there is a great deal of opportunity to move up the ladder of success, and the lack of alternatives produces frustration. Robert Quinn has shown statistically that both job satisfaction and mental health are poorer when a worker feels "locked-in" to his job.[9] Workers who feel there is little opportunity for mobility within their work organization, or little control over their job assignments, or little probability of getting another job elsewhere, characteristically suffer from tension, job dissatisfaction, and mental health problems.

Workers also are no longer confident that education provides a key to advancement. Robert Schrank and Susan Stein have claimed that whites who are blue-collar workers: (1) see the attack on the relevance of schools as an attack on their and their children's chances to "make it"; (2) feel that their school is being used for experiments in desegregation and are bitter that through compensatory education blacks are leap-frogging steps to ad-

vancement that they are still required to take; and (3) are frustrated by the fact that employers have raised the credential requirements for better jobs faster than they can gain them.[10]

Moreover, the impact of technology has been acutely felt by the blue-collar worker—not necessarily because it puts him out of a job, but because it lowers his status and satisfaction from the job. Schrank and Stein highlight the interplay between education and technology in the lives of blue-collar workers:

Knowledge, not skill, is the critical factor in modern technology. For example, a craftsman who can square off a piece of steel with a hand file may be a true artisan; but his artisanship is useless on a numerically controlled machine tool which needs someone who understands a system.[11]

Another major change that has been linked to the blues is the new composition of the blue-collar labor force. Traditionally, the ranks were filled by new European immigrants as the children of the old immigrants moved into white-collar jobs. Now, with unskilled immigration from Europe at an ebb, the children of blue-collar workers (both men and women) are becoming a second (or third) generation of blue-collar workers. This is an important factor in the recent increase in the blues, for working-class culture (like that of the middle class) dictates that people should be constantly improving their standard of living—children should do better materially than their parents.[12] This does not mean that the blue-collar worker's goal is to become an upper-middle-class intellectual. Rather, it is a reflection of the fact that a setback

[9] Quinn, Robert P., "Locking-in As a Moderator of the Relationship Between Job Satisfaction and Mental Health," Survey Research Center, University of Michigan, 1972.

[10] Schrank, Robert and Susan Stein, "Yearning, Learning and Status," in Sar A. Levitan, ed., *The Blue-Collar Workers: A Symposium on Middle America*, New York: McGraw-Hill, 1971.

[11] *Ibid.*

[12] This can be supported by Sheppard and Herrick's (*op. cit.*) study that showed young workers *in the same jobs* as older workers *with equal pay* to be less satisfied.

—to a worse job, to a smaller house, or to an older car—is a serious threat to those who have lived with the possibility of unemployment and failure. To follow in Dad's footsteps into the factory, then, is only acceptable if things are clearly much better there than they were for Dad.

Young blue-collar workers also are better educated than their parents. In 1960, 26% of white and 14% of black craftsmen and operatives had completed four years of high school. By 1969, 41% of whites and 29% of blacks in those jobs had completed a secondary education.[13] When we recall that decisive factors in job dissatisfaction are monotony, decreased chances for learning, and little need for exercising judgment and place these alongside the fact that blue-collar workers are better educated than ever before, we begin to see one of the real causes of their blues. These better-educated workers, quite clearly, are not so easily satisfied as their forebears with the quality of most blue-collar jobs—a fact verified by the Survey of Working Conditions.

Society's View of the Manual Worker. We must also recognize that manual work has become increasingly denigrated by the upper middle class of this nation. The problems of self-esteem inherent in these changing attitudes are further compounded by the impact of the communications media. For example, the images of blue-collar workers that are presented by the media (including school textbooks) are often negative. Workers are presented as "hard-hats" (racists or authoritarians) or as "fat cats" (lazy plumbers who work only twenty-hour weeks yet earn $400.00 a week). The view of the worker in the mass media is that he is the problem, not that he *has* problems.

Today, there is virtually no accurate dramatic representation—as there was in the 1930's—of men and women in working-class occupations. Instead, we have recently had the movie *Joe* and the television series about Archie Bunker. These stereotypes—ignoring the heterogeneity of blue-collar workers—do little to enhance the dignity of the worker or his job. For example, what does Archie do on the job? Is he ashamed of his job? Is that why he won't talk about it at home? Certainly, if he worked in an office we would see scenes of him at work. The negative view of blue-collar work on the show is reinforced by the fact that Archie's "socially enlightened" son-in-law is a future professional.

Research shows that less than one character in ten on television is a blue-collar worker, and these few are usually portrayed as crude people with undesirable social traits. Furthermore, portrayals tend to emphasize class stereotypes: lawyers are clever, while construction workers are louts. But it is not only the self-image of the worker that is being affected; television is conveying to children superficial and misleading information about work in society.[14] If children do, indeed, learn from television, they will "learn" that professionals lead lives of carefree leisure, interspersed with drama and excitement (never hard work), and that blue-collar workers are racist clods who use bad grammar and produce little of use for society.

The ramifications of the low societal view of the worker are extensive and related to the personal problems of workers: low self-esteem, alcoholism, and withdrawal from community affairs. Our interviews with blue-collar workers revealed an almost overwhelming sense of inferiority: the worker cannot talk proudly

---

[13] Schrank and Stein, *op. cit.*

[14] DeFleur, Melvin, "Occupational Roles As Portrayed on Television," *Public Opinion Quarterly*, Vol. 28, No. 57, 1964.

to his children about his job, and many workers feel that they must apologize for their status. Thus, the working-class home may be permeated with an atmosphere of failure—even of depressing self-degradation. This problem of esteem and identity is, perhaps, related to the recent rise in ethnic consciousness among the working class.

Statistical evidence indicates that the working class is composed heavily of Americans who identify themselves as "ethnics." In 1969, 46 million Americans identified themselves as members of some specific ethnic group; over 20 million of these people were in families earning between $5,000 and $10,000 a year.[15] The revival in ethnic identity has occurred mainly among second and third generation Polish, Italian, and Slavic workers in this income group. This "return" to ethnicity (the parents of these workers never abandoned their traditional roots) has occurred mainly in large, industrial, Northern cities—principally in Chicago, Detroit, Pittsburgh, Philadelphia, New York, and Boston. Significantly, working-class "ethnics" in these cities tend to hold jobs that are not intrinsically satisfying—jobs in heavy industry (steel, autos) which have low prestige, low autonomy, and little opportunity for growth. Thus, trapped in jobs that do not offer a high degree of self-esteem, many of these workers appear to have turned to their ethnic groups for a healthy self-concept. The clan, the tribe, or the ethnic group offers unquestioning acceptance and membership as it shields the individual from assaults on his self-esteem. In summary, the critical variable in ethnic discontent may be the nature of the jobs held by these workers.

White-Collar Privileges. Blue-collar discontent is exacerbated by distinctions between blue-collar and white-collar privileges on the job. For example, the blue-collar worker must punch time clocks, making it difficult for him to arrange his work schedule to manage such personal chores as visiting the doctor, getting his car repaired, and visiting the school to discuss his children's problems. More basically, 27% of all workers have no paid vacations, 40% have no sick leave,[16] and perhaps 70% will never receive a private pension check (even though large percentages may be employed in firms with pension plans).[17] Virtually all of those workers who are without these benefits are found among the ranks of non-professionals.

A problem related to management privileges is the general feeling among workers that their bosses abuse their disciplinary prerogatives, and that their unions do not challenge such "abuses." They often claim that work rules, particularly in the auto industry, are similar to military discipline. Some younger, more educated workers are even beginning to question the constitutionality of punishment at work without due process. For example, in some industries supervisors have the right to send offending workers home and dock their salaries for the time they were not permitted to work. Many such arbitrary dismissals occur when young, better-educated workers come into conflict with older, less-educated foremen, who rose to their job in a more authoritarian age. Other instances are due to unclear work rules. An autoworker explains his conflict with authority:

I'm a relief man and there's a lot of jobs I used to relieve that used to be easy, but now they're hard and sometimes you can't do everything, you know. And then the foreman comes up there and starts nagging you—you tell him you can't keep up with it. You can't

---

[15] U.S. Bureau of the Census, *Characteristics of the Population by Ethnic Origin*, 1970.
[16] Whiting, Basil, *The Suddenly Remembered American*, draft, Ford Foundation, 1971.
[17] *Wall Street Journal*, December 3, 1971, p. 4.

keep up with it and he still keeps nagging you and nagging you. And they have a lot of dual supervision out there now, where you got one foreman, your foreman who's supposed to tell you what to do, and then they got another foreman who comes along and tells you what to do. And that's not right—it gets confused.

Perhaps the most consistent complaint reported to our task force has been the failure of bosses to listen to workers who wish to propose better ways of doing their jobs. Workers feel that their bosses demonstrate little respect for their intelligence. Supervisors are said to feel that the workers are incapable of thinking creatively about their jobs.

In summary, the cause of the blue-collar blues is not bigotry, the demand for more money, or a changing work ethic. An autoworker explains the real genesis of the blues:

If you were in a plant you'd see—everybody thinks that General Motors workers have it easy, but it's not that easy. Some jobs you go home after eight hours and you're tired, your back is sore and you're sweatin'. All the jobs ain't that easy. We make good money; yeah, the money is real good out there, but that ain't all of it—cause there's really a lot of bad jobs out there.

Schrank hypothesizes that blue-collar blues "result from rising expectations of status and mobility and the apparent inability of the system to deliver." [18] But we believe that the system can deliver. The proposals we make later in this report for portable pensions, continuing education and retraining for workers, and for the redesign of work tasks are proper responses to the real problems of blue-collar workers. To do otherwise treats the symptoms, not the causes, of the blues. Great care, then, must be taken to interpret wisely the signs of discontent among workers. Increased industrial sabotage and sudden wildcat strikes, like the one at

Lordstown, portend something more fundamental than the desire for more money. Allegiance to extremist political movements may mean something other than hatred of those of another color.

White-Collar Woes

The auto industry is the *locus classicus* of dissatisfying work; the assembly line, its quintessential embodiment. But what is striking is the extent to which the dissatisfaction of the assembly-line and blue-collar worker is mirrored in white-collar and even managerial positions. The office today, where work is segmented and authoritarian, is often a factory. For a growing number of jobs, there is little to distinguish them but the color of the worker's collar: computer keypunch operations and typing pools share much in common with the automobile assembly-line.

Secretaries, clerks, and bureaucrats were once grateful for having been spared the dehumanization of the factory. White-collar jobs were rare; they had higher status than blue-collar jobs. But today the clerk, and not the operative on the assembly-line, is the typical American worker, and such positions offer little in the way of prestige. Furthermore, the size of the organizations that employ the bulk of office workers has grown, imparting to the clerical worker the same impersonality that the blue-collar worker experiences in the factory. The organization acknowledges the presence of the worker only when he makes a mistake or fails to follow a rule, whether in factory or bureaucracy, whether under public or private control. As Simone Weil wrote

For the bureaucratic machine, though composed of flesh, and well-fed flesh at that, is nonetheless as irresponsible and as soulless as are machines made of iron and steel.[19]

[18] Schrank and Stein, *op. cit.*
[19] Weil, Simone, *The Need for Roots*, 1952.

In a report on *The Quality of Working Life,* prepared for NATO, N. A. B. Wilson wrote

Lack of positive feedback and feeling of connection between the individual worker and the centers where decisions affecting him are made are inevitable to some degree in any large organization, but there is every reason to believe that they are especial hazards in government departments.[20]

Traditionally, lower-level white-collar jobs in both government and industry were held by high school graduates. Today, an increasing number of these jobs go to those who have attended college. But the demand for higher academic credentials has not increased the prestige, status, pay, or difficulty of the job. For example, the average weekly pay for clerical workers in 1969 was $105.00 per week, while blue-collar production workers were taking home an average of $130.00 per week.[21] It is not surprising, then, that the Survey of Working Conditions found much of the greatest work dissatisfaction in the country among young, well-educated workers who were in low-paying, dull, routine, and fractionated clerical positions. Other signs of discontent among this group include turnover rates as high as 30% annually and a 46% increase in white-collar union membership between 1958 and 1968.[22] A 1969 study of 25,000 white-collar employees in eighty-eight major companies showed a decline in the percentage of positive responses concerning several key factors of job satisfaction since 1965. For example, there was a 34% decline in the belief that their company would act to do

something about their individual problems.[23] These changing attitudes (and the failure of employers to react constructively to them) may be affecting the productivity of these workers: a survey conducted by a group of management consultants of a cross-section of office employees found that they were producing at only 55% of their potential. Among the reasons cited for this was boredom with repetitive jobs.[24]

Loyalty to employer was once high among this group of workers who felt that they shared much in common with their bosses—collar color, tasks, place of work. Today, many white-collar workers have lost personal touch with decision makers, and, consequently, they feel estranged from the goals of the organizations in which they work. Management has exacerbated this problem by viewing white-collar workers as expendable: because their productivity is hard to measure and their functions often non-essential, they are seen as the easiest place to "cut fat" during low points in the business cycle. Today, low-level white-collar workers are more likely to be sacrificed for the sake of short-term profitability than are blue-collar workers.

•   •   •

The Young Worker— Challenging the Work Ethic?

More than any other group, it appears that young people have taken the lead in demanding better working conditions. Out

[20] Wilson, N. A. B., "The Quality of Working Life: A Personal Report to the NATO Committee on Challenges of Modern Society," 1971.

[21] Gooding, Judson, *op. cit.*

[22] *Ibid.*

[23] *Ibid.*

[24] Stetson, Damon, "For Many Concerns: An Inadvertent 4-Day Week," *New York Times,* May 14, 1972.

[NOTE: Footnotes 25 to 29 occur in a section "Managerial Discontent," which has been omitted in this reprinting. Ed.]

of a workforce of more than 85 million, 22½ million are under the age of 30. As noted earlier, these young workers are more affluent and better educated than their parents were at their age. Factually, that is nearly all that can be generalized about this group. But it is asserted by such authors as Kenneth Keniston, Theodore Roszak, Charles Reich, and others, that great numbers of young people in this age group are members of a counter-culture. The President's Commission on Campus Unrest wrote that this subculture "found its identity in a rejection of the work ethic, materialism, and conventional social norms and pieties." Many writers have stressed the alleged revolt against work, "a new 'anti-work ethic' . . . a new, deep-seated rejection by the young of the traditional American faith in hard work." [30] But empirical findings do not always support the impressionistic commentaries.

It is commonly agreed that there is a difference between the in-mode behavior of youth and their real attitudes. Many young people do wear beads, listen to rock music, and occasionally smoke pot, but few actually live in communes (and these few may be working very hard), and even fewer are so alienated that they are unwilling to play a productive role in society. Daniel Yankelovich conducted national attitude studies of college students from 1968 to 1971 and found that two-thirds of college students profess mainstream views in general.[31] But their feelings in particular about work (and private business) are even more affirmative:

• 79% believe that commitment to a meaningful career is a very important part of a person's life.
• 85% feel business is entitled to make a profit.

• 75% believe it is morally wrong to collect welfare when you can work.
• Only 30% would welcome less emphasis on working hard.

While student feelings about work itself are generally high, Yankelovich found that attitudes towards authority are changing rapidly. In 1968 over half (56%) of all students indicated that they did not mind the future prospect of being "bossed around" on the job. By 1971 only one out of three students (36%) saw themselves willingly submitting to such authority. Equally important, while 86% of these students still believe that society needs some legally based authority to prevent chaos, they nevertheless see a distinction between this necessity and an authoritarian work setting.

Rising Expectations. Yankelovich also found a shift in student opinion on the issue that "hard work will always pay off" from a 69% affirmation in 1968 to a 39% affirmation in 1971. This certainly was, in part, indicative of the conditions in the job market for college graduates in 1971. But more basically, we believe, it highlights a paradox inherent in a populace with increasing educational achievement. Along with the mass media, education and its credentials are raising expectations faster than the economic system can meet them. Much of what is interpreted as anti-work attitudes on the part of youth, then, may be their appraisal of the kinds of jobs that are open to them.

The following case study of a young woman who is a recent college graduate illustrates the gap between expectations and reality:

I didn't go to school for four years to type. I'm bored; continuously humiliated. They sent me to Xerox school for three hours. . . . I realize that I sound cocky, but after you've been in the academic world, after

[30] *Economist*, April 30, 1972.
[31] Yankelovich, Daniel, *The Changing Values on Campus: Political and Personal Attitudes on Campus*, New York: Washington Square Press, 1972.

you've had your own class (as a student teacher) and made your own plans, and someone tries to teach you to push a button —you get pretty mad. They even gave me a goldplated plaque to show I've learned how to use the machine.[32]

The problem is compounded by the number of students who are leaving school with advanced degrees, like the young Chicago lawyer in the following case:

You can't wait to get out and get a job that will let you do something that's really important. . . . You think you're one of the elite. Then you go to a place like the Loop and there are all these lawyers, accountants, etc., and you realize that you're just a lawyer. No, not even a lawyer—an employee; you have to check in at nine and leave at five. I had lots of those jobs—summers—where you punch in and punch out. You think it's going to be different but it isn't. You're in the rut like everybody else.[33]

Today's youth are expecting a great deal of intrinsic reward from work. Yankelovich found that students rank the opportunity to "make a contribution," "job challenge," and the chance to find "self-expression" at the top of the list of influences on their career choice. A 1960 survey of over 400,000 high school students was repeated for a representative sample in 1970, and the findings showed a marked shift from the students valuing job security and opportunity for promotion in 1960 to valuing "freedom to make my own decisions" and "work that seems important to me" in 1970.[34]

Many of these student findings were replicated in the Survey of Working Conditions sample of young workers. For example, it seems as true of young workers as it is of students that they expect a great deal of fulfillment from work. But the Survey findings show that young workers are not deriving a great deal of satisfaction from the work they are doing. Less than a quarter of young workers reply "very often" when asked the question, "How often do you feel you leave work with a good feeling that you have done something particularly well?"

Age Group	Percentage Answering "Very Often"
Under 20	23
21–29	25
30–44	38
45–64	43
65 and over	53

Other findings document that young workers place more importance on the value of interesting work and their ability to grow on the job than do their elders. They also place less importance than do older workers on such extrinsic factors as security and whether or not they are asked to do excessive amounts of work. But the Survey documents a significant gap between the expectations or values of the young workers and what they actually experience on the job. Young workers rate their jobs lower than do older workers on how well their jobs actually live up to the factors they most sought in work. For example, the young value challenging work highly but say that the work they are doing has a low level of challenge.

It has also been found that a much higher percentage of younger than older workers feel that management emphasizes the *quantity* more than the *quality* of their work. Furthermore, it is shown that this adversely affects the satisfaction of younger workers. Such findings contradict the viewpoint that there is a weakening of the "moral fiber" of youth.[35]

[32] Starr, Joyce, "Adaptation to the Working World," 1972 (Contributed paper).
[33] *Ibid.*
[34] *Project Talent: Progress in Education, A Sample Survey*, American Institutes for Research, 1971.
[35] Sheppard and Herrick, *op. cit.*

Many young union members are challenging some basic assumptions about "a fair day's work for a fair day's pay." In the past, unions concerned themselves with establishing what a fair day's pay would be, while the employer's prerogative was to determine what constitutes a fair day's work. Young workers are now challenging both unions and management by demanding a voice in the setting of both standards, as the following case illustrates

Three young workers, aged twenty and twenty-one, were hired to clean offices at night. One evening the foreman caught one of the young janitors (who went to school during the day) doing his homework; another was reading the paper and the third was asleep with his feet up on a desk. The foreman exploded and gave them a written warning. The workers filed a grievance protesting the warnings: "We cleaned all the offices in five hours by really hustling and who the hell should get upset because we then did our own thing." One young worker said, "At school during study period I get my studies done in less than the hour and no one bugs me when I do other things for the rest of the time. We cleaned all those offices in five hours instead of eight. What more do they want?"

The union steward said he tried hard to understand what they were saying: "But the company has the right to expect eight hours work for eight hours pay. I finally got the kids to understand by taking them outside and telling them that if they got the work finished in five hours, then the company would either give them more work, or get rid of one of them. They're spacing it out nicely now and everyone's happy," he said, satisfied to have settled the grievance within the understood rules.[36]

The author of this study writes that the young workers were far from satisfied with the agreement. They wanted the

union to establish what had to be done and how much they would be paid to do it, and then they wanted the same freedom that professionals have to decide how to operate within the time and work frame allotted.

In summary, we interpret these various findings not as demonstrating a shift away from valuing work *per se* among young people, but as a shift away from their willingness to take on meaningless work in authoritarian settings that offers only extrinsic rewards. We agree with Willis Harman that:

The shape of the future will no more be patterned after the hippie movement and the Youth Revolution than the Industrial Age could have been inferred from the "New Age" values of the Anabaptists.[37]

New Values. A mistake is made, however, if one believes that the new attitudes toward authority and the meaning of work are limited to hippies. Judson Gooding writes that young managers, both graduates of business schools and executive trainees, "reflect the passionate concerns of youth in the 1970's—for individuality, openness, humanism, concern and change—and they are determined to be heard." [38]

Some young people are rejecting the corporate or bureaucratic worlds, while not rejecting work or the concept of work or profit. Gooding tells of one young former executive who quit his job with a major corporation because

You felt like a small cog. Working there was dehumanizing and the struggle to get to the top didn't seem worth it. They made no effort to encourage your participation. The decisions were made in those rooms with closed doors. . . . The serious error they made with me was not giving me a glimpse of the big picture from time to time, so I

[36] Haynes, John, "The New Workers: A Report," *New Generation*, Vol. 52, No. 4, Fall 1972.

[37] Harman, *op. cit.*

[38] Gooding, Judson, "The Accelerated Generation Moves Into Management," *Fortune*, March 1971.

could go back to my little detail, understanding how it related to the whole.[39]

This young man has now organized his own small business and designed his own job. As the publisher of a counter-culture newspaper, he might be considered a radical in his beliefs and life style, yet he says "profit is not an evil." Of course, many young workers do question the *use* of profits, especially those profits that they feel are made at the expense of society or the environment. Some businesses themselves are adopting this same attitude.

It may be useful to analyze the views of today's youth not in terms of their parents' values but in terms of the beliefs of their grandparents. Today's youth believe in independence, freedom, and risk—in short, they may have the entrepreneurial spirit of early capitalism. Certainly they are more attracted to small and growing companies, to small businesses and to handicrafts, than to the bureaucracy, be it privately or publicly owned. (The declining opportunity for such small-scale endeavors [documented in Chapter 1] probably contributes to both the job dissatisfaction of the young and their apparent lack of commitment to the kinds of jobs that are available.) On the other hand, their parents share a managerial ethic that reflects the need for security, order, and dependence that is born of hard times. Of course, this is being a bit unfair to the older generation and a bit over-generous with our youth, but it serves to get us away from the simplistic thinking that the "Protestant ethic has been abandoned." Who in America ever had the Protestant ethic and when? Did we have it in the thirties? Did the poor people or even middle-class people ever have it? It is argued by Sebastian

de Grazia that the Protestant ethic was never more than a myth engendered by the owner and managerial classes to motivate the lower working class—a myth which the latter never fully accepted.[40] Clearly, it is difficult to measure the past allegiance of a populace to an ideology.

But we *can* measure the impact of the present work environment on youth's motivation to work. For example, the Survey of Working Conditions found that youth seem to have a lower attachment to work than their elders on the same job. There are several reasons other than a change in the work ethic why this might be so. *First,* as we have already posited, young people have high expectations generated by their greater education. *Second,* their greater affluence makes them less tolerant of unrewarding jobs. *Third,* many new workers, particularly women, are voluntary workers. They are more demanding because they don't *have* to take a job. *Fourth,* all authority in our society is being challenged—professional athletes challenge owners, journalists challenge editors, consumers challenge manufacturers, the moral authority of religion, nation, and elders is challenged. *Fifth,* many former students are demanding what they achieved in part on their campuses a few years ago—a voice in setting the goals of the organization. The lecture has been *passé* for several years on many campuses—in colloquia and in seminars students challenge teachers. Managers are now facing the products of this progressive education. (One wonders what will happen when the children of today's open classroom, who have been taught to set their own goals and plan their own schedules, enter the workforce.)[41] *Sixth,* young blue-collar workers, who have grown up in an environment in

---

[39] *Ibid.*

[40] de Grazia, Sebastian, *Of Time, Work, and Leisure*, New York: The Twentieth Century Fund, 1962.

[41] See Chap. 5 in *Work in America* for a further discussion of this point.

which equality is called for in all institutions, are demanding the same rights and expressing the same values as university graduates. *Seventh,* there is growing professionalism among many young white-collar workers. They now have loyalty to their peer group or to their task or discipline, where once they had loyalty to their work organization.

In sum, it does not appear that young workers have a lower commitment to work than their elders. The problem lies in the interaction between work itself and the changing social character of today's generation, and in the failure of decision makers in business, labor, and government to recognize this fact.

The young worker is in revolt not against work but against the authoritarian system developed by industrial engineers who felt that "the worker was stupid, overly emotional . . . insecure and afraid of responsibility." [42] This viewpoint is summed up in Frederick Taylor's classic dictum to the worker:

For success, then, let me give one simple piece of advice beyond all others. Every day, year in and year out, each man should ask himself, over and over again, two questions. First, "What is the name of the man I am now working for?" and having answered this definitely, then, "What does this man want me to do, right now?"

The simplistic authoritarianism in this statement would appear ludicrous to the young worker who is not the uneducated and irresponsible person on whom Taylor's system was premised. Yet, many in industry continue to support a system of motivation that was created in an era when people were willing to be motivated by the stick. As an alternative to this approach, many personnel managers have offered the carrot as a motivator, only to find that young people also fail to respond to this approach.

From our reading of what youth wants, it appears that under current policies, employers may not be able to motivate young workers at all. Instead, employers must create conditions in which the worker can motivate himself. This concept is not as strange as it seems. From biographies of artists, athletes, and successful businessmen, one finds invariably that these people set goals for *themselves*. The most rewarding race is probably one that one runs against oneself. Young people seem to realize this. They talk less positively than do their elders about competition with others. But they do talk about self-actualization and other "private" values. Yankelovich found that 40% of students—an increasing percentage—do not believe that "competition encourages excellence," and 80% would welcome more emphasis in the society on self-expression.

Compared to previous generations, the young person of today wants to measure his improvement against a standard he sets for himself. (Clearly, there is much more inner-direction than David Riesman would have predicted two decades ago.) The problem with the way work is organized today is that it will not allow the worker to realize his own goals. Because of the legacy of Taylorism, organizations set a fixed standard for the worker, but they often do not tell him clearly why that standard was set or how it was set. More often than not, the standard is inappropriate for the worker. And, in a strange contradiction to the philosophy of efficient management, the organization seldom gives the worker the wherewithal to achieve the standard. It is as if the runner did not know where the finish line was; the rules make it a race that no worker can win.

It is problematic whether the intolerance among young workers of such poor

---

[42] Quoted in Paul Campanis, "You Are What You Work At," 1972 (Commissioned paper).

management signals temporary or enduring changes in the work ethic. More important is how management and society will reckon with the new emphasis that the workplace should lose its authoritarian aura and become a setting for satisfying and self-actualizing activity.

QUESTIONS

1. What is the function and role of work in our society? How do people differ in the meaning they attach to work?
2. Some authorities contend that there have been relatively recent shifts in prevailing attitudes toward work. Explain this point of view.
3. What is meant by a "social efficiency model"?
4. What factors contribute to dissatisfactions of blue-collar workers? Of white-collar? Of young workers?
5. In many respects the lot of American blue- and white-collar workers has improved substantially over the past 30 years. This is certainly true with respect to wages and fringe benefits. Yet we hear much more about worker alienation today than we did several years ago. Why is this so?

6.

Job Satisfaction: A Union Response

WILLIAM W. WINPISINGER

After some years of seeking legislative alternatives to collective bargaining, plus even more years of academic discussion and debate on the pros and cons of union responsibilities in relation to public rights, it now appears that labor's good friends in government, intellectual and academic circles have discovered an interesting new malady. They've already provided it with a name, a diagnosis and even a cure.

The name is the "blue-collar blues." The diagnosis is that because younger workers are brighter and better educated than their fathers they refuse to accept working conditions that past generations took for granted. The cure consists of a shot of psychic penicillin known as job enrichment.

There can be little doubt as to the existence of a rising tide of dissatisfaction, or alienation, among those who are increasingly and even sneeringly referred to as the Archie Bunkers of America.

Employers feel it in more absenteeism, more turnover and more strikes over working conditions. Politicians feel it in the perceptible shift of blue-collar workers from the principles of the New Deal to the philosophy of George Wallace. Unions feel it in the rising level of contract rejections and the growing number of defeats suffered by long-established business representatives and officers in union elections.

Just a couple of months ago *Time* magazine, in an essay on the work ethic, noted that according to a Gallup poll taken in 1971, 19 percent of all workers expressed dissatisfaction with their jobs. This was viewed with some pessimism by the learned editors of the magazine. If they had chosen to be optimistic they could just as validly have noted that 81 percent of all workers seem to be satisfied with their jobs.

There is, of course, no way to prove it but I feel reasonably certain that at no time in the entire history of man would Gallup have found 100 percent happiness and job satisfaction in the labor force. I doubt if 100 percent of the ancient Egyptians who built the pyramids, or 100 percent of the medieval craftsmen who constructed the great cathedrals, or 100 percent of the 19th century Irishmen who

Reprinted from the *AFL-CIO American Federationist*, Vol. 80, No. 2 (February 1973), pp. 8–10, by permission of the publisher.

William W. Winpisinger is a vice-president of the International Association of Machinists and Aerospace Workers.

laid the tracks for American railroads were so filled with job satisfaction that they consistently whistled while they worked.

The right to bitch about the job, or the boss, or the system, or even the union, is one of the inalienable rights of a free workforce. Whether workers today are generally happier than those in the so-called good old days is not provable one way or the other. Some claim the increasing atomization of work processes and the mind-deadening monotony of the modern assembly line cannot help but lead to anything except increasing alienation in the workforce. And yet the assembly line has been with us for a long time. The concept of the robotized worker, endlessly repeating one function, tightening the same bolt over and over, was already well established long before Charlie Chaplin satirized it in the movie *Modern Times* more than 40 years ago.

Strangely enough, Gallup's polls on worker dissatisfaction, which were started in 1949, consistently registered slow but steady increases in the level of worker satisfaction right up to 1969. Though workers throughout the 1950s and 1960s were never really affluent in the Galbraithian sense, they were making progress. On the whole, jobs were plentiful and the gap between what the average production worker earned and what the Bureau of Labor Statistics said he needed for a "modest but adequate" standard of living was narrowing. But then between 1969 and 1971 the overall rate of job satisfaction, according to Gallup, fell 6 percent. If this decrease were due to some substantial change in the nature of the jobs that people did I would have to agree with those who prescribe job enrichment as the answer to worker dissatisfaction.

Don't get me wrong. I am not opposed to efforts by management or industrial psychologists to make assembly-line jobs less monotonous and more fulfilling. But the point is—and it may not be too palatable to some in management or government or academic circles—that just as job dissatisfaction in the workplace yielded to trade union solutions in the past, such dissatisfaction can be decreased to the extent that trade union solutions are applied today.

One of the reasons that worker satisfaction declined in the late 1960s and early 1970s is that worker income, in relation to inflation and taxation and the purchasing power of the dollar that was earned by labor, also declined.

Because of government policies leading to rising unemployment, establishing one-sided controls on wages and permitting multinational corporations to export thousands of American jobs to Hong Kong, Taiwan and other low-wage areas, the gap between what the average worker earns and what his family needs for a decent standard of living has been growing. So it should come as no surprise to anyone that worker dissatisfaction is also growing.

The recent rash of strikes and other labor problems at the General Motors plant in Lordstown, Ohio, has been seized upon by those who write articles for learned journals as proof that even if the nature of the assembly line hasn't changed, the workforce has. As every student of industrial relations knows, the overwhelming majority of the workforce at Lordstown is young. On the basis of management's unhappy experiences with these kids, the experts have solemnly proclaimed the discovery of a new kind of workforce. They inform us that here is a generation that has never known a depression and thus has no interest in security; that grew up in a time of crass materialism and thus rejects the work ethic; that has been infected by the rebellion of youth and thus has no respect for authority. I have seen one scholarly analysis, in fact, that compares the "rebellion" at Lordstown in the early 1970s with the free speech movement at Berkeley in the early 1960s. And the conclusion was drawn that the nation's factories, like her colleges, would never be the same again.

Quite frankly, I submit that that kind of analysis overlooks one salient fact. The young workers at Lordstown were reacting against the same kind of grievances, in the same kind of way, as did generations of workers before them. They were rebelling against an obvious speedup; protesting safety violations; and reacting against working conditions that have been unilaterally imposed by a management that was determined to get tough in the name of efficiency. Anyone who thinks wildcats or slowdowns or even sabotage started at Lordstown doesn't know very much about the history of the American labor movement.

An almost identical series of incidents took place over much the same issues at Norwood, Ohio, at almost the same time but very few inferences were drawn about the changing nature of the workforce because, in this case, it was older workers who were involved.

Many people, including President Nixon, are viewing the decline of the work ethic in the United States with alarm. On the basis of my experience, which includes many day-to-day contacts with rank-and-file members of the Machinists, I can assure you that the work ethic is alive and well and living in a lot of good work places.

But what the aerospace workers and auto mechanics and machinists and airline mechanics and production workers we represent want, in the way of job satisfaction, is a wage that is commensurate with their skill.

If you want to enrich the job, enrich the pay check. The better the wage, the greater the job satisfaction. There is no better cure for the "blue-collar blues."

If you want to enrich the job, begin to decrease the number of hours a worker has to labor in order to earn a decent standard of living. Just as the increased productivity of mechanized assembly lines made it possible to decrease the workweek from 60 to 40 hours a couple of generations ago, the time has come to translate the increased productivity of automated processes into the kind of enrichment that comes from shorter workweeks, longer vacations and earlier retirements.

If you want to enrich the job, do something about the nerve-shattering noise, the heat and the fumes that are deafening, poisoning and destroying the health of American workers. Thousands of chemicals whose effect on humans has never been tested are being used in workplaces. Companies are willing to spend millions advertising quieter refrigerators or washing machines but are reluctant to spend one penny to provide a reasonably safe level of noise in their plants. And though we are now supposed to have a law that protects working people against some of the more obvious occupational hazards, industry is already fighting to undermine enforcement and the Nixon Administration has gone along with them by cutting the funds that are needed to make it effective.

If you want to enrich the jobs of the men and women who manufacture the goods that are needed for the functioning of our industrialized society, the time has come to re-evaluate the snobbery that makes it noble to possess a college degree and shameful to learn skills that involve a little bit of grease under the fingernails. The best way to undermine a worker's morale and decrease his satisfaction with himself and his job is to make him feel that society looks down on him because he wears blue coveralls instead of a white collar. I think it is ironic that because of prevailing attitudes many kinds of skilled craftsmen are in short supply while thousands of college graduates are tripping over one another in search of jobs.

Some of the most dissatisfied people I know are those who got a college degree and then couldn't find a position that lived up to their expectations. And that has been especially true the last few years. A lot of college-trained people are driving cabs today; they would have had a lot more job satisfaction and made a lot more money if they had apprenticed as auto mechanics.

If you want to enrich the job, give working people a greater sense of control over their working conditions. That's what they and their unions were seeking in the early 1960s when management was automating and retooling on a large scale. That's why we asked for advance consultation when employers intended to make major job changes. That's why we negotiated for clauses providing retraining and transfer rights and a fair share of the increased productivity that resulted from automation.

What workers resent—and what really causes alienation—are management decisions that rearrange job assignments or upset existing work schedules without reference to the rights of the workforce.

If you want to enrich the job, you must realize that no matter how dull or boring or dirty it may be, an individual worker must feel that he has not reached the end of the line. If a worker is to be reasonably satisfied with the job he has today he must have hope for something better tomorrow.

You know this is true in universities, in government and in management. Even an assembly line must have some chance of movement, even if it's only from a job that requires stooping down to one that involves standing erect. But here again, we are talking about a job problem for which unionism provides an answer. And the name of that answer is the negotiated seniority clause. Perhaps when workers

first negotiated the right to bid on better shifts, overtime or promotions on the basis of length of service, they weren't thinking in terms of "job enrichment," but were only trying to restrict management's right to allocate jobs and shifts and overtime on the basis of favoritism. But even if they weren't thinking in terms of "job enrichment," in actual practice that's what they got.

It's true that many young workers in their 20s resent the fact that while they have to tighten the same old bolt in the same old spot a thousand times a day the guys in their 40s are walking up and down the line with inspection sheets or running around the factory on forklifts.

They may resent and bitch about it now—but they also know that they are accumulating seniority which they can trade for a better job of their own some day.

These many ways in which jobs can be enriched may not be what management has in mind when it talks about job enrichment. On the basis of fairly extensive experience as a union representative, I find it hard to picture management enriching jobs at the expense of profits. In fact, I have a sneaking suspicion that "job enrichment" may be just another name for "time and motion" study. As labor historian Thomas Brooks said in a recent Federationist article, "Substituting the sociologist's questionnaire for the stopwatch is likely to be no gain for the workers. While workers have a stake in productivity it is not always identical with that of management. Job enrichment programs have cut jobs just as effectively as automation and stopwatches. And the rewards of productivity are not always equitably shared."

What some companies call job enrichment is really little more than the introduction of gimmicks such as doing away with time clocks or developing "work teams" or designing jobs to "maximize personal involvement"—whatever that means.

In conclusion let me say that I know there are those who worry about what the younger generation is coming to and wonder whether the rebellious young workers of today will be willing to fill their father's shoes in the factory jobs of tomorrow. We can't generalize from isolated examples but I was very interested in an NBC television documentary recently that studied the dissatisfaction of young workers. The part that interested me the most was the transformation in an assembly-line "hippie" who followed his electrician father's footsteps by becoming an apprentice and cutting his hair.

All the studies tend to prove that worker dissatisfaction diminishes with age. That's because older workers have accrued more of the kinds of job enrichment that unions have fought for— better wages, shorter hours, vested pensions, a right to have a say in their working conditions, the right to be promoted on the basis of seniority and all the rest. That's the kind of job enrichment that unions believe in.

QUESTIONS

1. How do Mr. Winpisinger's views on the causes of worker discontent compare with the causes given in the "Work in America" article?
2. Evaluate the author's prescription for actions to take to improve worker satisfaction.
3. Discuss the following statement which appears in the article. "I think it is ironic that because of prevailing attitudes many kinds of skilled craftsmen are in short supply while thousands of college graduates are tripping over one another in search of jobs."
4. Explain and evaluate the author's suspicion of management-initiated job enrichment.

PART IV

Employment and Development of People

"Employment and Development of people" is concerned with policies, issues, and techniques of manpower recruitment, selection, utilization, performance appraisal, and training and development. It is also concerned with the process of organization development. These activities are vital for acquiring, creating, and maintaining a competent workforce.

A. *Employment Policies and Selection.* A vital problem confronting those who establish employment qualifications is the weight that should properly be given to formal credentials such as education, licenses, and certificates. S. M. Miller in his article, "Breaking the Credentials Barrier," challenges prevailing beliefs (some say myths) about the ability of rigid selection hurdles to distinguish between potentially successful and unsuccessful employees. Acknowledging that education in the past has helped make our society more democratic, he holds that nowadays insistence upon educational credentials as a primary basis for entry into occupations may be a barrier to democracy.

The interview is the most universally used of all selection techniques, and it is also generally accorded the greatest relative weight. Although acknowledging that there has been insufficient coordinated research devoted to the interview, Eugene C. Mayfield has reviewed and interpreted nearly all the pertinent research conducted over the past fifty years. He relates just what is known about the reliability and validity of the interview and suggests further research needs.

Personnel testing is an intriguing subject for many executives. For some it holds promise of a quick cure for their manpower problems. Andrew H. Souerwine identifies several common fallacies about selection testing. He then goes on to explain the many problems that must be faced when installing a testing program. Among these are attitudes toward individuals, departmental relations, validation procedures, labor supply, expense, and discovering the real problems and their probable causes.

One of the most promising approaches to the evaluation and selection of people for managerial positions has been the assessment center. First used for picking officers in the British and German armies and by the United States Office of Strategic Services during World War II, the assessment-center technique is relatively new to American industry. The Bell System (AT&T) has pioneered its use in selecting management personnel. The article by Walter S. Wikstrom describes the use of assessment centers at the American Telephone and Telegraph Company.

B. *Equal Employment Opportunity and the Disadvantaged*. Public policy in the mid-1960's shifted from one of decades of benign neglect to one of positive government action to assist those who were disadvantaged and those who were victims of discrimination. On the antidiscrimination front, Title VII "Equal Employment Opportunity" of the Civil Rights Act of 1964 outlaws discrimination because of race, color, religion, sex, or national origin. As a result of amendments to this Act in 1972, the Equal Employment Opportunity Commission was given positive enforcement powers and can institute civil action in Federal courts to prohibit discrimination in employment.

In addition to its antidiscrimination activities the Federal government has also set up a great many programs to help disadvantaged people qualify for and obtain gainful employment. Programs have been set up in adult basic education, on-the-job and institutional skills training, counseling, and community services. Through the National Alliance of Busi-

nessmen, cooperative efforts between government and private business have been established to help the disadvantaged obtain jobs, learn job skills, and retain their places in the world of work.

In "Progress and Problems in Equal Employment Opportunity," William J. Kilberg explains some of the significant advances that have been made in equal employment opportunity through government legal action and consent decrees. In addition to focusing upon the historic American Telephone and Telegraph settlement, Mr. Kilberg covers a variety of issues, such as equal pay, testing, hiring quotas, and collective bargaining.

"IBM in the Ghetto: Anatomy of a Success" describes the successful establishment of a computer component assembly plant in the Bedford-Stuyvesant section of Brooklyn by the IBM Corporation. Practically all the employees were recruited from the local area. Despite initial fears about absenteeism, turnover, vandalism, and crime, these problems did not materialize. This article explains some of the reasons for IBM's successful experience.

C. *Performance Appraisal*. Philosophies and methods for evaluating the people in a given work force have undergone a considerable evolution since the early days of the personnel management movement in the 1920's. At first, a great deal of attention was devoted to the design of rating scales that carried numerical scores. Personality-trait rating and interpersonal comparisons were in vogue for many years. Later, emphasis was placed upon the need to identify and minimize such errors in rating as systematic bias, personal bias, the "halo" effect, and varying standards among different raters. Then, forced-distribution techniques (according to a normal curve) and forced-choice techniques (to minimize deliberate bias) were devised. Still later, emphasis was placed upon the need to communicate the rating to each employee. More recently, personnel specialists have advocated that more weight be given to actual performance and results on the job and less to personality traits. The best current thinking has led in the direction of appraisal by results and to a change in the relationship between boss and subordinate.

The article on performance appraisal, by Herbert H. Meyer, Emanuel Kay, and John R. P. French, Jr., reports findings from a significant research study conducted at the General Electric Company. These results and conclusions shed doubt upon the value of performance appraisal as commonly conducted in many organizations. Out of this research evolved a goal-setting method of appraisal where the boss is cast in the role of a counselor and helper rather than a judge. In personnel management circles this newer appraisal process is called "appraisal by results," "mutual goal-setting," or management by objectives.

D. *Training and Development.* Readings in this section are devoted to learning theories, psychologist B. F. Skinner's special learning and conditioning theories, and employee training.

It is my belief that there exists a fairly close relationship between the strength and viability of an enterprise and the amount of investment that top management purposefully commits to its human resources. The education and training of *all* the people in the organization is probably one of the most important kinds of human resource investments. Unfortunately, in too many organizations, allocations of talent, time, and money to this activity are insufficient.

David W. Brown reappraises existing training practices. In his article, "Is Your Training Department Working on the Wrong Problem?", he asks and answers several thought-provoking questions. For example, "Do we train our employees or do they learn in spite of us?" Brown believes that most learning takes place on the job, hence the training department ought to devote its attention to making on-the-job training more effective.

The article by Leslie E. This and

Gordon L. Lippett on learning theories and training covers an area too long neglected by educational psychologists. The authors provide a much needed interpretation of learning theories and principles so that these can be applied meaningfully by training directors in the design and implementation of their programs.

For over twenty-five years Harvard psychologist B. F. Skinner has researched and experimented with the conditioning of human behavior. His research with conditioning human behavior was preceded by many years of experimentation with controlling the behavior of animals. Skinner's work has relevance to both learning theory and motivation. In "Is It Skinner or Nothing?", John R. Murphy explains the principal parts of Skinner's theory, examines the criticisms that have been made of his formulations, and then discusses applications of Skinner's concepts.

E. *Organization Development.* To some people organization development is management development under another name. But in reality organization development is broader than management development and has more far-reaching goals. Organization development, often called simply OD, is a complex educational strategy designed to increase organizational effectiveness and health through planned intervention by a consultant using theory and techniques of applied behavioral science.

The article by W. Warner Burke clearly explains the concepts and methodologies of organization development and shows similarities and differences with management development. Burke points out that an important goal of OD is really to change the *culture* of an organization.

Many companies use T-group (T stands for training) or sensitivity training as a kind of basic training for managers and professionals who will then participate in on-going organization development activities in their firms. The leading force for the T-group laboratory training movement in the United States has been the National Training Laboratories (now called the NTL Institute for Applied Behavioral Science). In "Understanding Laboratory Education: An Overview," Clayton P. Alderfer describes and compares the three main forms of laboratory education (1) encounter groups, (2) T-groups, and (3) Tavistock conferences. He points out the quite different orientations of each. Then he discusses the strong criticisms that have been leveled at laboratory education by both laymen and professionals. Finally he talks about empirical research studies that have

sought to determine the effects of laboratory training activities.

The proof of the pudding is in the eating. Huse and Beer, in their "Eclectic Approach to Organizational Development," tell us about a series of OD activities that have been carried on in a manufacturing plant over a period of several years. In conducting these activities the authors were not committed to a single school of thought; rather they tried and used what seemed to work best. Results in terms of productivity, quality of product, absenteeism, and profits have been quite impressive.

7.

Breaking the Credentials Barrier

S. M. MILLER

Education has in the past helped make our society more democratic by emphasizing qualifications rather than connections. In this way, it has freed us considerably from the rule of nepotism and arbitrariness. Paradoxically, however, this same insistence on education is now becoming a barrier to democracy—particularly to our national effort to remake the social class structure of this country by reducing the number of its poor and underprivileged.

We have built this barrier through our emphasis on credentials. Indeed, we have become a credential society, in which one's educational level is more important than what he can do. People cannot obtain jobs that they could well fill because they lack educational qualifications. Negroes who dropped out of the educational steeplechase before obtaining a high-school diploma cannot get jobs. Employers do not feel that they are discriminating against these dropouts; they merely regard them as "unqualified." And they persist in their beliefs despite a growing body of evidence, analyzed by Ivar Berg at Columbia University, that the higher-educated have a worse record than the poorly educated at every occupational level—more absenteeism, turnover, dissatisfaction, and probably lower productivity. Indeed, few companies even know the connections between the educational level of their employees and their performance. They have not bothered to probe their records to find out if their beliefs accord with the results of their practice.

I focus on the exclusion of the low-educated, but the processes that we are concerned about build Chinese walls of exclusion around an increasing number of occupations. We have a new guild system of credentials, licenses, certificates—largely built on the base of education—which keeps people out of many occupational channels. There is increasingly, for many occupations, only one route in—that taken when young. Failing to take that route bars one forever from the possibilities of that occupation.

It is assumed that these credentialing procedures assure a better product—that those who receive the credentials can do much better in the occupation than those who do not; that those who successfully go through the steps needed to gain the credentials are better fitted for the occupation than those who are not interested in doing so or fail in the prescribed climb.

Reprinted by permission of The Ford Foundation. First given as an address before the American Orthopsychiatric Association in Washington, D.C., March 1967.

S. M. Miller is a Program Advisor in the National Affairs Division of The Ford Foundation.

I submit that we do not know if these two assumptions are true. To some extent they are undoubtedly untrue. And a broader assumption—that those who do not go through credentialing activities are unfit for the demands of the occupation—is clearly inaccurate. All of us know of individuals who cannot get jobs that they would be able to perform well because they lack the appropriate credentials—whether it is a high school diploma or a Ph.D.

The Reasons for Credentialism

Schools today are not a humanizing or an educational force as much as a credentialing agency, sorting people out who do not fit into the regular channels of educational development. Schools function to certify that someone is not harmful rather than to develop the potential of all. Many of the poverty and job-training programs serve the same function.

Why is credentialism growing? One reason is that we like to assume that our world is rational and scientific. We invest confidence in the present structuring of occupations as optimal; then the question becomes how best to fit people into these wisely constructed occupations.

Then we presume that we know enough to sort out "potential" and "ability" from their opposites. Consequently, we repose an enormous misplaced confidence in testing and educational achievement, even when we have quivers of doubt about their "real meaning." Objective measures seem to remove irrationality and discrimination in favor of universally applied, objective rules. Where there has been oversupply of labor and talent, then processes of exclusion on some basis will occur. But when shortages occur as now in many professions, maintenance of exclusion as the core process is obviously peculiar. Such peculiarity is undoubtedly based on some fear—a fear of having to make choices and exercise judgment.

This fear is related to the third reason for the spreading tide of credentialism. Increasingly, the results and achievements are difficult to measure in a service-growing society. Norms of production output are difficult to use in the professions or in government service. Ambiguity of purpose further compounds the measurement problems. If 70 per cent of patients seeing a physician have no ascertainable medical reason for being there, how does one measure the achievement and productivity of the physician? Our uncertainty about what is the product and how to measure effectiveness throws us back to the input—that is, what is the training of the occupational incumbent?

A fourth reason for emphasizing exclusion is the "marshal's baton" syndrome. Napoleon asserted that his military prowess was based not only on his kitchens but on his promotion outlook—every soldier carried a marshal's baton in his knapsack, ready to jump into a command position. In many occupations and organizations, the notion, at least for men, is frequently to employ only "top-notchers" who can move to the peak of the pyramid. Yet the possibilities of moving to the top are slim indeed. In many organizations there is enormous turnover; only a very few stay long, and yet the notion is of "long-distance promotability." Furthermore, as Robert K. Merton has pointed out, there is no possible definition of "top-notchers" nor an adequate number of them, so that organizations and professions are doomed to feel that they are being short-changed in their share of "top-notchers." The important thing in this context is that the "marshal's baton" syndrome serves to make it appear wise to exclude many, even when talent and ability are in short supply. And certainly it caters to the yearning for prestige to be able to say that the profession or organization has only top-qualified people.

A fifth reason for credentialism is the

importance of social appearance. As organizations and professions not only become more uncertain about criteria or performance, but require more intricate "teamwork," getting along with others, appearing "mature" and more acceptable to the public to be serviced, the desirability of insisting on educational credentials grows. For the credentials certify not educational achievement, but personal serviceability—that one knows how to get by, conform, manage. The educational failures—at whatever level—are social failures, bad risks.

Suggestions for Change

Does my attack on credentialism imply that there should be no standards of training, no qualifications for entrance into occupations? I do not think that these are the implications, but I do think my analysis implies the following:

There should be a general downgrading of the importance of education as the major credential. Experience and performance should gain greater importance. Many people will not be seriously considered for a job because they lack educational credentials; prospective employers will not even pause to investigate whether the low-educated can perform well. The absence of certificates results in automatic exclusion. Individuals should be judged on what they can do rather than where and how long they have gone to school.

If we treated experience and performance seriously, civil service regulations would be changed so that low education was not an automatic bar to many positions. Testing would be downgraded in favor of trying people in jobs and then assessing their performance. Since much of the job training today is not relevant to work, there should be a strong movement toward "Jobs first, training later." The absence of this practice means that many minority group members are now serving lifetime sentences of low income

and unemployment for their educational delinquencies.

"Dropout" is a label assigned at age sixteen; it persists through a lifetime. The consequence is that individuals who may have outgrown the issues which propelled them out of schools or who now have demonstrated and developed considerable skill are still economically disenfranchised because of their youthful educational difficulties. Once a dropout, always a dropout. As in many other aspects of American life, we need a de-labeling procedure which takes the curse off individuals who once ran afoul of conventional styles and were labeled and cast aside—whether the label is "dropout," "delinquent," or "mental patient."

We need deepened awareness of and respect for the abilities of those who have educational difficulties. We should not believe that our educational hurdles infallibly pick those who should be successes and unerringly cast aside those who should be failures. As we increasingly face the manpower problems of scarce talent, the great hope will be in the cultivation of talents among those who are now disadvantaged.

I do not wish to imply that every poor individual deserves and can use a marshal's baton. But many can. The failure is in cultivating these talents. We have much to learn here that we shall not learn if we persist in the new fashion of denouncing poor families for their deficiencies as educational environments. We then excuse the schools for their failure to learn how to adapt to and develop different varieties of students.

The first step of liberation from the shibboleths of invincible ignorance is to recognize the educational and occupational potential of many who have difficulty with educational systems as they are presently conducted.

We need new channels of credentialing and new points at which credentials can be expanded. While I am eager to see reduced emphasis on educational credentials, I am realistic enough to know that this kind of change is slow. Consequently, we must make it easier for individuals to obtain educational credentials.

Today, if one does not get twelve or sixteen or eighteen or twenty years of education in the orthodox way of continuous immersion without a break in the apparatus of formal education, one has much reduced chances of gaining credentials.

We should more effectively develop school programs and procedures so that once out does not mean permanently lost. Education and training will be increasingly a discontinuous process for the highly-educated in American society, as they will need new kinds of education at various points in their careers. The same attitude should prevail towards those who have not successfully weathered the educational system to high school or college graduation or beyond. They should be in practice re-entering and benefitting from education and training at various points in their lives.

To some extent the poverty programs are new credentialing systems in our society. Experience in the Job Corps or in the Neighborhood Youth Corps or in Manpower Development and Training Act programs may not be primarily important in terms of providing skills. Rather, employers may be more willing to hire youth who have gone through one of these self-selection and molding systems. Neighborhood Youth Corps experience may be a new way of getting a credential which employers will accredit and accept.

The Second-Chance University

By multiplying the number of credential channels, we make it easier for individuals to gain them. Those rejected by our educational system at age sixteen might be able to get needed credentials at age eighteen, twenty-two, or thirty. One should have second, third, fourth chances and ways of getting credentials. The more different ways of getting credentials, the fewer the people who would fail to get some brownie points needed for acceptance into the main economy.

What is needed is the idea of a Second-Chance University which permits "dropout" adults to get further and more useful opportunities to get credentials. Experience should be given educational credit; courses should be more relevant to activities—liberal-arts education need not be taught in traditional ways in order to reach traditional ends. While there is need for a formal structure to facilitate re-entry into the educational atmosphere, there is also need to recharge that educational atmosphere so that it is more hospitable and useful to those who have found the established educational practices less than useful or stimulating.

Every credential system should have an escape clause which permits the unusual person to be admitted to the realm of the elect. As professions tighten their qualifications, there is usually a "grandfather clause" which exempts oldtimers from meeting new qualifications. Similarly, at least 5 per cent of each year's entrants into a profession or other highly credentialed occupation should be individuals who have "qualified" in nonusual ways—by taking tests without the traditional educational prerequisites, or by getting credit for enriched experiences, for example. Some collective bargaining contracts have a similar provision: the company is allowed to hire back after a cutback up to 10 per cent of the labor force without paying attention to seniority; the other 90 per cent of the labor force must be rehired according to seniority. The company is permitted some margin of choice and selectivity to meet its production needs.

Without a minimum percentage, it is unlikely that a "creative minority" could in practice obtain unusual entrance into a field. Arbitrariness and favoritism could be avoided by a blue-ribbon panel of decision-makers.

The need here, as in so many other parts of our society, is for making pluralism possible in a complex society. We need a variety of social inventions to provide the structure and the reality of pluralism.

We should not assume that the present structuring of occupations is optimal. Many jobs, for example, call for too many different kinds of skills and too many time-consuming tasks; they should be broken down into finer tasks for many hands. Many jobs, too, should be enlarged so that those holding them can accept greater responsibility.

The emerging position of the nonprofessional is interesting here. The tasks of a professional job—like those of a social worker or nurse or teacher—can often be broken down into smaller units and combined in ways that permit less trained people to perform them. Sometimes the recombination produces services which the professional was not able to provide. These new positions could reduce the great unmeetable demand for professional services. With the tightening up of educational qualifications, it will be increasingly difficult to turn out an adequate number of professionals. As a consequence, the role of professional should increasingly be that of making it possible for less trained people to do effective work.

But this rational role is moving very slowly. There are grave limitations on what nonprofessionals are allowed to do; there is the absence of a career structure that permits many nonprofessionals to move into the middle class and into the elite stratum of the professional activity.

Professionals are increasingly becoming the gatekeepers of the welfare state, deciding on "professional" grounds who receives what kinds of services and who is allowed to perform various services. The pivotal importance of professional and organizational services has led many of the New Left students to focus on the professionals as the "enemy." While the assault is overdone and frequently misguided, there is something to the view that professions are hardening into barriers rather than aids. The guild-like features of professional occupations frequently are more visible than their commitment to broad social concerns, though there does seem to be important growth here. The emphasis on "competence" and "quality" frequently means a lack of attention to the poor or to those who do not easily fit into professional activities.

The slowness with which the nonprofessional is catching on—in being permitted to do broad jobs, in having chances to move up the occupational ladder—is indicative of the failure of professionals to reassess their roles today.

But I do not want to criticize professionals alone. For business deserves criticism here as well. Private enterprise could probably get needed labor (and at high productivity levels) if it restructured jobs so that the less trained could perform at least parts of them. The credentials problem is an issue vital to both the private and public sectors. The national interest of gaining decent employment for the low-educated and the poor could be joined with the private interest of profit.

In summary, we live in a pseudo-meritocracy where individuals are presumed to be selected for talent and placed into appropriate squares. Education becomes the major route to social mobility as the historic alternative routes are shut off. As social mobility becomes more important in our national policies, we narrow down the routes to it.

The general issue which the plight of the poor raises is that of a hardening and narrowing of society into fewer and fewer acceptable routes to economic improvement. We are slowly and rather hazily re-examining the core values and practices of our society. But we must press the search for equity and purpose rather than accept a patina of rationality through reliance on school processes in resolving our value choices.

QUESTIONS

1. How has education helped to make our society more democratic?
2. Do you think that education is being used as a criterion to legally practice discrimination on racial or other grounds?
3. How could shortages of talent in professions and other key occupations be alleviated by restructuring jobs?
4. Why is credentialism a growing phenomenon?
5. Do you agree that there should be a general downgrading of the importance of education as a major credential in favor of experience and demonstrated performance?

8.

The Selection Interview: A Re-evaluation of Published Research

EUGENE C. MAYFIELD

Summary

Over the last few years, the selection interview has been subjected to a great deal of criticism. Most of this criticism has stressed a general lack of evidence concerning the interview's reliability and validity. The present paper, while agreeing for the most part with prior criticism, attempts to take three further steps. First, the present limited knowledge is explained in terms of (a) a lack of comparability between studies and (b) an over-dependence on research results from other areas. Second, in spite of these shortcomings, there are numerous research findings which have received support from more than one study. These findings are summarized and discussed. Finally, a starting point for basic research on the selection interview which may lead to more profitable research in the future is presented.

Introduction

In 1915, one of the first studies concerned with the reliability of the selection interview appeared (Scott, 1915). In this study, six personnel managers interviewed 36 applicants for sales positions and ranked them in order of their estimated suitability for the job. The results, of course, are well known. The rankings made by the different personnel managers showed little relationship to each other. During the next 20 years, several other studies appeared in the literature showing similar results (Scott, Bingham, and Whipple, 1916; Hollingworth, 1922; Snow, 1924; Corey, 1933).

In 1916, Scott published another arti-

Reprinted from *Personnel Psychology*, Vol. 17, No. 3 (Autumn 1964), pp. 239–260, by permission of the author and publisher.

Eugene C. Mayfield is Second Vice-President and Director of Manpower Research, Life Insurance Marketing and Research Association, Hartford, Conn.

93

cle, this time concerned with the validity of selection interviews (Scott, 1916). In this study, the sales ability of 12 salesmen was rated by 13 executives. These ratings were then compared with the ratings the salesmen had received in earlier interviews. The relationship between the two sets of ratings averaged just slightly better than chance. Other early studies also threw doubt upon the validity of the interview (Kenagy and Yoakum, 1925; Moss, 1931). Only one study reported prior to 1930 showed the interview to have a high predictive validity (Clark, 1926). In this study, two investigators interviewed students and made predictions of semester grade averages. The resulting correlations were .66 and .73. However, Wagner (1949) pointed out a serious flaw in this study. The interviews were conducted late in the semester and the students were asked how they were doing in their schoolwork. Thus, the high correlations may have only meant that the students pretty well knew the grades they would get and were truthful enough to provide the interviewers with this information.

Since these early studies, a large number of articles have appeared which have been concerned with the selection interview. Many of these simply give opinions while a lesser number report actual experimental studies. Wagner (1949) reviewed the literature on the employment interview and found that out of 106 titles, only 25 concerned actual experiments. The writer has reviewed over 300 articles and has found a comparable situation to exist today.

Even with the relatively few experimental studies reported in the last 45 years, one would expect that a substantial amount of information has been gained concerning the interview. That this is not the case can best be shown by quoting the first two conclusions Wagner listed in his review of the literature. These are

1. A great deal of confusion exists as to what can and cannot be accomplished by the interview.
2. Research on the interview is much needed (Wagner, 1949, p. 42).

Things have not changed much since Wagner reached these conclusions in 1949. More recently England and Patterson suggested:

a moratorium on books, articles, and other writings about "how to interview," "do's and don't's" about interviewing, and the like, until there is sufficient research evidence about the reliability and validity of the interview as an assessment device to warrant its use in such work (England and Patterson, 1960, p. 57).

And Dunnette and Bass state

The personnel interview continues to be the most widely used method for selecting employees, despite the fact that it is a costly, inefficient, and usually invalid procedure. It is often used to the exclusion of far more thoroughly researched and validated procedures. Even when the interview is used in conjunction with other procedures, it is almost always treated as the final hurdle in the selection process. In fact, other selection methods (e.g., psychological tests) are often regarded simply as supplements to the interview.

The continued uncritical use of the personal interview offers a clear illustration of what is perhaps personnel management's prime problem—that is, the great resistance to carrying out fundamental research on its practices and techniques (Dunnette and Bass, 1963, p. 117).

Lack of Comparability Between Studies

One of the reasons for the apparent lack of useful knowledge about the selection interview is that most experimental studies have been undertaken to determine the validity of an interview in a particular situation. There is no question that this type of research is very practical and very necessary. However, it does not provide an answer to the question of why a given interview works or doesn't work. Therefore, such studies by themselves do not give us the information necessary to fully understand and improve interviews.

For example, Handyside and Duncan (1954) compared two promotion methods. One was a customary review with nominations being made. The other was a thorough analysis of the individuals being considered through the use of interviews, biographical data sheets, group discussions, and other procedures. The results showed that the second method was far superior and that each of the methods used turned out to be quite valid in predicting success. However, we are still unable to answer the question of why the interviews worked in this particular situation. All we are able to say is that, for some reason, they did appear to work well. The same limitation occurs in studies investigating the value of interviews in predicting the success of teachers (Shaw, 1952), armed service personnel (Newman, Bobbitt, and Cameron, 1946; Flanagan, 1947), and students (Moss, 1931; Sarbin, 1942; Putney, 1947).

Other difficulties arise when one tries to compare the results obtained from two or more different studies of this type. Since these studies have had the practical purpose of seeing if a given interview works, there has been little in the way of factorial designs involved. This problem was pointed out clearly by Yonge (1956) in the introduction to his article. For example, in some studies (Scott, Bingham, and Whipple, 1916; Bass, 1951) very little if any information was provided to the interviewers before their interview. In others (Shaw, 1952; Handyside and Duncan, 1954), a great deal of information was provided. Thus it is difficult to compare results since the interviews were not equivalent. As another example, it is generally felt that the more structured an interview is, the more reliable and valid

it is likely to be (Wagner, 1949; Bingham, Moore, and Gustad, 1959). For this reason, many of the studies appearing in the literature have been structured to varying degrees. However, in no study located was the amount of structure varied systematically to see what effect this would have on the results. Thus, it is difficult to determine the real effect of structuring an interview. It should also be noted that in studies where the interview was structured, the ratings made following the interview were almost always made on some sort of structured form. This brings up the question of whether it is the structure of the interview or the structure imposed on the rating form which leads to a higher reliability.

In addition to the varying amounts of structure in the rating form, different investigations have had the interviewers make final ratings on different traits or behavioral characteristics. For example, Shaw (1952) had the interviewers rate individuals on health and fitness, intellectual capacity and achievement, teacher interests, personal and social qualities—and then make an over-all rating. The study reported by Adams and Smeltzer (1936) placed the traits being rated under three main headings: physical characteristics, personality, and general aptitude for work. Campbell, Prien, and Brailey (1960), on the other hand, settled for one four-category final rating while Fearing and Fearing (1942) discuss the ten traits used for interview ratings by the civil service. This puts us into the position of trying to compare interviews when the outcomes were measured in different ways and of studying the results of interviewing without having taken any prior steps to determine what traits can be rated reliably. A recent study by Maas (1963) investigated the effect of rating scales per se and showed that by changing only the form of the rating scale, the reliability of the interview was greatly increased.

Still other factors make meaningful comparisons of studies difficult. For example, the interviews discussed in the literature are of different lengths. Kenagy and Yoakum (1925) worked with interviews one-half hour in length. Tupes (1950) investigated the value of one- and two-hour interviews, and Bugental (1953) studied ten-minute interviews. Since little work has been done investigating the effect of the length of the interview with other factors held constant, any comparison of results is difficult.

In addition to the varying length of the interviews, the types of positions for which predictions are being made varies a great deal. Many studies have been reported in which interviewees were being selected as teachers, students, army officers, truck drivers, salesmen, secretaries, and so forth. However, only one study was located where the validity of a particular type of interview was investigated with respect to a number of different occupations (McMurry, 1947). Since it is highly probable that the type of position a person is being selected for has an effect on the efficiency of the interview, more studies investigating the extent to which the validity of one type of interview generalizes to several occupations might provide us with valuable information.

Finally, the criteria of success used in the various studies lead to difficulty in interpretation. Crissy (1952) discusses this point in some detail. In brief, he points out the need to validate ratings trait by trait against criterion measures of these traits rather than against a measure of total job performance. That is, a rating of "cooperation" given by the interviewer should be validated against some measure of "cooperation on the job" rather than against a general measure of job success. This brings up another point which should be kept in mind when evaluating the research which has been done on selection interviewing. Frequently the validity of trait ratings has been assessed by using ratings on these same traits by close friends as the criterion. It is possible that such ratings may be so confounded with "halo" that they are of little value in this connection.

Dependence on Studies Carried Out in Other Fields

Even with the obvious difficulty of making generalizations from studies of the type just discussed, one frequently finds definite statements of procedures to follow to assure good selection interviewing. This would seem to indicate that studies are available which have been concerned with the interviewing process as well as with results per se and which have investigated the value of such procedures and techniques in actual interview situations. However, such studies are not as common as one would hope. Often it turns out that such statements of rules and procedures are based on generalizations from studies carried out in fields other than interviewing.

Let us, for example, investigate in some detail the studies which have led to the generally accepted recommendation that selection interviewers should refrain from using "leading" questions. The assumption behind this rule is that the interviewee will respond to such questions with the answer implied by the interviewer rather than with facts or with his true opinions.

The study most frequently quoted as supporting this rule is that by Muscio (1916). Muscio showed 25-second motion picture films to a group of men and women and later asked the subjects approximately 100 questions about the film. These questions were worded in different ways and Muscio compared the question form to the caution, suggestiveness, and reliability of the response. Striking differences became apparent. The question forms Muscio found to be best are still frequently accepted as a guide to how questions should be phrased (e.g., Bingham, Moore, and Gustad, 1959, p. 18). However, such a generalization from this study may not be justified. In Muscio's study, the subjects were asked about what they had observed in the motion picture. This is similar to having a third person ask an interviewer what he observed in the interview and is somewhat different than investigating the effect of questions asked the interviewee by the interviewer. In addition, a generalization from the observation of a 25-second motion picture film to a longer face-to-face interview would seem to be unwarranted.

Another study frequently cited as evidence that "leading" questions are poor is that by Greenspoon (1950). In this study it was found that the frequency of plural nouns could be increased, without the subject's knowledge, by reinforcing that response by saying, "Mmm-hmm." Later, Greenspoon (1954) showed the same result could be obtained by using a light or a 190-cycle-per-second tone in place of the verbal reinforcement. Other studies (e.g. Cohen et al., 1954) have shown similar results. These studies certainly lead to hypotheses which relate to an interview situation. However, before they can be accepted as actually applying to the selection interview, they need to be investigated further in a more realistic situation where the stimulus-response relationship is less restricted. For example, it is obvious that the response given to a question by an interviewee is not directly comparable to a simple plural noun response. Hildum and Brown (1956) were among the first to recognize this problem and a few studies (e.g., Verplank, 1955; Moos, 1963) have shown that such reinforcement can increase the frequency of occurrence of various classes of statements. However, these results still do not give a direct answer to the question of whether an interviewee will answer a

"leading" question with the answer implied by the interviewer.

The only interview situation where the effect of the form of the question itself has been subjected to detailed examination is in the opinion poll area. These studies have been well summarized by Hyman et al. (1954) and by Boyd and Westfall (1955). There is no doubt that the form of the question, in these cases, does influence the response. For example, it was shown in one study by Roslow, Wulfeck, and Corby (1940) that the question "Should members of the American Communist Party be deported?" led to different responses than the question "Should 'reds' and 'radicals' in the country be deported?" However, which response showed the true opinion of the subject was still in question. Thus, the preferred way of wording the question still seems to be in doubt. Other studies (e.g., Rice, 1929; Blankenship, 1940; Cahalan, Tamulonis and Verner, 1947; Shapiro and Eberhart, 1947) have shown that the interviewer's personal opinions will lead to different responses on the part of the respondent. Some studies attributed this result to unconscious "leading" by the interviewer. Others attribute it to the interviewer's interpretation of the interviewee's response. Which is actually the case, or if it is a combination of the two, cannot be completely determined on the basis of research which had been reported in the literature.

A few studies have concerned themselves with the truthfulness and reliability of replies obtained in counseling and opinion poll situations (e.g., Keating, Patterson, and Stone, 1950; Vaughn and Reynolds, 1951; Weiss and Dawis, 1960; Weiss et al., 1961). This would seem to be an excellent situation in which to compare the form of question to the truthfulness of the reply. However, in most cases these studies involved the use of interviewers' written records and there was no way to determine what form of question had originally been used to elicit these responses. In cases where it would have been possible to do so, such a comparison was not included in the experimental design. In summary, then, all we can really say is that the form of the question as well as interviewers' biases do influence the response given. The reason for this, or whether one form of questioning leads to more accurate replies in the interview situation, has not been determined as yet. Even if it could be determined from the studies which have been reported, it is possible that the results would not generalize from counseling and opinion poll situations to the selection interview.

We have just discussed the generally accepted rule that interviewers should not use leading questions. Many of the other rules normally given in "how to interview" books and pamphlets, when examined similarly, turn out to be generalizations from results obtained in situations quite removed from the selection interview. Such generalizations are of great value in forming hypotheses about the selection interview. However, they should be considered only as hypotheses until they are more thoroughly investigated.

Recent Approaches to Interview Research

There have been some recent approaches to the study of the interview which may lead to more profitable research in the future. The first of these is the division of the interview into units. Basically, this provides a microanalysis of the interview as opposed to the usual macroanalysis. Several types of units have been suggested as appropriate for this type of analysis and many studies using units have been undertaken (e.g., Chapple, 1949; Bales, 1950; Daniels and Otis, 1950; Borgatta and Bales, 1953; Muthard, 1953; Dipboye, 1954; Robinson, 1955;

Matarazzo, Saslow, and Matarazzo, 1956). Chapple (1949) related several such unit measures to the success of factory and department store personnel and found them to be valid in a concurrent validity study. However, since that time most of the studies using units have been concerned with the reliability of the units used and not of their validity. Only relatively recently have further attempts been made to relate such measures taken during an interview to other measures such as test scores (Matarazzo et al., 1958). The future will determine whether approaches of this type are profitable.

Another promising aspect of recent research is the increasing interest in studying the process of decision-making as it occurs in a selection interview, rather than in just looking at the results of the interview. The most complete study of this type was undertaken during the past 10 years at McGill University under the direction of E. C. Webster. Basically, this study is concerned with the procedures by which interviewers reach decisions from information obtained during an interview. There are many advantages to such an approach. For example, without knowing how decisions are made, one has little to guide his approach to increasing the reliability of selection interviews. However, if it can be shown that interviewers make different decisions after listening to the same interview because they pay attention to different information, then a definite approach could be taken—e.g., establishing methods which lead interviewers to attend to the same information. On the other hand, if it could be shown that such differences in final decisions occur because interviewers place different weight on the same information, a different approach to increasing interview reliability is indicated. The McGill studies have been reviewed by Webster (1959) and reports of the individual studies have appeared in recent journals (Springbett, 1958; Anderson, 1960;

Sydiaha, 1959, 1961, 1962; Rowe, 1963).

In summary, then, our knowledge of the selection interview is only a little more advanced than it was when Wagner reviewed the literature in 1949. However, it does appear that new approaches are becoming more prominent and results from long-term, coordinated research are beginning to appear in the literature. Results from such research may provide answers to many of the questions we now have.

Conclusions

In spite of the fact that there has been little coordinated research to date, there are enough consistent results to make a few fairly definite statements about what is and what is not true about the selection interview. Some of these provide only partial answers to more general questions and others raise more questions than they answer. However, the points mentioned below do give us some information on which to base further research.

1. The interview can be divided into various types of units, and this can be done reliably. Recently many studies have been reported in the literature which use this approach, several of which have been referred to earlier. Whether this approach will prove to be of benefit in understanding the interview process remains to be seen.

2. The intra-rater reliability of the interview appears to be satisfactory. Although little work has been done in this area, the three studies located which did investigate this aspect of the interview show the intra-rater reliability to be relatively high (Shaw, 1952; Pashalian and Crissy, 1953; Anderson, 1954). An interviewer reinterviewing the same interviewee, or listening to a tape of the original interview, after a time period arrives at approximately the same ratings he did originally. The degree to which memory played a part in the rela-

tionships found, however, is difficult to estimate.

3. An interviewer is consistent in his approach to different interviewees; the techniques he uses remain fairly constant. Some of the studies indicating this result are those by Goldman-Eisler (1952), Pashalian and Crissy (1953), Dipboye (1954), Danskin and Robinson (1954), Hoffman (1959), and Cavanagh et al. (1962). It also seems likely that an interviewer can be trained in the use of techniques. This conclusion is drawn from studies which show that people who have been trained in nondirective interviewing differ significantly in the techniques used from those trained in the directive approach (e.g., Porter, 1943). Studies of opinion polling (Hyman et al., 1954) also lead one to this conclusion.

4. A general suitability rating based on an unstructured interview with no prior information provided has extremely low inter-rater reliability, especially in an employment situation. This was originally shown by Scott (1915) and by other investigators more recently (e.g., Uhrbrock, 1948). In other words, the interview as normally conducted in a selection situation is of little value.

5. In an unstructured interview, material is not consistently covered. This is probably one of the causes of the unreliability of the interviews mentioned above. This fact was clearly shown by Pashalian and Crissy (1953) in their work with submariners. In this study it was found that out of 109 interviews, the following information was covered the percentage of times indicated:

Establishment of attendance at high school or college	86%
Marital status	75%
Reasons for leaving school—graduated, join the Navy, etc.	64%
Kinds of duty held in Navy	55%
Place(s) of duty in the Navy	50%

In general, it was found that the items most consistently covered were of the factual biographical type. The lowest consistency was found for items of the attitudinal type, such as attitude toward jobs held. Webster (1962) discusses a series of unpublished studies which also showed that different interviewers are frequently interested in different aspects of the applicant.

6. When interviewers obtain the same information, they are likely to interpret or weight it differently. This was clearly pointed out in a study by Wentworth (1953). Using a tape of an actual employment interview, he found that raters differed greatly as to how each of five items affected their impression of the applicant. Some items led to an extremely unfavorable impression on the part of some raters and to an extremely favorable impression on the part of others. Webster (1962) refers to studies where it was found that specific bits of information were given different interpretation and emphasis, especially with respect to personality characteristics. A study by Asch (1946) also supports this conclusion. The fact that different interviewers sometimes give different weight to the same information could also be a major cause of the unreliability of unstructured selection interviews.

7. Structured interviews, in general, provide a higher inter-rater reliability than do unstructured interviews. In almost all cases where a satisfactory reliability for the selection interview was reported, the interview was of a structured form. This same conclusion was reached by Wagner (1949) in his review of the literature. A study by Bass (1951) points out this fact clearly but also shows that the value of a structured interview form may be specific to a particular situation. In this study, a group of 64 upperclassmen were interviewed separately by eight interviewers. Two of these interviewers were from an insurance company and used the same guided interview form. Two others were from an office machine company and used another guided interview form. All four of these interviewers were evaluating the interviewee for a sales position with their own company. The ratings made on the candidates by the two insurance company representatives correlated .56 while those of the office machine company representatives correlated .74. These are higher than inter-rater reliabilities frequently reported in the literature. On the other hand, in two cases the same candidates had been rated by an insurance company representative and an office machine company representative. In these two cases, the correlations between the ratings made by the representatives were .24 and —.10.

This would seem to indicate that structuring an interview increases inter-rater reliability when interviewers from the same company use the same form, but that two different structured forms may lead to completely different ratings when used with the same interviewee. The reason for this is unknown at present, but it may result from different areas being covered, similar areas being covered in different ways, or because the men were being rated for different jobs.

8. Although the reliabilities of interviews may be high in given situations, the validities obtained are usually of a low magnitude. Examples of studies where this has been found are Moss (1931) and Dunlap and Wantman (1944). This indicates that along with the present emphasis on reliability, there should be more investigations of just what it is that is being measured reliably in selection interviews. It is recognized that such studies pose many practical difficulties, but they cannot be omitted from any comprehensive study of the interview. Without knowing what we can predict from an interview, and why we can predict it, it is unlikely any real gains can be made. Certainly reliability is an important factor and needs

to be studied in detail. But it should not be studied by itself in such a way that the validity problem is forgotten.

9. When an individual interviewer has tests of proven validity available, his predictions based on the interview and the test scores are generally no more (and frequently less) accurate than those based on the test scores alone. This has been shown in several studies (e.g., Sarbin, 1942; Conrad and Satter, 1946; Bloom and Brundage, 1947). Other related studies showing similar results have been reported by Meehl (1954). It would seem safe to assume, therefore, that where tests have a reasonably high relationship with success, the use of the typical individual face-to-face interview is of little, if any, value. It should be noted, however, that this statement is not necessarily true when more than one interviewer is used. Frequently when positive results are found for the interview when compared to tests, it turns out that a team approach had been used—either with all the interviewers working together as a "board" or with the interviewers interviewing the applicant independently of each other and then making a final group decision (e.g., Rundquist, 1947; Trankell, 1959). Although this is not conclusive evidence, it is possible that a team approach is a more promising interview method.

No investigations were located where the interview was used by itself on the applicants remaining after an original screening by tests. It is possible that such an approach would provide a different result than investigations of interviews *in conjunction with* tests and other information.

10. With respect to traits or characteristics which can be estimated reliably and validly from interviews, it seems that only the intelligence or mental ability of the interviewee can be judged satisfactorily. Wagner (1949) reports the reliabilities obtained in studies estimating intelligence to be .96, .87, .77, .62, and .90 and validities to be .58, .82, .45, .94, .51, and .70. No other trait or characteristic was judged so consistently or so well in a number of different studies. Two studies have appeared since Wagner's review which also support this conclusion. Hanna (1950) found that interviewers could estimate an individual's American Psychological Examination and OSU Psychological Test scores with validities of .71 and .66 respectively. Sperber and Adlerstein (1961) had clinical psychologists estimate interviewees' intelligence from transcripts and tape recordings of psychiatric interviews and obtained an average validity coefficient of .70.

On the other hand, there are two studies where little relationship was found between the estimate made by the interviewer and the individual's intelligence test scores (Magson, 1926; Driver, 1944). However, these appear to be the exception rather than the rule and the poor results might be due to restriction of range in the subjects' intellectual abilities or to some other factor outside the interview.

11. The form of the question does affect the answer obtained. This point was discussed in some detail earlier. It was pointed out that in spite of the many studies of this aspect of interviewing, we cannot answer definitely why and in what way the question form affects the answers.

12. The attitudes of interviewers do affect their interpretation of what the interviewee says. Rice (1929), in a classic study, showed that prohibitionist and socialist interviewers differed in their interpretation of the cause of destitution of social welfare cases. Hyman et al. (1954) summarize more recent studies from the area of opinion polling which also show such an effect to exist. However, no definite statement can be made as to what attitudes are the most biasing or the manner in which they change interpretations.

13. In the usual unstructured employment interview, the interviewer talks more than does the interviewee. This has

been shown by Uhrbrock (1933), Daniels and Otis (1950), and Anderson (1960). This finding shows that many interviewers violate the commonly stated rule that the interviewee should do most of the talking. Unfortunately, the rule itself has little factual evidence to support it. Anderson (1960) pointed out that the amount of time an interviewer talks may be related to his final decision to hire or reject, although the reason for this is not known. It may simply be that the interviewer makes his decision to hire early in the interview and then talks more because he is supplying information about the job to the interviewee. Or it may be that interviewers like "listeners."

14. Interviewers appear to be influenced more by unfavorable than favorable information. The first studies to show this result clearly were carried out at McGill University under the direction of E. C. Webster. Springbett (1958) found that an interviewer's impression was more likely to change from favorable to unfavorable than from unfavorable to favorable. He concluded that the active interview was primarily a search for negative data. Working with paper and pencil situations, Bolster and Springbett (1961) showed that it was easier to induce shifts in ratings toward rejection than toward acceptance and Rowe (1963) found that the mean rating given unfavorable items correlated higher with final decisions than did the mean rating of favorable items. As Bolster and Springbett point out, incidental findings from other studies also indicate a stronger reaction to negative information (Newman, Bobbitt, and Cameron, 1946; Bloom & Brundage, 1947; Crissy and Regan, 1951).

15. Interviewers tend to make their decisions early in an unstructured interview. One of the first studies to indicate this result was that by Driver (1944). He found that prolonging an interview past a certain point added little to an interviewer's ability to make a decision.

More recent studies also uphold this view. Springbett (1958) found that initial appraisal of information derived from an application form and the applicant's personal appearance appeared to be decisive for the final outcome of 85 per cent of interviews. Anderson (1960) found that the interviewer talked more and in a more friendly manner in the first half of interviews where the applicant was accepted than was true when the applicant was later rejected. This would imply that the interviewers had already made up their mind before the first half of the interview had been completed. Sydiaha, in an unpublished study (see Webster, 1962) obtained similar results, although his analysis was based on the entire interview. It might also be noted that a great deal of the decision is likely to be based on manner, facial expression, and personal appearance rather than on information obtained during the interview (Magson, 1926; Geidt, 1951; Springbett, 1958).

Future Research

The preceding conclusions are those which appear to have support from a number of experimental studies. Hundreds of other conclusions have been reported in the literature. However, it is generally found that these studies have not been replicated or that conflicting results have appeared. Even so, things do not appear quite as bad as many claim. We do know some things, and this knowledge can serve as a basis for, and be supplemented by, future research.

In what direction should we proceed with future research? There are, obviously, many avenues of approach available. Because of this fact, it would be difficult if not impossible to outline a complete research project which would answer all of the unanswered questions concerning the interview. It would, however, seem that the most profitable starting point of such a research project would be to investigate the decision-making process as it operates in the interview. Other approaches have provided us with the "what" answers. For example, research to date has told us that a structured interview form leads to higher inter-rater reliability. Research into the decision-making process may provide us with the "why" answers. Studies at McGill, undertaken with this objective in mind, have shown that in an unstructured interview (1) material is not covered consistently and (2) different interviewers are likely to weight the same information in different ways. These conclusions are supported by other studies, but only the McGill series was designed so that both results showed up. Here we may have an answer to part of the "why" question. That is, the structured interview may lead to a higher inter-rater reliability because (1) it makes it more likely that different interviewers get the same information and (2) it leads to a more equal weighting of information through the use of a structured rating form. Further investigation along these lines could supply us with information on what part each of the above plays and whether other factors are also leading to higher reliabilities. Having this information, we could then improve a structured guide by applying the methods which turn out to be the most important.

An approach with the objective of determining how decisions are reached may also be of value in studying the validity of these decisions. For example, it was pointed out that interviewers tend to emphasize negative information. Knowing that this affects the decision, we are now in a position to compare the results of this method of decision-making to that obtained when individuals are trained to weight the information in other ways.

In short, a careful study of the decision-making processes involved in the interview would provide answers to some of the questions discussed earlier. In addition, the results of such investigations would provide valuable guidelines for further research. The studies reviewed by Webster (1959) are a beginning step in this direction. Much more needs to be done.

REFERENCES

ADAMS, C. R. AND SMELTZER, C. H. "The Scientific Construction of an Interviewing Chart." *Personnel*, XIII (1936), 3–8.

ANDERSON, C. W. "The Relation Between Speaking Times and Decision in the Employment Interview." *Journal of Applied Psychology*, XLIV (1960), 267–268.

ANDERSON, R. C. "The Guided Interview As an Evaluative Instrument." *Journal of Educational Research*, XLVIII (1954), 203–209.

ASCH, S. "Forming Impressions of Personality." *Journal of Abnormal and Social Psychology*, XLI (1946), 258–290.

BALES, R. F. *Interaction Process Analysis: A Method for the Study of Small Groups.* Cambridge: Addison-Wesley, 1950.

BASS, B. M. "Situational Tests: I. Individual Interviews Compared with Leaderless Group Discussions." *Educational and Psychological Measurement*, XI (1951), 67–75.

BINGHAM, W. V. D., MOORE, B. V., AND GUSTAD, J. W. *How to Interview* (Fourth Edition). New York: Harper and Sons, 1959.

BLANKENSHIP, A. B. "The Effect of the Interviewer Upon the Response in a Public Opinion Poll." *Journal of Consulting Psychology*, IV (1940), 134–136.

BLOOM, B. F. AND BRUNDAGE, E. G. "Prediction of Success in Elementary Schools for

Enlisted Personnel." In D. B. Stuit (Editor), *Personnel Research and Test Development in the Bureau of Naval Personnel.* Princeton, N.J.: Princeton University Press, 1947, pp. 233–261.

BOLSTER, B. I. AND SPRINGBETT, B. M. "The Reaction of Interviewers to Favorable and Unfavorable Information." *Journal of Applied Psychology,* XLV (1961), 97–103.

BORGATTA, E. F. AND BALES, R. F. "The Consistency of Subject Behavior and the Reliability of Scoring in Interaction Process Analysis." *American Sociological Review,* XVIII (1953), 566–569.

BOYD, H. W. JR. AND WESTFALL, R. "Interviewers As a Source of Error in Surveys." *Journal of Marketing,* XIX (1955), 311–324.

BUGENTAL, J. F. T. "Explicit Analyses of Topical Concurrences in Diagnostic Interviewing." *Journal of Clinical Psychology,* IX (1953), 3–6.

CAHALAN, D., TAMULONIS, VALERIE, AND VERNER, HELEN W. "Interviewer Bias Involved in Certain Types of Opinion Survey Questions." *International Journal of Opinion and Attitude Research,* I (1947), 63–77.

CAMPBELL, J. T., PRIEN, E. P., AND BRAILEY, L. G. "Predicting Performance Evaluations." *Personnel Psychology,* XIII (1960), 435–440.

CAVANAGH, P., DRAKE, R. I., AND TAYLOR, K. F. "Youth Employment Service Interviews: Part 2. Differences Between Interviewers." *Occupational Psychology,* XXXVI (1962), 232–242.

CHAPPLE, E. D. "The Interaction Chronograph: Its Evolution and Present Application." *Personnel,* XXV (1949), 295–307.

CLARK, E. L. "Value of Student Interviews." *Journal of Personnel Research,* V (1926), 204–207.

COHEN, B. D., KALISH, H. I., THURSTON, J. R., AND COHEN, E. "Experimental Manipulation of Verbal Behavior." *Journal of Experimental Psychology,* XLVII (1954), 106–110.

CONRAD, H. S. AND SATTER, G. A. *The Use of Test Scores and Quality Classification Ratings in Predicting Success in Electricians' Mates School.* OSRD, 1945: Publications Board No. 13290. Washington: U. S. Department of Commerce, 1946.

COREY, S. M. "The Interview in Teacher Selection." *Journal of Educational Research,* XXVI (1933), 525–531.

CRISSY, W. J. E. "The Employment Interview—Research Areas, Methods, and Results." *Personnel Psychology,* V (1952), 73–85.

CRISSY, W. J. E. AND REGAN, J. J. "Halo in the Employment Interview." *Journal of Applied Psychology,* XXXV (1951), 338–341.

DANIELS, H. W. AND OTIS, J. L. "A Method for Analyzing Employment Interviews." *Personnel Psychology,* III (1950), 425–444.

DANSKIN, D. G. AND ROBINSON, F. P. "Differences in 'Degree of Lead' Among Experienced Counselors." *Journal of Counseling Psychology,* I (1954), 78–83.

DIPBOYE, W. J. "Analysis of Counselor Style by Discussion Units." *Journal of Counseling Psychology,* I (1954), 21–26.

DRIVER, R. S. "Research in the Interview." *Office Management Series,* No. 102. American Management Association, 1944, pp. 20–31.

DUNLAP, J. W. AND WANTMAN, M. J. *An Investigation of the Interview As a Technique for Selecting Aircraft Pilots.* CAA Airman Development Division, Report No. 33, 1944. Publications Board No. 50308. Washington: U. S. Department of Commerce, 1947.

DUNNETTE, M. D. AND BASS, B. M. "Behavioral Scientists and Personnel Management." *Industrial Relations,* II (1963), 115–130.

ENGLAND, G. W. AND PATTERSON, D. G. "Selection and Placement—The Past Ten Years." In H. G. Henneman, Jr., *et al.* (Editors), *Employment Relations Research: A Summary and Appraisal.* New York: Harpers, 1960, pp. 43–72.

FEARING, F. AND FEARING, F. M. "Factors in the Appraisal Interview Considered with Particular Reference to the Selection of Public Personnel." *Journal of Psychology*, XIV (1942), 131–153.

FLANAGAN, J. C. *AAF Aviation Psychological Program Research Reports*. Report No. 1. Washington: Government Printing Office, 1947.

GEIDT, E. H. "Judgment of Personality Characteristics from Brief Interviews." Unpublished Ph.D. thesis, University of California, 1951.

GOLDMAN-EISLER, FRIEDA. "Individual Differences Between Interviewers and Their Effect on Interviewees' Conversational Behavior." *Journal of Mental Science*, XCVIII (1952), 660–671.

GREENSPOON, J. "The Effect of Verbal and Mechanical Stimulae on Verbal Behavior." Cited as personal communication in Dollard, J. and Miller, N. E., *Personality and Psychotherapy*. New York: McGraw-Hill, 1950, 43–44.

GREENSPOON, J. "The Effect of Two Nonverbal Stimuli on the Frequency of Members of Two Verbal Response Classes." *American Psychologist*, IX (1954), 384 (Abstract).

HANDYSIDE, J. D. AND DUNCAN, D. C. "Four Years Later: A Follow-up of an Experiment in Selecting Supervisors." *Occupational Psychology*, XXVIII (1954), 9–23.

HANNA, J. V. "Estimating Intelligence by Interview." *Educational and Psychological Measurement*, X (1950), 420–430.

HILDUM, D. C. AND BROWN, R. W. "Verbal Reinforcement and Interviewer Bias." *Journal of Abnormal and Social Psychology*, LIII (1956), 108–111.

HOFFMAN, A. E. "An Analysis of Counselor Sub-Roles." *Journal of Counseling Psychology*, VI (1959), 61–67.

HOLLINGWORTH, H. L. *Judging Human Character*. New York: Appleton-Century-Crofts, 1922.

HYMAN, H. H. *et al. Interviewing in Social Research*. Chicago: University of Chicago Press, 1954.

KEATING, ELIZABETH, PATTERSON, D. G., AND STONE, C. H. "Validity of Work Histories Obtained by Interview." *Journal of Applied Psychology*, XXXIV (1950), 6–11.

KENAGY, H. G. AND YOAKUM, C. S. *The Selection and Training of Salesmen*. New York: McGraw-Hill, 1925.

MAAS, J. B. "The Patterned Scaled-Expectation Interview: Reliability Studies on a New Technique." *American Psychologist*, XVIII (1963), 438 (Abstract).

MCMURRY, R. N. "Validating the Patterned Interview." *Personnel*, XXIII (1947), 263–272.

MAGSON, E. H. "How We Judge Intelligence." *British Journal of Psychology*, Monograph Supplement No. 9, 1926.

MATARAZZO, RUTH G., MATARAZZO, J. D., SASLOW, G., AND PHILLIPS, JEANNE S. "Psychological Test and Organismic Correlates of Interviewer Interaction Patterns." *Journal of Abnormal and Social Psychology*, LVI (1958), 329–338.

MATARAZZO, J. D., SASLOW, G., AND MATARAZZO, RUTH G. "The Interaction Chronograph As an Instrument for Objective Measurement of Interaction Patterns During Interviews." *Journal of Psychology*, XLI (1956), 347–367.

MEEHL, P. L. *Clinical Versus Statistical Prediction: A Theoretical Analysis and a Review of the Evidence*. Minneapolis, Minn.: University of Minnesota Press, 1954.

MOOS, R. H. "The Retention and Generalization of Operant Conditioning Effects in an Interview Situation." *Journal of Abnormal and Social Psychology*, LXVI (1963), 52–58.

MOSS, F. A. "Scholastic Aptitude Tests for Medical Students." *Journal of the Association of American Medical Colleges*, VI (1931), 1–16.

MUSCIO, B. "The Influence of the Form of the Question." *British Journal of Psychology*, VIII (1916), 351–389.

MUTHARD, J. E. "The Relative Effectiveness of Larger Units Used in Interview Analysis." *Journal of Consulting Psychology*, XVII (1953), 184–188.

NEWMAN, S. H., BOBBITT, J. M., AND CAMERON, D. C. "The Reliability of the Interview in an Officer Candidate Evaluation Program." *American Psychologist*, I (1946), 103–109.

PASHALIAN, S. AND CRISSY, W. J. E. "The Interview: IV. The Reliability and Validity of the Assessment Interview As a Screening and Selection Technique in the Submarine Service." *MLR Report No. 216*, XII, No. 1, January, 1953.

PORTER, E. H., JR. "The Development and Evaluation of a Measure of Counseling Interview Procedures: Part II. The Evaluation." *Educational and Psychological Measurement*, III (1943), 215–238.

PUTNEY, R. W. "Validity of the Placement Interview." *Personnel Journal*, XXVI (1947), 144–145.

RICE, S. A. "Contagious Bias in the Interview: A Methodological Note." *American Journal of Sociology*, XXXV (1929), 420–423.

ROBINSON, FRANCIS P. "The Dynamics of Communication in Counseling." *Journal of Counseling Psychology*, II (1955), 163–169.

ROSLOW, S., WULFECK, W. H., AND CORBY, P. G. "Consumer and Opinion Research: Experimental Studies on the Form of the Question." *Journal of Applied Psychology*, XXIV (1940), 334–346.

ROWE, PATRICIA M. "Individual Differences in Selection Decisions." *Journal of Applied Psychology*, XLVII (1963), 304–307.

RUNDQUIST, E. A. "Development of an Interview for Selection Purposes." In G. A. Kelly (Editor), *New Methods in Applied Psychology*. College Park, Md.: University of Maryland Press, 1947, pp. 85–95.

SARBIN, T. R. "A Contribution to the Study of Actuarial and Individual Methods of Prediction." *American Journal of Sociology*, XLVIII (1942), 593–603.

SCOTT, W. D. "The Scientific Selection of Salesmen." *Advertising and Selling*, XXV (1915), 5–6 and 94–96.

SCOTT, W. D. "Selection of Employees by Means of Quantitative Determinations." *Annals of the American Academy of Political and Social Science*, LXV (1916).

SCOTT, W. D., BINGHAM, W. V. D., AND WHIPPLE, G. M. "Scientific Selection of Salesmen." *Salesmanship*, IV (1916), 106–108.

SHAPIRO, S. AND EBERHART, J. C. "Interviewer Differences in an Intensive Interview Survey." *International Journal of Opinion and Attitude Research* I (1947), 1–17.

SHAW, J. "The Function of the Interview in Determining Fitness for Teacher Training." *Journal of Educational Research*, XLV (1952), 667–681.

SNOW, A. J. "An Experiment in the Validity of Judging Human Ability." *Journal of Applied Psychology*, VIII (1924), 339–346.

SPERBER, Z. AND ADLERSTEIN, A. M. "The Accuracy of Clinical Psychologists' Estimates of Interviewees' Intelligence." *Journal of Consulting Psychology*, XXV (1961), 521–524.

SPRINGBETT, B. M. "Factors Affecting the Final Decision in the Employment Interview." *Canadian Journal of Psychology*, XII (1958), 13–22.

SYDIAHA, D. "On the Equivalence of Clinical and Statistical Methods." *Journal of Applied Psychology*, XLIII (1959), 395–401.

SYDIAHA, D. "Bales' Interaction Process Analysis of Personnel Selection Interviews." *Journal of Applied Psychology*, XLV (1961), 393–401.

SYDIAHA, D. "Interviewer Consistency in the Use of Empathic Models in Personnel Selection." *Journal of Applied Psychology*, XLVI (1962), 344–349.

TRANKELL, A. "The Psychologist As an Instrument of Prediction." *Journal of Applied Psychology*, XLIII (1959), 170–175.

TUPES, E. C. "An Evaluation of Personality-Trait Ratings Obtained by Unstructured Assessment Interviews." *Psychological Monographs*, LXIV (1950), No. 11 (Whole No. 317).

UHRBROCK, R. S. "Analysis of Employment Interviews." *Personnel Journal,* XII (1933), 98–101.

UHRBROCK, R. S. "The Personnel Interview." *Personnel Psychology,* I (1948), 273–302.

VAUGHN, C. L. AND REYNOLDS, W. A. "Reliability of Personal Interview Data." *Journal of Applied Psychology,* XXXV (1951), 61–63.

VERPLANCK, W. S. "The Control of the Content of Conversation: Reinforcement of Statements of Opinion." *Journal of Abnormal and Social Psychology,* LI (1955), 668–676.

WAGNER, R. "The Employment Interview: A Critical Summary." *Personnel Psychology,* II (1949), 17–46.

WEBSTER, E. C. "Decision Making in the Employment Interview." *Personnel Administration,* XXII (1959), 15–22.

WEBSTER, E. C. *Factors Pertaining to Decision Making in the Personnel Interview.* Final Report, Canadian Defence Research Board Grant 9435–53: April, 1962.

WEISS, D. J. AND DAWIS, RENE V. "An Objective Validation of Factual Interview Data." *Journal of Applied Psychology,* XLIV (1960), 381–385.

WEISS, D. J., DAWIS, RENE V., ENGLAND, G. W., AND LOFQUIST, L. H. *Validities of Work Histories Obtained by Interview.* Minneapolis, Minn.: University of Minnesota Press, 1961.

WENTWORTH, P. "How to Improve Employment Interviews." *Personnel Journal,* XXXII (1953), 46–49.

YONGE, K. A. "The Value of the Interview: An Orientation and a Pilot Study." *Journal of Applied Psychology,* XL (1956), 25–31.

QUESTIONS

1. Compare the results obtained from unstructured and structured interviews. How do you account for the difference?
2. Just how valid are selection interviews in general?
3. Some research has shown that an interviewer's impression of applicants is more likely to change from favorable to unfavorable than from unfavorable to favorable. Why is this so?
4. Considering what is known about the contribution of the interview to selection, what role in the entire selection process would you assign to it? Are there situations where the interview could be eliminated?

9.

More Value from Personnel Testing

ANDREW H. SOUERWINE

Ever since their rapid growth after World War II, programs in psychological testing have been under the scrutiny of the critical eyes of business executives. And well they should be! Millions of dollars are being spent annually on the sale of psychological tests, to say nothing of untold and incalculable sums consumed by industry for the development, administration, interpretation, and just plain maintenance of testing programs in individual companies. In all of these companies, experience with testing has brought a variety of reactions from "interesting," "helpful," "wouldn't be without it," and "let's have more of it," to "quackery," "waste of money," "a seed for conformity," and even to a frank and sometimes embarrassing admission of having a program and not knowing its value to the company. These reactions, in turn, have been recorded in the many articles written on the subject in the trade and professional journals.[1]

Test Your Opinion

A digest of this vast bibliography may lead to understandable confusion on the part of a person trying to make up his mind about the importance of psychological testing for use in his own company. All of the articles have at least some element of truth in them. The reader's problem is one of ferreting out fact from fiction, logic from emotion, reality from fantasy. This is no easy task. Perhaps it can be best solved by turning a spotlight on a series of incidents—all highly probable, and all reflecting certain problems in the development and use of psychological tests in business—and then discussing their implications. You may already have been in conversations like these.

1. *Quick Remedies.* At lunch one day with a group of executives, one of them says to you:

We have been having a lot of trouble lately with turnover in our transcriptionist

Reprinted from *Harvard Business Review*, Vol. 39, No. 2 (March–April 1961), pp. 123–130, by permission of the publisher. © 1961 by the President and Fellows of Harvard College; all rights reserved.

Andrew H. Souerwine is Professor of Industrial Administration and Director, MBA Program in Hartford, University of Connecticut.

[1] See, for example, Lewis B. Ward, "Problems in Review: Putting Executives to the Test," HBR July–August 1960, p. 6.

units. Just the other day we called in a consultant and talked to him about the kinds of tests he might have available for the selection of better girls for this job. We talked at some length about the job and about the qualities needed for this kind of work. The consultant assured us that he could develop a sound battery of selection tests and guaranteed us reduction in turnover within the year. I'm certainly glad that cat's finally off my back.

Would you agree with him?

2. *Interchangeability.* You are at lunch with executives from other companies. Learning that you are in personnel work, one of the men starts talking about an interesting experience he had. He says

A fellow came to my office about a year ago trying to sell me a program in testing. At first I was a little skeptical. Who needs tests? We're doing fine without them. But he asked me to give him ten minutes of my time and actually take the test. I figured I'd have nothing to lose, so I did. Y'know, that test is the most amazing thing. In just ten minutes that fellow told me more about myself than I hoped anybody would ever know about me.

I asked him to try it out on some of the other fellows in the office. Darned if they didn't have the same general reaction. That convinced us. We had one of our men take a course and learn more about the test. We just installed it about six months ago. Since that time, we've had little or no difficulty in selecting the right man. Almost to a man, we are told that the test really reveals a true picture of personality.

At this point, another in the group makes this observation:

I'm glad to hear you say that. I think our companies are quite similar. In fact, you will remember we cooperated in developing job descriptions. With that kind of experience, I think we'll get in touch with the outfit and talk with them, too.

Would you agree with them?

3. *"Tests Breed Conformity."* You

are in a meeting one day with a group of executives. They are talking about the new testing program which the technicians in the personnel department have just instituted. One executive says

Personally, I'm grateful we have such tests available to us now. They're going to be of some real help to me in making a decision. Of course, I think they've gone too far. One of the personnel department representatives was telling me today that they have considerable evidence that the company should not hire a clerk if she scores below a certain score on these tests. When you get to that point, you lose sight of the individual. Tests aren't perfect, and there's many a girl with a low score who could do a creditable job for us. After all, we know our department; we know what is needed and not needed. Tests are fine as guides, but we can't lose sight of the judgment that all of us have to exercise in a selection process.

A second executive comments on this view:

Well, I'm glad for the cutoff score. Decision making is easier, so I'm willing to go along with the test results. If they say "hire," I will. If they say "reject," well, I'll do that, too. Besides, people these days expect to be tested and they are willing to go along with whatever the test results tell us.

But a third man has this rejoinder:

Well, gentlemen, I must confess I'm scared. I don't like to get in the position of thinking that test results will be used for selection. This breeds conformity. Before we know it, we will have a group of girls around here who think alike, act alike, and maybe—fortunately or unfortunately—even *look* alike. Besides, as far as I can see, this is all money down the drain. You know as well as I do that these scores can be faked and influenced by so many things. If a girl has a good day or a bad day, it can affect her ability to get a job.

Would you agree with any of these men?

In the remainder of this article I shall discuss each of the three vignettes in turn.

But let me tip my hand in advance with this general conviction: if you agree wholeheartedly with any of these points of view, you are probably in for some problems in making a good decision regarding the development, the administration, or the use of testing programs in your company.

When to Test

The first vignette focuses on a problem which appears obvious once it is stated: the ability of tests to guarantee a quick remedy—in this case, a reduction in turnover. But the obvious is sometimes ignored, even by those with the best of intentions. The executive and the consultant are making an assumption that this turnover problem can be resolved through better selection procedures. In reality, however, the cause may be poor supervision, poor training, or poor work standards, to name just a few possibilities.

This is true of the many personnel problems facing a company—selection, placement, transfer, supervision, work flow, methods, benefits, salaries, training, working conditions, and absences. All can be the result of a variety of causes. When a problem exists in any of these areas, the first thing a company does is ask *why*. In all probability, there will be no one reason; therefore, there can be no one cure.

What cure *should* a company use? The solution is based on two major questions:

1. How much improvement can we expect by using this cure rather than some other one?
2. Will the cost of instituting this cure justify the amount of improvement?

Only when a company sees that it has a problem that may best be solved by developing a testing program, should it develop one—and then only if the estimated return justifies the estimated cost.

HIRING A SPECIALIST

The first vignette raises another problem, too. It is difficult (if not impossible) to guarantee results with any testing program. Granted, the competent professional is willing to make professional judgments. In all probability, if he has done an adequate preliminary study of the problem, he will be able to achieve some measure of improvement. But the effectiveness of any such program must rest on the facts obtained by relating test data to job performance. Hasty and unfounded predictions should be due cause for suspicion in the buyer.

Seeking the aid of a professional may, in itself, present a problem. It is somewhat disquieting for a company to buy a service, through a consultant or the employment of its own people, before it really knows whether testing will pay off. On the surface, this does not appear to be too businesslike. In order to avoid that "extra cost" before it knows what benefits might be derived, a company sometimes taps "that personnel man in the corner who seems to be interested in this sort of thing" and gives him the assignment of developing a testing program. This saving device usually ends up being costly.

Developing a testing program should not be a do-it-yourself project. It demands the use of competent, qualified personnel who are familiar with the myriad of technical details required for the adequate development and evaluation of selection devices.

Appraising the Value

In the second vignette we noticed the attitude that "the test works for me; therefore, it must be good," and the attitude that "it works in X company; therefore, it will work in ours." This suggests a different series of problems having to do mainly with questions regarding the value of any test used.

GULLIBLE'S TRAVELS

During my years of teaching in college and working in industry, I have demonstrated a technique known as "numerographology" which, I believe, bears on this point. Very briefly, it requires that a person write down in his own handwriting the first six-digit number that comes to mind. On this basis, I give a person an analysis, in a paragraph or two, of his major personality characteristics. Over the years, 98 percent of the people who have received an analysis through this technique have indicated that it is an unusually accurate and discerning means for analyzing personality.

Yet the technique is not for sale because, as a matter of fact, "numerographology" as a measuring instrument is extremely poor. Interestingly enough, all people get exactly the same description! As a demonstration, however, it has merit. Just because a lot of people are pleased with a particular test does not make it a good test. There are many reports of the gullibility of individuals, including executives and personnel managers.[2] A test may have the right-sounding name, it may have the personal testimony of many people, it may even make people feel good, but it can still be a highly useless test.

TROUBLES WITH STATISTICS

Where does a company turn to find support for the use of a given test? Most tests are accompanied by manuals, giving information on how to administer and score the tests; they should also include some information on the test's reliability and validity. These manuals, however, can be filled with statistics which are included primarily to impress rather than to shed light on the test's real worth. Hence, the manual might present tables which will indicate the difference in scores between those who are hired and those who are not hired. It may present data indicating that turnover has been reduced in a certain company during the first year of using this test. There may be tables showing how this test is related to other tests, similar and dissimilar; or how parts of this test are related to other parts.

But none of this information gives the company help on the question it really needs answered: Does this test measure the factor or factors which are related to job performance in our particular firm? What is even more to the point is the fact that the manual *cannot* give a company this information. Even a report in the manual on how well a test works in one company will not guarantee the same success in another. The only sure avenue is to use, and then to test, the test.

Determining Validity

There have been many articles written on what procedures a company should follow to determine the validity of the tests it uses. These steps can be enumerated very quickly:

1. Study the job.
2. Determine the factors needed for success.
3. Determine which factors can be tested and then develop or select the tests.
4. Administer the tests to applicants and hire without the benefit of test results, and/or administer the tests to a group of "good" and "poor" workers on that job.
5. Interpret the results; i.e., determine the extent to which test results are related to job performance.
6. Follow through and check the validity of the test results periodically.

The procedure sounds innocent enough. But problems in instituting it may be insurmountable for the company unless it is

---

[2] See Ross Stagner, "The Gullibility of Personnel Managers," *Personnel Psychology,* Autumn, 1958, p. 347.

forewarned and forearmed to deal effectively with them. Here are some of the key questions that come up:

Who determines what factors are essential on the job? At first glance, obtaining this information appears to be a rather modest requirement. All one need do is to observe the worker on the job and then make some reasonable guesses as to the characteristics needed for such performance.

But these observations are not done in a vacuum. They are made instead in a situation in which management, the employee, and in some cases, the union, may have some definite opinions. If all three parties agree, it is a happy situation. At least, it is about the best we can expect. If they do not agree, developing a testing program might be sidetracked before it starts. A personal experience may bear this out:

As a consultant to a small company, I was given the problem of developing techniques for the recruitment and selection of female college graduates for a particular job within the company. Through talks with management and with the college girls presently on the job, along with direct observation, I became thoroughly familiar with the duties of the position. A difference of opinion became apparent.

Management, on the one hand, felt that the job demanded the intelligence and the background of college graduates. The girls, on the other hand, were bored with their job and indicated that it could be done very well by women with a high school or, at best, a partial college background. Observation seemed to support the incumbents' opinion.

If we go along with management in this case and select college women, a program could be developed which has little chance of success, for we are now drawing from the wrong applicant population. If we do not accept management's point of view, then there again seems little value in developing a program. After all, management must support it if it is to be successful.

Who shall be tested? As indicated previously, a company has two choices in answering this question. First, it may elect to use present workers as its research group. If it does, it must be careful to lay the necessary groundwork before the researcher moves into a unit and starts testing the employees. Depending on the atmosphere which has been created in the company, employees may be understandably suspicious—they may fear for their future on the job. The actions of some unions may tend to magnify this problem. In addition, executives may have serious reservations about taking the necessary time out of the production schedule for the testing of employees, particularly if management feels that it is not receiving any direct benefits, such as information about specific employee performance.

The second way relates to the fact that all of the problems connected with present employees can be avoided by using an applicant population as the research group. This demands that the company hire on some basis other than test results, and at some later date relate the test results of these applicants to their job performance. From the researcher's point of view, such a procedure is ideal. But the manager who has a problem and who wants an answer may not want to wait a year or more to find out if the selection device is good or bad. Neither does management want to commit itself to hiring any more poor workers; it wants an answer—and right now.

What standards of performance shall be used in determining the usefulness of the tests? This is an age-old problem. At first glance, most companies feel that they are doing an excellent job of maintaining proper records of any employee's job performance and development. Unless these records are linked to some *objective* measures of performance, such as piece-rate production, number of days absent, or number of rejects, routine files on employees turn out to be a "by-guess-and-by-golly" kind of information regarding performance. To suggest to a company that new records must now be developed creates a problem which may appear insurmountable. "It's all right to institute some tests, but don't foul up our department's personnel records by changing them all round!" And yet change is crucial if such a company expects to learn anything about its testing program.

Even if management gets over this hurdle, there still remains the problem of what *kinds* of records to keep. We need not go into all of the problems related to merit evaluation, but it should be pointed out that they must be answered to the satisfaction of the company if suitable criteria are to be developed. As the complexity of the job increases, so do the problems in criteria development.

In our experience at The Travelers Insurance Companies, in developing selection tests for most clerical positions we rely primarily on the judgments of supervisors regarding the work performance of employees. We have judiciously avoided asking the supervisors to put a numerical weight on their judgments. Rather, through a personal interview with each of the supervisors over a period of time, we have obtained independent judgments on a sample of new employees. Supervisors were encouraged to refer to specific behavior on the job in arriving at their judgments. These independent supervisory ratings were then used as the criteria for research purposes.

Incidentally, we feel that this has a peripheral effect. Aside from giving us some information about new employees, it gives the supervisor another opportunity, apart from his annual merit evaluation, to take a closer look at his workers and to identify those who are not measuring up to expectations and those who are ready for more responsible jobs. This often results in correction talks with the employee or advancement for the employee at an earlier date.

Should management concern itself with the subject matter of the test? I recall reading a preliminary report regarding a brief test which one insurance company is developing, supposedly to determine the insurability of its automobile drivers below the age of 25. Someone raised a question regarding the use of such multiple-choice items on the test as "What kind of dog do you think would be the greatest cause of accidents?" or "With which of the following women would you most likely argue if you were involved with her in an automobile accident?"

On the face of it, questions like the foregoing appear to have little or nothing to do with the purpose of the test. From the practical business point of view, however, this should be of no real concern to the company. The important factor is one of knowing (and knowing in an empirical sense rather than feeling it intuitively) that the test items discriminate, in this case, between good and poor drivers.

But this does not mean that a company has no responsibility for the nature of the measuring instruments it uses. More than validity is at stake. Public relations, too, is a vital issue to consider. There may well be a point beyond which it is fruitless and even tactless to explore. This may be particularly true as the company ventures into personality testing, where, to date, the results for use in business have not been encouraging.

One cynic, who had apparently experienced some tortuous personal questioning, recently observed with tongue-in-cheek, but with a sharp needle-in-hand:

The moment some subaltern slips you a questionnaire asking such things as "Would you rather eat a banana split alone or with a jolly crowd?" pull this out of your pocket and have him fill it out for you:

1. How big is the Christmas bonus around here?
2. Would you classify your company as progressive or reactionary? That is, you aren't still sticking to two coffee breaks a day, are you?

3. The company pays for employee parking, of course?
4. Everybody has paid vacations, insurance plans, retirement programs, and all that stuff; but does this company have any real extras?
5. Whom do I see about arranging some sick leave during the duck-hunting season?

This kind of approach is guaranteed to have a startling effect in any company. That's a comforting thought indeed when you start reading the want ads again.

What are the tangential considerations? A company which subscribes to a testing program commits itself for a long period of time, not temporarily. As conditions change in labor supply—both in quantity and quality—and in business methods, the validity of a particular testing program is quickly affected. The question, therefore, becomes one not only of determining whether a test is good or not, but also of determining the extent to which a company is willing to support the many peripheral effects which are bound to arise from its commitments to such a program.

In this connection, the following considerations should be kept in mind:

Expense. Costs of a testing program are not only measured in the dollars needed to pay the salaries of the staff, but also in the effects that testing may have on the applicant, the employee, and the management. Reference has already been made to some of these effects, which may well, in the long run, cost more than the actual expense of administering the program.

Labor Supply. The establishment of a cutoff score on a test automatically reduces the number of people who may be considered for that particular job. If the testing program includes a series of tests, each with its own cutoff score, this will lead to an even smaller market of potential applicants for the job. The establishment of minimum test scores must, therefore, be related in some realistic fashion to the labor supply. A company cannot always afford to use that cutoff score which produces maximum validity.

Scope of Measurement. It is a generally accepted notion that no testing program can possibly measure all of the factors which are important for success on the job. This statement becomes more applicable as we move up to classification of jobs from the unskilled to the skilled to the supervisory and management levels. But even at the clerical level, after the company measures clerical aptitudes and typing skills and finds them to be above the minimum test standards, it must still make a decision regarding the motivations, the value systems, the attitudes of the applicants, and how these characteristics will enhance or detract from the basic skills.

The company cannot, therefore, use tests as a substitute, but rather only as a supplement to an already existing selection program. Highly valid tests can be offset by weaknesses in other areas of the selection process. Only the company can decide whether the cost for the addition of testing is the best place in the selection process to invest its money.

The Differences Within

We come now to the third vignette, which raises such attitudes as "I reserve the right to make the decision"; "I'm glad the tests decide for me"; and "Tests breed conformity." The comments made by the executives in this example reflect what has just been stated; namely, that the company atmosphere, attitudes, and value judgments have much to do, in the final analysis, with the success or failure of a testing program. A company can hire a highly competent consultant or staff man; it can develop excellent criteria and valid tests. But unless the testing program is carried on in an atmosphere which supports it and which understands it, it can be doomed to failure.

Hence, when the question of psychological testing first comes up, a company should take a hard, cold look at what it believes and is willing to support, not what it thinks it *should* do or *must* do.

LINE AND STAFF RELATIONS

Much has been written recently on this particular topic. There are those who believe that in the years to come staff functions will play an increasingly important part in the over-all operations of a company. Others talk in terms of staff *as opposed* to line, rather than staff *and* line functions.

A personnel testing program must, by its very nature, be developed and administered primarily through a staff department. If managers in line operations have no confidence in what staff departments are attempting to do, if they have an attitude that this should or could best be handled by line operators "who know what is really going on within the company," then it is doubtful that a testing program will have the support it needs to be as effective as it possibly can be.

VARIED ATTITUDES

What kinds of feelings and attitudes do executives have about testing? The following are outstanding:

"I can't give up my decision-making responsibilities to a testing program." The first executive in the third vignette indicated that he just could not go along with the results of the test and ignore other selection factors. Now, we can grant that there are many different factors which make for the success of individuals on the job. But if, through empirical study, a company determines that individuals with a certain test performance are, on the whole, not good employment risks, then management should be bound to the program and should not override these empirical findings by permitting their personal judgments to enter into a decision.

"I'm glad that tests can make the decision for me." On the other hand, the second executive in the example was equally wrong. Once an applicant scores above some empirically founded minimum standard, management must make an interpretation of test results. These results aid in the selection decision; they do not indicate that management *must* hire. When management gets to the point of thinking that tests can take away its responsibility to make a selection decision, it has developed a faith well beyond what is reasonable and justifiable.

"Tests can be faked." Often an argument which is used against installing a testing program leans heavily on the belief that tests can be faked. So can application blanks, letters of reference, and even information obtained through an interview. This argument implies that respondents will falsify tests at every opportunity, particularly when it comes to getting a job.

In the case of those positions that demand the evaluation of characteristics which psychology is willing to admit are not presently best evaluated through industrial test procedures (and here we can include most of the self-inventories and personality and attitude measures), certainly a company should think twice before utilizing them. But there are a myriad of tests that measure skills and abilities (apart from assessment of personality) which people either have or do not have, which can be measured reliably, and which can be objectively scored and related to whatever measures of performance a company desires.

"Tests breed conformity." Recent writings have argued that testing breeds the organization man, particularly at the supervisory and management levels where it selects out only those individuals who possess the qualities demanded by the corporation. There is little evidence to substantiate this claim. Undeniably, all people are different; and when it comes to the subtle personality characteristics which make for these differences—such

as motives, attitudes, values, and experiences—the variances are so great and the means to evaluate are still so relatively primitive that even if a company would desire all men with the same amount of the same drive, it would be difficult to select and recruit such a group.

But even more important is the fact that the very kind of man which a company now seeks for management positions denies the very probability of conformity. Management is becoming more aware of its need for the creative man, for the man with ability and drive to be imaginative, to develop new horizons in the industry, and to have the desire and the ambition to remove himself from the thundering herd of conformity and bureaucracy.

Management and People

Aside from their attitudes about testing, managers should also explore their feelings about people. A subtlety is involved here which, in my opinion, can make a real difference in the success of a program. Testing programs demand a fairly objective appraisal of individuals (an end that a company should move toward in all its evaluation procedures). Testing is not an invitation to consider applicants and employees as things in the environment which can be put through a mill. A decision cannot be reached without some person-to-person involvement on the part of the company.

On the one hand, as we have indicated, testing demands adherence to certain minimum standards empirically derived. On the other hand, failure to "pass" a test should rarely, if ever, be used as the sole basis for a discussion with an applicant who did not get the job he sought. It is difficult in such situations for the applicant to justify to himself or to others that the tests are any good at all. The test may, in fact, be valid. But we are talking here about feelings, and these feelings make a big difference when it comes to such things as public relations, employee morale, and relations with unions. Unless the company is tuned to these feelings before, during, and after the development of a testing program, installation of the program may have negative effects.

This concern for feelings sometimes takes the form of a claim that using tests is an invasion of privacy. Whether it is or not depends largely on the use to which the information is put. A company continuously has the problem of analyzing the materials with which it works, human or not.

Take the way a company carefully studies the manufactured product to determine its structure, and puts it under rigorous tests to check its overall effectiveness. In the same vein, a company seeks to obtain, in as valid a way as is possible, information about its people. Such records, of course, must remain confidential and be used only to the extent that they aid in evaluating the individual's potential effectiveness on the job. To do less than this indicates a lack of concern for the full development of people on the job. To do more than this implies a lack of respect for the individuality of the person.

Conclusion

In raising all of these questions, I am not suggesting that testing programs have no value. On the contrary! The evidence is much too weighty in support of the effectiveness of such programs in an industrial setting. I am urging, rather, that a company do more than focus on such factors as determining what the problem is, whether tests can help to resolve that problem, what program should be used in the development and evaluation of such tests, how much tests cost, effects on labor supply, and the like. While these areas must undoubtedly be considered, they will be of little value to the company that does not take a closer look at and gain insight into:

• Its departmental relations—particularly between line and staff functions.
• Its attitudes about people, both within and outside the company.
• Its feelings about objective measures of evaluation.
• Its desire for change.

Understandably, committing a company to a testing program can be disquieting. This is not only a matter of the general tendency to resist change. There is also a technical jargon which prevents complete understanding. And there is, to some degree, an accepted reliance on concepts or on other people rather than on one's own feelings in evaluating personnel. Testing means committing oneself to learning where the tests come from, what evidence the company has for making the statements it does, and how to evaluate more objectively the information it obtains on personnel. It means a willingness to become more critical of oneself, more aware of the overgeneralizations one makes about people, more aware of one's biases.

In short, over and above its concern for the mechanics of developing a testing program, a company must develop awareness of certain subtleties existing within its management ranks. These subtleties can be the overwhelming determinants for the success or failure of psychological testing in business.

QUESTIONS

1. Under what circumstances can selection testing make a contribution to the company?
2. Do you feel that psychological tests breed conformity in the organization?
3. Who should determine what factors are essential on the job? How?
4. Can testing give quick cures to management's problems?
5. Outline the principal issues management should face when installing a selection-testing program.

10.

Assessing Managerial Talent

WALTER S. WIKSTROM

Judging the managerial ability of subordinates is a continuing responsibility of almost every manager. When a man is to be brought into management ranks or promoted within them, one or more managers usually have to select a man who they believe will be able to perform successfully in the new job. The comments of managers suggest that it is not an easy task.

In the Bell Telephone System, and in a few other companies, some decided improvement has been achieved in the capacity of managers to select men with managerial talent and in the quality of the selections made. The device that has been used is the special assessment center.

The simplest definition of an assessment center is that it is a place where assessments are made. "Assessments," in this context, are the pooled judgments of several specially trained managers who use a variety of criteria to evaluate a man's performance as he goes through several different "test" situations. Usually some paper-and-pencil tests are also used, and an intensive interview is a normal part of the assessment procedure. It is this matter of multiple judgments based upon observations of performance in several situations that is the crux of the assessment center method.

The method is not new. Both the British and German armies have used it for the selection of officer candidates. In the United States, the World War II Office of Strategic Services used assessment centers to pick men for clandestine assignments behind enemy lines. Still, the technique has not been widely used to assess managerial potential.

How It Started in the Bell System

In 1956 the American Telephone and Telegraph Company began a long-term Management Study to uncover information about the personal development of men as they worked as managers within the Bell System. The study is still going on. As part of the study, AT&T operated assessment centers during the summers of 1956 through 1960 to obtain information about the backgrounds and abilities of young men just starting out in management careers in the System.

Reprinted from *The Conference Board Record*, Vol. 4, No. 3 (March 1967), pp. 39–44, by permission of The Conference Board.

Walter S. Wikstrom is Director, Organization Development Research, The Conference Board.

The first men assessed were recent college hires brought into the Michigan Bell operating company in 1956. While officials of that company did not have access to the assessments, they learned enough about the procedures to decide that the methods might be useful in selecting foremen from the ranks of skilled craftsmen employed by the firm. At the request of the Michigan company, the research staff in the parent organization modified the assessment procedures so that the center could be operated by specially trained line managers.

Today over fifty assessment centers are operating in various parts of the Bell System. They are used for the most part to help select men and women for the first (lowest) level supervisory positions. A few of the companies use assessment centers to assess men for positions at the fourth and fifth management levels, just below officer rank. Between five and six thousand men and women are now assessed annually.

The spread of the assessment center method in the System has occurred largely at the request of the operating companies. No pressure to adopt the method has been put upon the companies by AT&T. In fact, the parent company did not publicize the method within the System until several centers had already proven their value to the companies using them.

What Makes Assessment Different?

The parent company has said it is a wonder that selection, without prior assessment, is as successful as it is, in view of the many problems confronting a manager trying to pick a man to become a manager.

For one thing, the work of a craftsman is quite different from that of a manager. Yet, a manager trying to select a future foreman has to go by job performance as a craftsman. Further, the several men under consideration are apt to have worked at several different crafts. There is no standard basis of performance against which to judge the different men.

Another problem is that the manager probably can consider only a very few of the men who should be under consideration. Thus he may have only a limited idea of the range of talent that is available. He may pick the best man he knows of, but that may be far from the best man available.

An assessment center, on the other hand, can assess all the men who seem to have management potential or who indicate an interest in management work. Thus, any one man can be viewed against the background of all the available men. Judgments of their ability can be made on the basis of their performance on standardized tasks that call for managerial skills and abilities, not against the varying crafts at which they have been employed.

As used in the Bell System, an assessment is only information about potential ability; it is not a decision to promote. Promotions are still made by the responsible line officials in charge of the operations into which a man will be promoted. The information on the candidates received from an assessment center, however, can make the job of selecting the best man considerably easier and more often successful.

How Are Employees Nominated for Assessment?

Assessment begins when a man arrives at an assessment center. But most of the operating companies have spelled out procedures that begin before that, with the nomination of employees to attend.

The process begins, for example, when a foreman spots a telephone repairman who seems to have what it takes to be a foreman; or a supervisor notices a long-lines operator who might be a chief operator. Perhaps an employee himself has broached an interest in moving up into management. The employee is told that supervisory work requires skills that he has not had a chance to demonstrate on the job. Possibly even he does not really know whether or not he has what a management job requires. At the assessment center he will go through a number of exercises that call for the managerial skills of a supervisory position. Experienced line managers, specially trained in assessment procedures, will observe and evaluate his performance. The assessment results are given to him, if he wants them, and to the line management organization. Thus, the assessment will be available to superiors when he is considered for promotion.

After this explanation, the employee must decide whether or not he wishes to go. If he does, he is scheduled to attend a center operated by his company when next there is an opening.

What Happens at an Assessment Center?

Assessment is a half-week process, with a dozen men going through at a time. In addition to the situational exercises in which they participate, the men take a few paper-and-pencil tests and have a lengthy interview with one of the staff assessors.

The interview is an important part of the procedure. It is a "depth" interview, but not in the clinical psychology sense. It is conducted by a line manager, not a psychologist. The interviewer encourages the man to talk about his work experience and his educational preparation, about his experiences growing up and his personal goals and plans. He is questioned about his understanding of the nature of management work and about his reasons for wanting to be part of management. It is a much more searching interview than the average manager is apt to conduct when selecting men for promotion to a foreman's position.

Three paper-and-pencil tests are normally administered at the centers. One is a general test of mental ability (*School and College Ability Test,* Educational Testing Service), a test of ability to reason (*Critical Thinking,* Educational Testing Service—no longer published) and a test on knowledge of current affairs (*Contemporary Affairs Test*). The last test is designed to reveal the breadth of a man's interests by showing the degree to which he is familiar with events in the world around him. A new version is developed annually by the parent company with the aid of a consultant.

If interviews and tests were all that were involved in the assessment procedures, they would not be significantly different from much personnel selection. What is distinctive, whether in the Bell System companies or in the wartime OSS, is the use of situational exercises for observing the prospects.

The Situations

During his time at an assessment center, a Bell System man participates in four situational exercises. One is the "IN-Basket" exercise. Basically it is a structured experience in managing.

IN-BASKET EXERCISE

A man is assigned a desk with a collection of papers in the desk's "IN" basket. The stack includes memos, letters, reports and the other communications that would be typical in the daily mail of a supervisor in the System. He also is given a copy of the union contract, an organization chart for his segment of the hypothetical company he is working for, and other background material, as well as blank stationery.

For a couple of hours he reads, analyzes and acts upon the situations that the contents of his "IN" basket reveal. He dictates memos, answers letters, jots notes about follow-up actions he must take. He determines the priorities to be met in dealing with the problems in the basket. He decides what to delegate and to which "subordinate." For several hours he "manages."

At the end of the exercise, a member of the staff conducts a systematic interview about his performance, questioning him about his reasons for the actions he took and the decisions he made. The assessor writes a report evaluating the managerial judgment shown by the man as he tackled this sample of managerial work.

OTHER SITUATIONS

The other situations involve groups of six men observed by one or more of the staff. (To make several judgments available for the final assessment, different observers are used for the different exercises.) A business game requires the men to run a toy company, profitably if possible. They buy various component parts that can be assembled in a number of ways to make different toys. The men must actually assemble real parts to make real toys; this game does not involve merely making decisions about what to do. The prices they must pay for components change during the game. So do the prices that the "market" will pay for the various finished toys.

The men must determine the best mix of products in the light of material costs and prevailing prices. They have to determine proper inventory levels of components and finished goods. They must set up an efficient organization for analyzing data, reaching decisions and producing toys.

The observers take note not only of the decisions that are taken by the group, but also of the interaction among the men as they work on the problem. They note signs of leadership, analytical ability, competitive spirit and risk-taking, and other characteristics that the men display.

Another situation requires the men to play the roles of supervisors meeting to agree upon a man for a promotion. Each man is given a background description of

a "subordinate" whom he is to sponsor. Since only one "'promotion" is available, the men must compete to see which man can persuade the others to select his "subordinate."

The exercise begins with each man in turn making a short prepared presentation on the merits of his "candidate." During this phase of the exercise the observers look for skill in communicating clearly, concisely and persuasively.

After hearing all the presentations, the six "supervisors" discuss the merits of the "candidates" and eventually agree on a ranking of the "candidates" in the order of their suitability for the promotion. The observers watch the interplay of the men as they deal with the shifting, competitive situation. Afterward, the assessors prepare written reports on each of the men: his success in achieving the goal (the rank of his "candidate"), his ability to persuade and negotiate, the way in which he sized up the situation and adapted his approach to the behavior of the other men he was dealing with. In addition to this narrative report, each man is rated and ranked on his contribution to the group's work and on his own success.

For this exercise there is no single "best way" that the assessors are looking for. Some groups approach a deadlock as several dominant men attempt to steamroller one another, Good management may mean someone breaking the deadlock. Another group may founder until one man leads the discussion so as to get all the information considered and evaluated and a decision arrived at. The "right" behavior depends upon what is going on in the group meeting. The task of the assessors is to size up the situation during the meeting and the way in which each man responds to it.

Another group discussion exercise involves a labor dispute. Each man is required individually to dig out pertinent "facts"about the dispute by questioning a member of the staff. Since the staff members provide information only when it is specifically requested, the men must be astute in deciding what facts they need to understand the dispute. With information in hand, the men independently decide how the dispute should be handled. During this phase of the exercise, the assessors look for evidence of a man's fact-finding ability, the logic of his thinking and his decisiveness.

The six men then meet in a group discussion to try to arrive at a common decision, with the staff observing the interaction. During this group phase, the assessors look for the same characteristics as they do in the previously mentioned "promotion" exercise.

The Staff Arrives at the Assessment

The work of the assessment center staff does not end when the half-week of interviews, tests and exercises is over. The men who have been under observation return to their jobs but the six staff members and the director spend the remainder of the week carefully considering the behavior of each man in each of the situations. They must agree upon an over-all assessment.

Each man is considered separately. His test scores are reviewed. The observers read their reports on his behavior in the situational exercises, including the ratings on effectiveness and his rank in the group he worked with. The report of the interview is read. Then each staff member independently rates the man on twenty characteristics that are believed relevant to success as a manager.

Among these characteristics are management abilities, such as ability to plan and to organize, to communicate, to reach a decision, and to use information effectively. More personal characteristics are also considered, such as flexibility, breadth of interest, and leadership.

Finally, the staff discusses the ratings that each member has given the man; the entire group then assigns him to one of four categories: "more than acceptable," "acceptable," "less than acceptable," and "unacceptable." The director then prepares a summary report that includes the over-all assessment of promotability and discusses the strengths and weaknesses of the man as seen in the various situations at the center.

The subjects of all this work are also given the chance to learn about the assessment. Eighty-five percent of the men who have been through the centers in the operating companies have asked for a report on how they did. This report is usually given face-to-face by one of the center staff who travels to the men in order to provide this personal feedback. The feedback has been valuable in prompting acceptance of the centers by the men who have been assessed.

In many cases men have learned about some easily correctable weakness that has been uncovered; they can then take steps to prepare for future management work. Other men learn that they are seen as having good potential for advancement. Even when a craftsman has learned that he does not seem to have management ability, he usually has not indicated resentment toward the center process. The attitude of most of the men seems to be that they have been given a fair chance to show what they can do. Their acceptance of the results is eased up by the fact that the results in no way reflect upon their abilities as skilled craftsmen; their prestige is not threatened by the suggestion that they may not be good managers.

Who Are the Staff Members?

The staff of the assessment centers is drawn from experienced managers of proven ability from levels above that for which promotions are being considered. Thus, in the case of centers judging men for promotion into first-line supervision, the assessors would come from the second-level of management and the director of the center would be a third-level man.

Assignment to a center is temporary, usually for a six-month period. Directors generally serve for two years. It is thought that the knowledge of operations that these temporary staffs bring is a major factor in the success of the centers.

Although the director of a center reports to a fourth-level manager in his company's general personnel department, the other staff members remain on the payroll of their former units throughout their temporary assignments.

Success as a manager is the chief requirement that must be met in selecting men for these assignments. Assessors are selected by their line supervisors and come from the same departments and areas as the men who are to be assessed. Beyond that, the companies seek men who seem to be perceptive in dealing with others, who seem to be able to establish rapport in talking with men and who have natural ability to understand what makes a man tick. Communications ability is required, both oral and written. Oral communication is important because the overall assessments are arrived at in conference with other assessors; reports of observations must be made clearly and concisely. The ability to write clearly is important for the many written reports of observations that will be required from a staff assessor during his term of service.

A three-week training period introduces the new staff members to the work that they will be doing. The training may be provided by men from the parent corporation, by an experienced man in the operating company or by an experienced director. The new men learn about the tests that are part of the procedure, and what the results mean. They study the situations and they will observe and brush up their interviewing skills. Perhaps as important as anything they they learn, they have a chance to get to know one another, to size each other up and learn how to evaluate each other's judgments.

The third week of the training period is usually a dummy run through an assessment program with twelve subjects who are not actually being assessed. Here they practice the procedures and iron out any snags.

The companies have found that no special expertise is required. The skills can be acquired, although they improve with experience. And after six months of work, fatigue usually begins to take its toll. The work is extremely grueling, according to those who have served as assessors. Close attention is required whenever a man is being interviewed or a group is being observed. Written reports must be prepared quickly and yet with precision and clarity. Long hours of discussion are needed for the assessors to reach agreement on the assessments of the men who have been observed. After six months of this work the typical assessor is drained.

Rotation Keeps Job Knowledge Fresh

The companies see another advantage in rotating this assignment among experienced managers. An assessor is never more than six months from the actual operations for which he is assessing potential managers. He can assess in terms of the actual behavior requirements of a job with which he is familiar. If a team of managers were given a permanent assignment to an assessment center, the companies believe they would almost certainly lose touch with the gradually changing requirements of supervisory positions. They would then be picking men to handle the jobs as they existed in the past, not as they exist in the present.

To preserve this element of practical judgment, the assessors are left free to use their judgment and experience in evaluating what they observe at the centers. As indicated above, at one stage in the procedure each assessor must rate each man on some twenty characteristics.

But that is merely to assure that the assessors will not overlook something that might be important. If, in the judgment of an assessor, one or more of these characteristics is not really important to success as a supervisor, he can ignore them when he makes his over-all assessment of a man's managerial ability. In a sense, the procedure dictates what will be considered, while the assessors determine whether or not it will be considered important.

What Benefits Have Resulted?

The assessment center method of selecting potential managers has spread through the Bell System because of its demonstrated worth in the companies that used it at the start. In the opinion of management in those companies, a higher proportion of good men were being promoted when those making the promotions had the benefit of assessments of the candidates.

A study of the value of assessment centers was conducted in the Michigan operating company, the first unit in the System to use assessment centers in the selection of plant department foremen. The study compared the performance of the last forty men promoted before the opening of the center with the performance of the first forty men promoted after assessment data were available. Of the first group, only one third were considered to be doing a better than satisfactory job; a third were considered to have potential to advance at least one more level. But of the group promoted after assessment data were fed into the selection process, two thirds were rated as doing a better than satisfactory job and two thirds were thought to have potential for further advancement. The selection batting average had been doubled through the use of assessments.

Findings consistent with those of the Michigan study, although less dramatic,

have come from a study of the operation of assessment centers in four operating companies. The study was done by the personnel research unit of the American Telephone and Telegraph Company. In all but one of the four companies, foremen who had been chosen after the assessment centers were in operation were doing a better job than foremen chosen prior to assessment. The difference was modest but real. More significantly, perhaps, there was a large difference between these groups in terms of potential for further advancement. Far more of the foremen who had been chosen after assessment were seen to have potential to advance than was true of those foremen whose promotion came before the assessment program was begun.

In those cases where results ran counter to the rest it was often found that assessors had been lenient in their ratings. They had given far more assessments of "acceptable" than was typical of most assessors. This had the effect of letting more men of questionable ability be promoted with an acceptable rating from the center. This suggests to these companies that assessors should apply fairly stringent standards so that line management is forced to take a careful look at questionable cases.

As noted earlier, a poor assessment is not a kiss of death. Men who are assessed as "less than acceptable" or "unacceptable" may still be promoted if their line superiors believe that the assessment is not an accurate reflection of ability or if they believe that a real weakness uncovered during assessment has been overcome. Of course, when a poor assessment has been given a man, his whole record is given a very careful going over and far fewer men in these groups are eventually promoted than is true of the men with higher ratings.

In the parent company's study of the four operating companies, 5 per cent of men who had been rated "unacceptable" had been promoted anyway; of these, nearly half were thought to be doing well. Thus line superiors had been able to select from this group a fairly large number of men who could succeed.

A Related Study

For Bell System companies there is another bit of evidence for this selection process. It comes from the Management Progress Study being conducted by the parent company. In connection with this study, special assessment centers[1] were conducted in the summers of 1956 through 1960. The subjects were 422 young men on first-level management jobs in six Bell System companies. Two-thirds of the men were recent college graduates and one-third were former craftsmen who had been promoted into supervisory positions.

One part of the over-all assessment made at these centers was a prediction that a man would or would not reach middle management within ten years. Although at most, eight years have elapsed since these assessments were made, the research unit has conducted a preliminary study of the validity of those predictions. Of those men who have already reached middle-level positions in the System, 78 per cent had been predicted to do so. Of those who had not advanced beyond their first-level jobs, 95 per cent had been assessed as not having potential for advancement. Inasmuch as the assessments have not been reported to anyone in the System, they cannot have had the effect of self-fulfilling prophecies. Bell sees this as evidence that assessment centers are able to make remarkably accurate judgments of potential for advancement.

How Much Does All This Cost?

Assessment is a fairly expensive operation. The parent company has estimated that it costs about $400 to assess one man. That figure includes the costs of operating the center; the salary, travel and living expenses at the center of the men being assessed; and other related expenses.

Weighed against the costs of employing poor managers (which the Bell System has not tried to estimate) the System companies figure that they are making a wise investment when they spend money to help select better men. They believe that it is worth $400 a man to get a markedly better managerial group.

QUESTIONS

1. What is an assessment center, and how does it differ from ordinary selection methods?
2. What happens at an assessment center?
3. What are the advantages and disadvantages of assessment centers?

---

[1] These centers were "special" in that they were staffed by psychologists, used tests different from those used in the operating centers and different, though similar, situational exercises. The assessments have not been available to anyone in the system other than the research personnel in the parent company.

11.

Progress and Problems in Equal Employment Opportunity

WILLIAM J. KILBERG

The contract compliance program set up under Executive Order 11246, as amended, uses the government's procurement process to require equal employment opportunity (EEO) by Federal contractors and subcontractors and federally assisted construction contractors and subcontractors. The thrust of that Program is to increase the utilization of minorities and females throughout an employer's work force pursuant to nondiscrimination and affirmative action objectives.

Our position, which has been fully supported by the courts, emphasizes the legitimate concern of the Government to ensure that the work force needs of the Nation are met. It is a privilege, not a right, to do business with the Government. Before the Government grants that privilege, it is going to exact certain commitments, among them a commitment to nondiscrimination and affirmative action in employment.

Using the concept of goals and time-tables, employers are asked to review their personnel policies, practices, and procedures to ensure that they're fair and valid; to take affirmative action to increase the relevant labor pools from which they recruit and promote; and to make good faith efforts to meet these targets, which the employers themselves set in the nonconstruction area, for minority and female utilization throughout their work forces.

It would be inconsistent to recognize the need for remedying employment underutilization without at the same time meeting the concomitant need of nondiscrimination. We have said that underutilization is the result of discrimination. But indeed, it might not be a result of a particular employer's discrimination. Rather, it could result from discrimination in education, housing, health care, transportation, or any number of discriminatory facets of our society.

The *Bethlehem Steel* Decision[1] of January 1973 is significant in that it is

Reprinted from the *Labor Law Journal*, Vol. 24, No. 10 (October 1973), pp. 651–661 by permission of the publisher and author.

William J. Kilberg is Solicitor of Labor, United States Department of Labor.

[1] *In the Matter of Bethlehem Steel Corp.*, Decision of the U. S. Secretary of Labor, Docket No. 102–68, January 15, 1973, EMPLOYMENT PRACTICES GUIDE ¶ 5128.

the first decision under the administrative hearing process set up under the Executive Order to recognize that the definition of discrimination is expansive and requires a concomitant expansive reading of the remedial relief that's required. Accordingly, the *Bethlehem* Decision substituted a plantwide seniority system for a department or division seniority system which had the effect of perpetuating prior discrimination.

In *Bethlehem,* the Office of Federal Contract Compliance in the Department of Labor alleged that there existed a class of individuals who were suffering the present effects of prior discrimination. Therefore, it was agreed that this should be treated as present discrimination. We also recognized that full relief would require providing these individuals an opportunity to move into their rightful place, i.e., where they would have been but for the employer's initial discrimination in job assignment and seniority strictures.

The AT&T Settlement

The AT&T[2] settlement agreement and consent decree, following on the heels of *Bethlehem,* is dramatic evidence of how quickly the Government was able to grasp this new dimension and further expand relief to include back-pay, coverage of professional employees, and some new legal concepts, particularly the concept of restitution. These concepts were tied together to meet the demands of the Executive Order, the Equal Pay Act, and Title VII of the Civil Rights Act of 1964, as amended.

The fact that two separate EEO agencies of the Government, the Department of

Labor and the Equal Employment Opportunity Commission, were able to get together and sit down and bargain in good faith with the largest private employer in the United States and reach a settlement of this dramatic proportion is a very significant event.

The Department had begun equal pay actions against various components of the Bell Systems four to five years before the instant AT&T case came to fruition. There was also a contract compliance action undertaken pursuant to the Executive Order Program by the General Services Administration, which was the Contract Compliance Agency for the Bell System and other utilities.

The Concept of Restitution

I think one of the most dramatic and far-reaching aspects of the relief in AT&T was the concept of restitution. This involved considerations of what the Company during our negotiations called "the would have beens and the should have beens." In AT&T there are some 300,000 telephone operators, alone, across the United States. We said that some proportion of those operators, but for the Company's personnel policies, practices, and procedures, which we alleged were discriminatory, would have been, or should have been, or might have been in craft jobs. Obviously, we didn't know which ones.

The Company said, "which ones—tell us which ones and we'll talk relief."

We said, "We don't know and you don't know, but some percentage of them would have been, or should have been, or might have been."

What we did was tie in a definition of

2 Agreement by the American Telephone and Telegraph Company, its associated Bell Telephone Companies, the Equal Employment Opportunity Commission, and the U.S. Department of Labor, January 18, 1973, EMPLOYMENT PRACTICES GUIDE ¶1860. The provisions of the agreement were embodied in a consent decree entered in the U.S. District Court, Eastern District of Pennsylvania, Civil Action No. 73-149, January 18, 1973. Model Affirmative Action Program for the Bell System appears at EMPLOYMENT PRACTICES GUIDE ¶ 1861.

who those "would have beens" and "should have beens" were with the Company's affirmative action steps. Since we didn't know at that point precisely what the Company's goals should be, they had to decide on their goals by doing an analysis of fifteen job classifications in 700 facilities. Looking at the number of job openings that the Bell System has in a given year in craft jobs, it was legitimate to expect the Company to transfer approximately 10,000 women over a two-year period from operator and clerical jobs into craft jobs.

And so we said, "Those will be the 'would have beens' and 'should have beens' and we'll transfer them on the basis of an interest minimum qualification."

The Company said, "Well, how shall we pay them?" and "What shall we pay them?"

This is something we anguished over together for some period of time. The Company had done some studies to determine what their pay rates were and what they would have been getting if employed in craft positions. We set up a system which would pay women depending upon when they transferred and whether they then remained on the job for a period of time. We said that those that transferred in the first six months will get $100.00, those who transfer in the second six months will get $200.00, in the third $300.00, in the fourth $400.00

Thus, an incentive was provided to members of the "affected class" to transfer out of non-craft, non-management jobs into craft jobs. A concomitant incentive was provided for the Company to transfer them. The faster they were transferred, the less it cost the Company. There was also some equity involved. Those persons (predominantly women but also some minorities) who transferred later had waited longer to be transferred, so they deserved a greater sum of money: We developed a system which would yield a rapidly integrated work force and, I think, the rapid transformation of a large bureaucratic organization from one which resisted such change to one that would not only accept it but also would be in a posture of supporting it because it would be a fully integrated work force in a rather short period of time.

Equal Pay Concepts

Another aspect of the agreement, which I think is fascinating, involves some equal pay concepts and also raises some other novel questions. There were seven and a half million dollars in relief in this agreement. This relief could have been achieved under either Title VII, the Equal Pay Act, or the Executive Order, depending upon how the EEO aspects of the women transferees are viewed.

Some background information on the Bell System is needed here. A few years back the Bell Company said, "All right, we are going to allow women to transfer into craft jobs. But, when they transfer among craft jobs or from non-craft into craft jobs, they receive the previous rate of pay plus a differential."

Anomalous situations can occur. A woman earning $100.00 a week who transfers from a clerical or operator position with a 10 percent differential would receive a total of $110.00. A man transferring from a less skilled craft to the very same position, if he formerly earned $200.00 a week, would receive $220.00 to do the same work. It is possible that a woman with greater seniority in a particular craft could earn substantially less than the man transferring into that craft even though she might be his supervisor. These dollar figures are not accurate, of course, merely illustrative.

Under Title VII, or under the Executive Order, that situation would involve remedying the employment problems of an affected class, a group of persons who are suffering the present effects of prior discrimination involving discriminatory placements of female applicants as operators or clericals based solely on the criteria of sex. This differential wage payment system, which on its face is nondiscriminatory, has a discriminatory impact in fact. The only reason that the woman earns less than the man is the initial job placement. Her previous pay rate becomes a barrier to her being where she would have been but for the Company's initial discrimination.

On the other side of the coin, viewing this as Equal Pay Act violation, one would first look at the particular jobs where men and women are doing substantially equal work and the women make less than the men.

We would say to the Company, "What excuse have you got for this? Have you got something that falls within the exceptions stated in the Equal Pay amendments to the Fair Labor Standards Act?"

The employer would say, "Yes, it's based on a wage differential which is the way we promote people and the way we pay them."

"Yes," we'd say, "but the difference in wages was itself based on a discriminatory placement and, therefore, would not be an acceptable defense under the Equal Pay Act."

Thus, the two statutes have the same effect.

Determining the Unit Involved

Michigan Bell had an overwhelming majority of women in the job classification of switchroom helpers. During World War II, as was common with so many companies, the Bell System hired women for formerly male jobs. When the war ended they sent the women home and they rehired the men. Michigan Bell, however, found that women were very good workers and they kept them on as switchroom helpers.

The EEOC, in doing their massive two-year study of the Bell System for their

Federal Communications Commission Case, found that the women at Michigan Bell, as switchroom helpers, were earning substantially less than men performing the same job throughout the rest of the Bell System. This posed an interesting problem for us. Under the Equal Pay Act, we are limited to comparing jobs within a Company. Thus, the question arises whether Michigan Bell is a separate Company from the other Bell Companies.

The Michigan Bell problem can be approached from a Title VII vantage point. Title VII remedies (and this is true of the Executive Order as well) have normally called for integration of jobs and job opportunity. For example, those women who were switchroom helpers would be given an opportunity to move into other craft jobs. We have always maintained that companies have a right to dirty, miserable, low-paying jobs. What they don't have a right to do is to assign people to these jobs on the basis of race or sex.

It was finally agreed that the Michigan Bell Company would raise the rates of those women working as switchroom helpers to the average rate earned by men in other Bell Companies. That's an equal pay remedy, really, under a Title VII guise, because a very difficult legal question would have arisen under the Equal Pay Act.

The Situation in Retail Stores

Other questions arise, particularly in the retail store situation. For example, an employer has women selling women's clothing and men selling men's clothing. The women earn substantially less than the men, and our opinion is that it's substantially equal work, although not all employers would agree on this.

What if the employer says, "All right. I have three women selling women's clothing and I have three men selling men's clothing. Tomorrow I'm going to hire three women to sell men's clothing and three more men to sell women's clothing. I will pay those women who are presently selling women's clothing two years' worth of backpay [which is the statute of limitations under the Equal Pay Act if it is not a wilful violation] and I'm home free."

This too seems to present an anomalous situation. The employer is going to pay women backpay for a two-year period of time to compensate them for the difference between what they earn selling women's clothing and what they would have earned selling men's clothing. But for the future they will earn less while doing exactly the same job.

Under Title VII, one might say, using the same theory of continuing discrimination, "But for your initial job discrimination in job placement (i.e., sending these women to sell women's clothing), they might have been selling men's clothing; therefore, you have to raise their wages to what they would have been."

What if the employer, instead of hiring three new women and three new men transferred the three women selling women's clothing to the men's wear department and hired six new persons to sell women's clothing, three women and three men? This poses an interesting question and shows the continuing viability of the Equal Pay Act and the need for interchange of ideas between Equal Pay and Title VII theories. This situation is not too far different from the situation we faced in the *Miller Brewing*[3] case in the 7th Circuit, where the Court held that a company cannot engage in evasive tactics to avoid raising a wage rate which had its basis in sex discrimination (only one step from a "taint" theory).

Unions and EEO Settlements

AT&T raises a question, it seems to me, of how the Government should deal with unions in a settlement situation. The Executive Order requires that they be given a right to be heard. If we go to a hearing, they have a right to intervene and, indeed, the Steelworkers did intervene in the Bethlehem Case.

The Equal Pay Act has presented problems in bringing unions into cases involving questions of backpay because of a feeling that persons discriminated against ought not to contribute to their own relief. If women are members of the union, and if indeed the union is somewhat responsible and should contribute to the backpay owed to these women, then we'll have the strange situation of seeing these women pay for their own relief out of their union dues.

Clearly, unions have a right to be heard with regard to their legitimate interests in protecting their members. In the AT&T Case we tried to resolve this by setting up parameters for the parties to bargain. Essentially what we did was agree to the minimums and to the broad framework of what relief was required.

We said, "You can't give any less than this but you can give more."

We did this with regard to seniority. We imposed company-wide seniority. We did not impose system-wide seniority. We said the parties could bargain about that. We set up transfer plans. There were differences we tried to protect, and we carved out things that already were in collective bargaining agreements, such as posting notices to protect posting and bidding systems so where they existed they would remain. Where they didn't exist, the parties could bargain about them. We tried to walk a very difficult line: to give neither the employer nor the union something they would not have otherwise obtained through collective bargaining.

Perhaps the parameters for an agreement, or a parameter within which the

[3] *Hodgson v. Miller Brewing Company*, (CA-7 1972) 457 F. 2d 221, 4 EPD ¶ 7691.

parties may bargain, should be established before the agreement is entered into. Perhaps the parties should bargain without parameters.

This has been done in some cases under the Executive Order where we have said to the employer and the union, "Go to it, come back to us with what you've got and we'll tell you if it's any good."

You give them some ground rules such as "We have to have this. We have to have that, because this is what we are trying to remedy."

I think the latter is preferable. But when you get into a situation with many unions, as in AT&T where we had primarily two large ones (the Communication Workers and the International Brotherhood of Electrical Workers), they sometimes have conflicting interests. In AT&T, there were interests of other aggrieved parties who had come into the FCC Hearings and also wanted to be heard. We felt that we would have a three-ring circus and we just couldn't have bargaining among so many parties.

But, this is certainly a legitimate question: How are the unions going to protect their rightful interests? The Communication Workers have filed a motion to intervene in Philadelphia, where we filed the AT&T consent decree, and we're waiting for a decision from Judge Higgenbotham as to whether they should be a party to the case.

If they are permitted to intervene, there is a question of whether they should be a party plaintiff or a party defendant. It's the position of the Government that the relief the Communication Workers are asking for would, if anything, make them properly a party defendant. We cannot see them as a party plaintiff.

Counterclaims Against Unions

Then there is the question of counterclaim and contribution. This could happen if the Company should choose to counterclaim against the Communication Workers for a contribution of some portion of the monetary relief. It is not unthinkable in view of Judge Merhige's decision of April 30, 1973 in *Gilbert v. General Electric*,[4] involving GE's asserted right of contribution from IUE for sex discrimination liability. As I noted earlier, under the Equal Pay Act, we have consistently taken the position that the wage obligation falls exclusively on the employer—and the statute makes clear that the definition of employer does not include unions (except as to its own employees). Employees ought not to contribute to their own relief.

Pursuing this line of thought, what ought the relationship be between employers and unions with regard to equal employment opportunity problems? It seems to me that the question must be divided into two parts: (1) before the Government gets involved and (2) after the Government gets involved.

Before the Government gets involved one has to look at the law under the National Labor Relations Act. In a recent decision involving the *Jubilee Manufacturing Company*,[5] an attempt is made to distinguish between employer discrimination *per se,* which the Board says is not actionable, and employer discrimination which has an effect on Section 7, NLRA rights, which is actionable.

In the *Hughes Tool*[6] and *Miranda*[7] cases, we see a clear line of opinions which hold that certain union discrimination is a violation of Section 8(b) (1)

---

[4] *Gilbert v. Electric Company*, (DC Va. 1972) 347 F. Supp. 1058, 5 EPD ¶ 8011, 8663, 8664, 6 EPD ¶ 8749, 8750.

[5] *Jubilee Manufacturing Company*, 202 NLRB 2, 1973 CCH NLRB ¶ 25,127.

[6] *Hughes Tool Company*, 104 NLRB 318.

[7] *Miranda Fuel Company, Inc.*, 140 NLRB 181, 1962 CCH NLRB ¶11,848; (CA-2 1963) 326 F. 2d 172, 48 LC ¶ 18,646.

of the National Labor Relations Act. In the *Mansion House*[8] case, where the Fifth Amendment was raised by the 8th Circuit, the court held broadly that an employer is not required to bargain with a union which maintains discriminatory policies. Presumably, this would also hold true in the 8th Circuit for a union which refuses to bargain with an employer who discriminates, although the Court's ruling may be read narrowly to limit itself to the recognition stage.

Read together, these cases seem to fall into a pattern that makes some sense. The Board has control over union conduct directly because the Board gives the union its imprimatur of legality and it certifies unions (something it does not do for employers). But the Board can and does properly regulate the employer's relationship with the union. So it doesn't seem strange for the Board to be in a posture whereby union discrimination is *per se* a violation of the Act based upon the union's duty of fair representation. But employer discrimination is a violation only when it has a discernible effect on Section 7 rights.

EEO and Collective Bargaining

Having said this, questions still remain. If an existing contract which one party is desirous of changing, ostensibly because the bargaining agreement allegedly requires the employer to take actions in a personnel context which are violative of Title VII, the Equal Pay Act, or the Executive Order, to what extent will the Board recognize *Mansion House* in the bargaining context? What has to be proved in a *Mansion House* context? How far in bargaining does either party have to go?

What is the role of the Federal equal employment opportunity agencies, particularly if one party asks an agency to intervene in the bargaining process and make a determination of illegality? Does the Board have to find that discrimination has occurred?

This raises another question. It brings me to Section 301 of the Taft–Hartley Act. Assume in that context that an employee challenges the validity of a contract because it does not conform with Government-imposed provisions in like situations.

For example, an employee may read the AT&T case and say, "Ah-hah! We have the same situation in my company and what's more the seniority system is written into the collective bargaining agreement as it was in AT&T."

Is the judge, under Section 301, required to hold a Title VII-like trial to determine if the same situation exists in the case at bar as existed in AT&T?

Put broadly, should the courts, under Section 301 of the Taft–Hartley Act, and the National Labor Relations Board, under the National Labor Relations Act, limit their concern on questions of race and sex discrimination to issues of fair representation and to questions of certification and revocation of certification? Such questions are going to have to be faced by the courts.

What about the situation after the Government becomes involved? The Southern District of Georgia has declared in the *Union Camp*[9] case, that after attempted bargaining, the employer could unilaterally implement an affirmative action plan required by the Government. The employer need not take the issue to arbitration and need not bargain for less than was required.

[8] *Mansion House Center Management Corp.*, 190 NLRB 78. 1971 CCH NLRB ¶ 23,036; (CA-8 1972) 466 F. 2d 1283, 69 LC ¶ 13,012; (CA-8 1973) 70 LC ¶ 13,407; 195 NLRB 37, 1972 CCH NLRB ¶ 23,861; (CA-8 1973) 5 EPD ¶ 8454.

[9] *Savannah Printing Specialities and Paper Products Local Union 604 v. Union Camp Corp.*, (DC Ga. 1972) 350 F. Supp. 632, 5 EPD ¶ 8551.

In the Philadelphia Plan litigation, *Contractors Association of Eastern Pennsylvania v. Secretary of Labor*,[10] in which the Supreme Court denied certiorari in October, 1972, we were able to get a decision from the Third Circuit saying that a collective bargaining agreement cannot override the equal employment opportunity requirements of statutory law, or Executive Order 11246. Under Board law, after impasse, the employer can unilaterally implement his last offer. The union, of course, can strike.

If an affirmative action program is approved by the Government, arguably at least, there is a Title VII exclusion from the Norris/LaGuardia Act, which may enable the employer to enjoin an employee walkout directed at blocking implementation of the affirmative action plan. If there is no affirmative action plan, and we have had situations like this, the Government, through the Department of Justice, or, I assume at this point, the Equal Employment Opportunity Commission, can move to enjoin the union's actions in striking, if the Government can show that the employer's actions were necessary for compliance with equal employment opportunity laws.

My final point involves the role of unions with regard to the collective bargaining process in equal employment matters. Seniority is not, *per se,* discriminatory. I think a tremendous amount of confusion has arisen because of some of those cases where we've had to attack seniority systems. Neither is an apprenticeship system, *per se,* discriminatory.

One of the ironies of this whole field, I think, is that unions and representatives of minority groups have a lot more in common than they realize. Both are concerned about employer discretion. The union is concerned that if the employer has too much discretion he might discriminate because of union membership or activity; while minorities and women are concerned that an employer with too much discretion might discriminate against them on the basis of race or sex. Procedures, such as seniority and testing, that eliminate this discretion where it should not appropriately apply are things which are not bad on their face.

Hiring Quotas

There is a recent decision in New York in the *Lathers Local 46*[11] case. That case, it seems to me, raises many difficult questions about quotas. It seems that it raises questions involving an apparent lack of concern on the part of the court, that I read into the case, with the availability of the requisite numbers of skilled minorities, which the court said must be hired.

I think there were various economic factors, including unemployment rates and the like, which were not considered. It was a case where a local union was sued, refused to obey the order of the court, was very recalcitrant and the court finally threw up its hands and ordered, I think, some very desperate measures. It is just that sort of thing which we want to avoid. We do not want to throw the baby out with the bathwater.

Apprenticeship in the construction trades is a good thing, if it is properly designed and implemented. It can provide necessary and meaningful training opportunities. We don't want to bring people onto construction jobs who will be safety hazards.

[10] *Contractors Association of Eastern Pennsylvania v. Schulz,* (DC Pa. 1970) 311 F. Supp. 1002, 2 EPD ¶ 10,192; (CA-3 1971) 442 F. 2d 159, 3 EPD ¶ 8180; 92 S. Ct. 98, 404 U. S. 854, 4 EPD ¶ 7526.
[11] *U.S. v. Lathers Local 46,* (DC NY 1971), 2 EPD ¶ 10,226; (DC NY 1971) 328 F. Supp. 429, 3 EPD 8249; (DC NY 1972) 341 F. Supp. 694, 4 EPD ¶ 7749; (CA-2 1973) 471 F. 2d 408, 5 EPD ¶ 8104; (U. S. S. Ct. 1973) cert. denied, 5 EPD ¶ 8597.

Testing and EEO

In the AT&T agreement we settled a very thorny testing question. The Company and the Government disagreed as to whether the Company's tests were in fact validated. AT&T had validated its tests some years ago and, in fact, it was one of the first companies to undertake a nationwide validation of its testing. The problem was that we thought they did it wrong because we thought the mechanism they used to validate the test was itself questionably based on 1972 standards.

We reached an agreement whereby the Company would be allowed to continue using its tests, provided the Company did not use these tests as a defense to a failure to meet the goals for minority and female utilization. AT&T may have other good faith defenses which it could use but it could not use the test itself in order that we would remove any question of the disparate impact of the test on the Bell System's employment policies. But we have allowed the tests to remain in place provisionally.

Federal EEO Coordination

I think there is something else that comes out of the AT&T case, and that is the general need for Federal EEO coordination. This is a very real and serious problem which was recognized by the Congress in the Equal Employment Opportunity Amendments of 1972 to the Civil Rights Act of 1964. Aware of the multiplicity of forums, the Congress established an Equal Employment Opportunity Coordinating Council to discuss common problems and eliminate conflict and duplication. The Council includes the Department of Labor, the Department of Justice, the EEOC, the Civil Rights Commission, and the Civil Service Commission.

We have had one major case since AT&T, which required coordination among the agencies and that is with Delta Airlines.[12] There, the Department of Labor, operating pursuant to its authority under Executive Order 11246, as amended, and the Department of Justice operating pursuant to its authority for pattern and practice cases under Title VII joined together and successfully resolved differences which both agencies had with Delta Airlines.

I think such coordination is going to have to be the approach of the future. Employers do not wish to be whipsawed and neither do the various Government agencies. I think in the AT&T context, the Company bargained in good faith with us. The period between our sitting down with AT&T until the time an agreement was reached and a consent decree filed was only five months. Now, it is true that there were years of effort behind that from the EEOC, from the Department of Labor under its Equal Pay Act authority, and from the General Services Administration, under its contract compliance authority under the Executive Order. But I really think the key to the Company's willingness to talk was the assurance that could be given that, at least insofar as the Federal Government was concerned, those elements of difference which we had and which we brought to the bargaining table, were now resolved and we would not again sue the Company on those issues.

Of course, private suits are not precluded and the State agencies are still taking action. Indeed, we just reached a $436,000 Equal Pay settlement with New England Bell on issues not resolved with AT&T. I personally feel that every employer has the right to believe that when

---

[12] *United States v. Delta Airlines*, (DC Ga. 1973), EMPLOYMENT PRACTICES GUIDE ¶ 5152.

he deals with an agency of the Government, he's dealing with the United States Government and he doesn't have to distinguish among us. I can't expect any employer to understand the bureaucracy. I've been in Government for four years and I don't understand it.

Conclusion

These matters are interlocking. I think that one of the most beneficial and dramatic aspects of the AT&T case, was the fact that it was resolved by agreement. The fact that the agreement was reached in a relatively short period of time and that there was a good deal of good faith bargaining on the part of the Company and on the part of the unions with which we spoke auger well.

I think it's a rational agreement which holds together, which recognizes the legitimate concerns of the unions and the legitimate concerns of the employer, and which produces some strong and very necessary relief for minorities and females throughout the Bell System. It is this kind of agreement and this kind of process which I think the Government would like to see in many other cases.

We did it again in Delta, and I think we'll do it again in other cases to come. I think this is the proper approach for resolution of many of these very difficult EEO questions. Such an approach can ensure the rights of minority and female workers while preserving the legitimate aspects of the employer's personnel policies, practices, procedures, and the union's interests in the collective bargaining process and agreement.

QUESTIONS

1. What do you think of the desirability of financial restitution for women and minority employees as applied in the American Telephone and Telegraph Company case? If a company is not currently discriminating in regard to equal pay treatment or promotions but has done so in the past, should that company provide restitution?
2. In devising remedies for discriminatory practices, as in the case of lower wages for women than men for the same kind of work, do you think the union should be liable for any of the cost of the relief for the affected employees where there has been a collective bargaining relationship?
3. In working toward elimination of discrimination do you think the Federal government should require that employers adopt quotas on the number and percentage of women and blacks it will hire over a period of years?
4. How might a company's selection tests deny equal job opportunities to minorities? Discuss.

12.

IBM in the Ghetto: Anatomy of a Success

ROBERT SCHRANK and SUSAN STEIN

Since July 1968 IBM has operated a computer component assembly plant in the Bedford-Stuyvesant section of Brooklyn. It is IBM's only manufacturing facility in a central city and, most importantly, the only major industry to locate in the area in recent years. IBM's experience in Brooklyn, contrary to the projections of many of its hesitant supporters, has been positive and profitable. Some of the remaining difficulties we saw grow mostly out of problems that any large corporation has in trying to deal with a lumbering city bureaucracy—not out of the plant's location in Bedford-Stuyvesant. The plan's success suggests that we may need to reconsider some of the issues around black capitalism, central city development, and the minority community labor pool.

The plant opened its doors with 200 workers and now employs approximately 400 people, evenly divided between production and nonproduction workers. About 75 percent of the work force is male and almost all the employees were recruited from the area and have remained there.

From the outset the plant has produced external computer cables and two power packs—one for keypunch machines and one for verifiers. It formerly took 2½ and 3 hours, respectively, to produce the power packs. An engineering change recently combined the two power packs into one unit requiring only 1 hour to produce. For this work employees originally were paid a minimum of $85 per week. Average starting salary now is $100 per week, with opportunities for advancement.

After more than 3 years 75 percent of the original year's production staff still is working for IBM, as are 95 percent of the nonproduction staff. Turnover, a key problem in the early months, has been reduced by two-thirds. Absence runs approximately 5 percent, which relates favorably to other IBM facilities. Sixty production workers are enrolled in IBM-sponsored in-plant training after hours and a considerable number of production

Reprinted from *Manpower*, Vol. 4, No. 5 (May 1972). *Manpower* is published by the U.S. Department of Labor.

Robert Schrank is a project specialist and Susan Stein is a program officer with the Ford Foundation.

and administrative staff take outside education programs, with the costs being paid by IBM's tuition refund plan.

Contrary to what many expect, the atmosphere in the plant is like that in most other manufacturing plants. It is not being run as a social experiment; it is required to deliver quality products according to a schedule. As a supplier of essential computer components to eight other plants, the Brooklyn facility's ability to meet production schedules is critical to its survival.

Because of the plant's central city location, in the early months of operations visitors might have sensed management concern over absenteeism, turnover, vandalism, pilferage, drugs, drinking, crime, and similar problems often associated with the ghetto. Undoubtedly, this was a reflection of both the observer's and management's preconceptions of the problems a central city plant would encounter. Today the visitor senses less management concern and frustration with minority group or central city problems and more concern with the city's bureaucracy and the failure of other companies to follow IBM's suit.

What have been the key elements in IBM's Bedford-Stuyvesant success and are they unique? In spite of much publicity to the contrary, the company found a reliable work force in the community. At the outset management selected 155 persons after personal interviews and testing. Forty percent of the first recruits had no high school diploma, 16 percent had been in prison, 22 percent had been unemployed for 6 weeks or longer in the previous year. Other employers in the area decried these characteristics, citing their experiences with high turnover, absenteeism, and the like. The word got around that the available work force just wasn't reliable.

Work Force Proves Capable

IBM found differently. The workers stayed and worked well—so well that the hiring policy was loosened. Hiring and replacement in the last year, raising the work force to 400, has been based primarily on evidence of some past work experience. Prospective employees are not automatically disqualified because of felony convictions, nor does IBM use tests, except to assess secretarial skills. The constant stream of applicants at IBM's doors springs mostly from contacts made by persons working in the plant (an employee tells a friend, etc.).

IBM's experience supports what many Bedford-Stuyvesant residents have been saying for some time. There is a stable work force in the area and it responds to decent jobs at decent pay. The IBM employees are neither the cream nor the hard core of what is available. They simply are a fair sampling of the diversity of skills available in any community.

In this respect, IBM Bedford-Stuyvesant plant manager Halvan I. Lieteau stresses the importance of not generalizing about the available labor pool from the experience of marginal companies paying minimum wages. He does not categorize local residents as people who are ignorant of how to get and hold a job. Instead, he stresses their capabilities. Lieteau's experience suggests that many Bedford-Stuyvesant residents know all too well the deficiencies of many of the jobs available to them and for those reasons do not pursue substandard jobs or leave them as soon as they can meet immediate financial needs.

Businessmen and industrial managers often complain about being unable to find reliable workers in the ghetto. They point to the large number of entry-level job openings and the equally large number of unemployed poor. In one recent article a company director was interviewed because of his vociferous complaints about the lack of applicants for jobs at his plant. It turned out that the company had a chicken feather cleaning factory which needed a man for its midnight to 8 a.m. shift. The job paid $1.60 per hour and involved working in a cloud of dust and feathers.

It was not the kind of job that attracts many applicants.

Lieteau attributes his positive experience to the fact that IBM offers respectable work, in a decent setting, for good pay. He feels certain that others with similar offerings will find similar response.

A second key element has been the extensive support IBM gave the plant in its early stages. This support, while hard to document, probably included the consulting time of high-priced management and production experts, operational assistance, supervision by experienced and proven workers, and a personnel philosophy carefully articulated and tested elsewhere. In fact, almost any kind of help on any matter was only as far away as the nearest phone. And, of course, the status of the IBM name must not be overlooked.

It is important to realize, however, that most large companies—probably all of Fortune's 500—routinely offer this type of assistance to new branch operations. An infant operation never is expected to spring to life in full armor like Athena. A period of testing, adjustment, and subsidy is anticipated. But this normal nurturing process often is forgotten in dealing with many central city problems. Instant solutions are demanded in central city manufacturing plants while long-term development is tolerated in middle class suburban areas.

This impatience may have more to do with our prejudices and biases than with reality. It must be realized that ghetto enterprises often require 2 to 3 years to mature, which means that large profitable companies have an edge over the private individual entrepreneur. The lone businessman usually cannot wait 3 years to make a profit. This ability to wait can be a critical factor lacking in many black capitalism type projects. In our haste to see more minority owned or operated businesses, we too often ignore the realities of small business history and place too great expectation on the small entrepreneur.

A third factor in IBM's Bedford-Stuyvesant success is the type of work done in the Brooklyn plant. It is clean, highly labor-intensive work involving small physical units that require minimum trucking and storage space. Storage space may be a critical factor in plant costs in a central city location. Other important factors in the type of work are that IBM is in a growth industry—electronics—and the materials and processes used in the Brooklyn plant do not bring the odor and aura of a glue factory or a rubber plant into a residential area.

None of these three elements—a reliable work force, adequate support, and a suitable type of work—is remarkable or unique to IBM's Brooklyn plant. Certainly other companies might successfully undertake similar efforts. What prevents them from doing so—apart from the stereotypes of inner-city problems? The answer, in many cases, is reluctance to begin a frustrating engagement with city bureaucracies over building codes, licensing, equipment purchase, plant construction, land acquisition, and similar matters.

Land often is available in central cities for industrial use, but adequate parcels of it cannot be assembled in any reasonable time. Zoning, ownership, purchase, and title laws can draw out land acquisitions to 4 to 5 years. If a company is lucky enough to find land or even a usable building, getting it through the myriad of applicable codes can be a frustrating and costly process.

One experience IBM had with its Brooklyn plant—although involving a relatively minor matter—illustrates the kind of frustration that can result from having to deal with antiquated city governments. In purchasing fire hoses for the Brooklyn plant, IBM officials consulted with the local fire department authority. This resulted in purchase of what the local department inspector and the manufacturer claimed to be "the latest thing in fire hoses—(used) in all the top downtown buildings." Soon after the hoses were purchased a higher level in the fire department authority said they were unsuitable and produced a different set of instructions. Such lack of clarity about regulations, often typical of big city bureaucracies, creates the "who wants to get involved in that lunacy" syndrome and helps explain why major corporations avoid central city locations.

Strong Support Required

Another issue raised by IBM's experience is the need for extensive financial and management support to new ghetto enterprises. Much of the effort to create minority entrepreneurs may be weakened because of limited capacity to underwrite the heavy financial burdens of early development. In the case of the individual entrepreneur, he can borrow only so much money himself. He has to make it quickly or die.

The community economic development corporation has a different problem—one of divided loyalties. Many minority leaders who emerged in the sixties built their community base through social programs for youth, the elderly, the unemployed, the untrained, and similar groups. They are now moving into large-scale economic development.

These entrepreneurs clearly have an edge over the individual small businessman, in both the technical assistance at their command and backup financing. But they have a problem in their dual role as businessmen and social program operators or community leaders. When faced with heavy losses and continual difficulties, only so much money and effort can be expended on righting entrepreneurial ventures before social programs suffer. In some cases, entrepreneurial success may even depend on some antisocial efforts such as reducing the work force or raising prices in businesses backed by the community development organization.

In these respects, a company like IBM has many advantages in developing viable central city enterprises. This is not an argument against black capitalism. What IBM's experience does suggest, however, is that major industrial corporations may have the greatest potential for employment and in turn for real impact on central city minority unemployment. Black capitalism should be stimulated and supported for its own sake, not for its role in alleviating the problems of the central city or the poor.

Finding other IBMs will not be easy. Cities will need to offer distinct advantages over suburban plant locations. This means creating financial incentives, assembling and holding land in industrial parks, improving public transportation and consolidating and rationalizing building codes. Admittedly, eliminating the tangle of municipal red tape will require hand-to-hand combat with some entrenched interests and bureaucracies.

The point is that these are not impossible tasks and the unemployment level in central cities is not resistant to change. The problems are neither too complex nor too extensive to be approached. Working with the IBM model, it may be possible to interest other corporations in central city locations—not just as a social responsibility but as an efficient corporate operation.

QUESTIONS

1. Many companies fear that they will be beset with problems of low productivity, high costs, vandalism, absenteeism, and turnover if they locate a plant in an urban

ghetto. What factors, mentioned in the article, were influential in making the IBM operation in the Bedford-Stuyvesant section of Brooklyn a success?

2. Prepare a list of the major actions which the management of a company should take to establish and operate a program of employing the disadvantaged.

3. How can the management of a firm justify to its stockholders a major effort to employ disadvantaged people?

13.

Split Roles in Performance Appraisal

HERBERT H. MEYER, EMANUEL KAY, AND JOHN R. P. FRENCH, JR.

In management circles, performance appraisal is a highly interesting and provocative topic. And in business literature, too, knowledgeable people write emphatically, pro and con, on the performance appraisal question.[1] In fact, one might almost say that everybody talks and writes about it, but nobody has done any real scientific testing of it.

At the General Electric Company we felt it was important that a truly scientific study be done to test the effectiveness of our traditional performance appraisal program. Why? Simply because our own experience with performance appraisal programs had been both positive and negative. For example:

• Surveys generally show that most people think the idea of performance appraisal is good. They feel that a man should know where he stands and, therefore, the manager should discuss an appraisal of his performance with him periodically.

• In actual practice, however, it is the extremely rare operating manager who will employ such a program on his own initiative. Personnel specialists report that most managers carry out performance appraisal interviews only when strong control procedures are established to ensure that they do so. This is surprising because the managers have been told repeatedly that the system is intended to help them

Reprinted from *Harvard Business Review*, Vol. 43, No. 1 (January–February 1965), pp. 123–129, by permission of the publisher. © 1965 by the President and Fellows of Harvard College; all rights reserved.

At the time of this article Herbert H. Meyer and Emanuel Kay were both with the Behavioral Research Service of the General Electric Company. John R. P. French, Jr., was Program Director at the Research Center for Group Dynamics, Institute for Social Research, University of Michigan.

[1] Douglas McGregor, "An Uneasy Look at Performance Appraisal," HBR, May–June 1957, p. 89; Harold Mayfield, "In Defense of Performance Appraisal," HBR, March–April 1960, p. 81; and Alva F. Kindall and James Gatza, "Positive Program for Performance Appraisal," HBR, November–December 1963, p. 153.

141

obtain improved performance from their subordinates.

We also found from interviews with employees who have had a good deal of experience with traditional performance appraisal programs that few indeed can cite examples of constructive action taken —or significant improvement achieved— which stem from suggestions received in a performance appraisal interview with their boss.

Traditional Program

Faced with such contradictory evidence, we undertook a study several years ago to determine the effectiveness of our comprehensive performance appraisal process. Special attention was focused on the interview between the subordinate and his manager, because this is the discussion which is supposed to motivate the man to improve his performance. And we found out some very interesting things—among them the following:

• Criticism has a negative effect on achievement of goals.
• Praise has little effect one way or the other.
• Performance improves most when specific goals are established.
• Defensiveness resulting from critical appraisal produces inferior performance.
• Coaching should be a day-to-day, not a once-a-year, activity.
• Mutual goal setting, not criticism, improves performance.
• Interviews designed primarily to improve a man's performance should not at the same time weigh his salary or promotion in the balance.
• Participation by the employee in the goal-setting procedure helps produce favorable results.

As you can see, the results of this original study indicated that a detailed and comprehensive annual appraisal of a subordinate's performance by his manager is decidedly of questionable value. Furthermore, as is certainly the case when the major objective of such a discussion is to motivate the subordinate to improve his performance, the traditional appraisal interview does not do the job.

In the first part of this article, we will offer readers more than this bird's-eye view of our research into performance appraisal. (We will not, however, burden managers with details of methodology.) We will also describe the one-year follow-up experiment General Electric conducted to validate the conclusions derived from our original study. Here the traditional annual performance appraisal method was tested against a new method we developed, which we called Work Planning and Review (WP&R). As you will see, this approach produced, under actual plant conditions, results which were decidedly superior to those afforded by the traditional performance appraisal method. Finally, we will offer evidence to support our contention that some form of WP&R might well be incorporated into other industrial personnel programs to achieve improvement in work performance.

Appraising Appraisal

In order to assure a fair test of the effectiveness of the traditional performance appraisal method, which had been widely used throughout General Electric, we conducted an intensive study of the process at a large GE plant where the performance appraisal program was judged to be good; that is, in this plant:

• appraisals had been based on job responsibilities, rather than on personal characteristics of the individuals involved;
• an intensive training program had been carried out for managers in the use of the traditional appraisal method and techniques for conducting appraisal interviews;
• the program had been given strong backing by the plant manager and had been policed diligently by the personnel staff so that over 90 per cent of the exempt employees had been appraised and interviewed annually.

This comprehensive annual performance appraisal program, as is typical, was designed to serve two major purposes. The first was to justify recommended salary action. The second, which was motivational in character, was intended to present an opportunity for the manager to review a subordinate's performance and promote discussion on needed improvements. For the latter purpose, the manager was required to draw up a specific program of plans and goals for the subordinate which would help him to improve his job performance and to qualify, hopefully, for future promotion.

INTERVIEW MODIFICATIONS

Preliminary interviews with key managers and subordinates revealed the salary action issue had so dominated the annual comprehensive performance appraisal interview that neither party had been in the right frame of mind to discuss plans for improved performance. To straighten this out, we asked managers to split the traditional appraisal interview into two sessions—discussing appraisal of performance and salary action in one interview and performance improvement plans in another to be held about two weeks later. This split provided us with a better opportunity to conduct our experiment on the effects of participation in goal planning.

To enable us to test the effects of participation, we instructed half the managers to use a *high participation* approach and the other half to use a *low participation* technique. Thus

Each of the "high" managers was instructed to ask his appraisee to prepare a set of goals for achieving improved job performance and to submit them for the manager's review and approval. The manager also was encouraged to permit the subordinate to exert as much influence as possible on the formulation of the final list of job goals agreed on in the performance improvement discussion.

The "low" managers operated in much the same way they had in our traditional appraisal program. They formulated a set of goals for the subordinate, and these goals were then reviewed in the performance improvement session. The manager was instructed to conduct this interview in such a way that his influence in the forming of the final list of job goals would be greater than the subordinate's.

CONDUCTING THE RESEARCH

There were 92 appraisees in the experimental group, representing a cross section of the exempt salaried employees in the plant. This group included engineers; engineering support technicians; foremen; and specialists in manufacturing, customer service, marketing, finance, and purchasing functions. None of the exempt men who participated as appraisees in the experiment had other exempt persons reporting to them; thus they did not serve in conflicting manager-subordinate roles.

The entire group was interviewed and asked to complete questionnaires (a) before and after the salary action interview, and (b) after the delayed second discussion with their managers about performance improvement. These interviews and questionnaires were designed to achieve three objectives:

1. Assess changes in the attitudes of individuals toward their managers and toward the appraisal system after each of the discussions.

2. Get an estimate from the appraisee of the degree to which he usually participated in decisions that affected him. (This was done in order to determine whether or not previous lack of participation affected his response to participation in the experiment.)

3. Obtain a self-appraisal from each subordinate before and after he met with his manager. (This was done in order to determine how discrepancies in these self-appraisals might affect his reaction to the appraisal interview.)

Moreover, each salary action and performance improvement discussion was observed by outsiders trained to record essentially what transpired. (Managers preferred to use neither tape recorders nor unseen observers, feeling that observers unaffiliated with the company—in this case, graduate students in applied psychological disciplines—afforded the best way of obtaining a reasonably close approximation of the normal discussions.) In the appraisal for salary action interviews, for example, the observers recorded the amount of criticism and praise employed by the manager, as well as the reactions of the appraisee to the manager's comments. In the performance improvement discussions, the observers recorded the participation of the subordinate, as well as the amount of influence he seemed to exert in establishing his future success goals.

CRITICISM AND DEFENSIVENESS

In general, the managers completed the performance appraisal forms in a thorough and conscientious manner. Their appraisals were discussed with subordinates in interviews ranging from approximately 30 to 90 minutes in length. On the average, managers covered 32 specific performance items which, when broken down, showed positive (praise) appraisals on 19 items, and negative (criticism) on 13. Typically, praise was more often related to *general* performance characteristics, while criticism was usually focused on *specific* performance items.

The average subordinate reacted defensively to seven of the manager's criticisms during the appraisal interview (that is, he reacted defensively about 54 per cent of the time when criticized). Denial of shortcomings cited by the manager, blaming others, and various other forms of excuses were recorded by the observers as defensive reactions.

Constructive responses to criticism were *rarely* observed. In fact, the average was less than one per interview. Not too surprising, along with this, was the finding that the more criticism a man received in

the performance appraisal discussion, the more defensively he reacted. Men who received an above-average number of criticisms showed more than five times as much defensive behavior as those who received a below-average number of criticisms. Subordinates who received a below-average number of criticisms, for example, reacted defensively only about one time out of three. But those who received an above-average number reacted defensively almost two times out of three.

One explanation for this defensiveness is that it seems to stem from the overrating each man tended to give to his own performance. The average employee's self-estimate of performance *before* appraisal placed him at the 77 percentile. (Only 2 of the 92 participants estimated their performance to be below the average point on the scale.) But when the same men were asked *after* their performance appraisal discussions how they thought their bosses had rated them, the average figure given was at the 65 percentile. The great majority (75 out of 92) saw their manager's evaluation as being less favorable than their self-estimates. Obviously, to these men, the performance appraisal discussion with the manager was a deflating experience. Thus, it was not surprising that the subordinates reacted defensively in their interviews.

CRITICISM AND GOAL ACHIEVEMENT

Even more important is the fact that men who received an above-average number of criticisms in their performance appraisal discussions generally showed *less* goal achievement 10 to 12 weeks later than those who had received fewer criticisms. At first, we thought that this difference might be accounted for by the fact that the subordinates who received more criticisms were probably poorer performers in general. But there was little factual evidence found to support this suspicion.

It was true that those who received an

above-average number of criticisms in their appraisal discussions did receive slightly lower summary ratings on overall performance from their managers. But they did not receive proportionally lower salary increases. And the salary increases granted were *supposed* to reflect differences in job performance, according to the salary plan traditionally used in this plant. This argument, admittedly, is something less than perfect.

But it does appear clear that frequent criticism constitutes so strong a threat to self-esteem that it disrupts rather than improves subsequent performance. We expected such a disruptive threat to operate more strongly on those individuals who were already low on self-esteem, just as we expected a man who had confidence in his ability to do his job to react more constructively to criticism. Our group experiment proved these expectations to be correct.

Still further evidence that criticism has a negative effect on performance was found when we investigated areas which had been given special emphasis by the manager in his criticism. Following the appraisal discussion with the manager, each employee was asked to indicate which one aspect of his performance had been most criticized by the manager. Then, when we conducted our follow-up investigation 10 to 12 weeks later, it revealed that improvement in the most-criticized aspects of performance cited was considerably *less* than improvement realized in other areas!

PARTICIPATION EFFECTS

As our original research study had indicated, the effects of a high participation level were also favorable in our group experiment. In general, here is what we found:

Subordinates who received a high participation level in the performance interview reacted more favorably than did those who received a low participation level. The "highs" also, in most cases, achieved a greater percentage of their improvement goals than did their "low" counterparts. For the former, the high participation level was associated with greater mutual understanding between them and their managers, greater acceptance of job goals, a more favorable attitude toward the appraisal system, and a feeling of greater self-realization on the job.

But employees who had traditionally been accustomed to low participation in their daily relationship with the manager did not necessarily perform better under the high participation treatment. In fact, those men who had received a high level of criticism in their appraisal interviews actually performed better when their managers set goals for them than they did when they set their own goals, as permitted under the high participation treatment.

In general, our experiment showed that the men who usually worked under high participation levels performed best on goals they set for themselves. Those who indicated that they usually worked under low levels performed best on goals that the managers set for them. Evidently, the man who usually does not participate in work-planning decisions considers job goals set by the manager to be more important than goals he sets for himself. The man accustomed to a high participation level, on the other hand, may have stronger motivation to achieve goals he sets for himself than to achieve those set by his manager.

GOAL-SETTING IMPORTANCE

While subordinate participation in the goal-setting process had some effect on improved performance, a much more powerful influence was whether goals were set at all. Many times in appraisal discussions, managers mentioned areas of performance where improvement was needed. Quite often these were translated into specific work plans and goals. But this was not always the case. In fact, when we looked at the one performance area which each manager had emphasized in the appraisal interview as most in need of improvement, we found that these items actually were translated into specific work plans and goals for only about 60 per cent of our experiment participants.

When performance was being measured 10 to 12 weeks after the goal-planning sessions, managers were asked to describe what results they hoped for in the way of subordinate on-the-job improvement. They did this for those important performance items that had been mentioned in the interview. Each manager was then asked to estimate on a percentage scale the degree to which his hoped-for changes had actually been observed. The average per cent accomplishment estimate for those performance items that *did* get translated into goals was 65, while the per cent estimate for those items that *did not* get translated into goals was about 27! Establishing specific plans and goals seemed to ensure that attention would be given to that aspect of job performance.

SUMMATION OF FINDINGS

At the end of this experiment, we were able to draw certain tentative conclusions. These conclusions were the basis of a future research study which we will describe later. In general, we learned that:

Comprehensive annual performance appraisals are of questionable value. Certainly a major objective of the manager in traditional appraisal discussions is motivating the subordinate to improve his performance. But the evidence we gathered indicated clearly that praise tended to have no effect, perhaps because it was regarded as the sandwich which surrounded the raw meat of criticism.[2] And criticism itself brought on defensive reactions that were essentially denials of responsibility for a poor performance.

Coaching should be a day-to-day, not a once-a-year, activity. There are two main reasons for this:

1. Employees seem to accept suggestions for improved performance if they are given in a less concentrated form than is the case in comprehensive annual appraisals. As our experiment showed, employees become clearly more prone to reject criticisms as the number of criticisms mount. This indicates that an "overload phenomenon" may be operating. In other words, each individual seems to have a tolerance level for the amount of criticism he can take. And, as this level is approached or passed, it becomes increasingly difficult for him to accept responsibility for the shortcomings pointed out.

2. Some managers reported that the traditional performance appraisal program tended to cause them to save up items where improvement was needed in order to have enough material to conduct a comprehensive discussion of performance in the annual review. This short-circuited one of the primary purposes of the appraisal program—that of giving feedback to the subordinates as to their performance. Studies of the learning process point out that feedback is less effective if much time is allowed to elapse between the performance and the feedback. This fact alone argues for more frequent discussions between the manager and the subordinate.

Goal setting, not criticism, should be used to improve performance. One of the most significant findings in our experiment was the fact that far superior results were observed when the manager and the man *together* set specific goals to be achieved, rather than merely discussed needed improvement. Frequent reviews of progress provide natural opportunities for discussing means of improving performance *as needs occur,* and these reviews are far less threatening than the annual appraisal and salary review discussions.

Separate appraisals should be held for

[2] See Richard E. Farson, "Praise Reappraised," *Harvard Business Review,* September–October, 1963, p. 61.

different purposes. Our work demonstrated that it was unrealistic to expect a single performance appraisal program to achieve every conceivable need. It seems foolish to have a manager serving in the self-conflicting role as a counselor (helping a man to improve his performance) when, at the same time, he is presiding as a judge over the same employee's salary action case.

New WP&R Method

This intensive year-long test of the performance appraisal program indicated clearly that work-planning-and-review discussions between a man and his manager appeared to be a far more effective approach in improving job performance than was the concentrated annual performance appraisal program.

For this reason, after the findings had been announced, many GE managers adopted some form of the new WP&R program to motivate performance improvement in employees, especially those at the professional and administrative levels. Briefly described, the WP&R approach calls for periodic meetings between the manager and his subordinate. During these meetings, progress on past goals is reviewed, solutions are sought for job-related problems, and new goals are established. The intent of the method is to create a situation in which manager and subordinate can discuss job performance and needed improvements in detail without the subordinate becoming defensive.

BASIC FEATURES

This WP&R approach differs from the traditional performance appraisal program in that:

• There are more frequent discussions of performance.
• There are no summary judgments or ratings made.
• Salary action discussions are held separately.

• The emphasis is on mutual goal planning and problem solving.

As far as frequency is concerned, these WP&R discussions are held more often than traditional performance appraisal interviews, but are not scheduled at rigidly fixed intervals. Usually at the conclusion of one work planning session the man and manager set an approximate date for the next review. Frequency depends both on the nature of the job and on the manager's style of operating. Sometimes these WP&R discussions are held as often as once a month, whereas for other jobs and/or individuals, once every six months is more appropriate.

In these WP&R discussions, the manager and his subordinate do not deal in generalities. They consider specific, objectively defined work goals and establish the yardstick for measuring performance. These goals stem, of course, from broader departmental objectives and are defined in relation to the individual's position in the department.

COMPARISON SETTING

After the findings of our experiment were communicated by means of reports and group meetings in the plant where the research was carried out, about half the key managers decided they would abandon the comprehensive annual performance appraisal method and adopt the new WP&R program instead. The other half were hesitant to make such a major change at the time. They decided, consequently, to continue with the traditional performance appraisal program and to try to make it more effective. This provided a natural setting for us to compare the effectiveness of the two approaches. We decided that the comparison should be in the light of the objectives usually stated for the comprehensive annual performance appraisal program. These objectives were (a) to provide knowledge of results to employees, (b) to justify reasons for salary action, and (c) to motivate and help employees to do a better job.

The study design was simple. Before any changes were made, the exempt employees who would be affected by these programs were surveyed to provide baseline data. The WP&R program was then implemented in about half of the exempt group, with the other half continuing to use a modified version of the traditional performance appraisal program. One year later, the identical survey questionnaire was again administered in order to compare the changes that had occurred.

ATTITUDES AND ACTIONS

The results of this research study were quite convincing. The group that continued on the traditional performance appraisal showed no change in *any* of the areas measured. The WP&R group, by contrast, expressed significantly more favorable attitudes on almost all questionnaire items. Specifically, their attitudes changed in a favorable direction over the year that they participated in the new WP&R program with regard to the

• amount of help the manager was giving them in improving performance on the job;
• degree to which the manager was receptive to new ideas and suggestions;
• ability of the manager to plan;
• extent to which the manager made use of their abilities and experience;
• degree to which they felt the goals they were shooting for were what they *should* be;
• extent to which they received help from the manager in planning for *future* job opportunities;
• value of the performance discussions they had with their managers.

In addition to these changes in attitudes, evidence was also found which showed clearly that the members of the WP&R group were much more likely to have taken specific actions to improve performance than were those who continued with the traditional performance appraisal approach.

Current Observations

Recently we undertook still another intensive study of the WP&R program in order to learn more about the nature of these discussions and how they can be made most effective. While these observations have not been completed, some interesting findings have already come to light—especially in relation to differences between WP&R and traditional performance appraisal discussions.

PERCEIVED DIFFERENCES

For one thing, WP&R interviews are strictly man-to-man in character, rather than having a father-and-son flavor, as did so many of the traditional performance appraisals. This seems to be due to the fact that it is much more natural under the WP&R program for the subordinate to take the initiative when his performance on past goals is being reviewed. Thus, in listening to the subordinate's review of performance, problems, and failings, the manager is automatically cast in the role of *counselor*. This role for the manager, in turn, results naturally in a problem-solving discussion.

In the traditional performance appraisal interview, on the other hand, the manager is automatically cast in the role of *judge*. The subordinate's natural reaction is to assume a defensive posture, and thus all the necessary ingredients for an argument are present.

Since the WP&R approach focuses mainly on immediate, short-term goals, some managers are concerned that longer range, broader plans and goals might be neglected. Our data show that this concern is unfounded. In almost every case, the discussion of specific work plans and goals seems to lead naturally into a consideration of broader, longer range plans. In fact, in a substantial percentage of these sessions, even the career plans of the subordinates are reviewed.

In general, the WP&R approach appears to be a better way of defining what is expected of an individual and how he is doing on the job. Whereas the traditional performance appraisal often results in resistance to the manager's attempts to help the subordinate, the WP&R approach brings about acceptance of such attempts.

Conclusion

Multiple studies conducted by the Behavioral Research Service at GE reveal that the traditional performance appraisal method contains a number of problems:

1. Appraisal interviews attempt to accomplish the two objectives of
• providing a written justification for salary action;
• motivating the employee to improve his work performance.
2. The two purposes are in conflict, with the result that the traditional appraisal system essentially becomes a salary discussion in which the manager justifies the action taken.

3. The appraisal discussion has little influence on future job performance.

4. Appreciable improvement is realized only when specified goals and deadlines are mutually established and agreed on by the subordinate and his manager in an interview split away from the appraisal interview.

This evidence, coupled with other principles relating to employee motivation, gave rise to the new WP&R program, which is proving to be far more effective in improving job performance than the traditional performance appraisal method. Thus, it appears likely that companies which are currently relying on the comprehensive annual performance appraisal process to achieve improvement in work performance might well consider the advisability of switching to some form of work-planning-and-review in their industrial personnel programs.

QUESTIONS

1. What are the purposes of the appraisal interview?
2. One of the findings of the research reported in this article was that separate appraisals should be held for different purposes. Why should there be a conflict between salary action and goal-setting interviews?
3. In this research it was found that criticism has a negative effect upon goal achievement. Why is this so?
4. What are the principal features of the "work planning and review" program developed at General Electric?
5. Evaluate traditional performance appraisal programs in the light of findings reported in this article.

14.

Is Your Training Department Working on the Wrong Problem?

DAVID W. BROWN

How effective is your company's training program? John Hannon reported in a recent *Training and Development Journal* article that most managers rate their training program no better than poor or average. Only one in ten of those surveyed consider their program to be excellent. The survey also said that the most economical and practical training method was "supervised learning by doing." [1] In spite of the considerable effort made in recent years to improve learning through the use of video tape, programmed instruction and other modern techniques, most industrial training takes place on the job under the direction of the employee's immediate supervisor.

Norman R. F. Maier in *Psychology in Industry* says that the acceptance by management of need for training has been accomplished despite the fact that there have been very few studies published demonstrating the value of formal training programs. [2]

After observing and participating in business "training" for a number of years, it seems to me that it is time to carefully reappraise training practices.

- Do we train our employees or do they learn in spite of us?
- Do industrial supervisors over-rate their ability to train?
- Can we improve learning by removing the emotional blocks which prevent it from occurring?
- Man has a powerful drive to learn and to know. Are we using it properly?

How Effective Is Industrial Training?

At best it is difficult and frustrating. This story may provide some clues as to why this is so.

Reprinted from *Training and Development Journal*, Vol. 23, No. 5 (May 1969), pp. 16–20, by permission of the publisher.

David W. Brown is Manager of Manufacturing, Pyrofilm Resistor Company, Cedar Knolls, N.J.

[1] "How Companies Look at Training, Sobering Results of a New National Survey," John W. Hannon, *Training and Development Journal*, Jan. 1968.

[2] *Psychology in Industry*, Norman R. F. Maier, Houghton Mifflin Co., 1955, p. 320.

The production operator was in trouble. She was helixing film resistors (putting a spiral in the cylindrical surface of the resistor) and she was losing one out of every ten resistors because the mechanical set up was incorrect. The foreman, hurrying past on his way to a meeting, saw the pile of resistors in her scrap box, and stopped to talk with her. After watching four or five cycles of the operation it was clear what the problem was.

He said with good humor, "You have your stop set in too close, that's why the resistors are not spiraling up to value. Here, let me move it out half a turn for you. Now, see what's happened? No more scrap. I thought you understood that when I went over it in the training class. Do you see how I fixed it?"

The operator was embarrassed. She smiled and said, "Thanks." The foreman went off to his meeting satisfied that he was really training his employees. ("Training of employees is the responsibility of the immediate supervisor.")

As soon as he was out of sight, the operator turned to the operator at the next machine and said, "What did he do to fix my machine?"

I saw that happen in a department considered by management to be well run, and operating well within budget. She didn't learn anything. He was sure he had "trained" her. You're skeptical? Unusual case? On the contrary, this incident is fairly typical of training in American industry.

Most workers in business and industry are not doing highly engineered jobs, in the conventional industrial engineering sense. They are doing specialized unique jobs where the operator himself helps create his own job and where he is in many cases the best qualified person to train a replacement.

Furthermore, mechanization and automation are reducing the number of highly-populated jobs which are suitable for very thorough industrial engineering analysis and formal training programs. We are seeing an increase in service and technical jobs where the employee has more freedom and contributes more to the development of his own job. Formal training programs in practice do not train more than a small percentage of industrial workers.

On-the-Job Training

Most training is directed by the employee's immediate supervisor. In theory, the supervisor trains his new employee. Actually the supervisor delegates most of the actual training to senior subordinates, a practice that is sometimes called on-the-job training, or learning by doing. An experienced supervisor can do most jobs in his department reasonably well, but because the time required for training is so long, he does not have the time to personally coach each new man. After explaining department policies and the work of the department, the supervisor takes the new man on a brief tour and introduces him around, and then puts him with an experienced employee to learn the job so that he can get back to his other problems. The senior employee, with the advantage of long experience on the job, knows the subtle tricks that make the difference between a fumbling performance and a superior one, and is supposed to transfer this skill to the new man.

The senior operator however is not a trained teacher. He has trouble organizing the subject matter and communicating ideas to the new man. He may lack understanding of the technical background of the operation. He may not be very interested in how fast the new employee learns. The quality of the training is uncertain.

Let's get a little more personal. Who trained you to do your present job? Probably no one. Probably like most of us, you worked it out by yourself. Because you were ambitious and highly motivated you observed the good and bad practices of others doing similar work, and read all you could, and got some good coaching from senior members of your profession, and perhaps even learned something at school.

The point is that you weren't "trained" by your employer. You learned to do your job by your own initiative. And that is the way most people in business and industry learn their jobs, including the industrial worker who theoretically gets "trained" by his supervisor. Actually the amount of actual useful learning that occurs as a result of "training" is minor compared to the amount picked up in ingenious subtle ways by the employee himself. We don't train our employees; they learn in spite of us.

Supervisors As Teachers

Here is another story:

The production manager and the chief engineer were concerned about the number of errors by operators who were performing an evaporation operation used in the manufacture of electronic components. They reasoned that a talk by a knowledgeable specialist might help, so they arranged for the engineer who did the initial development work on the process to talk to the operators about vacuum systems and the principle of evaporation. The production manager was impressed by the clarity of the talk and the down-to-earth nature of the material covered. Both he and the lecturer were pleased at how it had gone.

The next day the production manager received the verdict from the shop. The foreman reported, somewhat hesitantly, that the operators didn't understand what he said; he talked over their heads. Furthermore, the material he covered was not helpful to them.

The foreman hesitated before disillusioning the boss. A good foreman of course recognizes his responsibility to be frank with his superior, but as the episode with the spiraling operator shows, it is expecting a lot from human clay to count on production workers telling the boss the blunt truth about the quality of his training programs.

Most industrial supervisors grossly overrate their ability to train. One of the simplest methods of improving training is to increase the use of tests. The engineer and the production supervisor should have started out by defining what information they wanted the operators to learn. They then could have drawn up a simple written test to be given at the end of the talk so that they could find out whether they had accomplished their objectives.

The foreman who tried to train the spiraling operator could have improved the learning experience by testing. He could have set up the machine improperly after he was finished instructing her and then asked her to correct the set up.

You probably overrate your effectiveness as a trainer. Certainly if you don't test as a routine matter after each training incident, I can guarantee that you overrate yourself.

Please note that I am advocating tests as a method of evaluating the *learning* and not the *learner*. In most industrial situations the student has enough ability to learn the job. The question is does management have the skill to cause learning to take place?

Emotion and Learning

Well, if it is true that we don't really teach people, that our fumbling attempts to train them are almost irrelevant, what can we do to improve learning? There are emotional blocks which get in the way between the teacher and the learner. The skill of the supervisor in recognizing and dealing with these emotional factors is crucially important to learning.

Unfortunately, many adults have been taught by parents, teachers, or supervisors that to ask questions is to risk being thought of as stupid or overly aggressive. One emotional factor that must be dealt with therefore is the unwillingness we have to expose our ignorance, especially to a superior. Employees will go to any length to avoid admitting to the boss that they don't understand what he is talking about, especially if the boss thinks the employee should understand it.

That's why it is so important when training subordinates to explain thoroughly and then test to be sure the matter is understood. If the subordinate does not get it the first time he will almost never on his own initiative raise the subject at a later date. If he feels that the subject matter is important, he will go to a peer and ask for clarification. If he feels that the matter is not important he will forget about it and hope he doesn't get caught. Most supervisors have had the experience of hearing a subordinate say, "Yes, I remember our talking about that but I guess I didn't understand it." When this happens the supervisor should take the opportunity to discuss with the employee their mutual failure to communicate. It is difficult for most people to admit to the boss that they don't understand what he is talking about. The supervisor should with patience and understanding refuse to tolerate evasive action; he should require that information be transferred in a cooperative distortion-free atmosphere.

Threats to Learning

Sit in a class of executives attending a lecture. Listen to the questions. There are three kinds. The rarest is the simple, frank admission of confusion or request for clarification. The question comes only from a very self-confident relaxed person. The second and more common question is from an intelligent, aggressive trainee, who is out to show everyone else how smart he is. He asks questions like, "Yes, that certainly makes sense, but isn't it true in certain circumstances. . . ." Lecturers love this intelligent kind of question because it shows that they really are putting the material over well.

The third kind of question is the most common and the most tragic. It is not asked. The average guy in the room understands about three-quarters of what is going on, but he hates to ask a stupid question because he knows that if he does everyone will *know* he is just an average guy. Most students in lectures believe in the old saying: "It is better to remain silent and appear stupid than speak and remove all doubt." Good politics but poor learning. It is almost impossible to eliminate this problem when you are teaching a group, but there are ways to minimize it. Small discussion groups, for example, are less threatening than formal lectures. Training by a peer is less threatening than training by a supervisor; this is one important reason for the popularity of on-the-job training.

Programmed learning, video tape and slide/sound programs all have the potential advantage of being relatively threat-free. With programmed learning the trainee is expected to answer most of the questions correctly which has the effect of building up the learner's self-confidence. These techniques, however, are expensive to use on low-population jobs, and are relatively inflexible.

Pride an Obstacle

Another emotional factor which blocks learning is pride. An aggressive subordinate will try to become independent of the boss as quickly as possible. He wants to run his own show. He sometimes goes to ridiculous lengths to avoid asking for advice from the boss until he has a good solution to the problem. Then he can go in with the problem solved.

I'm sure you are familiar with the old army doctrine of completed staff-work, which says that the staff man is responsible for carrying through so thoroughly on a problem that all that is required is the superior's signature on the necessary orders to put into effect the best possible solution to the problem. It is of course legitimate for a superior to expect subordinates to solve their own problems. But the subordinate must not distort this principle to the point where he avoids using his boss as a valuable source of information.

Teachers' Emotions

There are also emotional factors which affect the teacher and reduce his effectiveness. One of the most common problems is fear of competition—fear that when the trainee is fully proficient he may replace the trainer or reduce his value to the organization. It is difficult for an employee to disclose all the tricks of his craft to a newcomer. His relative value to the organization is reduced if a dozen people all can do the job as well as he can. This factor is particularly common where the trainer is ambitious, or is a self-taught, skilled specialist. A manager who is training an ambitious younger subordinate sometimes finds it difficult to open up completely with the subordinate, even though he really wants to develop the younger man. These are normal, human reactions which should be faced up to frankly.

When a senior employee is asked to train a newcomer, his attitude may range all the way from friendliness through apathy to frank hostility. It is extremely important for the supervisor to accurately gauge the attitude of the trainer. The trainer may feel that this is extra work for which he is not being properly compensated. He may find the trainee unpleasant on a personal level. He may feel that time devoted to training will reduce his production for the day and result in criticism from the boss. He may feel that his boss wants production first, and training second.

The supervisor who finds that senior operators are reluctant trainers should consider some recognition to compensate the trainer for the burdens of the work—a special title, a badge, a special uniform, more money, etc.

Emotional attitudes are extremely important factors in the exchange of information. They can have unfortunate effects on the behavior of both trainers and trainees.

The Excitement of Learning

Once the negative emotional blocks to learning are dealt with, we have access to a vast, virtually unexplored, positive resource. We are born with an intense curiosity about the world around us. There is tremendous excitement in the act of comprehension. We want to learn.

We use only a small fraction of the potential of the human brain, perhaps 5 to 10 per cent. It has been said that the brain has a capacity infinitely greater than that of the largest computer. The innate capacity to learn is not much of a problem in industry. There is adequate intellectual capacity in most people to learn their jobs rapidly and to do them well.

Intelligence tests frequently tell more about a person's habits with regard to learning than about his intellectual capacity. A very young child is naturally inquisitive and persistent in pursuit of knowledge. He asks questions without regard for what others will think and is excited by his search. Encourage this as he grows up and he will appear intelligent. Take the same child and place him for a few crucial years in an environment where asking questions results in peer disapproval and where teachers and parents are impatient with persistent questions. Train him to turn away from knowledge and his intelligence will appear to suffer.

Is it possible that the difference between the outstanding employee and the mediocre one is that the former has habits of inquisitiveness and curiosity, while the latter has an emotional blindfold on which makes him afraid to reach out for new knowledge?

Conclusions

1. Learning in industry is like an iceberg. Most learning occurs out of sight. Formal training is highly visible but is relatively unimportant compared with what the employee picks up on his own.

2. Most learning takes place on the job. The Training Department should spend a large share of its resources in making this learning more effective. This should take priority over formal training programs with limited objectives, like management training classes and sales training classes.

3. Supervisors and coaches should be taught how to teach and how to tell whether learning is taking place.

4. Emotional attitudes on the part of teacher and student are extremely important in industrial life. Supervisors must be trained to recognize and deal constructively with normal emotional factors which prevent learning from occurring.

5. The great challenge for us is to create a climate in which our associates can recover a child-like eagerness for learning. When our employees are able to display an intense uninhibited curiosity about their environment we will have made significant progress towards the achievement of a well-trained effective work force.

QUESTIONS

1. What do you think of the author's suggestions for the use of testing in training programs?
2. Discuss the emotional blocks to learning covered by the author. How can these be overcome?
3. Do you agree that major emphasis ought to be given to improving on-the-job training activities in industry as compared with formal classroom training?
4. Who is most suitable to be the on-the-job trainer? The supervisor? Someone else? Why? What should be his qualifications and responsibilities?

15.

Learning Theories and Training

LESLIE E. THIS and GORDON L. LIPPITT

Attempts are often made to distinguish between training and education. Some educators feel that training directors are not engaged in education. Most training directors believe they are. Educators tend to make this distinction: training is narrow in scope and involves only learning that is directly related to job performance, while education is concerned with the total human being and his insights into, and understanding of, his entire world. These attempts to distinguish between training and education seem petty inasmuch as both are concerned with the process of human learning.

Berelson and Steiner define learning as "Changes in behavior that result from previous behavior in similar situations. Mostly, but by no means always, behavior also becomes demonstrably more effective and more adaptive after the exercise than it was before. In the broadest terms, then, learning refers to the effects of experience, either director or symbolic, on subsequent behavior." [1]

For the training director, learning would seem to imply these kinds of things:

a. Knowing something intellectually or conceptually one never knew before.

b. Being able to do something one couldn't do before—behavior or skill.

c. Combining two knowns into a new understanding of a skill, piece of knowledge, concept, or behavior.

d. Being able to use or apply a new combination of skills, knowledge, concept, or behavior.

e. Being able to understand and/or apply that which one knows—either skill, knowledge, or behavior.

Since the training director is concerned with learning, it follows that he should be concerned with learning theory. Training directors often talk about the learning theory that underlies their training. However, most of us do not have a good understanding of learning theories and their application to our training efforts. It is through the eyes of the training director

Reprinted from *Training and Development Journal* (two-part article) Vol. 20, No. 4 (April 1966), pp. 2–11; Vol. 20, No. 5 (May 1966), pp. 10–18, by permission of the publisher.

Leslie E. This is Chief, Employee Development and Safety Branch, Agricultural Research Service, U.S. Department of Agriculture, Washington, D.C. Gordon L. Lippitt is Professor of Behavioral Sciences at George Washington University, Washington, D.C., and President of Leadership Resources, Inc.

[1] Berelson, Bernard and Steiner, Gary A., "Human Behavior—An Inventory of Scientific Findings," Harcourt, Brace and World, Inc., 1964.

156

that the authors have ventured into an overview of learning theory.

As they design training programs, training directors are confronted by many factors about which they must make decisions:

a. *Desired Outcomes for the Learning Experience.* This can range from complex comprehension of organizational dynamics to simple manual skills.

The *managers* who underwrite training programs normally stipulate an entirely different set of training outcomes. These usually are identified as reduction of costs; increased productivity; improved morale; and a pool of promotional replacements. Sometimes these are confused by training directors as outcomes of training that are affected by learning theory. It seems to us that these may be results of training but that learning theory does not directly relate to these as outcomes.

b. *Site for Learning.* Training directors are concerned whether learning best occurs on the job; in a classroom; on organizational premises or off organizational premises; university or other formal site; cultural island; or at home.

c. *Learning Methods.* These are on a continuum from casual reading to intense personal involvement in personal-relationship laboratories.

d. *Grouping for Learning.* Our grouping of learners can involve all combinations from dyads to audiences of 1,500.

As we work with, and manipulate, the kinds of variables listed above, we tend to confuse them with learning theory. For example, a training director will say "My theory of learning is that employees learn best when placed in small discussion groups at a training site removed from the plant." What is not clear to most training directors is that the variables identified above result in a myriad of devices and techniques that stem from, and are most effectively utilized by, a given learning theory. In and of themselves they are not learning theory.

Theory vs. Corollaries

Just as we confuse learning theory with the variables discussed, the use of the terms "learning theory" and "learning theory corollaries or principles" can be confusing. Usually the learning theory can be stated very broadly—for example, "Learning occurs when a stimulus is associated with a response." From this generalization about how learning occurs, a number of specific learning laws, rules, or statements are derived—for example, "Repetition of a response strengthens its connection with a stimulus." Thus, the statement, "problems are difficult to solve when they require the use of the familiar in an unfamiliar way" is a corollary of the Behaviorist Learning School Theory. It is the learning theory corollaries that most often serve as the application guides to the trainer.

Some research findings about learning seem to be unrelated to any particular learning theory and will be found in the literature as isolated pieces of research. Two examples follow:

a. Sleep immediately following learning results in more retention than when the subject stays awake after learning (even if he gets the same amount of sleep before the retention test).

b. Simple facts do not seem to be learned during sleep, even when they are presented throughout the night by tape recording.

We have discussed corollaries in detail because a training director sometimes chances upon one or more of these and incorporates them into his training design. He then says "Here is the learning theory that I am employing in my training activity." Sometimes the corollaries he employs have been borrowed from, or are derived from, several learning theories and so would appear to be inconsistent. However, this may be quite valid. This is so because the content and training objectives for a given training program may include both skill and conceptual training. Each of these kinds of training would tend to borrow techniques from different learning theories.

Our major point here, however, is that training directors frequently confuse a learning theory corollary with a basic learning theory. A learning theory is always greater than the corollary. In using the corollary, the training director is often unaware of the major learning theory which lies behind it.

What Is Motivation?

As one plows into the learning theory literature, one is confronted by the problem of motivation. Can you motivate a learner to learn? Is understanding learning motivation a prime requisite of the training director and instructor? Immediately one runs into difficulty. It becomes obvious that learning theorists do not agree on what motivation is or how it is accomplished. Generally speaking, you find these premises:

a. The learner must be self-motivated.

b. The trainer must motivate the learner through an effective learning climate.

c. We do not know enough about causes of motivation to discuss its role in the learning process.

Most training directors believe there is a factor called motivation. They seem to be evenly split as to whether the learner must be self-motivated or whether the training situation or trainer motivates the learner. Those who believe that learning must be self-motivated usually believe the trainer must provide the conditions under which self-motivation can occur. In practice, there is little to distinguish the training designs of trainers who subscribe to differing philosophies. Designed conditions under which self-motivation can occur look very much like the designs of those who attempt to motivate learners.

As the training director explores learning theory, he is confronted with another discouraging task. If anything is in print discussing, in layman terms, individual or comparative learning theories we have not found it. Learning theories are to be found in courses in educational psychology and require a strong background in psychology, research, and statistics to understand them. Some of the differences seem to a training director to be very subtle. It is extremely discouraging to attempt to understand either the individual theories or the difference between the schools embracing several theories.

Animal Experiments Valid?

The first thing that strikes the training director is that most of the research on learning theory has been accomplished using animals and fowls for subjects. Several authors comment that at least 95 per cent of learning research has been accomplished on data received from experiments of rats, chickens, pigeons, monkeys, dogs, and cats.

It is also interesting to note that research on animals and fowls inevitably occurs under one or both of two conditions: the animal or fowl is very hungry or is sex deprived. It may very well be that training directors have been overlooking some excellent motivational factors in this area.

Two other immediate problems present themselves. First, it is often difficult to distinguish learning theories differentiated as to general schools. Second, it is even more difficult to distinguish between individual learning theories within the general schools.

This difficulty is compounded because of the technical language and equations used to express the theories or proportions of the theories. Usually aspects of the theories are stated mathematically and then expressed in prose. Neither of these is done in such a way that a training director can easily comprehend them. He is then faced with the problem of trying to determine what the technical language expresses and restating it in words he can understand.

Learning Theory Schools

Generally, learning theories seem to fall into six general schools.

The first school is known as the *Behaviorist School*. Primarily, these theories hold that learning results from the rewards or punishment that follows a response to a stimulus. These are the so-called S-R Theories.

E. L. Thorndike was one of the early researchers into learning. Generally he held that learning was a trial-and-error process. When faced with the need to respond appropriately to a stimulus, the learner tries any and all of his response patterns. If by chance one works, then that one tends to be repeated and the others neglected. From his research he developed certain laws to further explain the learning process—for example, the Law of Effect: if a connection between a stimulus and response is satisfying to the organism, its strength is increased—if unsatisfying, its strength is reduced.

E. R. Guthrie basically accepted Thorndike's theory, but did not accept the Law of Effect. He came up with an "S-R Contiguity Theory" of learning. His position was that the moment a stimulus was connected to a response—the stimulus would thereafter tend to elicit that response. Repeating the connection would not strengthen the association. Thus, if I am learning a poem and learn it sitting down, I can probably recall that poem best when sitting rather than standing. Generally he did not attach much significance to reward and punishment—responses will tend to be repeated simply because they were the last ones made to a stimulus.

Clark Hull introduced a new concept —not only were a stimulus and response present in learning—but the *organism* itself could not be overlooked. The response to a stimulus must take into account the organism and what it is thinking, needing, and feeling at the moment. We now had the S-O-R concept.

B. F. Skinner is usually identified with the Behaviorist School. Rather than construct a theory of learning, he seems to believe that by observation and objective reporting we can discover how organisms learn without the need of a construct to explain the process. He depends heavily upon what is called operant conditioning. He makes a distinction between "Respondent" and "Operant" behavior. Respondent behavior is that behavior caused by a known stimulus—operant behavior is that behavior for which we can not see or identify a stimulus, though one may, and probably does, exist. If we can anticipate an operant behavior, and introduce a stimulus when it is evidenced, we can provide the occasion for the behavior by introducing the stimulus—but the stimulus does not necessarily evoke the behavior. Thus the emphasis on learning is on correlating a response with reinforcement. This is at the heart of programmed instruction—a correct response is reinforced.

Other researchers have developed variations of the theories described above. Some assume that the organism is relatively passive but that the response is in the repertoire of the learner. Other theorists pay particular attention to instrumental conditioning. They assume that the organism acts on his environment and that the response may not be in his repertoire. Still others talk about mediating responses in which a period of time may elapse between the stimulus and the response—or the response may be a series of responses that stretch over a period of time. For example, a man may be desirous of mar-

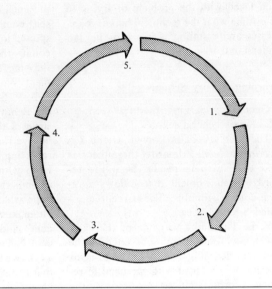

Equilibrium

1. The learning situation is presented to the individual.

2. He moves away from equilibrium.

3. But attempts to move back to equilibrium.

4. He organizes the new material in an effort to integrate and systematize it.

5. He moves to equilibrium.

FIGURE 1[3]

rying a girl but will work for ten years to save enough money to support her adequately before proposing.

Gestalt School

The second grouping is the *Gestalt School*. These theorists believe that learning is not a simple matter of stimulus and response. They hold that learning is cognitive and involves the whole personality. To them, learning is infinitely more complex than the S-R Theories would indicate. For example, they note that learning may occur simply by thinking about a problem. Kurt Lewin, Wolfgang Kohler, E. C. Tolman and Max Wertheimer are typical theorists in this school. They reject the theory that learning occurs by the building up, bit by bit, of established S-R connections. They look at the phenomenon of insight, long-coming or instantaneous. To them, "the whole is more than the sum of the parts."

"Central in Gestalt theory is the Law of 'Pragnanz' which indicates the direction of events. According to this law, the psychological organization of the individual tends to move always in one direction, always toward the 'good' Gestalt, an organization of the whole which is regular, simple, and stable.[2]

"The Law of 'Pragnanz' is further a law of equilibrium. According to it, the learning process might be presented as follows: The individual is in a state of equilibrium, of 'good' Gestalt. He is confronted by a learning situation. Tensions develop and disequilibrium results. The individual thus moves away from equi-

[2] Kurt Koffka, "Principles of Gestalt Psychology," Harcourt, Brace, 1935, p. 110.
[3] Marsh, Pierre J. "Selected Learning Theories: Their Implications for Job Training." Master's Thesis, George Washington University, School of Business and Public Administration, Washington, D.C., August 6, 1965, pp. 56–57.

librium but at the same time he strives to move back to equilibrium. In order to assist this movement back to the regular, simple, stable state, the learning situation should be structured so as to possess good organization (e.g., simple parts should be presented first; these should lead in an orderly fashion to more difficult parts). The diagram in Figure 1 represents the movement toward equilibrium in the learning process."

A third school is the *Freudian School.* This is a difficult school to capsulize. "It is no simple task to extract a theory of learning from Freud's writings, for while he was interested in individual development and the kind of re-education that goes on in psychotherapy, the problems whose answers he tried to formulate were not those with which theorists in the field of learning have been chiefly concerned. Psychoanalytic theory is too complex and, at least at the present time, too little formalized for it to be presented as a set of propositions subject to experimental testing." [4]

A fourth school is the *Functionalists.* These seem to take parts of all the theories and view learning as a very complex phenomenon that is not explained by either the Gestalt or the Behaviorist theories. Some of the leaders in this school are John Dewey, J. R. Angell, and R. S. Woodworth. These men borrow from all the other schools and are sometimes referred to as "middle of the roaders."

A fifth so-called school is those who subscribe to *Mathematical Models.* To these researchers, learning theories must be stated in mathematical form. Some of these proponents come from different learning theory schools but tend to focus on mathematical models such as the Feedback Model, Information-Theory Model, Gaming Model, Differential Calculus Model, Stochastic Model, and the Statistical Association Model. As one tries to understand this school, it occurs to one that they seem to have no theory of their own but are expressing research findings of other theorists in mathematical terms.

A sixth school is more general in nature and can best be characterized by calling it *Current Learning Theory Schools.* These are quite difficult to classify and seem to run the range of modifying Gestalt Theories, modifying Behavioral Theories, accommodating two pieces of both theories, assuming that training involves the whole man—psychological, physiological, biological, and neurophysiological. Some of these are the Postulate System of MacCorquodale and Meehl and the Social Learning Theory of Rotter.

Current Research

Some of the more exciting kinds of current research seem to be in the neurophysiological interpretations of learning. One example of this was shown on a national television program, "Way Out Men," February 13, 1965. In this research, flatworms are trained to stay within a white path. If they deviate from the white path, they receive an electrical shock. After the flatworms learn to stay within the prescribed path, they are then chopped up and fed to a control group of worms. This control group learns to stay within the white path in about half the learning time. This has led some theorists to talk about the possibility of eventually feeding students "professorburgers."

Additional research is going on in this area and we have recently seen two or three other related pieces of research. It seems to indicate a key as to where memory and instincts are stored so that they can be transmitted to offspring. One is intrigued by this research when one re-

---

[4] Hilgard, Ernest R. "Theories of Learning," Appleton-Century-Crofts, Inc., 1956, p. 290.

members popular beliefs such as "Eating of the Tree of Knowledge," eating fish is a good brain food, and the practice of cannibals eating the brain of an educated man to become smart or to eat the heart of a brave man to become courageous.

Transfer of Learning

One of the problems that often confront a training director is the transfer of learning. Some of the major ways in which learning theories attempt to provide for the transfer of that which is learned to the work situation are the following:

1. *Actually doing the "that" which is being learned.* In this instance, we believe transfer is best when learning occurs on or in live situations. This is so because little or no transfer is needed—what is learned is directly applied. Instances employing this technique are on-the-job training, coaching, apprenticeship, and job experience.

2. *Doing something that is similar to that which is to be learned.* This transfer principle is applied when we use simulated experiences—the training experience and techniques are as similar to the job as possible. Sometimes we let the trainee discover the principles and apply them to his job. In other instances, particularly in skill training, he works on mock-ups which closely resemble the actual equipment on which he will work. Other techniques employed would include role playing, sensitivity training, and case studies.

3. *Reading or hearing about that which is to be learned.* In this instance, the trainer or a book gives the trainee the principles and then discusses and illustrates them. The trainee must now figure out the ways in which what he has heard or read applies to his job and how he can use it. Illustrative training techniques would be lectures, reading, and most management and supervisory training programs featuring the "telling" method.

4. *Doing or reading about anything on the assumption it will help anything to be learned.* In this instance there is an assumption that a liberalized education makes the trainee more effective in whatever job he occupies or task he is to learn. This might be termed the liberal arts approach. It assumes that a well-rounded, educated person is more effective, and more easily trained in specifics, if he understands himself, his society, his world, and other disciplines. Obviously, this would be a somewhat costly way of training. It would involve perceptual living and generalized education.

Much research has gone into the transfer of learning. Most of this occurs in the S-R Theories. It seems to be less of a problem in the other major theories. This is quite understandable as one compares the theories of learning. For example, the S-R Theories become quite concerned with questions like "Will the study of mathematics help a person learn a foreign language easier and more quickly?" This has led to much research regarding the conditions under which the transfer of learning best occurs. It is also applicable to conceptual learning. For example, will learning how to delegate responsibilities to children be useful in the delegation process in the work organization?

Adult Learning

Recent research at the University of Nebraska indicated:

1. The average older adult in an adult education program is at least as intellectually able, and performs as well, as the average younger participant.

2. Adults who continue to participate in educative activity learn more effectively than similar adults who do not. This would simply seem to indicate that learning skills require practice to be maintained.

3. Adults learn far more effectively when they are permitted to learn at their own pace.[5]

Conditions for Learning

The concerns about motivating individuals to learn, and the recognition that there is such a thing as a learning process, have led training directors and training psychologists to explore the condition under which learning seems best to occur. Numerous lists of conditions for learning exist. They vary depending on the learning theory school to which the author subscribes. However, there is a remarkable acceptance of some general conditions that should exist for effective learning regardless of the learning theory employed. One of these composite lists follows.

1. *Acceptance that all human beings can learn.* The assumption, for example, that you "can't teach an old dog new tricks" is wrong. Few normal people at any age are probably incapable of learning. The tremendous surge in adult education and second careers after retirement attests to people's ability to learn at all ages.

2. *The individual must be motivated to learn.* This motivation should be related to the individual's drives.

    a. The individual must be aware of the inadequacy or unsatisfactoriness of his present behavior, skill, or knowledge.

    b. The individual must have a clear picture of the behavior which he is required to adopt.

3. *Learning is an active process, not passive.* It takes action and involvement by and of the individual with resource persons and the training group.

4. *Normally, the learner must have guidance.* Trial and error are too time-consuming. This is the process of feed-

back. The learner must have data on "how am I doing" if he is to correct improper performance before it becomes patternized.

5. *Appropriate materials for sequential learning must be provided:* cases; problems; discussion; reading. The trainer must possess a vast repertoire of training tools and materials and recognize the limitations and capacities of each. It is in this area that so many training directors get trapped by utilizing the latest training fads or gimmicks for inappropriate learning.

6. *Time must be provided to practice the learning;* to internalize; to give confidence. Too often trainers are under pressure to "pack the program"—to utilize every moment available to "tell them something." This is inefficient use of learning time. Part of the learning process requires sizable pieces of time for assimilation, testing, and acceptance.

7. *Learning methods, if possible, should be varied to avoid boredom.* It is assumed that the trainer will be sufficiently sophisticated to vary the methods according to their usefulness to the material being learned. Where several methods are about equally useful, variety should be introduced to offset factors of fatigue and boredom.

8. *The learner must secure satisfaction from the learning.* This is the old story of "you can lead a horse to water. . . ." Learners are capable of excellent learning under the most trying of conditions if the learning is satisfying to one or more of their needs. Conversely, the best appointed of learning facilities and trainee comfort can fail if the program is not seen as useful by the learner.

9. *The learner must get reinforcement of the correct behavior.* B. F. Skinner and the Behaviorists have much to say on this score. Usually learners need fairly

---

[5] Knox, Alan B., and Sjogren, Douglas. "Research on Adult Learning," *Adult Education,* Spring 1965, pp. 133–137.

immediate reinforcement. Few learners can wait for months for correct behavior to be rewarded. However, there may well be long-range rewards and lesser-intermediate rewards. We would also emphasize that rewarded job performance when the learner returns from the training program must be consistent with the learning program rewards.

10. *Standards of performance should be set for the learner.* Set goals for achievement. While learning is quite individual, and it is recognized that learners will advance at differing paces, most learners like to have bench marks by which to judge their progress.

11. *A recognition that there are different levels of learning and that these take different times and methods.* Learning to memorize a simple poem is entirely different from learning long-range planning. There are, at least, four identifiable levels of learning; each requiring different timing, methods, involvement, techniques, and learning theory.[6]

At the simplest level we have the skills of motor responses, memorization, and simple conditioning.

Next, we have the adaption level where we are gaining knowledge or adapting to a simple environment. Learning to operate an electric typewriter after using a manual typewriter is an example. Third, is the complex level, utilized when we train in interpersonal understandings and skill, look for principles in complex practices and actions, or try to find integrated meaning in the operation of seemingly isolated parts.

At the most complex level we deal with the values of individuals and groups. This is a most subtle, time-consuming, and sophisticated training endeavor. Few work organizations have training programs with value change of long-standing,

cultural or ethnic values as their specific goal. Many work organizations, however, do have training programs aimed at changing less entrenched values.

The reader will recognize that this listing of conditions under which people learn contains concepts and principles from most of the learning theory schools. Most training directors are generalists, and seldom do their training programs focus on a constant single-objective outcome. It is perhaps inevitable that his own guiding training concepts and principles will be a meld from many theories. It is important however, that he understand the theories of learning so that he is using those concepts and principles which can best assure he will accomplish his organization's training objectives in specific training programs.

As the training director explores learning theory, he finds the following points of view:

a. There are individual exponents of a given theory who insist that their theory alone accounts for the way people learn.

b. There are those who insist that we do not know what learning theory is and that learning theorists do not contribute to the real problems of training.

c. There are those who will be frank in saying to a training director, "You are heavily on your own. Learning theory in its present state will not materially help you. Experiment. If it works and gets you the results you want—don't worry about what learning theory lies behind your success."

It is encouraging to note that some social scientists are aware of this breach between research and practice:

". . . Knowledge is not practice and practice is not knowledge. The improvement of one does not lead automatically to the improvement of the other. Each

---

[6] Composite drawn from: (a) Lippitt, Gordon L., "Conditions of Learning Affecting Training," unpublished notes; and (b) Miller, Harry L., "Teaching and Learning in Adult Education," Macmillan Publishing Co., Inc., 1964.

can work fruitfully for the advancement of the other but also, unfortunately, each can develop separately from the other and hence stuntedly in relation to the other." [7]

"It should be clear that the linking of social theory to social practice, as well as the development of a practice-linked theory of the application of social science knowledge to practice, is an intellectual challenge of the first magnitude. But it is one that many social scientists—particularly those who rarely leave the university system—have neglected." [8]

"Lewin is credited with remarking that one can bridge the gap between theory and reality only if one can tolerate 'constant intense tension.' Roethlisberger and his colleagues described these tensions all too well for the person trying to improve

the practice of administration when they wrote on 'Training for a Multidimensional World' [9] which I have already recommended to anyone seriously planning to enter this field." [10]

In relating learning theory to learning goals, learning theory corollaries, and the designed learning experience or training program, here is a model that is useful in visualizing their interrelationship and their time sequence:

Two points are critical regarding the model in Figure 2:

a. The model describes either a single training program or a series of training programs separated by a span of months or even years.

b. The lines indicate that the process is not a single revolution—but a continuous process. In the life of a single training

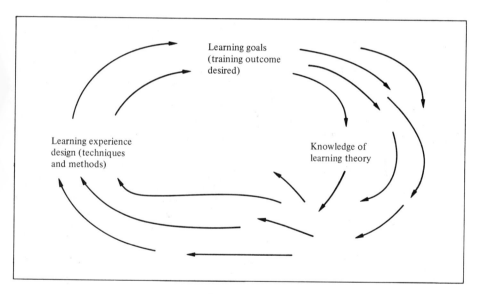

Learning goals
(training outcome
desired)

Learning experience
design (techniques
and methods)

Knowledge of
learning theory

FIGURE 2

[7] Roethlisberger, Fritz J., in introduction to Clark, James V. "Education for the Use of Behavioral Science," Institute of Industrial Relations, University of California, Los Angeles, Calif., 1962, p. 4.

[8] Clark, James V., *op. cit.*, p. 89.

[9] Roethlisberger, Fritz J., and others; "Training for Human Relations: An Interim Report," Division of Research, Harvard Business School, Boston, Mass., 1954, Chapter 9.

[10] Clark, James V., *op. cit.*, p. 91.

program, the learning goals may be modified—or the design, learning corollaries, or even the learning theory employed may undergo on-the-scene modification if they are not producing the desired learning goals.

The model does not exist in a vacuum, nor is the choice of its component parts a matter of whim, preference, or intellectual selection. It is always related to the forces within the organization, the trainees, the trainers, and the situation, as is indicated in Figure 3.

If we accept (1) that effective training always takes into account the major forces impinging upon it and (2) that trainees have insights into factors that facilitate their learning, then it follows that we should listen attentively to trainee observations. Some of the more frequently mentioned are:

a. Participants almost always rate very high, as a training benefit, their interactions with each other. This seems particularly true in heterogeneous groups.

A simplified mathematical statement of this model is

$$\text{Learning Goal}(s) = \frac{\text{Present state of the organization} + \text{present state of trainees} + \text{recognized need for change}}{\text{Appropriate learning theory} + \text{appropriate training design} + \text{supportive climate for changed trainee behavior}}$$

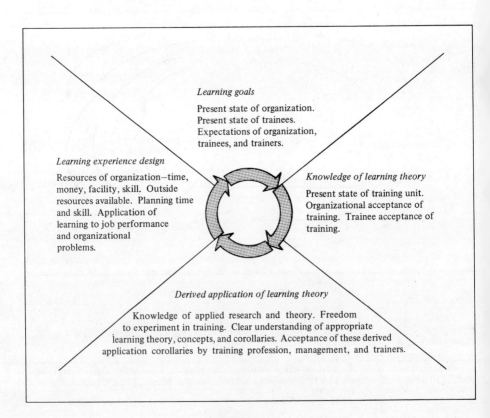

Learning goals

Present state of organization.
Present state of trainees.
Expectations of organization,
trainees, and trainers.

Learning experience design

Resources of organization—time, money, facility, skill. Outside resources available. Planning time and skill. Application of learning to job performance and organizational problems.

Knowledge of learning theory

Present state of training unit. Organizational acceptance of training. Trainee acceptance of training.

Derived application of learning theory

Knowledge of applied research and theory. Freedom to experiment in training. Clear understanding of appropriate learning theory, concepts, and corollaries. Acceptance of these derived application corollaries by training profession, management, and trainers.

FIGURE 3

They comment that they have become aware that their problems are not peculiar; it has been helpful to learn about other programs; they have learned from each other; and they have become more perceptive and broadened in the understanding of their role. We have, in the past, looked upon this as a minor side benefit of heterogeneous training. We are now inclined to believe this may be one of the major benefits of such training.

b. Participants always complain that they need time to internalize, digest, reflect, and be left alone. We usually answer by scheduling more night meetings. Perhaps we need to experiment with two hours of training and six hours of internalization.

c. Participants like "bull sessions."

d. Participants say they need more recreation to release some of their emotional and physical energy.

e. The use of dyad conversations seems useful—even if these are forced. They seem to serve a helpful purpose of reaction, clarification, and feedback.

f. Time for reading pertinent articles and books seems to have excellent payoff. Training directors generally feel that managers would not accept training time being used for reading purposes.

g. Some limited experimentation seems to indicate that it is desirable to attempt to bring all participants up to a minimum level of knowledge before placing them in a training program. This can be accomplished by preliminary reading or programmed instruction.

No Single Theory

We are inclined to think that listening to the comments of participants as to what *they* believe enhances their learning and designing training programs to meet these expressed needs might have very excellent payoff in training programs even if the training director could not find support for the technique within existing learning theories. What we suspect is that there is no *single* learning theory that should be embraced by a training director or a training program.

This feeling seems to be supported as one surveys the current trends in training programs. These trends would seem to borrow from most of the Schools of Learning Theory. To illustrate, the authors believe that the following trends can be identified:

1. A trend toward a focus on *improved performance* rather than on increased individual knowledge.

2. A trend to *train situations* rather than individuals.

3. A trend to see training as the way *management gets its job done* rather than a function of the training department.

4. A trend toward building up *in-house* capabilities rather than dependence on outside experts.

5. A trend toward insistence on *evaluation* of training rather than accepting it on faith.

6. A trend toward designing learning that will focus on *learning-how-to learn.*

7. A trend toward training that is *reality-based* as against training that is highly unrelated to the learners' life experience.

8. A trend toward training that has an *action-learning* base rather than [being] based on one-way communication.

9. A trend toward training that provides *reinforcement* and followup experience for trainees rather than "graduating" them from a training program.

10. A trend to depend more on the learning to be *self-motivated by the learner* rather than imposed on the learner by the trainers.

11. A trend for training to be *goal-oriented* rather than vague assurance that it will be "good for you."

12. A trend toward greater *homogeneity* in the persons being trained.[11]

[11] Lippitt, Gordon L. "Changing Trends in Organized Development," Talk before the Public Administrative Society, University of Michigan.

Fitting Specific Needs

There would appear to be different learning techniques and conditions that are applicable to different kinds of training and learning. The training programs within a work organization are not all aimed at the same kind of learning. Perhaps different learning theories apply according to the nature of the subject to be taught and learned, the nature of the organization, the nature of the trainees, and the available teaching resources. This would indicate that no single learning theory can be applied across-the-board to all learning activities.

We suggest the following format as one that would be useful to a training director:

Step 1: What is the learning outcome desired? This will indicate what is to be taught—orientation, problem solving, decision making, knowledge, memorization, changed attitude, changed behavior, manual skill, creativity, self-insight, lessened resistance to change, person-to-person relationships, group-to-group relationships, technical knowledge, communication, self-development, executive development, or understanding principles and theory.

Step 2: Based on what is to be taught, select the learning theory most applicable to that content; i.e., Behavioral Theory, Cognitive Theory, Functionalism, Mathematical Model, Psychiatric, Neurophysiological, or total man and environment.

Step 3: The basic learning theory should be utilized by examining the derived Corollary Theories and principles useful in effectively training toward the desired end. For example; knowing others better, knowing related programs better, reflection time, informal interaction, exercise, recreation, advance preparation, immediate reward, delayed reward, learning plateau, practice-rest-practice, reading with recitation, meaningful material,

"A-na" phenomena, immediate use, material known previously, important material, pleasant material, concept formation, concrete concept, part–whole versus whole–part, positive instances versus negative instances, general to specific, maturation task relatedness, fatigue factor, and motivation.

Step 4: These considerations would then suggest specific decisions on the following factors:

a. The learning site—on-the-job; classroom-organizational premises; classroom-off organizational premises; university or other formal site, cultural island, or home.

b. The grouping. (1) Related to size —one, dyad, trio, groups 5–8, groups 9–15, groups 16–30, and audience style —any number. (2) Related to relationships of participants—all male, all female, mixed sex; little experience, much experience, mixed experience; old, young, mixed age groups; known to each other, not known to each other; same organization—vertical, horizontal, diagonal; other organization—homogeneous, mixed; same educational level, mixed educational level; and same task or mixed tasks.

c. The learning methods to be employed—lecture, panel, symposium, debate, laboratory, programmed instruction, experience, coaching, job progression, job rotation, job enlargement, apprenticeship, situational training, personal reading, correspondence, liberal arts, formal school, formal outside program, workshop, conference, institute, seminar, visitation, or discussion groups.

d. The training aids to be used— movies, instantaneous replay movies, telephone—loudspeaker, TV, role play, exercises, in-basket, gaming, film strips, slides–transparent, tape recorder, blackboard, newsprint easel, flannel board, magnetic board, self-administered instruments, tests and quizzes, case studies—no printed discussion, case studies—printed discussion, case studies—incident process, experiments, models—mockups, and group-generated data.

e. The type of resource persons or instructors—written material, experience, instrumentation, self, organizational technical expert, outside technical expert, organizational resource people, professors, industrial resource people, training department, supervisor, or peers.

f. How much attention needs to be paid to transfer of learning: direct transfer; live, stimulated reality; principle to be applied; no direct application; known stimuli—opposite response; familiar to be used in unfamiliar way; or principle to be learned and applied.

Change on the Job

As training directors, we strive very hard to establish response patterns that hopefully will be carried over and continued in the work situation. This is at the heart of one of the criticisms managers level at training programs—the behavior of participants back in the work situation too often seems relatively unchanged.

As one examines this phenomenon, one is struck that most training programs in the conceptual areas of supervision and management lean very heavily upon Theory "Y" assumptions. We do not know of any programs that pointedly train toward Theory "X" assumptions. Conversely, organizations still have a goodly amount of Theory "X" assumptions underlying both their operations and supervisory and management practices.[12]

This raises two questions:

1. In our zeal to get away from the mechanistic approach to organizational dynamics, we have underplayed the role of these factors in the total organization as they affect training outcomes. We have tended to train as if such realities did not exist and as if the only dynamics that were operable were the human factors in the training. This has created a breach between the training office, the operating people, and management.

2. The S-R phenomenon not only operates within the training situation but is very much operable within the work situation. People react in the direction of the rewards they receive. The S-R patterns initiated in a training session have very little chance of survival when they come up against different S-R patterns of rewards in the work situation. For example, among the work situation S-R patterns rewarded are the following: "Research paper production gets you promoted—not supervisory ability or a skill." "Promotions depend on who you know—not what you know." "I don't give a damn how your people feel—we've got a job to do." "OK, you've been to a training program. Say something new." "Seniority is what really counts around this place."

Reward Patterns

If a S-R pattern, initiated in a training program, is to be maintained in the work situation, then it must be rewarded by the organization. If the pattern is in conflict with rewarded patterns, the newly learned patterns do not have much chance to survive. We believe that this accounts for a great deal of supposedly poor results of training. The training is not in harmony with the reward patterns of the organization. As training directors, we would have much better success if we would train according to the pattern rewarded, and apparently desired by the organization.

The research into learning theory has

---

[12] McGregor, Douglas. "The Human Side of Enterprise," McGraw-Hill, 1960. Chapters 3 and 4, pp. 33–57 for detailed explanation.

indicated a need that has not been recognized fully by the training profession. We are amazed that a critically needed overview of the field of learning theory has not been written to assist the training director. We need an identification of the existing learning theories that appear to be best researched and validated, the statement and comparison of these theories in language that the training director can comprehend and understand, and suggested guidelines for ways in which the training director can utilize these learning theories to the enhancement of his training activities. We believe such a publication is long overdue and would be highly welcomed by almost all training directors. We believe it would add much to the professionalization of the training job. More importantly it would very well make our training programs more effective in meeting the needs of our organizations.

Helpful Guidelines

Beyond the implications for training directors that this exploration into learning theory has suggested, there seem to be some guidelines from such an exploration that are useful to a manager:

1. The sophistication needed to understand and utilize the implications of learning theory has much to say about the kinds of qualifications and skills a training director should bring to the job. The naive assumption that the bestowal of title and salary makes one a training director is tragic. Similarly, the managerial assumption that an employee who has the knack of making cute speeches or who once taught elementary school is training director material is inadequate. We would even go further and suggest there are some questionable implications of taking an employee who never managed even a small subunit and entrusting him with the training of other managers.

2. We have already commented on why we believe much of our training is not effective. Operational and organizational climate must support the training received. In addition, managers need to be much more realistic and expect that very few entrenched S-R responses can be changed in a week's training program.

3. We need to relook at the anxiety about evaluation of training. We are not even sure how people learn and this creates real problems in trying to evaluate the effectiveness of our learning process efforts. We know people do learn but we are not sure why. When one looks at the tremendous number of complicated, tenuous, and conceptual ideas that are discussed within the span of one week in the average supervisory or management training program, it seems naive in the least to expect that very much by way of established new patterns of behavior could possibly emerge. The expectations of management are too high, and we as training directors have promised too much.

Enchantment of Theory

We see no other trap. As we become concerned with learning theory, we must expect to find conflicting theories and conflicting practices within the profession. We must keep our focus on our objectives and not become seduced by enchantment with the theories.

"Theories . . . attempt to organize existing knowledge, they attempt to provide guiding threads or hypotheses toward new knowledge, and they may also furnish principles by which what is known can be used. This practical outcome is seldom central in the thinking of the constructor of theory, and it is not surprising, therefore, that the person seeking advice from the learning theorist often comes away disappointed.

". . . It turns out, however, that many of the quarrels of the theorists are internal ones, not very important in relation to immediate practical problems; there are, in fact, a great many practically important experimental relationships upon which the theorists are in substantial agreement. . . . If the theoretical differences are irreconcilable, and one position eventually wins out over the other, there will ultimately be an effect upon practice. But advice for practical people today need not wait for the resolution of these theoretical controversies." [13]

This, then, is the challenge to those of us desiring to meet the critical problem of developing effective training programs to meet the changing manpower needs of today's organizations.

REFERENCES

Bass, Bernard M. and Vaughan, James A. "Psychology of Learning for Managers." Graduate School of Business, University of Pittsburgh.

Berelson, Bernard and Steiner, Gary A. "Human Behavior—An Inventory of Scientific Findings." Harcourt Brace, and World, Inc., 1964.

Blake, Robert R., Mouton, Jane S., Barnes, Louis B., and Greiner, Larry E. "Breakthrough in Organization Development." *Harvard Business Review*, Vol. 42, Nov.–Dec. 1964, pages 133–155.

Boudreaux, Edmond and Megginson, Leon C. "A New Concept in University Sponsored Executive Development Programs." *Training Directors Journal*, Vol. 18, Nov. 1964, pages 31–41.

Bradford, Leland P., Gibb, J. R., and Benne, K. D. "T-Group Theory and Laboratory Method." John Wiley and Sons, 1964.

Goldiamond, Israel. "Justified and Unjustified Alarm over Behavioral Control." In: Milton, Ohmer. "Behavior Disorders: Perspectives and Trends." J. B. Lippincott, 1965, pages 237–262.

Green, Edward J. "The Learning Process and Programmed Instruction." Holt, Rinehart, and Winston, Inc., 1962.

Grose, Robert F. and Birney, Robert C. "Transfer of Learning." D. Van Nostrand Co., Inc., 1963.

Guerin, Quintin W. "A Learning Theory Model." *Training Directors Journal*, Apr. 1965, pages 40–45.

Harris, Theodore L., and Schwahn, Wilson E. "Selected Readings on the Learning Process." Oxford University Press, 1961.

Hilgard, Ernest R. "Theories of Learning." Appleton, Century, Crofts, Inc., 1948.

Marsh, Pierre J. "Selected Learning Theories: Their Implications for Job Training." Master's thesis submitted August 6, 1965. School of Business and Public Administration. George Washington University: Washington, D. C.

Miller, Harry L. "Teaching and Learning in Adult Education." Macmillan Publishing Co., Inc., 1964.

Morton, Robert B., and Bass, Bernard M. "The Organizational Training Laboratory." *Training Directors Journal*, Oct. 1964, Vol. 18, pages 2–15.

National Society for the Study of Education. Yearbook. 63d. ed. Pt. I. "Theories of Learning and Instruction." Hilgard, Ernest A. (edited by). University of Chicago Press, 1964.

Rothschild, William E. "Practicing Managerial Skills." *Training Directors Journal*. Nov. 1964, pages 23–30, Vol. 18.

[13] Hilgard, Ernest R. "Theories of Learning," p. 485.

SKINNER, B. F. "Pigeons in a Pelican," *The American Psychologist*, Vol. 15, No. 1, Jan. 1960, pages 28–37.

WESCHLER, I. R. AND SCHEIN, E. H. "Issues in Human Relations Training." (Sel. Reading Ser. 5) Memorial Issue. National Training Laboratories, 1962.

WRIGHT, A. R. "Translating Creativity Findings to Industrial Training Programs." *Human Relations Training News*. Summer 1964, pages 5–7.

QUESTIONS

1. What are the six learning theories discussed in this article?
2. Why do the authors say, "What we suspect is that there is no *single* learning theory that should be embraced by a training director or a training program"?
3. Give guidelines or conditions for learning that should be understood by trainers when designing a learning experience or program.
4. Discuss the problem of transfer of learning from the learning situation to the work situation. What factors inhibit "change on the job"?

16.

Is It Skinner or Nothing?

JOHN R. MURPHY

The public response to B. F. Skinner's *Beyond Freedom and Dignity*[1] reveals a good deal more about the public than it does about Skinner or this work; and it reveals a good deal more about management's perceptions of training than you and I can afford to ignore.

The response has been more extensive, more uniformly antagonistic and more intensely stated than that touched off by any other book during 1971. Skinner has been the subject of a *Time* magazine cover story, a *New York Times* interview, editorial and cover book review, a *Newsweek* education column and countless other reviews. He has guest appeared on Today, Dick Cavett, David Frost, Firing Line, and CBS Morning News. The book was widely circulated as a condensation in *Psychology Today*. The American Psychological Association gave him its annual award. *Time* quoted his colleagues' description as "the most influential psychologist in the country." The book has been number 3 on the best-seller list. But you get the idea.

This would be a remarkable achievement for any semi-technical book, but on top of that:

• The author has been almost entirely out of the public limelight since the early 1960's.
• What image did survive associated ("pigeon-holed?") him with "short step/immediate-feedback," dull rote learning, and the replacement of tail-fins by teaching machines as the nation's hardware sex symbol. Who among us has not damned him with the faint praise, "Well, at least we learned to specify behavioral objectives out of that PI thing."
• The targets of the most heated attacks are positions which Skinner presented (and presented more forcibly) years ago.

Any one of these should have given publisher Alfred Knopf great qualms. But against these odds the spectacular commercial success and critical reaction have occurred, and that suggests that somehow Skinner has struck a sensitive nerve. But this extraordinary emotional reaction has diverted attention away

Reprinted from *Training and Development Journal*, Vol. 26, No. 2 (February 1972), pp. 2–8, by permission of the publisher.
John R. Murphy is Chairman, Training Research Forum, Oyster Bay, New York.

[1] Skinner, B. F., *Beyond Freedom and Dignity*, Alfred Knopf, New York, 1971.

173

from the only issues that make much practical difference *today*: How much of it is relevant to training? How much of it works? Under what conditions?

To answer that we need to examine:

1. Skinner's fundamental position on *the* cause of behavior (because that will be the acid test of your willingness to implement principles of learning which he derives from it).

2. The most consistent critical reactions (because they are the objections you and I will also encounter) and an imputed Skinnerian rebuttal (because we can't overcome those objections with just our own fancy footwork).

3. The principles of learning which he has developed experimentally and what they tell us about designing training (because if we can't use this technology to increase our reliability in predicting and delivering behavior, we are not about to go very far in the business world).

Skinner on Learning

At a Training Research Forum seminar in 1971, Dr. Skinner brought literally every learning principle he has ever stated back to a six-word premise:

"BEHAVIOR IS DETERMINED BY ITS CONSEQUENCES"

Period. That's it. Either you buy that or you don't. If you don't, stop reading —there is not much here you can use effectively. If you do, then the other controversial, painful conclusions in *Beyond Freedom and Dignity* follow inescapably from it. Perhaps a lot of the emotionalism about behaviorism springs from discomfort with that unforgiving go/no-go switch. Even if you say, "I believe that *some* behavior is determined by its consequences," the kindly doctor will shoot from the hip with five quick questions and you're dead—shot with your own bullets. "Face it," the man

says, "Thursday's behavior is caused by Wednesday's consequences of Tuesday's behavior."

If behavior is determined by its consequences, then the way to change behavior is to change the consequences and rearrange the *"contingencies* of the reinforcement." The question is not only "what *is* the consequence," but "in what way (by what contingency) is the consequence (reinforcement) *related* to the behavior?"

This represents a significant change in emphasis for Skinner, and in fact, much of the current criticism is still aimed at the "stimulus-response" straw-man of the early 1960's. He is concerned by that misperception, because it clouds what he now sees as a more critical concept, the role of *consequences* as the only real shaper of behavior. He now emphasizes that "Learning does not occur because behavior has been primed (stimulated); it occurs because behavior, primed or not, is *reinforced.*"

Critics on Skinner

Unfortunately, the critical response to the book has focused on the academic issue of whether man is inherently autonomous and whether it is ethical to "manipulate" him (just in case it turns out he wasn't autonomous after all). That focus is unfortunate, because the argument leads nowhere and draws attention away from the real issue:

what evidence is there that behavior is controlled by its consequences, and how can that make us more effective in helping people to learn, and more reliable when we make commitments to develop a specific level of human performance?

Time's definition of behavioral technology may be the most rational summary statement made by the press: "Behavioral technology is a developing science that aims to change the environment rather than people, that seeks to alter actions rather than feelings, and that shifts the customary psychological emphasis on the world inside men to the world outside them." [2]

But from that point on, there is a high content of emotional static because "Skinner's program runs counter to the traditional humanist image of man as an autonomous individual possessed of a measure of freedom and personal dignity." [3] Novelist Arthur Koestler's not very helpful response is typical: "(Behavioral technology is) . . . a pseudoscience . . . a monumental triviality that has sent psychology into a modern version of the dark ages." [4] You do have to agree that, if the Koestlers see that much power in behavioral technology as a "triviality," it's certainly understandable that they would not want to recognize it as having any great substance.

The most consistent specific criticisms seem to derive from the autonomy hang-up:

1. "You shouldn't have to bribe or manipulate people with frequent and scheduled bursts of reinforcement."

Skinner attributes much of the criticism of his work, and, for that matter, much of the ineffectiveness of our social programs, to the non-scientific concept, "should." John Cline, project director for Project Alpha (one of the performance contracts in public education) expressed his own exasperation with criticism of his use of rewards in the classroom to reinforce learning: "We hear from people that the kid should *want* to succeed. Well, goddamn yeah, he *should*. But he *doesn't*." [5]

2. "People aren't pigeons."

As far as I know, Skinner has never admitted to an inability to discriminate people from pigeons. What he does say is that "what is common to pigeon and man is a world in which certain contingencies of reinforcement prevail. The schedule of reinforcement which makes a pigeon a pathological gambler is to be found at a racetrack and a roulette table —where it has a comparable effect." [6]

3. "Even if there is some validity to Skinner's position, he makes it impossible to deal with because he insists that his is the only truly scientific way to study behavior and learning."

Well, Skinner argues, what are its alternatives? "Let's evaluate behavioral technology . . . only in comparison with what is done in other ways. What, after all, have we to show for non-scientific good judgment or common sense or the insights gained through experience?" If you believe, with Skinner, that we have here the rudiments of a new science-based technology, then is there any more reason to accept *other* explanations for his experimentally-derived results than the physicist has for agreeing with Aristotle's view that an object falling toward earth increases its velocity because it became more "jubilant" as it neared the ground? Once you have documented the relationship between behavior and its consequences, can you allow for other superstitions and theories which propose undocumented counter positions?

But then, even the critic goes on to say that "the most terrifying thing about Skinner's claim that he is probably right . . . the behavioral technology capable of eliminating man's inner core of subjectivity is for all practical purposes currently available." [7]

[2] *Time*, 20 Sep. 1971.
[3] Rubenstein, Richard L., (book review) *Psychology Today*, Sep. 1971.
[4] *Time, op. cit.*
[5] Cline, John, "Learning COD—Can the Schools Buy Success?" *Saturday Review*, 18 Sep. 1971.
[6] Skinner, B. F., *The Technology of Teaching*, Meredith Corp., 1968.
[7] Rubenstein, *ibid.*

4. "Even though man is autonomous and can't be controlled by others, it's still unethical to do so."

Skinner takes the usually acceptable scientific position that he is merely a systematic observer of what is already going on, the everyday reality which is already much as he describes it. People may be unaware of what they are doing, but conditioning and reconditioning of behavior are going on all the time. "The fundamental mistake" which he attributes to the humanists and inner-man devotees, "is to assume that their methods leave the balance of control to the individual, when in fact they leave it to other conditions."

WHAT'S IN IT FOR US TRAINING TYPES?
Two things:

• We need to get better operational control of Skinner's conclusions about how people learn, because we're not going to become reliably productive in the business world until we do.
• Skinner's critics have done us a service, by verbalizing in a cogent manner the partially-hidden assumptions our top-management people often have about the whole concept of planned behavior change.

Trainers and Unreliability

Seven years have slipped away since Colonel Ofiesh asked, "Can the science of learning be applied to the art of pedagogy? . . . Can the studies of learning be applied to training and education? . . . the effort to apply what we know (?) about learning to the art of teaching has been a colossal failure." [8] And I would argue that we're not much further ahead in 1972.

Let's stop looking at this as a rhetorical question—it isn't. The value of a science is that it permits one to predict outcomes.

In the corporation, the success of the marketing or production vice president is based on his ability to predict (budget) and deliver some quantified economic value. The issue of whether he does so on the basis of "science" doesn't come up because he usually predicts tolerably well and seldom is asked to produce a scientific basis for his prediction. If we want to play with the big boys, the name of the game is *predict* (i.e., take accountability for) results and deliver. By and large, we can't do that very well now, and the only light spot on the horizon I see is the opportunity to harness learning theory. If we don't soon command some learning theory and its applications to reliable predictions, we've got about the same chance of getting management to entrust the training department with vital responsibility as has the employees' picnic committee.

Aside from the emotional fluff, what is there in Skinner's work that the trainer can use to increase his reliability and effectiveness? Back to catechism lesson one:

"Behavior Is Determined by Its Consequences"

The progression of logic continues as follows:

1. Behavior change (learning) can be achieved only by changing the consequences and their contingent relationship with the behavior in question.
2. The task of teaching thus becomes arranging contingencies of reinforcement.
3. The role of training in an organization can then be defined:

Training is the function in an organization which identifies, develops and maintains those behaviors required for the organization to reach its goals. Where changes in

---

[8] Ofiesh, Col. Gabriel D., *Programmed Instruction, a Guide to Management,* American Management Assn., New York, 1965.

behavior are required, they are achieved by arranging the contingencies of reinforcement under which people learn. This may be accomplished through traditional training programs, or through changes in the operating system if that happens to be where the controlling contingencies are located. This function may be dispersed throughout the organization (to line supervisors, to other staffs, etc.) depending on their natural access to the contingencies involved.[9]

4. Learning manifests itself only when an organism modifies its behavior in response to a given stimulus.

5. Learning proceeds with three kinds of responses:

  a. Discrimination (between classes).

  b. Concept formation (i.e., generalization among classes based on similarity of some characteristic).

  c. Chaining (a series of responses in which the reinforcer of one response, becomes the stimulus for the next response).

6. Behavior which has reinforcing consequences (reward) is more likely to occur again.

7. Behavior which has aversive consequences (punishment) is less likely to occur again; but the relative power of punishment in changing behavior is miniscule compared with the power of positive reinforcement.

8. Behavior which goes unreinforced is eventually extinguished.

9. Confirmation to the learner that he has modified his behavior toward a desired outcome is reinforcing to him.

10. The major difference between learners is the rate at which learning occurs, not the way in which it occurs.

11. One of the critical contingencies is the time lapse between behavior and its reinforcement. When the consequences of behavior occur immediately, the chances of that behavior occurring again

are greater than if there is a delay of as little as one day. "No one is ever actually reinforced by remote consequences, but rather by mediating reinforcers which have acquired their power through some connection with them." Since most of the reinforcers in the business world are not very immediate (compensation, promotion, formal acclaim), a central task of training is to *mediate the remote reinforcers* (make the ultimate consequences of behavior more immediate).

For example, the ultimate reinforcer of newly-trained selling behavior is sales closed and other follow-on rewards. Usually these occur some days after the behavior is introduced in the sales training session, and are relatively weak reinforcers of behavior occurring in training. A Skinnerian solution would be to simulate reality by paying the salesman off in cash or other tangible values right in the training setting as he exhibits each new approximation to the desired behavior.

In fact, we could generalize from this to say that Skinner's approach to the problem of transfer would put the highest emphasis on simulating the job situation—its stimuli, its reinforcers, the contingency relationship between response and consequence, and any other important inputs to the individual in that job.

Communications skills are often "taught" by taking the trainee through an example or a role play. The trainee may indeed engage in the behavior which someone defines as "effective communication," but "if the behavior is entirely under the control of the instructor or role partner, it is probably not being brought under the control of stimuli which will be encountered in similar problems on the job."

12. While the *transfer* of behavior to the job depends on bringing it under the

[9] Training Research Forum, March 1971.

control of stimuli in training that are similar to those on the job, the need to provide for the *maintenance* of that behavior over long periods of time imposes another requirement. Even if the learner's supervisor is supportive of the new behavior, he is not a very reliable reinforcer for two reasons:

First, he has neither the skills nor the time to discriminate and reinforce the desired behavior on an effective schedule.

Second, his predictability as a reinforcer is pretty shaky because his own behavior will change in response to the effect his reinforcement has on the learner. The supervisor and learner may start an escalation of mutual reinforcement that is impossible to predict and allow for.[10]

Because of this, Skinner stresses the importance of "making a person dependent on *things* rather than on other people." In other words, build into the environment mechanisms which are triggered when reinforcible behavior occurs. For a salesman, for example, the ideal built-in reinforcer would be a firm order on those calls in which he uses the appropriate behavior. That ideal can in fact be realized if the salesman has been prepared in training to maintain the behavior even if it is reinforced in only a small percent of the occasions in which he uses it.

Where the sales trainer lacks the confidence to rely on that ideal situation, others must be built in. If, for example, the salesman files a written contact report on each call, he might indicate the calls on which he felt he had done a better than usual job of using the particular skill. The sales manager's secretary could be trained to recognize reinforcible reports (a far simpler task than recognizing the degree of the behavior itself). She would flag it for the sales manager who would send it back to the salesman with a short comment recognizing the specific behavior and encouraging him to continue and develop its use.

13. In addition to the accuracy and immediacy of the reinforcement, the other major contingency is the "*schedule of reinforcement.*" This concept recognizes that it is impractical (and often undesirable) to reinforce *every* appropriate response, and offers several alternative schedules of the relationship between behavior and reinforcement. Two special situations are worth knowing about:

The Variable-Ratio Schedule. This is the gambler's schedule and the most powerful of all behavior shapers. Reinforcement of the desired behavior occurs randomly. Since the learner does not know which response will be reinforced, he will make the response (put the quarter in the slot machine or keep each production unit within specs) many, many times regardless of the infrequency of reinforcement (a jackpot or a satisfactory quality control check). He is "hooked" as they say, and a bare minimum of reinforcement will sustain that behavior for long periods of time.

Stretching the Ratio. This technique ought to be a central objective of any training design. It also deals with the problem of sustaining behavior on the job with the relatively small number of reinforcements available there, as opposed to the 1–1 ratio which is possible in the training situation. Stretching the ratio means that the 1–1 training ratio is gradually stretched to 5–1 or 100–1, or whatever approximation of the job condition can be achieved—*before the learner leaves the training experience.*

14. And this gem: "To *acquire* behavior, the learner must *engage* in behavior." Read that one again.

---

[10] See Carl Semmelroth, "The Regulation of Behavior by the Behavior of Others," *NSPI Journal*, Vol. IX, No. 8.

Applications to Training Design

These learning principles can be used to design and evaluate training by examining the following variables:

1. The stimuli presented on the job.
2. The responses to those stimuli.
3. The consequences of those responses.
4. The contingencies of reinforcement/consequences (their relationship to the response).
5. Items 1–4 in the *training* experience.
6. Items 1–4 in the redesigned job situation.

The questions the behaviorist asks about these variables include:

1. Are the descriptions of each element clear enough to discriminate whether or not it has occurred?
2. Do the elements in the learning situation approximate as closely as possible those of the redesigned job situation?
3. To the extent that the training stimulus and response cannot simulate the work stimulus and response, does the training develop behavior which will enable the worker to adapt to these discrepancies on the job?
4. Have the punishing or interfering consequences of the behavior on the job been minimized?

A WAY TO BEGIN

Probably the most successful application of reinforcement theory with dollar payoff has been the work of Ed Feeney, Vice President, Systems Performance, at Emery Air Freight. Feeney's process and spectacular results have been documented elsewhere for ASTD members. For our purpose, a short probing sequence which is the key to his success is a good starting point. Given evidence that some specific performance indicator needs to be improved, Feeney asks

1. What is the standard of performance?
2. Does the employee know the standard?

3. How well does the employee *think* he is doing?
4. How well does his supervisor think he is doing?
5. What aversive consequences of the desired behavior may be suppressing it?
6. What is reinforcing the undesired behavior?
7. What natural or contrived reinforcers are at hand in the immediate work environment to begin reinforcing the desired behavior?
8. What aversive consequences of the undesired behavior are at hand?
9. What learner responses are already available in embarking on a program of progressive approximation to the desired behavior?
10. What schedule of reinforcement is most efficient for developing and maintaining the desired behavior?
11. What reinforcers are available to reward the worker's supervisor for reinforcing the worker's new behavior?

An important benefit of this approach is that it sidesteps the philosophical issue about autonomous man. It comes across as a straight-forward, workmanlike business problem analysis. If the jargon is left out, managers don't feel uncomfortable in proceeding this way, and Emery Air Freight has over $2,000,000 in increased profit, tied directly to this approach, to prove it.

Autonomous Man and Your Chief Executive Officer

Not all company situations, however, will let you get that far without raising the issue of whether man is or ought to be controlled by things outside himself. If an organization has been infected by the "motivation" virus it will be more difficult to overcome the religious fervor about "building a fire under a man" to get him to "realize his potential," and like that.

I like Tom Gilbert's analysis:
"These programs have been sold through articulate and appealing ration-

ales. Mostly, their appeal has been the historical appeal of the 'psychology of personality'—theories about the 'inner man.' They promise to show the executive how to better understand the basic and innermost motives and attitudes of himself and others—and they also seem to promise that such intimate knowledge will lead the executive to being a more effective manager. The appeal of motivational hierarchies, sensitivity training, attitudes that can be plotted on a grid, and the like, has been similar to the appeals of psychoanalysis and religion—these programs really began with Freud and modern theologists who have promised power and peace through inner knowledge. But if the appeal has been as great, the success is equally hard to evaluate . . . We don't get very far by choosing attitudes and inner motives as variables, not because those things don't exist, but because we can't directly manipulate them—and perhaps we have no business trying to. Thus, we look to what we can directly affect: a man's environment . . . his patterns of reinforcement, the feedback of information, those events that interfere with his performance, and the quality of the stimuli to which he is expected to respond . . . This may have the side effects of changing a man's attitudes, his motivation—but these results are in fact side effects, not directly manipulable materials." [11]

At the Training Research Forum Seminar, we asked Skinner to illustrate the difference between his position and those of the various human relations and motivation alchemists. Their problem, he responded is that "they try to deal with things *in the person.* Our 'knowledge' of people keeps us from looking scientifically at the shaping factors which occurred in their past." Graphically, he sees behavior as the starting point for both himself and motivationalists.

But, they make the mistake of trying to infer from the behavior "what is going on inside" the person that "motivates" him to behave so. "These attempts to explain behavior by recourse to inner-man attributes are no explanation *until someone explains the explanation.*" Skinner has very little patience with the cognitive (or as he calls them, the "mentalism") group. To him, "the important objection to 'mentalism' is that the world of the mind steals the show. Behavior is not recognizable as a subject in its own right." What's more, he says, "those who object most violently to the manipulation of behavior make the most vigorous efforts to manipulate minds."

"The Way I Did It"

The immediate problem which mentalism presents to the training man is that it seems to be widely shared by businessmen generally and by successful (top-level) managers especially. The successful executive likes to attribute his success to his own volition, hard work, perseverence, spirit, etc., and often assumes that people, being autonomous, are responsible for their own development—or lack of it. You really can't change behavior in any fundamental way, except that maybe you can "motivate" people to see the light (definition: "the way I did it") by appealing to that inner-man potential we all are supposed to have. The consequence of this view for management's confidence in training is clear to us all.

Now the issue has spectacular visibility again because Skinner's critics have convincingly articulated the autonomous man concept and presumably reinforced that belief of our top management people. We need to recognize the intensity of that view and find a strategy for dealing with it, or *we are not going to be given the chance to use behavioral technology* ex-

---

[11] Gilbert, Thomas S., unpublished paper, 1971.

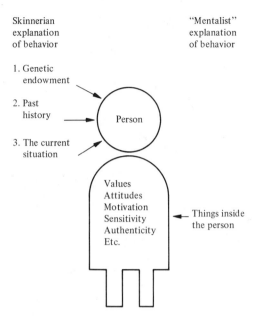

Skinnerian
explanation
of behavior

"Mentalist"
explanation
of behavior

1. Genetic
endowment

2. Past
history

Person

3. The current
situation

Values
Attitudes
Motivation
Sensitivity
Authenticity
Etc.

Things inside
the person

FIGURE 1   Skinner proposes that observable behavior can be usefully explained only by going directly to the three causes "outside" the man. The mentalists propose that the key is in characteristics which they attribute to the "inner man."

tensively as the basis for improving our reliability and effectiveness.

One response to the humanists/mentalists, on their own terms, has been made by Geary Rummler of Praxis Corporation. He points out that the so-called "humanists" have, in fact, less concern for the human than the behaviorist. Referring to Skinner's diagram of the causes of behavior, Rummler says that the behaviorist "proceeds on the assumption that the employee basically wants to do a good job, and given half a chance and reasonable support will probably do so." [12] (What's that? You didn't know that Skinner was the original theory Y man?) The trainer's task is to construct contingencies of reinforcement which can help him learn the job behavior and others which help him maintain it.

The humanist, on the other hand, sees a performance gap and instantly jumps right on the *man*. "Let's find out what's *wrong with him*. Let's fix him up inside so that he has good values and attitudes." This seems to be not only a less optimistic view of man than the behaviorist approach, but it is what leads us to our irrelevant and ineffective attempts to "motivate" this troublesome person. The focus on the *consequences* of the person's behavior is more effective since the whole point of behavioral research is that *that* is what causes behavior. As Skinner says, "No one directly changes a mind . . . what we change in each case is a *probability of action*."

Or, as an anonymous psychologist put it, "How do I know what I think until I feel what I do?" [13]

We began with three questions, "How

---

[12] Rummler, Geary, Personal Strategy Clinic No. 1 (Training Research Forum), Jan. 1971.
[13] Quoted anonymously by Jerome Bruner, *The Process of Education*, Random House, New York, 1963.

much of this is relevant to training? How much of it works? Under what conditions?"

How Relevant? Skinner's learning theory is relevant to training in direct proportion to your acceptance of our behaviorist definition of training. If you are comfortable with that approach, then this theory of reinforcement is not only relevant, it is probably the only way to carry it off.

How Much of It Works? If you can accept the proposition that "Behavior is determined by its consequences," then any change in the consequences (and contingencies of reinforcement) of behavior "works" in the sense that it will change behavior. How *well* it works depends on your skill in getting answers to the Skinner and the Feeney analysis questions.

Under What Conditions? Aye, there's the rub.

The necessary conditions are not scientific or esoteric. They are about the same ones that make or break our present programs:

1. You have to know what you are doing. With reinforcement theory there's no "winging it." Only Dr. Fred can shoot from the hip without shooting himself in the foot. So, learn baby, learn!

2. You need access to the consequences of the present and the desired behavior —wherever they fall in the organizational structure.

3. You will want to assure that your management people have some knowledge of what you are doing and your basis for it. Don't try to implement these concepts behind a smoke screen of pretending you're not. That means you will need to deal with the "inner-man motivation" beliefs which are so comfortable to top management.

4. Since the three preceding requirements are tough ones, the fourth is what the humanist will call "courage" and "tenacity," and what B. F. Skinner would call "arranging enough positive reinforcement for yourself to neutralize the aversive consequences of a lot of hard work and high risk."

QUESTIONS

1. What are the essential elements of psychologist B. F. Skinner's theory of motivation of behavior?
2. Do you agree with the author that a supervisor cannot be as effective a reinforcer as some "thing" or mechanistic reinforcer?
3. Do you agree with the assertion that people generally like to gamble for a payoff or reward that is uncertain or probabilistic?
4. Regarding "the inner or autonomous" versus the "externally conditioned" man argument, does the practical trainer or the manager have to really accept one point of view and reject the other in order to help improve the performance of others?
5. Give examples of how a trainer can apply Skinner's concepts in the classroom. How can these be applied in an on-the-job learning situation?

17.

A Comparison of Management Development and Organization Development

W. WARNER BURKE

The growth of organization development (OD) has been accompanied by a predictable confusion about its conceptualization and practice. Many people have conducted or have been involved in "pieces" of OD for several years. Others claim to have been "conducting OD" when, in fact, what they have been conducting is laboratory training for members of their organization. Still others, after hearing some explanation of organization development, will declare that they have heard nothing new, and that such events are everyday occurrences in their organization.

It is quite possible that none of these claims is unjustified, since OD does consist of a variety of activities including laboratory training. Persons who examine the way they conduct their everyday operation, especially in the area of human relations, may be behaving according to some principles and practices of organization development.

But OD is more than the conduct of training laboratories. It can be defined as a *planned process* of cultural change. This process consists of two phases: (a) diagnosis and (b) intervention. OD begins with a diagnosis of the current organizational culture, i.e., an identification of the norms, procedures, and general climate of the organization. This identification process becomes more diagnostic as a distinction is then made between those standards of behavior, procedures, and so on which seem to facilitate the organization's reaching its

Reproduced by special permission from *The Journal of Applied Behavioral Science*, Vol. 7, No. 5, September–October 1971, pp. 569–579, published by the NTL Institute for Applied Behavioral Science.

W. Warner Burke is Director, Executive Programs and Executive Director, OD Network, NTL Institute for Applied Behavioral Science.

183

objectives (while meeting the needs of its members) from those which do not facilitate the attainment of its goals.[1] Following this diagnostic phase, interventions are planned to change those norms which are seen as barriers to effective individual and organizational functioning.

In summary, although persons may be involved in events that are properly labeled as OD technology, such activities are not considered *organization development* if they are not part of a planned effort at changing the organization's culture.

Dimensions of Comparison

One way to clarify a relatively new concept, principle, or practice is to compare it with something more familiar. In this article, management development will serve as a counterpoint. This will be doubly useful, since OD is confused more with management development than with any other concept or practice.

Management development is practiced in various ways: managers are systematically shifted from one kind of job to another to learn different facets of organizational life; managers take psychological tests and then have sessions with a counselor who helps them interpret their test scores; managers receive clinical counseling by psychologists working in the role of management consultants. A more common practice, however, is to provide managers with education: managers attend company training programs, are sent away for several months to attend an "advanced executive" course at a school of business administration, or they enroll in brief training programs such as three-day workshops on management systems or one-week sensitivity training

programs. This educational approach to management development will be used as the primary counterpoint in the comparison with OD.

Several dimensions are critical to both of these developmental strategies for change in organizations. They are: *reasons for use, typical goals, interventions for producing change, time frame, staff requirements,* and *values.* In order to clarify OD and to pinpoint some of the practical concerns of this strategy for change, it will be contrasted with management development along each of these six dimensions. A summary of these comparisons is provided in Figure 1.

REASONS FOR USE

Leaders in organizations often turn to OD (provided they know about it) when there are difficult problems to be solved. As Beckhard (1969) says, somebody or something is "hurting" and there is a *felt need* to make some organizational changes in such areas as (a) organizational structures and roles, (b) intergroup conflict or collaboration, (c) methods of problem solving, and (d) the way the organization handles acquisitions and mergers, to name only a few.

A management development program may be established to deal with these same needs, but the orientation typically focuses more on individuals than on the organization. The needs are usually diagnosed as managers' lack of skill and expressed in this way: "Our managers need to be brought up to date on the latest thinking and techniques."

The primary reason for using OD is a need to improve some or all of the *systems* that constitute the total organization. The main reason for using some form of management development is a need to improve some aspect of the *manager.*

---

[1] This general objective of OD, a stronger integration of the goals of the organization with those of individual members, has been discussed by Argyris (1964) and outlined in NTL Institute's *News and Reports* issue on "What Is OD?"—1968, 2 (3).

FIGURE 1. **A Comparison of Organization Development and Management Development**

CATEGORY	ORGANIZATION DEVELOPMENT	MANAGEMENT DEVELOPMENT
Reasons for Use	Need to improve overall organizational effectiveness Typical examples of tough problems to be solved: • Interunit conflict • Confusion stemming from recent management change • Loss of effectiveness due to inefficient organizational structure • Lack of teamwork	Need to improve overall effectiveness of manager Managers do not know company policy or philosophy Managers are void in certain skills Managers seem to be unable to act decisively
Typical Goals	To increase the effectiveness of the organization by— • Creating a sense of "ownership" of organization objectives throughout the work force • Planning and implementing changes more systematically • Facilitating more systematic problem solving on the job To reduce wasted energy and effort by creating conditions where conflict among people is managed openly rather than handled indirectly or unilaterally To improve the quality of decisions by establishing conditions where decisions are made on the basis of competence rather than organizational role or status To integrate the organization's objectives with the individual's goals by developing a reward system which supports achievement of the organization's mission as well as individual efforts toward personal development and achievement	To teach company values and philosophy To provide practice in management skills which lead to improved organizational effectiveness To increase ability to plan, coordinate, measure, and control efforts of company units To gain a better understanding of how the company functions to accomplish its goals
Interventions for Producing Change	Education and problem solving on the job; learning while problem solving and solving problems while learning Following a diagnosis, utilization of one or more of the following techniques:	Sending of manager to some educational program Job rotation of managers Specialized training "packages"

FIGURE 1. (Continued)

CATEGORY	ORGANIZATION DEVELOPMENT	MANAGEMENT DEVELOPMENT

	• Team building
	• Training programs
	• Intergroup confrontations
	• Data feedback
	• Technostructural interventions
	  Change in organizational
	  structure
	  Job enrichment
	  Change in physical environment
	  (social architecture)
		Courses and/or conferences
		Counseling
		Reading of books and articles

Time Frame	Prolonged	Short, intense
Staff Requirements	Diagnostician Catalyst/Facilitator Consultant/Helper Knowledge and skill in the dynamics of planned change Experience in the laboratory method of learning	Teacher/Trainer Program Manager Designer of training programs Knowledge in the processes of human learning
Values	Humane and nonexploitative treatment of people in organizations Theory Y assumptions Collaboration Sharing of power Rationality of behavior Openness/candor/honesty Importance of surfacing and utilizing conflict Right of persons and organizations to seek a full realization of their potential Explicitness of values as a value in itself	Competition Belief that "education is progress" Belief that managers need challenging periodically Manager's right to have time for reflection and renewal Belief that individual should "fit" organization's needs Right of person to seek full realization of his potential

TYPICAL GOALS

To avoid repetition, the reader can refer to Figure 1 for a listing of goals for both OD and management development. Other sources for statements of OD objectives are NTL Institute's *News and Reports*, 1968, issue which covered "What Is OD?" and the recent book by Beckhard (1969). Management development objectives have also been discussed elsewhere (Burr, 1967; French, 1970).

Management development is a program of developing managers who will be able to contribute more to their organization; OD is a continual process of developing social conditions so that the manager can make these contributions. Although the strategies have different objectives, they are complementary, not incompatible.

INTERVENTIONS FOR PRODUCING CHANGE

In OD there are at least five major categories of interventions: team building, intergroup problem solving, data feedback, technostructure, and training. Team building is probably the cornerstone of OD and is utilized most often. Team building does not necessarily involve conducting a T Group with an organizational "family" unit, although this is one approach (Blake, Mouton, & Blansfield, 1962). Other forms concentrate on improving the "task work" of the team, e.g., goal-setting, decision-making, or problem-solving techniques (cf. Beckhard, 1969; Burke & Hornstein, in press; Schein, 1969).

Intergroup problem-solving interventions are well known (Blake, Shepard, & Mouton, 1964; Harrison, 1967) and may be adapted to OD quite easily (Beckhard, 1969). These interventions may be quite useful when there is unproductive conflict between organizational units, such as sales and production in industry or administration and faculty in a university.

Data feedback as an intervention for change is discussed at some length in Hornstein, Bunker, Burke, Hornstein, and Lewicki (1971). The method which has had most use is the survey feedback procedure developed by Mann (1957). This procedure has as its primary component the analysis and discussion of self-generated data by members of overlapping organizational units.

Technostructural interventions refer to changes in the structure of an organization or of a person's job. An example of the latter is Herzberg's (1968) job enrichment technique; Trist's (1960) sociotechnical change (e.g., modifying work flow patterns) is an example of the former. Technostructural interventions may also include the modification of environment: e.g., changing the physical arrangement of an office to affect human interaction patterns.[2]

Naturally, training can often be a useful OD intervention. The intervention may take the form of (a) skill training for all levels of management (e.g., conducting appraisal interviews); (b) more education in substantive areas (e.g., systems analysis); or (c) further education in organizational management in general (e.g., attending a 16-week "executive course" at a major university). In the OD context, a training program is most useful when it is designed to meet a *diagnosed need* in the organization. For more specific examples of this relationship see Buchanan's (1962) discussion of the use of training laboratories in OD.

Training is probably the major subcategory of management development in use today. Other facets of management development include job rotation, counseling, and career development—but the major focus is on educating the manager. The major strategy for change in management development is to improve the manager's knowledge and skill and, to some extent, to modify his attitudes. The major strategy for change in OD is to change the organization's *culture* from one which deals with problems "as we have always done" to a culture which (a) takes full advantage of the human resources available, and (b) allows for a process to develop which will ensure that the organization can plan and implement needed change at all levels rather than having to "adjust" to change already in progress.

TIME FRAME

Since OD is a *process*, not a program, there is an implied timelessness. This im-

---

[2] See Steele's (1971) discussion of this approach, which is sometimes referred to as social architecture.

plication is no accident. OD is a process of continual organizational renewal. The process is one of constantly examining the way the organizational systems are functioning and looking for ways of improving these functions. Management development, on the other hand, usually takes the form of some program which has a beginning and an end.

Staff Requirements

The primary areas in which an OD specialist should have competence—or the areas which should be represented in an internal OD department or group—are these:

• Ability to diagnose problems of an organizational nature accurately.
• Ability to function as a facilitator or catalyst for groups in the organization.
• Understanding of and skill in the consultative process; the ability to give help which is useful.
• Understanding of the dynamics and realities of planned change.
• Skill and knowledge in experience-based learning methodology.

The specialist in management development should also have skill and knowledge in the technology of experience-based learning, in particular, and some understanding of human learning, in general. Other areas of competence which should be represented are (a) lecturing and various methods of training which are not necessarily experience based, (b) program management, (c) managerial counseling, and (d) career development.

Values

The major general value which OD represents is the humane and nonexploitative treatment of people in organizations. All other values of OD seem to relate, in one way or another, to this primary value of human dignity.

A listing of some of the more specific values of OD is found in Figure 1. Most of these are self-explanatory, but an elaboration of several is probably in order.

McGregor's motivational statements about man, which he labeled "Theory Y," are not only based on some psychological principles of human behavior but also imply certain values as well (e.g., man is not inherently lazy; he seeks rather than shuns responsibility).

While OD does not necessarily advocate the restructuring of all organizations according to the democratic process, a goal of power sharing (e.g. decentralizing decision making to the lowest point of relevant information in the organization) does have a value connotation. There is "something bad," OD practitioners believe, in a condition where *all* power is vested in one individual.

A value of surfacing conflict and dealing with it has always been a part of OD. This particular value is beginning to be modified from one of "it's good to resolve conflict" to one of "it's good to resolve conflict some of the time, but not always." Some OD practitioners have found that old conflicts they had once helped "to resolve" sometimes reappear, and that they either need to be reworked or that they can be recognized as unsolvable and therefore "lived with."

An interesting development in OD is the emphasis on making values themselves more explicit. Today many OD practitioners are advocating that organizations and their members be more explicit about the values they represent. This advocacy usually becomes operationalized when the practitioner is working with an organization in the area of goal setting or mission.

In management development there is still a value premium on competition. This emphasis may not be at the expense of collaboration, but the latter certainly takes a back seat. Managers are trained to beat their market competitors as part of the free enterprise system in our country. But this norm (value) of competition also extends internally to the managers' organizational team where it can frequently negate overall organizational effectiveness. To keep this competitive edge, management development practitioners believe that managers should be challenged periodically and that they should have a chance for reflection.

The last two values of management development mentioned in Figure 1 are somewhat contradictory, but they are found in some management development programs. Specifically, lip service is given to *"self*-actualization," but what the organization's authority figures really want is a better fit of the individual to the *organization's* goals and objectives. In organizations which are quite explicit about this latter value and norm, if the manager does not want to "fit," he can look for a job elsewhere. Other organizations give more than lip service to a manager's developing his potential by reinforcing efforts made in that direction.

While there are some value conflicts between OD and management development, or at least in the way management development is practiced in certain organizations, there is also overlap and compatibility (e.g., the right of a person [and

an organization] to seek full realization of his [its] potential).

Concluding Comment

In an effort to clarify the nature of OD, a method of comparing it with a more common change strategy, management development, has been chosen. While this comparison technique may be useful for clarification, the method should not dictate the message. The two strategies for change are not incompatible. On the contrary, management development and OD are quite complementary. Management development should be one of several intervention techniques available to an OD effort.

Management development programs should *respond* to diagnosed needs in the organization. This is not to say that other OD interventions cannot be developed as a result of some management development program. Either strategy can develop from the other. The point is that an appropriate OD intervention, whether it be a management development program or a change in the organizational structure, is one which originates from study and diagnosis of current, relevant data.

REFERENCES

ARGYRIS, C. *Integrating the individual and the organization.* New York: Wiley, 1964.
BECKHARD, R. *Organization development: Strategies and models.* Reading, Mass.: Addison-Wesley, 1969.
BLAKE, R. R., MOUTON, JANE S., & BLANSFIELD, M. G. The logic of team training. In I. R. Weschler and E. H. Schein (Eds.), *Issues in training.* Selected Readings Series, No. 5. Washington, D.C.: National Training Laboratories, associated with the National Education Association, 1962. Pp. 77–85.
BLAKE, R. R., SHEPARD, H. A., & MOUTON, JANE S. *Managing intergroup conflict in industry.* Houston: Gulf, 1964.
Buchanan, P. C. Training laboratories in organization development. In I. R. Weschler and E. H. Schein (Eds.), *Issues in training.* Selected Readings Series, No. 5. Washington, D.C.: National Training Laboratories, associated with the National Education Association, 1962. Pp. 86–92.
BURKE, W. W., & HORNSTEIN, H. A. (Eds.) The social technology of organization development. Washington, D.C.; NTL Learning Resources Corporation, in press.
BURR, R. B. Management development. In R. L. Craig and L. R. Bittel (Eds.), *Training and development handbook.* New York: McGraw-Hill, 1967. Pp. 363–395.

FRENCH, W. L. *The personnel management process* (Rev. Ed.). New York: Houghton Mifflin, 1970.

HARRISON, R. Training designs for intergroup collaboration. *NTL Training News,* 1967, *11* (1), 1–3.

HERZBERG, F. One more time: How do you motivate employees? *Harvard Bus. Rev.,* 1968, *46,* 53–62.

HORNSTEIN, H. A., BUNKER, BARBARA B., BURKE, W. W., HORNSTEIN, MARION G., & LEWICKI, R. J. *Social intervention: A behavioral science approach.* New York: Free Press, 1971.

MANN, F. C. Studying and creating change: A means to understanding social organization. In C. M. Arensburg and W. Ellison Chalmers (Eds.), *Research in industrial human relations.* New York: Harper, 1957.

NTL INSTITUTE FOR APPLIED BEHAVIORAL SCIENCE. What Is OD? *News and Reports,* 1968, 2 (3).

SCHEIN, E. H. *Process consultation: Its role in organization development.* Reading, Mass.: Addison-Wesley, 1969.

STEELE, F. I. Organization development and sticks and stones. In H. A. Hornstein, Barbara B. Bunker, W. W. Burke, Marion G. Hornstein, and R. J. Lewicki. *Social intervention: A behavioral science approach.* New York: Free Press, 1971.

TRIST, E. L. *Socio-technical systems.* London: Tavistock Institute of Human Relations, 1960.

QUESTIONS

1. What are the principal methodologies of organization development?
2. How do management development and organization development differ? In what respects are they similar?
3. Mr. Burke states that organization development is a process, not a program. Explain.
4. Compare the prevailing value in organizations of interpersonal competition with the organization development value of collaboration. What are the implications of each?
5. What is meant by the culture of an organization? Do you think really long lasting and true cultural change can be achieved? How is the culture of an organization affected by the culture of the society at large?

18.

Understanding Laboratory Education: An Overview

CLAYTON P. ALDERFER

Laboratory education—learning about human behavior through experiences in group activities—is simultaneously an evolving educational technology, a loosely defined philosophy, and a social movement. Most of its practitioners believe that human interactions can be better understood and more effectively carried out, and, as a consequence, more gratifying to the participants. Thus, laboratory education offers the promise of radically changing the way we understand and act in human relationships. Much of this promise has been realized.

But not all of the aspirations have been fully achieved. The failures, the incompleteness, and the sense of even greater possibilities have led many persons to be critical of laboratory education. Some of these criticisms are based on carefully collected data which have been subjected to thorough analysis. Other evaluations have been severely biased and often sensationalistic, whether the conclusions were positive or negative. This article reviews the current status of laboratory educa-

tion, with an emphasis on identifying major areas of conflict and explaining why the disagreements take the form that they do.

Common Processes of Learning

The term "laboratory education" refers to a set of assumptions and practices. The various forms of laboratory education include a number of common elements such as acceptance of experience-based learning technology, recognition of the role of emotions in human relationships, and utilization of the small group (10 to 12 persons) as a central component in training designs.

The learning laboratory usually takes place on a "cultural island." Participants are taken away from their normal day-to-day activities to a setting where the learning experiences occur. Frequently this new setting is naturally beautiful, but at the very least it is different and thereby provides the participant with both safety from former distractions and a setting

Reprinted from *Monthly Labor Review*, Vol. 93, No. 12 (December 1970), pp. 18–27.

Clayton P. Alderfer is Associate Professor of Organizational Behavior, Department of Administrative Sciences, Yale University.

that does not necessarily reinforce his usual ways of behaving. A second component of the laboratory involves the use of unstructured or semistructured learning tools. The staff usually attempts to design a set of experiences that serve to heighten certain aspects of human behavior and emotions. Participants learn by becoming actively involved in these activities and by developing skills which allow them to observe both themselves and others during these experiences. A person is asked to engage himself in the unfolding events and later to step back and try to see the patterns in his own and others' behavior. Much of the sense of excitement and high level of emotionality comes from the participant's becoming involved. Experiential learning is based on the assumption that experience precedes intellectual understanding. A continuing challenge in designing laboratories is to achieve that optimal degree of involvement which allows a person to flavor the richness of human interaction but is not so compelling that he loses all sense of what is happening.

A key element in almost all laboratory designs is the small group, typically quite unstructured and serving as a primary group for most participants during the varied laboratory program. One or two staff members meet regularly with the small group to aid participants' learning.

Variations in Laboratory Methods. Differences among various laboratory methods tend to emerge around the nature of the small group activities. Three frequently used names for the small groups are encounter groups, T groups, and self study groups. The professional organizations most closely identified with these group labels are, respectively, Esalen Institute, National Training Laboratories Institute for Applied Behavioral Science, and Tavistock Institute of Human Relations. The varied names for the group provide clues about the different nature of the learning experiences offered and of the

whole laboratories which utilize the particular type of group. Differences (which tend to be of degree only) include relative focus on intrapsychic, interpersonal, intragroup, or intergroup phenomena; emphasize the personal in comparison to the professional qualities of the staff; and explicitly include the place of thinking in laboratory activities.

Reliable data on the extent of laboratory training are difficult to come by. Table 1 gives estimates, provided by leaders in the three areas, on the number of participants. In actual practice there are many more laboratories than those covered by these estimates. Warner Burke, Director, Center for Organization Studies, NTL, estimates that the 1970 NTL figure represented about 5 percent of the laboratories conducted in the United States. The overwhelming majority are being conducted independently of the NTL by business firms, educational institutions, church groups, and so on. But though the table understates the actual number of participants it does illustrate the rapid growth in laboratory education.

Encounter Laboratories. The encounter group, the Esalen Institute, and personal growth laboratories in general tend to focus primarily on learning about the individual. Encounter groups tend to produce experiences where a person examines himself in new and different ways, aided by others. A participant in this kind of experience is encouraged to look inward to himself, to become more in touch with his fantasy life, and to become more aware of his physical activities. Part of the emphasis on body movement includes attention to nonverbal communications. A person may learn to attend more fully to his own nonverbal communications, to read others' signs more adequately, and to practice being more effective in his body language. Psychodramatic techniques are often used in laboratories of this kind. Frequently the focus in these exercises is on interpersonal relationships that have been troublesome for people in the past. Other group members are asked to volunteer to be "stand-ins" for or representatives of a key person in a participant's life history. Staff members help set the stage for these encounters, sometimes actively taking part themselves, and almost always leading the discussion and working through of the events after they happen.

TABLE 1. Participants in Experiential Laboratories Sponsored by Three Organizations in the United States

Sponsoring Group	Approximate Number of Participants*		
	1962	1965	1970
Esalen		600	11,000
National Training Laboratories	900		2,400
Tavistock		100	250

*These estimates were provided by Richard Price and Stuart Miller of Esalen; Warner Burke and Patricia Walton of National Training Laboratories; and Edward Klein of Tavistock.

Personal growth laboratories contain more components than the encounter group, however. Various exercises in body movement and artistic expression are frequently employed. It is not uncommon for the staff to include members of the performing arts such as modern dance or theater. Some of the key writings which give greater detail, flavor, and rationale for these methods include Schutz (1967), Murphy (1967), Perls (1969), and Rogers (1969).[1] John Weir is another key figure in the development of encounter laboratories, but to this writer's knowledge he has not written of his ideas or developments.

There can be little doubt that many persons who attend encounter-oriented laboratories have joyful, freeing experiences. The ever increasing popularity of the Esalen Institute and personal growth laboratories testifies to this (Murphy, 1967; Shepard, 1970). Yet these experiences have also been validly criticized. With the focus of the laboratories on freeing people and making them more expressive, little of their learning experience is directed toward examining the consequences of excessive self-expression. Because the laboratories produce potent effects so rapidly, they also tend to spawn disciples very readily (Lakin, 1969). It is not uncommon for participants to start their own groups and "turn on" their friends after as few as one or two group experiences. Within the laboratory itself, participants may be tempted to engage in personality analyses of each other for which they are ill-equipped (Argyris, 1967).

Staff members tend to be central in the learning processes and often are charismatic figures. They frequently seem magical in the techniques they employ and in the effects they can have on some people (Haigh, 1968). As a consequence some participants tend to copy the manifest qualities of staff members' behavior without careful or thoughtful examination of what or how they are learning.

Another factor which is likely to work against a more critical examination of the learning processes by participants is the tendency for an anti-intellectual bias to develop. While the laboratories are a potent counterforce to our culture's excessive reliance on rational intellective activities, they seem to forget that thinking is also part of the human potential. Encounter laboratories give relatively little attention to how thinking and talking can be reincorporated into a person's behavioral repertoire after he has become more emotionally and physically free.

Although all laboratories find the boundary between education and therapy

[1] Authors and their works are listed in the bibliography following the text.

to be a fine one, perhaps the line is thinnest in the encounter laboratories (Jenkins, 1962). Many staff members for encounter laboratories are also practicing psychotherapists. The new techniques which have developed through encounter laboratories have also had an impact on the practice of psychotherapy, and the latter has affected the laboratories (Burton, 1969).

Both the beauty and the limitations of the encounter approach are captured in the frequently quoted words of Frederick S. Perls:

> I do my thing, and you do your thing.
> I am not in this world to live up to your expectations.
> And you are not in this world to live up to mine.
> You are you and I am I,
> And if by chance we find each other, it's beautiful.

The sense of individuality and freedom in these words is unmistakable. But missing is the recognition that commitments can be reached by mutuality and that a superordinate goal may sometimes require the suppression of certain individual needs in order for others to be expressed.

T Group Laboratories. The T group (for human relations training) and the National Training Laboratories Institute at its outset were developed to increase the human relations skills which people brought to their leadership, group, and organizational relationships. Bradford, Benne, and Lippitt, the men whose original conversations led to the founding of NTL, were social psychologists who were interested in both research and action (Bradford, 1967). The initial focus of learning was on interpersonal and intragroup phenomena. National Training Laboratories has grown considerably over the years, however, and today it conducts laboratories focused on individual growth and intergroup relations. Nevertheless, the initial focus on interpersonal and intragroup phenomena

still conditions much of what T groups and NTL are about.

T group laboratories often tend to be focused on the interpersonal impact that members make on each other. In the unstructured T groups, members examine their leadership, membership, and other roles. They see the consequences of different kinds of leadership styles and attempt to learn about the complex interrelationships between group processes and group effectiveness.

A T group leader acts as a person who is also a professional. He does not deny that he is more experienced and knowledgeable than most group members, but he does not act in such a way as to increase the natural distance between himself and group members. He is likely to discuss his own feelings when he sees that as useful to himself and others. He attempts to establish relationships of mutuality between himself and group members. Recognizing that some members of a group will assume that he is like other key figures in their lives, he is willing to examine the impact of his own behavior on others, but he is also likely to ask group members to concentrate on his group behavior when giving feedback. He is likely to assume that people learn not only from what he says but also from how he behaves.

The T group tradition has produced a considerable amount of empirical research (for example, *The Journal of Applied Behavioral Science*) and theorizing (Bradford, Gibb, and Benne, 1964; Argyris, 1962, 1969). The quality of this work has sometimes been questioned by thoughtful critics (Dunnette and Campbell, 1968; House, 1967), with good reason. Frequently laboratory education research has consisted of poorly designed studies from which the investigators have drawn unjustified conclusions. Control groups have often been missing. Measuring instruments have been poorly designed. More recently, investigators have addressed directly the special problems of research on laboratory education and are now utilizing research designs which offer greater promise in terms of the kinds of conclusions one might draw (Rubin, 1967; Harrison, 1970; Alderfer and Lodahl, 1971).

Democratic values have played an important part in much of the thinking that has influenced T group theory and practice (Whyte, 1953). The impact of democratic practices has undoubtedly been a strong factor in accounting for the wide diversity of practice, the high degree of innovation, and the strong sense of collaboration and commitment experienced by many members of the NTL system. Nevertheless, the profusion of democratic values has also served as a means for avoiding some more difficult issues.

In a long overdue action, National Training Laboratories has recently begun to develop the organizational machinery for accrediting group leaders. For a long time NTL had been unofficially granting credentials to practitioners by publishing lists of those persons who were elected to positions of Professional Member, Associate, or Fellow (Schein and Bennis, 1965). In order not to emphasize its exclusiveness, however, NTL consistently maintained the public position that it was not an accrediting agency. Now the focusing of public attention on the quality of group leadership and NTL's eminence in the field has led the organization to change its course.

National Training Laboratories' initial focus was toward interpersonal and intragroup phenomena. For some time there was a tendency for the key learnings from this level of analysis to be transferred uncritically to larger units, such as intergroup relations and larger social systems. A key paper in this line of thought was by Slater and Bennis (1964), who proclaimed "Democracy Is Inevitable." More recently, Bennis (1970) has revised his original thinking, and NTL has become increasingly involved with intergroup concerns, especially those surrounding racism in our society.

Tavistock Conferences. The self-study group has evolved from a tradition which traces its roots to modern psychoanalytic theory of object relations (Klein, 1959). During World War II, British psychoanalyst W. R. Bion discovered that groups were a useful way to treat psychiatric casualties from the war. His group work led to his writing of *Experiences in Groups* (1959), a book that has become a classic in the field and a key theoretical work for leaders of Tavistock study groups. Although Tavistock theories have evolved from the psychoanalytic tradition, the conferences are directed to learning, not therapeutic goals (Rice, 1965).

Authority relationships form a key element in the learning process of self-study groups. Tavistock staff members, who are called consultants, remain distant and remote in their relationships with group members. They think about their behavior in terms of "staying in role," with the intent of contributing to the group's exploration of relations within the group. In carrying out their roles, the consultants are very punctual in entering and leaving group meetings, dress in relatively formal attire, and intervene in group activity only when they believe it will promote learning. Their statements tend to be metaphorical and they consistently point out how members seem to be relating to them, often as surrogates for other key figures such as parents, siblings, lovers, and the like (Astrachan and Klein, 1961; Redlich and Astrachan, 1969).

Tavistock laboratories also focus on intergroup relations through the use of exercises which ask participants to negotiate among groups in order to make a decision or carry out a task. These activities serve to underline the impact of individual, subgroup, and group boundaries. The analysis of boundaries plays a key role in Tavistock theory and methods. One of the key learnings is the types of fantasy and mythmaking that groups indulge in with respect to each other across group boundaries. A. K. Rice's work (1965, 1969) on laboratory design and on individual, group, and intergroup transactions as boundary crossings is the major conceptual work in this area.

Staff members direct their interventions to the group rather than to any individual. The latter's behavior or statements, however, are assumed to express group concerns unless contradicted by others. Thus, whenever a person speaks in the group he is viewed as speaking for the group and his statement is viewed as representing some element of the group opinion.

Little in the staff behavior allows one to determine the degree to which the interventions cause the study group behavior or merely reflect it. Consultants rarely discuss their own feelings with the group, although they do use their feelings as an important source of data for understanding group events (Rice, 1965). It might be expected that group members would focus much of their attention on the consultant when he intervenes in the group activity yet behaves in a relatively inaccessible manner. Important questions can be raised about the generality of the learning about leadership that participants achieve in study groups. It is one thing to learn that persons develop vivid and hostile fantasies about persons who appear to be leaders yet deny the role, who behave in distant ways and speak metaphorically about their perceptions of the group. It may be a mistake, however, to assume that reactions of this sort are representative of typical reaction to authority figures regardless of how they behave.

Tavistock consultants do not suggest that their behavior is a model for group members to follow. Yet a question can be raised as to whether modeling occurs nonetheless. There is research to support the notion that modeling or imitation is a general human learning process (Bandura and Walters, 1963). If modeling does occur in study groups, then it would appear that the Tavistock style of study group would teach participants to be leaders who do not share their feelings, remain personally distant from the group, talk in metaphors, focus attention on themselves by their mode of intervention, and hold quite strictly to the prescribed definition of their roles.

This writer has serious questions about whether these types of learning are very useful for small group effectiveness. However, there are times when learning of this kind is realistic. Leaders of large social systems cannot be seen regularly by more than a few members. They frequently serve as spokesmen for the group. To come to terms with leaders in this kind of role, group members have little choice but to rely on their fantasies and therefore to project and transfer their reactions from prior relationships. Learnings from study group and intergroup activities in a Tavistock laboratory can be very enlightening with regard to multiple group functioning in large scale social systems.

Comparison of Laboratory Approaches

The primary learning and dangers differ among the three approaches to laboratory education. For encounter group laboratories, the primary target is individual expression and artistic creativity. A danger in this approach is that participants may learn to act out their impulses without realistically considering the consequences of their behavior for themselves and for others. T group laboratories primarily aid learning about mutuality, trust, and collaboration. There is a danger that democratic values and behavior may be applied in situations where they are not realistic or appropriate. Moreover, differences among individuals with regard to task or professional competence may be ignored because they tamper with the norm that everyone is equal. Tavistock laboratories promote learning about authority relationships and the functions of group boundaries. It is possible that consultant behavior in the study group may become a model for nonmutuality when this kind of behavior is neither necessary nor effective.

The common theme in the criticisms of each of these approaches to learning by experience is that the particular approach may lead to unwarranted generalization. Learning which evolves from a particular approach does not apply to all situations. At first glance it would appear that this caution is clear to understand and easy to apply. But the learning processes of laboratory education do not lend themselves readily to a norm of moderation. Overattention to concerns about being too self-expressive can prevent a person from taking the risks which would enable him to become more free and spontaneous. Fear of being overwhelmed by a pseudodemocratic horde may prevent a person from exposing enough of himself to really find out what can be gained by sharing more of himself with the group. The need to feel competent or free of tension may inhibit a person from exposing himself to his fantasies about distant leaders or engaging in the turbulent processes of intergroup negotiations. It is difficult to write critically about the different approaches to laboratory education without unintentionally colluding with the very human processes—fear, hostility, fantasy, and so on—that prevent persons from learning about themselves and their complex relations with others.

The kinds of laboratory education described in this article represent efforts to apply behavioral science concepts to increase learning about human relationships. Each of the laboratories exists as an educational setting. However, although all approaches aim to transfer learning to non-laboratory settings, an active role for the staff in promoting transfer typically ends with the conclusion of the laboratory. Additional developments in the direct utilization of behavioral science knowledge for organizational change through the use of experiential methods will be the subject of a future article.

Public and Professional Criticism

During the past several years, a number of articles have been devoted to laboratory education, both in widely circulated newspapers and magazines and in professional journals. Not all of this coverage has been comprehensive or unbiased. Some has been blatantly slanted and inaccurate. The purpose of this section is to alert the reader to some of the forms that public and professional criticism has taken and to caution him against putting too much credence in sensationalistic accounts.

Newspapers and Magazines. The front page of the *Wall Street Journal* on July 14, 1969, carried a story with the headline, "Some Companies See More Harm Than Good in Sensitivity Training— Frank Exchanges Sometimes Hamper Work; Sessions Can Produce Breakdowns —A Tough Boss Turns Meek." The lead paragraph was, "Last year a big New York consumer products company sent Mrs. D, a product manager, to a week-long sensitivity training program. She got so sensitive she quit the company." In this article, a number of key academic authorities were cited to support the author's slant, but the full range of professional opinion was not presented. In a number of instances the writer obtained opinions from persons who had participated in symposia or debates on laboratory education but chose to present only the critical side of the controversy. He cited Marvin Dunnette and John Campbell

(1968) on the subject of research findings but did not include Chris Argyris (1968) who had raised questions with them about research procedures. Warren Bennis (1966) has written extensively about the conditions under which laboratory methods are likely to result in constructive organizational change but nowhere was his work included.

In contrast to the above article, *Today's Health* featured a discussion of laboratory education from a more balanced perspective. The title of this article was "Sensitivity Training: Fad, Fraud, or New Frontier." The lead paragraph in the piece was, "Here's a comprehensive, up-to-the-minute look at a new dimension in human relations—its problems (misguided do-gooders), its bizarre aspects (T group bums looking for thrills), and its outlook (potential for good)." This article, too, had a bit of sensationalism, for it only included pictures of encounter labs where the participants were engaged in active nonverbal behaviors. But for one who was willing to read the text, author Ted J. Rakstis provided a sampling of informed opinion, both inside and outside the medical profession as well as inside and outside the laboratory education profession. Cautions, criticisms, and potentials all received attention and discussion. The reader looking for a final definitive opinion would not be satisfied by Rakstis' piece, but one looking for a delineation of the issues so he could make more informed choices would be aided by it.

Psychiatrists. An issue on which one might expect psychiatrists to agree concerns the impact of laboratory education on mental health. They do not, and the December 1969 issue of the *American Journal of Psychiatry* shows a broad range of differences. At one extreme, there is the paper by Ralph Cranshaw who asked, "How Sensitive Is Sensitivity Training?" He reported three cases of psychiatric problems which arose in conjunction with persons attending labor-atory programs, and he noted that his colleagues had encountered similar cases. He argued that the responsibilities of laboratory trainers had not been fully defined and implied that the practitioners of sensitivity training could be justly accused of irresponsible experimentation with human beings. He charged that education in the form of sensitivity does not include the concepts of freedom, truth, and empathy in its operation. In his conclusion he stated, "The medical profession can say, to those who will listen, that sensitivity training is insensitive to the individual for he is not seen as a whole person."

There were some very questionable qualities about the Cranshaw paper. With an n = 3 sample the writer seemed willing to generalize to the entire operation of sensitivity training. One of the three cases was under treatment with Cranshaw prior to attending the laboratory which preceded his hospitalization for emotional difficulties. Cranshaw did not raise such questions as whether the hospitalization might have occurred regardless of the laboratory experience, whether his own efforts at treatment might have hastened the need for hospitalization, or whether the hospitalization was a constructive or destructive experience for the client. When arguing that freedom, empathy, and truth are not part of the code of operations for sensitivity training, Cranshaw was simply not fully informed. Key writings in the field by Argyris (1962), Bennis (1966), and Bradford *et al.* (1964) have consistently emphasized these values.

The way Cranshaw approached his critique was unfortunate because the issues he raised with regard to possible harm to participants, areas of responsibility among trainers, and the necessity for free choice for participants are important. They can be handled adequately only by continually confronting them. The errors in logic and fact in his presentation, however, probably reduce the kind of positive effect which his points could have.

At the other extreme of psychiatric reaction is the paper by Cadden and others (1969), who reported their experiences with a voluntary program of laboratory education for incoming medical students. They found no evidence that the group experiences precipitated emotional illnesses. In contrast, they noted that the laboratory experiences aided several students in becoming aware of their need for psychiatric consultation. The overall need for psychiatric consultation among first year students, however, was reduced in comparison to preceding years because the groups made it possible to handle certain situational crises more effectively. They also noted that the laboratory program seemed to improve student-faculty communication. The contrast with Cranshaw's reactions could hardly be more marked.

There is no reason to assume that only one of the two critiques is accurate, however. Both refer to rather specific cases. One underlines the dangers; the other shows realized potential. It would be a serious error to assume that because some laboratories are poorly conducted or some individuals poorly handled, all similar activities share these outcomes. It would be equally unfortunate to assume that because one system found benefits for individuals and groups, all systems will also benefit without careful planning and competent execution.

T Group Trainers. The inhouse controversies which were featured in the Landmarks issue of *The Journal of Applied Behavioral Science* (1967, 3(2)) focused on the differences in approach to laboratory education. In the one case, Argyris (1967), who has consistently contributed to T group practice, theory, and research, raised issues with the encounter group wing of NTL. He found many of the trends in personal growth laboratories to be running counter to the initial goals and concepts of the National

Training Laboratories. Several NTL trainers responded to Argyris' issues, but there was little consensus among their responses. Some, such as Kingsbury (1967) and Shepard (1967), sharply disagreed with him. Others such as Coffey (1967) and Work (1967) essentially agreed with him. Those who disagreed were more active in conducting personal growth laboratories than those who agreed.

In the same edition, Bass questioned whether the T group with its focus on openness and collaboration provided a full enough range of learnings to permit transfer to organization level issues. He was particularly concerned with learnings about competing interest groups, distant leaders, and organizational demands which sometimes require suppressing individual and small group interests. Few of the commentators on the Bass paper agreed with all of the premises of his arguments, but most agreed in whole or in part with his general conclusions.

Major areas of disagreement emerged within the NTL tradition when the interpersonal and intragroup focus became more oriented to the individual and when the inadequacies of using only collaborative models in large social systems became apparent. The inhouse controversies closely paralleled the various emphases featured among the different types of laboratory education programs. The potential payoff from constructive dialogue among practitioners from the various orientations is high, because the strengths and limitations of the approaches are often complementary.

Empirical Research and Ethical Questions

Most thoughtful discussions of laboratory education pay some attention to what has been or can be offered by empirical research. Many of the controversial issues could be clarified, differentiated, and possibly even resolved if the appropriate empirical studies were carried out. Ideally, research produces unambiguous answers to precisely defined questions. Practically, this rarely happens. During the past several years there have been two independent efforts to review the research literature on laboratory education (House, 1967; Campbell and Dunnette, 1968). These reviews reached some, though not identical, agreement in their conclusions. However, several of the commentators on laboratory education have written as if there was no research or that one could not draw conclusions from it (Gottschalk and Pattison, 1969; Rakstis, 1970).

House (1967) stated his major conclusions as follows: "It has been shown that T group training is not only capable of inducing anxiety, but the anxiety is an intended part of the training. Such induced anxiety may have the very unrewarding effect of unsettling, upsetting, and frustrating those subjected to it. The method may also have the intended effect of inducing more consideration for subordinates, less dependence on others, less demand for subservience from others, and better communication through more adequate and objective listening."

Campbell and Dunnette (1968) concluded: "The evidence, though limited, is reasonably convincing that T-group training does induce behavioral changes in the 'back home' setting. . . . It still cannot be said with any certainty whether T groups lead to greater or lesser changes in self-perceptions than other types of group experience, the simple passage of time, or the mere act of filling out a self-description questionnaire. . . ."

House (1967) laid greater emphasis on the role of anxiety and tension in the learning process of laboratory education than Campbell and Dunnette (1968) did. Meanwhile, Campbell and Dunnette (1968) gave more attention to the inadequacies of current research designs than House did. They also differentiated more precisely than House between be-

havioral and attitudinal changes as a result of laboratory education. Reading House, one would probably feel relatively sure that important changes came from laboratory education, but the reader would also be encouraged to examine whether the costs of the changes were worth the payoff. Reading Campbell and Dunnette, one would probably be less certain about the type of changes, especially with regard to attitudes, that could be credited to laboratory education. One would also be alerted to many of the methodological errors that have been made in laboratory education research.

Elsewhere, this writer has commented on the House and Campbell–Dunnette reviews (Alderfer, 1970). House tends to underemphasize the fact that most important or significant change processes include anxiety. The key question concerns whether the participants and staff are equipped to deal with the tensions effectively, not with whether they should exist. Poor instruments and inadequate controls do contaminate many laboratory education research studies. It is also true, however, that studies frequently had different sources of invalidity and yet reached the same conclusions. Studies with better designs had ways of checking sources of error even though they could not completely control them. My conclusion, therefore, was that the two reviews were conservative both with respect to the potential dangers in the methods and with respect to the kind of payoffs that could be expected.

Most of the research reviewed to date has been directed toward seeing whether T group laboratories result in behavior and attitude changes for participants when they return to work settings. There has been far less research, if any, on similar or related questions for encounter and Tavistock laboratories. Much of the public concern over laboratory education has been tied directly or indirectly to personal growth laboratories. The lack of empirical research on these very potent learning settings should be changed. A similar point applies to the Tavistock laboratories, and there are indications that research of this kind is being carried out (Astrachan and Klein, 1970).

Lakin's (1969) delineation of ethical issues in laboratory education offers a paradigm for thinking through many of the needed researches. We need to study more about the processes that lead persons to attend laboratories, including questions of how to identify persons who might be harmed and who are most likely to benefit. The work of Steele (1968) and Rubin (1967) offers promise in this direction, but it is only a bare beginning. We need to know more about the effect of various design components, staff behavior, and laboratory processes, such as that offered by the research of Argyris (1962), Culbert (1968), Harrison and Lubin (1965), Bolman (1970; 1971), Schmuck et al. (1969), Lubin and Zuckerman (1969), and Alderfer and Lodahl (1971). But the number of questions that could be addressed is much greater than the answers so far provided. Quite a few studies have been addressed to assessing the outcomes of laboratory education, but still more with better designs and instrumentation are needed. Especially important are questions with regard to changes in interpersonal and intergroup behavior as a result of laboratory programs. What we know about laboratory-induced changes in behavior exists almost entirely at the individual level.

Both the critics and the advocates of laboratory education are people. They have their own unique combinations of needs, values, abilities, and personal styles. They participate in interpersonal relationships with each other. They belong to overlapping and competing groups. Their reactions (including this author's) to laboratory education are bound to be influenced by these factors.

Questions of knowledge, professional competence, and ethical behavior are closely intertwined. When it is well known that a particular behavioral pattern is harmful, a professional who consciously or unconsciously undertakes such a pattern should be questioned on ethical grounds. So often the issues are not clear, however. Sometimes conservative members of a profession or of a competing profession raise ethical questions about innovations because they fear that they will soon have to revise or change some of their own well-established ideas or behavior if the new concepts are proven valid. The value of innovation for its own sake should never be a reason for infringing on the freedom or individuality of human beings. Nor should the inertia of tradition serve to block the responsible experimentation that is so necessary if we are to become more effective in coping with the many social problems that we face in today's world.

These issues define some very fine lines to draw. Reasonable and competent professionals have disagreed and will continue to disagree on specific cases. The important conditions for public welfare and for professional growth are that issues of professional practice be subject to continual examination by those who are equipped to do so, that theory development and empirical research go along with new developments in professional practice, and that the outcomes of these dialogues be shared among the professions and with the public.

BIBLIOGRAPHY

ALDERFER, C. AND LODAHL, T. M., "A quasi-experiment on the use of experiential methods in the classroom," *Journal of Applied Behavioral Science*, 1971, in press.
ALDERFER, C., "Subcultures in behavioral science and the interpretation of research

on experiential methods," *Proceedings of the Twenty-second Annual Winter Meeting, IRRA*, 1969, 98–108.

ARGYRIS, C., "Conditions for competence acquisition and therapy," *Journal of Applied Behavioral Science*, 1968, 4, 147–178.

ARGYRIS, C., *Interpersonal Competence and Organizational Effectiveness* (Homewood, Ill., Dorsey, 1962).

ARGYRIS, C., "Issues in evaluating laboratory education," *Industrial Relations*, 1968, 8, 28–40.

ARGYRIS, C., "On the future of laboratory education," *Journal of Applied Behavioral Science*, 1967, 3, 153–183.

ASTRACHAN, B. M. AND KLEIN, E. B., "Learning in groups," *Journal of Applied Behavioral Science*, 1971, in press.

BANDURA, A. AND WALTERS, R. H., *Social Learning and Personality Development* (New York, Holt, Rinehart, and Winston, 1963).

BASS, B. M., "The anarchist movement and the T-group: some possible lessons for organizational development," *Journal of Applied Behavioral Science*, 1967, 3, 211–227.

BENNIS, W. G., *Changing Organizations* (New York, McGraw-Hill, 1966).

BENNIS, W. G., "A funny thing happened on the way to the future," *American Psychologist*, 1970, 25, 595–608.

BOLMAN, L., "Some effects of trainers on their T groups," *Journal of Applied Behavioral Science*, 1971, in press.

BRADFORD, L. P., "Biography of an institution," *Journal of Applied Behavioral Science*, 1967, 3, 127–143.

BURTON, A. (ED.), *Encounter* (San Francisco, Jossey-Bass, 1969).

CADDEN, J. J., FLACH, F. F., BLAKESLEE, S., AND CHARLTON, R., "Growth in medical students through group process," *American Journal of Psychiatry*, 1969, 126, 862–873.

CALAME, B. E., "The truth hurts," *Wall Street Journal*, July 14, 1969, 1.

CAMPBELL, J. P. AND DUNNETTE, M. D., "Effectiveness of T-group experiences in managerial training and development," *Psychological Bulletin*, 1968, 70, 73–104.

COFFEY, H. S., "Some fundamental issues raised," *Journal of Applied Behavioral Science*, 1967, 3, 184–185.

CRANSHAW, R., "How sensitive is sensitivity training?" *American Journal of Psychiatry*, 1969, 126, 868–873.

CULBERT, S. A., "Trainer self-disclosure and member growth in two T-groups," *Journal of Applied Behavioral Science*, 1968, 4, 25–46.

DUNNETTE, M. D. AND CAMPBELL, J. P., "Laboratory Education: impact on people and organizations," *Industrial Relations*, 1969, 8, 1–27.

GOTTSCHALK, L. A. AND PATTISON, E. M., "Psychiatric perspectives on T-groups and the laboratory movement: an overview," *American Journal of Psychiatry*, 1969, 126, 823–839.

HAIGH, G. V., "A personal growth crisis in laboratory training," *Journal of Applied Behavioral Science*, 1968, 4, 437–452.

HARRISON, R., "Problems in the design and interpretation of research on human relations training," *Journal of Applied Behavioral Science*, 1971, in press.

HARRISON, R. AND LUBIN, B., "Personal style, group composition, and learning," *Journal of Applied Behavioral Science*, 1965, 1, 286–301.

HOUSE, R. J., "T-group education and leadership effectiveness: a review of the empiric literature and a critical evaluation," *Personnel Psychology*, 1967, 20, 1–32.

JENKINS, D. H., "Ethics and responsibility in human relations training," In Weschler, I. R. and Schein, E. H., *Issues in Human Relations Training* (Washington, NTL–NEA, 1962), 108–113.

KINGSBURY, S., "An open letter to Chris Argyris," *Journal of Applied Behavioral Science*, 1967, 3, 186–199.

KLEIN, M., *Our adult world and its roots in infancy*. Tavistock Pamphlet No. 2.

LAKIN, M., "Some ethical issues in sensitivity training," *American Psychologist*, 1969, 24, 923–928.

LUBIN, B. AND ZUCKERMAN, M., "Level of arousal in laboratory training," *Journal of Applied Behavioral Science*, 1969, 5, 483–490.

MURPHY, M., "Esalen: where it's at," *Readings in Psychology Today*. (Delmar, Calif., C.R.M., 1967), 410–415.

PERLS, F. S., *Ego, Hunger, and Aggression* (New York, Random House, 1969).

RAKSTIS, T., "Sensitivity training: fad, fraud, or new frontier," *Today's Health*, 1970, 48(1), 20–25, 86.

REDLICH, F. C. AND ASTRACHAN, B., "Group dynamics training," *American Journal of Psychiatry*, 1969, 125, 1501–1507.

RICE, A. K., "Individual, group, and intergroup processes," *Human Relations*, 1969, 22, 565–584.

RICE, A. K., *Learning for Leadership* (London, Tavistock, 1965).

ROGERS, C. R., "The group comes of age," *Psychology Today*, 1969, 3, 27–31; 58–61.

RUBIN, I., "The reduction of prejudice through laboratory training," *Journal of Applied Behavioral Science*, 1967, 3, 29–50.

SCHEIN, E. H. AND BENNIS, W. G., *Personal and Organizational Change Through Group Methods* (New York, Wiley, 1965).

SCHMUCK, R. A., RUNKEL, P. J., AND LONGMEYER, D., "Improving organizational problem solving in a school faculty," *Journal of Applied Behavioral Science*, 1969, 5, 455–482.

SCHUTZ, W. C., *Joy: Expanding Human Awareness* (New York, Grove Press, 1967).

SHEPARD, H. A., "In defense of clumsiness," *Journal of Applied Behavioral Science*, 1967, 3, 204–205.

SHEPARD, H. A., "Personal growth laboratories: toward an alternative culture," *Journal of Applied Behavioral Science*, 1970, 6, 259–268.

SLATER, P. E. AND BENNIS, W. G., "Democracy is inevitable," *Harvard Business Review*, 1964, 42(2), 51–59.

STEELE, F. I., "Personality and the laboratory style," *Journal of Applied Behavioral Science*, 1968, 4, 25–46.

WHYTE, W. F., *Leadership and group participation* (New York State School of Industrial and Labor Relations, May 1953).

WORK, H. H., "To Chris Argyris," *Journal of Applied Behavioral Science*, 1967, 3, 208–209.

QUESTIONS

1. Compare and contrast the educational designs of encounter groups, T group laboratories, and Tavistock conferences.
2. Do you think that the kind of behavior learned in laboratory training can be readily transferred to a corporate organization setting? Discuss.
3. Why has there been controversy, among laymen and professionals alike, over laboratory education?
4. Relate laboratory education, especially T-group training, to organization development.

19.

Eclectic Approach to Organizational Development

EDGAR F. HUSE and MICHAEL BEER

In one sense this article might be called a success story. The manufacturing plant to be described achieved striking increases in production and efficiency during the period of our study. The important thing about the experience, however, is not what was achieved but *how* it was achieved. The approach taken by management could, in our opinion, be used with similar results in countless other situations —service organizations as well as manufacturing facilities, nonprofit institutions as well as business corporations, small companies as well as large ones. There is probably more flexibility and managerial "freedom of choice" in the approach described here than in any other that has been offered. Ability and a sense of commitment are required to make the approach work, but no unusual talents are necessary.

In fact, no one segment of the approach will seem novel to HBR subscribers; many of the specific methods have been well described in past articles,[1] and all have been used with success many times in industry and other fields. Therefore the plant managers did not break new ground when they employed job enrichment, job participation, the project manager or "integrator" approach, and other such concepts.

What this management group did that was different was to employ and integrate a *wide variety* of OD approaches in order to improve the quality and profitability of operations. The managers were not married to any one approach in particular. Their experience demonstrates how an executive or team of managers can use an assortment of methods and concepts to solve operating problems. That is the lesson we shall emphasize in this article.

In fairness to the reader, we must stress

Reprinted from the *Harvard Business Review*, Vol. 49, No. 5 (September–October 1971), pp. 103–113, by permission of the publisher. © 1971 by the President and Fellows of Harvard College; all rights reserved.

Edgar F. Huse is Professor of Management and Chairman, Organizational Studies Department, School of Management, Boston College. Michael Beer is Manager of Organizational Research and Development at Corning Glass Works.

[1] See HBR's *Organizational Development Series*, Parts I, II, and III.

that there are no simple "off the shelf" formulas that a manager can uncritically apply without first carefully diagnosing his organization and its problems as they exist at a specific point in time. (Many times this diagnosis should be made with the help of a personnel man or an outside behavioral scientist.) An approach that works extremely well in one situation may not work or may be less effective in a different situation, even though the problems may appear to be very similar. As an example, job enrichment for factory workers has been effective in many situations. However, we know of an organization which has used OD concepts to reduce manufacturing costs by almost 45% in less than a year, but the technology of the organization has basically precluded the use of job enrichment at the level of the production worker.

Another point that needs to be stressed is that a unified approach to OD changes the entire culture of an organization over time, increasing the interest of employees in new work methods and experimentation. The quotations in the ruled insert suggest the general attitudes that materialized at the plant we studied. This means that a technique or approach may not be effective at one point in time but may be highly effective at a later point where the receptivity of individuals has changed. For this reason, too, each situation must be diagnosed separately.

Elements of Approach

The OD program was started in 1966 in one plant of a corporation with about 50 plants; most of the OD work was accomplished in 1968 and 1969. The factory manufactured a variety of electrical and electronic instruments for medical and laboratory use. The range of products has considerably expanded and now varies from relatively simple to highly complex electronic devices; for instance, one instrument now in manu-

Typical Reactions to OD

Assembly worker: "You get involved in your job here and want to come to work because you know what you have to do and the goals you have to meet."

Engineer: "I disagreed with this organizational development approach when I first got here and thought it was for the birds. The thing that convinced me was the way we got those new products into production. Because of the problems involved, in any other company where I've worked before we would have had a real fiasco."

First-line supervisor: "I hate to say it, and I'm not going to do it, but I honestly think that I could be off the production floor for a whole month and my girls would still make the schedule without my being there."

Graduate student after a field trip to the plant: "I'm glad we went on a plant tour instead of having the plant manager come to lecture to us. If I hadn't seen it myself, I wouldn't have believed it. I tried to explain to my father (an executive in another firm) and he asked me if I had been smoking pot."

facture contained more than 500 parts and 12 different printed circuit boards with electronic readouts of blood analyses.

At the time the study began, the plant followed the familiar structural model; it had a plant manager and such departments as manufacturing, personnel, plant engineering, quality assurance, and materials control. The organization had grown considerably in size since the project started, including the addition of marketing and product development groups which before were reporting to different parts of the parent company.

At the very beginning, there were approximately 35 hourly employees, mostly unskilled or semiskilled women with high school educations. There were approximately 15 technical and clerical personnel and 8 salaried professional and managerial personnel. Because of the nature of the product, the plant was basically, but not completely, an assembly organization.

The fact that at the beginning the plant was relatively small and that a majority of the production workers were women causes some difficulties in generalizing the findings. Yet it is our view that the processes of management developed in this plant are not only applicable to larger plants and different technologies, but should be even more effective in larger organizations with other kinds of operations.

The economic performance of the plant is shown in Parts A, B, and C of Exhibit I.

MEANS OF CHANGE

The OD approach which continues to be used at the plant has been eclectic since the very beginning. It is based on four basic beliefs:

1. The operating manager is very concerned about doing a good job and works hard at it. He is far more concerned about results than about "theory" as such.

2. If a spirit of enquiry and experimentation can be developed in an organization, the operating manager will try new approaches and will continue to use those that help him to get his job done better. Conversely, he will drop or cease using an approach which, for him, is not helpful, at least as he perceives it.

3. The role of behavioral scientists (or change agents) should be to help the operating manager do his job better (by acting as resource people), but not to tell him how to do his job.

4. A variety of approaches to improvement have their place in an organizational development program, and neither the manager nor the change agent should become wedded to any single tool or technique. (For example, although sensitivity training has been used widely in industry as an instrument for change, it has not yet been used at this plant and, indeed, may never be used unless it appears appropriate at a particular point in time.)

The resource people available to operating managers during the period of the study consisted primarily of a team of three individuals available for counseling, raising questions, consulting, and giving feedback. These people were the two authors and the plant personnel man. A fourth member of the team was a researcher whose main responsibility was to interview and gather data in the organization for diagnostic, feedback, and research purposes.

The basic approach was for the two "outside" change agents to work with individual managers and supervisors, helping them to solve specific ongoing problems or to initiate small experiments in management. The emphasis was on helping with current problems and establishing a climate for experimentation. The result was that some managers soon began to apply some new concepts. Since most of the early experiments were successful, managers' interest and motivation to change grew steadily.

While the change agents were interested in using "theory" so they could better fit the nature and kind of their help into longer-term objectives for change and development, discussions of theory, when held, were incidental to solving immediate job problems. Indeed, encouraging a spirit of experimentation may be more important than theory in projects of this type.

Changes in Task and Structure

The OD program at the plant has produced (a) changes that relate to tasks and organizational structure as well as (b) changes that relate to the more individualized behavior and relationships of persons and groups. Although we will be talking about these two areas as though they are separate, it should be noted that work on both proceeded simultaneously and, more importantly, that they are highly interdependent. Improvement in the one facilitates improvement in the other. For example:

• Improvement in interpersonal trust and cooperation facilitates the possibility of structural changes; and structural changes, if done properly, facilitate the development of interpersonal trust and cooperation. Thus, initial attempts at job enrichment may be extremely difficult in unionized plants that distrust management.

• It is not enough for a manager to improve his understanding of his own behavior and his relationships with others. For one thing, the high rate of transfer and promotion of managerial personnel in many organizations considerably reduces the effects of organizational change based only on changes in individuals and relationships. Moreover, the organizational structure has not only a great deal of influence on the effectiveness of production efforts,[2] but also a great deal of effect on the behavior of individuals (e.g., trust or distrust between production and R&D). All this suggests that effective OD programs must be simultaneously concerned with tasks and organizational structure *as well as* the relationships of individuals and groups, especially if change is to last after employees shift jobs.

Although the managers used a number of OD approaches, three in particular will be noted in this section:

1. *Job enrichment*—This is the concept of changing the structure of jobs to provide individuals with more opportunity to handle work with responsibility for *planning, doing,* and *evaluating* their own work. The purpose is to create more interesting and challenging work and to increase employee involvement and motivation.

2. *Autonomous or integrated work teams*—This concept means creating cohesive work groups around interrelated or interdependent jobs. The purpose is to create further meaning in work through identification with a particular group and/or product.

3. *The principle of the "integrator"*— Integrators are used to bring together more closely work groups with differing goals and objectives—e.g., marketing, product development, plant engineering, manufacturing, and other functional groups.

Now let us look at some of the results achieved, first in four departments, then in the plant as a whole.

HOT PLATE DEPARTMENT

In this department employees assembled a number of different models of hot plates. This department had been organized into the normal assembly-line operation, and management was satisfied with productivity. Applying job enrichment principles, the first-line supervisor and an engineer came up with a design that was radically different from the assembly line. Each girl was to assemble the entire hot plate. The manager explained that, in the future, each girl was expected to do the entire job. No other changes were made in the department or in its personnel.

The girls reacted positively to the change. As one girl remarked, "Now, it is *my* hot plate." There was a drop in controllable rejects (those within the control of the workers) from 23% to 1% in the next six months. Absenteeism dropped from 8% to less than 1% in the same period of time. As for productivity,

[2] See John J. Morse and Jay W. Lorsch, "Beyond Theory Y," HBR May–June, p. 61.

A. Plant efficiency (as measured by speed in learning production tasks)
Learning rate

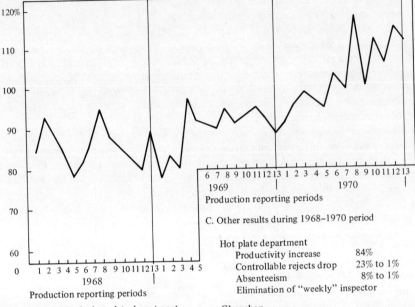

Production reporting periods

B. Productivity in the hot plate department
Productivity index

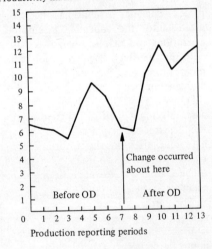

Production reporting periods

C. Other results during 1968–1970 period

Hot plate department
Productivity increase	84%
Controllable rejects drop	23% to 1%
Absenteeism	8% to 1%
Elimination of "weekly" inspector	

Glass shop
Productivity increase	20%

Materials control department
Parts shortage list reduced from 14 IBM pages
to 1 page

Instrument department
Four new products introduced in eight months
with only a slight drop in overall
productivity. New product efficiency*
now never less than	80%
Productivity increase	17%
Quality increase	50%
Absenteeism reduced	50%

Supervision
Elimination of job of manufacturing manager
Elimination of 1/3 of first-line supervisory jobs†

Incremental profit
One of the best among 50 plants
in corporation

*Measured in terms of speed in learning new production tasks.
†Vacant jobs not filled after promotion of individuals.

EXHIBIT 1   Economic impact of OD.

there was a gain of 84% in the second half of the year (see Part B of Exhibit I).

In this department, all routine final inspection was eventually turned over to the assembly workers themselves. A full-time quality control job has since been eliminated.

Why was job enrichment emphasized by the managers in this case? The fact that the task was principally assembly work made job enrichment feasible, but actually that fact was not the main reason. The managers chose this approach because it appealed to them; because of their backgrounds and interests, they "felt comfortable" with it. At another time, they might have chosen a different approach—say, more participation in decision making. And if other personnel had been in charge at the time, different OD principles might have been used—with similar gains in productivity and quality. In other words, job enrichment was not dictated by the economics of the situation; it was elected by the individuals involved.

GLASS SHOP

In this department the girls used lathes to form tubing and other shapes for electrodes. After discussion, the supervisor decided to form teams as a technique for increasing productivity. His approach was very simple. What he did was to go to different groups and tell the girls something like this:

"Look, I think we ought to organize in teams, and you four girls are responsible for the 'X' electrodes. You are responsible for the total task. I want you girls to know that we're going to need 500 of these the next accounting period, and it's up to you to decide who's going to do what, how you're going to do it, and how you schedule it."

When this approach did not work as well as expected, the supervisor revised it (with the help of the advisers). An increase in productivity of about 20% resulted before long. There were immediate and lasting changes in the involvement and commitment of employees and their interest in the work. On occasion, the girls would stay in the cafeteria after punching out so as to discuss schedules and manufacturing problems over a cup of coffee. One afternoon, one of the workers commented to one of the authors, "Isn't it silly for a bunch of us housewives to stay here after work worrying about how we are going to make the schedule? We should be home cooking dinner for our families."

Although the approach caused some difficulties which took work and time to iron out, the teams met the schedule, pooled efforts, and swapped jobs as necessary. The supervisor no longer had to assign work at the beginning of the day to each employee, as was traditionally done in most manufacturing plants.

The choice of OD approach was again dictated not by economics or technology but by the manager's personal choice. With different personalities, other methods probably would have been chosen.

MATERIALS CONTROL

This department had responsibility for the functions of purchasing, inventory control, plant scheduling, and expediting, with various people specializing in each. Before OD, the plant was plagued with parts shortages which caused production delays. In addition, some inventories were too high.

After experimenting successfully with job enrichment on individual cases, the department manager decided to change his organizational structure. He then worked out a plan of action. Rather than have each group specialize in a particular functional area, he decided to organize his department on the basis of product lines. Each group would have total project responsibility for a particular product line or department, including all the functions of purchasing, scheduling, inventory control, and expediting.

Since this was a radical change, he moved slowly, discussing it thoroughly and considering implications and alternative approaches. When he made the move people were ready. In three months (with sales constant) parts-shortage lists were reduced from 14 pages to less than 1 page (the pages were IBM printouts). Later, as more complex instruments were introduced and sales increased, the absolute number of shortages went up although the relative amount still showed a considerable net decrease.

Employee reaction was positive. As one person put it:

"It gives you a great sense of satisfaction to know that you have been a part of coordinating the back-up work for an entire department."

INSTRUMENT ASSEMBLY

In the instrument department, which assembles complex electronic devices, there have been both successes and failures in OD. At the outset, some things were tried which the workers were not adequately prepared for. For example, the supervisor tried to get employees to choose their own work teams and found them unwilling to do so. As a result, the approaches did not work. But some months later, a new supervisor took over the department. He began by building trust, explaining the reasons for schedule changes, and involving his people in the planning process. He also began working toward what he calls the "total job concept," which is what we have earlier called job enrichment. Over the last year, he has been able to implement this concept so that he now has housewives individually doing complete assemblies of complex instrument systems with up to 500 parts and 12 printed circuit boards.

In addition, four major new instruments were introduced into the department during eight months. Yet overall departmental productivity was reduced by only a slight amount (usually significant drops in productivity occur in such circumstances). One of the new products, an extremely complex one, was introduced to the manufacturing floor without drawings, because of delays in design. Nevertheless, the plant made the time commitment.

At a later date, the plant accountant generated figures regarding the effect on productivity of the total job concept program. He did not use one of the new products (since there was no prior history) but used a standard model which had been in production for two years prior to the change to job enrichment. He found that:

• Productivity was up 17% (this increase was the equivalent of about $1,500 per year per worker).
• Quality was up 50%.
• Absenteeism was reduced by over 50%.

Now many calibrations and checks previously performed by "weekly" technicians and quality control inspectors are being performed by the production workers themselves. There is an interest in what the *organization* is doing. As one of the workers put it:

"I'm interested in the team and what we can do in terms of our production goal. Sometimes I sit at home and think of how we can better the goal and how we can improve."

Some have questioned how far job enrichment can progress. Our studies suggest that productivity of the assembly worker increases up to the level of complexity where one person can assemble a single instrument in a normal working day. Beyond this level, teams may need to work together to assemble more complex instruments.

MATRIX ORGANIZATION

The OD program led to plantwide changes in organization as well as changes within departments. One of the most interesting ones was the development of so-called "integrators" to help with production.[3] This development has occurred in two stages.

In the first stage of OD the plant manager felt that, because of the complexity of problems at lower levels, the daily production meeting, attended by his staff, was not as productive as it could be. He felt that many of the decisions could be pushed downward and that his time and the time of his staff could be put to better use in longer-range planning. In addition, there were communications failures, delays, and misunderstandings as the managers served as "communications carriers" to and from their own departments.

Discussions led to the formation of a matrix organization. Each first-line production supervisor was to be an "integrator" for a team consisting of representatives from each of the departments involved with his production department. Such a team might consist of a technician from the quality assurance department, a technician or engineer from engineering, and a representative from the appropriate product-line team in materials control. While the approach is still not a complete success, it is slowly improving. One of the main reasons for problems immediately after the change was the failure to prepare individuals effectively for their new roles and to provide them with new and better skills in carrying out the matrix approach. What is impressive has been the ability of all concerned to diagnose and discuss the lack of complete success with candor and honesty and to formulate plans for improvement.

Now a second-stage, modified approach is being used to integrate such sections of the organization as marketing, product development, plant engineering, manufacturing, and materials control. As new products move through marketing, product development, and manufacturing, teams are brought together to integrate the work of the separate units and departments. Work teams might include R&D, marketing, materials control, and production people. Interviews conducted in the plant in December 1970 indicate that this approach is working well. As one individual in manufacturing put it:

"We have never had new products move so smoothly into the plant before. We've been able to solve the problems that used to plague us in the past. We have our conflicts, but they are brought out in the open and ironed out before it is too late and everybody is locked in. For the first time, we are really integrated. I don't think that we'll ever have another problem like the 'Model X'. . . ."

FEWER MANAGERS

As decision making has been pushed downward and more responsibility has been picked up by technicians and production workers, a significant change has occurred in the level and numbers of managerial personnel. For example:

When the study started, there was a plant manager, a manufacturing manager, and, reporting to him, first-line supervisors (foremen). When the manufacturing manager was promoted to plant manager, the vacancy was not filled by a substitute. Again, when a first-line supervisor was promoted to another plant, the other two first-line supervisors requested that he not be replaced.

As a result of cases like the foregoing, OD resulted in a one-third reduction of the first-line supervisory force and the

---

[3] See Paul R. Lawrence and Jay W. Lorsch, "New Management Job: The Integrator," HBR November–December 1967, p. 142.

complete reduction of an additional layer of supervision at a time when the manufacturing work force increased.

Effect on Behavior

How did the OD program affect the actions and attitudes of individuals and groups? Let us examine several different types of change that resulted, continuing to bear in mind that the behavioral effects went hand in hand with the changes produced in operations and organization structure.

IMPROVED COMMUNICATIONS

OD led to a general opening of communications channels so that a level of trust could be developed to assist with the other changes. But this was only part of the story; some specific changes in practice and procedure were introduced by management.

Departmental Meetings. The individual supervisors began, with relatively little training, a series of monthly meetings between each boss and his subordinates, including first-line supervisors with production employees. The initial format was simply for the supervisor to tell subordinates what was going on in the plant and in his department. He discussed the monthly objectives of the plant, how it was doing with regard to its objectives, how the department objectives fit in with the plant objectives, and the like.

At the beginning, these meetings were rather stiff with little communication. But this pattern changed radically; the participants became truly involved in two-way communications. In addition, particularly at the production-worker level, the content of communications changed from "mini-gripes" to "mega-gripes"; that is, the discussions, questions, and comments changed from very specific topics such as vacation and sick-leave policies to areas of broader concern such as: What is our product being used for?

Some Limitations of This Study

The OD program was carried out in one plant of a large multiplant organization. The interface between the parent corporation and the plant has not always been easy. Most large corporations (and the parent organization of this plant is no exception) have well-established policies and practices. An OD program may at times cause stresses and strains with established practices and procedures. To give only one example, how does management reward workers who have doubled their production when it operates under an established pay-rate system which is not directly geared to productivity? How does the usual job evaluation program reflect the fact that hourly assembly workers are now doing the calibration and inspection previously required of weekly paid technicians? We do not yet have answers to such problems. However, there is evidence that the changes that have occurred in the plant have influenced thinking in the larger organization.

Who is using it? What do they think of it? Are our quality standards high enough? How are we going to make schedule?

This shift, particularly among production people, took some time to evolve, because all of the production workers had come from more traditional companies. As one worker put it:

"In the last company I worked for, things were different. You were told what to do and you did it. No one told you anything about the company and what you were working on, and no one asked you anything about 'nothing.' "

Coffee with the Boss. The plant manager set up a weekly communications meeting with a continuously rotating group of hourly and weekly employees to close the communications loop at the top. The same kind of shift occurred in these meetings as in the meetings just described.

Other Approaches. Over time it became evident that all levels of employees wanted more information about their jobs, how their jobs fitted into the organization, and how the business was doing. Plant tours were initiated to show employees from one department what was happening in other departments. Significantly, after a time, hourly employees began to give the tours in their own departments, first to other workers and, eventually, to visitors (including vice presidents of the parent organization).

In addition, charts were placed at the major traffic point in the plant. Revised monthly, the charts showed actual versus budgeted progress in key areas, such as sales and plant effectiveness. For proprietary reasons, actual dollar figures were not used—comparisons were in units instead. On one visit, one of the authors was reviewing the charts when an assembly worker went by and remarked: "Don't they look good? We're proud of where we are." And, indeed, she had a right to be proud.

The process of increased and improved communication just described may sound deceptively easy. It was not. To those of us involved in planning the projects, the process of change seemed agonizingly slow. We would often meet in utter frustration when we realized how few obvious changes had taken place. In addition, there were problems connected with being a part of a large corporation.

LEADERSHIP AND SUPERVISION

There is no doubt that leadership and supervision have an important impact on the motivation, commitment, adaptability, the satisfaction of employees. As changes resulted from OD, supervisors increasingly became participative, supportive, and willing to delegate. The changes were carried out by the supervisors and managers of the plant and were, therefore, reflections of their changing values and leadership style.

Perhaps the most interesting aspect in the development of participative management was the early difficulty encountered in understanding and applying the concept. After early discussion of the approach, some individuals were interpreting it to mean a "be warm and friendly to everyone, regardless of the situation" type of approach. That is, concern for people was being emphasized to the exclusion of concern for task and production. Occasionally, the early confusion of a manager resulted in "wild" swings in style from laissez-faire to directiveness. When warmness and friendliness did not work for him, his increased frustration would erupt in a new, tough, and quite unexpected (from the employee's point of view) approach to a problem. These swings reflected a trial-and-error learning process on the manager's part, much like an attempt to groove a new golf swing.

The search for an appropriate style of management on a continuum between "hard" and "soft" reflects a common confusion about participative management. This approach, as the managers gradually learned, is an integration of concern for people *and* concern for production through mutual involvement by boss and subordinate in goal setting and through mutual decisions affecting subordinates. Directive leadership is actually easier for the manager because he can "go by the book." Participative management is tougher, both on him and on subordinates, because the direction and control come from within the individual as a result of a sense of commitment. Let us illustrate:

Production and other goals are mutually planned by the plant manager and his staff. Goals for each department are derived from the plant goals, and individual or team goals are derived (with the help of production workers) from the department goals. In a presentation to higher-level management, the plant manager told the higher-level manager he thought that every worker in the plant had a clear idea of what his goals were for the next accounting period. The goals were consistently tough. Participative management is not "soft."

The plant has a relatively high rate of involuntary turnover. Action is taken consistently to terminate an employee when appropriate. Performance is the criterion for firing and, together with seniority, for promotion. Managers are frank with employees about the reasons for termination. This practice surely reflects concern for people, but it also carries with it the assumption that people are interested in doing a good job and are mature enough to understand the reasons for both promotions and terminations. Parenthetically, evaluation is two way, since a "Rate Your Boss" form is frequently used to give direct feedback from employees to supervisors.

The "culture" produced by OD has enhanced the ability of managers and employees to look at themselves realistically and to take individual responsibility for difficult decisions that are often bucked upward in more traditional organizations. One employee's comment may help to show the degree and kind of change in leadership and supervision which have occurred in the plant:

"Since I've been working here, my husband is a much better supervisor in his plant. I tell him what he should do to make his people more interested in what they are doing, based on what our supervisors do here."

During late 1970 and early 1971, as was happening in most companies, sales were declining and the plant was producing products faster than they could be sold. As a result, management decided that a layoff or reduction was economically necessary. After a number of alternatives were considered, these were openly discussed with the assembly workers. The final decision (to reduce the number of workweeks in the month for individual employees) was actually applauded by the work force.

GROUP PROCESSES

Another problem at the plant had to do with the interdependence of departments in accomplishing plant objectives and the fact that differences between department goals and time horizons often created intergroup conflict. The later use of integrators contributed to the solution here, but earlier approaches were also helpful.

One such approach was to build more communication bridges between departments. Early in the OD program, plant professional and supervisory personnel felt that the relationships between different departments needed to be improved. As a result, a first meeting was held with the plant and department managers to discuss perceptions of their own and other departments. During that meeting, frank discussions were carried on regarding what were seen as the good and bad points of each department. Even the change agents were discussed. (For example, we were told that we were not providing sufficient, definitive answers, and that we were not performing as much in the role of directive "experts" as the plant supervisory personnel felt that we should.)

After the session, the managers decided that follow-up meetings of the same type should be held and that the format and style of these meetings should be expanded. As an example, cross-departmental meetings were established on a periodic basis. In these meetings certain personnel of a department would meet, in turn, with people of each other department to discuss expectations, perceptions, and strong and weak points. Although it is difficult to quantify the results, the general agreement was that they were extremely helpful. As one monthly employee put it, "Before we had these meetings, I really wasn't concerned about the people in 'X' department except to feel that they weren't doing their job. After we held the interdepartmental meetings, I began to understand some of their problems. I began to listen to them and to work with them."

A second approach had to do with group development. There is substantial evidence to indicate that cohesive work teams have strong effects on the performance of individuals. How could the manager develop teams to increase trust, communication, and support of the organization?

The plant manager and his staff formed themselves into a "board of directors" for the plant. As a group they would meet monthly to discuss a plant problem and develop a team solution to it. Then the individual managers asked the change agents to sit in on the meetings that they had with their own subordinates. After a meeting, the change agents would lead a discussion of how the session went and how it might have been more effective. This included private, personalized feedback to both managers and subordinates regarding their own performance. However, sensitivity training was never used. This technique was discussed, but the plant staff felt that it did not need or want such an approach. Indeed, sufficient openness developed to make T-groups unnecessary; the efforts and risks taken by some individuals in soliciting feedback from their peers met the need instead.

Conclusion

The experience of the plant we studied shows that OD is a powerful means of increasing organizational effectiveness, whether measured in terms of profitability, productivity, labor cost, or other ways. The OD program employed by management was based on these assumptions:

• Operating managers will continue to use those techniques and approaches that help them get their jobs done better.
• No single organizational development technique can be completely effective by itself.
• Employees desire responsibility, challenging work, and an opportunity to grow and develop.

Jobs, communications, and organizational structure, to identify just a few dimensions of the OD program, were shaped by the managers to allow employees to satisfy their work needs. The result was increased involvement in work, commitment to the organization, motivation, and personal growth. Moreover, the plant grew in effectiveness. In 1970, for example, it was recognized as one of the best among about 50 other corporate plants in its "incremental profit" (a term for dollars made on sales above budgeted sales). Again, voluntary turnover among hourly employees has been consistently below that for the area; productivity and quality have improved as changes have been made in department after department; the plant handles more volume with less supervision and indirect labor; and management has been able to introduce new and highly complex products quickly, without drops in productivity.

Business leaders do not need to be told how important such gains are in the current industrial environment. Employees are demanding more meaningful involvement in work and organization. Accelerating change is placing a great premium on a company's ability to adapt to new markets and technologies. The traditional, bureaucratic form of organization is being challenged as it has never been before. OD is becoming more than a means to improvement and superior performance. It is becoming a means to survival.

QUESTIONS

1. Explain the point made by the authors about "tasks and organization structure" and "individual behavior and relationships of persons and groups." How important is each of these to the organization development effort?
2. Identify and explain all the specific actions that were instituted in this plant. How were the climate and organizational situation changed?
3. The authors speak of an "eclectic approach to organizational development." Can you identify any over-all theory of management that was being applied in this plant? Explain.

PART V

Motivation and Management of People

Part V deals with topics in organizational behavior. We are here concerned with systems of management, motivation, leadership and supervision, morale, participative management, communication, administrative justice, and value systems underlying organizational life.

A. *Systems of Management.* A variety of characteristic modes or styles of managing people exists in the world of work. These patterns of management largely determine outcomes in terms of organizational performance and employee satisfaction.

The thinking of the late Douglas McGregor has had a profound impact upon organization theorists and management practitioners. His Theory X and Theory Y constructs have probably been discussed more widely in the past fifteen years than any other single management theory. In his essay McGregor presents the essence of two contrasting views about the nature of man and the leadership role of management. According to McGregor, knowledge of motivational principles and an understanding of the conditions of modern life both point to serious deficiencies in the conventional style of management. He proposes management by self-control and self-direction.

In "Evolving Models of Organizational Behavior," Keith Davis relates man's psychological hierarchy of needs with models of organizational behavior. The beliefs and assumptions about human behavior and leadership that managers hold serve as guides, often subconscious, of their daily styles of behavior. Davis states that managerial practices have been evolving from the autocratic model to a custodial model and then to a supportive model. A very recent trend is toward a collegial model. Each successive model activates higher-order human drives and is more democratic.

B. *Motivation.* Both the student of administration and the manager must be intensely concerned with the mainsprings of man. What conditions or forces impel people to produce in an organizational setting? Is motivation something that is primarily internally generated, or is man shaped mainly by external forces? What role do money and other incentives play in the total motivational situation?

In the first article in this section Frederick Herzberg explains the distinction between those factors that lead to real satisfaction and those factors that lead to job dissatisfaction. He labels the former "motivators" and the latter "hygienic" factors. He then explains how jobs can be redesigned to provide for a greater array of motivating factors and thus generate improved performance.

The practicing executive in private business typically has strong faith in the efficacy of money as a motivator of employee performance. Yet behavioral scientists have often demonstrated and asserted that money is not nearly so important a work incentive as managers claim. What lies behind this apparent contradiction? David C. McClelland, who has spent years studying achievement motivation and its ramifications, gives us some answers in his article, "Money As a Motivator: Some Research Insights."

Some exciting things have been happening at the Emery Air Freight Company. The next selection tells us how this company, through the efforts of Edward J. Feeney, Vice President, System Performance, has improved performance in several important operations through application of B. F. Skinner's concepts of positive reinforcement. Through such management techniques as performance audit, performance standards, positive reinforcement, and continuous feedback of results the company has experienced dramatic and lasting increases in work performance.

Dru Scott in her article, "Motivation from the TA Viewpoint," explains the concepts of transactional analysis so that they can be useful in a work organization setting. She explains that people spend their time in a variety of activities that can be classified into withdrawal, rituals, pastimes, psychological games, activities, and intimacy. She then explains the meaning of the three ego states of one's personality: Parent, Adult, and Child.

C. *Leadership and Supervision.* It has long been recognized that the behavior of the supervisor in relationships with his work group has a great deal to do with the performance and satisfactions of that group. Likewise, the education and skills of the supervisor are paramount in determining his and his unit's performance. The articles in this section deal with these dimensions of the leadership role.

Drawing upon empirical research evidence, Robert T. Golembiewski demonstrates why there is no one leadership style that is best for all circumstances. Analyzing autocratic, group-centered, and free-rein styles, he shows how situational factors such as personality, task, intelligence, and group characteristics interact with style to determine the performance of the work unit.

Rensis Likert shows how research findings on motivation can be used to augment productivity in modern organizations. His proposals and concepts are based upon many applied research investigations conducted by the Institute for Social Research of the University of Michigan. The article by Dr. Likert was presented at a conference of public administrators. The research findings and interpretations have general application and are pertinent to both the public and private sectors of the economy.

D. *Morale–Attitude Studies.* Executives must be concerned about the esprit de corps, attitudes, satisfactions, and discontents of their employees. These factors often affect job performance and usually affect attendance, turnover, and labor stability. Over and above the utilitarian reasons for interest in these matters, management ought to care about the general well-being of the personnel in the organization. This may be justified on the basis of humanitarianism, ethical values, or social responsibility.

Executives can appraise the state of morale by observation, interviews, grievance analysis, exit interviews, and through the use of outside consultants who may utilize a variety of devices. A widely used method of measuring employee attitudes is the formal questionnaire survey. M. Scott Myers discusses the pitfalls of traditional survey practices and then explains a procedure that has worked successfully for feeding back results to all levels in the organization. Employee involvement in achieving corrective action is emphasized.

E. *Participative Management.* The concept of member participation in the functions and decisions of an enterprise —that is, task and ego involvement—is a central issue in the writings of many organization theorists. Participation programs can take many forms: self-managed work teams, consultative management, labor-management cooperation, committee management, and others. But the central theme of all forms is that employees exercise at least some voice in the decisions of their organizational unit.

Frederick Chaney and Kenneth Teel describe a highly successful program, conducted over a four-year period, of worker participation in goal setting and performance improvement at Autonetics, a division of North American Rockwell Company. They point out the critical importance of providing ample coaching and guidance for front-line supervisors to enable them to adequately conduct employee problem-solving meetings. An unusual aspect of this program is that it succeeded without strong top management involvement.

The article by Harold M. F. Rush, "A Nonpartisan View of Participative Management," demonstrates the close connection between organization development and participative management. He reports the findings of a survey of 45 companies that are committed to the use of organization development policies and methodologies and 108 non-organization development firms. He then compares their management practices in regard to attitude surveys, group problem solving, goal setting, communication, conflict resolution, team building, and other related organization-building activities.

F. *Communication.* Communication transmits information and understanding from person to person. Managers spend much of their time engaged in face-to-face and written communication. Considerable trouble and conflict can and do result from inadequate or distorted communication.

Alfred Vogel points out the strong desires of employees to speak up about job-related problems, yet they are often reluctant to do so. Management attitudes and practices contribute largely to this failure of upward communication. The author shows how management interest in communication has progressed through three stages: (1) management communicates one-way to the employees, (2) management surveys employee attitudes and problems, and (3) management asks for ideas in initiating and implementing change. This third stage calls for a mutual exchange in an atmosphere of trust and respect.

G. *Administrative Justice.* As the structure and governance of work organizations evolve we find a number of forces that are leading toward constitutionalism. By constitutionalism we mean that the rights and responsibilities of citizens (i.e., employees and managers) are spelled out in policy documents, procedure statements, collective-bargaining agreements, and formalized grievance procedures. All of these policies and pro-

219

grams, which are largely internal to the organization, are formulated in the context of a growing body of statute and common law that protects the rights of working men and women. In recent years, thoughtful leaders in both private and public enterprises have given increasing thought to the need for systems of administrative justice in managing work forces.

In his article on discipline in unionized organizations, Dallas Jones devotes special attention to the responsibilities of the first-line supervisor and to his interaction with the personnel-industrial relations staff. Jones also discusses the corrective or human-relations aspects of discipline along with the legalistic components.

In his article, "When Workers Are Discharged—An Overview," Robert W. Fisher explains the types of job protection and due process procedures available to employees who are threatened with discharge. Those with most complete appeal procedures are unionized and governmental personnel. In addition, all workers, whether unionized or government or private sector nonunion, are protected by law against discriminatory discharge be-cause of race, color, sex, religion, age, or national origin. The largest group of personnel unprotected against arbitrary or capricious discharge are the millions in nonunion establishments whose particular cases may fall outside the fair employment practices jurisdiction.

H. *Value Systems in Organizational Life.* Managers seldom openly acknowledge or articulate their philosophical underpinnings or values. Yet these are crucial in determining their day-to-day behavior and the way they lead their organizations. Oftentimes writers and consultants in the field of organizational behavior also fail to explicitly state their values. Robert Tannenbaum and Sheldon A. Davis in "Values, Man, and Organizations" make a real contribution by clearly and forthrightly stating a set of values that they feel ought to guide the conduct of people in work organizations. Although it is Tannenbaum and Davis who are enunciating these values, they make it clear to the reader that these viewpoints are rather widely held by both organization theorists and organization-development practitioners. These beliefs are basically humanistic in orientation.

20.

The Human Side of Enterprise

DOUGLAS McGREGOR

It has become trite to say that the most significant developments of the next quarter century will take place not in the physical but in the social sciences, that industry—the economic organ of society —has the fundamental know-how to utilize physical science and technology for the material benefit of mankind, and that we must now learn how to utilize the social sciences to make our human organizations truly effective.

Many people agree in principle with such statements, but so far they represent a pious hope—and little else. Consider with me, if you will, something of what may be involved when we attempt to transform the hope into reality.

I

Let me begin with an analogy. A quarter century ago basic conceptions of the nature of matter and energy had changed profoundly from what they had been since Newton's time. The physical scientists were persuaded that under proper conditions new and hitherto unimagined sources of energy could be made available to mankind.

We know what has happened since then. First came the bomb. Then, during the past decade, have come many other attempts to exploit these scientific discoveries—some successful, some not.

The point of my analogy, however, is that the application of theory in this field is a slow and costly matter. We expect it always to be thus. No one is impatient with the scientist because he cannot tell industry how to build a simple, cheap, all-purpose source of atomic energy today. That it will take at least another decade and the investment of billions of dollars to achieve results which are economically competitive with present sources of power is understood and accepted.

It is transparently pretentious to sug-

Reprinted from *Leadership and Motivation, Essays of Douglas McGregor*, edited by Warren G. Bennis and Edgar H. Schein with Caroline McGregor by permission of The M.I.T. Press, Cambridge, Massachusetts. Copyright © 1966 by The Massachusetts Institute of Technology. First published in *Adventure in Thought and Action*, Proceedings of the Fifth Anniversary Convocation of the School of Industrial Management, M.I.T., April 9, 1957.

The late Douglas McGregor was Professor of Industrial Management and Sloan Fellows Professor at the Massachusetts Institute of Technology.

221

gest any *direct* similarity between the developments in the physical sciences leading to the harnessing of atomic energy and potential developments in the social sciences. Nevertheless, the analogy is not as absurd as it might appear to be at first glance.

To a lesser degree, and in a much more tentative fashion, we are in a position in the social sciences today like that of the physical sciences with respect to atomic energy in the thirties. We know that past conceptions of the nature of man are inadequate and in many ways incorrect. We are becoming quite certain that, under proper conditions, unimagined resources of creative human energy could become available within the organizational setting.

We cannot tell industrial management how to apply this new knowledge in simple, economic ways. We know it will require years of exploration, much costly development research, and a substantial amount of creative imagination on the part of management to discover how to apply this growing knowledge to the organization of human effort in industry.

May I ask that you keep this analogy in mind—overdrawn and pretentious though it may be —as a framework for what I have to say this morning.

Management's Task: Conventional View

The conventional conception of management's task in harnessing human energy to organizational requirements can be stated broadly in terms of three propositions. In order to avoid the complications introduced by a label. I shall call this set of propositions "Theory X":

1. Management is responsible for organizing the elements of productive enterprise—money, materials, equipment, people—in the interest of economic ends.
2. With respect to people, this is a process of directing their efforts, motivating them, controlling their actions, modifying their behavior to fit the needs of the organization.

3. Without this active intervention by management, people would be passive—even resistant—to organizational needs. They must therefore be persuaded, rewarded, punished, controlled—their activities must be directed. This is management's task—in managing subordinate managers or workers. We often sum it up by saying that management consists of getting things done through other people.

Behind this conventional theory there are several additional beliefs—less explicit, but widespread:

4. The average man is by nature indolent—he works as little as possible.
5. He lacks ambition, dislikes responsibility, prefers to be led.
6. He is inherently self-centered, indifferent to organizational needs.
7. He is by nature resistant to change.
8. He is gullible, not very bright, the ready dupe of the charlatan and the demagogue.

The human side of economic enterprise today is fashioned from propositions and beliefs such as these. Conventional organization structures, managerial policies, practices, and programs reflect these assumptions.

In accomplishing its task—with these assumptions as guides—management has conceived of a range of possibilities between two extremes.

The Hard or the Soft Approach?

At one extreme, management can be "hard" or "strong." The methods for directing behavior involve coercion and threat (usually disguised), close supervision, tight controls over behavior. At the other extreme, management can be "soft" or "weak." The methods for directing behavior involve being permissive, satisfying people's demands, achieving harmony. Then they will be tractable, accept direction.

This range has been fairly completely explored during the past half century, and management has learned some things from the exploration. There are difficulties in the "hard" approach. Force breeds counterforces: restriction of output, antagonism, militant unionism, subtle but effective sabotage of management objectives. This approach is especially difficult during times of full employment.

There are also difficulties in the "soft" approach. It leads frequently to the abdication of management—to harmony, perhaps, but to indifferent performance. People take advantage of the soft approach. They continually expect more, but they give less and less.

Currently, the popular theme is "firm but fair." This is an attempt to gain the advantages of both the hard and the soft approaches. It is reminiscent of Teddy Roosevelt's "speak softly and carry a big stick."

Is the Conventional View Correct?

The findings which are beginning to emerge from the social sciences challenge this whole set of beliefs about man and human nature and about the task of management. The evidence is far from conclusive, certainly, but it is suggestive. It comes from the laboratory, the clinic, the schoolroom, the home, and even to a limited extent from industry itself.

The social scientist does not deny that human behavior in industrial organization today is approximately what management perceives it to be. He has, in fact, observed it and studied it fairly extensively. But he is pretty sure that this behavior is *not* a consequence of man's inherent nature. It is a consequence rather of the nature of industrial organizations, of management philosophy, policy, and practice. The conventional approach of Theory X is based on mistaken notions of what is cause and what is effect.

"Well," you ask, "what then is the *true* nature of man? What evidence leads the social scientist to deny what is obvious?" And, if I am not mistaken, you are also

thinking, "Tell me—simply, and without a lot of scientific verbiage—what you think you know that is so unusual. Give me—without a lot of intellectual claptrap and theoretical nonsense—some practical ideas which will enable me to improve the situation in my organization. And remember, I'm faced with increasing costs and narrowing profit margins. I want proof that such ideas won't result simply in new and costly human relations frills. I want practical results, and I want them now."

If these are your wishes, you are going to be disappointed. Such requests can no more be met by the social scientist today than could comparable ones with respect to atomic energy be met by the physicist fifteen years ago. I can, however, indicate a few of the reasons for asserting that conventional assumptions about the human side of enterprise are inadequate. And I can suggest—tentatively—some of the propositions that will compose a more adequate theory of the management of people. The magnitude of the task that confronts us will then, I think, be apparent.

II

Perhaps the best way to indicate why the conventional approach of management is inadequate is to consider the subject of motivation. In discussing this subject I will draw heavily on the work of my colleague, Abraham Maslow of Brandeis University. His is the most fruitful approach I know. Naturally, what I have to say will be overgeneralized and will ignore important qualifications. In the time at our disposal, this is inevitable.

Physiological and Safety Needs

Man is a wanting animal—as soon as one of his needs is satisfied, another appears in its place. This process is unending. It continues from birth to death.

Man's needs are organized in a series of levels—a hierarchy of importance. At the lowest level, but preeminent in importance when they are thwarted, are his physiological needs. Man lives by bread alone, when there is no bread. Unless the circumstances are unusual, his needs for love, for status, for recognition are inoperative when his stomach has been empty for a while. But when he eats regularly and adequately, hunger ceases to be an important need. The sated man has hunger only in the sense that a full bottle has emptiness. The same is true of the other physiological needs of man—for rest, exercise, shelter, protection from the elements.

A satisfied need is not a motivator of behavior! This is a fact of profound significance. It is a fact that is regularly ignored in the conventional approach to the management of people. I shall return to it later. For the moment, one example will make my point. Consider your own need for air. Except as you are deprived of it, it has no appreciable motivating effect upon your behavior.

When the physiological needs are reasonably satisfied, needs at the next higher level begin to dominate man's behavior—to motivate him. These are called safety needs. They are needs for protection against danger, threat, deprivation. Some people mistakenly refer to these as needs for security. However, unless man is in a dependent relationship where he fears arbitrary deprivation, he does not demand security. The need is for the "fairest possible break." When he is confident of this, he is more than willing to take risks. But when he feels threatened or dependent, his greatest need is for guarantees, for protection, for security.

The fact needs little emphasis that, since every industrial employee is in a dependent relationship, safety needs may assume considerable importance. Arbitrary management actions, behavior that arouses uncertainty with respect to continued employment or which reflects favoritism or discrimination, unpredictable administration of policy—these can be powerful motivators of the safety needs in the employment relationship *at every level* from worker to vice president.

Social Needs

When man's physiological needs are satisfied and he is no longer fearful about his physical welfare, his social needs become important motivators of his behavior—for belonging, for association, for acceptance by his fellows, for giving and receiving friendship and love.

Management knows today of the existence of these needs, but it often assumes quite wrongly that they represent a threat to the organization. Many studies have demonstrated that the tightly knit, cohesive work group may, under proper conditions, be far more effective than an equal number of separate individuals in achieving organizational goals.

Yet management, fearing group hostility to its own objectives, often goes to considerable lengths to control and direct human efforts in ways that are inimical to the natural "groupiness" of human beings. When man's social needs—and perhaps his safety needs, too—are thus thwarted, he behaves in ways which tend to defeat organizational objectives. He becomes resistant, antagonistic, uncooperative. But this behavior is a consequence, not a cause.

Ego Needs

Above the social needs—in the sense that they do not become motivators until lower needs are reasonably satisfied—are the needs of greatest significance to management and to man himself. They are the egoistic needs, and they are of two kinds:

1. These needs that relate to one's self-esteem—needs for self-confidence, for

independence, for achievement, for competence, for knowledge.

2. Those needs that relate to one's reputation—needs for status, for recognition, for appreciation, for the deserved respect of one's fellows.

Unlike the lower needs, these are rarely satisfied; man seeks indefinitely for more satisfaction of these needs once they have become important to him. But they do not appear in any significant way until physiological, safety, and social needs are all reasonably satisfied.

The typical industrial organization offers few opportunities for the satisfaction of these egoistic needs to people at lower levels in the hierarchy. The conventional methods of organizing work, particularly in mass-production industries, give little heed to these aspects of human motivation. If the practices of scientific management were deliberately calculated to thwart these needs—which, of course, they are not—they could hardly accomplish this purpose better than they do.

Self-fulfillment Needs

Finally—a capstone, as it were, on the hierarchy of man's needs—there are what we may call the needs for self-fulfillment. These are the needs for realizing one's own potentialities, for continued self-development, for being creative in the broadest sense of that term.

It is clear that the conditions of modern life give only limited opportunity for these relatively weak needs to obtain expression. The deprivation most people experience with respect to other lower-level needs diverts their energies into the struggle to satisfy *those* needs, and the needs for self-fulfillment remain dormant.

III

Now, briefly, a few general comments about motivation:

We recognize readily enough that a man suffering from a severe dietary deficiency is sick. The deprivation of physiological needs has behavioral consequences. The same is true—although less well recognized—of deprivation of higher-level needs. The man whose needs for safety, association, independence, or status are thwarted is sick just as surely as is he who has rickets. And his sickness will have behavioral consequences. We will be mistaken if we attribute his resultant passivity, his hostility, his refusal to accept responsibility to his inherent "human nature." These forms of behavior are *symptoms* of illness—of deprivation of his social and egoistic needs.

The man whose lower-level needs are satisfied is not motivated to satisfy those needs any longer. For practical purposes they exist no longer. (Remember my point about your need for air.) Management often asks, "Why aren't people more productive? We pay good wages, provide good working conditions, have excellent fringe benefits and steady employment. Yet people do not seem to be willing to put forth more than minimum effort."

The fact that management has provided for these physiological and safety needs has shifted the motivational emphasis to the social and perhaps to the egoistic needs. Unless there are opportunities *at work* to satisfy these higher-level needs, people will be deprived; and their behavior will reflect this deprivation. Under such conditions, if management continues to focus its attention on physiological needs, its efforts are bound to be ineffective.

People *will* make insistent demands for more money under these conditions. It becomes more important than ever to buy the material goods and services that can provide limited satisfaction of the thwarted needs. Although money has only limited value in satisfying many higher-level needs, it can become the focus of interest if it is the *only* means available.

The Carrot and Stick Approach

The carrot and stick theory of motivation (like Newtonian physical theory) works reasonably well under certain circumstances. The *means* for satisfying man's physiological and (within limits) his safety needs can be provided or withheld by management. Employment itself is such a means, and so are wages, working conditions, and benefits. By these means the individual can be controlled so long as he is struggling for subsistence. Man lives for bread alone when there is no bread.

But the carrot and stick theory does not work at all once man has reached an adequate subsistence level and is motivated primarily by higher needs. Management cannot provide a man with self-respect, or with the respect of his fellows, or with the satisfaction of needs for self-fulfillment. It can create conditions such that he is encouraged and enabled to seek such satisfactions *for himself*, or it can thwart him by failing to create those conditions.

But this creation of conditions is not "control." It is not a good device for directing behavior. And so management finds itself in an odd position. The high standard of living created by our modern technological know-how provides quite adequately for the satisfaction of physiological and safety needs. The only significant exception is where management practices have not created confidence in a "fair break"—and thus where safety needs are thwarted. But by making possible the satisfaction of low-level needs, management has deprived itself of the ability to use as motivators the devices on which conventional theory has taught it to rely—rewards, promises, incentives, or threats and other coercive devices.

Neither Hard nor Soft

The philosophy of management by direction and control—*regardless of whether it is hard or soft*—is inadequate to motivate, because the human needs on which this approach relies are today unimportant motivators of behavior. Direction and control are essentially useless in motivating people whose important needs are social and egoistic. Both the hard and the soft approach fail today because they are simply irrelevant to the situation.

People deprived of opportunities to satisfy at work the needs that are now important to them behave exactly as we might predict—with indolence, passivity, resistance to change, lack of responsibility, willingness to follow the demagogue, unreasonable demands for economic benefits. It would seem that we are caught in a web of our own weaving.

In summary, then, of these comments about motivation:

Management by direction and control—whether implemented with the hard, the soft, or the firm but fair approach—fails under today's conditions to provide effective motivation of human effort toward organizational objectives. It fails because direction and control are useless methods of motivating people whose physiological and safety needs are reasonably satisfied and whose social, egoistic, and self-fulfillment needs are predominant.

IV

For these and many other reasons, we require a different theory of the task of managing people based on more adequate assumptions about human nature and human motivation. I am going to be so bold as to suggest the broad dimensions of such a theory. Call it "Theory Y," if you will.

1. Management is responsible for organizing the elements of productive enterprise—money, materials, equipment, people—in the interest of economic ends.

2. People are *not* by nature passive or resistant to organizational needs. They

have become so as a result of experience in organizations.

3. The motivation, the potential for development, the capacity for assuming responsibility, the readiness to direct behavior toward organizational goals are all present in people. Management does not put them there. It is a responsibility of management to make it possible for people to recognize and develop these human characteristics for themselves.

4. The essential task of management is to arrange organizational conditions and methods of operation so that people can achieve their own goals *best* by directing *their own* efforts toward organizational objectives.

This is a process primarily of creating opportunities, releasing potential, removing obstacles, encouraging growth, providing guidance. It is what Peter Drucker has called "management by objectives" in contrast to "management by control."

And I hasten to add that it does *not* involve the abdication of management, the absence of leadership, the lowering of standards, or the other characteristics usually associated with the "soft" approach under Theory X. Much on the contrary. It is no more possible to create an organization today which will be a fully effective application of this theory than it was to build an atomic power plant in 1945. There are many formidable obstacles to overcome.

Some Difficulties

The conditions imposed by conventional organizational theory and by the approach of scientific management for the past half century have tied men to limited jobs which do not utilize their capabilities, have discouraged the acceptance of responsibility, have encouraged passivity, have eliminated meaning from work. Man's habits, attitudes, expectations—his whole conception of membership in an industrial organization—have been conditioned by his experience under these

circumstances. Change in the direction of Theory Y will be slow, and it will require extensive modification of the attitudes of management and workers alike.

People today are accustomed to being directed, manipulated, controlled in industrial organizations and to finding satisfaction for their social, egoistic, and self-fulfillment needs away from the job. This is true of much of management as well as of workers. Genuine "industrial citizenship"—to borrow again a term from Drucker—is a remote and unrealistic idea, the meaning of which has not even been considered by most members of industrial organizations.

Another way of saying this is that Theory X places exclusive reliance upon external control of human behavior, whereas Theory Y relies heavily on self-control and self-direction. It is worth noting that this difference is the difference between treating people as children and treating them as mature adults. After generations of the former, we cannot expect to shift to the latter overnight.

V

Before we are overwhelmed by the obstacles, let us remember that the application of theory is always slow. Progress is usually achieved in small steps.

Consider with me a few innovative ideas which are entirely consistent with Theory Y and which are today being applied with some success.

Decentralization and Delegation

These are ways of freeing people from the too-close control of conventional organization, giving them a degree of freedom to direct their own activities, to assume responsibility, and, importantly, to satisfy their egoistic needs. In this connection, the flat organization of Sears, Roebuck and Company provides an interesting example. It forces "management by objectives" since it enlarges the number of people reporting to a manager until he cannot direct and control them in the conventional manner.

Job Enlargement

This concept, pioneered by I.B.M. and Detroit Edison, is quite consistent with Theory Y. It encourages the acceptance of responsibility at the bottom of the organization; it provides opportunities for satisfying social and egoistic needs. In fact, the reorganization of work at the factory level offers one of the more challenging opportunities for innovation consistent with Theory Y. The studies by A. T. M. Wilson and his associates of British coal mining and Indian textile manufacture have added appreciably to our understanding of work organization. Moreover, the economic and psychological results achieved by this work have been substantial.

Participation and Consultative Management

Under proper conditions these results provide encouragement to people to direct their creative energies toward organizational objectives, give them some voice in decisions that affect them, provide significant opportunities for the satisfaction of social and egoistic needs. I need only mention the Scanlon Plan as the outstanding embodiment of these ideas in practice.

The not infrequent failure of such ideas as these to work as well as expected is often attributable to the fact that a management has "bought the idea" but applied it within the framework of Theory X and its assumptions.

Delegation is not an effective way of exercising management by control. Participation becomes a farce when it is applied as a sales gimmick or a device for kidding people into thinking they are important. Only the management that has

confidence in human capacities and is itself directed toward organizational objectives rather than toward the preservation of personal power can grasp the implications of this emerging theory. Such management will find and apply successfully other innovative ideas as we move slowly toward the full implementation of a theory like Y.

Performance Appraisal

Before I stop, let me mention one other practical application of Theory Y which —though still highly tentative—may well have important consequences. This has to do with performance appraisal within the ranks of management. Even a cursory examination of conventional programs of performance appraisal will reveal how completely consistent they are with Theory X. In fact, most such programs tend to treat the individual as though he were a product under inspection on the assembly line.

Take the typical plan: substitute "product" for "subordinate being appraised," substitute "inspector" for "superior making the appraisal," substitute "rework" for "training or development," and, except for the attributes being judged, the human appraisal process will be virtually indistinguishable from the product-inspection process.

A few companies—among them General Mills, Ansul Chemical, and General Electric—have been experimenting with approaches which involve the individual in setting "targets" or objectives *for himself* and in a *self*-evaluation of performance semiannually or annually. Of course, the superior plays an important leadership role in this process—one, in fact, that demands substantially more competence than the conventional approach. The role is, however, considerably more congenial to many managers than the role of "judge" or "inspector" which is forced upon them by conventional performance. Above all, the individual is encouraged to take a greater responsibility for planning and appraising his own contribution to organizational objectives; and the accompanying effects on egoistic and self-fulfillment needs are substantial. This approach to performance appraisal represents one more innovative idea being explored by a few managements who are moving toward the implementation of Theory Y.

VI

And now I am back where I began. I share the belief that we could realize substantial improvements in the effectiveness of industrial organizations during the next decade or two. Moreover, I believe the social sciences can contribute much to such developments. We are only beginning to grasp the implications of the growing body of knowledge in these fields. But if this conviction is to become a reality instead of a pious hope, we will need to view the process much as we view the process of releasing the energy of the atom for constructive human ends—as a slow, costly, sometimes discouraging approach toward a goal which would seem to many to be quite unrealistic.

The ingenuity and the perseverance of industrial management in the pursuit of economic ends have changed many scientific and technological dreams into commonplace realities. It is now becoming clear that the application of these same talents to the human side of enterprise will not only enhance substantially these materialistic achievements but will bring us one step closer to "the good society." Shall we get on with the job?

QUESTIONS

1. What are the assumptions of "Theory X" about people at work? About managing people?
2. What are the assumptions of "Theory Y" about people at work? About managing people?
3. How do the assumptions and practices discussed in question 1 and 2 relate to Maslow's motivational fundamentals?
4. What style or styles of management have you personally experienced or observed? Describe the consequences of these styles.

21.

Evolving Models of Organizational Behavior

KEITH DAVIS

The affluent society of which John Kenneth Galbraith wrote a decade ago has become even more affluent.[1] There are many reasons for this sustained improvement in productivity, and some of them are advancing technology, available resources, improved education, and a favorable economic and social system. There is, however, another reason of key significance to all of us. That reason is management, specifically the capacity of managers to develop organizational systems which respond productively to the changing conditions of society. In recent years this has meant more complex administrative systems in order to challenge and motivate employees toward better teamwork. Improvement has been made by working smarter, not harder. An increasingly sophisticated knowledge of human behavior is required; consequently, theoretical models of organizational behavior have had to grow to absorb this new knowledge. It is these evolving models of organizational behavior which I wish to

discuss; then I shall draw some conclusions about their use.

The significant point about models of organizational behavior is that the model which a manager holds normally determines his perception of the organizational world about him. It leads to certain assumptions about people and certain interpretations of events he encounters. The underlying model serves as an unconscious guide to each manager's behavior. He acts as he thinks. Since his acts do affect the quality of human relations and productivity in his department, he needs to be fully aware of the trends that are occurring. If he holds to an outmoded model, his success will be limited and his job will be harder, because he will not be able to work with his people as he should.

Similarly, the model of organizational behavior which predominates among the management of an organization will affect the success of that whole organization. And at a national level the model which prevails within a country will influence

Reprinted from *Academy of Management Journal*, Vol. 11, No. 1 (March 1968), pp. 27–38, by permission of the publisher.

Keith Davis is professor of Management, Arizona State University.

[1] John Kenneth Galbraith, *The Affluent Society* (Boston, Mass.: Houghton Mifflin, 1958).

the productivity and economic development of that nation. Models of organizational behavior are a significant variable in the life of all groups.

Many models of organizational behavior have appeared during the last 100 years, and four of them are significant and different enough to merit further discussion. These are the autocratic, custodial, supportive, and collegial models. In the order mentioned, the four models represent a historical evolution of management thought. The autocratic model predominated 75 years ago. In the 1920s and 1930s it yielded ground to the more successful custodial model. In this generation the supportive model is gaining approval. It predominates in many organizations, although the custodial model probably still prevails in the whole society. Meanwhile, a number of advanced organizations are experimenting with the collegial model.

The four models are not distinct in the sense that a manager or a firm uses one and only one of them. In a week—or even a day—a manager probably applies some of all four models. On the other hand, one model tends to predominate as his habitual way of working with his people, in such a way that it leads to a particular type of teamwork and behavioral climate among his group. Similarly, one model tends to dominate the life of a whole organization, but different parts therein may still be pursuing other models. The production department may take a custodial approach, while supportive ideas are being tried in the office, and collegial ideas are practiced in the research department. The point is that one model of organizational behavior is not an adequate label to describe all that happens in an organization, but it is a convenient way to distinguish one prevailing way of life from another. By comparing these four models, we can recognize certain important distinctions among them.

The Autocratic Model

The autocratic model has its roots deep in history, and certainly it became the prevailing model early in the industrial revolution. As shown in Table 1, this model depends on power. Those who are in command must have the power to demand, "You do this—or else," meaning that an employee will be penalized if he does not follow orders. This model takes a threatening approach, depending on negative motivation backed by power.

In an autocratic environment the managerial orientation is formal, official authority. Authority is the tool with which management works and the context in which it thinks, because it is the organizational means by which power is applied. This authority is delegated by right of command over the people to whom it applies. In this model, management implicitly assumes that it knows what is best and that it is the employee's obligation to follow orders without question or interpretation. Management assumes that employees are passive and even resistant to organizational needs. They have to be persuaded and pushed into performance, and this is management's task. Management does the thinking; the employees obey the orders. This is the "Theory X" popularized by Douglas McGregor as the conventional view of management.[2] It has its roots in history and was made explicit by Frederick W. Taylor's concepts of scientific management. Though Taylor's writings show that he has worker interests at heart, he saw those interests served best by a manager who scientifically de-

[2] Douglas McGregor, "The Human Side of Enterprise." in *Proceedings of the Fifth Anniversary Convocation of the School of Industrial Management* (Cambridge, Mass.: Massachusetts Institute of Technology, April 9, 1957). Theory X and Theory Y were later popularized in Douglas McGregor, *The Human Side of Enterprise* (New York: McGraw-Hill, 1960).

TABLE 1   Four Models of Organizational Behavior

	AUTOCRATIC	CUSTODIAL	SUPPORTIVE	COLLEGIAL
Depends on	Power	Economic resources	Leadership	Mutual contribution
Managerial orientation:	Authority	Material rewards	Support	Integration and teamwork
Employee orientation:	Obedience	Security	Performance	Responsibility
Employee psychological result:	Personal dependency	Organizational dependency	Participation	Self-discipline
Employee needs met:	Subsistence	Maintenance	Higher-order	Self-realization
Performance result:	Minimum	Passive cooperation	Awakened drives	Enthusiasm
Morale measure:	Compliance	Satisfaction	Motivation	Commitment to task and team

Source: Adapted from Keith Davis, *Human Relations at Work: The Dynamics of Organizational Behavior* (3rd ed.; New York: McGraw-Hill, 1967), p. 480.

termined what a worker should do and then saw that he did it. The worker's role was to perform as he was ordered.

Under autocratic conditions an employee's orientation is obedience. He bends to the authority of a boss—not a manager. This role causes a psychological result which in this case is employee personal dependency on his boss whose power to hire, fire, and "perspire" him is almost absolute. The boss pays relatively low wages because he gets relatively less performance from the employee. Each employee must provide subsistence needs for himself and his family; so he reluctantly gives minimum performance, but he is not motivated to give much more than that. A few men give higher performance because of internal achievement drives, because they personally like their boss, because the boss is a "natural-born leader," or because of some other fortuitous reason; but most men give only minimum performance.

When an autocratic model of organizational behavior exists, the measure of an employee's morale is usually his compliance with rules and orders. Compliance is unprotesting assent without enthusiasm. The compliant employee takes his orders and does not talk back.

Although modern observers have an inherent tendency to condemn the autocratic model of organizational behavior, it is a useful way to accomplish work. It has been successfully applied by the empire builders of the 1800s, efficiency engineers, scientific managers, factory foremen, and others. It helped to build great railroad systems, operate giant steel mills, and produce a dynamic industrial civilization in the early 1900s.

Actually the autocratic model exists in all shades of gray, rather than the extreme black usually presented. It has been a reasonably effective way of management when there is a "benevolent autocrat" who has a genuine interest in his employees and when the role expectation of employees is autocratic leadership.[3] But these results are usually only moderate ones lacking the full potential that is available, and they are reached at considerable human costs. In addition, as explained earlier, conditions change to require new behavioral models in order to remain effective.

As managers and academicians became familiar with limitations of the autocratic model, they begin to ask, "Is there a better way? Now that we have brought organizational conditions this far along, can we build on what we have in order to move one step higher on the ladder of progress?" Note that their thought was not to throw out power as undesirable, because power is needed to maintain internal unity in organizations. Rather, their thought was to build upon the foundation which existed: "Is there a better way?"

The Custodial Model

Managers soon recognized that although a compliant employee did not talk back to his boss, he certainly "thought back"! There were many things he wanted to say to his boss, and sometimes he did say them when he quit or lost his temper. The employee inside was a seething mass of insecurity, frustrations, and aggressions toward his boss. Since he could not vent these feelings directly, sometimes he went home and vented them on his wife, family, and neighbors; so the community did not gain much out of this relationship either.

It seemed rather obvious to progressive employers that there ought to be some way to develop employee satisfactions and adjustment during production—and in fact this approach just might cause more productivity! If the employee's in-

securities, frustrations, and aggressions could be dispelled, he might feel more like working. At any rate the employer could sleep better, because his conscience would be clearer.

Development of the custodial model was aided by psychologists, industrial relations specialists and economists. Psychologists were interested in employee satisfaction and adjustment. They felt that a satisfied employee would be a better employee, and the feeling was so strong that "a happy employee" became a mild obsession in some personnel offices. The industrial relations specialists and economists favored the custodial model as a means of building employee security and stability in employment. They gave strong support to a variety of fringe benefits and group plans for security.

The custodial model originally developed in the form of employee welfare programs offered by a few progressive employees, and in its worst form it became known as employer paternalism. During the depression of the 1930s emphasis changed to economic and social security and then shortly moved toward various labor plans for security and control. During and after World War II, the main focus was on specific fringe benefits. Employers, labor unions, and government developed elaborate programs for overseeing the needs of workers.

A successful custodial approach depends on economic resources, as shown in Table 1. An organization must have economic wealth to provide economic security, pensions, and other fringe benefits. The resulting managerial orientation is toward economic or material rewards, which are designed to make employees respond as economic men. A reciprocal employee orientation tends to develop emphasizing security.

---

[3] This viewpoint is competently presented in R. N. McMurry, "The Case for Benevolent Autocracy," *Harvard Business Review* (Jan.–Feb., 1958), pp. 82–90.

The custodial approach gradually leads to an organizational dependency by the employee. Rather than being dependent on his boss for his weekly bread, he now depends on larger organizations for his security and welfare. Perhaps more accurately stated, an organizational dependency is added atop a reduced personal dependency on his boss. This approach effectively serves an employee's maintenance needs, as presented in Herzberg's motivation-maintenance model, but it does not strongly motivate an employee.[4] The result is a passive cooperation by the employee. He is pleased to have his security; but as he grows psychologically, he also seeks more challenge and autonomy.

The natural measure of morale which developed from a custodial model was employee satisfaction. If the employee was happy, contented, and adjusted to the group, then all was well. The happiness-oriented morale survey became a popular measure of success in many organizations.

LIMITATIONS OF THE CUSTODIAL MODEL

Since the custodial model is the one which most employers are currently moving away from, its limitations will be further examined. As with the autocratic model, the custodial model exists in various shades of gray, which means that some practices are more successful than others. In most cases, however, it becomes obvious to all concerned that most employees under custodial conditions do not produce anywhere near their capacities, nor are they motivated to grow to the greater capacities of which they are capable. Though employees may be happy, most of them really do not feel fulfilled or self-actualized.

The custodial model emphasizes economic resources and the security those resources will buy, rather than emphasizing employee performance. The employee becomes psychologically preoccupied with maintaining his security and benefits, rather than with production. As a result, he does not produce much more vigorously than under the old autocratic approach. Security and contentment are necessary for a person, but they are not themselves very strong motivators.

In addition, the fringe benefits and other devices of the custodial model are mostly off-the-job. They are not directly connected with performance. The employee has to be too sick to work or too old to work in order to receive these benefits. The system becomes one of public and private paternalism in which an employee sees little connection between his rewards and his job performance and personal growth; hence he is not motivated toward performance and growth. In fact, an overzealous effort to make the worker secure and happy leads to a brand of psychological paternalism no better than earlier economic paternalism. With the psychological variety, employee needs are dispensed from the personnel department, union hall, and government bureau, rather than the company store. But in either case, dependency remains, and as Ray E. Brown observes, "Men grow stronger on workouts than on handouts. It is in the nature of people to wrestle with a challenge and rest on a crutch . . . The great desire of man is to stand on his own, and his life is one great fight against dependency. Making the individual a ward of the organization will likely make him bitter instead of better."[5]

As viewed by William H. Whyte, the employee working under custodialism becomes an "organization man" who belongs to the organization and who has

---

[4] Frederick Herzberg, Bernard Mausner, and Barbara Snyderman, *The Motivation to Work* (New York: John Wiley and Sons, 1959).

[5] Ray E. Brown, *Judgment in Administration* (New York: McGraw-Hill, 1966), p. 75.

"left home, spiritually as well as physically, to take the vows of organizational life." [6]

As knowledge of human behavior advanced, deficiencies in the custodial model became quite evident, and people again started to ask, "Is there a better way?" The search for a better way is not a condemnation of the custodial model as a whole; however, it is a condemnation of the assumption that custodialism is "the final answer"—the one best way to work with people in organizations. An error in reasoning occurs when a person perceives that the custodial model is so desirable that there is no need to move beyond it to something better.

The Supportive Model

The supportive model of organizational behavior has gained currency during recent years as a result of a great deal of behavioral science research as well as favorable employer experience with it. The supportive model establishes a manager in the primary role of psychological support of his employees at work, rather than in a primary role of economic support (as in the custodial model) or "power over" (as in the autocratic model). A supportive approach was first suggested in the classical experiments of Mayo and Roethlisberger at Western Electric Company in the 1930s and 1940s. They showed that a small work group is more productive and satisfied when its members perceive that they are working in a supportive environment. This interpretation was expanded by the work of Edwin A. Fleishman with supervisory "consideration" in the 1940s[7] and that of Rensis Likert and his associates with the "employee-oriented supervisor" in the 1940s and 1950s.[8] In fact, the *coup de grace* to the custodial model's dominance was administered by Likert's research, which showed that the happy employee is not necessarily the most productive employee.

Likert has expressed the supportive model as the "principle of supportive relationships" in the following words:

The leadership and other processes of the organization must be such as to ensure a maximum probability that in all interactions and all relationships with the organization each member will, in the light of his background, values, and expectations, view the experience as supportive and one which builds and maintains his sense of personal worth and importance.[9]

The supportive model, shown in Table 1, depends on leadership instead of power or economic resources. Through leadership, management provides a behavioral climate to help each employee grow and accomplish in the interests of the organization the things of which he is capable. The leader assumes that workers are not by nature passive and resistant to organizational needs, but that they are made so by an inadequate supportive climate at work. They will take responsibility, develop a drive to contribute, and improve themselves, if management will give them

---

[6] William H. Whyte, Jr., *The Organization Man* (New York: Simon and Schuster, 1956), p. 3.

[7] An early report of this research is Edwin A. Fleishman, *"Leadership Climate" and Supervisory Behavior* (Columbus, Ohio: Personnel Research Board, Ohio State University, 1951).

[8] There have been many publications by the Likert group at the Survey Research Center, University of Michigan. An early basic one is Daniel Katz et al., *Productivity, Supervision and Morale in an Office Situation* (Ann Arbor, Mich.: The University of Michigan Press, 1950).

[9] Rensis Likert, *New Patterns of Management* (New York: McGraw-Hill, 1961), pp. 102–103.

half a chance. Management's orientation, therefore, is to support the employee's performance.

Since performance is supported, the employee's orientation is toward it instead of mere obedience and security. He is responding to intrinsic motivations in his job situation. His psychological result is a feeling of participation and task involvement in the organization. When referring to his organization, he may occasionally say "we," instead of always saying "they." Since his higher-order needs are better challenged, he works with more awakened drives than he did under earlier models.

The difference between custodial and supportive models is illustrated by the fact that the morale measure of supportive management is the employee's level of motivation. This measure is significantly different from the satisfaction and happiness emphasized by the custodial model. An employee who has a supportive leader is motivated to work toward organizational objectives as a means of achieving his own goals. This approach is similar to McGregor's popular "Theory Y."

The supportive model is just as applicable as the climate for managers as for operating employees. One study reports that supportive managers usually led to high motivation among their subordinate managers. Among those managers who were low in motivation, only 8 per cent had supportive managers. Their managers were mostly autocratic.[10]

It is not essential for managers to accept every assumption of the supportive model in order to move toward it, because as more is learned about it, views will change. What is essential is that modern managers in business, unions, and government do not become locked into the custodial model. They need to abandon any view that the custodial model is the final answer, so that they will be free to look ahead to improvements which are fitting to their organization in their environment.

The supportive model is only one step upward on the ladder of progress. Though it is just now coming into dominance, some firms which have the proper conditions and managerial competence are already using a collegial model of organizational behavior, which offers further opportunities for improvement.

The Collegial Model

The collegial model is still evolving, but it is beginning to take shape. It has developed from recent behavioral science research, particularly that of Likert, Katz, Kahn, and others at the University of Michigan,[11] Herzberg with regard to maintenance and motivational factors,[12] and the work of a number of people in project management and matrix organization.[13] The collegial model readily adapts to the flexible, intellectual environment of scientific and professional organizations. Working in substantially unprogrammed activities which require effective teamwork, scientific and professional employees desire the autonomy which a collegial model permits, and they respond to it well.

The collegial model depends on management's building a feeling of mutual contribution among participants in the organization, as shown in Table 1. Each employee feels that he is contributing

[10] M. Scott Myers, "Conditions for Manager Motivation," *Harvard Business Review* (Jan.–Feb., 1966), p. 61. This study covered 1,344 managers at Texas Instruments, Inc.

[11] Likert describes a similar model as System 4 in Rensis Likert, *The Human Organization: Its Management and Value* (New York: McGraw-Hill, 1967), pp. 3–11.

[12] Herzberg et al., *op. cit.*

[13] For example, see Keith Davis, "Mutuality in Understanding of the Program Manager's Management Role," *IEEE Transactions on Engineering Management* (Dec., 1965), pp. 117–122.

something worthwhile and is needed and wanted. He feels that management and others are similarly contributing, so he accepts and respects their roles in the organization. Managers are seen as joint contributors rather than bosses.

The managerial orientation is toward teamwork which will provide an integration of all contributions. Management is more of an integrating power than a commanding power. The employee response to this situation is responsibility. He produces quality work not primarily because management tells him to do so or because the inspector will catch him if he does not, but because he feels inside himself the desire to do so for many reasons. The employee psychological result, therefore, is self-discipline. Feeling responsible, the employee disciplines himself for team performance in the same way that a football team member disciplines himself in training and in game performance.

In this kind of environment an employee normally should feel some degree of fulfillment and self-realization, although the amount will be modest in some situations. The result is job enthusiasm, because he finds in the job such Herzberg motivators as achievement, growth, intrinsic work fulfillment, and recognition. His morale will be measured by his commitment to his task and his team, because he will see these as instruments for his self-actualization.

Some Conclusions About Models of Organizational Behavior

The evolving nature of models of organizational behavior makes it evident that change is the normal condition of these models. As our understanding of human behavior increases or as new social conditions develop, our organizational behavior models are also likely to change. It is a grave mistake to assume

that one particular model is a "best" model which will endure for the long run. This mistake was made by some old-time managers about the autocratic model and by some humanists about the custodial model, with the result that they became psychologically locked into these models and had difficulty altering their practices when conditions demanded it. Eventually the supportive model may also fall to limited use; and as further progress is made, even the collegial model is likely to be surpassed. There is no permanently "one best model" of organizational behavior, because what is best depends upon what is known about human behavior in whatever environment and priority of objectives exist at a particular time.

A second conclusion is that the models of organizational behavior which have developed seem to be sequentially related to man's psychological hierarchy of needs. As society has climbed higher on the need hierarchy, new models of organizational behavior have been developed to serve the higher-order needs that became paramount at the time. If Maslow's need hierarchy is used for comparison, the custodial model of organizational behavior is seen as an effort to serve man's second-level security needs.[14] It moved one step above the autocratic model which was reasonably serving man's subsistence needs, but was not effectively meeting his needs for security. Similarly the supportive model is an effort to meet employees' higher-level needs, such as affiliation and esteem, which the custodial model was unable to serve. The collegial model moves even higher toward service of man's need for self-actualization.

A number of persons have assumed that emphasis on one model of organizational behavior was an automatic rejection of other models, but the comparison with man's need hierarchy *suggests that each model is built upon the accomplish-*

[14] A. H. Maslow, "A Theory of Human Motivation," *Psychological Review* (L. 1943), 370–396.

ments of the other. For example, adoption of a supportive approach does not mean abandonment of custodial practices which serve necessary employee security needs. What it does mean is that custodial practices are relegated to secondary emphasis, because employees have progressed up their need structure to a condition in which higher needs predominate. In other words, the supportive model is the appropriate model to use *because* subsistence and security needs are already reasonably met by a suitable power structure and security system. If a misdirected modern manager should abandon these basic organizational needs, the system would quickly revert to a quest for a workable power structure and security system in order to provide subsistence-maintenance needs for its people.

Each model of organizational behavior in a sense outmodes its predominance by gradually satisfying certain needs, thus opening up other needs which can be better served by a more advanced model. Thus each new model is built upon the success of its predecessor. The new model simply represents a more sophisticated way of maintaining earlier need satisfactions, while opening up the probability of satisfying still higher needs.

A third conclusion suggests that the present tendency toward more democratic models of organizational behavior will continue for the longer run. This tendency seems to be required by both the nature of technology and the nature of the need structure. Harbison and Myers, in a classical study of management throughout the industrial world, conclude that advancing industrialization leads to more advanced models of organizational behavior. Specifically, authoritarian management gives way to more constitutional and democratic-participative models of management. These developments are inherent in the system; that is, the more democratic models tend to be necessary in order to manage productively an advanced industrial system.[15] Slater and Bennis also conclude that more participative and democratic models of organizational behavior inherently develop with advancing industrialization. They believe that "democracy is inevitable," because it is the only system which can successfully cope with changing demands of contemporary civilization in both business and government.[16]

Both sets of authors accurately point out that in modern, complex organizations a top manager cannot be authoritarian in the traditional sense and remain efficient, because he cannot know all that is happening in his organization. He must depend on other centres of power nearer to operating problems. In addition, educated workers are not readily motivated toward creative and intellectual duties by traditional authoritarian orders. They require higher-order need satisfactions which newer models of organizational behavior provide. Thus there does appear to be some inherent necessity for more democratic forms of organization in advanced industrial systems.

A fourth and final conclusion is that, though one model may predominate as most appropriate for general use at any point in industrial history, some appropriate uses will remain for other models. Knowledge of human behavior and skills in applying that knowledge will vary among managers. Role expectations of employees will differ depending upon cultural history. Policies and ways of life

---

[15] Frederick Harbison and Charles A. Myers, *Management in the Industrial World: An International Analysis* (New York: McGraw-Hill, 1959), pp. 40–67. The authors also state on page 47, "The design of systems of authority is equally as important in the modern world as the development of technology."

[16] Philip E. Slater and Warren G. Bennis, "Democracy Is Inevitable," *Harvard Business Review* (March–April, 1964), pp. 51–59.

will vary among organizations. Perhaps more important, task conditions will vary. Some jobs may require routine, low-skilled, highly programmed work which will be mostly determined by higher authority and provide mostly material rewards and security (autocratic and custodial conditions). Other jobs will be unprogrammed and intellectual, requiring teamwork and self-motivation, and responding best to supportive and collegial conditions. This use of different management practices with people according to the task they are performing is called "management according to task" by Leavitt.[17]

In the final analysis, each manager's behavior will be determined by his underlying theory of organizational behavior, so it is essential for him to understand the different results achieved by different models of organizational behavior. The models used will vary with the total human and task conditions surrounding the work. The long-run tendency will be toward more supportive and collegial models because they better serve the higher-level needs of employees.

QUESTIONS

1. Show how the four models of organizational behavior discussed in the article seem to be sequentially related to man's psychological hierarchy of needs.
2. Why is it difficult in the modern, complex organization for a top executive to be authoritarian in the traditional sense?
3. For what types of situations is each style of management likely to be most prevalent?
4. From your personal work experience describe the model of organizational behavior you have encountered.
5. Why do you think there has been a tendency toward more democratic models?

---

[17] Harold J. Leavitt, "Management According to Task: Organizational Differentiation," *Management International* (1962), No. 1, pp. 13–22.

22.

One More Time: How Do You Motivate Employees?

FREDERICK HERZBERG

How many articles, books, speeches, and workshops have pleaded plaintively, "How do I get an employee to do what I want him to do?"

The psychology of motivation is tremendously complex, and what has been unraveled with any degree of assurance is small indeed. But the dismal ratio of knowledge to speculation has not dampened the enthusiasm for new forms of snake oil that are constantly coming on the market, many of them with academic testimonials. Doubtless this article will have no depressing impact on the market for snake oil, but since the ideas expressed in it have been tested in many corporations and other organizations, it will help —I hope—to redress the imbalance in the aforementioned ratio.

Motivating with KITA

In lectures to industry on the problem, I have found that the audiences are anxious for quick and practical answers, so will begin with a straightforward, practi cal formula for moving people.

What is the simplest, surest, and mos direct way of getting someone to do some thing? Ask him? But if he responds tha he does not want to do it, then that call for a psychological consultation to deter mine the reason for his obstinacy. Tel him? His response shows that he doe not understand you, and now an exper in communication methods has to be brought in to show you how to ge through to him. Give him a monetary in centive? I do not need to remind the reader of the complexity and difficulty involved in setting up and administering an incentive system. Show him? Thi means a costly training program. We need a simple way.

Every audience contains the "direct ac tion" manager who shouts, "Kick him!" And this type of manager is right. The surest and least circumlocuted way of get

Reprinted from the *Harvard Business Review*, Vol. 46, No. 1 (January–February 1968) pp. 53–62, by permission of the publisher. © 1968 by the President and Fellows of Harvard College; all rights reserved.

Frederick Herzberg is Professor of Management, University of Utah.

ting someone to do something is to kick him in the pants—give him what might be called the KITA.

There are various forms of KITA, and here are some of them:

Negative Physical KITA. This is a literal application of the term and was frequently used in the past. It has, however, three major drawbacks: (1) it is inelegant; (2) it contradicts the precious image of benevolence that most organizations cherish; and (3) since it is a physical attack, it directly stimulates the autonomic nervous system, and this often results in negative feedback—the employee may just kick you in return. These factors give rise to certain taboos against negative physical KITA.

The psychologist has come to the rescue of those who are no longer permitted to use negative physical KITA. He has uncovered infinite sources of psychological vulnerabilities and the appropriate methods to play tunes on them. "He took my rug away"; "I wonder what he meant by that"; "The boss is always going around me"—these symptomatic expressions of ego sores that have been rubbed raw are the result of application of:

Negative Psychological KITA. This has several advantages over negative physical KITA. First, the cruelty is not visible; the bleeding is internal and comes much later. Second, since it affects the higher cortical centers of the brain with its inhibitory powers, it reduces the possibility of physical backlash. Third, since the number of psychological pains that a person can feel is almost infinite, the direction and site possibilities of the KITA are increased many times. Fourth, the person administering the kick can manage to be above it all and let the system accomplish the dirty work. Fifth, those who practice it receive some ego satisfaction (one-upmanship), whereas they would find drawing blood abhorrent. Finally, if the employee does

complain, he can always be accused of being paranoid, since there is no tangible evidence of an actual attack.

Now, what does negative KITA accomplish? If I kick you in the rear (physically or psychologically), who is motivated? *I* am motivated; *you* move! Negative KITA does not lead to motivation, but to movement. So:

Positive KITA. Let us consider motivation. If I say to you, "Do this for me or the company, and in return I will give you a reward, an incentive, more status, a promotion, all the quid pro quos that exist in the industrial organization," am I motivating you? The overwhelming opinion I receive from management people is, "Yes this is motivation."

I have a year-old Schnauzer. When it was a small puppy and I wanted it to move, I kicked it in the rear and it moved. Now that I have finished its obedience training, I hold up a dog biscuit when I want the Schnauzer to move. In this instance, who is motivated—I or the dog? The dog wants the biscuit, but it is I who want it to move. Again, I am the one who is motivated, and the dog is the one who moves. In this instance all I did was apply KITA frontally; I exerted a pull instead of a push. When industry wishes to use such positive KITAs, it has available an incredible number and variety of dog biscuits (jelly beans for humans) to wave in front of the employee to get him to jump.

Why is it that managerial audiences are quick to see that negative KITA is *not* motivation, while they are almost unanimous in their judgment that positive KITA *is* motivation? It is because negative KITA is rape, and positive KITA is seduction. But it is infinitely worse to be seduced than to be raped; the latter is an unfortunate occurrence, while the former signifies that you were a party to your own downfall. This is why positive KITA is so popular: it is a tradition; it is in the

American way. The organization does not have to kick you; you kick yourself.

MYTHS ABOUT MOTIVATION

Why is KITA not motivation? If I kick my dog (from the front or the back), he will move. And when I want him to move again, what must I do? I must kick him again. Similarly, I can charge a man's battery, and then recharge it, and recharge it again. But it is only when he has his own generator that we can talk about motivation. He then needs no outside stimulation. He *wants* to do it.

With this in mind, we can review some positive KITA personnel practices that were developed as attempts to instill "motivation":

1. *Reducing Time Spent at Work.* This represents a marvelous way of motivating people to work—getting them off the job! We have reduced (formally and informally) the time spent on the job over the last 50 or 60 years until we are finally on the way to the "6½-day weekend." An interesting variant of this approach is the development of off-hour recreation programs. The philosophy here seems to be that those who play together, work together. The fact is that motivated people seek more hours of work, not fewer.

2. *Spiraling Wages.* Have these motivated people? Yes, to seek the next wage increase. Some medievalists still can be heard to say that a good depression will get employees moving. They feel that if rising wages don't or won't do the job, perhaps reducing them will.

3. *Fringe Benefits.* Industry has outdone the most welfare-minded of welfare states in dispensing cradle-to-the-grave succor. One company I know of had an informal "fringe benefit of the month club" going for a while. The cost of fringe benefits in this country has reached approximately 25 per cent of the wage dollar, and we still cry for motivation. People spend less time working for

more money and more security than ever before, and the trend cannot be reversed. These benefits are no longer rewards; they are rights. A 6-day week is inhuman, a 10-hour day is exploitation, extended medical coverage is a basic decency, and stock options are the salvation of American initiative. Unless the ante is continuously raised, the psychological reaction of employees is that the company is turning back the clock.

When industry began to realize that both the economic nerve and the lazy nerve of their employees had insatiable appetites, it started to listen to the behavioral scientists who, more out of a humanist tradition than from scientific study, criticized management for not knowing how to deal with people. The next KITA easily followed.

4. *Human Relations Training.* Over 30 years of teaching and, in many instances, of practicing psychological approaches to handling people have resulted in costly human relations programs and, in the end, the same question: How do you motivate workers? Here, too, escalations have taken place. Thirty years ago it was necessary to request, "Please don't spit on the floor." Today the same admonition requires three "please"s before the employee feels that his superior has demonstrated the psychologically proper attitudes toward him.

The failure of human relations training to produce motivation led to the conclusion that the supervisor or manager himself was not psychologically true to himself in his practice of interpersonal decency. So an advanced form of human relations KITA, sensitivity training, was unfolded.

5. *Sensitivity Training.* Do you really, really understand yourself? Do you really, really, really trust the other man? Do you really, really, really, really cooperate? The failure of sensitivity training is now being explained, by those who have be-

come opportunistic exploiters of the technique, as a failure to really (five times) conduct proper sensitivity training courses.

With the realization that there are only temporary gains from comfort and economic and interpersonal KITA, personnel managers concluded that the fault lay not in what they were doing, but in the employee's failure to appreciate what they were doing. This opened up the field of communications, a whole new area of "scientifically" sanctioned KITA.

6. *Communications.* The professor of communications was invited to join the faculty of management training programs and help in making employees understand what management was doing for them. House organs, briefing sessions, supervisory instruction on the importance of communication, and all sorts of propaganda have proliferated until today there is even an International Council of Industrial Editors. But no motivation resulted, and the obvious thought occurred that perhaps management was not hearing what the employees were saying. That led to the next KITA.

7. *Two-Way Communication.* Management ordered morale surveys, suggestion plans, and group participation programs. Then both employees and management were communicating and listening to each other more than ever, but without much improvement in motivation.

The behavioral scientists began to take another look at their conceptions and their data, and they took human relations one step further. A glimmer of truth was beginning to show through in the writings of the so-called higher-order-need psychologists. People, so they said, want to actualize themselves. Unfortunately, the "actualizing" psychologists got mixed up with the human relations psychologists, and a new KITA emerged.

8. *Job Participation.* Though it may not have been the theoretical intention,

job participation often became a "give them the big picture" approach. For example, if a man is tightening 10,000 nuts a day on an assembly line with a torque wrench, tell him he is building a Chevrolet. Another approach had the goal of giving the employee a *feeling* that he is determining, in some measure, what he does on his job. The goal was to provide a *sense* of achievement rather than a substantive achievement in his task. Real achievement, of course, requires a task that makes it possible.

But still there was no motivation. This led to the inevitable conclusion that the employees must be sick, and therefore to the next KITA.

9. *Employee Counseling.* The initial use of this form of KITA in a systematic fashion can be credited to the Hawthorne experiment of the Western Electric Company during the early 1930's. At that time, it was found that the employees harbored irrational feelings that were interfering with the rational operation of the factory. Counseling in this instance was a means of letting the employees unburden themselves by talking to someone about their problems. Although the counseling techniques were primitive, the program was large indeed.

The counseling approach suffered as a result of experiences during World War II, when the programs themselves were found to be interfering with the operation of the organizations; the counselors had forgotten their role of benevolent listeners and were attempting to do something about the problems that they heard about. Psychological counseling, however, has managed to survive the negative impact of World War II experiences and today is beginning to flourish with renewed sophistication. But, alas, many of these programs, like all the others, do not seem to have lessened the pressure of demands to find out how to motivate workers.

Since KITA results only in short-term

movement, it is safe to predict that the cost of these programs will increase steadily and new varieties will be developed as old positive KITAs reach their satiation points.

Hygiene vs. Motivators

Let me rephrase the perennial question this way: How do you install a generator in an employee? A brief review of my motivation-hygiene theory of job attitudes is required before theoretical and practical suggestions can be offered. The theory was first drawn from an examination of events in the lives of engineers and accountants. At least 16 other investigations, using a wide variety of populations (including some in the Communist countries), have since been completed, making the original research one of the most replicated studies in the field of job attitudes.

The findings of these studies, along with corroboration from many other investigations using different procedures, suggest that the factors involved in producing job satisfaction (and motivation) are separate and distinct from the factors that lead to job dissatisfaction. Since separate factors need to be considered, depending on whether job satisfaction or job dissatisfaction is being examined, it follows that these two feelings are not opposites of each other. The opposite of job satisfaction is not job dissatisfaction but, rather, *no* job satisfaction; and, similarly, the opposite of job dissatisfaction is not job satisfaction, but *no* job dissatisfaction.

Stating the concept presents a problem in semantics, for we normally think of satisfaction and dissatisfaction as opposites—i.e., what is not satisfying must be dissatisfying, and vice versa. But when it comes to understanding the behavior of people in their jobs, more than a play on words is involved.

Two different needs of man are involved here. One set of needs can be thought of as stemming from his animal nature—the built-in drive to avoid pain from the environment, plus all the learned drives which become conditioned to the basic biological needs. For example, hunger, a basic biological drive, makes it necessary to earn money, and then money becomes a specific drive. The other set of needs relates to that unique human characteristic, the ability to achieve and, through achievement, to experience psychological growth. The stimuli for the growth needs are tasks that induce growth; in the industrial setting, they are the *job content*. Contrariwise, the stimuli inducing pain-avoidance behavior are found in the *job environment*.

The growth or *motivator* factors that are intrinsic to the job are: achievement, recognition for achievement, the work itself, responsibility, and growth or advancement. The dissatisfaction-avoidance or *hygiene* (KITA) factors that are extrinsic to the job include: company policy and administration, supervision, interpersonal relationships, working conditions, salary, status and security.

A composite of the factors that are involved in causing job satisfaction and job dissatisfaction, drawn from samples of 1,685 employees, is shown in Exhibit 1. The results indicate that motivators were the primary cause of satisfaction, and hygiene factors the primary cause of unhappiness on the job. The employees, studied in 12 different investigations, included lower-level supervisors, professional women, agricultural administrators, men about to retire from management positions, hospital maintenance personnel, manufacturing supervisors, nurses, food handlers, military officers, engineers, scientists, housekeepers, teachers, technicians, female assemblers, accountants, Finnish foremen, and Hungarian engineers.

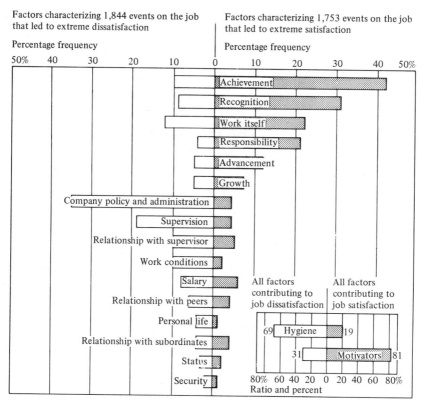

EXHIBIT 1   Factors affecting job attitudes, as reported in 12 investigations.

They were asked what job events had occurred in their work that had led to extreme satisfaction or extreme dissatisfaction on their part. Their responses are broken down in the exhibit into percentages of total "positive" job events and of total "negative" job events. (The figures total more than 100 per cent on both the "hygiene" and "motivators" sides because often at least two factors can be attributed to a single event; advancement, for instance, often accompanies assumption of responsibility.)

To illustrate, a typical response involving achievement that had a negative effect for the employee was, "I was unhappy because I didn't do the job successfully." A typical response in the small number of positive job events in the Com-

pany Policy and Administration grouping was, "I was happy because the company reorganized the section so that I didn't report any longer to the guy I didn't get along with."

As the lower right-hand part of the exhibit shows, of all the factors contributing to job satisfaction, 81 per cent were motivators. And of all the factors contributing to the employees' dissatisfaction over their work, 69 per cent involved hygiene elements.

ETERNAL TRIANGLE

There are three general philosophies of personnel management. The first is based on organizational theory, the second on industrial engineering, and the third on behavioral science.

The organizational theorist believes that human needs are either so irrational or so varied and adjustable to specific situations that the major function of personnel management is to be as pragmatic as the occasion demands. If jobs are organized in a proper manner, he reasons the result will be the most efficient job structure, and the most favorable job attitudes will follow as a matter of course.

The industrial engineer holds that man is mechanistically oriented and economically motivated and his needs are best met by attuning the individual to the most efficient work process. The goal of personnel management therefore should be to concoct the most appropriate incentive system and to design the specific working conditions in a way that facilitates the most efficient use of the human machine. By structuring jobs in a manner that leads to the most efficient operation, the engineer believes that he can obtain the optimal organization of work and the proper work attitudes.

The behavioral scientist focuses on group sentiments, attitudes of individual employees, and the organization's social and psychological climate. According to his persuasion, he emphasizes one or more of the various hygiene and motivator needs. His approach to personnel management generally emphasizes some form of human relations education, in the hope of instilling healthy employee attitudes and an organizational climate which he considers to be felicitous to human values. He believes that proper attitudes will lead to efficient job and organizational structure.

There is always a lively debate as to the over-all effectiveness of the approaches of the organizational theorist and the industrial engineer. Manifestly they have achieved much. But the nagging question for the behavioral scientist has been: What is the cost in human problems that eventually cause more expense to the organization—for instance, turnover, absenteeism, errors, violation of safety rules, strikes, restriction of output, higher wages, and greater fringe benefits? On the other hand, the behavioral scientist is hard put to document much manifest improvement in personnel management, using his approach.

The three philosophies can be depicted as a triangle, as is done in Exhibit 2, with each persuasion claiming the apex angle. The motivation-hygiene theory claims the same angle as industrial engineering, but for opposite goals. Rather than rationalizing the work to increase efficiency, the theory suggests that work be *enriched* to bring about effective utilization of personnel. Such a systematic attempt to motivate employees by manipulating the motivator factors is just beginning.

The term *job enrichment* describes this embryonic movement. An older term, job enlargement, should be avoided because it is associated with past failures stemming from a misunderstanding of the problem. Job enrichment provides the opportunity for the employee's psychological growth, while job enlargement merely makes a job structurally bigger. Since scientific job enrichment is very new, this article only suggests the principles and practical steps that have recently emerged from several successful experiments in industry.

JOB LOADING

In attempting to enrich an employee's job, management often succeeds in reducing the man's personal contribution, rather than giving him an opportunity for growth in his accustomed job. Such an endeavor, which I shall call horizontal job loading (as opposed to vertical loading, or providing motivator factors), has been the problem of earlier job enlargement programs. This activity merely enlarges the meaninglessness of the job. Some examples of this approach, and their effect, are:

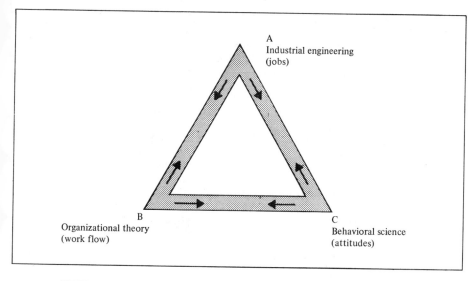

A
Industrial engineering
(jobs)

B
Organizational theory
(work flow)

C
Behavioral science
(attitudes)

EXHIBIT 2   "Triangle" of philosophies of personnel management.

- Challenging the employee by increasing the amount of production expected of him. If he tightens 10,000 bolts a day, see if he can tighten 20,000 bolts a day. The arithmetic involved shows that multiplying zero by zero still equals zero.
- Adding another meaningless task to the existing one, usually some routine clerical activity. The arithmetic here is adding zero to zero.
- Rotating the assignments of a number of jobs that need to be enriched. This means washing dishes for a while, then washing silverware. The arithmetic is substituting one zero for another zero.
- Removing the most difficult parts of the assignment in order to free the worker to accomplish more of the less challenging assignments. This traditional industrial engineering approach amounts to subtraction in the hope of accomplishing addition.

These are common forms of horizontal loading that frequently come up in preliminary brainstorming sessions on job enrichment. The principles of vertical loading have not all been worked out as yet, and they remain rather general, but I have furnished seven useful starting points for consideration in Exhibit 3.

A SUCCESSFUL APPLICATION

An example from a highly successful job enrichment experiment can illustrate the distinction between horizontal and vertical loading of a job. The subjects of this study were the stockholder correspondents employed by a very large corporation. Seemingly, the task required of these carefully selected and highly trained correspondents was quite complex and challenging. But almost all indexes of performance and job attitudes were low, and exit interviewing confirmed that the challenge of the job existed merely as words.

A job enrichment project was initiated in the form of an experiment with one group, designated as an achieving unit, having its job enriched by the principles described in Exhibit 3. A control group continued to do its job in the traditional way. (There were also two "uncommitted" groups of correspondents formed to measure the so-called Hawthorne Effect —that is, to gauge whether productivity and attitudes toward the job changed artificially merely because employees sensed that the company was paying more at-

PRINCIPLE	MOTIVATORS INVOLVED
A. Removing some controls while retaining accountability	Responsibility and personal achievement
B. Increasing the accountability of individuals for own work	Responsibility and recognition
C. Giving a person a complete natural unit of work (module, division, area, and so on)	Responsibility, achievement, and recognition
D. Granting additional authority to an employee in his activity; job freedom	Responsibility, achievement, and recognition
E. Making periodic reports directly available to the worker himself rather than to the supervisor	Internal recognition
F. Introducing new and more difficult tasks not previously handled	Growth and learning
G. Assigning individuals specific or specialized tasks, enabling them to become experts	Responsibility, growth, and advancement

EXHIBIT 3   Principles of vertical job loading.

tention to them in doing something different or novel. The results for these groups were substantially the same as for the control group, and for the sake of simplicity I do not deal with them in this summary.) No changes in hygiene were introduced for either group other than those that would have been made anyway, such as normal pay increases.

The changes for the achieving unit were introduced in the first two months, averaging one per week of the seven motivators listed in Exhibit 3. At the end of six months the members of the achieving unit were found to be outperforming their counterparts in the control group, and in addition indicated a marked increase in their liking for their jobs. Other results showed that the achieving group had lower absenteeism and, subsequently, a much higher rate of promotion.

Exhibit 4 illustrates the changes in performance, measured in February and March, before the study period began, and at the end of each month of the study period. The shareholder service index represents quality of letters, including accuracy of information, and speed of response to stockholders' letters of inquiry. The index of a current month was averaged into the average of the two prior months, which means that improvement was harder to obtain if the indexes of the previous months were low. The "achievers" were performing less well before the six-month period started, and their performance service index continued to decline after the introduction of the motivators, evidently because of uncertainty over their newly granted responsibilities. In the third month, however, performance improved, and soon the members of this

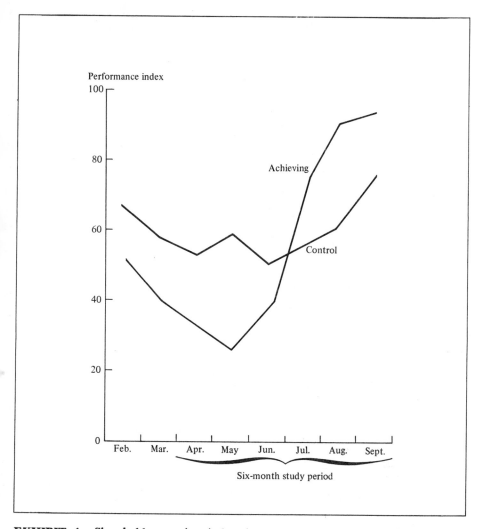

EXHIBIT 4 Shareholder service index in company experiment. [Three-month cumulative average.]

group had reached a high level of accomplishment.

Exhibit 5 shows the two groups' attitudes toward their job, measured at the end of March, just before the first motivator was introduced, and again at the end of September. The correspondents were asked 16 questions, all involving motivation. A typical one was, "As you see it, how many opportunities do you feel that you have in your job for making worth-while contributions?" The answers were scaled from 1 to 5, with 80 as the maximum possible score. The achievers became much more positive about their job, while the attitude of the control unit remained about the same (the drop is not statistically significant).

How was the job of these correspondents restructured? Exhibit 6 lists the suggestions made that were deemed to be horizontal loading, and the actual vertical

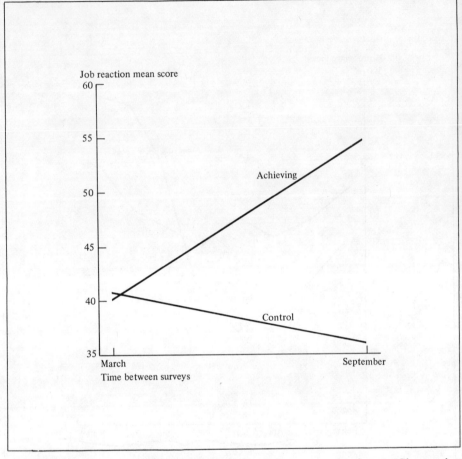

Job reaction mean score

EXHIBIT 5   Changes in attitudes toward tasks in company experiment. [Changes in mean scores over six-month period.]

loading changes that were incorporated in the job of the achieving unit. The capital letters under "Principle" after "Vertical loading" refer to the corresponding letters in Exhibit 3. The reader will note that the rejected forms of horizontal loading correspond closely to the list of common manifestations of the phenomenon on page 247.

Steps to Job Enrichment

Now that the motivator idea has been described in practice, here are the steps that managers should take in instituting the principle with their employees:

1. Select those jobs in which (a) the investment in industrial engineering does not make changes too costly, (b) attitudes are poor, (c) hygiene is becoming very costly, and (d) motivation will make a difference in performance.

2. Approach these jobs with the conviction that they can be changed. Years of tradition have led managers to believe that the content of the jobs is sacrosanct and the only scope of action that they have is in ways of stimulating people.

Horizontal Loading Suggestions (Rejected)	Vertical Loading Suggestions (Adopted)	Principle
Firm quotas could be set for letters to be answered each day, using a rate which would be hard to reach.	Subject matter experts were appointed within each unit for other members of the unit to consult with before seeking supervisory help. (The supervisor had been answering all specialized and difficult questions.)	G
The women could type the letters themselves, as well as compose them, or take on any other clerical functions.	Correspondents signed their own names on letters. (The supervisor had been signing all letters.)	B
All difficult or complex inquiries could be channeled to a few women so that the remainder could achieve high rates of output. These jobs could be exchanged from time to time.	The work of the more experienced correspondents was proofread less frequently by supervisors and was done at the correspondents' desks, dropping verification from 100% to 10%. (Previously, all correspondents' letters had been checked by the supervisor.)	A
The women could be rotated through units handling different customers, and then sent back to their own units.	Production was discussed, but only in terms such as "a full day's work is expected." As time went on, this was no longer mentioned. (Before, the group had been constantly reminded of the number of letters that needed to be answered.)	D
	Outgoing mail went directly to the mailroom without going over supervisors' desks. (The letters had always been routed through the supervisors.)	A
	Correspondents were encouraged to answer letters in a more personalized way. (Reliance on the form-letter approach had been standard practice.)	C
	Each correspondent was held personally responsible for the quality and accuracy of letters. (This responsibility had been the province of the supervisor and the verifier.)	B, E

EXHIBIT 6 Enlargement vs. enrichment of correspondents' task in company experiment.

3. Brainstorm a list of changes that may enrich the jobs, without concern for their practicality.

4. Screen the list to eliminate suggestions that involve hygiene, rather than actual motivation.

5. Screen the list for generalities, such as "give them more responsibility," that are rarely followed in practice. This might seem obvious, but the motivator words have never left industry; the substance has just been rationalized and organized out. Words like "responsibility," "growth," "achievement," and "challenge," for example, have been elevated to the lyrics of the patriotic anthem for all organizations. It is the old problem typified by the pledge of allegiance to the flag being more important than contributions to the country—of following the form, rather than the substance.

6. Screen the list to eliminate any *horizontal* loading suggestions.

7. Avoid direct participation by the employees whose jobs are to be enriched. Ideas they have expressed previously certainly constitute a valuable source for recommended changes, but their direct involvement contaminates the process with human relations *hygiene* and, more specifically, gives them only a *sense* of making a contribution. The job is to be changed, and it is the content that will produce the motivation, not attitudes about being involved or the challenge inherent in setting up a job. That process will be over shortly, and it is what the employees will be doing from then on that will determine their motivation. A sense of participation will result only in short-term movement.

8. In the initial attempts at job enrichment, set up a controlled experiment. At least two equivalent groups should be chosen, one an experimental unit in which the motivators are systematically introduced over a period of time, and the other one a control group in which no changes are made. For both groups, hygiene should be allowed to follow its natural course for the duration of the experiment. Pre- and post-installation tests of performance and job attitudes are necessary to evaluate the effectiveness of the job enrichment program. The attitude test must be limited to motivator items in order to divorce the employee's view of the job he is given from all the surrounding hygiene feelings that he might have.

9. Be prepared for a drop in performance in the experimental group the first few weeks. The changeover to a new job may lead to a temporary reduction in efficiency.

10. Expect your first-line supervisors to experience some anxiety and hostility over the changes you are making. The anxiety comes from their fear that the changes will result in poorer performance for their unit. Hostility will arise when the employees start assuming what the supervisors regard as their own responsibility for performance. The supervisor without checking duties to perform may then be left with little to do.

After a successful experiment, however, the supervisor usually discovers the supervisory and managerial functions he has neglected, or which were never his because all his time was given over to checking the work of his subordinates. For example, in the R&D division of one large chemical company I know of, the supervisors of the laboratory assistants were theoretically responsible for their training and evaluation. These functions, however, had come to be performed in a routine, unsubstantial fashion. After the job enrichment program, during which the supervisors were not merely passive observers of the assistants' performance, the supervisors actually were devoting their time to reviewing performance and administering thorough training.

What has been called an employee-centered style of supervision will come about not through education of supervisors, but by changing the jobs that they do.

Concluding Note

Job enrichment will not be a one-time proposition, but a continuous management function. The initial changes, however, should last for a very long period of time. There are a number of reasons for this:

• The changes should bring the job up to the level of challenge commensurate with the skill that was hired.
• Those who have still more ability eventually will be able to demonstrate it better and win promotion to higher-level jobs.
• The very nature of motivators, as opposed to hygiene factors, is that they have a much longer-term effect on employees'

attitudes. Perhaps the job will have to be enriched again, but this will not occur as frequently as the need for hygiene.

Not all jobs can be enriched, nor do all jobs need to be enriched. If only a small percentage of the time and money that is now devoted to hygiene, however, were given to job enrichment efforts, the return in human satisfaction and economic gain would be one of the largest dividends that industry and society have ever reaped through their efforts at better personnel management.

The argument for job enrichment can be summed up quite simply: If you have someone on a job, use him. If you can't use him on the job, get rid of him, either via automation or by selecting someone with lesser ability. If you can't use him and you can't get rid of him, you will have a motivation problem.

QUESTIONS

1. According to Frederick Herzberg, what is the difference between "movement" of an individual and motivation?
2. Considering your own experiences and observations of others, how do you regard the findings on job attitudes shown in Exhibit 1?
3. Distinguish between hygienic factors and motivators.
4. How does job enrichment apply motivational principles?
5. Do you agree with Herzberg that employees should not be involved in the redesign of their own jobs?

23.

Money As a Motivator: Some Research Insights

DAVID C. McCLELLAND

For nearly half a century, industrial psychologists have been demonstrating that money isn't nearly so potent a motivating force as theory and common sense suggest it ought to be. Elton Mayo's 1922 study of work output in a Philadelphia textile mill set the tone of what was to follow. Management had found that incentive payment schemes had not succeeded in increasing work or decreasing turnover in a department where the jobs were particularly monotonous and fatiguing. Mayo found, on the other hand, that allowing the men to schedule the work for themselves brought dramatic increases in productivity. Where money incentives hadn't proven effective, psychic rewards worked.[1]

Over and over again, later students[2] of industrial psychology emphasized the same point. Money isn't everything. Its meaning is in the eye of the beholder. It functions only as a symbol representing more important psychological factors in the work situation.

Why, then, in spite of all the evidence, do people still take money so seriously as a motivator? In the first place, money obviously is very important: Work, unless it is volunteer or "play," involves a contract between two parties "guaranteed" by the payment of money. The pay may symbolize the psychological realities of the contract imperfectly—which may be all the psychologists are saying. The employee may think he is working for it,

Reprinted from *The McKinsey Quarterly* (Fall 1967), pp. 10–21, by permission of the publisher and author.

David C. McClelland is Professor of Psychology, Department of Social Relations, Harvard University.

[1] Cf. S. W. Gellerman, *Motivation and Productivity*, American Management Association, New York, 1963.

[2] Cf. R. Likert, "A Motivational Approach to a Modified Theory of Organization and Management" in *Modern Organization Theory* (M. Haire, ed.), John Wiley & Sons, New York, 1959; F. Herzberg, B. Mausner, & B. Snyderman, *The Motivation to Work* (2nd ed.), John Wiley & Sons, New York, 1959; W. F. Whyte, *Money and Motivation*, Harper & Row, Publishers, New York, 1955; D. McGregor, *The Human Side of Enterprise*, McGraw-Hill, New York, 1960; for review of these studies see Gellerman, *op. cit.*

and the manager may think he is using it to get the employee to work, but both are only partly right. To understand the situation better, particularly if we wish to manage motivation or behavior, we must penetrate beyond the money itself and consider what it really represents to employer and employee.

Money Misconceptions

But it is not just man's tendency to confuse symbols with realities that leads him to talk as if money were an end in itself. There are at least three other reasons why he does so. In the first place, no idea is more deeply entrenched in contemporary American psychology than the notion that in the end all learning is based on a few simple material rewards. I suspect practically all top managers today learned in Psychology I that there are so-called primary material rewards, such as food and water, and that all other rewards are "secondary," getting their "motivating value" from learned associations with the primaries. Money obviously falls into the secondary category.

This notion involves some major misconceptions, and there is no good reason why it should continue to shape the thinking of men who are interested in managing motivation. But it has persisted because of its appealing simplicity, and because the alternatives to it are hard to formulate so neatly.

Let me, however, illustrate one of these alternative approaches by a quick analogy. Think of what goes on in a man's mind as if it were a computer printout of a lot of miscellaneous material. In commonsense terms, a lot of thoughts buzz through a man's head during any given time. As anyone who has tried to do content analysis of computer printouts knows, the periods or other punctuation marks are of key importance. That is, if you are to search and simplify what is otherwise a bewildering mass of material, it is first necessary to break it up into units within which co-occurrences can be noted.

In real life, rewards or incentives are like punctuation marks. They break up sequences or call attention to them. In psychological terms, they are attention-getting, affect-producing mechanisms, rather than substitutes for something else. As such they are of tremendous importance in producing organization or order in thought and action. Note, however, that they are only one possible type of attention-getting mechanism. Bright lights and colors, changes in rest periods, reorganizations of work flow—all sorts of things—can also get attention.

In short, rather than being some kind of a substitute for simpler material rewards, money is more sensibly regarded as *one of a class* of attention-getters. And, like other members of its class, it can lose its attention-getting power with repetition.[3]

A second reason why managers go on thinking that money is a prime motivator is that most of them are highly achievement-oriented; in the psychologist's terms, they are "high in *n* Ach." (See editor's note, p. 263.) We know that such men attach special significance to money rewards. They are strong believers in steeply increasing financial rewards for greater accomplishment. Because they themselves are particularly interested in some concrete measure that will sensitively reflect how well they have done, it is easy and natural for them to mistake this idea for a related one—namely, that the more money you offer someone the harder he will work.

Obviously, believing in more pay for more work is simply not the same as say-

[3] See J. Kagan, "On the Need for Relativism," *American Psychologist,* 1967, pp. 22, 131–142.

ing that more pay will lead *to* more work. But the fallacy in this reasoning is not only logical but psychological, for other experimental evidence shows that even men who score high in *n* Ach are not themselves spurred to greater efforts by money incentives. While they attribute greater importance to money as a motivator, it doesn't motivate *them* to work harder.

The apparent explanation: They seek financial reward, not for its own sake, but because it tells them how well they are doing. As Saul Gellerman has pointed out, the incentive value of top executive salaries must lie primarily in their "merit badge" quality, since high taxes result in rather minor differences in take-home pay at this level of compensation. So managers believe money is important in motivating others because they mistakenly think it motivates themselves. Actually, while it *is* more important to them as a measure of accomplishment, it doesn't really motivate them. And it doesn't motivate others either, except indirectly—as workers and others are ready to point out whenever they are asked.

Finally, the third reason why managers keep coming back to money as a way of motivating people is because at the practical level it is the one thing they can manipulate rather easily. After all, it is part of their job to motivate the people working for them, to get more work out of people, or at the very least to make sure that people aren't loafing. The higher their achievement motivation, the more they will want to show an improvement in the quality or quantity of the work done by their people. They may listen patiently to the psychologist and sociologists who seek to convince them that money isn't important for its own sake, but then what can they do to change those other psychological factors which are sup-

posedly more important? Payment plans are real and manipulable. Plans for dealing with psychological factors often seem nebulous.

What, then, does all this add up to? Are we left with the conclusion that the nature of incentive plans makes no difference at all? Hardly. It is one thing to say that psychological factors will modify how incentive plans work; it is quite another to conclude that variations in incentive plans do not make any difference.

What we need is a change in orientation. The problem is managing motivation —not managing work, but managing the *desire* of men to work. This means seeing incentive plans as a particular means of achieving specific objectives within the larger framework of the work situation.

The Work Variables

It has recently been shown[4] that a work situation involves four sets of variables which must be accurately diagnosed before a "prescription" can be written for improvement:

1. The motives and needs of the persons working at the task.
2. The motivational requirements of the task they have to perform.
3. The motives (or strengths and limitations) of the manager.
4. The organizational climate.

Once a manager knows where he stands on these variables in a particular work situation, he is in a position to do various things. For example, if he finds that most of his workers are strongly achievement-oriented, while the tasks to be performed are assembly-line work that doesn't satisfy this motivation, he has an obvious mismatch. To bring the interests of the people into line with the motivational requirements of the job, he can get

---

[4] G. H. Litwin and R. A. Stringer, *Motivation and Organization Climate*, Harvard University Press, Cambridge, Mass., 1967.

a different type of worker or change the nature of the task.

Our focus here, however, is narrower: Given different settings on these four types of variables, how can management use payment plans to help motivate men? Obviously, there can be no simple sovereign payment system that will work best for all people under all conditions. But we can give illustrations.

Variations in the Motives of Workers. Whether workers or managers are high or low in achievement motivation makes a real difference in the effectiveness of financial incentives. Several studies have shown that offering additional financial rewards for doing a task does not make strongly achievement-oriented people work harder or better.[5] A group of aggressive, achievement-minded salesmen would certainly be angry if their extra efforts were not recognized with a much greater financial reward; yet offering them bonuses is not what produces the extra effort. This may seem like a psychological distinction without a difference, but the interpretation of the meaning of the bonus plan genuinely affects performance, as a later example will show.

People with relatively low achievement motivation, on the other hand, *will* work harder for increased financial rewards. It is not the task itself that interests them, however, nor does the money they get by doing it interest them primarily as a measure of accomplishment. Rather, it has other values for them.

Two consequences flow from this simple fact. First, if there is any way to get the reward without doing the work, they will naturally tend to look for it. This means that managers who rely primarily

on money to activate people who are low in achievement motivation will have a much harder job of policing the work situation than they would if the work satisfied certain other motivational needs. This conclusion will hardly come as news to managers who have been struggling with employee incentive plans over the past generation.

The second implication is that such employees will have to want something that the money can buy. Obviously, there are lots of important things that money *can't* buy: tolerable working conditions, friendship, and job security, to name a few. As a number of studies have shown, even the material possessions that most middle-class managers assume everyone wants, such as a home of one's own, are in fact not wanted by many of the people he is trying to motivate. It follows that if a manager must deal largely in financial incentives for these people, he will have to give some thought to creating psychological wants that money will satisfy— such as more education for children, a happier retirement, a more exciting (and expensive) vacation, etc.

But money can also have other values for people who are most strongly motivated by needs for social approval and solidarity with others in the work group. One study found, somewhat to the experimenters' surprise, that girls who scored high in *n* Affiliation (see editor's note, p. 263) actually worked harder for money prizes than girls who scored low on this factor, whereas there had been no difference between the two types of girls when the extra incentives were not offered.[6] Evidently the money helped to create a general expectancy on the girls'

[5] J. W. Atkinson and W. R. Reitman, "Performance As a Function of Motive Strength," *Journal of Abnormal and Social Psychology*, 1956, pp. 53, 361–366; J. W. Atkinson (ed.), *Motives in Fantasy, Action and Society*, D. Van Nostrand Co., Princeton, N. J., 1958; C. P. Smith, "The Influence of Testing Conditions on Need for Achievement Scores and Their Relationship to Performance Scores," in *A Theory of Achievement Motivation* (J. W. Atkinson and N. T. Feather, eds.), John Wiley & Sons, New York, 1966, pp. 277–297.
[6] Atkinson and Reitman, *op. cit.*

part that they should work hard to please the experimenters. The moral again is simple: For a working force that scores high on this factor, incentive plans and payments should be framed in terms of working together for the common good, not—as achievement-oriented managers nearly always assume—of working for one's own gain.

Finally, another study showed that college students who scored high in *n* Power (see editor's note, p. 263), spend more money on prestige supplies—expensive liquor, college insignia, powerful motorcycles or cars, etc.—in other words, on things which will make them feel or seem big, strong, powerful and respected.[7] If a manager finds his staff scores high in *n* Power, then, he ought to administer his financial incentives in different ways, perhaps even presenting some of them in the form of prestige supplies—such as a trip to Europe or a new Cadillac—for especially outstanding performance.

One simple lesson to be learned from all these studies is that the motivational characteristics of the staff make a lot of difference. Even with the cost of incentives held constant, their form and meaning have to be shaped to fit the needs of the people they are designed to influence.

Variations in the Motivational Requirements of Tasks. Researchers have suggested some simple measuring devices for the motivational requirements of different tasks.[8] For instance, the job of an assembly-line worker has more "affiliation" than "achievement" elements, because workers must interact with each other: Successful task accomplishment depends on the cooperation of co-workers, stable working relationships over time, etc. If this is so, how can incentive

plans help? Actually they are more likely to hinder, because most incentive plans are based on the assumption that all tasks primarily involve achievement. And in fact such plans usually make less than 10 per cent of the people into "rate-busters," while they make the rest of the work force angry because the extra incentives reinforce behavior which is in direct opposition to the affiliation requirements of the task.[9] Such "gung-ho" achievers often disrupt normal working patterns and lower average productivity over the long run.

Even at the sales level this can be true. While, generally speaking, successful salesmen are strongly achievement- and power-oriented and low in affiliation needs, at least one sales situation has been identified in which the very best salesmen scored only moderately high in achievement orientation, quite a bit higher in affiliation orientation than most salesmen, and lower in power orientation.[10] These particular salesmen were involved in a task which, in the researchers' words, required "a much greater emphasis on co-ordinating the efforts of the sales and service function, and on building long-term close customer relationships involving a high degree of trust, than on entrepreneurial selling." Here an incentive plan based on sales volume alone could easily attract the wrong men (those too high in *n* Ach) into sales, or influence existing salesmen to neglect the long-term consumer relationships that experience shows to be necessary for success in this job. Money payments have to fit not only the characteristics of the people in a work force, but also the nature of the jobs they have to perform.

Variation in the Motives of Managers.

[7] D. G. Winter, "Power Motivation in Thought and Action," unpublished Ph.D. thesis, Harvard University, 1967.

[8] Litwin and Stringer, *op. cit.*

[9] Whyte, *op. cit.*

[10] G. H. Litwin and J. A. Timmons, *Motivation and Organization Climate: A Study of Outstanding and Average Sales Offices*, Behavioral Sciences Center, Boston, Mass., 1966.

As we have seen, unless the manager understands his own motives, he may project them onto others. It is all too easy for a manager, in making plans for other people, to assume that they are like himself. But if he knows what *he* wants, he may be able to avoid falling into the trap. He may, for example, even be able to see when his own motivations are leading him to propose new ideas that have little chance of success. I have sometimes wondered how many personnel managers think up new incentive plans in order to convince *their* superiors that they are high achievers, deserving of a special bonus. Actually, a personnel man ought to be specially rewarded for picking and keeping outstanding men, but such day-to-day performance may be less promptly noticeable and rewardable than the installation of a brand-new incentive plan. Here again, the pay system may tend to distort the personnel job by treating and rewarding it as a straightforward achievement proposition.

Beyond such considerations, a manager must understand himself well enough to know what he can or should do in a given organizational situation. Thus he may discover that, while his staff is heavily affiliation-oriented and therefore wants and needs many signs of approval and friendship, he himself is rather aloof, priding himself that he got where he is today by not wasting time with "the boys." This kind of self-understanding should help him create the kind of climate that will make the incentive system work under a given set of conditions.

Variations in Climate. Two researchers, G. H. Litwin and R. A. Stringer, have identified some nine different dimensions on which organizational climates can vary.[11] They hypothesize that each of these variables has different effects on the organization. For example, a high degree of *structure* (rules, regulations, going through channels), reflecting an emphasis on power and control, should reduce affiliation and achievement needs among its employees, but at the same time make them more power-oriented. Similarly, a high degree of risk or challenge in the tasks to be performed should arouse achievement motivation but have little or no effect on workers' affiliation or power needs.

Consider how these climatic factors may operate when the incentive system is held constant. In one study[12] four outstanding sales offices were contrasted with four average sales offices, not only in terms of climate differences as perceived by the salesmen, but also in terms of actual observations of how managers interacted with their men during the day.

The incentive system in all offices was the same and men in the outstanding and the average offices were equally satisfied with it. Yet other climate variables apparently made for very different performance averages. The outstanding offices, as perceived by their salesmen, had more structure, evoked more identity and loyalty, and were warmer and friendlier. The salesmen from these outstanding offices also felt that higher standards were being set and that they were more often rewarded by the manager for their efforts than criticized for nonperformance. Their views were substantiated by observation of managers in the two types of offices. Those in the outstanding offices gave almost twice as much praise and encouragement as the managers from the average offices. To quote from the study.

the outstanding manager makes it a habit to compliment a man sincerely on a job well done; a personal thank-you is always given over the phone and in person. He might also drop the man a note of congratulation and thanks for a successful sale. He also typically

[11] Litwin and Stringer, *op. cit.*
[12] Litwin and Timmons, *op. cit.*

thanks the customer in the same manner and makes a real effort to visit the new installation with the salesman and compliment the salesman's efforts before the customer. In contrast, the average manager's attitude is that "these men are on very large commissions and that's what makes them hustle. They know they can go out on any day of the week and get a raise just by selling another piece of equipment. Oh, I *might* buy them a drink, but it's money that motivates these guys." [13]

Once again we see that nonfinancial, situational factors are important, but with a difference. Furthermore, we have a nice illustration of how too exclusive a concern for money can distract a manager's attention from other psychological variables that he ought to be taking into account.

Incentive Plan Variables

But it is no use repeating that everything depends on the way financial plans are perceived. If variations in the incentive plan really matter, we should be able to discover just what difference they make by investigating them while holding situational variables constant. Until such specific studies have been made, we cannot generalize very confidently about the important variables in the incentive plan itself. But on the basis of some theory and laboratory research it may be permissible to speculate about three of these variables: the probability of success (winning the incentive award), as perceived by participants in the plan; the size of the incentive offered; and the nature of the response-reward relationship.

Probability of Success. Experimental evidence indicates that moderate probabilities of winning an incentive reward

produce better performance than either very low or very high probabilities. [14] In general, one researcher has shown, a person who has one chance in two of getting a reward will work harder than if he has a lower or higher probability of getting it, regardless of the strength of his achievment motivation or the size of the money incentive. [15] A study of my own confirmed the fact that students will work harder when the odds are lower than three chances out of four. [16] The generalization seems likely to hold for financial incentive plans, though the optimum probability for winning a special reward obviously would need to be worked out for each particular situation. John W. Atkinson's estimate that it is somewhere around the one-chance-in-two level is not a bad place to start. [17]

We know two further facts about this phenomenon. First, strongly achievement-oriented individuals work best under odds as slim as one in three, or even longer. [18] Thus, an incentive plan for a strongly achievement-oriented sales force should obviously offer a different set of odds from a plan designed for a group of clerical workers who score low in *n* Ach.

Second, we know that the perceived probability of success changes with experience. This is probably why achievement-oriented people work better under somewhat longer odds than the average person. They know from past experience that they tend to be more successful than the average person in tasks they undertake. Therefore, what to the outside observer is a one-in-three chance of winning for an average worker is correctly perceived by the high achiever as a one-in-two chance for him.

Many of the difficulties that incentive

13 *Ibid.*, p. 13.
14 See Atkinson, *op. cit.*; Atkinson and Feather, *op. cit.*
15 Atkinson, *op. cit.*, p. 296.
16 D. C. McClelland, *The Achieving Society*, D. Van Nostrand Co., Princeton, N. J., 1961.
17 Atkinson, *op. cit.*
18 *Ibid.*; see also McClelland, *op. cit.*

plans get into flow from the fact that experience changes the perceived probability of success. Suppose a salesman or a worker exposed to a new incentive plan works extra hard and gets a special bonus. Then what does he do in the next time period? If he notices that a lot of other people have made it, and if he makes it again, he may fear that management will raise the normal standard. Management, on its side, may wonder how it can keep the perceived probability of success at the optimal level without raising standards as individuals get better at their jobs. Most managers are unhappy if incentive plans stop working after a while. Yet, theory suggests that, because experience changes perceived probability of success, plans would have to be changed regularly in order to keep expectancies of winning at an optimal level for producing performance.

Size of Incentive. Offered $2.50 for the best performance, a group of college students solved more arithmetic problems than when they were offered only $1.25— regardless, again, of their level of achievement motivation, or the odds under which they were attempting to win the prize.[19] Obviously, then, size of reward makes a difference.

Just as obviously, "size" is a relative matter—relative, that is, to one's own starting point and to what other people are getting. Five hundred dollars is much more of an incentive to a $5,000 wage earner than to a $50,000 executive. Almost certainly, the increment in money necessary to create a "just noticeable incentive" is some kind of constant fraction of the base. But, again, this function has yet to be determined for real-life situations. It would probably be easier to work out in a personnel recruiting context, where the incentive effect of additional pay is more obvious than that of incentives offered for increased output in a given work setting.

Many authors have recently turned their attention to how large a man perceives an incentive to be, in comparison not with his own starting level but rather with what others like him are getting.[20] Here, oddly enough, the yardstick seems to be more absolute than relative. That is, for a man earning $50,000, $500 may not seem like much of an incentive relative to his own past earnings, but it could become an important incentive if it puts him clearly ahead of another man whom he sees as a competitor.

One other finding relates to the size of incentives. In a couple of studies, managers receiving middle-level compensation scored higher in n Ach than either lower- or higher-paid managers.[21] The data are hard to interpret with any certainty, but they are suggestive. One can infer that the managers with relatively low compensation (here, less than $20,000 a year) are those in the 35–50 age range who just haven't "made it." They are less successful, less achievement-oriented, and less rewarded. But why should the higher-paid manager (here, $25,000 a year and up) also be lower in achievement motivation? Older men, who may also get higher salaries, tend to become less achievement-oriented, but in this study age was controlled. Do the findings mean, then, that high financial rewards may lower motivation to achieve? Or do they mean that while high achievement motivation is necessary to get to the top, other motives are necessary for performing really well once one has gotten there?

Interestingly enough, the same pattern has been found in society: The middle-class people "on the way up" score high-

[19] Atkinson, *op. cit.,* p. 293.
[20] See R. L. Opsahl and M. D. Dunnette, "The Role of Financial Compensation in Industrial Motivation," *Psychological Bulletin,* 1966, pp. 66, 94–118.
[21] See Atkinson, *op. cit.,* p. 269.

est in *n* Ach, whereas those from lower-
and upper-class backgrounds are less
achievement-oriented.[22] This might mean
that very large financial rewards tend to
decrease achievement motivation, perhaps not because they satisfy so many
needs in the traditional sense but because
they lead people to get interested in other
things. At any rate, the possibility that
very large rewards decrease motivation
is intriguing and would seem to deserve
further investigation.

The Response-Reward Relationship.
Even in seniority systems where a man
gets more pay as he grows older, the tacit
assumption is that, with greater experience on the job, he is presumably doing
the job better, even though it would be
impractical to try to measure exactly how.
This suggests the first variable in the incentive situation: how specifically the
desired response is defined. If a person
doesn't know what he is supposed to do
to earn the reward, he will obviously be
less able to do it. So, in general, the supposition is that the more clearly specified
the behavior, the greater the incentive
value of the reward.

In some jobs—selling, for example—
desired performance is relatively easy to
define, while in others, such as the job of
a personnel manager, it is quite difficult.
In any case, it seems probable that successful incentive plans involve goals
worked out as specifically as possible in
advance, between superior and subordinate, so that the subordinate will know
whether he is achieving his goals.

Two types of errors are commonly
made in specifying the response for which
the reward is offered. First, the manager
may assume that the task primarily involves work output and may specify the
expected responses in those terms,
whereas a careful job analysis would

show that other factors are important to
success. A case in point is the sales offices
mentioned previously, where too much
emphasis on selling interfered with service functions and actually lowered performance.

Second, the manager may believe he
is rewarding better performance from his
staff, when in fact he is primarily rewarding other kinds of behavior, such as being
loyal to him or "not rocking the boat." A
comparative study of two large business
organizations in Mexico provides an interesting illustration.[23] In Company A,
where rewards were clearly given for
better performance, men with high
achievement motivation got significantly
more raises over a three-year period.
However, in Company P, where men
were highly regarded if they were loyal
to the boss and stayed in line, men who
scored high in *n* Power were more often
promoted. Company A was growing
much more rapidly than Company P. Yet
the president of Company P declared that
he was interested in better performance
from his top executives and couldn't understand why his company was not growing faster. He did not realize, though his
subordinates did, that he was actually dispensing financial rewards primarily for
loyalty to himself.

Another important characteristic of
the response is whether it is expected
from a group or from individuals. Should
incentives be prorated on the basis of
group performance, as in profit-sharing
plans, or given for individual performance alone? No easy generalization is
yet possible, though everyone agrees that
each work situation should be carefully
analyzed to see which type of performance it is most appropriate to reward in
a given case. For example, where the staff
is strongly affiliation-oriented and the job

[22] B. C. Rosen, "Race, Ethnicity, and the Achievement Syndrome," *American Sociological Review*, 1959, pp. 24, 47–60.

[23] J. D. W. Andrews, "The Achievement Motive in Two Types of Organizations," *Journal of Personality and Social Psychology*, June 1967.

requires lots of interpersonal cooperation, some kind of group incentive plan would obviously be more effective than one rewarding individual excellence.

Still another important variable is the delay between the response and the reward. How often should bonus reviews be held—monthly, semi-annually, or annually? Most studies with lower animals in simple learning situations suggest that the shorter the delay, the greater the incentive value of the reward. Applying this principle to the design of an industrial incentive plan could lead to "atomizing" expected improved responses so that a person could accumulate "points" every time he showed a better response, the points to be totaled and cashed in for money at regular intervals. The difficulty of measuring performance in a given work situation will almost certainly decide how often and how immediately rewards can be given. Generally speaking such variations in timing are probably less important than the other variables mentioned, since most adults, and certainly most managers, are able to work for rewards deferred at least a month, and often a year or even longer.

In summary, then, money is one tool among many for managing motivation. It is a treacherous tool because it is deceptively concrete, tempting many managers to neglect variables in the work situation and climate that really affect productivity. In the near future, there will be less and less excuse for neglecting these variables, as the behavioral sciences begin to define them and explain to management how they can be manipulated just as one might change a financial compensation plan.

Incentive plans will continue to play an important role in the overall management framework. But the effective manager will also need to diagnose the needs of his staff, the motivational requirements of their jobs, his own motives, and the climate of the present organizational setup. Then he can rationally plan how to improve productivity by improving the climate; by developing certain motives in key people; by making a better match between the needs of the people and the needs of the job; or, finally, by specifically gearing incentive plans to the organizational situation.

A Note on Terminology
[Editor, *McKinsey Quarterly*]

Over the past decade, psychologists and students of management have given increasing attention to needs for achievement, affiliation, and power as sources of human motivation. They have found these concepts useful for both explaining and changing human behavior, particularly in work situations.

The *need for achievement*, probably the most widely studied of the three, is the need to optimize one's performance and to attain a standard of excellence in any endeavor. In common descriptive usage, this need is usually referred to by a general term such as "achievement motivation" or "achievement orientation"; considered as a specific quantitative variable, it is termed "*n* Achievement" or "*n* Ach" and measured by analyzing the content of oral or written stories for achievement-linked ideas. It is this potentially measurable aspect of achievement motivation that psychologists have in mind when they say that a person is "high in *n* Ach."

Likewise, the *need for affiliation*, or for warm and supportive human relationships—in a word, friendship—may be termed "affiliation motivation" in a general sense, and "*n* Affiliation" or "*n* Aff" when used as a measurable variable. Scores for "*n* Aff," like those for "*n* Ach," are obtained by verbal-content analysis.

Power motivation—or "*n* Power" as it is called when reference is to the measurable variable—refers to the need to control or influence others, directly or indirectly.

It is theoretically possible, then, to rate anyone for *n* Ach, *n* Aff, and *n* Power; the combined scores would reflect the individual's important motivational characteristics, as understood by behavioral science today.

Interested readers will find a more detailed discussion of these concepts in Dr. McClelland's book *The Achieving Society* (D. Van Nostrand Company, Inc., Princeton, N.J., 1961).

QUESTIONS

1. Explain what the author means by the statement, "Money isn't everything. Its meaning is in the eye of the beholder."
2. It is all too easy for the manager, in making plans for other people, to assume that they are like himself. Comment.
3. Explain the following:
   a. Achievement needs
   b. Affiliation needs
   c. Power needs
4. Under what conditions would a pay incentive plan be most successful?
5. Summarize the principal conclusions regarding the use of money as a motivator.

24.

At Emery Air Freight: Positive Reinforcement Boosts Performance

AMACOM

At Emery these days, P.R. stands for *positive reinforcement,* not public relations, and the payoffs from applying Skinner's ideas to the motivation of employees exceed the wildest claims ever made by public relations practitioners for the results of their art. One example: Small shipments intended for the same destination fly at lower rates when shipped together in containers rather than separately. By encouraging employees to increase their use of containers (from 45 per cent to 95 per cent of all possible shipments), Emery has realized an annual saving of $650,000.

"With savings this large we can't afford to worry about charges that we're manipulating our employees," says Edward J. Feeney, Vice-President—System Performance, the man primarily responsible for introducing P.R. at Emery. Continues Feeney: "Actually, the charge that you're manipulating people when you use positive reinforcement—I prefer myself to say that you're shaping their behavior —is a hollow one to start with. People in business manipulate their employees all the time—otherwise they would go bankrupt. The only questions are, how effective are you as a manipulator and what ends do you further with your manipulation? Our end is improved performance, and we've been damned effective in getting it." Feeney emphasizes that his approach and that of Emery's management generally is pragmatic, not doctrinaire. They're sold on the merits of Skinner's ideas, not because of their internal logic or the eloquence with which they are frequently proposed, but because so far at least they have paid off handsomely in each area Emery has seen fit to apply them.

Importance of Performance Audit

Emery has been selective in its application of P.R.; it's a powerful tool that should be employed where it's most needed and where the potential for improvement is the greatest. These are things that Feeney feels strongly can't be left to intuition or guesswork—hence the necessity for a performance audit before you institute P.R. in a given area. Emery doesn't want to be in the position of the corporation that targeted tardiness reduction as the object of a major effort. Before the drive, tardiness averaged ½ of 1 per cent; after the drive, ¼ of 1 per cent. Big deal! Emery has a different magnitude of payoff in mind.

Take the example of container utilization that we mentioned. Executives at Emery were convinced that containers were being used about 90 per cent of the times they could be used. Measurement of the actual usage—a measurement made by the same managers whose guesses had averaged 90 per cent—showed that the actual figure was 45 per cent, or half the estimate. Feeney saw no reason, given the proper motivational climate, why employees couldn't consistently meet a standard of 95 per cent and save Emery $650,000 annually—which, of course, subsequently happened.

The performance audit fulfills two primary purposes. First, it indicates the areas in which the biggest potential profit payoffs exist—the areas in which Emery should focus its attention; second, it convinces previously skeptical managers on quantitative grounds that no words can contravene and there is need for substantial improvement.

The performance audit would be justified for the second effect alone—convincing managers that improvement is needed and persuading them to cooperate with a program designed to bring about the improvement. "Most managers genuinely think that operations in their bailiwick are doing well; a performance audit that proves they're not comes as a real and unpleasant surprise," says Feeney.

We also suspect that an unpleasant surprise of some magnitude is necessary to secure the cooperation of a goodly number of managers in implementing a program that, with its concentration on praise and recognition as motivators and the elimination of censure, runs contrary to the beliefs and practices of a working lifetime.

On the other hand, Feeney emphasizes the importance of cushioning the blow if you want to enlist their cooperation. "We structure the performance audit so that the managers are heroes for making the audits, and we reassure them that irrespective of the current level, they will look good if they can improve."

What about the performance standards set as a part of each performance audit? How are they set? What do they signify? Sometimes, as in the case of the customer service department with its goal of customer call-backs within 90 minutes of the initial telephone query, the department had to set the goal in advance of the audit study. On study, it appeared reasonable and it was left unchanged. Sometimes there is no standard, and one has to be set on the basis of observation and common sense.

The latter usually indicates the impracticality of setting perfection or 100 per cent performance as your standard. For example, the ideal in answering phone calls from customers would be for the customer never to get a busy signal that might lead him to call one of Emery's competitors. The problem is that studies have shown that in any given hour, five minutes, although not the same five minutes, is always going to account for 35 per cent of the calls during the hour. Hence, it's much too costly to staff a switchboard with the number of operators necessary to prevent busy signals during those peak five minutes.

Emery has experimented, with a measure of success, with having employees set the standards for their own jobs. It was done in the customer service office in Chicago. The employees set a higher standard: not just giving customers a progress report within 90 minutes, but having *all* the requested answers to customer queries within that time—and they have presently reached this standard, although they fall short of the 90 to 95 per cent achieved on progress reports. The problem, as Feeney sees it, is in giving the employees all the data they need to hit on a reasonable standard—a very time-consuming process. Otherwise, employee-set standards either will be unrealistically high or unacceptably low. Either way, both the company and the employees lose out. The standard that is too low deprives the employee of self-satisfaction and the company of work that it is paying for; the standard that is too high, achievable only once in while by virtue of extraordinary effort or luck, will leave the employee frustrated and embittered. Sooner or later —and it's usually sooner—his performance will revert to a lower level than before he participated in setting the unattainable standard.

Providing Praise and Recognition— Avoiding Censure

In those areas in which Emery uses P.R. as a motivational tool, nothing is left to chance. Each manager receives two elaborate programmed instruction workbooks prepared in-house and geared to the specific work situation at Emery. One deals with recognition and rewards, the other with feedback. Under recognition and rewards, the workbook enumerates no less than 150 kinds, ranging from a smile and a nod of encouragement, to "Let me buy you a coffee," to detailed praise for a job well done.

Of all forms of praise, the most effective, according to Feeney, is praise for the job well done—expressed in quantitative terms. Not "Keep up the fair work, Murray," as shown on TV, or even "Great

going, Joe—keep it up," but "Joe, I liked the ingenuity you showed just now getting those crates into that container. You're running pretty consistently at 98 per cent of standard. And after watching you, I can understand why."

In bestowing praise and recognition, Emery follows Skinner pretty closely. There is the same emphasis on reinforcing specific behavior; the same insistence that the behavior be reinforced as soon as possible after it has taken place; the same assertion that you reinforce frequently in the beginning to shape the desired behavior, but that as time goes on, maintaining the desired behavior requires progressively less frequent and unpredictable reinforcement. As Skinner wrote, in reference to Emery's application of his ideas, "You don't need to maintain a system of contrived reinforcers indefinitely. People get the impression that I believe we should all get gumdrops whenever we do anything of value. There are many ways of attenuating a system of reinforcement. . . . But the main thing is to let noncontrived reinforcers take over."

At the gumdrop stage of P.R., Feeney urges supervisors to supply praise and recognition at least twice a week during the early weeks or months of behavior shaping. It's impractical to require them to provide P.R. more frequently—they are too busy, they would forget, etc. Once the desired behavior has been established, managers have more discretion—the key point being the unpredictability of the reinforcement, not the frequency. Keep P.R. coming on a descending scale of frequency—but keep the employee guessing as to when or whether he's going to be praised or recognized.

At least in the early days of shaping behavior, it's difficult to determine which deserves the most credit for the improvement in performance—providing praise and recognition or withholding censure and criticism. Particularly in those cases where the manager seldom praised before —even when he had good reason—the switchover from censure to praise produces instant, almost miraculous results. Performance improves dramatically, and along with it, employee morale and superior-subordinate relations.

What do you do with the employee when praise, recognition, and feedback don't work? Do you contrive to refrain from criticising his or her work? At what point do you throw in the sponge?

Feeney's general answer was that P.R. worked with nine employees out of ten. On those occasions where it appeared not to be working, investigation usually revealed that below standard performance was not the employee's fault—factors such as the wrong tools or work overload were responsible. And once they were corrected, the employee responded as positively to praise and recognition as anyone else. He cited several instances, not among the rank-and-file, where a custom-tailored program of P.R. salvaged men who were 30 days short of being fired.

Even with the below-par employee, the manager takes the positive note. He would probably ignore a day or a week in which no improvement took place, preferring to wait for a period of slight improvement—say from 70 to 75 per cent. Then he might follow-up his praise of the improvement by asking the man what he thought could be done to improve further. Everything he said from there on would be an attempt to solve the problem and provide the manager with additional opportunities for reinforcement.

All in all, we got the impression of a program that failed, on the few occasions when it did, not because of employee resistance, but because of supervisory intransigence—the boss was unable or unwilling to apply it, especially with the so-called problem employee—and a few

supervisors have left Emery in consequence.

Feedback is easier to institutionalize than praise and rewards. A written report is a tangible artifact that you can see. But even with feedback you have occasional lapses, Feeney cautions, in any areas where it isn't mandatory. Some managers loathe paperwork; others are too busy to extend the measure of praise and recognition indicated by the feedback or they don't recognize behavior that deserves positive reinforcement. "The biggest problem with the program occurs," adds Feeney, "when managers stop asking for feedback and stop offering recognition and rewards because there's been no recognition of their efforts from above —their boss hasn't asked, 'Why didn't I see your performance report?' or extended any reward or recognition himself. In other words, the program breaks down whenever there are no consequences and no positive reinforcement for the manager who is supposed to implement it."

**Beyond Gumdrops—
Continuous Feedback**

Skinner talks about the necessity of letting the noncontrived reinforcers take over in any program of P.R.—which, in our view, explains the crucial importance at Emery, and probably in any industrial setting, of continuous feedback. Emery, in each area where it has utilized P.R., has required each employee to keep a record himself of what he or she has accomplished each and every day. In customer service, for example, each representative ticked off daily on a sheet how long it had taken to reply to each call. It took no special skill to compare this with the standard of 90 minutes. Similar sheets, all relatively simple and all recorded by the employees themselves, were instituted in all departments covered by P.R.

Noncontrived reinforcers they were

not. Emery provided the sheets, gave no option on filling them out, and defined the terms of frequency. But we think this is an example of a contrived reinforcer laying the essential groundwork—providing the time framework for noncontrived reinforcers to mature and take over. Let's postulate three basic stages of development: (1) A period in which frequent P.R. by the supervisor plus continuous feedback leads to rapid progress towards the desired behavior; (2) a period in which infrequent P.R. by the boss is accompanied by continuous feedback— itself, of course, a species of P.R.; (3) a period in which the supervisor is only a very occasional source of P.R. and feedback is overwhelmingly the principal source of contrived reinforcement.

Feeney emphasizes the effect of feeding back on improved performance. "We found that when we provided daily feedback only one week out of four or one out of five, performance in the periods without feedback reverted to the previous level or was almost as bad." There's no question that feedback is the critical variable in explaining the success of the program, he adds.

What is continuous feedback, and what is its relation to Skinner's requirement that, in any program of P.R., "The main thing is to let noncontrived reinforcers take over?" The noncontrived reinforcer clearly is the conviction on the employee's part that they are doing a good job, a fair day's work. But how are they to know? Part of the answer is observable— they've been busy, the customers have seemed satisfied, maybe the boss has extended P.R. More conclusive, if they're in doubt, they can look at the sheets and see at a glance exactly how they stand in reference to the standard. In other words, the internal or natural reinforcer—the conviction and satisfaction of a job well done—is corroborated and itself powerfully reinforced by the evidence of a

sheet on which the work accomplished is compared daily with the standard for the job.

Feeney tells a story that illustrates both the necessity for continuous feedback and the way in which previous consequences determine present behavior. Emery requires any employee who receives a package damaged during shipment from an airline to fill out a fairly time-consuming form. At a certain installation, he pointed out to the boss that without feedback and P.R. the employees wouldn't bother—the reinforcements they got from filling out the form were all negative. The paperwork was time-consuming and boring, they were likely to get some flack from airline representatives who would in their own good time find ways of hitting back, they were taking time from their number one priority—getting the shipment delivered on time. A check revealed that no damage forms were turned in. However, a physical check of cartons showed several damaged, one with a hole punched in the side, another that looked as if a hand had reached into the top and taken something out, etc. Feeney feels that his colleague, at this point, got the message. The only way around the problem of getting the damaged slips filled out was to (1) specify the desired behavior—i.e. set the standard; (2) require the employee to provide continuous feedback—keep daily records on how many cartons were damaged and submit them to his supervisor; and (3) whenever feasible, positively reinforce the behavior—when the feedback showed that it was justified.

Money and Positive Reinforcement

Skinner includes money in his list of positive reinforcers, as long as it is linked to specific behavior. The weekly paycheck doesn't positively reinforce; it's a negative reinforcer. You work to avoid the loss of the standard of living supported by the paycheck. On the other hand, piece-rate payments geared to specific on-the-job behavior are positive reinforcers; so are commissions paid to salesmen. Just as effective, Skinner argues, would be to take a leaf from gambling and introduce a lottery into industry, with each employee geting a weekly lottery ticket that might pay off in a weekly drawing. Here it's paying off unpredictably but in the long run on a determined schedule that provides the positive reinforcement.

Emery does not use money as a positive reinforcer. Several reasons seem to underlie the choice. First, Emery has no employees on incentive payments, not even salesmen; there is therefore no built-in necessity to link dollar payments to improved performance. Second, management holds the belief that performing up to standard is what it has a right to expect from each employee in return for his paycheck. The savings achieved through the program have helped to make it possible for Emery to pay as much or more than its competitors, and offer equal or bigger benefits—facts not lost on its employees. Finally, Emery's experience suggests that praise and recognition, especially self-recognition through feedback, are enough. In some areas, employees have consistently performed up to standard for more than three years. The savings for Emery in consequence have been substantial, despite the omission of money as a positive reinforcer.

At first blush this seems surprising. Interestingly, AT&T had a similar experience with a job-enrichment program that also substantially increased employee productivity and performance. In an AT&T experiment with 120 women answering stockholder inquiries, various measures were taken to give employees more responsibility and control over their jobs. The response was uniformly positive, with one exception—a girl who quit because she wasn't getting more money

for a more responsible job. She felt that she was worth more to the company and should be paid more. That only one employee out of 120 expected to get paid more as a consequence of the program that improved the value of their services calls for a little explaining. So does the continuing success of P.R. at Emery.

There are several possible explanations. People know a good thing when they see it. The programs at both AT&T and Emery have improved the intrinsic nature of the job as seen by the employees themselves—that's sufficient reward.

Also, many studies have shown that employees have a crude but keen sense of distributive justice on the job. They may do less than what they themselves consider a fair day's work for a large number of reasons, even though they frequently feel guilty about it. On the other hand, they resent and resist any attempt to exact more than their perception of a fair day's work in return for what they are paid. Improve the job—in Emery's case, provide via praise, recognition, and continuous feedback the evidence of a job well done—and eventually you will develop what Skinner would call the natural reinforcer of job satisfaction. This, in turn, guarantees that the employee will want to live up to his own standard of a fair day's work. In other words, part of the success of P.R. at Emery is that the standards set for employees were seen by them as reasonable to begin with. The missing element was any positive incentive to reach them. The weekly paycheck was ineffective—Skinner is correct—it took praise, recognition, and feedback to do the job. Similarly, at AT&T, job enlargement and job enrichment provided the incentives to improved performance that hitherto were lacking.

A story that Feeney tells illuminates the problem. A Harvard Business School student on a summer assignment with Emery was helping with a performance audit on one of the loading docks. In the process he managed to gain the confidence of a union steward, who told him in so many words that any problems Emery had with the workers were not due to money—they were well paid. The one thing they weren't getting paid was attention. Many of them worked at night with a minimum of supervision and recognition. A situation in which employees feel fairly paid in relation to the work expected of them but in which money is almost the sole recognition received is ripe for improvement via positive reinforcement.

Proof of the Pudding

At present, P.R. is fully operative in three areas at Emery—in sales and sales training, operations, and containerized shipments. The benefits in all three are impressive, and they have been sustained for periods of from three to four years. We can forget about the Hawthorne effect in explaining the success of P.R. at Emery.

In sales training, each salesman completes a programmed instruction course on his own, with plenty of feedback structured into the course to let him know how he is doing. In addition, sales managers apply P.R. in their day-to-day relations with salesmen, and sales reports provide the indispensable feedback. Sales have gained at a more rapid rate since P.R. entered the sales picture, and Feeney feels that it deserves some of the credit for the increased rate.

The relationship between P.R. and improved customer service, part of operations, is undeniable. Before P.R., standards were met only 30 to 40 per cent of the time; after P.R., the figure was 90 to 95 per cent. Most impressive is the rapidity of the improvement and its staying power. In the first test office, for example, performance skyrocketed from 30 per cent of standard to 95 per cent in a single day. Staying power? After

almost four years, performance in the vast majority of Emery customer service offices still averages 90 to 95 per cent.

In containerized shipping operations the story is the same: With P.R., container use jumped from 45 per cent to 95 per cent—with the increase in 70 per cent of the offices coming in a single day.

There were few cases in which feedback was temporarily interrupted because of managerial changes and other reasons. Whenever this occurred, performance slumped quickly by more than 50 per cent, only to return rapidly to the 95 per cent level once the feedback was resumed.

All in all, Emery has saved over $3 million in the past three years. No doubt about it: Positive reinforcement pays.

On the basis of this kind of success, Emery has big plans to expand the use of P.R. It's already been extended to overall dock operations. Emery's route drivers are covered and measured on items such as stops per hour and sometimes on shipments brought back versus shipments dispatched. Eventually P.R. will be introduced wherever it's possible to measure work and set quantifiable standards. Feeney and his group will set their priorities, of course, on the basis of what performance audits tell them about the potential for improvement and savings.

When you have scored the kind of success that Emery has you're not quick to innovate. However, thought is being given to the introduction in certain areas of different rewards and schedules, including having the computer acknowledge behavior and even using some kind of financial reward as positive reinforcer.

What Does Emery Prove?

More precisely, what does Emery prove about the feasibility of behavior modification through positive reinforcement? The question must be asked and answered at several levels. At the first and most apparent level, the answer is easy: In those areas in which Emery has used P.R., behavior modification has been instant, dramatic, sustained, and uniformly in the desired direction. There also seems little doubt that P.R. deserves most of the credit for the dramatic improvement in performance.

A few qualifiers are in order. Positive reinforcement so far has been used selectively for Emery in areas where work could be measured and quantifiable standards set if they didn't already exist, and areas where observation showed that the existing level of performance was far below the standard. This last point applies equally to the customer-service representatives and the dock loaders, but is less true for the salesmen—their performance was lower than Emery felt it should be, but not in the same category as the other two employee groups.

Also Emery has yet to arrive at the point where the natural reinforcers—in this case an internally generated sense of job satisfaction—have taken over. After three to four years of P.R., praise and recognition from the boss are applied infrequently and unpredictably, but the other contrived reinforcer, continuous feedback, is still administered daily. In fact, Emery's past experience has been that whenever it stopped providing continuous feedback, performance rapidly reverted to the previous low levels. On the other hand, this experience occurred during the early days of supplying positive reinforcement. Perhaps now Emery could stop providing continuous feedback and maintain the current high levels of performance. We can only guess.

At another level we have to take into account the context in which P.R. has been used at Emery. We have to consider whether or not special conditions exist at Emery that favor the successful application of positive reinforcement. How far are we justified in claiming that what has worked at Emery will work equally well in a different organization with a different

product, a different climate, and different problems?

On the basis of the available evidence, we can't go overboard in generalizing from Emery's undeniable success in applying positive reinforcement to solve its performance problems. That Emery has no incentive programs and is therefore spared the complexity and the conflict habitually generated in manufacturing situations where standards, performance, and earning are inextricably linked; that Emery has so far restricted P.R. to areas in which it has been possible to positively reinforce one employee without producing adverse consequences for any other employee; and that Emery, during the period it has applied P.R., has been a rapid-growth organization, able to offer far more than the usual opportunities for growth and promotion are factors that provide a partial measure of the conditions, by no means common in organizations, that have fostered an atmosphere conducive to the application of positive reinforcement.

The second condition we mentioned is something Emery has worked at. Feeney emphasized that Emery was careful not to set individuals or groups competing against each other to see which came closest to meeting the standard. Instead, managers were coached to urge employees to think in terms of what they were doing now compared to what they have done in the past. Comments Feeney, "If you set individuals or teams competing against each other, there's only room for one first—but lots of losers. If you want to know the effect of this kind of competition on performance, all you need is to look at what happens at the end of the baseball season to the performance of the team that's 32 games behind."

Whether the conditions we have described are indispensable to the successful application of P.R. or merely helpful we have no way of determining. The problem is lack of evidence. Emery is the only company to date to have applied P.R. on a fairly broad scale over a fairly long period of time. Even with Emery, neither this report nor a previous article in *Business Week* (Dec. 28, 1971) can claim to be the kind of objective in-depth study that's called for. A few other organizations—among them Cole National in Cleveland, Michigan Bell Telephone, and Ford Motor Co.—are in the early stages of experimenting with positive reinforcement, and more organizations are giving serious thought to using positive reinforcement. More than 200 have contacted Feeney since Emery's work with P.R. received public recognition.

Will positive reinforcement work? Feeney believes that the question has already been answered with a resounding affirmative. He cites upwards of 1000 case studies involving mental patients, delinquent children, and problem pupils in which P.R. resulted in dramatic improvement in behavior. The only questions remaining, as he sees it, are questions of methodology and application.

Of course, none of these episodes took place in an industrial setting. Until we have a lot more evidence—both from Emery and from other sources—any conclusions about the use of P.R. in industry have to be tentative.

One last level of consideration. Positive reinforcement as the answer to organizational problems of productivity and performance has a plethora of rivals. A generation of theorists and practitioners has systematically overturned stones in search for a formula or method for converting low-producing groups or individuals into high-producing ones. A partial enumeration would include job enrichment and job enlargement, organization development in all its varied guises, Theory Y, participative management, team development, the Scanlon Plan, autonomous leadership. We could go on —but we won't. How does P.R. stack up against these other and we think com-

peting approaches to improving productivity and performance?

At this point it's impossible to give a conclusive answer. We have seen the problems with the evidence on the results of positive reinforcement. Similar problems exist with the results of every other technique for improving productivity and performance. There's little objective evidence available, and what evidence there is abounds in caveats—the technique will work under the proper circumstances, the parameters of which are usually not easily apparent.

Take the entire field of organization development. An exhaustive search of the literature on the subject by Professor George Strauss of the University of California Business School at Berkeley turned up exactly three research studies worthy of the name. What did they prove? That under the proper circumstances OD can increase productivity, though perhaps not as much as conventional techniques such as purchasing new equipment, job simplification, and "weeding out" inefficient operators. So far, the search for a sure-fire all purpose formula for turning low-producing groups into high-producing ones appears to be almost as elusive as the search for the philosopher's stone that would turn everything it touched into gold.

Which leads us to what conclusion as to the merits of positive reinforcement relative to its rivals? With the customary caveats, we feel that P.R. has much to recommend it. As an approach, it deserves more recognition and application that it has hitherto received. It suffers from its sponsorship: Positive reinforcement has a bad name with businessmen and with the general public because of its association with Skinner, his alleged totalitarian leanings, his denial of free will, and the inescapable fact that his theory of human behavior is rooted in his experiments with pigeons. People instinctively resent a theory that seems to suggest that they're not much brighter than pigeons and can be controlled in similar ways.

We understand the problem, but it's unfortunate that it has prevented the more extensive application of positive reinforcement. On the basis of what little we can observe, P.R. is easier, less complex, and less expensive to introduce than most of its rivals, while the results are at least as impressive as those achieved by any of them.

Feeney is probably correct: A lot of managers practice positive reinforcement without knowing it. He cites, for example, Vince Lombardi, who provided endless feedback on performance to his players and who after a really bad defeat never uttered a word of criticism in the locker room. True, but until more organizations consciously and systematically apply positive reinforcement, it will never get the recognition that it appears to deserve.

QUESTIONS

1. What are the principal elements of Emery Air Freight's program of motivation and performance improvement?
2. Make a list of as many forms of positive reinforcement as you can that may be used in a work situation. Include both tangible and intangible types.
3. Compare positive reinforcement with criticism and punishment for shaping behavior.
4. B. F. Skinner states that present behavior is shaped by the consequences of one's previous behavior. Discuss.
5. Do you think that Emery Air Freight's reluctance to foster interpersonal competition is desirable? Discuss.

25.

Motivation from the TA Viewpoint

DRU SCOTT

If you find people in your organization are not listening to admonitions about "being aware that certain behaviors may inadvertently function as disincentives to production," try Transactional Analysis (TA). General theories of TA have been widely popularized by books like the late Dr. Eric Berne's *Games People Play*, Harris' *I'm OK—You're OK*, and James and Jongeward's *Born to Win*, but the specific uses of TA in organizations are not so well known.

It does have those uses, though; during six years of working with a variety of governmental and corporate managers, the author has seen TA unlock motivational problems that have plagued their organizations for years. Colorful, easy-to-understand terms are just one way TA can help bridge the gap between motivational theory and practice, As one seasoned line manager put it, "TA isn't one of those wishy-washy, nicey-nicey methods. It's practical and it makes sense. TA is a welcome relief from just hearing about loving people into productivity."

TA puts handles on ideas that have appeared in textbooks for years but have only recently been on the scene in organi-

zational problem solving. It skilfully combines new research with traditional concepts and provides a useful framework for a variety of management theories. Although it was originally a therapy-based method, it is also an excellent training method. The transition from a therapeutic to an organizational setting requires careful adaptations, but we are beginning to realize the full promise of applying TA to the challenge of channeling people's motivations into organizational outlets, while satisfying their individual needs.

Studies of the importance of stroking and stimulation conducted in the 1940s by René Spitz are now receiving increasing attention from managers and executives. Dr. Spitz found that babies who were not touched and stroked, even though they were adequately fed, diapered, and kept warm, did not grow normally. This research, combined with evidence that battered children are more likely to survive than completely neglected children, points out the vital role of strokes—positive or negative. More recently, Dr. Berne focused new attention on the life-long human need for strokes.

Reprinted by permission from *Personnel*, January–February 1974 © 1973 by Dru Scott. All rights reserved.

Dru Scott is president of Dru Scott Associates, San Francisco, California.

Since a stroke is any unit of recognition, it can take many forms—strokes can be positive, negative, or mixed. Positive strokes include remarks like these:

"You did a good job on that report."

"Thank you for making sure we met the deadline."

"I'm glad you're working in our department."

Some examples of negative strokes are:

"I wish we'd never hired you."

"Jones, not you again!"

"Of course, you wouldn't be able to handle anything this difficult."

"You did it all wrong again."

In addition to the clearly positive or negative forms of recognition, some strokes contain a little of both. Such mixed, or crooked, strokes might sound like these:

"Pretty good job for an old man."

"You really look good for a change."

"You do such a nice job with routine work."

Receiving strokes of some kind is of prime importance to a healthy person, regardless of age, place, or even job—no matter how senior we are, how much education we have, or what our past accomplishments are.

How People Work for Strokes

Strokes are usually sought in early childhood and then in later life according to a certain hierarchy. Positive strokes are the most encouraging to growth, negative strokes are better than none at all; but the absence of strokes is usually crippling. Here's an example of the hierarchy at work that shows how the wrong behavior can get more strokes, even though negative, than the right behavior.

Of five sales people who work for one manager, four turn in their sales reports on time every week. The other sales person consistently turns in late reports, week after week, month after month. In this situation, it is obvious that the delinquent performance is most likely to get the most attention. The person who produced what the manager didn't want (late data) ended up getting the most strokes. Granted, they were negative—a bawling out, exasperated glances, and nagging—but they were strokes.

On the other hand, what kind of recognition was given to the four sales people who supplied the needed information without any prodding? They got neither positive nor negative strokes from a boss who was preoccupied with late reports. The result was that gradually the pattern changed. One by one, the four reliable sales people began to turn their reports in late, or with obvious mistakes, because "it doesn't seem to make any difference."

Six months later the sales manager could be heard complaining at executive staff meetings, "I don't know what happened; I used to be able to count on four of my people but now, everybody's late." Of course, what happened is that he had reinforced undesirable behavior by his negative strokes.

A Stroking Success Story

Frequently, the managers acclaimed as "born leaders" give positive strokes without deliberate planning or conscious awareness. Take the case of the manager who never had a problem about his section heads' or employees' being on time—in fact, they usually came in early, though this was certainly not true in the rest of the company—and they consistently produced quality work. What was behind the early starts and the high morale?

For one thing, the boss regularly arrived an hour early and opened his office door, and his staff learned to expect this open-door time, when they could drift into his office for a few minutes to say something like, "Oh, by the way, that system down in production really turned out well." It was a time to go in and report project successes and talk about work in general. Managers and employees alike grew to know that between 8 and 9 they could count on some positive strokes for a job well done.

This boss was doing three things right. First, he created a climate in which people could directly ask for and receive positive strokes. And he encouraged staff members to exchange positive strokes. Second, he gave more positive strokes for getting results and solving problems than he did for excuses and low productivity. Third, he organized the department so that his staff members had an opportunity to get strokes from the work itself. They were assigned total responsibility for a system, rather than a specialized responsibility in a number of systems, and the responsibility included each staff member's being the first to measure the success of the system.

Thus, his people's energies were directed to getting the job done, not invested in wondering about "When am I finally going to get some appreciation around here?" or complaining about "Why don't I get any recognition?" or in unconsciously manipulating people and the work to get negative recognition (which is only a shoddy and inefficient substitute for positive strokes). This manager made effective use of his and his staff's time and energies. Building in ready sources of strokes increased motivation. And by consistently associating strokes with results, that organization consistently got the right results.

Positive Strokes from Work Itself

Work can be a major source of strokes. When work is designed so that people get high-intensity, long-lasting gratification from it, they need fewer low-intensity strokes through ritualized, nonproductive conversations. This, of course, does not mean that morning greetings and general chit-chat will stop altogether, or that

they should. Rather, it means that people who are getting high-intensity strokes from work and are motivated by what they are doing will naturally spend less time collecting low-intensity strokes by standing around the Xerox machine catching up on the news.

According to the TA concept, work or activity is just one of the six ways we spend time; the other five are withdrawal, rituals, pastimes, psychological games, and intimacy. Each method of structuring time provides a way to give, get, or avoid strokes, which may be of either low or high intensity and of either narrow or wide availability. It is the multiplication of stroke intensity by stroke availability that determines stroke satisfaction—and stroke satisfaction means motivation. Thus, the formula for this relationship is $SI \times SA = SS$. The following six descriptions of the way we spend time all bring that formula into play.

Withdrawal means leaving the situation, either mentally or physically, and avoiding strokes. The worker on a factory assembly line may withdraw into a dream world of hunting or of fishing or of some new household project. The person hidden behind a newspaper in the company cafeteria may be primarily concerned with avoiding strokes, not with gathering information.

Rituals permeate almost every aspect of organizational life. The "Hello, how are you" of the secretary as she comes in in the morning and the company-sponsored retirement party are both examples of rituals. Rituals produce strokes of light intensity, but high availability.

Pastimes are ways of spending the time talking about everyday topics. They are conversations a person can engage in almost impersonally, about the weather, who won the football game, and other casual topics. Pastimes are merely a way of getting strokes from almost anyone. They rate low on the intensity scale and high on availability. Because of the low intensity, employees who get most of their strokes this way will need to spend a lot of time to get a full quota of stroke satisfaction.

Psychological games always include (1) a hidden meaning, (2) a set of repetitive moves, (3) a switch or unexpected turn of events, and (4) a predictable payoff. Games waste time and do not solve problems, but some say that we spend from 50 to 90 per cent of our waking hours playing games. A reason for this could be the double highs that games provide—high intensity and high availability. Although games can provide intense strokes, however, there is usually a putdown or negative aspect.

The game of Blemish illustrates the point. The Blemish player looks over a report, project, or person until he finds something wrong—a too-wide left margin, computations on the wrong-color paper, or a slightly wrinkled collar. The Blemish player's objective is not to solve a problem or improve a situation, but to find something wrong, so there's no stopping him by correcting the fault to which he has called attention. He just moves on. Colleagues and subordinates usually figure out ways to cope with this person, of course. They spend time planning which little mistake to plant or make bets on how many minutes and seconds it will take him to find a mistake.

Here's another example of a game, this one built around phoney persecutor, victim, and rescuer roles. Nancy, a division manager, opens a staff meeting with this question: "What do you think we should do to lower the rate of absenteeism —it's way up?"

One response is, "Well, I think we should give cash awards to people who don't take time off."

Nancy counters with, "You know, George, that sounds like a good idea, but we are far exceeding the amount we expected to spend on awards, and you know this is a tight money year. I do like to have your ideas, though."

Another reply: "Have you thought about writing up commendations for the company newspaper for people who have the best attendance?" Nancy comes back with, "You know, Helen, that sounds good on the surface, but I'm afraid that it would just eat up more time than it would be worth. We'd be spending money on paper and really not solving the problem."

"Well, have you thought about calling in the employee for disciplining each time he's absent?"

"Bill, that's a good idea and I think the people really deserve to be disciplined when they have been absent too much. But it seems to me that if we spend all of our time in those interviews we won't be able to get the work done."

So the game ends with a frustrated silence on the part of Nancy's would-be rescuers. She sounds as if she is asking for help, but actually she is just proving that "my people can't help me, but it's good for them to keep on trying."

Activities or work means anything we do dealing with the material reality of life. Although we're most concerned here with things people are paid to do, activities are not necessarily paid for, for instance, gardening, stamp collecting, and photography, hobbies that promise strokes of high intensity and high availability.

Intimacy is the last way of getting and giving strokes. An open, authentic relationship between people who feel comfortable about themselves and each other can be a deep source of positive strokes, but, although the reward for sharing secret dreams and hopes is high, so is the risk. Intimacy provides high-intensity positive strokes, but most people limit their availability.

The increase in motivation and productivity is long-lasting when the strokes are derived from the work itself. Sometimes, however, it is desirable to increase the number of strokes that come from the people involved; for instance, if the work is boring but cannot be made more interesting, the managers and supervisors may need to concentrate on giving more strokes to their employees.

One company that provides household cleaning help solved an old problem in a new way. The problem was keeping capable domestic help, even when the pay was adequate. The work itself usually provides few opportunities for strokes. The one-day-a-week worker in a large house may never feel the satisfaction of finishing a job, and the worker may lack a sense of client or product, since the houseworker typically never sees the people who use and enjoy the clean and orderly house. Another stroke-limiting factor is working alone in an empty house, completely cut off from the opportunity to get strokes from others.

This company successfully solved the problem by dropping the traditional one-person-to-one-house-a-day schedule and sending teams of two housekeepers to two homes a day. Turnover decreased and favorable feedback from customers increased. This time, increasing the strokes from people turned the trick when increasing the strokes from the work itself was less feasible.

The Ego States: Who's Saying What?

During recent months the terms "Parent," "Adult," and "Child" have increasingly been cropping up in conversations across the country. When the terms are capitalized, as they are in the TA context, they stand for three major parts of personality, the Parent ego state, Adult ego state, and Child ego state.

The ready acceptance of the concepts is largely due to the practicality of the TA framework. Most people quickly confirm, "Yes, sometimes I do act like my mother or father" (Parent); "Yes, I do make rational decisions based on current information" (Adult); "Yes, sometimes I do feel just as I did when I was a little kid" (Child).

Eric Berne distinguished the Parent, Adult, and Child ego states from the super ego, ego, and id by pointing out that Parent, Adult, and Child are identifiable sources of thinking and feeling and behaving within each person. One way of expressing this difference is to say that the Parent, Adult, and Child each contains real people with real names and addresses. The Parent contains what a young child learned from the authority figures that were significant to him. In one person, the names and addresses might be those of his father and mother, in another, those of an older brother and sister. The name and address in the Adult ego state would be that of the person himself as a grown-up who rationally gathers data, processes it, and makes decisions. The Child ego state would contain the name and address of the person himself as a small child.

The Parent ego state is the collection of all the values, opinions, and how-to instructions from authority figures in early childhood. Someone responding from his Parent ego state might sound like this:

"What do you mean, a new system? We've always done it this way."

"How can you work at such a messy desk? Everyone knows you should put everything away immediately."

"I don't want to see anyone around here not looking busy."

"Be sure and wear overshoes when you go out to the plant site. You know you'll catch your death of cold if you don't."

"It's a well-known fact. Women can't supervise."

A person expressing his Parent ego state may use a set of gestures copied exactly from his Parent figures. Parent gestures depend, of course, on each person's particular background, but frequently indications of Parent behavior are finger-shaking critically, arms crossed over the chest, with impatient toe-tapping, an exasperated sigh, or fingers drumming on the table top. Also characteristic are words like should, ought, must, never, and always.

The Adult ego state is the rational thinking aspect of each person. Through it people can estimate probabilities, postpone gratification, make new decisions, and solve problems. And, of great importance, people change at will through the Adult state. Here are examples of Adult responses:

"Here's an announcement of a new system. I'm going to see how it was developed and tested."

"I'm interested in what you produce, not what your desk looks like."

"I've noticed that he rarely looks rushed, but he always finishes his projects on schedule."

"Since you're going out to the plant site, were you aware that heavy rains are predicted for this afternoon?"

"I wonder if there is enough life insurance to cover all the expenses."

Eye contact, open posture, straightforward listening are all characteristic of the Adult ego state, and so are questions such as, "What is your thinking about this?" "What are the facts?" "What is the best decision?" "How can we solve this problem?"

The Child ego state is the source of deep feeling, creativity, spontaneity, rebellion, adaptation, and affection. It's the little girl or boy each person once was. It is also the source of feeling OK or not-OK about oneself. Here are some examples of Child responses:

"Wow, I'm curious about this new system we've been hearing about."

"It must be kind of fun to let your papers stack up and spill over like that."

"I look so harried and concerned while I'm talking on the phone, but no one ever knows I'm calling my bookie."

"I'll get my feet wet any time I please."

"Gee, it's scary to think about someone in your family dying."

Tipoffs that someone is functioning in his Child ego state are downcast eyes, shrugged shoulders, whining voice tones, and words like "I dunno," "Gee," and "Wow."

Stroking Parent, Adult, and Child

People who are turned on to their work are people who are taking care of all three ego states. This means an acceptance that we are sometimes rational, sometimes judgmental or nurturing, and sometimes childlike and creative, compliant and rebellious. It also means we need to feel all right about receiving and asking for OK strokes in each area. (An OK stroke is one that is directed at a constructive part of someone's personality at an appropriate time.)

Strokes for the Parent, of course, depend on satisfying each person's unique Parent messages, but some common sources are doing work that is important, knowing the organization produces a worthwhile product, doing something that is good for someone else, working hard, and earning enough money to be secure.

Strokes for the Adult usually involve demonstrating respect for a person's thinking ability. A stroke might be asking for advice and considering it, helping someone solve a problem himself, or letting people take on responsibility.

Since the Child ego state contains the specific feelings, ways of coping, and adapting we each experienced as a youngster, the best strokes for the Child vary from person to person. One way of identifying what kind of Child strokes people will respond to is to find out what they wanted when they were young but never got enough of. One manager remembered immediately—"a room by myself." He had grown up in a household of six children, but only three bedrooms.

While a private office for him wasn't possible, some movable colored room dividers established a sense of territory that was pleasing to his Child ego state, and the simulated "room by myself" had a good effect on his productivity.

Other strokes for the Child might be signaled by the person's pleasure in feeling needed or the company of other people at work. His curiosity might be satisfied by new projects to develop, or he might respond positively to bright, colorful walls or carpeting.

Matching Strokes with Needs

During a period of rapid change, the Parent and Child ego state may not be getting enough strokes. Remedying this lack may entail more OK touches that give a lift, like unexpected doughnuts at coffee break time; avoiding conditions that might activate critical Parent messages, like dirty work areas; and not forgetting expected rituals, like greetings or opportunities to socialize.

Strokes and needs can be matched in other ways. One department manager decided his management by objectives program was floundering because meeting objectives provided strokes only for the Adult, rational part of his staff members —it didn't provide "feeling" strokes for the Child. Now each management team that reaches its six-month objectives gets a company-paid, luxurious holiday weekend. And team members also get their pictures in the company magazine. ("Look, Ma, I made it" is still a strong stroke for many of us.)

But stroking can be misdirected, too. In a company actively encouraging upward mobility, one woman complained to her manager, "You're always telling us you want women to move up, yet when I, for one, do something well, you rarely say anything about the good results or the way I handled the work. You just say, 'Atta girl. You're a nice gal to have

around.' " She obviously needed strokes for her Adult, but she was being offered only strokes for her Child.

What people are stroked for, what kind of strokes they get, and how they get them continue to affect an organization's time and energy investments. To repeat, if an organization does not facilitate OK positive strokes, people will figure out ways to manipulate people and the work to get negative strokes. And forcing people to fall back on time-wasting, nonproductive games to get strokes is also a poor alternative to giving positive strokes.

When Strokes Are in Short Supply

The larger and older the organization, the more difficult it may be to elicit strokes. Pats on the back may be reduced to an interoffice memo or a once-a-year bonus. And in organizations of all sizes some employees may feel almost immoral about needing and asking for strokes: "I know I shouldn't need it, but I really wish somebody would tell me every once in a while that I'm doing a good job." Here, the manager should help the person feel that it is all right to ask directly for strokes.

The process of helping people feel all right about giving themselves strokes is even more difficult, particularly if someone has learned a Parent message that blocks out most positive Child strokes— messages such as, "Don't get a big head"; "stop fishing for a compliment"; "nice girls aren't pushy"; or "real men don't need praise."

Helping people become aware of the implications of such messages may be all that is necessary. Encouraging employees to take the initiative for strokes for their total personality may have some surprising results. In one accounting office a usually restrained bookkeeper announced to his supervisor, "I feel down this morning. I think about five minutes of nurturing would get me started." Five minutes of "You're doing a great job and we all appreciate the kind of work you're doing," accompanied by a cup of coffee, were the strokes he needed. Had he not asked for the strokes directly, he might have wasted three or four hours of time and energy complaining about the work, telling someone else how no one appreciated him, and taking four long coffee breaks.

Soft-Pedaling the Jargon

A word of caution: Be careful about using TA language with people who don't know its specific meanings. Game, Parent, Adult, Child, and stroke are useful terms, but only in their place. I shudder when I remember hearing an enthusiastic but misguided man telling a co-worker. "The trouble with you is you have a rotten Parent."

If you decide it would help solve a problem to level with someone, it might be wise to explain the situation more in terms of "I feel" or "I see such-and-such happening" and less in terms of "You make me . . ." or "You always. . . ." Concentrate on current, observable behavior, rather than on past happenings or intentions. Specifically, focus on what the person is doing right now that relates to accomplishing the goals of the job. Rather than, "You're too Parent, and you're always giving me negative strokes," your feedback might properly be, "I feel put down when you stand over my desk and slam down a report in front of me."

In summary, Transactional Analysis is a useful tool for understanding what motivates people on the job. People do work to get recognition. If they do not get positive recognition, or positive strokes, they will invest time and energy to get negative recognition—negative strokes. Giving positive ones is more efficient, obviously, but it should be remembered that the more boring and routine the work and the less personal contact with management, the higher the probability that people will get strokes through nonproductive methods such as rituals and small talk. In any case, long-term motivation depends on each person's getting healthy recognition for each part of the personality—Parent, Adult, and Child ego states.

QUESTIONS

1. What meaning do "strokes" have for employees? How can these influence their behavior?
2. Do you see any relationship between the stroking discussed in this article and the reinforcement discussed in the article "At Emery Air Freight: Positive Reinforcement Boosts Performance"?
3. How can "strokes" be matched to the Parent, Adult, and Child ego states in dealing with people?
4. Many individuals, including managers, acknowledge that people have a need for recognition or stroking, yet they also acknowledge that they themselves seldom provide it for their subordinates or co-workers. How can you explain this apparent contradiction?

26.

Three Styles of Leadership and Their Uses

ROBERT T. GOLEMBIEWSKI

Managers who have tried to keep track of research and thinking on the subject of leadership may well sympathize with the centipede that was asked how it managed its legs, for this innocent question, the limerick tells us, reduced the unfortunate creature to lying "distracted in a ditch considering how to run."

The question asked in the leadership literature—"How does one lead men?"—is every bit as disconcerting as the one put to the centipede. Nevertheless, the parallel between them is not quite exact. The centipede, until he had to think about it, was only doing what came naturally and doing it well. Leadership in the work situation, however, does not belong to the order of instinctive behavior. Doing what comes naturally in striving for leadership often leaves much to be desired.

Though management has tended to be all too receptive to endorsements for this, that, or the other leadership approach, its interest has sound foundations. In the first place, a considerable body of evidence shows that the productivity of a work unit is affected by the kind of leadership the unit receives. In the second, decisions about what style of leadership to adopt must to some extent be made for the company as a whole rather than being left to the intuitions of individual managers. Still, management's interest has not been satisfied, for the evidence supporting any one leadership style can always be countered, and frequently is, by evidence supporting its precise opposite. The bewildered organization that has tried and abandoned one style after another may well be pardoned for asking, "Where do we go from here?"

Fortunately, it is beginning to look as if a theory based on empirical findings is at last in the making. No one yet knows exactly what its ultimate content will be, but its outlines can now be perceived and —even more important—can be put to use to improve managerial practice.

At this point, it may be useful, therefore, to review the research findings that

Reprinted by permission of the publisher from *Personnel*, July–August 1961 issue. © 1961 by the American Management Association, Inc.
Robert T. Golembiewski is Research Professor of Political Science and Management, University of Georgia.

283

form the skeleton of this theory and to examine their practical implications. But before doing so, it is necessary to define the term "leadership"—though this in itself is a question that has stirred up endless controversy. For the purposes of this article, however, "leadership" will be taken to mean the consistent ability to influence people in desired ways.

On the classification of leadership styles, fortunately, there is more agreement. Most authorities recognize three basic types: "leader-centered," or "autocratic"; "group-centered," or "democratic"; and "individual-centered," or "free rein."[1] The supposedly modern view, of course, is that the group-centered style is the most conducive to productivity. By contrast, the traditional view admits only the leader-centered style, regards the group-centered style as a plaything of psychologists, and dismisses the free-rein style as constituting not leadership, but rather its surrender.

Each in Its Place

Supporters of any all-or-nothing view have one thing in common: they will often be surprised to find that the research literature does not consistently support any one leadership style. The reason for this lies not in any failing of the research itself but in the simple fact that there is no "best" style. Indeed, the question "Which kind of leadership should we use?" prevents any useful answer. The question should be, rather, "Which kind of leadership *when?*"

This "when," it is worth pointing out, constitutes an integral part of the question, for every scientific formulation must at some point specify the conditions

it covers. Even the well-tested law explaining what happens when objects are dropped holds true only for objects that are heavier than air. If the objects are dropped at certain points in space, moreover, they will "fall up" (float).

This approach provides a partial explantation of the apparent chaos of the research literature. Many studies that seem to contradict each other are simply accounts of leadership phenomena under different conditions. Studies based upon observation of similar conditions, on the other hand, have yielded a pattern of consistent results.

Fortunately, leadership study has now taken on a "situational" approach. The main point of this approach has been well expressed in popular terms by Auren Uris, who advises the would-be leader as follows: "The skill with which you apply the three basic tools of leadership—autocratic, democratic, and free-rein techniques—determines your personal success as a leader."[2]

What, then, are the conditions that should be taken into account in the choice of a leadership style? There are many. Four among them, however—personality, task characteristics, task roles, and group characteristics—are particularly important and have been explored in a number of research studies. A separate examination of each of these conditions should provide some guidelines for translating such advice as Uris' into action.

Personality. As the advocates of group-centered leadership often fail to realize, not all people can function well under the same kind of leadership. There are, for example, many people whose personalities make them unfitted for a group- or individual-centered style.[3] Such a person

[1] For a typical treatment, see A. Uris, *How to Be a Successful Leader.* McGraw-Hill Book Company, Inc., New York, 1953, pp. 32–39.

[2] *Ibid.,* p. 31.

[3] Many personnel men are aware of these personality effects and therefore recruit only from those groups of people whose general social training seems likely to produce the personality characteristics appropriate to the organization's leadership style. Thus some companies seek out rural workers because of their alleged amenability to formal discipline.

was Administrator H, described in Harold Lasswell's *Psychopathology and Politics*.[4] A childhood marked by unfortunate sexual experiences and domination by an overbearing, prudish father had left him sharply, though unconsciously, ambivalent toward authority. Consequently, he worked well under supervision but invariably became careless when he was given substantial freedom on the job.

Needless to say, giving free rein to a subordinate like H would bring nothing but trouble, though over the long run his personality might possibly change enough to permit a looser kind of supervision. Studies of "'authoritarianism'" confirm these common-sense conclusions about how to deal with men like Administrator H. Authoritarians behave in ways that reveal compulsive conformity based upon a view of the world as menacing and unfriendly. Though they are not necessarily people of low intelligence, they think in relatively few channels from which they cannot be moved. In addition, they seek security through the exercise of authority or, better still, through surrender to some powerful authority figure.

Studying authoritarianism in military groups, Medalia formulated and tested the following two hypotheses:[5]

1. People with strong authoritarian tendencies will be more likely to accept formal military leaders with the conventional traits of the "good officer" than will people with weak authoritarian tendencies.

2. People with strong authoritarian tendencies will be more likely to re-enlist than will people with weak authoritarian tendencies.

The data that emerged from his study are shown on Table 1. Not only do these findings support both hypotheses but, when one takes into account certain technical factors in the study that tended to obscure any relations, they suggest a very strong relation between personality and leadership style.

The practical advantages of adapting leadership style to personality characteristics seem clear from this study. In the groups analyzed, it could mean a 23 per cent increase in the acceptance for the formal leader by his subordinates and a 14 per cent increase in the intent to re-enlist. These figures indicate the need for developing a valid diagnostic indicator of the leadership style to which an individual will respond best. Comparable changes in a business organization would certainly prove well worth the cost of meshing leadership style and personality factors.

A word of qualification must, however, be inserted here. Most people have wide "response repertoires." That is, they are able to perform the wide range of behaviors required by the various styles of leadership despite their personal preference for a particular style.

This adaptability was demonstrated by Berkowitz in an experiment with a communication network that channeled a great deal of information to some positions and very little to others.[6] Half the subjects were assigned to communication positions in which they would have to act in ways that were not congruent with their personalities; submissive people were placed in central positions, dominant people in peripheral positions. The other half were assigned to the positions appropriate to their personalities. Though the two kinds of subjects at first performed quite differently, Berkowitz found, the "misplaced" subjects generally

---

[4] *The Political Writings of Harold D. Lasswell.* The Free Press, Glencoe, Ill., 1951, pp. 127–35.

[5] N. Z. Medalia, "Authoritarianism, Leader Acceptance, and Group Cohesion," *Journal of Abnormal and Social Psychology*, LI, No. 2 (1955), pp. 207–13.

[6] L. Berkowitz, "Personality and Group Position," *Sociometry*, XIX, No. 4 (1956), pp. 210–22.

TABLE 1   Relation of Authoritarianism in Members of a Military Group to Acceptance of Formal Heads and Intent to Re-enlist

LEADER ACCEPTANCE	AUTHORITARIANISM			DIFFERENCE BETWEEN HIGH AND LOW
	High	*Medium*	*Low*	
Above Median	59%	52%	36%	+23
Below Median	41	48	64	−23
Total	100%	100%	100%	
Intent to Re-enlist				
Yes or Undecided	38%	34%	24%	+14
No	62	66	76	−14
Total	100%	100%	100%	

managed to adjust to the demands of their positions by the last of the three trials in the experiment.

Berkowitz' experiment, however, was brief. The findings of other research projects indicate that if it had continued, the subjects in the final group would ultimately have displayed reactions ranging from dissatisfaction to attempts at sabotaging the work process. Just when it is that such reactions begin to appear will be determined by circumstances and personalities. But when they do hit, they hit hard.

A manager, then, may vary his style of leadership, but he cannot force people to act forever in ways that are uncongenial to their personalities. This imposes a difficult task upon the manager and the organization—ascertaining the behavior preferences of the individual subordinates and then arranging the work so as to allow them to carry out their tasks in the manner they prefer. Unless this is done, the formal head will remain just that, rather than being accepted by his men as their leader.

Task Characteristics. The second major condition affecting the usefulness of any given leadership style is the nature of the task to be performed. Though little work has so far been done in classifying tasks, it should be adequate here to note that tasks may be distinguished in terms of (1) the obviousness of the solution to the problem or of the work itself and (2) the amount of cooperation the task requires.

Unfortunately, research to date has for the most part assumed that all tasks are quite complex and require a great deal of interpersonal cooperation. Because socioemotional factors affect performance most strongly when the task is of this kind, the leader-centered style, which tends to generate emotional flare-ups, usually shows up poorly under these circumstances, while the group-centered style shows up well.

Many tasks, however, do not have these assumed characteristics. One of Deutsch's experiments illustrates the value of distinguishing between kinds of tasks.[7] The prediction to be tested was that internally cooperative groups would be more effective than internally competitive groups. When groups of both kinds attempted to solve human relations and puzzle problems, it was found, the "cooperative" groups did indeed perform better on a number of measures of effectiveness, in-

[7] M. Deutsch, "The Effects of Cooperation and Competition upon Group Process," in *Group Dynamics: Research and Theory*, ed. D. Cartwright and A. Zander. Row, Peterson and Company, Evanston, Ill., 1953, pp. 319–53. See especially tables 23.5, 23.7, 23.9, and 23.11.

cluding quantitative and qualitative output, member satisfaction with group functioning and output, and amount of aggressive behavior. But on several measures the differences between the two kinds of groups were more marked for the human relations problem than for the puzzle problem. It seems as if the objectively demonstrable nature of the puzzle solution made it difficult for members of the "competitive" groups to block each other in subtle ways. (Certainly, the nature of the task would have made direct blocking seem ridiculous.) The open-endedness of the human relations problem, on the other hand, gave them ample opportunity to run each other ragged.

In terms of leadership style, these data suggest that the leader-centered style is particularly inappropriate to tasks that have more than one possible solution and that require a considerable amount of interpersonal cooperation. More important still, the data seem to leave little room for the leader-centered style even on tasks with just the opposite characteristics, for, as has already been noted, the group-centered style generally proved the more effective not only for the human relations problem but for the puzzle problem as well. In actual business and industrial situations, it should also be pointed out, emotional tensions can affect performance adversely at any number of points in the operation—at far more points than in Deutsch's experimental situation. Moreover, the marked preference most people show for the group-centered style furthers its claim to being the more useful of the two.

This does not mean, however, that the leader-centered style should be rejected out of hand. A situation in which most of the operators are strongly authoritarian and the task is a simple one requiring little cooperation is obviously tailor-made for authoritarian leadership.

The Role of Intelligence

Calling a task "simple" of course implies some relation between the task itself and the intelligence of the people who are to perform it. The importance of taking this relation into account in deciding upon a leadership style has been demonstrated by a simple experiment with a game based on "Twenty Questions." [8] As Table 2 indicates, though all the subjects worked on essentially the same task, the "Brights" did their best under a group-centered style, and the "Dulls," under a leader-centered style. The relation was especially marked for the "Dulls," whose problem-solving efficiency was only half as high under group-centered leadership as under authoritarian leadership.

Regulating work assignments by task and personality characteristics may seem like a great deal of bother, but the 100 per cent performance difference for the "Dulls" suggest that the extra bother will more than pay its own way. Indeed, business would most likely find it profitable to subsidize the research necessary for the development of even more precise ways of differentiating people than those now available. The "Brights" in this experiment—to give just one illustration of the value of this greater precision—probably included some authoritarian subjects. (Though low intelligence is frequently accompanied by high authoritarianism, high intelligence is not so frequently accompanied by low authoritarianism.) Excluding the authoritarians from the "Bright" sample would probably have had two effects: the performance of the remaining "Brights" under group-centered conditions would have improved, and that

[8] A. D. Calvin et al., "The Effect of Intelligence and Social Atmosphere on Group Problem-Solving Behavior," *Journal of Social Psychology*, XLV, First Half (1957), pp. 61–74.

TABLE 2   Effects of Leadership Style and Members' Intelligence upon Group Performance in "Twenty Questions" Game

MEMBERS' INTELLIGENCE AND LEADERSHIP STYLE		MEASURES OF PERFORMANCE	
		Median No. of Questions Asked per Problem	Per Cent of Problems Solved
Bright	Group-centered	15.5	100.0
	Leader-centered	18.5	87.5
Dull	Group-centered	31.0	37.5
	Leader-centered	24.5	75.0

of the "Brights" under leader-centered conditions would have deteriorated. In the industrial situation, both the individual and management could profit from a more comfortable "fit" of employees to their tasks.

Task Roles. Still another question to be considered in choosing a leadership style is "Who does what?"—that is, "What are the roles of the leaders and followers?" Though the very notion of leadership implies a set of roles different from those of followership, just what functions are covered by each set cannot be rigidly prescribed. Indeed, the distribution of functions is often the product of social consensus, and may vary even among work teams performing the same operation in the same organization.

Roles do, however, fall into three broad categories: roles peculiar to the superior, roles peculiar to the subordinate, and "mixed" roles, whose functions are performed by either or both. The general argument here, by way of preview, is that each of these three classes implies a different leadership style.

Evidence indicates that supervisors who are successful in influencing their subordinates' behavior in the desired directions —that is, supervisors who are leaders— work at sharpening these differences in roles. In a study by Kahn and Katz, su-

pervisors of section gangs on a railroad and supervisors of clerical sections in an insurance company were asked how much of their time was usually spent in supervisory matters, and how much in other matters.[9] Their answers, shown in Table 3, revealed that the supervisors with low-producing sections were two or three times more likely to perform the same duties as their men, or to perform the paperwork aspects of their jobs, than the supervisors with high-producing sections.

These findings can be explained by a little common-sense reasoning: The behavior of the low-producing supervisors reflects either a lack of consensus about roles in their work groups or their own failure to respect an existing consensus. Whatever the case, conflict is likely, and must inevitably result in productivity losses.

Not only should the superior differentiate his function from those of his subordinates, but he should, of course, perform certain *specific* functions. The amount of planning he does, for example, is directly related to the productivity of his section. Some interesting data on this score were obtained by asking foremen in a tractor factory whether they were able to plan their work ahead as much as they liked.[10] Though their answers, given in Table 4, suggest that the high-producing

[9] R. L. Kahn and D. Katz, "Leadership Practices in Relation to Productivity and Morale," in Cartwright and Zander, *op. cit.*, p. 615.
[10] *Ibid.*, p. 619.

TABLE 3   Time Spent in Supervising in Relation to Section Productivity

SECTION PRODUCTIVITY	50% OR MORE OF TIME SPENT IN SUPERVISING %	LESS THAN 50% OF TIME SPENT IN SUPERVISING %	NOT ASCERTAINED %	TOTAL %
Insurance company				
High	75	17	8	100
Low	33	59	8	100
Railroad				
High	55	31	14	100
Low	25	61	14	100

foremen actually did more planning than the low-producing foremen, it should be noted that the foremen were talking about the fulfillment of their planning expectations, not about how much planning they actually did or how much they thought necessary. It seems reasonable to assume that high-producing foremen were more aware of the importance of planning than the others. Thus their less-than-complete satisfaction may reflect high hopes rather than low accomplishment. If this is so, then they must have been even more active in planning their work than the table suggests.

Tables 3 and 4 deal with but two of the three categories of roles outlined above: roles peculiar to the subordinate and roles peculiar to the superior. There is, however, substantial evidence of the harm that superiors do in failing to respect the third category of roles: those whose performance is "mixed." The conflict generated by supervisory insensitivity to this third category is, of course, the subject of much of the human relations literature.

But what leadership styles do these three categories demand? As the provisional model in Table 5 shows, it seems likely that the superior's roles are best handled with a leader-centered style, and the subordinate's roles with a free-rein style. This does not, however, mean that the superior should surrender all his power over certain functions. On the contrary, every role assumes a set of guide-lines for behavior, and the three leadership styles are merely different techniques for developing and enforcing them. When the guidelines are violated—whatever the leadership style under which they were developed—the supervisor is put into a decisive position.

If, for example, a worker insisted on tightening bolts with his teeth, his fellow workers and his supervisor would undoubtedly be scandalized and would agree that the worker's freedom in deciding how to perform this operation did not extend quite so far as all that. Group pressure—especially in a work unit operating under group-centered leadership—might encourage him to change his ways. But the supervisor would still be on the spot, formally and socially. He would have to supplement this pressure and perhaps take formal action. When violations of the behavioral guidelines are winked at, the supervisor invariably comes off a loser.

The supervisor who would be a leader, then, must have a deft touch. A useful criterion for determining when to step in can be found in the concept of "relevance," that is, in how the issue ranks in terms of its importance to, say, the employees, the organization as a whole, or the boss.

The more relevant an issue is to the group, experimental evidence shows, the more willing the group is to accept a relatively authoritarian way of dealing with it. Thus a leader who is strongly sup-

TABLE 4   Foremen's Perception of Opportunity for Planning in Relation to Section Productivity

| SECTION PRODUCTIVITY* % | FOREMAN'S RESPONSES | | | |
	Can Plan Ahead As Much As Needed %	Sometimes Have Trouble Planning Far Enough Ahead %	Can Seldom or Never Plan Ahead %	TOTAL %
97–101	37	42	21	100
91–96	51	32	17	100
86–90	29	41	30	100
80–85	29	46	25	100
50–79	14	40	46	100

* Productivity is expressed as per cent of standard.

ported by this group may depend primarily on free-rein and group-centered styles, which encourage member involvement. When a relevant issue arises, however, he will exercise substantial influence, and, in fact, the group will expect him to do so. (The leader-centered superior with a work unit of authoritarians will, of course, hold a tight rein on most matters and therefore need not have such a delicate touch. But such situations are rare.)

An issue may, of course, be relevant to the formal organization but not to the group. If, for example, the work unit neglects its responsibilities to the company on the question of the level of production, the superior may have to use a leader-centered style despite the group's reluctance to have him do so. On less relevant matters, however, we would do well to balance it with a group-centered or free-rein style, which would reduce any tension generated by the leader-centered style. The "relevance" concept, in other words, supplements the model in Table 5, for an unanticipated relevant item may appear in any one of the three categories. The handling of such items will in the long run determine whether the formal head continues to function as a leader or loses his control over the group.

Group characteristics. Discussing the relevance of an issue for a work group implies that the group has developed certain common standards of its own and on its own. This characteristic of groups— the tendency to develop group norms and group goals—may be accompanied by fairly powerful mechanisms for imposing the group's will upon its members and upon the outside world. The group therefore plays a large part in determining the success of the various leadership styles. Group properties have, of course, been examined at length in the social science literature, and this author has sketched their broad implications for organization performance elsewhere.[11]

One aspect worth considering here is the degree to which the group as a group accepts its formal head. If the group feels that its supervisor is not fulfilling its needs, it may find itself a more satisfactory leader from within its own ranks. This should not be a matter of indifference to industrial managers, for the emergence of an informal leader who acts as spokesman for a work unit is often asso-

[11] R. T. Golembiewski, "The Small Group and Public Administration," *Public Administration Review*, XIX, No. 3 (1959), pp. 149–56.

TABLE 5   A Provisional Model of Roles and Appropriate Leadership Styles

CATEGORY OF ROLES	TYPICAL FUNCTION	GENERALLY APPROPRIATE LEADERSHIP STYLE
1. Roles peculiar to the superior	Setting general goals	Leader-centered
2. "Mixed" roles	Relocating machines on which individuals have worked for many years	Group-centered
3. Roles peculiar to the subordinate	Deciding how to use a tool	Free-rein

ciated with low productivity. In the Kahn and Katz study, workers in railroad section gangs were asked, "Is there some one man in the section who speaks up for the men when they want something?" Fewer than one in six respondents in the high-producing sections answered *yes,* while over half the respondents in the low-producing sections did so.[12]

Must the Leader Be Liked?

Such data as these, however, should not be taken as an endorsement of group-centered leadership. All three styles are equal to the task of winning informal acceptance for the formal head, though under different conditions. Moreover, the supervisor is not always well advised to try to raise his informal status to the level of his formal status. He must consider, among other things, the nature of his group's norms, which he will have to respect if he is to gain informal acceptance. If, as is by no means uncommon, the norms favor low output, his attempt to gain high informal status may force him to compromise his formal position.

The dangers of such an attempt are illustrated in a study of aerial bombardment crews by Adams.[13] Each member of each crew was ranked on several measures of status within the crew—formal rank, popularity, reputed flying ability, and so on. When the formal ranks of the members of any crew were quite similar to their ranks on the other measures, Adams found, the crew as a whole did well on "social performance" (harmony, intimacy, and the like). The crews that showed up best in these two respects, however, were not the best in "technical performance" (e.g., bombing accuracy). These findings seem reasonable. The popularity of the formal leaders of these crews was probably based in part upon their respect of a norm opposed to outstanding technical performance. Obviously, it did not make them particularly effective in their formal position. On the contrary, their closeness with their men helped the crews resist the demands of the "outside" organization.

A supervisor inheriting a work unit with a low-output norm faces a difficult task in choosing a style of leadership. If he employs a free-rein style, he will most likely succeed only in supporting the group norm. At the other extreme, the use of a leader-centered style may well harden the group's resistance to the formal organization. Even if the supervisor succeeds in breaking the group norm, he will most likely arouse antagonisms

[12] Kahn and Katz, *op. cit.,* p. 616.
[13] S. Adams, "Status Congruency As a Variable in Small Group Performance," *Social Forces,* XXXII, No. 1 (1953), pp. 16–22.

bound to affect the work process sooner or later.[14] (One major exception must be noted here: Groups of authoritarians, as has already been pointed out, will generally respond well to a leader-centered style. But this offers little practical consolation, given the apparent rarity of such groups.) Finally, it is the group-centered style, paradoxical though it may seem, that offers the best chance of success in changing a low-output norm, and group-centered leadership has actually proved useful in a number of instances. The reason for this seems to be that low output is a means by which the members of a work unit protect themselves against some perceived threat. A group-centered style often acts to make the group members feel less threatened and thus reduces their need for the low-output norm. But this is not inevitable.

In sum, every leadership style stands liable to failure in the attempt to develop and enforce a more acceptable output norm. If none of them works, the supervisor has no choice but to stop being a practicing psychologist and recommend that the unit be broken up.

Concluding Notes

The difficulties of choosing a leadership style, then, are great even if only a single condition is considered. From the two preceding paragraphs alone it should be clear that the question of how to lead any given work group is far more complex than is recognized by any existing

generalizations, all of which call for a single leadership style. To compound this complexity, however, the four sets of conditions discussed in this article always appear in combination, so that some elements in a situation may favor one style while some elements favor another.

In fact, our increasing knowledge of the complexity of the question has outmoded the traditional designations of leadership styles. These designations, which suggest exclusive categories, ought to be modified so as to express the ways in which leadership styles continuously change in response to changing situations. The suggestions presented above outline the nature of the necessary changes. Needless to say, though these suggestions are consistent with the available research findings, they will need further verification before they can be considered rules for action.

Finally, it must be noted that the foregoing discussion has centered on the question "What are the conditions under which various leadership styles are most useful?" and has, in effect, neglected the question "What *should be* the dominant leadership style?" This neglect should not be taken as indicating that the question of value is unimportant. Rather, it recognizes that in practice the choice of a leadership style implies, and is preceded by, a value choice. In the field of leadership, as in every other, the use of empirical regularities must always be guided by considerations of what ought to be.

[14] Such a situation is analyzed in R. T. Golembiewski, "O & M and the Small Group," *Public Administration Review*, XX, No. 4 (1960), pp. 205–12.

QUESTIONS

1. How does the author define the following?
   a. Leadership
   b. Autocratic leadership
   c. Group-centered leadership
   d. Free-rein leadership

2. Show how situational factors can determine which leadership style is most effective. Give the principal situational factors or conditions.
3. How does differentiation of task roles affect productivity of a work group? What tasks should the leader concentrate on?
4. For an effectively functioning group is it necessary that the leader be liked? Explain.

27.

Improving Management Through Continuing Research

RENSIS LIKERT

An important change is occurring today in the art of management comparable to that occurring in the art of medicine. Both medicine and management are arts since both require decision and action even though the information available to the practitioner is both incomplete and imperfect.

The art of medicine has long been based on the knowledge acquired by clinicians. Clinical judgment has been the foundation upon which medical practice has been based. During the past decade or two, a new source of knowledge has appeared. Quantitative, systematic research is now coming to be accepted as the soundest foundation upon which to base the art of medicine. Whenever the results from clinical judgment and quantitative research do not agree, the research findings are accepted increasingly as the more valid.

We are witnessing a comparable fundamental change in the art of management.

Quantitative, systematic research is beginning to be substituted for practitioner judgment in providing the foundations upon which the art of management is based. This is an important change and will enable management to perform better because the basic concepts underlying managerial processes and procedures are more valid.

I shall not try to present specific research findings in this short paper. Instead, I shall limit myself to general conclusions based on research done by the Institute for Social Research of The University of Michigan and studies by other investigators. The Institute has done over 30 major studies and has collected data from over 50,000 non-supervisory employees and from several thousand supervisors and managers.

I want to stress that while all these research studies provide impressive support for the general conclusions which I shall present, they do not provide abso-

Rensis Likert is former Director of the Institute for Social Research, The University of Michigan, and also Professor Emeritus of Psychology and Sociology.

lute proof for them. The conclusions are my interpretations of the data.

I believe that in those broad areas of business management concerned with how best to organize, coordinate, and manage human effort, the results of quantitative research are supplying new concepts more powerful and effective than those which they are replacing. If these basic concepts are found to be applicable to government (a logical supposition since managing people in a government agency is essentially the same process as managing them in a business organization), they will have major implications for public administration.

Management Assumptions

One traditional and central assumption which research is progressively and seriously undermining is the notion that buying a man's time gives the employer control over the employee's behavior. Most organizations base their standard operating procedures upon this assumption. But the plain facts are that the highest producing managers in American industry do not, on the average, believe in its validity nor do they base their managerial behavior upon it. They recognize the great importance of the economic motives, but they seek to harness the economic motives to the non-economic motives so that all these motives reinforce and strengthen one another. High-producing managers have discovered that the non-economic motives which may and sometimes do lead to the restriction of production can equally well be used to encourage production.

Another assumption which research findings are progressively dispelling is the belief that if an organization is to obtain the highest productivity and lowest costs continuously over time, that organization must put direct, hierarchical pressure upon its employees to produce at specific levels. An increasing body of

research findings dealing with widely different kinds of work show that high levels of direct, hierarchical pressure from production are more often associated with low rather than high productivity. A high degree of pressure is associated with low productivity. A low degree of pressure is associated with high productivity.

Part of the relationship between pressure and productivity is attributable, no doubt, to the greater attention that management gives to poorly producing units. There is evidence, however, that significant amounts of the causation is in the opposite direction. Data show that when high-producing managers take over a new low-producing department, they do not change their style of leadership. They do not put pressure on these employees for production but may actually reduce it, even though they, themselves, have high performance goals.

There is also evidence that (for periods of two or three years) direct, hierarchical pressure for high or increased productivity does result in impressive increases in productivity. This hierarchical pressure may take many forms, such as manpower cuts, budget cuts, timing jobs, setting standards, and pressing for production levels which meet the standards. The research findings show, however, that such pressure adversely affects the attitudes and loyalties of both supervisory and non-supervisory employees and their confidence and trust in their superiors and in the organization. Pressure seems to cause employee reactions and attitudes to become progressively resentful, hostile and bitter. These unfavorable attitudes lead to greater absence and turnover and to greater pressure on high-producing employees to restrict output. They are a source of more grievances, slowdowns and strikes.

In achieving its impressive, relatively immediate increases in productivity, direct hierarchical pressure liquidates valuable human assets. If the costs of hostile employee reactions, including strikes, were charged (as they should be) against the productivity increases, these increases would often be less impressive and profitable than they are now considered to be.

Although direct, hierarchical pressure for high productivity and low costs has these serious consequences, it does not follow that it is desirable for a manager to have low productivity goals. Quite the contrary! The highest producing managers have higher productivity goals than do other managers, but they do not attempt to achieve high productivity by putting direct, hierarchical pressure on their units.

The principles and procedures used by the highest producing managers provide other new foundations for the art of management. In presenting some of these briefly, I want to remind you again that what I say is *my* interpretation of substantial research findings and is not the last word. We, as yet, do not have sufficient corroborative evidence to establish, beyond all doubt, the validity of all the conclusions.

Principles Based on Research

A most important principle[1] reflected in the behavior of the highest producing managers is *a supportive orientation* toward other members of the organization. Indications of the extent of this supportive behavior can be obtained by asking subordinates such questions as the following:

a. To what extent does your superior try to understand your problems and do something about them?

b. How much is your superior really interested in helping you with your personal and family problems?

c. To what extent is he interested in helping you get the training which will assist you in being promoted?

d. To what extent does your superior try to keep you informed about matters related to your job?

e. How much confidence and trust do you have in your superior?

How much do you feel he has in you?

f. Does your superior ask your opinion when a problem comes up which involves your work?

Does he value your ideas and seek them and endeavor to use them?

A second general principle used by the highest producing managers is *the involvement of subordinates* in decisions affecting them. High-producing managers, in comparison with other managers, involve their subordinates more in work-related decisions and in this process more often use the work group rather than individual employees as the decision-making unit. Work group meetings, either formal or informal, are used more frequently by the highest producing managers than by other managers and the ideas and thinking of the men are taken more seriously and used more fully. This use of group-decision processes develops more loyalty among the men toward each other, more cooperative behavior and greater teamwork, and more commitment to implementing the decisions made and the goals set.

A third general principle of the highest producing managers is that they have *higher performance goals* and greater concern for achieving them than do other managers. As seen by their subordinates, the highest producing managers "pull for the men and the company and not for the company only." These managers establish a reciprocal responsibility. The supportive behavior of these managers and the decision-making processes which they use result in subordinates establishing high performance goals for themselves. High performance goals of the

---

[1] For a more complete statement of this and other principles see Rensis Likert, *New Patterns of Management*, (New York: McGraw-Hill, 1961), Chapters 8, 11, 12 and 13.

subordinates coupled with their greater loyalty toward each other and toward their superior contribute to high productivity by the work group with a minimum of waste. These work groups accomplish more with less feeling of pressure or strain than do other groups.

The approach used by these highest producing managers to achieve high productivity takes time to pay off. They are trying to establish organizations in which high productivity and low costs are a continuous, not a short range, phenomenon. They accomplish this objective by building organizations which, in comparison with others, have better communication, better decision-making based on this better communication, greater capacity to coordinate the efforts of the members of the organization, more favorable and cooperative attidues, greater identification with the organization and greater concern in achieving the organization's goals. In field experiments involving hundreds of employees, we find it takes at least a year or two for this approach to achieve high levels of productivity and low costs. But once excellent levels of performance are reached they are usually maintained.

Implications for Public Administration

What are the implications of all this for public administration and the operation of the Federal Government? If further research in business establishes beyond doubt the validity of the general conclusions I have briefly described, and if similar research in government yields the same over-all pattern of findings, these results would require substantial changes in some of the major efforts now being pursued to increase productivity and reduce costs in Federal agencies.

There is, in my judgment, sufficient evidence in support of the general conclusions which I have presented to indicate that we should take a hard and questioning look at some of the steps now being taken to reduce the costs of government, and to examine critically the assumptions upon which these steps are based and the evidence supporting these assumptions.

The steps to which I refer are those which involve in one form or another direct, hierarchical pressure on the personnel in agencies to increase their productivity. These include such procedures as across-the-board manpower cuts or budget cuts. These cuts of, say, 2 to 5 per cent are usually made with the expectation that the agency will still perform the same volume of services after the cut as prior to it. Other procedures involve measuring productivity or output, setting standards and pressing to have employees produce at the specified level. Perhaps some of you have experienced such pressures or even applied them.

In making these comments about measuring productivity, I hope I am not misunderstood. I am not suggesting that efforts to measure productivity are undesirable. I hold the opposite point of view most strongly. It is very important to develop sound measurements of productivity, output and costs, and I trust that these efforts will be continued and extended. My concern is focused on how the measurements of productivity are used. My hope is that productivity measurements as they become available will be used in the way the highest producing managers in business and industry use such data and not in the way that the less productive managers use them.

From available research findings, I would expect that direct, hierarchical pressure within the Federal Government will yield, on the average and over the long run, the same pattern of results as it appears to be yielding in business. That is, such pressure will be associated with low, rather than high, productivity. These direct pressure procedures may well yield in government, as in business, appreciable increases in productivity and lowering of costs for about a two year period. Accompanying these favorable productivity changes, however, are likely to be serious adverse changes in the organization. Loyalties will decrease, confidence and trust will decrease, concern for achieving the organization's objectives will decrease, there will be greater pressure to restrict production, absence and turnover will increase, good people will leave the organization, quality of work will slip or be harder to maintain, and hostilities, resentments, unfavorable attitudes will increase.

Such changes in the organization will mean, of course, that the increases in productivity achieved from the direct, hierarchical pressure were obtained at a serious cost to the organization. Substantial human assets of the organization, such as loyalty, confidence and trust, undistorted and efficient communication and high performance goals, are adversely affected. The cost of this liquidation of human assets—perhaps in the form of the dollar costs required to rebuild them—should be charged against the greater productivity obtained by means of the hierarchical pressure. To ignore the substantial dollar costs when an effective organization is "mined" in this way is not sound nor accurate accounting and leads to erroneous conclusions. Until all the legitimate costs are measured and properly charged, all productivity increases cannot be considered actual improvement nor real savings.

If such steps as direct, hierarchical pressure are not likely to yield sustained increases in productivity (in Federal agencies), what alternative courses of action can be recommended? I should like to recommend two:

First, that research be undertaken in governmental agencies to test whether the general conclusions which I have suggested are valid and applicable;

Second, that measurements be taken regularly not only of productivity, output, costs and similar end-result variables but also of all the major variables which need to be measured to obtain accurate information as to an organization's strengths and weaknesses and as to its performance characteristics and capabilities.

Let me elaborate on each point briefly. The civilian payroll of the Federal Government is, I believe in excess of 14 billion dollars. If a fraction of a per cent of that amount were made available for the kind of research I have been discussing, the applicability to government of the general conclusions emerging from research in business and industry could be tested and validated or modified within a relatively short period of time. Such research would establish far sounder foundations upon which to base the art of public administration than now exists. This would lead to better administration, greater productivity, and lower costs. Based on the results obtained in business organizations when research findings are applied, increases in productivity many times greater than the sums spent on the research could reasonably be expected. I believe that all persons seriously interested in reducing the costs of government should examine carefully the promise which this approach offers.

Using Proper Variables

Turning now to my second recommendation. There are three broad classes of variables that need to be measured if one wishes to have accurate information about an organization. These are the causal variables, the intervening variables and the end-result variables. The *causal* variables are the independent variables such as the structure of the organization and management's policies, decisions, strategies, and behavior. The *intervening* variables reflect the internal state and health of the organization. Examples of the intervening variables of interest here include: the loyalties, attitudes, motivations, performance goals, perceptions, and skills of all members of the organization and the organization's capacity for effective interaction, communication, and decision making. The *end-result* variables are the dependent variables which reflect the results achieved by the organization, such as its productivity, costs, scrap loss, and total output.

All three of these broad classes of variables need to be measured at periodic intervals if one wishes to understand the current state of an organization, its performance capacity, and the character of its current operation. The periodic measurements of these variables, and observations of the changes and trends in them would, for example, actually reveal the consequences of productivity increases when accompanied by the liquidation of some of the human assets. Such information would enable more accurate and hard-headed accounting and avoid the erroneous conclusions often drawn today from short-range trends.

There is an even more important use of the measurements of all three classes of variables. If made regularly available to each administrator or supervisor, these measurements would motivate him to improve his managerial performance and would provide him with powerful resources for enabling him to recognize and diagnose his inadequacies as a manager, to discover what changes he should make in his behavior, and to learn from the measurements whether the corrective steps he has tried to take have actually yielded the improvement he seeks.

This single use of these measurements, particularly the measurements of the causal and intervening variables, in "feedback" processes, coupled with intelligent and supportive coaching, could readily yield improvements in productivity and costs many times greater than the amount which I suggest be spent for research.

The art of public administration plays a key role in our effectiveness as a nation. Improvement in this art, as I have endeavored to show, can be greatly accelerated by building sounder foundations based on rigorous, quantitative research. The encouragement and support of this research offers, in my judgment, the most constructive approach to providing adequate and efficient administration while keeping the costs of government at a minimum. I sincerely hope we will see a substantial increase in the amount of this research conducted both by government agencies themselves and also conducted for them by university and similar research organizations.

QUESTIONS

1. What changes are taking place in the art of management? Do you agree with the trend?
2. Discuss the effects of direct, hierarchical management pressure for production upon the performance of the organization and upon the people.
3. Discuss the implications for public administration of Likert's findings and recommendations.
4. There are three broad classes of variables that need to be measured if one wishes to have accurate information about an organization and its performance capabilities. What are these and how can they be used?

28.

How Attitude Surveys Can Help You Manage

M. SCOTT MYERS

Ever since managers learned that behavior is related to attitudes, they have been interested in measuring and changing attitudes. Most large companies in the last two or three decades have at least experimented with attitude surveys, and many of them administer them routinely as a part of their ongoing industrial relations program. Unfortunately, attitude surveys are often administered without thoughtful analysis of what their purposes should be. Like many other programs such as performance reviews, suggestion systems and communication programs, they often administer them because "other progressive companies do," and value them as symbols of progressive management.

The Traditional Way

Let's review the traditional fate of an attitude survey. A typical attitude questionnaire is a form containing approximately a hundred items of the type illustrated in Figure 1.

Forms are administered to employees, usually by an outside consultant, and responses to each item are calculated and tabulated by job classification, shift, plant location and various other categories. The report is generally sent to top management where it is reviewed behind the closed doors of an executive conference room. Though such a report always contains much positive information, it inevitably contains such information which is seen as "negative," "ungrateful" or "disloyal." Managers, who naturally have strong proprietary interests in the company, usually find it difficult to understand why employees express anticompany feelings and feel hurt when employees question their motives and competence.

Relative Importance of Items

The inability to determine the relative importance of the items complicates their interpretation. Which, for example, is the most serious problem—50 per cent don't

---

Reprinted from *Training and Development Journal*, Vol. 21, No. 10 (October 1967), pp. 34–36; 38–41, by permission of the publisher.
M. Scott Myers is an organization development consultant.

like the cateferia, 30 per cent are dissatisfied with the hours of work, or 20 per cent believe favoritism exists in their department? Just blindly following percentages could be misleading, as the cafeteria may be a less important problem than favoritism. So, managers often hang on the dilemma of trying to identify the real problems which deserve their attention and, even if they agree, trying to plan remedial action. Traditionally, they conclude their review by saying, "I am sure there is an important message here for us that can help us become more effective as managers. But, this stuff is dynamite and we've got to be careful who sees it." They adjourn their meeting without an action plan and put off doing anything further until it is safe to file the report away forever in the personnel department archives.

When they administered the questionnaires, they promised to give employees the results of the survey. But, since it is "dangerous" for employees to see *all* the data, they publish a report which reads something like this:

The attitude survey administered in the Ajax Company seven months ago has been analyzed, and much useful information has been obtained from this survey. It was gratifying to note that most of you were very positive in your attitudes toward the company, our fringe benefits, the cafeteria and hours of work. Ninety per cent of you said you were proud to work at Ajax!

A few felt there was opportunity for improvement in the administration of the performance review and wage and salary program. Surprisingly, very few were acquainted with their opportunities for advancement, but many had confidence in top management. Some of you felt that favoritism was a problem in your department, but most of you thought your supervisor was qualified for his job.

This information is very useful because it indicates a need to clarify career opportunities in Ajax and policies governing growth with the company, and it stresses our need to continue our efforts in supervisory training. No company is perfect, of course, but we believe ours is better than most, and we are doing everything in our power to make Ajax the kind of company you want it to be.

We would like to take this opportunity to thank all of you for your useful suggestions, and hope to ask you from time to time for additional suggestions.

With the publication of this report in the company newspaper, management has "done its duty," and fulfilled the need for feedback. Such a white-washed report usually deceives no one but the managers, and employees don't react to this insult to their intelligence only because they are accustomed to it, and they really didn't expect much else. This type of management behavior is so commonplace that many employees have come to accept it as the traditional behavior of managers; and, while they resent it, they apparently have come to believe that since so many managers act this way, there must be some reason for it. Managers, and employees themselves, do not often realize that complaints, grievances, absenteeism, tardiness, malingering, picketing, slowdowns, strikes, etc., are primarily symptoms of mismanagement.

The Involvement Approach[1]

Attitude surveys needn't follow this traditional pattern. They have potential for serving a number of constructive purposes, as illustrated by the attitude measurement program now being applied in several operations in Texas Instruments.

Every year a questionnaire of the type illustrated in Figure 1 is administered to a 10 to 20 per cent sample of employees throughout the company. Profiles, as il-

[1] The author wishes to acknowledge the key role played by Earl Weed, Corporate Personnel Director, in guiding the introduction of the involvement approach in Texas Instruments.

	Agree	?	Disagree
The hours of work here are O.K.	( )	( )	( )
I'm paid fairly compared with other employees.	( )	( )	( )
My supervisor has always been fair in his dealings with me.	( )	( )	( )
I have confidence in the fairness and honesty of management.	( )	( )	( )
I work in a friendly environment.	( )	( )	( )
I know how my job fits in with other work in this organization.	( )	( )	( )
My supervisor welcomes our ideas even when they differ from his own.	( )	( )	( )
I'm proud to work for this company.	( )	( )	( )
Favoritism is a problem in my area.	( )	( )	( )
I have very few complaints about our lunch facilities.	( )	( )	( )

FIGURE 1   Typical attitude survey items.

lustrated in Figure 2, are prepared from the results and delivered to each of approximately 160 department managers. The heavy solid line shows the company average for this year and is the same on every profile. The thin solid line is this year's department results and the dotted line is last year's department results. These detailed profiles, which fill 22 pages for each department, enable the manager to compare his department's results for each item to the total company results and to his last year's profile.

When first administered in TI, attitude survey results were fed back in top-to-bottom sequence, beginning with the president, thereby putting middle managers in an uncomfortable defensive position. To avoid this conflict situation, the reporting procedure was changed to issue reports directly to department heads. This enabled them to analyze the results, plan corrective action and report both the results and action plans upward, thereby making it a more positive experience. Though the department head's situation was improved by this new procedure, lower levels of supervision and nonsuper-

visory employees were sometimes put on the defensive and were not always in agreement with the department head's interpretation of survey results. The final and logical step in the development of the program was to change the procedure to involve nonsupervisors in the analysis of results, as illustrated in Figure 3.

Now, upon receipt of the profiles (on Vu-graph transparencies), the department head presents and discusses them in general terms to a group meeting of all members of his department, and then hands them to a committee of hourly employees (or non-supervisory salaried employees for salaried groups) for detailed analysis and recommendations. Committee members may be selected by a manager, selected by an appointed committee chairman or formed by an informal group process. Committee members usually number about six, and are authorized to meet as often as required on company time to analyze the results. A member of the personnel department orients the committee members and then leaves them to function as an autonomous group, returning to the group only if requested.

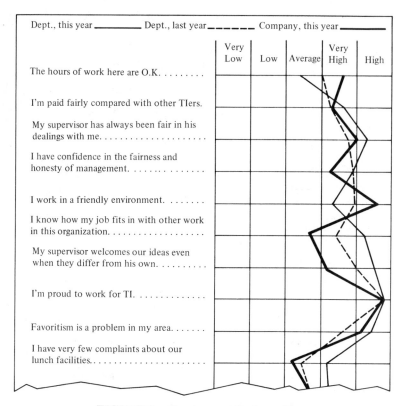

	Very Low	Low	Average	Very High	High
The hours of work here are O.K.					
I'm paid fairly compared with other TIers.					
My supervisor has always been fair in his dealings with me.					
I have confidence in the fairness and honesty of management.					
I work in a friendly environment.					
I know how my job fits in with other work in this organization.					
My supervisor welcomes our ideas even when they differ from his own.					
I'm proud to work for TI.					
Favoritism is a problem in my area.					
I have very few complaints about our lunch facilities.					

Dept., this year ——————— Dept., last year ——————— Company, this year———————

FIGURE 2 Employee attitude profile.

Typically, a committee will meet in four or five 2-hour sessions, questioning fellow employees between sessions to gain information and insights in preparation for the next meeting. Committee members finally prepare a written report for the department head, summarizing their interpretation of the survey results and recommendations for improvements. The department head shares these findings with middle and lower managers, and together they formulate corrective action.

Face-to-Face Meetings

The department head meets with the committee to discuss their recommendations and clarify points of misunderstanding. This face-to-face meeting is most successful in an atmosphere of informality, approval and authentic relationships. Unfortunately, the more threatening managers usually have the worst problems and are least successful in getting committee members to level with them. However, committee members acting as spokesmen for their peers are able to say things which they wouldn't say individually.

Serious misunderstandings are often clarified through these meetings. For example, one department head, in a spirit of angry resignation said, "From reading your report, it seems that I have no recourse but to fire Bill and Peter (foremen)." Committee members hastily replied, "Oh no, we wouldn't want that to happen; we believe they can change." Needless to say, with this vote of confidence, these two foremen made sincere

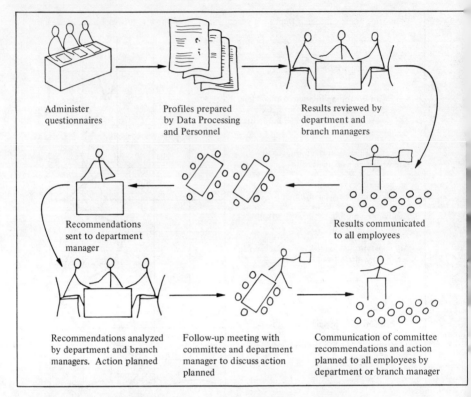

Administer
questionnaires

Profiles prepared
by Data Processing
and Personnel

Results reviewed by
department and
branch managers

Recommendations
sent to department
manager

Results communicated
to all employees

Recommendations analyzed
by department and branch
managers. Action planned

Follow-up meeting with
committee and department
manager to discuss action
planned

Communication of committee
recommendations and action
planned to all employees by
department or branch manager

FIGURE 3 Attitude survey flow chart.

efforts to become more effective and, though their enthusiasm was not immediately translated into supervisory competence, their earnest efforts evoked the forbearance of their subordinates.

Finally, a meeting is held with all members of the department to explain the results of the survey, the committees' recommendations and actions to be taken. Usually, this presentation consists of three parts:

1. A description of actions to be taken immediately.
2. Actions to be taken at some future, specified time.
3. Recommendations which cannot be implemented, or must be deferred, and the reason why.

The involvement of employees in the analysis of survey results serves many purposes. First, it is direct feedback of survey results to those who participated in the survey, ungarnished by value judgments of managers. Second, the appeal for help in solving company problems reflects a philosophy of confidence in, and respect for, the individual which is most likely to evoke behavior which earns this trust. Third, it is a form of vertical job enlargement which takes the employee out of restrictive unthinking repetition and affords an opportunity for initiative. Finally, recommendations made by the persons closest to the problem have been more valid than those of managers and staff people.

Summary

In summary, the attitude survey can serve the manager in three basic functions:

Committee Report for XYZ Department

Problems	*Recommendations*
1. New employees are sometimes hired for good jobs that old employees are qualified to fill.	1. Post job openings on bulletin boards and explain procedure for bidding on these jobs.
2. Sometimes employees are not told till Friday night that they are expected to work on Saturday.	2. Give at least two days' notice of the requirement to work on weekends.
3. Some believe that salary comparisons with other companies do not take into consideration overtime pay practices in effect in other companies.	3. Define the normal work week for salaried personnel which serves as the basis for salary comparisons with other companies
4. We sometimes read about company events in local newspapers before we hear about them in the company.	4. Let employees hear first about company events through department meetings, newspaper, bulletins and supervisors.
5. We are often pulled off a job before it's finished and put on another rush job.	5. Better planning and more consideration on the part of supervision could correct most of this.
6. Some items on attitude survey are confusing.	6. Give Corporate Personnel a list of confusing items with suggested changes.
7. Because the attitude survey is done on a sample basis, a lot of people feel "left out."	7. Increase the size of the samples or explain why you can't.

FIGURE 4 Problems and committee suggestions.

1. It provides the manager with measures of managerial effectiveness—through trend data with which he can check his progress from year to year, and by enabling him to compare his department with the rest of the company and with other companies.

2. It identifies problems and evolves workable solutions for solving them.

3. It serves as a medium for involving employees in the analysis and solution of problems, thereby contributing to their personal and professional growth.

QUESTIONS

1. Why is it often difficult to interpret attitude survey findings? How may this dilemma be resolved?
2. Why do some managements feel impelled to give a meaningless and bland report of the survey findings to their work force?
3. Describe and evaluate the procedure recommended by the author.
4. Are there risks associated with openness and frankness in discussing survey findings with employees?

29.

Participative Management:
A Practical Experience

FREDERICK B. CHANEY and KENNETH S. TEEL

In recent years, increasing numbers of employees have pressured for greater involvement and relevance in their day-to-day, on-the-job activities. Like today's college students, many have openly resisted authoritarian, "do as you're told" management practices. Instead, they have demanded a voice in determining what they are to do, how they are to do it, and even how they are to be evaluated. In short, more and more employees have insisted on being in on decisions that affect them and on being involved in what they consider to be meaningful work.

To meet these demands, many companies have adopted participative management practices. Some, like Harwood and Texas Instruments, have been highly successful. Others, not so well publicized, have been unsuccessful. Most, undoubtedly, have fallen somewhere between the two extremes. To show how participative management techniques can be successfully introduced and used on a

continuing basis, this article describes the authors' four years of experience in implementing and applying such techniques at Autonetics, a division of North American Rockwell.

Before describing how to use participative management techniques, it seems appropriate to discuss briefly why a company might wish to use them. Obviously, no profit-oriented company exists solely to satisfy its employees' personal needs; rather, it has at least two fundamental goals—to survive and to make a profit. Effective use of participative management techniques can help reach these goals. When employees have "a piece of the action," they identify more closely with the company; they develop greater esprit de corps; and, perhaps most important, they work harder to achieve goals they have helped to establish. In other words, participative management can bring about increased employee motivation.

At the same time, involving employees in identifying and solving production

Reprinted by permission of the publisher from *Personnel*, November–December 1972, ©
1972 by AMACOM, a division of American Management Associations.
   Frederick B. Chaney is president of Continuing Education Corporation. Kenneth S. Teel is
Professor of Manpower Management at California State University.

problems can result in improved technical solutions. Employees who face problems on a day-to-day basis often develop a clearer understanding of the nature of the problems and sounder ideas of how they might be solved than do experts brought in to deal with them. Providing a supportive environment in which employees are encouraged to express their ideas can make available to the company a reservoir of previously untapped technical expertise.

Despite these logical and persuasive theories and apparent advantages, at Autonetics it was decided that pilot studies should be conducted before any systematic attempt to introduce participative management throughout the production facility.

The Pilot Studies: Quality Assurance

The first study was conducted in an electronics inspection department. There, supervisors of two equivalent groups were given six hours of instruction in principles and techniques of employee motivation and performance improvement, supplemented by one hour of individual counseling by the staff psychologist on the specific goal-setting techniques to be used. After this training, the supervisors met with their subordinates and encouraged them to establish goals for a reduction in paperwork errors, which were excessive and were causing delays in shipping the end product. One supervisor met with his inspectors as a group for approximately one hour each week for four weeks; the second supervisor held a series of short individual conferences during the same period. Both participative techniques resulted in establishment of goals of 50 per cent reductions in paperwork errors, but, during the three-month evaluation period, reductions in errors of approximately 75 per cent were obtained by the first group, whereas the second group showed no significant improvement.

Experience gained in this study indicated that it was impossible to make a clear-cut distinction between group and individual goal setting. Employees were generally reluctant to establish individual goals until they knew how their own performance compared with the department average. So, in reality, goals set in individual supervisor-employee conferences were strongly influenced by the performance of the group as a whole. Furthermore, both supervisors indicated a strong preference for the group procedure, because it required less time to cover the same number of employees and it provided an opportunity for employees to exchange ideas on how the goals might be met. These findings, along with the apparent superiority of the group goal-setting process, led to a decision to use the group process in all subsequent studies.

One other finding that emerged from this initial study: it was extremely difficult and somewhat artificial to try to get employees to establish more challenging goals without discussing the factors that limited group performance. Group problem solving seemed to be a prerequisite to goal setting—employees must be given a chance to identify and solve problems inhibiting performance before they could be expected to set and meet more ambitious goals.

The Pilot Studies: Manufacturing

The second study was carried out to evaluate the combined effectiveness of group problem solving and goal setting in a typical manufacturing operation. Five supervisors in electronics assembly took an eight-hour training course in participative management, covering traditional topics such as principles of motivation, performance measurement, feedback, and communications, as well as the group problem-solving and goal-setting processes. The supervisors were also given practice in the use of discussion leadership techniques and individual counseling by staff psychologists after each meeting.

Next, each supervisor conducted a series of eight biweekly, half-hour meetings with his employees. Quantitative data on quantity and quality of production were obtained for three of the five groups. (Similar data were not available for the other two.) Two months after initial goal setting, one group had increased its output from 12 to 17 cables per week and had reduced its defect rate from eight to less than three per cable. A second group, by changing from a stationized assembly line, in which each person performed a series of specialized tasks, to an individual-build approach, in which each built the complete circuit board, reduced production time from 5.5 to 4.2 hours per board and defect rates by 50 per cent. A third group reduced assembly time per system by 50 per cent and defect rates by 40 per cent. Improved performance by this group alone resulted in a saving of approximately $20,000 in five months.

Getting the Bugs Out of the Program

Even though these early attempts in manufacturing were quite successful, several problems were noted:

• The supervisors appeared to need more individual guidance in conducting their initial sessions than had originally been assumed. Several found that they were unable to create the proper atmosphere or to supply the information requested by their subordinates during their first few group meetings. Two commented that they would have stopped the meetings after the first two or three if they had not received additional counseling by the staff psychologist for an average of two hours per week.
• The formal classroom instruction seemed to be of little value in preparing supervisors for the group sessions. Instead, the most effective training seemed to occur in the group meetings themselves—"learning by doing"—and in the individual supervisor-psychologist coaching sessions held immediately after each training session.
• All of the participating supervisors stated that their superiors did not fully understand and therefore did not adequately support the use of participative techniques. As a matter of fact, some of the superiors openly expressed doubts about the value of the meetings and questioned whether supervisors should pull their employees off the production line to take part in such meetings. This finding clearly demonstrated that more effort was needed to orient higher levels of management before any attempt to introduce participative management at lower levels.

To overcome these deficiencies, the implementation program was modified before participative management was launched throughout most of the production areas, and in some engineering organizations. The key elements in the revised program were these:
• Management orientation
• Supervisory seminars
• Supervisor-group meetings, emphasizing performance measurement, problem solving, and goal setting
• Coaching of supervisors by staff psychologists
• Management follow-up

Since the revised program proved to be markedly successful, the discussion that follows might be considered a how-to-guide for an organization interested in establishing its own participative management program.

Step 1: Management Orientation

Two informal discussion meetings were held by staff psychologists with the managers to whom the supervisors participating in the program reported to ensure that the managers both understood and supported the program. The rationale underlying the use of participative management was described; the successful pilot studies were detailed; the concepts to be presented to the supervisors were reviewed; the overall program was outlined; suggestions were solicited as to how the program might be tailored to meet the special needs of each department; and questions were answered.

It was emphasized that (1) change occurs slowly and the managers, therefore, should not expect overnight "miracles," and (2) the supervisors would have to devote considerable time to preparing for, holding, and following up on the group meetings and might need temporary help during the early phases of the program. An attempt was made to get the managers to agree to support the program for three months and postpone evaluating it until the end of that period.

In over 90 per cent of the cases, this step resulted in a management commitment to support the program. In the few cases where it did not, no further attempt was made to implement the program in the managers' bailiwicks.

Step 2: Supervisory Seminars

In four informal, one hour seminars, a staff psychologist and five to eight supervisors discussed in depth the principles and techniques of effective communications, leadership, problem solving, and goal setting. The psychologist served primarily as a discussion leader, encouraging the supervisors to raise questions and to offer suggestions about making participative management work for them. He also attempted to set an example by conducting the seminars in the way he hoped the supervisors would conduct their own group meetings; to underscore that point, part of the final seminar was devoted to a critique of the techniques the psychologist had used as discussion leader.

Step 3: Supervisor–Group Meetings

Next, each supervisor met with his employees, as a group, once a week for 12 weeks, even though some of the supervisors still felt inadequately prepared to conduct group meetings. There were two reasons for this go-ahead: First, previous research had clearly shown that supervisors, like almost anyone else, learn best by doing. Second, if the supervisors had been given the option of having additional training until they felt fully ready to start the new program, some might have chosen an excessive amount, thereby causing serious delays and accompanying administrative complications.

To help the supervisors feel more secure, a staff psychologist attended each group meeting, serving strictly as a resource person and observer. He answered questions directed to him by the supervisor, but always referred group members' questions to the supervisor, to reinforce the fact that the supervisor was not just the designated, but the actual, discussion leader. He also made detailed notes on the supervisor's and the group's behavior, which he used as the basis for his individual coaching session with the supervisor after each meeting.

After the initial 12 weekly meetings, supervisors were encouraged to continue them, although less frequently, as meaningful problem-solving sessions, rather than routine get-togethers. Most supervisors held monthly or quarterly meetings, or scheduled them on an as-needed basis.

The first two or three group meetings were devoted primarily to identifying possible ways in which group performance could be measured objectively and quantitatively, and to selecting the most appropriate ones for tracking subsequent performance. Thus, the group members themselves played the major role in determining how their work would be evaluated.

The selected measures were used to identify areas in which group performance was above, at, or below expectations, and several meetings were then devoted to in-depth analyses of problem areas. Group members were encouraged to identify factors inhibiting production, suggest ways in which they might be handled, and, with the help of industrial engineers who served as consultants, select modifications of work methods and procedures to be adopted on a trial basis. As feedback became available on the success of the modified approaches, further changes were made if they were indicated; thus, problem solving continued through all of the meetings, and the group members remained alert to the significance of the problem identification-problem solving-feedback loop.

By the sixth or seventh meeting, most groups had established goals calling for significant improvements in performance; in those groups that had not, the staff psychologist urged the supervisor to try to get the group to agree on firm goals by the ninth meeting, for several reasons. After all, performance data had been available on a weekly basis from the third meeting on, so each group had ample information on which to base its goals. Furthermore, long-time research had pretty well proved that participation gets sound performance results only when a group makes decisions and sets firm goals. However, research had also shown that people work harder and perform better when they shoot for goals that are within their reach. Thus, it was up to the supervisor both to encourage his group to set goals and to see that the goals set were attainable. (Actually, most supervisors found themselves having to hold back the group from setting "pie in the sky," instead of realistic goals.)

STEP 4: COACHING OF SUPERVISORS

Before and after each of the first 12 group meetings, the supervisor and staff psychologist met privately for a coaching-critique session. Before the meetings, the psychologist reviewed the supervisor's performance in previous meetings, sug-

gested ways in which he might improve his effectiveness as a discussion leader, discussed the specific purposes of the forthcoming meeting, and answered any questions the supervisor had. In short, he served as a personal professional adviser in helping the supervisor prepare for the meeting. Immediately after the meeting he went over the supervisor's performance, pointing out what he had done well or poorly and suggesting ways in which he might do better next time.

The supervisors and the staff psychologists agreed that this individual coaching-feedback was the most valuable single element in preparing the supervisors, both intellectually and attitudinally, for effective use of participative management techniques. They also agreed, however, that after the first 12 meetings, the psychologist should attend subsequent meetings and provide further coaching only at the invitation of the supervisor. As far as the authors are aware, this participative management implementation program at Autonetics is the only one that gives so much emphasis to the systematic use of coaching.

STEP 5: MANAGEMENT FOLLOW-UP

After the first 12 group meetings, a second meeting was held with the managers to whom the supervisors reported. With the help of a staff psychologist, the supervisors described their experiences in the group meetings, explained changes that had been made to improve performance, reviewed the goals that had been set, showed the progress that had been made toward those goals, described their own and their employees' reactions to the program, and answered questions raised by the managers. In this way, the meeting effectively closed the loop, providing direct feedback to the managers on how well participative management had worked in their own organizations, and a suitable occasion for the managers to reinforce the behavior of the supervisors by public praise of those who had successfully used participative techniques.

How Well Did the Program Work— and Why?

During the four years the authors were involved in the Autonetics program, quantitative performance data were obtained for 40 groups. Of these, 27 showed statistically significant performance gains; 12 showed no significant changes; and one showed a significant decline. The 27 averaged 20–30 per cent increases in production, along with 30–50 per cent decreases in errors, and they also exhibited more positive attitudes (via a questionnaire survey) toward the company after being involved in the program. It therefore seems reasonable to conclude, generally, that the overall program was successful. Participative management is no panacea. It will not solve all management problems; it may not achieve any gains at all in some cases. Nevertheless, the two-out-of-three batting average reported here suggests that the odds are heavily in favor of a well-planned and carefully-conducted implementation program. Furthermore, the dollar value of the gains achieved in the successful groups should, as it did in this instance, far exceed the total cost of the program for all groups, successful or not-so-successful.

Detailed analyses of the data and observations of the individual groups lead to a number of more specific conclusions:

A Little No Better Than None. Unless the supervisor succeeds in generating a fairly high level of participation in his group, the chances of achieving worthwhile performance gains are extremely low—a prediction borne out by a study conducted by one of the authors as part of the overall implementation program at Autonetics.

Six groups were ranked by level of participation, on the basis of observations made independently by two staff psychologists. The two rankings were identical, so the top two groups were categorized as high in participation, the next two as medium, and the last two as low. Performance and attitude data were also obtained for two equivalent groups in the same organization in which participative techniques were not used. Attitude measures for all groups were obtained by computing the percentage of positive responses to a 30-item job related questionnaire.

It was found that medium to high levels of participation resulted in significant improvements in both attitudes and performance. Even low levels of participation resulted in more positive attitudes, but they did not evince any tangible performance benefits over the three-month period covered by the study. Expressed positive attitudes showed an almost linear improvement with increased participation, ranging from 35 per cent for the no-participation groups to 80 per cent for the high. On the other hand, performance showed no noteworthy changes for the no- and low-participation groups, but highly significant improvements for both the medium and high groups. The gains achieved by the high-participation groups, however, were almost twice as great as those of the medium groups.

Supervisors the Key Element. Observation of both those groups in which participation was successful and those in which it was not revealed that the individual supervisor was the crucial factor. His attitudes and behavior strongly influenced the level of participation achieved; the level of participation, in turn, determined the extent of the gains achieved.

The "successful" supervisors by words and actions made clear their genuine interest in employee ideas and feelings. They created an open, supportive atmosphere; they identified areas where they needed help; they actively solicited employee comments; they listened attentively to those comments, without making snap judgments; and they provided feedback at every meeting about what they were doing to implement employee suggestions.

Most of the "unsuccessful" supervisors, on the other hand, went through the motions of asking for employee comments and suggestions but actually did not pay much attention to them. Employees were quick to see that they were simply taking part in another exercise and typically offered only superficial or negative comments.

Discussions with several of these supervisors brought out two major reasons for their ineffective use of participative techniques. Some had used authoritarian management techniques for so long that they were convinced that they had sole responsibility for making decisions affecting the group; under pressure from higher management, they apparently subscribed to the participation idea, but did not really involve their employees in the decision-making process. The other reason was that a few who were relatively new to supervision felt insecure and were reluctant to reveal their own weaknesses by asking their employees for help in solving work-group problems.

As was pointed out earlier, participative management is not for everyone. If the supervisor is not sold on participation or if he is insecure, he would probably be better off using other management techniques.

It Helps, but Participation Doesn't Have to Start with the Boss. All of the supervisors in this program were at the first level, and most of them, particularly in the factory, worked for superiors who used rather authoritarian management techniques. Nevertheless, as we have seen, two out of three were able to obtain significant improvements in employee performance and attitudes by using partic-

ipative techniques, and several of their bosses have since begun to follow the participative approach. Thus, successful implementation occurred from the bottom up, rather than in the more traditional top-down direction. (Of course, the management orientation at the outset established at least a hands-off, wait-and-see management commitment to what the supervisors were about to try.)

A top-down program undoubtedly would have been faster, and it might have been more effective, but it might also have had only token acceptance, which would have died out as soon as another management technique received the blessing of top executives. At Autonetics, demonstrating the value of the program at the first level proved to be highly effective in enlisting strong top-level support for continuing and expanding it.

Group Goal Setting Not a Must. Under certain circumstances—for example, when firm contractual commitments have already been established—it may not be possible to allow a group to set its own production goals. Even then, though, participation can be used both to gain group acceptance of the predetermined goals and to identify ways in which those goals can best be met. In one such case, the supervisor personally set a new production goal at the level demanded by contract but succeeded in obtaining a high level of participation by explaining fully why that goal had to be met, by showing a real interest in getting the employees' help in identifying and solving the problems facing the group, and by putting into effect many of their suggestions for changes in work methods and procedures. The success of his approach was evidenced by the fact that his employees surpassed a goal that was twice what their production had averaged during the two and a half months prior to the first group meeting.

It is evident that group goal setting is

not a requisite for successful use of participation. What is a requisite, however, when the supervisor sets the goals—and perhaps particularly then—is his positive attitude in dealing with the group.

Participative vs. Permissive Management. Some critics of participative management have contended that it is too permissive, that it results in the supervisor's abandoning his prerogatives and relegating his responsibilities to the group. Apparently, these critics have confused participative with laissez-faire management. True participative management requires that the supervisor work closely and actively with his employees to plan, organize, coordinate, and control the work of the group. The supervisor shares his responsibilities with the group—he does not surrender them.

Furthermore, he often has to provide firm guidelines to keep group meetings focused on appropriate topics; he has to provide information on requirements imposed on the group by the larger organization of which it is a part; he has to take the lead in deciding which of the group's suggestions should be implemented and in seeing that they are implemented; and he has to establish a system for providing regular feedback on how well the group is doing.

In short, true participative management is an active, goal-oriented process in which the supervisor works *together* with his employees to identify and solve the problems they share. By so doing, he makes them feel more important and thereby creates an environment in which they not only produce more but also are more satisfied with their work.

A Prognosis of Cautious Optimism

The implementation program described here was successful in a large majority of the cases in one large company. With management commitment and perhaps some minor modifications to meet the requirements of a particular organization, it should be just as successful in other companies, regardless of their size.

Participative management offers no simple, easy solution to all organizational problems; for managers and supervisors who are willing to work hard at it, however, it does offer high probabilities of payoff in both increased production and improved employee attitudes. Participative management is a practical way of integrating individual and organizational goals. It gives employees opportunities to play active roles in planning, coordinating, and controlling their own work, and thus makes employees' work more meaningful and relevant. For the modern manager having to deal with a workforce demanding more voice in shaping its own activities and destiny, participative management seems to offer a promising route to the satisfaction of employee needs and, at the same time, increased company profits. Who can fault that combination?

QUESTIONS

1. Why might a company's management decide to install a participative management program?
2. Discuss the problems involved in setting performance goals for or with hourly employees.
3. What problems face the front-line supervisor who wants to manage his department by a participative management system?

4. "Some critics of participative management have contended that it is too permissive, that it results in the supervisor's abandoning his prerogatives and relegating his responsibilities to the group." Discuss and evaluate this quotation from the article.

5. Some authorities claim that participative management works best when it is implemented by top management and works its way downward through to the lower levels of the organization. Yet this process apparently did not occur at Autonetics. How would you explain the success of this program which operated without apparent real top-management involvement?

30.

A Nonpartisan View of Participative Management

HAROLD M. F. RUSH

"Alienation" is a word that seems to appear today whenever there is a discussion of the characteristics of America's workforce. Social critics frequently attribute the alienated workers' discontent to the "dehumanization of work," and many a polemic has been directed against the poor quality of the working life. Indeed, the problem of poor motivation—when it's argued to result in lowered productivity—is obvious cause for concern among the business community and to the nation as a whole. This year that concern became official with the report of a special inquiry by HEW into the problem of worker alienation.[1]

While it is generally agreed that a large part of the working population is apathetic —disenchanted by the work it does—a similar concensus on the remedy for the situation is wanting. Some see the solution as a matter of shortening the hours or lessening the number of days worked in order to provide more leisure or elective time for workers. Others prescribe revisions of work sequences in several kinds of job design, hoping to enlarge or enrich the jobs people hold. Still others recommend greater worker involvement in the decisions that affect them through the practice of "participative management."

Participation is a recurring theme in the management literature of the past two decades, for the concepts of employee participation are cardinal tenets of the behavioral science or "organization development" school of managing. Partisans of participative management often display missionary zeal as champions of a new order in which employees join with management in setting goals, solving problems, and managing tasks and jobs on an everyday basis.

Still, the question remains: is participative management an ideal or a reality? In pursuit of an answer, The Conference Board recently completed a study of methods designed to improve the effec-

Reprinted from *The Conference Board Record*, Vol. 10, No. 4 (April 1973), pp. 34–39, by permission of The Conference Board.

Harold M. F. Rush is a member of The Conference Board Management Research unit.

[1] *Work in America* (Cambridge, Mass., The MIT Press, 1973).

tiveness of business organizations.[2] The 147 U.S. and Canadian firms that participated in the study were designated, by a panel of nationally known behavioral science theorists and practitioners, as "OD companies or "non-OD companies"—that is, as firms that actually practice the concepts of organization development or as those that do not. Each company was surveyed in detail about several kinds of corporate activities, and the responses of the OD and non-OD companies were compared.

Although the sample was small—45 OD and 102 non-OD companies—and the possibility of "rater bias" must be taken into account, there is good reason to conclude from the results of the study that the OD companies do, in fact, try more often than non-OD companies to translate the concepts of participation into actual practice. And this would seem to confirm the differences in the relative value placed upon participative management philosophy by the two groups of companies.

Measuring Participation

Participation may occur in any number of circumstances and at any or all hierarchical levels of the organization. However, although there is widespread intellectual acceptance of the concept of participation as a means of humanizing work and of gaining greater employee motivation, in most instances, according to the survey, participation occurs only at the upper levels of the organization. Still, proponents of the participative style management insist that the concept be applied wherever appropriate, in all jobs and at all levels of the organization. And for them, the "acid test" of commitment to real participation is the involvement of employees at the rank-and-file level of the

organization. Thus, measuring degrees of involvement becomes important.

The most commonly used methods of assessing employee attitudes is through some kind of systematic attitude measurement. This is usually accomplished by a detailed survey administered at periodic intervals, or at a time of change in policy or practice. Of the 102 non-OD companies participating in The Conference Board's study, only 38% report the use of such surveys, compared with 71% of the OD companies. Only 16% of the non-OD companies include employees at all levels in these surveys, while 29% of the OD companies cover the whole organization in their surveys.

Moreover, of those companies that do not include the entire organization, 31% of the OD companies report that white collar, nonmanagerial employees are surveyed, and 27% say they include blue collar employees. White collar employees are included in attitude surveys by only 19% of the non-OD companies, and blue collar employees by just 15% (Table 1).

What happens to the information after it is collected varies from company to company. Generally it is used to assess the fundamental climate of the organization —the problems employees encounter in the course of their work, their understanding of goals and objectives that determine the quantity, pace, and quality of their work, and the nature of the interpersonal relationships that are considered so vital to the work environment. Sometimes management may compare these attitudes with attitudes at another point in time, or may assess employee acceptance of changes effected or anticipated. Whatever the uses of the attitude surveys, most behavioral scientists agree that the persons participating in the surveys have a right to know the results, whether or not the findings put the company and

[2] Harold M. F. Rush, *Organization Development: A Reconnaissance*, to be published by The Conference Board, spring 1973.

management in a favorable light. Thus, it is interesting to note that only a third of the non-OD companies The Conference Board studied give such feedback to their employee participants, while more than 60% of the OD companies regularly furnish results to those surveyed (Table 1).

A psychologist employed by a large international chemical company complained about his company's use of attitude survey data. "Too often," he stated, "we ask for employee attitudes and opinions in great detail, but in most cases, once we have the data, nothing is done with it. And this is because the employees are telling management things that management doesn't want to hear, so management ignores the findings. Then they wonder why we continue to have discontent, grievances, and strikes. It would be better not to ask the employees what they believe and feel than to ask them and do nothing. For this reason, I wish we didn't go through the motions of collecting attitudinal data. At least we wouldn't be insulting the employees."

That such survey data can be extremely valuable is a feeling shared by many of the managers who responded to The Board's questions. They believe that sources of dissatisfaction uncovered by elaborate surveys in which employees speak candidly, and with anonymity, may be a most valuable source of information about working conditions and practices for management. Some even believe that the survey data can be used as a basis for modifications, corrections, or improvements by the employees themselves, since those closest to the problem have a better grasp of its entirety and are most capable of correcting it—an obvious example of the application of shared responsibility. More than half of the OD companies, compared with only 8% of the non-OD companies, report using attitude survey data as the basis for improving employee work situations (Table 1).

TABLE 1 Attitude Survey Practices

	Non-OD Companies (N = 102)	OD Companies (N = 45)
Company conducts systematic surveys	39 (38%)	32 (71%)
Surveys include all organizational levels	16 (16%)	13 (29%)
Surveys include nonmanagement, "white collar" employees	19 (19%)	14 (31%)
Surveys include "blue collar" employees	15 (15%)	12 (27%)
All those surveyed received feedback	34 (33%)	28 (62%)
Work groups use survey data for own improvement	9 (8%)	23 (51%)

Group Problem Solving

It is common knowledge that the growth and effectiveness of individuals and organizations are closely tied to their ability to identify and solve the problems they encounter. In business firms these problems may be related to the economic or material aspects of the organization, or they may take the form of interpersonal problems between peers, subordinates, and superiors as they relate to each other in the work environment. Often the problems are both economic and interpersonal.

Working on the premise that "all of us know more than any one of us knows," many organizations undertake problem identification and resolution in a group setting. Here, ideally, several perspectives and kinds of expertise can be brought to bear upon the problem. Further, this participative-group approach to problem solving is undertaken on the assumption that people will be more committed to overcoming a problem if they have helped to decide upon the strategy to be used.

How frequently is the approach taken? Nearly half of the non-OD companies in The Board's study responded that they use participative-group methods of problem solving, and virtually all the OD companies report similar methods (Table 2). But a more pronounced difference between the designated groups appears when we analyze the composition of the problem solving groups. Forty percent of the OD companies report that they use group methods for problem solving at all levels within the organization, wherever appropriate. This contrasts sharply with the 6% of the non-OD firms that report involvement of all levels and jobs in the group problem solving process.

Among those companies that do not use participative-group methods at all levels, seven firms (16%) in the OD group of companies do at least involve lower management and rank-and-file employees in the activity. Four firms (4%) in the non-OD group do the same.

Although a large number of non-OD companies report using some participative-group methods for problem solving, few carry the process into the lower levels of the organization. Thus, the participatory approach remains confined to the upper ranks of management and among scientific and professional employees. By comparison, a majority of the OD firms include employees at lower levels.

Goal Setting

In the matter of goal setting, a process closely allied to problem solving, appropriateness of participation is considered a

TABLE 2   Poblem Solving and Goal Settiing

	NON-OD COMPANIES (N = 102)	OD COMPANIES (N = 45)
Company uses participative-group methods of problem solving	48 (47%)	44 (98%)
All levels participate in problem solving	7 (6%)	18 (40%)
Lower management and rank and file participate in problem solving	4 (4%)	7 (16%)
Rank and file help to set short-range goals	0 (0%)	14 (31%)

key variable. For example, lower levels of the corporate hierarchy are thought to have neither the perspective nor the expertise to establish the long-range goals of the organization. The appropriate level for this kind of goal setting is clearly at the top of the organization, where responsibility and accountability for the larger goals and objectives lie.

In the setting of short-range goals, however, it is thought practicable to include those persons responsible for achieving them. For these goals not only have shorter time spans, but their achievment can be more easily controlled through the efforts of employees at the work group level. Behavioral scientists posit, moreover, that it is not only appropriate but most desirable in terms of motivation that the employees who have responsibility for working towards short-range goals have a voice in establishing the goals.

Of course, work groups do not set goals at random. Short-range goals are established within the larger framework of long-range corporate goals, even in the most permissive or participative organizations. Further, the level of employees who help to set short-range goals is highly dependent upon the scope and nature of the goals under consideration. The Conference Board study reveals that while participation in the setting of short-range goals may take place at all levels of supervision, it is noticeably lacking at the rank-and-file employee level. Even among the OD companies, only 14 firms—less than a third of the OD company sample—report the involvement of rank-and-file in short-range goal setting (Table 2). But, even that small number of companies stands in marked contrast to the non-OD companies, *none* of which report involvement at that level.

Communication

In a very real sense, comunication is the lifeblood of an organization's operation. Communication is also, for behavioral scientists as well as practitioners, a major focus of organization development programs. They speak of communication in terms of the *process*, as distinguished from the media. Thus communication for them includes everything that transpires whenever people attempt to convey information, ideas, or feelings, and feedback is an integral component of it. The exercises they use to improve communication among individuals and groups most often take place in face-to-face small group settings, and the emphasis is on experiential learning, rather than intellectual or "head-level" learning.

The Conference Board study shows that such exercises take place almost exclusively at the managerial levels of the companies. Seventeen (17%) of the non-OD companies report experience-based communication activities, but only two of them include all employee levels in their programs. Two others conduct special exercises to improve communication exclusively among rank-and-file employees. While 38 (84%) of the OD companies, on the other hand, conduct experience-based activities, only twelve include all organizational levels. Eight of the OD companies (18%) hold communication improvement activities at the rank-and-file level. Exercises to improve communication between rank-and-file employees and their superiors, first-line supervision, are reported by only 3% of the non-OD sample, while the figure is 18% for the OD sample (Table 3).

Conflict Resolution

Companies particularly interested in organizational development often undertake special exercises to bring interpersonal conflict out in the open—to identify its sources and deal with the issues. Increasingly the emphasis in these exercises is less on resolution than on management of conflict, but, the primary aim is to bring conflicting parties together in a situation which allows them to deal with their problems in an atmosphere of objectivity. Here, it is hoped, that hitherto unexpressed and unexamined resentment or animosity, which so often impede communication and collaboration, can be aired and perhaps "evaporated."

The Conference Board's inquiry into conflict resolution activities yielded mixed results. Among the non-OD companies, less than one-fourth of them report having adopted this behavioral technique. Among the OD companies, however, almost three-fourths claim they make some kind of special effort to resolve or manage conflict (Table 3). As was true in the case of experience-based communication techniques, there is little evidence that

TABLE 3 Communication Improvement and Conflict Resolution

	NON-OD COMPANIES (N = 102)	OD COMPANIES (N = 45)
Companies using experiential exercises to improve communication process	17 (17%)	38 (84%)
Communication exercises include all organizational levels	2 (2%)	12 (27%)
Communication exercises *within* rank and file groups	2 (2%)	8 (18%)
Communication *between* rank and file and first-line supervision	3 (3%)	8 (18%)
Company has conflict resolution activities	22 (22%)	33 (73%)
Conflict resolution involves rank and file	0 (0%)	1 (2%)

companies are concerned with personal conflict among lower level employees. Only one of the OD companies reported conflict resolution exercises for rank-and-file employees, and none of the non-OD companies reported its use at that level (Table 3).

Team Building

Proponents of the behavioral science approach stress the importance of cooper-ative and collaborative team effort. To critics who decry this approach by citing the old saw about a camel being a horse designed by a committee, they point out that, in a modern company, people work in a social setting where groups are a fact of life. Therefore, they believe a man-agerial style that capitalizes upon the existence of groups is preferable to a style characterized by dealing on a one-to-one basis with subordinates.

Behavioralists insist, moreover, that co-hesiveness, common purpose, open com-munication, and real collaboration are what must be striven for if a "group" is to design the horse rather than the camel —acknowledging that an aggregation of people does not automatically make a group, nor a committee a team. They say that, in the ideal organization develop-ment model, real teams can play a crucial role in achieving organizational effective-ness.

Team building can, and does, accord-ing to our study, take many forms. Most often it consists of special meetings be-tween a supervisor and the "work family" that reports to him. Frequently these meetings are held away from the work site and employ the services of a profes-sional "third party" who observes the in-teractions and helps guide the activities of the participants. The work teams identify and deal with, in specific terms, any problems that seem to impede their effectiveness—whether these be related to interpersonal communication, inadequate equipment or systems, poor work process design, attendance and turnover, produc-tivity, or a host of other concerns. The ground rules include getting the problems and issues "out on the table" and working them through until a satisfactory solution is achieved.

While team building could be con-sidered appropriate and effective at any level of the organization, since people must interact in one way or another in the course of their jobs, it nevertheless has not yet seen widespread use at lower levels. Only 20% of the OD companies include rank-and-file employees in team building, and only 4% of the non-OD companies do so (Table 4).

Intergroup Relations

The aim of intergroup building is like that of team building—to help people to work together better—but this practice involves bringing together two interfacing work groups where collaboration is considered vital. These groups may be units from the same department or they may be from different functional segments of the organization—research and development with manufacturing, for example, or manufacturing with sales. But they are brought together to explore and attempt to resolve a problem related to their cooperation or lack thereof.

In their meetings the two groups identify and analyze specific barriers to collaboration and effectiveness. Usually teams with representatives from both groups are formed, and these propose solutions to the barriers or undertake action projects to improve the intergroup effort.

There is as little incidence of intergroup building as of team building among rank-and-file employees investigated by The Board's study. It takes place in only four of the non-OD companies, and among the OD companies it occurs in only five instances (Table 4).

Task Forces

Task forces, ad hoc groups, and other "temporary systems" are used widely in business firms. They are called by many different names, but their common trait is their temporary nature, although "temporary" may refer to one week or several years. Their membership varies. They may be a "horizontal slice" of the organization—a peer group; they may be a

TABLE 4   Teams and Task Forces

	Non-OD Companies (n = 102)	OD Companies (n = 45)
Team building for rank and file	4 (4%)	9 (20%)
Intergroup building for rank and file	4 (4%)	5 (11%)
Task forces include rank and file	10 (10%)	20 (44%)

"vertical slice" of the organization—persons within a department or function with direct reporting relationships, and usually representing several hierarchical levels; or they may be a "diagonal slice" of the organization—representatives of several reporting levels and kinds of jobs.

At any rate, they represent a company's attempt to bring to bear several kinds of expertise and differing perspectives on a problem, or to provide the various organizational levels and functions the opportunity to have some influence on the project.

Companies that practice organization development often see another value in the use of task forces—their tendency to "democratize." In other words, by creating relationships and shared responsibility among individuals who are not "officially" peers, a kind of leveling takes place which seems to foster cooperation and creativity. Especially in the vertical- or diagonal-slice task forces, there is a built-in mechanism for upward and downward communication, because members come from multiple organizational levels. It is not surprising, then, that the OD companies studied include rank and file in task forces with greater frequency than non-OD companies—44% of the OD companies, versus 10% of the non-OD companies (Table 4).

Autonomous Work Groups

Among the many remedies offered to counter worker alienation is one that carries the concepts of participation beyond the traditional means of involving employees in decisions that affect them—the autonomous work group. The term can be somewhat misleading, since autonomy is a relative thing in large business organizations, and since work groups are neither totally self-sufficient nor self-contained. However, a few companies have experimented with organizing such work groups, and these have been composed of persons and jobs with common linkages and dependencies brought together with the idea that they will develop into self-managing micro-organizations.

Clearly, these so-called autonomous work groups exist within the framework of the larger organization and their goals and objectives are determined within the objectives of the total organization. However, they do have a pronounced degree of independence that exceeds that of work groups in more traditional organization structures. Members frequently set their their own schedules, handle the division of labor within the work group, and inspect and evaluate their own output. They also control their own personnel problems such as attendance and productivity. They may even select and train new members.

Each member of the group is accountable to the rest of the group for his own behavior and contribution, while the group as a *whole* is accountable to management, and its performance is evaluated on this basis. Since there is no boss within the group, they are sometimes referred to as "leaderless" work groups.

Sometimes the autonomous work groups are established only among scientific and professional employees, but they also are formed occasionally among production workers and other lower level employees. In fact, thirteen (29%) of the OD companies The Board surveyed report

TABLE 5   Autonomous Groups and Peer Evaluations

	Non-OD Companies (N = 102)	OD Companies (N = 45)
Company has autonomous "leaderless" work groups	7 (7%)	13 (29%)
Rank and file perform peer evaluations	1 (1%)	4 (9%)

the existence of autonomous work groups at the rank-and-file level. Among the non-OD companies, seven firms (7%) report that they have such groups (Table 5).

Peer Evaluation

Members of autonomous work groups not only evaluate each other's performance, but they may also seek to regulate each other's behavior and performance. Another form of peer evaluation can occur in work settings that do not have autonomous work groups. Some companies have experimented with this, asking employees to evaluate other employees with whom they presumably have sufficient contact to permit judgment of their performance. Their evaluations may then be used in regular performance reviews, or when an employee is being considered for a raise in pay or a promotion to a higher-level job. There is little evidence, however, that peer evaluations are used widely at *any* level, though a few firms studied—one of the non-OD companies and 4 of the OD companies—have used them even with rank-and-file employees (Table 5).

From the foregoing indications there is evidence that some companies at least are trying to employ the minds as well as the hands of lower-level employees. (Participation in matters such as collecting money in United Fund campaigns or deciding upon the cafeteria menu is, of course, quite a different matter from participation in making decisions that affect on-the-job performance.) It may simply be a matter of believing a maxim of the behavioral scientists: creativity, imagination, and ingenuity in solving organizational problems are not the special province of the better educated and higher-level elite of the organization. Instead, they are qualities widely distributed among the population.

QUESTIONS

1. Of what value are attitude surveys and what should be done with the information collected?
2. In what ways can nonsupervisory employees become involved in setting goals?
3. How are team-building activities conducted? What is the purpose of team building?
4. What are autonomous work groups? Where can they be used?
5. Sketch out the major differences in the ways in which firms are managed by a participative or organization development system and by a traditional bureaucratic system.

31.

Why Don't Employees Speak Up?

ALFRED VOGEL

Communications is enjoying one of its periodic revivals in management circles, but the emphasis today is somewhat different from what it was in the past. One can identify three stages in the evolution of industrial communications:

Phase I: One-way communications down. Vast sums have been and are being spent in developing the formal apparatus of information supply—employee magazines and newspapers, films, newsletters and bulletins, informational meetings. Most companies expect their supervisors to be active disseminators of information, and some even spend money instructing them on how to do it. Countless surveys have shown that employees do appreciate being kept informed and that they will listen when management communicates intelligently and forthrightly on matters of vital interest to the company.

The basic assumption, however, behind the one-way approach is that if employees know what management knows about company problems, they will exert themselves to help lick them. Information will lead to understanding, and understanding will result in purposeful action. Recognition that things often don't work out that way has caused many managements to abandon the simplistic, one-way-street approach to communications.

Phase II: Management seeks to find out what employees are thinking. Information gathering or feedback is today a conspicuous feature of the communications system in many, many companies. Management takes stock of employee attitudes and knowledge in order to predict reactions to possible alternatives or to determine how an action has been received. Through supervisors' reports, comprehensive attitude surveys and quickie checkups, or informal chats with employees, management gains a tactical sense of employees' gripes and concerns.

Feedback systems, though unquestionably useful, are incomplete. They isolate the employee from the decision-making process and thus often fail to enlist his whole-hearted cooperation in making solutions work.

Phase III: Management asks employees to help in initiating and implementing change. With the rise of such theories as

Reprinted by permission from *Personnel Administration*, Vol. 30, No. 3 (May–June 1967). Copyright 1967, Society for Personnel Administration, 485–87 National Press Bldg., 14th and F Streets, N.W. Washington, D.C. 20004.

Alfred Vogel is a specialist in communications and management–employee relations research with the Opinion Research Corporation.

"participative management" and with increasing recognition that employees often have something valuable to contribute (beyond the accepted limits of their normal job duties), many companies now are actively seeking ways of getting employees to participate more in decisions affecting them.

The basic assumption here is that employees should be treated as respected partners in searching for better ways to achieve goals—rather than as enemies of progress who have to be cajoled, forced or manipulated into doing the "right" things. In short, upward communications and mutual exchange have become the focus of much of the current interest management has in communications.

The Research on Upward Communications

In the past two years, Opinion Research Corporation has conducted a two-phased study among employees and their immediate bosses to explore the climate for upward communications in industry. The results of these studies do, we believe, shed some light on the questions raised at the beginning of this article.

Before going into the results, a few words about the research itself are needed. Included in the research were 265 engineers and scientists, 499 white-collar employees, 1,049 hourly employees, and 344 of their immediate supervisors in eight companies—a metropolitan bank, a manufacturer of household products, a producer of paper products, the branch store of a major retailer, two chemical companies and two public utilities. At three of the companies, hourly employees were represented by unions.

The Employee Desire to Be Heard

The desire to be heard is, as one would expect, widespread among employees. In quantified terms, about 90 per cent of the employees say that it is "very" or "fairly" important to them to be able to discuss their ideas about work problems with higher management (people above their immediate boss). Job occupation or sex makes little difference: the desire is as strong in the production worker as in the engineer or clerical employee, and it is as strong among women as among men.

There are important differences, however, in the character of this desire. Engineers, for example, have high interest in helping to make important work decisions. Hourly employees see communications with management mainly as a way of facilitating the work; they want to tell management about obstacles to performance which, in their view, management should do something to remove. Differences in such matters as educational achievement, social background, career aspirations, and concepts of the work role probably account for those differences in expectations regarding the function of communications.

Many employees find it difficult to get the ear of management. Although the results differ from company to company, over half the employees studied complained of lack of opportunity to make contact with those above their immediate supervisor.

Obstacles to Upward Communications

Most knowledgeable people in management as well as social scientists have long recognized that such factors as fear of retaliation and remoteness of management from employees make employees reluctant to speak up. In these studies we have tried to develop some preliminary quantitative parameters—to find the degree that employees feel inhibited by the potential obstacles to communications in the job situation.

Obstacle Number One: Many employees fear that expressing their true feelings about the company to their boss could be dangerous. The boss is often seen as untrustworthy, a man to whom it is dangerous to talk with full candor.

"An employee who told his immediate supervisor everything he felt about the company would probably get into a lot of trouble."

	PER CENT AGREEING WITH THIS STATEMENT
All employees	54
Engineers and scientists	50
White-collar employees	50
Hourly employees	59

Although important differences exist from company to company, as they do on all the issues in the study, what's interesting is that many scientists and engineers, on whom management depends for innovation and who are usually thought to be "close" to management, don't trust their bosses.

Obstacle Number Two: The fairly widespread belief that disagreeing with the boss will block promotion. In the eyes of employees, management retaliation can probably take many forms. A major one certainly is fear that speaking frankly will kill one's chances of advancement. Many employees in some companies do in fact believe that the way to get ahead is to be a "yes-man."

"The best way to get ahead in this company is not to disagree very much with your boss." Nonsupervisory employees

	TRUE	HARD TO DECIDE	UN-TRUE
Household products company	54%	14	27
Retail store	43%	14	36
Chemical company	42%	17	38
Utility company	32%	14	54
("No opinion" omitted)			

Fear of retaliation is one of the roots of the problem. Free exchange can never become a reality in a corporation as long as employees believe that freedom to speak up means only freedom to agree. No wonder that so much information management gets from employees is unreliable—they are often afraid to speak the truth.

The results discussed so far reflect bad supervisory listening practices—intolerance, narrowmindedness, arbitrary exercise of authority. But in a larger sense, they may indicate a more fundamental difficulty. Since lower managers often take their cues from those above, higher management in many cases has apparently not convinced lower management that the company is receptive to criticism and to the new and different. We know from other studies that *supervisors stifle criticism and frank expression of views because they think it makes them look bad in the eyes of their superiors.*

Obstacle Number Three: The widespread conviction that management is not interested in employee problems. For many employees, management is remote, shut off, preoccupied with its own concerns and therefore out of touch with employee values and worries.

"Many problems important to an employee are not considered important by management."

	PER CENT AGREEING WITH THIS STATEMENT
All employees	72%
Engineers and scientists	61%
White-collar employees	70%
Hourly employees	80%

As many observers[1] have pointed out, all communication involves a transaction —a something for something exchange.

---

[1] See "The Obstinate Audience," Raymond A. Bauer, in *The American Psychologist,* May 1964.

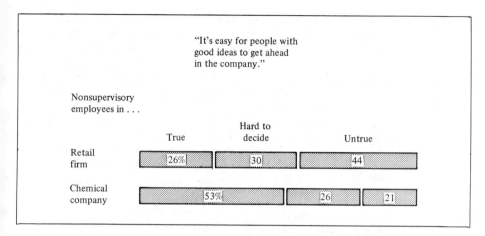

"It's easy for people with good ideas to get ahead in the company."

Nonsupervisory employees in . . .

People are not passive recipients of messages. One price management often pays for not convincing employees that it is concerned with their problems is that employees close their minds to management concerns.

Obstacle Number Four: The feeling that employees are not rewarded for good ideas. Some companies have a lot of work to do convincing employees that they will be rewarded for their ideas.

Note, however, the contrast [shown in the figure] between the retail firm and the chemical company, a firm with a long history of trying to improve communications, on the issue of whether good ideas are rewarded.

Many companies have employee suggestion systems to solicit ideas for improving technical or mechanical processes. Suggestion systems are usually not appropriate for spotting problems having to do with breakdowns in relations between people or for generating ideas to improve management-employee cooperation. Suggestion systems tap ideas of physical but not social invention.

Obstacle Number Five: Lack of supervisory accessibility and responsiveness. In the studies we have done, employees do not give their supervisors high grades on various facets of the upward communications job. For example, typically only

about a third of the employees rate their boss as "good" on being easy to see with a problem and only about a quarter rate him "good" on such matters as ability to handle complaints and encouraging suggestions. On the other hand, majorities of employees are apt to rate their boss "good" on matters having to do with job knowledge and operating problems.

Supervisors in part disagree. The vast majority believe they are readily accessible to employees. At the same time, however, many do admit to lack of skill in performing the upward communications task and ask for more training in specifics.

Per cent of supervisors saying they need more training in

Communications—particularly in how to listen	72
How to handle employee problems and complaints	67
How to lead group discussions	57

Obstacle Number Six: The conviction that higher management doesn't take prompt action on problems. Prompt management responsiveness to employee problems and concerns is unquestionably a key element in successful upward communications because it completes or closes the cycle of interchange.

Many employees do not have a high opinion of management performance in response to employee demands for action on their problems.

And in companies where employees have a low opinion of management responsiveness, it is worth looking into the cause. Typically, these include:

• Lack of machinery for getting problems to the attention of management quickly.
• Failure to allocate clearly responsibilities for taking prompt action.
• Failure to keep employees informed of what is being contemplated or of action taken.

The Supervisor As Listener

Many supervisors have apparently learned to recognize good communications techniques. For example, when asked to nominate the most important ingredients of good communications, they are apt to cite such factors as encouraging open discussion, discussing work-related matters with clarity, keeping in touch with employee thinking, being a good listener. Relatively few supervisors will cite such things as expressing oneself forcefully, not passing out too much information, communicating solely through channels. Supervisors recognize that mutual exchange is essential. They know what they should be doing.

The question is: do supervisors listen with understanding to employees' points of view? The evidence from our studies is that many supervisors are often out of tune with the thinking of employees and do not have adequate understanding of employee values and needs.

For example, the supervisors of one group of essentially "homogeneous" employees (people relatively similar in social background, education, job status and aspirations, etc.) seriously underesti-

mated the expressed need of these employees to make the most of their talents, to work in a congenial environment and to have good working conditions.

More seriously, when employees are asked to describe the things about their immediate supervisors that cause them the most trouble on the job, bad listening practices head the list by a long way. Typical complaints about poor listening include descriptions of the boss as capable but arrogant, unavailable to listen, closed-minded, unwilling to talk things over with employees.

The purpose of this article is not to indict management or supervision on its listening practices. In some companies, management does appear to listen well; in others there are serious problems. But the findings do indicate that the inadequacies in upward communications discussed here are fairly widespread, not merely myths invented by personnel people or social scientists to justify self-seeking efforts to steer management attention to the need to improve communications.

Summing Up

In our opinion, this research shows that better communications between supervisors and employees is possible for those companies willing to work at it. Employees have a fairly keen desire for upward communications (one that would probably grow under proper encouragement and removal of frustrations and obstacles). And there is economic payoff, in the form of profitable new ideas and ways of doing things, for management in getting a better two-way flow of ideas going (but this is a story in itself).

Communications devices and techniques abound. New ones aren't necessary. The task for management is to establish conditions that encourage supervisors and employees to speak freely to each other. This can't be accomplished overnight. In some cases, hoary company

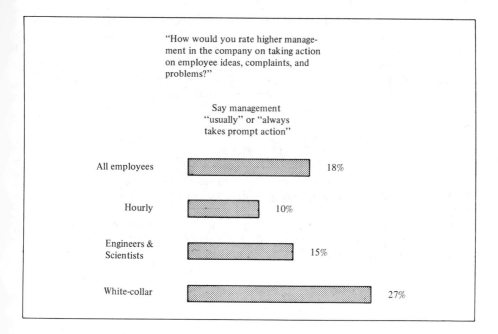

"How would you rate higher management in the company on taking action on employee ideas, complaints, and problems?"

Say management "usually" or "always takes prompt action"

All employees 18%

Hourly 10%

Engineers & Scientists 15%

White-collar 27%

traditions will have to be overcome—an often tedious, difficult and uncertain process.

It is far easier, of course, to state the conditions that appear to encourage better communications throughout the organization than to bring these conditions into being. Knowledge of these conditions is a necessary first step to implementation, however. They include:

Frankness Within Management. Establish genuine two-way communications between all levels of management. When critical discussion is choked off at higher levels of the company, it ceases to flow at lower levels.

Supervisor Accessibility. Develop an awareness among managers that the keys to better listening are accessibility and responsiveness. Employees don't want to be heard all the time. But when they do have a problem, they need the assurance that their boss will listen and act.

Welcome for the New and Different. Tolerate all kinds of ideas, those that are foreign, silly or hostile as well as those that management considers constructive, i.e., those that it is willing to accept. Looking with disfavor on employees for thinking differently leads to closed minds.

Visible Benefits. Visibly reward those who have creative new ideas. This is the strongest encouragement management can give.

Acceptance of Criticism. Regard criticism as healthy and normal, lack of criticism as dangerous and undesirable, an indication that employees have given up trying to get through to management.

Sensitivity to Employees. Be willing to wrestle with the thorny problem of interpreting what a man is really trying to say. A gripe about working conditions may mask a belief that the boss doesn't appreciate the individual's job performance.

Some companies appear to be moving in the right direction. An important element in some of the more advanced management development programs is to make managers more aware of their subordinates' needs and to improve their listening skills.

No one can be put in charge of two-way communications. It is an active process and takes active interest and encouragement by management to achieve.

Good listening by managers is a basic condition of such communications. Yet, employees must be convinced that not only are they free to speak, but that it's worth doing—that new ideas are adopted, people with unconventional ideas get ahead, conflict and criticism that sharpen issues are not suppressed or ignored but viewed as necessary parts of the process of increasing organizational strength and improving performance.

QUESTIONS

1. Why are employees often reluctant to freely express their ideas to their supervisors?
2. Do you feel that most managers genuinely want to hear what is on employees' minds?
3. What are the potential dangers of inadequate upward communication?
4. What can management do to increase the upward flow of information and tap useful employee ideas and criticisms?

32.

The Supervisor and the Disciplinary Process in a Unionized Setting

DALLAS L. JONES

An important and persistent problem in the unionized firm is that of discipline. Although in recent years other aspects of the management-union relationship, such as work rules, have attracted widespread attention, it is highly probable that most firms spend as much or more time with disciplinary matters than with any other type of grievance.[1, 2]

The reasons for the importance of discipline are not difficult to find. For the company, the building and maintaining of a disciplined work group is one of the foremost management responsibilities in the successful operation of the business. Without a disciplined work force—one in which employees are meeting established standards of conduct and performance—no organization can survive. Every or-

ganization must be vitally concerned with discipline at all times.

Discipline is of no less importance to the individual and to the group. Disciplinary action threatens the individual's employment status; even a written reprimand can have possible serious future consequences for employment standing. Employee reaction to discipline also results because of its effect upon his ego. The group is also concerned if the disciplinary action involves a matter which may adversely affect them or if they believe the action to be unfair. Because of this great concern with discipline, the union is forced to challenge most disciplinary matters—sometimes even when it would prefer not to do so.[3]

It is for these reasons that discipline is

Reprinted by permission from *Personnel Administration*, Vol. 26, No. 1 (January–February 1963). Copyright 1963, Society for Personnel Administration, 485–87 National Press Bldg., 14th and F Streets, N.W., Washington, D.C. 20004.

Dallas L. Jones is Professor of Industrial Relations, Graduate School of Business Administration, University of Michigan.

[1] This article is based in large part upon a larger study of mine, *Arbitration and Industrial Discipline* (Ann Arbor, Michigan, Bureau of Industrial Relations, 1961), particularly Chapters 1, 6 and 9. Permission to utilize this material was granted by the Bureau of Industrial Relations.

[2] Disciplinary cases constitute the majority of cases that go to arbitration under the rules of the American Arbitration Association.

[3] *Arbitration and Industrial Discipline*, Chapter 7, pp. 127–142.

so important. It is also because discipline is so important that there is no area in which the skill of the supervisor is more essential. To understand his problems, and consequently his approach to disciplinary matters in the unionized firm, it is necessary to understand the situation in which he operates.

Framework of Discipline in the Unionized Firm

Disciplinary policy in the unionized firm must recognize two important factors: First, fear has a lesser role than it formerly did in developing a cooperative, disciplined work group; and second, disciplinary policy and action must be shaped to meet the standards set by the labor agreement and arbitration. Modern disciplinary policy must attempt to blend the psychological-sociological principles of effective leadership and "corrective discipline" with the legal principles of "due process" which have arisen with the development of the labor agreement and arbitration.[4]

Management's task of developing a disciplined work force is much different than it was a few decades ago. Then, a disciplined work group was often attained through fear. Management could pursue such a disciplinary policy because there were no legal restrictions to prohibit it and the moral and economic beliefs tended to support it.

Even without the rise of large scale industrial unionism, it is doubtful that this type of discipline could have long continued in the face of a better educated work force and a changing public opinion. Unionism, however, gave it a quick death for once a union is established in the plant, fear as a motivational device becomes of decreased importance. This is not to say that fear has no part in the disciplinary process, for obviously fear does exist when people know they can be disciplined for failure to meet established standards—fear thus acts as a deterrent. But fear can only be used to produce the acceptable minimum; it cannot be used to force people to do more. Moreover, unionism can reinforce informal group obstruction tactics. To achieve the cooperative work group the supervisor wants and requires, he must today be more than just a disciplinarian—he must be a leader.

The supervisor's approach must thus be one whereby the group regards him as fair and supportive. They must regard his as one who is a source of help rather than fear, who does not play favorites, and whose disciplinary actions are based upon cause and carried out in such a manner so as not to give the impression of "getting even" for an improper act. This is the "corrective discipline" approach, which in essence is a leadership, problem-solving approach which requires great skill on the part of the supervisor.

The second task, that of developing a disciplinary policy shaped to meet the standards of the labor agreement and arbitral review, is no less difficult. Today, some 95 per cent of all labor agreements contain arbitration provisions. The vast majority of these agreements give to the arbitrator the power to reverse penalties and usually to modify penalties if the arbitrator finds there has not been "cause" for discipline or if the penalty is too severe.[5] Although the arbitrator is legally

---

[4] The term discipline by "due process" is that of Orme W. Phelps, *Discipline and Discharge in the Unionized Firm* (Berkeley, University of California, 1959), pp. 2–4.

[5] Even when the labor agreement does not explicitly provide that discipline shall be for cause, most arbitrators hold that discipline must be for cause; otherwise, one of the fundamental purposes of the labor agreement—negotiated job rights—would be modified. Most arbitrators also hold, in the absence of specific language or stipulation by the parties, that they have the right to modify penalties as well as to reverse them.

limited to interpreting the agreement, the right to determine cause gives him considerable discretion. Because of this power, the arbitrator has had a tremendous impact upon industrial discipline. Briefly then, what are some of the requirements of a disciplinary policy set by arbitration?

As Arthur Ross has said, arbitrators did not turn to contract law for their disciplinary principles, but turned instead "to modern concepts of enlightened personnel administration sprinkled with elements of procedural due process in criminal cases." [6] From "enlightened personnel administration," most arbitrators have accepted the premise that discipline should be corrective and not punitive— that before an employee can be discharged, unless he has committed a so-called major offense, he should be given a chance to modify his behavior through the imposition of lesser penalties. Moreover, in determining the penalty, such factors as length of service and disciplinary record must be considered. Arbitrators have helped, therefore, to establish corrective discipline principles.

Equally as important has been the establishment of procedural requirements which form an important element of due process because they are essential safeguards in the protection of individual rights. In general, there must be charges as to the nature of the misconduct, the reasons for the penalty, and full opportunity for the individual to utilize the grievance procedure. Significant also has been the shifting of the burden of proof from the individual to the employer who must show both the fact of wrongdoing and the need for discipline.

Substantively, justification for a penalty is not simply a matter of proving the em-

ployee guilty of the misconduct charged. It must also be shown that the rule under which the employee is disciplined has as its objective the efficient functioning of the plant and that the penalty assessed is justified in terms of the offense and the employee's past record. Moreover, the penalty must not be discriminatory and must be consistent with other actions taken by management for the same offense. Although, theoretically at least, there do not have to be uniform penalties, there does have to be consistency of action; that is, a determination upon the part of management to enforce the rules. Management's part in the practice of levying penalties and enforcing the rules is thus very important.

The impact of arbitration upon disciplinary policy has indeed been great. Although the company has the basic right to set policies and to assess penalties, the arbitrator can in effect nullify a policy by refusing to uphold a penalty assessed under it. Disciplinary policy thus has to be formulated and carried out with arbitration in mind.

This need has led to considerable centralization of the labor relations function. Because of the requirement that penalties be assessed under rules in harmony with the principles of the labor agreement, and because there must be some consistency in the assessment of penalties if the penalty is to stand the test of arbitration, disciplinary power in many companies has been taken from the supervisor and placed in the hands of staff specialists or of higher line supervision.[7] Even where this has not been done, and supposedly the supervisor has disciplinary power, he relies so much upon the "advice" of the staff specialist that "advice" becomes something more than that in most cases.

---

[6] Arthur M. Ross, "The Arbitration of Discharge Cases: What Happens After Reinstatement," *Critical Issues in Labor Arbitration*, Jean T. McKelvey, ed. (Washington, Bureau of National Affairs, Inc., 1957), p. 24.

[7] In the two companies included in my study, higher supervision levied penalties in one and the personnel staff in the other.

This is true even though the staff specialist may not be trying to usurp the supervisor's authority.[8] The reason is simple: if there is any doubt regarding whether the penalty will be upheld by the arbitrator, it is very likely to be reversed at a higher step of the grievance procedure when the staff assumes control.

The staff at higher levels of the grievance procedure usually will not process a grievance to arbitration that does not have a reasonable chance to be decided in the company's favor. Not only does the staff believe that a reversal of the company's action is detrimental to discipline, but the staff also believes that such a decision adversely affects the prestige of management as well as the standing of the staff in the organization.[9] The result is that the staff is constantly exerting pressure upon the supervisor to make certain that before he takes disciplinary action there is ample evidence against the individual and that the action is consistent—in other words, to "build up a case" against the individual so that the penalty will stand the test of arbitral review if it is challenged by the union.

The supervisor then must work between the pressure of his work group below and the staff department above. He must secure cooperation from his group, and he must be cognizant of the "due process" requirements of the labor agreement. How then does he approach his problem? Is he so much concerned with the legal requirements of due process that he becomes less concerned with the individual and the corrective aspects of discipline?

The Disciplinary Process

The overwhelming impression given by most supervisors is that they are more concerned with due process problems— that is, they take a "legalistic" approach to discipline rather than a "corrective" approach. Supervisors emphasize the need to "build up a case"—to make certain that the penalty will stand if challenged by the union. Building up a case for the supervisor means, among other things, calling attention to disciplinary breaches, maintaining records, taking prompt action and rigorously observing employee rights in doing so. This response of the supervisor should not be surprising—he is, as noted above, under pressure from the staff to do so. Moreover, if he does not have a case and his action is reversed, he is placed in an embarrassing situation with his work group.

But it is a mistake to assume that most supervisors *act* only in these terms. Building up a case usually becomes important only beyond the initial stages of the disciplinary process. If discipline is regarded in the broad and corrective sense as training, then much of what the supervisor does is discipline. A supervisor will speak to an individual regarding his faults or mistakes. In so doing, the supervisor will not only point out the individual's error, but he will in effect reprimand, even though not in the formal sense, and suggest ways of correction. The supervisor will use different approaches with different individuals depending upon his analysis of the individual and the nature of

---

[8] I have found that in many companies the right to discipline is more a theoretical right than an actuality. The foreman, except for very minor actions, consults with the staff and then follows their advice. See also Charles A. Myers and John G. Turnbull, *Line and Staff in Industrial Relations*, Pigors, Myers and Malm, eds. (New York, McGraw-Hill, 1959), pp. 63–81.

[9] There was no evidence in my study to indicate that management does lose prestige— unless, of course, too many cases are reversed. *Arbitration and Industrial Discipline*, Chapter 4, pp. 76–96.

the situation. In the majority of instances, neither the individual nor the supervisor will regard this action as discipline, and for most individuals this type of action is all that is required—no formal disciplinary action is required.

Nor do most supervisors, in spite of pressure from above, automatically assess penalties for rule violations when from the legal point of view they should do so —although it is difficult to get them to admit that this is so.[10] Instead, many supervisors take a truly problem-solving approach. They attempt to take such action, based upon their analysis of the individual and the problem, that will deal with the immediate situation in a manner that will benefit the individual while at the same time considering its effect upon the group. As a result, there may or may not be a formal penalty.

This approach to discipline by the supervisor should not be unexpected for, as noted above, under present industrial conditions a supervisor cannot be effective if he acts simply as a disciplinarian. How far a supervisor will go in utilizing this approach, however, is dependent upon several factors: the confidence of the supervisor in himself, his confidence in his group, and his relationship with the union steward. Some supervisors lack the confidence to take actions that are not according to the "book" and find safety in using the legal approach. A supervisor must also have assurance that his group will not view such an action as favoritism. And last, a supervisor must have some assurance from the union steward, either explicit or implicit, that the action will not be used as precedent in future cases. Thus, supervisors will vary in their use of

the corrective approach, some will use it for only very minor infractions whereas others will go much further.

But if the individual does not respond to corrective action at this early stage of the disciplinary process, the supervisor changes from a "corrective" to a "legal" approach. The individual is now regarded by the supervisor as a potential troublemaker. In order to protect himself in the event it becomes necessary to levy more severe penalties, he begins to formalize reprimands and to maintain records. In other words, he begins to build up a case.

It is at this point that the staff begins to play a more active role. The supervisor consults with the staff, formally or informally, to make certain that the penalty will stand arbitral review. Although such factors as the seriousness and circumstances of the disciplinary breach, the individual's prior record and his length of service are considered, factors which are important in the corrective approach, the emphasis is upon selecting a penalty that will meet the legal test of "just cause" rather than upon correction as such. Although no precise formula can be developed to apply to every case, there does develop a rather uniform code with penalties assessed within narrow limits and often below the maximum that could be imposed. Penalties assessed in this manner erect a defense against union challenges of inconsistency or discrimination and build arbitral acceptance of the disciplinary action. The disciplinary system becomes "progressive" discipline and quite often "price lists," formal or informal, are built up—i.e., known penalties for rule violations. Correction be-

---

[10] Supervisors dislike to admit that they do not "go by the book" because of the emphasis upon "building a case." The author has found that it is only in case discussions when he takes the "legalistic" approach will supervisors begin to question it and refer to their own experiences. Most supervisors also find that the human relations approach is more satisfying. See R. F. Maier and Lee E. Danielson, "An Evaluation of Two Approaches to Discipline in Industry," *The Journal of Applied Psychology*, XL, No. 5 (1956), pp. 319–323.

comes a byproduct of the system and not its central objective.

The disciplinary process is thus a combination of both the corrective and the legalistic approaches. In the early stages, correction is dominant; in the latter stages legalism becomes most important. The question can be asked, what are the values of this approach for all concerned?

For the individual, the progressive approach has both limitations and values. The evidence clearly indicates that many individuals would benefit by more severe penalties at an early stage of the disciplinary process.[11] On the other hand, the individual does receive certain definite benefits. He is freed from the possibility or even the appearance of arbitrary action. As Lloyd Reynolds has said, freedom from arbitrary disciplinary action makes of him a free man in the shop.[12] Consideration is also given to his length of service and past record in assessing penalties. When progressive penalties are applied, the individual is placed on warning that his behavior is not acceptable. He is thus given the opportunity to change it, although he is seldom given all the help that a truly corrective approach requires. In a very real sense, correction becomes a by-product of the system. If the individual changes his behavior, and he is given the opportunity to do so, well and good; if he does not, then management has a case which will stand the test of arbitration.

Management also receives certain other values from this approach—values which are not always recognized because of the cumbersomeness and the abuses which can develop under due process. First, while it does take time, a troublesome employee can usually be dismissed. Thus the deterrent aspect of discipline is maintained. But second, and more important,

progressive discipline helps to build the type of work force management desires.

If there were widely varying penalties, employees would be suspicious. They would find it difficult to understand why one individual is disciplined more severely than another—even though based upon the premise that it would be more corrective. Consistent progressive penalties, on the other hand, carry an appearance of fairness even though this might not be true in terms of what is best for the individual. The evidence also clearly indicates that when there are known rules of conduct and progressively severe penalties are applied to offenders, there is employee acceptance that the disciplinary action is justified. In addition, when progressive penalties are consistently applied, employees know what to expect, and this too builds up acceptance of disciplinary action as well as emphasizing its deterrent quality. The result is often the attainment of the positive attitudes which management desires.

Consistent, progressive action also builds up union acceptance of disciplinary action. There is always considerable pressure upon union officials by the membership to represent a disciplined individual if he desires it even when the membership believes that the disciplinary action is fair. But when the action is consistent, the union can often make just a token protest because they can point out to the membership that there is little hope of receiving a favorable decision from the arbitrator. The leadership is thus able to take a position which benefits both the company and the union.[13]

Development of Supervisors

The supervisor has the most important role in the disciplinary process. How-

---

[11] See Dallas L. Jones, *op. cit.*, Chapter 3, pp. 35–74.

[12] Lloyd G. Reynolds, Labor Economics and Labor Relations, (3rd ed.; Englewood Cliffs, N. J.: Prentice-Hall, Inc., 1959), p. 207. See also Dallas L. Jones, *op. cit.*, Chapter 3, pp. 35–74.

[13] See Dallas L. Jones, *op cit.*, Chapter 7, pp. 127–142.

ever, because the disciplinary process has changed so greatly, he requires much more skill in the handling of disciplinary problems. It is also necessary that he receive full understanding and help from the staff.

Supervisory training programs must include knowledge of the legal requirements set by arbitration—without such knowledge the supervisor would be placed in an untenable position. But a training program must go much farther. Supervisors are not always given adequate instruction into the meaning and implications of the corrective discipline approach. It has been the author's experience that too often disciplinary training is separated from leadership training and that disciplinary training is concerned primarily with techniques and "legal" rulings. Techniques are important, but only when backed up with understanding. Fortunately, many supervisors have been able to bridge the gaps in such training—but why not help them do it?

It is also important that the staff under-stand the problems of supervisors and that the staff support them.[14] Thus, one of the constant complaints of supervisors is the staff will "trade" away one grievance for another, even when there is a solid "case." Undoubtedly such complaints are exaggerated, but there are enough verified instances to give them color. On other occasions, there is a lack of communication as to why a grievance has been settled in a particular way or even as to what has happened. Perhaps the most disconcerting experience for a supervisor is to be told by the steward that a grievance has been settled in a given manner before he is informed by his own organization.

Space does not permit a more complete discussion of the training needs of the supervisor and the type of staff relationship that is required to help him carry out his difficult job. This analysis of the disciplinary process should, however, emphasize the attention that should be given by personnel administrators to these problems.

QUESTIONS

1. What is discipline, and why is it so important?
2. What due process elements of discipline have arbitrators tended to establish and support?
3. Show how the disciplinary process is a combination of the corrective and the legalistic approaches.
4. What kind of relationship should exist between the supervisor and the personnel staff?
5. What should be the content of a training program for supervisors dealing with discipline?

[14] A brief but excellent article on this subject is Maynard N. Toussaint, "Line–Staff Conflict: Its Causes and Cure," *Personnel*, May–June, 1962.

33.

When Workers Are Discharged: An Overview

ROBERT W. FISHER

Most 19th century U.S. employers would have been astonished at the suggestion that a decision to discharge a worker should be reviewed for fairness. They believed the employer-employee relationship conveyed upon them unfettered discharge power.[1] In the famous 1827 conspiracy case, *Commonwealth* v. *Moore and others*, the prosecutor made this clear:

[the employers] had an undisputed right to discharge any workman . . . when they conceived that his continuance was no longer conducive to their interest . . . they were at perfect liberty to dismiss every journeyman [tailor]. . . .

To those who argued that the employer was justified in firing the tailors *because* they had demanded more money, another commonwealth attorney objected:

the discharge was a matter of perfect right, without the assignment or even existence of

reason. Let him be without reason . . . let it be caprice. Still it was a right, with which no man or set of men must be permitted to interfere. . . .[2]

This argument sums up the "common law" employment relationship in which the employer is perfectly free to fire any employee. The employee is perfectly free to quit. This relationship evolved out of small, person-to-person, artisan industries and an economy dominated by agriculture. As the economy grew, most workers came to know they would never become employers in the artisan tradition. They would remain skilled workers, operatives, or laborers working for someone else. The changed economic situation made the relative rights of employers and employees conscious points of dispute. The automatic assumption of employer sovereignty was questioned. Did the English common

Reprinted from *Monthly Labor Review*, Vol. 96, No. 6 (June 1973), pp. 4–17.

Robert W. Fisher is an economist and senior editor, *Monthly Labor Review*, Bureau of Labor Statistics.

[1] Lawrence Stessin, *Employee Discipline* (Washington, D.C., The Bureau of National Affairs, Inc., 1960), pp. 2–3.

[2] John R. Commons and others, eds., *A Documentary History of American Industrial Society, Volume IV: Labor Conspiracy Cases* (Cleveland, Ohio, Arthur H. Clark Co., 1910); (Reprint edition, New York, Russell & Russell, 1958), pp. 172 and 238.

law which fit nicely an artisan/agricultural setting really suit America in the second half of the 19th century? [3]

When the 20th century opened, the typical U.S. employment relationship had tipped from the artisan/agricultural to the industrial. This accelerated movement toward a new view of the employer's power to dismiss. As one commentator put it: "Discharge on caprice and without compunction [had] taken on an antisocial flavor." [4] Nonetheless, employers continued to dismiss workers freely when they transgressed employer work rules, or pushed for higher wages, shorter hours, and a voice in the employment relationship. [5]

The situation changed abruptly during the Great Depression. The worst economic plunge in the Nation's history temporarily set back "management rights" adherents, brought new public support to proponents of "worker rights," and resulted in the passage of the National Labor Relations Act in 1935.

Supporters of management rights have urged basically that all rights in the employment relationship not won by contract or forbidden by law belonged to employers. Supporters of worker rights argued that labor possessed some "inherent" rights quite apart from contracts or laws. [6] From one point of view, the National Labor Relations Act came into being as a public curb on management rights.

The act gave workers a publicly sanctioned right to organize and bargain collectively. The U.S. Supreme Court upheld the act in 1937 and cleared the way for unions to organize millions of additional workers. (About 3.7 million were organized at the time of passage, almost 9 million by 1940.[7]) For union workers, employment tenure was no longer controlled solely by employers. For the more numerous nonunion workers, employers still generally had unilateral power until the development of fair employment practices legislation, mainly after World War II, began to place further limitations on it.

Why Workers Are Discharged

Today, workers are fired for reasons ranging from the bankruptcy of their employer to personal fault. There is little appeal from dismissals brought on by business failure or production cutbacks even if the worker is blameless. However, discharges for personal reasons—incompetence, insubordination, absenteeism, loafing, fighting, gambling, using intoxicants or being intoxicated on the job, stealing, destroying company property, highly individualistic grooming or dress, and similar reasons—may be challenged. However, an effective right to contest a firing is largely reserved to employees of unionized firms, most Federal and State Government employees, and many employees of local governments.

Most workers and unions would probably agree with employers that incompetence, insubordination, absenteeism, drinking, gambling, fighting, and so on

[3] See Orme W. Phelps, *Introduction to Labor Economics*, 4th ed. (New York, McGraw-Hill Book Co., 1967), ch. 5; Richard B. Morris, *Government and Labor in Early America* (New York, Columbia University Press, 1941). For a concise review of United States labor history, see *A Brief History of the American Labor Movement*, Bulletin 1000 (Bureau of Labor Statistics, 1970).

[4] Lawrence Stessin, *Employee Discipline*, p. 20.

[5] See, for example, Irving Bernstein, *A History of the American Worker: The Lean Years* (Boston, Houghton Mifflin Co., Publishers, 1970), pp. 1–43.

[6] See James C. Phelps, "Management's Reserved Rights: An Industry's View," and Arthur J. Goldberg, "Management's Reserved Rights: A Labor View." *Management Rights and the Arbitration Process* (Washington, The Bureau of National Affairs, Inc., 1956), pp. 102–29.

[7] *A Brief History of the American Labor Movement*, p. 65.

are appropriate grounds for *discipline* of some sort, though not necessarily discharge. But labor and management tend to disagree, sometimes sharply, over discharges for the following: engaging in a wildcat strike, being garnished or arrested, belonging to a controversial organization, advocating an unpopular cause, being "disloyal" to the employer, and so on.

Dismissal of a member of a racial, ethnic, or religious minority, a woman, or an older worker also may provoke much heat and sometimes flame in the employment relationship. Whatever reason is given for the discharge, the fired worker may feel discriminated against, particularly if discharge actions appear to affect only members of his or her group. Employers are likely to be more upset than in the usual disputed discharge because of the imputation of prejudice and unfairness.

Collectively, managers and supervisors still tend to view discharge as a necessary tool in maintaining work discipline. Over time, they have accepted some "due process" restraints growing out of law and contract on their right to discharge workers. Workers—at least those in highly formalized employment situations—have lost some of their apprehension about dismissal except during periods of economic distress. Even workers in these situations, however, have made it clear they still consider dismissal too important to be left solely to employers' discretion.

The general drift has been toward placing checks on discharge in the form of deliberative reviews which prune arbitrary from justified discharges. Within the general movement, government, labor, and business continue to grope for a fair institutional formula for discharge. How much dismissal power should employers have?

How much protection from discharge do workers need? What is society's role in mediating between conflicting interests?

I. The Contractual Shield

A worker's protection from dismissal varies greatly depending on whether he is a union member, a Federal Government employee, a State or local government employee in jurisdictions with merit systems, or other worker. Union members and Federal workers, and many State and local employees, work in what are called "fully structured" situations.[8] That is, they are usually employed under detailed, specific work rules and regulations and have clearly defined legal rights with respect to discharge and other terms and conditions of employment. Nonunion workers in large firms work in "partly structured" situations. That is, they are employed under detailed personnel practices set up by the employer. By contrast, workers employed in small nonunion firms, public employees under patronage systems, or workers employed by private individuals are in "unstructured" situations. Their only protection from discharge resides in Federal, State, or local laws that forbid or control discharge for specific reasons.

Protection from discharge in the U.S. economy is comprehensive in union contracts but is limited to organized groups of workers—about a third of the nonsupervisory work force. Protection in laws is limited to discharges for specific reasons but is comprehensive in coverage of the work force. The most important laws in this area are labor relations, antidiscrimination, and civil service laws.[9]

The discussion begins with the best protected workers: union members. It then

[8] Orme W. Phelps, *Introduction to Labor Economics*, pp. 45–48.
[9] Other laws—such as the Wage and Hour Law of 1938, the Age Discrimination in Employment Act of 1967, and the Consumer Protection Act of 1969—provide some protection against arbitrary discharge in specific situations.

treats laws that protect union and non-union workers. These laws may be characterized as (1) those directed toward preventing certain practices—unfair anti-unionism or discrimination based on race or color—and (2) those that protect identifiable groups of workers—Federal, State, and local government employees. It concludes with a consideration of suggestions for improving safeguards and how discharge is handled in selected other countries.

CONTRACTUAL REACH

A law's sweep often stops at political, geographic, or industrial boundaries. Even national laws, such as the National Labor Relations Act (amended in 1947 by the Labor Management Relations Act), halt before certain factors—small size, intrastate activity, and so forth. One feature of union contracts is that they attempt to impose similar if not identical protections for members across political, geographic, and industrial limits.

Discharged union members generally know exactly where to look for help: the grievance procedure. A typical contract clause that enables union members to have discharges reviewed reads: "Grievances growing out of discharge, layoff, promotion, demotion, hiring, rehiring, and transfer, shall be subject to the grievance procedure. . . ." [10]

Most contracts also provide that workers may be discharged only "for just cause" or "for cause." This repudiates the common law view that an employer should be free to fire workers without cause. Just cause means the employer must have a good reason for firing an employee. Ironically, union contracts which usually seek to protect workers

from discharge provide for discharge in at least one instance: when a new hire refuses to join the union within a prescribed period under a union security provision.

HOW THE PROCEDURE WORKS

A Bureau of Labor Statistics study found grievance procedures provided in almost all union contracts that affect 1,000 workers or more. [11] Another Bureau study found arbitration mandated in about 19 of 20 contracts. [12] The grievance procedure under the contract is the means by which a discharge is measured against just cause. In the first part of the procedure, management and labor attempt to reconcile their differences over the dismissal. In the second, which becomes operative only when the parties fail to agree, an arbitrator or arbitration panel is granted authority to make binding disposition of the dismissal case.

The Bureau study of grievance procedures also determined that contractual time limits for processing a grievance ranged from a week to a year. Most fell within a week to 2 months. Time requirements generally depend on the number and complexity of the steps in a particular procedure.

The typical grievance moves through three, four, or more steps. Dismissal cases present a special problem in that the worker is no longer on the payroll. Such cases are generally handled by the union steward and higher union officials. However, the worker does present his story directly to union officials, at the arbitration hearing, and may be invited to tell it at a labor-management conference. As in most negotiating situations, agreement at any step is final and binding. In dismis-

[10] *Major Collective Bargaining Agreements: Grievance Procedures,* Bulletin 1425–6 (Bureau of Labor Statistics, 1966), p. 20, quote from the contract between the West Virginia Pulp and Paper Co. and the Interstate Papermakers.

[11] *Major Collective Bargaining Agreements: Grievance Procedures,* Bulletin 1425–1 (Bureau of Labor Statistics, 1964), p. 1.

[12] *Major Collective Bargaining Agreements: Arbitration Procedures,* p. 5.

sals, the first part of the grievance procedure may be truncated with the case going directly to arbitration.

ARBITRATION AND CONTRACTS

Private arbitration under union contracts has been given a firm legal underpinning by the courts. In the Labor Management Relations Act of 1947, Congress expressed preference for private rather than public settlement of disputes. It singled out arbitration, mediation, and conciliation as means to this end. This expression of confidence in private resolution was based on the success of wartime arbitration.

Ten years later, the U.S. Supreme Court in effect approved of arbitration in some key cases. In *Lincoln Mills* (1957), the High Court held that Federal courts could enforce agreements between unions and management, including agreements to arbitrate disputes. This was another change from practice under the common law: "At common law, agreements to arbitrate future disputes were not generally enforceable." [13]

Another controversial point remained: If labor and management agreed to arbitrate, could either withhold a specific issue? In a landmark series of cases involving the Steelworkers union in 1960, the Supreme Court ruled that *all* issues were arbitrable except those expressly withheld in the contract.[14] One labor relations scholar objected that the courts might make themselves "rubber stamps" for the decisions of private arbitrators.[15] Generally, the court has held its ground. However, the courts have split over whether an arbitration finding on racial discrimination is conclusive.[16]

PATH OF GRIEVANCES

When a worker is fired, he may file a grievance with his union which, weighing strategic and tactical elements, must decide whether to take it up with management. So long as the firing is questionable, the union will probably press for reinstatement. Unless management agrees to reinstate (or the union abandons the case in the face of new evidence), the grievance will move through the grievance procedure. At the end of the line, arbitration is usually triggered by written notification by the union, although management too can ask for arbitration.

A list of arbitrators is secured from either the Federal Mediation and Conciliation Service or the American Arbitration Association, or, in some cases, such as the New York City apparel industry or the automobile industry, the discharge goes to a permanent arbitrator. Employer and union in effect approach each other from opposite ends of the list, alternately striking off names of arbitrators least acceptable to them. Ideally, they agree on the last one. (The list is always odd in number.) Sometimes, however, one or the other may look over a list and decide right away they want another. When a panel of three arbitrators or more is to be chosen, each side may pick an arbitrator with the chairman (and swing member) chosen either by a process of elimination or by the members already selected.

An arbitration hearing is a sort of court proceeding with the robes removed and

[13] R. W. Fleming, *The Labor Arbitration Process* (Urbana, University of Illinois Press, 1965), p. 22.

[14] *United Steelworkers* v. *Warrior and Gulf Navigation Co.*, 363 U.S. 574 (1960); *United Steelworkers* v. *Enterprise Wheel and Car Corporation*, 363 U.S. 593 (1960); and *United Steelworkers* v. *American Manufacturing Co.*, 363 U.S. 564 (1960).

[15] Harry Wellington, *Labor and the Legal Process* (New Haven, Yale University Press, 1968), pp. 122–23.

[16] See, for example, *Newman* v. *Avco Corp.*, 451 F. 2d 743 (1971) and *Alexander* v. *Gardner-DeVow Co.* (1972).

the sleeves rolled up. The arbitrator is judicial without being judge-like. One current complaint about the process is that arbitrators increasingly resemble judges, giving rules of procedure precedence over the needs of good industrial relations.[17]

RELATIONS BETWEEN FORUMS

When an arbitrator's decision is in, the grievance normally ends. There are times, however, when other forums get involved. The boundaries between private grievance arbitration and public adjudication are fluid. The mandates of laws, contracts, court rulings, and custom overlap and sometimes conflict, resulting in the occasional intrusion of public forums into private procedures. Sometimes participants in private proceedings will ask for public intervention.

The Reluctant Union. Usually the employer is the obstacle to satisfactory resolution of a worker's dismissal grievance. Occasionally, however, the union may stand in his way. Why, in some instances, might it not press for reinstatement? Unions tend not to press grievances they believe (1) cannot be won, (2) involve rivals within the union, or (3) are without merit.[18] Since unions must pay half the cost of usually costly arbitration, their sometime selectivity is more understandable. In any event, a union must make discretionary judgments regularly. As a consequence, unions' behavior has occasionally raised the issue of "fair representation" in court cases and in proceedings

before the National Labor Relations Board.

A worker can present his grievance directly to his employer under section 9 of the Labor Management Relations Act, but that would not be too promising a route in a discharge case. The employer has rendered a verdict on the value of the employee's services unlikely to be reversed by a one-to-one conference.

Recognizing the reality of half-hearted or grudging representation of workers by unions (who "own" the worker's grievance under law and contract), Federal courts have for over a quarter of a century insisted unions must represent all workers in the bargaining unit fairly. As exclusive representative, it is their duty. The courts found this duty in the Railway Labor Act in the 1940's and 1950's in cases involving workers who refuse to join a union and black workers and members of other minorities. The courts also have found it in the language of section 9 of the Labor Management Relations Act.[19]

But while the courts have been crystal clear about the union's duty, they have been ambiguous about how to carry it out. They insist that the worker and the union exhaust the steps in the privately negotiated grievance procedure. Beyond that lies a question mark. One scholar has held that in balancing workers' rights against unions' needs for orderly control of transactions with management, the courts have given higher priority to orderly control.[20]

[17] See William J. Kilberg, "The FMCS and arbitration: problems and prospects," *Monthly Labor Review*, April 1971, p. 41; and James F. Power, "Improving arbitration: roles of parties and agencies," *Monthly Labor Review*, November 1972, p. 21. See also "New directions in grievance handling and arbitration," a group of 5 articles in *Monthly Labor Review*. November 1972, pp. 3–30.

[18] *Major Collective Bargaining Agreements: Grievance Procedures*, p. 17.

[19] Legal scholars consider these cases important: *Steele v. Louisville & Nashville R.R.*, 323 U.S. 192 (1944); *NLRB v. Wallace*, 323 U.S. 248 (1944); *Elgin, Joliet & Eastern Ry. Co. v. Burley*, 325 U.S. 711 (1945); *Syres v. Oil Workers*, 350 U.S. 892 (1955); *Ford Motor Co. v. Huffman*, 345 U.S. 330 (1953); and *Manuel Vaca v. Niles Sipes*, 368 U.S. 171 (1967).

[20] See Benjamin Aaron, "The Individual's Legal Rights As an Employee," *Monthly Labor Review*, June 1963, pp. 666–73.

With the NLRB. In some decisions in the 1960's, the National Labor Relations Board called a union's failure to represent workers evenhandedly an unfair labor practice. That position would permit the Board to enumerate remedial actions for unions to take.

The Board's approach was rebuffed in a 1962 case but sustained in 1964 and 1966.[21] These results indicate the courts, following the Supreme Court's lead, will go along with linking unfair labor practices to certain flagrant instances of unfair representation. Such an instance would be a union discriminating against minority or women members or nonmembers. Where the issues are less clear cut or where the web of discrimination can be spun with greater deviousness, both the courts and the National Labor Relations Board have been more cautious.

A more settled relationship between NLRB and contract grievances are the grounds under which the Board will review arbitration decisions. Like the courts, the Board generally keeps hands off arbitration decisions under contracts. It will intervene only if convinced the arbitration proceeding was unfair, the arbitration award conflicts with the purposes of the Labor Management Relations Act, or the parties had not agreed to accept the arbitrator's decision as final and binding.[22] The Board's position does not prevent an employee (or union or employer) from appealing issues to it—such as unfair labor practice charges—that are not or

cannot be dealt with in an arbitration proceeding.

With the EEOC. Relations between contract grievances and public handling of employment discrimination cases are uneasy and unsettled, partly due to the recency of the Equal Employment Opportunity Act and the general lack of judicial precedents. In one case, a Federal circuit court ruled that workers can file a grievance under a union contract grievance procedure and file a court suit in the future so long as they do not get "duplicate" relief. This decision and others have given the worker appealing for redress for unfair treatment because of race, color, religion, sex, or national origin another forum in which to have his contractual and Title VII rights aired.[23]

With Civil Service Laws. Under Executive Order 11616 which controls Federal union-management relations, Federal workers *cannot* appeal discharges under the grievance procedure of a union contract. They must use the civil service's statutory appeals procedure governing "adverse actions," of which discharge is one. They may, however, have union representation in the appeals process.

The situation is less clear at State and local levels because there are so many jurisdictions with separate laws and regulations. However, the concept of "binding arbitration"—a central ingredient in private labor-management contracts—has run into trouble. One researcher noted that attempts to use it in public employ-

---

[21] See *Miranda Fuel Co.* and *Michael Lopuch* (140 NLRB No. 7, 1962), first decided in 1959 (125 NLRB No. 53) and reconsidered; 362 F. 2d 172, 180 (C.A. 2 1963); see *Monthly Labor Review*, March 1963, pp. 305–306; *Hughes Tool Co.* (147 NLRB 1573, 1964); *United Rubber Workers, Local 12* v. *NLRB* (368 F. 2d 12, C.A. 5, 1966), see *Monthly Labor Review*, February 1967, p. 61. See also *Local 1367, International Longshoremen's Association* (C.A. 5, 1966).

[22] See Jay W. Waks, "Arbitrator, Labor Board, or Both," *Monthly Labor Review*, December 1968, pp. 1–5. For a recent statement of the NLRB position, see *Collyer Insulated Wire* and *Local 1098, Brotherhood of Electrical Workers* (192 NLRB No. 150), *Monthly Labor Review*, November 1971, pp. 64–66.

[23] *Bowe* v. *Colgate Palmolive Co.* (416 F.2d 711, C.A. 7, 1969).

ment disciplinary cases have been frustrated in State courts.[24] The courts' reasoning has been that appeals procedures mandated by law cannot be discarded for a negotiated process unless the law is changed.

To obey the law and at the same time receive an independent opinion on a grievance, unions and public employers at some State and local government levels use "advisory arbitration." In it an arbitrator is engaged by both parties. He renders a "decision" in the case. The decision "advises" the parties of a sensible resolution of the dispute. Even if union, employer, or both reject the advice and resolution has to emanate from the statutory procedure, the arbitrator's views, as those of a seasoned individual with no ax to grind, can form the basis for a compromise.

After Reinstatement

The payoff for the fired worker—whether union or nonunion, minority or majority, woman or man—is reinstatement to the job. But what happens to fired workers who get their jobs back? Researchers have not supplied the last word but they have uncovered important clues. All the studies are limited in scope, partly due to the existence of a multitude of cases scattered over time and throughout the country.[25]

The earliest study (covering 1950–55) explored the dismissal and reinstatement of 207 employees of 145 establishments.

It was discovered that a worker's length of service and work profile before discharge were the critical elements in his success after reinstatement under arbitration. Arbitrators took particularly hard looks at cases involving senior employees (more than 5 years' service) and employees with previously good work records. These workers were more likely to be reinstated than junior employees and more likely to keep out of trouble after being restored to their respective jobs.

The later studies covered 1959, 1962–64, and 1969–70. (Two of them dealt with reinstatement under the Labor Management Relations Act rather than under private arbitration.) They tended to confirm the earlier findings. Complaints of supervisory harassment after reinstatement came largely from either junior employees or those who had poor work profiles to begin with. Junior employees had an image problem. So did workers with a string of disciplinary woes. Management possessed few clues as to what type of worker the often-disciplined workers were. Thus both were likely to be terminated again. Workers higher in seniority and with good work records tended to make it.

II. Major Legal Protections

Those who are not protected from unfair discharge by a union contract are sometimes shielded by the law. Labor relations and antidiscrimination laws are

[24] Charles P. Fischbach, "Grievance Arbitration in Public Employment Disciplinary Cases," *Labor Law Journal*, December 1971, pp. 780–87.

[25] Arthur M. Ross, "The Arbitration of Discharge Cases: What Happens After Reinstatement," *Critical Issues in Labor Arbitration* (Washington, The Bureau of National Affairs, Inc., 1957); see *Monthly Labor Review*, June 1957, pp. 677–88; Dallas Jones, *Arbitration and Industrial Discipline* (Ann Arbor, University of Michigan, 1961); and Les Aspin, "Legal Remedies Under the NLRA: Remedies Under 8(a) (3)," *IRRA Series: Proceedings* of the Twenty-Third Annual Winter Meeting (Madison, Wis., 1971), pp. 264–272; see *Monthly Labor Review*, March 1971, pp. 57–59. See also Thomas J. McDermott and Thomas H. Newhams, "Discharge-Reinstatement: What Happens Thereafter," *Industrial and Labor Relations Review*, July 1971, pp. 526–40.

the most significant of those that prohibit dismissal of workers for specific reasons. These laws reflect public policy determinations that dismissal should not be allowed for union activity, or because of one's race, color, religion, sex, or national origin. (Other laws prohibit discharge for being over 40 years old, for being garnished under certain circumstances, for complaining of wage-hour violations, and so forth.) By contrast, review of discharges for personal reasons—incompetence, absenteeism, and so on—have been left to arrangements hammered out by private parties, typically unions and employers. However, Federal civil service law and regulations and those of some States and localities do provide comprehensive protection from discharge, calling for a review of the dismissal regardless of the reason given for it.[26] In addition, any employee covered by a labor relations or antidiscrimination statute can turn to that statute if he feels his discharge for say absenteeism is actually for a prohibited reason such as union activity or color.

LABOR RELATIONS

The National Labor Relations Act (amended in 1947 and 1959) has served as the prototype for those labor relations acts enacted at State or local levels. The NLRA itself drew on the Railway Labor Act passed in 1926.[27] What follows will be largely confined to principles and procedures in the national law.

The NLRA permits workers to "form, join, or assist" labor organizations, to engage in collective bargaining through "representatives of their own choosing," and to engage in other "concerted activities" to carry on collective bargaining. Employers may not "interfere with, restrain, or coerce" workers carrying on protected activity. Of course, the strongest restraint is dismissal. The law provides procedural safeguards against such retaliatory dismissals. The act also forbids unions' pressuring employers to fire or otherwise mistreat a member in disfavor with the union, or to conduct union business in such a way (such as job assignments at hiring halls) so as to encourage nonmembers to join the union. That is, workers may carry on union activities but they may also "refrain" from doing so.[28]

The investigatory, conciliatory, and adjudicatory functions of the National Labor Relations Board are familiar to labor relations specialists, companies, and unions that have dealt with or may deal with the NLRB, but not so familiar to the general public nor, as recent events show, to some State and local governments struggling with new labor relations issues in the public service. When the NLRB receives a worker's charge that he was discharged for union (or other protected) activity, its local office investigates. If this investigation finds the *charge* meritorious, an NLRB *complaint* is issued. The Board's regional office tries to resolve the situation. If it fails, the charge goes to an NLRB administrative law judge[29] who conducts a hearing at which the worker and his representative and the employer

---

[26] Some jurisdictions do not provide the strict rules governing discharge that are contained in Federal Civil Service procedures.

[27] In labor relations, the Railway Labor Act covers railroad and airline workers. The law provides that they settle disputes privately "in conference," but also provides for the National Railroad Adjustment Board which arbitrates disputes over rights under an agreement. The adjustment board is divided into four divisions which handle grievances for (1) operating employees, (2) shop employees, (3) all non-operating employees except shop, waterborne, and supervisory employees, and (4) all other railroad employees. The 1936 amendment which placed airlines under the act permits airlines and their employee unions to use either private arbitration or set up public adjustment boards.

[28] Sections 7 and 8 of the National Labor Relations Act.

[29] Officials who performed a similar function prior to 1971 were called trial examiners.

and his representative present their cases. The hearing judge issues his findings and recommends a settlement to the NLRB. In its order, the Board may adopt the administrative law judge's position, modify it, or arrive at its own conclusions. It accepts briefs from the parties' attorneys and may take oral argument before reaching a decision. If the company, employee, or the organizing union disagree with the Board, they can appeal to a Federal appellate court. The latter may uphold, modify, or refuse to enforce the Board's order. If any party is dissatisfied with the appellate decision, he can appeal to the U.S. Supreme Court. Some hotly contested cases of discriminatory discharges have shuttled between the NLRB, the appeals courts, and the Supreme Court for years.[30]

ANTIDISCRIMINATION

Laws prohibiting discrimination against workers because of their race, color, religion, sex, or national origin provide another kind of protection against arbitrary dismissal. The impetus for these laws came from public policy to end discrimination against minority group and women workers, but they actually protect all workers—union and nonunion, men and women, public and private.

The strange career of such laws saw the first ones, still in operation, enacted immediately after the Civil War. A roughly 70-year hiatus followed. Then in 1940 Executive Order 8587 was issued, the first national action against job discrimination since Reconstruction. Since then, State and local jurisdictions have enacted such laws, and a number of Federal Executive Orders have been issued. The most comprehensive curb on employment discrimination—Title VII of the Civil Rights Act—was enacted in 1964.

Because laws and orders have emanated from national, State, and local jurisdiction over a considerable period,

workers can contest employment discrimination, including unfair dismissal, on several grounds. Among the most important are the 14th Amendment to the U.S. Constitution, the Civil Rights Acts of 1866 and 1871, the Age Discrimination in Employment Act of 1967, Executive Order 11478 (1972), Title VII of the Civil Rights Act of 1964 (amended in 1972), and various State and local laws. The 14th Amendment and the two 19th century laws permit the worker to go directly to court. While a forceful remedy, it raises problems for the impecunious. All the others generally require that the worker exhaust the steps in an administrative procedure which loosely resembles the investigatory and conciliatory steps pursued by the NLRB. While administrative procedures also take time, they have the advantage of shifting the costs of investigation, conciliation, and court suit from the worker to the administrative agency. Of course, the worker may retain an attorney anyway and may have to go to court at his own expense if the decision reached in the administrative procedure does not suit him.

The administrative procedures of the Equal Employment Opportunity Commission, established under Title VII, will be used to illustrate the general procedures pursued by most equal or fair employment practices agencies. Workers in private, State, or local government employment who believe they have been discharged (or otherwise unfairly handled in employment) because of race, color, religion, sex, or national origin can appeal their dismissal to the EEOC. The Commission has 7 regional offices and 32 district offices. The local offices investigate, determine merit, and attempt to resolve meritorious complaints.

Before the 1972 amendments, the worker had to take his own case to Federal court if the Equal Employment

[30] See *Monthly Labor Review*, January 1964, pp. 65–66, and May 1968, pp. iii–iv.

Opportunity Commission failed to resolve it to his satisfaction. Under the amendments, the Commission can now take cases to court, lifting a financial burden from the worker. The Commission also investigates cases against State and local government employers, but the U.S. Justice Department takes them to court when necessary. The 1972 law permits private organizations or individuals to bring charges on behalf of others. These changes are expected to improve the worker's chances of achieving a settlement without a court test.[31]

Discharge cases made up a significant part of the Commission's workload of charges in fiscal year 1971, the latest data of this type available:

TYPE OF COMPLAINT	PER CENT DEALING WITH DISCHARGE
Race or color	33.2
Religion	46.1
Sex	15.4
National origin	37.0
All other	23.0

Forty-three States, the District of Columbia, Puerto Rico, the Virgin Islands, and a number of cities also have enacted laws against discrimination. Thirty-five States' procedures meet Federal standards. The Equal Employment Opportunity Commission defers to these States, permitting them to handle cases within their area first.[32] In some of the laws, discriminatory discharge is specifically prohibited. In others, it is barred by implication because the acts forbid mis-treatment of workers on discriminatory grounds.

Prohibitions against discriminatory discharges (and similar unfair treatment) are clear in the law but cloudy in application. Indeed, difficulties in imputing or proving illegal motives have contributed to a recent shift in emphasis from motives to results. In the opinion of the Equal Employment Opportunity Commission (which administers Title VII), the rule emerging from recent court decisions is this: Regardless of motive, if an employer's practices or policies tend to exclude identifiable groups, such as minorities and women, then the practice or policy is illegal unless business necessity is proved.[33]

Expanding Coverage. Title VII's coverage of workers has been protean in its 8 years of existence. It started out applying to firms with 100 workers or more, unions with 100 members or more (or that ran hiring halls), employment agencies that deal with covered firms, and so on. Following the 1972 amendments, the law applies to firms with 15 workers or more, employment agencies that deal with covered firms and joint apprenticeship programs of covered firms and unions. The amendments also extended protection to State and local government employees and placed authority for handling discrimination charges in the Federal service in the hands of the U.S. Civil Service Commission. Like other employees, Federal workers can take their complaints to court after 180 days.

CIVIL SERVANTS

The Federal Civil Servants Act of 1883 signaled the start of a merit system for

---

[31] A worker is free to file a court suit if the Commission does not resolve his complaint or file a court suit on his behalf within 180 days. The Commission is required to notify him when the 180-day period ends. The worker then has 90 days in which to file suit. Courts can appoint attorneys for complainants who cannot get one.

[32] Section 706 of Title VII, Civil Rights Act of 1964, as amended in 1972.

[33] The U.S. Supreme Court's decision in *Willie Griggs* v. *Duke Power Co.* (1971) is the most important.

most Federal employees. They were no longer subject to instant dismissal for reasons having nothing to do with the job, including who won the election. Between the 1880's and the first World War, many States and localities adopted similar laws.

Civil service appeals placed some "due process" safeguards on dismissal (and other disciplinary) actions. Public managers cannot fire subordinates and not bother about reasons, good or bad. They have to warn a worker before discharge and justify the action to managerial superiors, to a civil service commission, and, in some cases, in Federal, State, or local courts. The procedures, at least at the Federal level, have grown more complex and detailed over the years. Each step must be followed in letter and spirit or a discharge can be overturned on procedural grounds. Among the 80 million plus workers in the U.S. economy, only union workers have similar detailed, legalistic protections.

Despite their legalistic trappings, however, civil service appeals systems, even those for Federal workers, remain essentially unilateral. Those deciding whether a discharge is proper are all management employees. This built-in one-sidedness, the example of grievance procedures in private industry, and other factors (such as professional lobbying for pay increases) have led growing numbers of government workers to join labor organizations. The recent upsurge has been dramatic. Between 1956 and 1968, over half the growth in union membership (about 2.1 million) was among government workers. By 1970, union membership in the public sector exceeded 2.6 million, almost tripling the 1956 level.[34]

Where contracts are won, unionized Federal Government employees can now bargain about many of the terms and conditions of employment. However, dismissals generally must still be appealed through the applicable mandated appeals process.

Today, discharge under the common law is handled much as it was in the 19th century. It still applies to all employer-employee relationships not specifically governed by statutes. And it applies to those parts of even "statutory" employment relationships where there is no legislative guidance. Under the common law, employers can still fire employees for any reason or for no reason.[35] Employees can quit with or without cause. Employers may sue an employee for damages if his quitting causes losses on materials or similar setbacks. Conversely, the employee can sue to recover damages for "wrongful discharge." The employee cannot win reinstatement under the common law, because one of its tenets is that neither employer nor employee should be made to suffer an undesired relation with the other. In the modern setting, this laissez faire relationship applies mostly to individual contracts for hire and in small, nonunion private firms. However, this reasoning informs much of employer-employee relations in the United States and other nations.

III. With All Deliberate Speed

The boards, courts, commissions, and grievance procedures that place due process controls on discharge all suffer from delay—too much time, too much money. Even though, in some forums, accelerated procedures can be adopted, such as going straight to arbitration under a union contract, considerable time passes before a decision is reached. Foreign processes are

[34] Harry P. Cohany and Lucretia M. Dewey, "Union membership among government employees," *Monthly Labor Review*, July 1970, pp. 15–20.
[35] See "Discharge in the Law of Arbitration," *Vanderbilt Law Review*, December 1966, p. 81.

also bothered by the lapse of time between claim and adjudication. The dilemma is that a swift decision may be unjust or may seem to be unjust; a just decision may take too long.

A consequence of their importance to industrial relations is that boards, courts, commissions, and grievance procedures have been showered with suggestions for improving the handling of worker grievances of which the most pressing is discharge. Most suggestions are tended to speed up things, thereby winning more worker confidence as well as trimming costs.

ON LABOR RELATIONS

Some critics propose separation of the National Labor Relations Board's judicial from its administrative functions as one way to speed up its operations. They suggest that the Board's judicial functions either be placed in a new labor court of some sort or be taken over by regular Federal courts. (Some urge that the NLRB be abolished in favor of labor courts in the manner of some European countries.) They argue that decentralization of consideration of cases would result in greater speed. Rebutters of these proposals question whether courts could act any faster. They hold that legalism— briefs, pretrial motions, transcripts, postponements, weighing evidence, formal decisions, appeal provisions—consumes time regardless of the type of forum. Defenders of the proposals urge that several forums, despite legalism, could act swifter than one forum.

Other critics hold the NLRB can be streamlined and pepped up without basic alteration. They would pass more power to administrative law judges, whose decisions would be final unless at least two Board members objected. Another idea is that Board orders be self-enforcing unless a party to the order petitions for review within 30 days. Those who hold these views often suggest that the one speedup that would require no change except in policy is for the NLRB to make greater use of its injunctive powers to get discharged workers back on the job immediately.[36]

Another recent proposal dealing with a change in policy or direction rather than in function would reallocate manpower and other resources among the NLRB's various activities.[37] With regard to discriminatory dismissals, these critics propose that discharge cases (which make up the "bulk" of charges filed with the NLRB) be handled as quickly as "priority cases"—those involving secondary boycotts, proscribed picketing, and "hot cargo" contractual arrangements.

Fair Employment. The Equal Employment Opportunity Commission is still relatively new. Nonetheless, proposals to speed up its handling of discriminatory discharge cases (and other law violations) are already being heard. In 1972, the Congress granted the EEOC power to go directly to Federal court with cases it could not resolve through conciliation. (Before, it had to ask the U.S. Justice Department to bring suit and then only in cases involving a "pattern or practice" of discrimination.) Supporters of added power hope the threat of court test will spur settlements in conciliation. Operationally, the agency has been adding district offices to speed handling of cases and is exploring other changes to speed things up, such as consolidation of charges against the same employer for blanket handling.

Union Grievances. In a 1971 article, the former General Counsel of the Federal Mediation and Conciliation Service re-

---

[36] For a summary and analysis of alternatives, see Fritz L. Lyne, "The National Labor Relations Board and Suggested Alternatives," *Labor Law Journal*, July 1971, pp. 408–23.

[37] William Gomberg and Bernard Samoff, "Improving Administrative Effectiveness of the NLRB," *Labor Law Journal*, April 1973, pp. 201–220.

commended that the backlog building up on seasoned arbitrators be reduced by use of "apprenticeship training" for new arbitrators, schedules of fees geared to encourage use of fledgling arbitrators, and, if necessary, Government publication of new arbitrators' opinions to give them exposure. He advocated jettisoning briefs, stenographic records, formal written awards, and other legalistic paraphernalia except in complicated cases. And he expressed a need for further experimentation with "conference" or "advisory" arbitration in which large numbers of "routine" cases are disposed of in a relatively short time.[38]

What should be done for workers when the union refuses to press their grievance? There have been three general proposals on this. One urges mandatory handling of all workers' grievances. A second urges mandatory handling of "critical" worker grievances—those involving discharge, seniority, and pay. The last would leave the handling of grievances entirely to the union's discretion.[39]

Supporters contend the requirement to handle all grievances would remove the possibility of invidious or irrelevant considerations affecting the union's behavior. Critics demur that it might also further clog grievance channels. Supporters of the second proposal hold that it would tend to prune borderline grievances while preserving a worker's critical job interests. Those who are skeptical argue that now discharge, pay, and seniority are generally the critical interests, but at some future time other interests may be more critical or at least as important. The problem of defining what is critical and who would define it would be a recurring headache.

The third alternative approximates the prevailing court view. It acknowledges that unions have a duty to represent all workers in the bargaining unit fairly, but argues that unions (and management) should be free to weigh each case. Moreover, supporters argue that few unions would fail to press critical interests. Critics doubt this, pointing out that a major reason for recent scholarly concern about individual worker's rights in grievance procedures has been occasioned by some unions' arbitrary decisions.

The stately pace of grievances has prompted some unions to look at their contractual arrangements. Notable among these, the Steelworkers and the major steel companies undertook in their 1971 contract to experiment with accelerated arbitration in what they call "routine" arbitration cases. Strict time limits are imposed on the length of the hearing and the time from hearing to decision.[40] More developments can be expected because there are frequent reports of worker dissatisfaction with the functioning of grievance procedures.

OTHER NATIONS' SYSTEMS

Like the United States, other countries are groping for the right formula on dismissals and other discipline. While it is generally agreed that employers cannot have an entirely free hand, a reluctance to provide means to force reinstatement is also evident. Often the law will provide money as an alternative to forced re-employment.

Great Britain. Prior to passage of the British Industrial Relations Act in 1971, workers widely resorted to the "unofficial" or wildcat strike to protest what they considered unfair dismissal. If the union steward, who wielded unusual power compared with his U.S. counterpart, could not resolve the dispute, the workers

[38] William J. Kilberg, pp. 43–45.

[39] Alfred W. Blumrosen, "Legal Protection for Critical Job Interests: Union-Management Activity Versus Employee Autonomy," *Rutgers Law Review*, Summer 1959, pp. 631–65.

[40] Ben Fischer, "Arbitration: the steel industry experiment," *Monthly Labor Review*, November 1972, pp. 7–10.

walked out. Many unofficial strikes were caused by dismissal disputes.[41]

Under the new law, which provides legal sanctions for previously informal British labor relations, workers can appeal unfair dismissal to industrial tribunals. These tribunals can recommend reinstatement but cannot compel it. However, the tribunals can compel the employer to pay the discharged worker appropriate compensation if the employer will not take the worker back.[42]

France. Labor courts in France are the oldest institutions of their kind in the world, having been established in the early 19th century. They are composed of equal numbers of representatives of labor and management viewpoints drawn from the occupational, industrial, and geographic areas covered by a court. A professional judge is introduced only in deadlocks. French workers can appeal their dismissals to the labor courts where they are "judged by their peers." [43] There are problems, however. (1) The courts have not been established for all geographic areas, industries, or occupations. Hence, some workers must take their grievances to regular courts. (2) There are no appellate labor courts so workers dissatisfied with the decision of their peers must turn to professional judges in the regular courts who may not be versed in labor issues. (3) Finally, and most important for the dismissed worker, the labor courts (and ordinary courts) cannot order his reinstatement. Thus dismissed workers with grievances bring suit for damages only.

West Germany. The German system of labor courts, which began in 1926 and survived the upheavals of National Socialism and World War II, continues to dominate the labor law system of the Federal Republic of Germany.[44] The law is everywhere in West German labor relations, ranging from the Labor Courts Act of 1926 to the Collective Bargaining Act of 1949 and the Act on Protection Against Dismissals of 1951.

Fired workers may appeal their dismissals to labor courts if they were fired with proper notice, or if fired "on the spot" directly to a panel of the Federal Labor Court. This court is the top of the three-level court system which includes regular labor courts and appellate labor courts. The courts determine if the dismissal was "socially justified," that is, if the firing was appropriate "with respect to the personality or conduct of the employee, or urgent needs of the plant. . . ." The courts may order reinstatement and backpay under this German equivalent of the "just cause" provisions which appear in private U.S. labor-management contracts. The picture in West Germany with regard to dismissals (and labor relations in general) is complicated by inevitable conflicts in a system dominated by labor courts but with significant authority residing in collective bargaining agreements and in a system of employer-employee relations which is distinct from unions and employer associations: the "works councils."

Sweden. Swedish labor law leaves the handling of discharges largely to provisions in union contracts. These cover two-thirds of Swedish workers. Contracts have sharp teeth because the work rules in collective agreements are enforceable in labor courts. Swedish law, like U.S. law,

---

[41] Frederic Meyers, *Ownership of Jobs: A Comparative Study* (Los Angeles, Institute of Industrial Relations, University of California, 1964), pp. 27–28.

[42] Norman Robertson and K. Ian Sams, "The new legal framework for Britain's industrial relations," *Monthly Labor Review*, March 1972, pp. 48–52.

[43] Xavier Blanc-Jouvan, "The Settlement of Labor Disputes in France," in Benjamin Aaron, ed., *Labor Courts and Grievance Settlement in Western Europe* (Berkeley, Calif., University of California Press, 1971), pp. 1–80.

[44] See Thilo Ramm, "Labor Courts and Grievance Settlement in West Germany," in Benjamin Aaron, ed., *Labor Courts and Grievance Settlement in Western Europe*, pp. 81–157.

protects workers from arbitrary dismissal because of union activity. In addition, employers cannot dismiss workers for going into military service, performing their "civic duties, getting married, or becoming pregnant." [45]

The worker tries to adjust grievances at the first management level. If unsatisfied he may ask the union to argue the case with higher levels of management. If it is not resolved at company level, the case goes to the Joint Labor Market Council for the area. In practice, few cases go beyond union and management.

Japan. The Japanese system of job protection reflects that nation's traditional paternalistic employer-employee relationship and, since World War II, the influence of American-style industrial relations.[46] Thus a worker with tenure is considered a lifetime employee, but discharge is possible for reasons specified in the labor-management contract. Typical causes for dismissal are absenteeism, insubordination, incompetence, immorality on the job, falsification of records, and similar behavior. (These are also reasons for discharge in the United States.) Procedures for appeals from or indemnification for discharge are spelled out in the labor contract. In general, the handling of discharge and other discipline is left mainly in private hands.[47]

DRAWING THE LINE

As this brief illustrative survey of other countries' practices shows, there is a general reluctance to reinstate dismissed workers. The idea is that once an employee has been fired, a fruitful reestablishment of the employment relationship is difficult at best. Like some of its industrialized counterparts, the United States does provide for reinstatement of workers discharged for specific reasons. Also, employers in large nonunion firms have set down detailed rules governing separation. The most fully protected American workers are union members. Reinstatement of workers in the manner in which it commonly occurs under U.S. union contracts is relatively unique in industrialized countries.[48]

By contrast, the situation of nonunion workers in small U.S. firms more closely resembles that of their 19th century counterparts than their 20th century union or Federal Government mates. Even in small firms, however, employers are a good deal more sensitive about the impact and importance of discharge. And Federal, State, and local laws on labor relations and discrimination do provide some protection from unfair dismissal. Nonetheless, when it all boils down, nonunion workers in small firms may generally be fired without cause. They must rely upon the costly common law remedy of damages as their only path to redress. As one researcher has put it, their grip on the job is precarious because the employer has almost total sway over it.[49] Their situation is uneasy, particularly in times of economic distress.

But the difficulty of drawing a proper line between managers' needs for authority and workers' needs to be free of arbitrary, discriminatory, and capricious dis-

---

[45] *Labor Law and Practice in Sweden*, Report 285 (Bureau of Labor Statistics, 1964), pp. 27–30. See also Folke Schmidt, "The Settlement of Employment Grievances in Sweden," in Benjamin Aaron, ed., *Labor Courts and Grievance Settlement in Western Europe*, pp. 159–246.

[46] See Robert Evans, Jr., "Japan's labor economy—prospect for the future," *Monthly Labor Review*, October 1972, pp. 3–8.

[47] *Labor Law and Practice in Japan*, Report 376 (Bureau of Labor Statistics, 1970), pp. 18–20, 29–32.

[48] Benjamin Aaron, ed., "Introduction," *Labor Courts and Grievance Settlement in Western Europe*, pp. xix–xx.

[49] Frederic Meyers, *Ownership of Jobs: A Comparative Study*, pp. 7, 100.

charge remains. The proposals concerning the American system of processing complaints of workers (or their representatives) against employers and of employers against workers or their representatives indicate something of the complexity of the problem. What is best for either union or employer is likely to be less than optimal for the worker. What is best for all three remains elusive.

Future developments probably will continue along the main lines of the past. As a matter of public policy, prohibitions against dismissals for other reasons will be added to those regarding union activity and discrimination as the Nation continues to shed 19th century ideology. Unions will keep on pushing to narrow the grounds for dismissal under contracts.

Other Problems. Workers, mostly those outside of unions, are often unaware of their legal rights when discharged. They may automatically seek their old jobs back since workers, particularly in nonunion companies, are sometimes given another chance. This is most likely if the reasons for discharge are marginal. If rebuffed, the worker looks for another job.

Nonunion workers may have their job rights explained to them by unions, civil rights and civil liberties organizations, or governmental units. They may repair to the law for redress. Union members and civil servants may use their grievance and appeals procedures. However, regardless of the law, or administrative procedure, it takes a highly persistent worker to pursue his or her job rights through layers of management, commissions, boards, and courts—and often an intrepid one to return to a job after being fired.

QUESTIONS

1. Explain the evolution of job rights of employees from the early nineteenth century, when employers could fire an employee for any reason or no reason at all, up to the situation at the present time. Give major causes for changes which have occurred. Are there still situations in which an employer can fire employees for any reason or no reason at all?
2. Would it be possible to effectively operate our modern industrialized society without substantial job rights protected by law and contract?
3. a. How are unionized worker grievances of discharges processed through a grievance procedure? What is the role of arbitration?
   b. Should employees in nonunion organizations be accorded the same rights to due process review in discharge cases? How might this be accomplished?
4. Why might it be difficult for an administrative law judge to determine whether a discharge was for "just cause or for union activity, race, color, sex, or age?"
5. Do you find merit in the labor court or industrial tribunal system which is used in some European countries?
6. How can one balance the manager's need to maintain discipline and authority with the employees' need to be free of arbitrary, discriminatory, and capricious discharge?

34.

Values, Man, and Organizations

ROBERT TANNENBAUM and SHELDON A. DAVIS

Introduction

We are today in a period when the development of theory within the social sciences will permit innovations which are at present inconceivable. Among these will be dramatic changes in the organization and management of economic enterprise. The capacities of the average human being for creativity, for growth, for collaboration, for productivity (in the full sense of the term) are far greater than we have recognized . . . it is possible that the next half century will bring the most dramatic social changes in human history.[1]

For those concerned with organization theory and with organizational development work, this is an exciting and challenging time. Probably never before have the issues at the interface between changing organizations and maturing man been so apparent, so compelling, and of such potentially critical relevance to both. And to a considerable extent, the sparks at the interface reflect differences in values both within organizations and within man—human values which are coming loose from their moorings, whose functional relevance is being re-examined and tested, and which are without question in transition.

Many organizations today, particularly those at the leading edge of technology, are faced with ferment and flux. In increasing instances, the bureaucratic model—with its emphasis on relatively rigid structure, well-defined functional specialization, direction and control exercised through a formal hierarchy of authority, fixed systems of rights, duties, and procedures, and relative impersonality of human relationships—is responding inadequately to the demands placed upon it from the outside and from within the organization. There is increasing need for experimentation, for learning from experience, for flexibility and adaptability, and for growth. There is a need for greater inventiveness and creativity, and a need for collaboration among individuals and groups. Greater job mobility and

Reprinted from *Industrial Management Review*, Vol. 10, No. 2 (Winter 1969), pp. 67–86, by permission of the Industrial Management Review Association.
    Robert Tannenbaum is Professor of Behavioral Science, Graduate School of Business Administration, University of California, Los Angeles; and Sheldon A. Davis is Vice President and Director of Industrial Relations, TRW Systems Group of TRW Inc.

[1] See Bennis (1).

355

the effective use of temporary systems seem essential. An environment must be created in which people will be more fully utilized and challenged and in which people can grow as human beings.

In his recent book, *Changing Organizations*, Warren Bennis has pointed out that the bureaucratic form of organization "is becoming less and less effective, that it is hopelessly out of joint with contemporary realities, and that new shapes, patterns, and models . . . are emerging which promise drastic changes in the conduct of the corporation and in managerial practices in general." [2] At least one of the newer models, the one with which our recent experience is most closely connected, is organic and systems-oriented. We felt that, for the present at least, this model is one which can suggest highly useful responses to the newer demands facing organizations.

At this historical juncture, it is not just organizations which are in flux. Man, perhaps to an extent greater than ever before, is coming alive; he is ceasing to be an object to be used, and is increasingly asserting himself, his complexity, and his importance. Not quite understanding why or how, he is moving slowly but ever closer to the center of the universe.

The factors underlying man's emergence are complex and interrelated. They include higher levels of educational attainment, an increased availability of technology which both frees man from the burdens of physical and routine labor and makes him more dependent on society, an increasing rate of change affecting his environment which both threatens and challenges him, and higher levels of affluence which open up opportunities for a variety and depth of experiences never before so generally available.

The evidences of this trend are many. They are to be found, for example, in the gropings within many religions for more viable modes and values. They are to be found in the potent thrusts for independence of minorities everywhere, and in the challenges of our youths who find our values phony and often materialistically centered. They are to be found in the involvement of so many people in psychotherapy, in sensitivity training, and in self-expression activities in the arts and elsewhere. They are also to be found in the continuing and growing interest in writings and ideas in the general direction of the humanistic-existential orientation to man.

Organizations are questioning and moving away from the bureaucratic model, in part because man is asserting his individuality and his centrality, in part because of growing dissatisfaction with the personally constraining impact of bureaucracies. In this flux, organizations and man must find a way with each other. In our view, this way will be found through changing values—values which can hopefully serve the needs for effectiveness and survival of organizations and the needs for individuality and growth of emergent man. Those concerned with organization theory and with organizational development have, in our judgment, a most important role to play in this quest.

Values in Transition

Deeply impressed with the managerial and organizational implications of the increasing accumulation of knowledge about human behavior. Professor Douglas McGregor formulated his assumptions of Theory Y.[3] According to him, these assumptions were essentially his interpretations, based upon the newer knowledge and on his extensive experience, of the nature of man and of man's motivation.

[2] See Bennis (1).
[3] See McGregor (5).

In our view, McGregor was overly cautious and tentative in calling the Theory Y tenets "assumptions" and in limiting them to being his "interpretations." In trying to be "scientific," he seemed reluctant in his writing to assert explicitly as *values* those elements (including the Theory Y assumptions) which so much affected his organizational theory and practice. He was not alone in his reluctance. Perhaps the most pervasive common characteristic among people in laboratory training and in organizational development work is their values, and yet, while organizational development academicians and practitioners are generally aware of their shared values and while these values implicitly guide much of what they do, they too have usually been reluctant to make them explicit.

We want here not only to own our values but also to state them openly. These values are consistent with McGregor's assumptions and in some instances go beyond this. They are not scientifically derived nor are they new, but they are compatible with relevant "findings" emerging in the behavioral sciences. They are deeply rooted in the nature of man and are therefore basically humanistic. As previously suggested, many of the values underlying the bureaucratic model and its typical implementation have been inconsistent with the nature of man, with the result that he has not been fully utilized, his motivation has been reduced, his growth as a person stunted, and his spirit deadened. These outcomes sorely trouble us, for we believe organizations can in the fullest sense serve man as well as themselves.

Growing evidence strongly suggests that humanistic values not only resonate with an increasing number of people in today's world, but also are highly consistent with the effective functioning of organizations built on the newer organic model.[4] As we discuss a number of these values below, we will provide some face validity for their viability by illustrating them with cases or experiences taken from our involvements with or knowledge of a number of organizations which recently have been experimenting with the interface between the organizational and humanistic frontiers described above. The illustrations come primarily from TRW Systems, with which we have had a continuing collaboration for more than four years. Other organizations with which one or both of us have been involved include Aluminium Company of Canada, Ltd., U. S. Department of State, and the Organizational Behavior Group of Case Institute of Technology.

We clearly recognize that the values to which we hold are not absolutes, that they represent directions rather than final goals. We also recognize that the degree of their short-run application often depends upon the people and other variables involved. We feel that we are now in a period of transition, sometimes slow and sometimes rapid, involving a movement away from older, less personally meaningful and organizationally relevant values toward these newer values.[5]

Away from a View of Man As Essentially Bad Toward a View of Him As Basically Good. At his core, man is not inherently evil, lazy, destructive, hurtful, irresponsible, narrowly self-centered, and the like. The life experience which he has, including his relationships with other peo-

---

[4] This contention is supported by the further discussion of Theory Y by McGregor (6); by the discussion of System 5 by Likert (4); and by the discussion of 9, 9 management by Blake and Mouton (2).

[5] On reading an earlier draft of this paper, a corporation executive commented: "I think the perspective is wrong when the impression is created that these values are widespread. They are probably spreading from an infinitesimal fraction to a tiny fraction of the world's population, but at an accelerating rate."

ple and the impact on him of the organizations with which he associates, can and often do move him in these directions. On the other hand, his more central inclination toward the good is reflected in his behavior as an infant, in his centuries-long evolution of ethical and religious precepts, and in the directions of his strivings and growth as a result of experiences such as those in psychotherapy and sensitivity training. Essentially man is internally motivated toward positive personal and social ends; the extent to which he is not motivated results from a process of demotivation generated by his relationships and/or environment.

We have been impressed with the degree to which the fairly pervasive cultural assumption of man's badness has led to organizational forms and practices designed to control, limit, push, check upon, inhibit, and punish. We are also increasingly challenged by the changes in behavior resulting from a growing number of experiments with organizational forms and practices rooted in the view of man as basically good.

Within an organization it is readily apparent to both members and perceptive visitors whether or not there is, in general, an atmosphere of respect for the individual as a person. Are people treated arbitrarily? Are there sinister coups taking place? How much of the time and energy of the members of the organization is devoted to constructive problem solving rather than to playing games with each other, back-biting, politicking, destructive competition, and other dysfunctional behavior? How does management handle problems such as the keeping of time records? (Some organizations do not have time clocks and yet report that employees generally do not abuse this kind of a system). One of the authors can remember a chain of retail stores which fired a stock clerk because he had shifty eyes, although he was one of the best

stock boys in that chain. There are all kinds of negative assumptions about man behind such an incredible action.

For a long period of time, two senior engineers, Taylor and Durant, had real difficulty in working together. Each had a negative view of the other; mutual respect was lacking. Such attitudes resulted in their avoiding each other even though their technical disciplines were closely related. A point in time was reached when Taylor sorely needed help from Durant. Caught up in his own negative feelings, however, he clearly was not about to ask Durant for help. Fortunately, two of Taylor's colleagues who did not share his feelings prodded him into asking Durant to work with him on the problem. Durant responded most positively, and brought along two of his colleagues the next day to study the problem in detail. He then continued to remain involved with Taylor until the latter's problem was solved. Only a stereotype had kept these men apart; Taylor's eventual willingness to approach Durant opened the door to constructive problem solving.

Away from Avoidance or Negative Evaluation of Individuals Toward Confirming Them As Human Beings. One desire frequently expressed by people with whom we consult is: "I wish I knew where I stand with my boss [with this organization] [with my colleagues] [with my subordinates]. I'd really like to know what they think of me personally." We are not referring to the excessively neurotic needs of some persons for attention and response, but rather to the much more pervasive and basic need to know that one's existence makes a difference to others.

Feedback that is given is generally negative in character and often destructive of the individual instead of being focused on the perceived short-comings of a given performance. It seems to be exceedingly difficult for most of us to give positive feedback to others—and, more specifically, to express genuine feelings of affection and caring.

When people are seen as bad, they need to be disciplined and corrected on the issue only; when they are seen as good, they need to be confirmed. Avoidance and negative evaluation can lead individuals to be cautious, guarded, defensive. Confirmation can lead to personal release, confidence, and enhancement.

A senior executive reported to one of us that he did not get nearly as much feedback as he wanted about how people thought about him as a person and whether or not they cared for him. He reported that one of the most meaningful things that had happened to him in this regard occurred when the person he reported to put his arm around him briefly at the end of a working session, patted him on the shoulder, and said, "Keep up the good work," communicating a great deal of warmth and positive feelings toward the person through this behavior. This event had taken place two years ago and lasted about five seconds, yet it was still fresh in the senior executive's memory and obviously has had a great deal of personal meaning for him. In our culture, most of us are grossly undernourished and have strong need for the personal caring of others.

Away from a View of Individuals As Fixed Toward Seeing Them As Being in Process. The traditional view of individuals is that they can be defined in terms of given interests, knowledge, skills, and personality characteristics: they can gain new knowledge, acquire additional skills, and even at times change their interests, but it is rare that people really change. This view, when buttressed by related organizational attitudes and modes, insures a relative fixity of individuals, with crippling effects. The value to which we hold is that people can constantly be in flux, groping, questing, testing, experimenting, and growing. We are struck by the tremendous untapped potential in most individuals yearning for discovery and release. Individuals may rarely change in core attributes, but the range of alternatives for choice can be widened, and the ability to learn how to learn more about self can be enhanced.

Organizations at times question whether it is their responsibility to foster individual growth. Whether or not it is, we believe that for most organizations, especially those desiring long-term survival through adaptability, innovation, and change, it is an increasing necessity. Further, evidence suggests that to have people in process requires a growth-enhancing environment. Personal growth requires heatlhy organizations. This value, then, carries with it great implications for work in organizational development. In organizations, people continuously experience interpersonal difficulties in relating to the other people with whom they must work. Some reasons for the difficulties are that people listen very badly to each other, attribute things of a negative nature to another person, and make all kinds of paranoid assumptions, with the result that communication breaks down rather severely.

There have been many instances within TRW Systems of people, who, in the eyes of others around them, produce some fairly significant changes in their own behavior. Most of these changes have been reported quite positively. In some cases there have been rather dramatic changes with respect to how a person faces certain kinds of problems: how he handles conflicts, how he conducts staff meetings, etc. In those cases, an individual who is perceived as having changed quite often reports that these changes are personally rewarding, that he feels better about himself and more optimistic and expansive about life.

TRW Systems is committed to a continuation and improvement of its Career Development program, which places considerable emphasis on the personal and professional growth of its members. Although the original commitment was perhaps largely based on faith, experience gained in recent years strongly suggests that one of the most productive investments the organization can make is in the continuing growth of its members and in the health of the environment in which they work.

Away from Resisting and Fearing Individual Differences Toward Accepting and Utilizing Them. The pervasive and long-standing view of man as bad takes on even more serious implications when individual differences among men appear —differences in race, religion, personality (including personal style), specialties, and personal perceptions (definitions of truth or reality). A bad man poses sufficient problems but a strange bad man often becomes impossible.

Organizations and individuals are frequently threatened by what they consider questioning of or challenge to their existing values and modes, represented by the presence of alternative possibilities. And they choose to avoid the challenge and the related and expected conflicts, discomforts, and the like which might follow. As a result, they achieve drabness, a lack of creativity, and a false sense of peace and security. We firmly believe that the existence of differences can be highly functional. There is no single truth, no one right way, no chosen people. It is at the interface of differences that ferment occurs and that the potential for creativity exists. Furthermore, for an organization to deny to itself (in the name of harmony or some similar shibboleth) the availability of productive resources simply because they do not conform to an irrelevant criterion is nothing short of madness. To utilize differences creatively is rarely easy, but our experience tells us

that the gains typically far outweigh the costs.

In the play *Right You Are [If You Think You Are]* Pirandello makes the point that truth in a particular human situation is a collection of what each individual in the situation sees. Each person will see different facets of the same event. In a positive sense, this would lead us to value seeing all the various facets of an issue or problem as they unfold in the eyes of all the beholders and to place a positive value on our interdependence with others, particularly in situations where each of us can have only part of the answer or see part of the reality.

An organization recently faced the problem of filling a key position. The man whose responsibility it was to fill the position sat down with five or six people who, due to their various functional roles, would have a great deal of interaction with the person in that position and with his organization. The man asked them to help him identify logical candidates. The group very quickly identified a number of people who ought to be considered and the two or three who were the most logical candidates. Then the group went beyond the stated agenda and came up with a rather creative new organizational notion, which was subsequently implemented and proved to be very desirable. After this took place, the executive, who had called the meeting in order to get the help for the decision he had to make, reported that it was very clear to him that doing the job became much easier by getting everyone together to share their varying perceptions. This meant that he had more relevant data available to him in making his decision. Furthermore, the creative organizational concept only came about as a result of the meeting's having taken place.

In most organizations persons and groups with markedly different training, experience, points of view, and modes of operating frequently bump into each other. Project managers face functional performers, mechanical engineers face electrical engineers, designers face hardware specialists, basic researchers face action-oriented engineers, financial specialists face starry-eyed innovators. Each needs to understand and respect the world of the other, and organizations should place a high value upon and do much to facilitate the working through of the differences which come into sharp focus at interfaces such as these.

Away from Utilizing an Individual Primarily with Reference to his Job Description Toward Viewing Him As a Whole Person. People get pigeon-holed very easily, with job description (or expectations of job performance) typically becoming the pigeon hole. A cost accountant is hired, and from then on he is seen and dealt with as a cost accountant. Our view is that people generally have much more to contribute and to develop than just what is expected of them in their specific positions. Whole persons, not parts of persons, are hired and available for contribution. The organizational challenge is to recognize this fact and discover ways to provide outlets for the rich, varied, and often untapped resources available to them.

One of many personal examples that could be cited within TRW Systems is that of a person trained as a theoretical physicist. Having pursued this profession for many years, he is now effectively serving also as a part-time behavioral science consultant (a third-party process facilitator) to the personnel organization within the company. This is an activity for which he had no previous formal training until a new-found interest began asserting itself. The organization has supported him in this interest, has made a relevant learning opportunity available to him, and has opened the door to his per-forming an additional function within the organization.

An organizational example involves the question of charters that are defined for particular sub-elements of the organization: divisions, staffs, labs, etc. What are their functions? What are they supposed to do? To state the extreme, an organizational unit can have very sharply defined charters so that each person in it knows exactly what he is supposed to do and not do. This can lead to very clean functional relationships. Another approach, however, is to say that the *core* of the charter will be very clear with discrete responsibilities identified, but the outer edges (where one charter interacts with others) will not be sharply defined and will deliberately overlap and interweave with other charters. The latter approach assumes that there is a potential synergy within an organization which people can move toward fully actualizing if they can be constructive and creative in their interpersonal and intergroup relations. Very different charters are produced in this case, with very different outcomes. Such charters must, by definition, not be clean and sharply described, or the innovative and coordinated outcomes that might come about by having people working across charter boundaries will not occur.

Away from Walling-Off the Expression of Feeling Toward Making Possible Both Appropriate Expression and Effective Use. In our culture, there is a pervasive fear of feelings. From early childhood, children are taught to hide, repress, or deny the existence of their feelings, and their learnings are reinforced as they grow older. People are concerned about "losing control," and organizations seek rational, proper, task-oriented behavior, which emphasizes head-level as opposed to gut-level behavior. But organizations also seek high motivation, high morale, loyalty, team work, commitment, and creativity, all of which, if they are more than words, stem from personal feelings. Further, an individual cannot be a whole person if he is prevented from using or divorced from his feelings. And the energy dissipated in repression of feelings is lost to more productive endeavors.

We appreciate and are not afraid of feelings, and strongly believe that organizations will increasingly discover that they have a reservoir of untapped resources available to them in the feelings of their members, that the repression of feelings in the past has been more costly, both to them and to their members, than they ever thought possible.

One of the relevant questions to ask within an organization is how well problems stay solved once they are apparently solved. If the feelings involved in such problems are not directly dealt with and worked through, the problem usually does not remain solved for very long. For example, if two subordinates are fighting about something, their supervisor can either intervene and make the decision for them or arbitrate. Both methods can solve the immediate difficulty, but the fundamental problem will most likely again occur in some other situation or at some other time. The supervisor has dealt only with the symptoms of the real problem.

The direct expression of feelings, no matter what they are, does typically take place somewhere along the line, but usually not in the relevant face-to-face relationship. A person will attend a staff meeting and experience a great deal of frustration with the meeting as a whole or with the behavior of one or more persons in it. He will then talk about his feelings with another colleague outside the meeting or bring them home and discuss them with or displace them on his wife or children, rather than talking about them in the meeting where such behavior might make an important difference. To aid communication of feelings, participants at a given staff meeting could

decide that one of the agenda items will be: "How do we feel about this meeting; how is it going; can it be improved?" They could then talk face-to-face with each other while the feeling is immediately relevant to the effective functioning of the staff group. The outcomes of the face-to-face confrontation can be far more constructive than the "dealing-with symptoms" approach.

Away from Maskmanship and Game-Playing Toward Authentic Behavior. Deeply rooted in existing organizational lore is a belief in the necessity or efficacy of being what one is not, both as an individual and as a group. Strategy and outmaneuvering are valued. Using diplomacy, wearing masks, not saying what one thinks or expressing what one feels, creating an image—these and other deceptive modes are widely utilized. As a result, in many interpersonal and intergroup relations, mask faces mask, image faces image, and much energy is employed in dealing with the other person's game. That which is much more basically relevant to the given relationship is often completely avoided in the transaction.

To be that which one (individual or group) truly is—to be authentic—is a central value to us. Honesty, directness, and congruence, if widely practiced, create an organizational atmosphere in which energies get focused on the real problems rather than on game-playing and in which individuals and groups can genuinely and meaningfully encounter each other.

Recently, two supervisors of separate units within an organization got together to resolve a problem that affected both of them. At one point in their discussion, which had gone on for some time and was proving not to be very fruitful, one of them happened to mention that he had recently attended a sensitivity training laboratory conducted by the company. At that point, the other one mentioned that sometime back he had also attended a laboratory. They both quickly decided "to cut out the crap," stop the game they were playing, and really try to solve the problem they had come to face. Within a very short period of time, they dramatically went from a very typical organizational mode of being very closed, wearing masks, and trying to outmaneuver each other, to a mode of being open and direct. They found that the second mode took less energy and that they solved the problem in much less time and were able to keep it solved. But, somehow, at least one of them had not felt safe in taking off his mask until he learned that the other one had also gone through a T-Group.

When people experience difficulty with others in organizations, they quite often attribute the difficulty to the fact that the other person or group is not trustworthy. This attitude, of course, justifies their behavior in dealing with the other. On numerous occasions within TRW Systems, groups or individuals who are experiencing distrust are brought together and helped to articulate how they feel about each other. When the fact that "I do not trust you" is out on the table, and only then, can it be dealt with. Interestingly, it turns out that when the feeling is exposed and worked through, there are not really very many fundamentally untrustworthy people. There certainly are all kinds of people continuously doing things that create feelings of mistrust in others. But these feelings and the behavior that triggers them are rarely explored in an effort to work them through. Instead, the mistrust escalates, continues to influence the behavior of both parties, and becomes self-fulfilling. Once the locked-in situation is broken through and the people involved really start talking to each other authentically, however, trust issues, about which people can be very pessimistic, become quite workable. This has happened many, many times in organizational development efforts at TRW Systems.

Away from Use of Status for Maintaining Power and Personal Prestige Toward Use of Status for Organizationally Relevant Purposes. In organizations, particularly large ones, status and symbols of status can play an important role. In too many instances, however, they are used for narrowly personal ends, both to hide behind and to maintain the aura of power and prestige. One result is that dysfunctional walls are built and communication flow suffers.

We believe that status must always be organizationally (functionally) relevant. Some people know more than others, some can do things others cannot do, some carry more responsibility than others. It is often useful for status to be attached to these differences, but such status must be used by its holder to further rather than to wall off the performance of the function out of which the status arises. An organization must be constantly alert to the role that status plays in its functioning.

It is relatively easy to perceive how status symbols are used within an organization, how relatively functional or dysfunctional they are. In some organizations, name dropping is one of the primary weapons for accomplishing something. A person can go to a colleague with whom he is having a quarrel about what should be done and mention that he had a chat with the president of the organization yesterday. He then gets agreement. He may or may not have talked with the president, he may or may not have quoted him correctly; but he is begging the question by using a power figure in order to convince the other person to do it his way. In other organizations, we have observed that people very rarely work a problem by invoking the name of a senior executive, and that, in fact, those who do name-drop are quickly and openly called to task.

At TRW Systems, with only minor exceptions, middle- and top-level executives, as well as key scientists and engineers, are typically available for consultation with anyone in the organization on matters of functional relevance to the organization. There is no need to use titles, to "follow the organization chart," to obtain permission for the consultation from one's boss or to report the results to him afterwards. As a result, those who can really help are sought out, and problems tend to get worked at the point of interface between need on the one hand and knowledge, experience, and expertise on the other.

Away from Distrusting People Toward Trusting Them. A corollary of the view that man is basically bad is the view that he cannot be trusted. And if he cannot be trusted, he must be carefully watched. In our judgment, many traditional organizational forms exist, at least in part, because of distrust. Close supervision, managerial controls, guarding, security, sign-outs, etc., carry with them to some extent the implication of distrust.

The increasing evidence available to us strongly suggests that distrusting people often becomes a self-confirming hypothesis—distrusting another leads to behavior consciously or unconsciously designed by the person or group not trusted to "prove" the validity of the distrust. Distrust begets distrust. On the other hand, the evidence also suggests that trust begets trust; when people are trusted, they often respond in ways to merit or justify that trust.

Where distrust exists, people are usually seen as having to be motivated "from the outside in," as being responsive only to outside pressure. But when trust exists, people are seen as being motivated "from the inside out," as being at least potentially self-directing entities. One motivational device often used in the outside-in approach involves the inculcation of guilt. Rooted in the Protestant ethic, this device confronts the individual with "shoulds," "oughts," or "musts" as rea-

sons for behaving in a given way. Failure to comply means some external standard has not been met. The individual has thus done wrong, and he is made to feel guilty. The more trustful, inside-out approach makes it possible for the individual to do things because they make sense to him, because they have functional relevance. If the behavior does not succeed, the experience is viewed in positive terms as an opportunity to learn rather than negatively as a reason for punishment and guilt.

Organizations which trust go far to provide individuals and groups with considerable freedom for self-directed action backed up by the experience-based belief that this managerial value will generate the assumption of responsibility for the exercise of that freedom. In California, going back about twenty-seven years, a forward-looking director of one of our state prisons got the idea of a "prison without walls." He developed and received support for an experiment that involved bringing prisoners to the institution where correctional officers, at that time called guards, carried no guns or billy clubs. There were no guards in the towers or on the walls. The incoming prisoners were shown that the gate was not locked. Under this newer organizational behavior, escape rates decreased, and the experiment has become a model for many prisons in this country and abroad.

An organizational family embarked upon a two-day team-development lab shortly after the conclusion was reached from assessment data that the partial failure of a space vehicle had resulted from the non-functioning of a subsystem developed by this team. At the outset of the lab, an aura of depression was present but there was no evidence that the team had been chastized by higher management for the failure. Further, in strong contrast with what most likely would have been the case if they had faced a load of guilt generated from the outside, there was no evidence of mutual destructive criticism and recriminations. Instead, the team was able in time to turn its attention to a diagnosis of possible reasons for the failure and to action steps which might be taken to avoid a similar outcome in the future.

During a discussion which took place between the head of an organization and one of his subordinates (relating to goals and objectives for that subordinate for the coming year), the supervisor said that one of the things he felt very positive about with respect to that particular subordinate was the way he seemed to be defining his own set of responsibilities. This comment demonstrated the large degree of trust that was placed in the subordinates of this particular supervisor. While the supervisor certainly made it clear to this individual that there were some specific things expected of him, he consciously created a large degree of freedom within which the subordinate would be able to determine for himself how he should spend his time, what priorities he ought to have, what his function should be. This is in great contrast to other organizations which define very clearly and elaborately what they expect from people. Two very different sets of assumptions about people underlie these two approaches.

Away from Avoiding Facing Others with Relevant Data Toward Making Appropriate Confrontation. This value trend is closely related to the one of "from maskmanship toward authenticity," and its implementation is often tied to moving "from distrust toward trust."

In many organizations today there is an unwillingness to "level" with people, particularly with respect to matters which have personal implications. In merit reviews, the "touchy" matters are avoided. Often, incompetent or unneeded employees are retained much longer than is justified either from the organization's or

their own point of view. Feelings toward another accumulate and at times fester, but they remain unexpressed. "Even one's best friends won't tell him."

Confrontation fails to take place because "I don't want to hurt Joe," although in fact that non-confronter may be concerned about being hurt himself. We feel that a real absurdity is involved here. While it is widely believed that to level is to hurt and, at times, destroy the other, the opposite may often be the case. Being left to live in a "fool's paradise" or being permitted to continue with false illusions about self is often highly hurtful and even destructive. Being honestly confronted in a context of mutual trust and caring is an essential requirement for personal growth. In an organizational setting, it is also an important aspect of "working the problem."

A quite dramatic example of confrontation and its impact occurred in a sensitivity training laboratory when one executive giving feedback to a colleague said to him that he and others within the organization perceived him as being ruthless. This came as a tremendous jolt to the person receiving the feedback. He had absolutely no perception of himself as ruthless and no idea that he was doing things which would cause others to feel that way about him. The confrontation was an upending experience for him. As a result, he later began to explore with many people in the organization what their relationship with him was like and made some quite marked changes in his behavior after getting additional data which tended to confirm what he had recently heard. In the absence of these data (previously withheld because people might not want to hurt him), he was indeed living in a fool's paradise. A great deal of energy was expended by other people in dealing with his "ruthlessness," and a considerable amount of avoidance took place, greatly influencing the productivity of everyone. Once this problem was exposed and worked through, this energy became available for more productive purposes.

Away from Avoidance of Risk-Taking Toward Willingness to Risk. A widely discernible attribute of large numbers of individuals and groups in organizations today is the unwillingness to risk, to put one's self or the group on the line. Much of this reluctance stems from not being trusted, with the resulting fear of the consequences expected to follow close upon the making of an error. It often seems that only a reasonable guarantee of success will free an individual or group to take a chance. Such a stance leads to conformity, to a repetition of the past, to excessive caution and defensiveness. We feel that risk-taking is an essential quality in adaptable, growthful organizations; taking a chance is necessary for creativity and change. Also, individuals and groups do learn by making mistakes. Risk-taking involves being willing "to take the monkey on my back," and it takes courage to do so. It also takes courage and ingenuity on the part of the organization to foster such behavior.

At TRW Systems, the president and many of the senior executives were until recently located on the fifth floor of one of the organization's buildings, and part of the language of the organization was "the fifth floor," meaning that place where many of the power figures resided. This phrase was used quite often in discussion: "the fifth floor feels that we should. . . ." In working with groups one or two levels below the top executives to explore what they might do about some of the frustrations they were experiencing in getting their jobs done, one of the things that dominated the early discussions was the wish that somehow "the fifth floor" would straighten things out. For example, a group of engineers of one division was having problems with a group of engineers of another division, and they stated

that "the fifth floor" (or at least one of its executives) ought to go over to the people in the other division and somehow "give them the word." After a while, however, they began to realize that it really was not very fruitful or productive to talk about what they wished someone else would do, and they began to face the problem of what they could do about the situation directly. The discussion then became quite constructive and creative, and a number of new action items were developed and later successfully implemented—even though there was no assurance of successful outcomes at the time the action items were decided upon.

Away from a View of Process Work As Being Unproductive Effort Toward Seeing It As Essential to Effective Task Accomplishment. In the past and often in the present, productive effort has been seen as that which focused directly on the production of goods and services. Little attention has been paid to the processes by which such effort takes place; to do so has often been viewed as a waste of time. Increasingly, however, the relevance to task accomplishment of such activities as team maintenance and development, diagnosis and working through of interpersonal and intergroup communication barriers, confrontation efforts for resolution of organizationally dysfunctional personal and interpersonal hangups, and assessment and improvement of existing modes of decision-making is being recognized. And, in fact, we harbor growing doubts with respect to the continued usefulness of the notion of a task-process dichotomy. It seems to us that there are many activities which can make contributions to task accomplishment and that the choice from among these is essentially an economic one.

Within TRW Systems, proposals are constantly being written in the hope of obtaining new projects from the Department of Defense, NASA, and others. These proposals are done under very tight time constraints. What quite often happens is that the request for the proposal is received from the customer and read very quickly by the principals involved. Everybody then charges off and starts working on the proposal because of the keenly felt time pressure. Recently, on a very major proposal, the proposal manager decided that the first thing he should do was *spend a couple of days* (out of a three-month period of available time) meeting with the principals involved. In this meeting, they would not do any writing of the proposal but would talk about how they were going to proceed, make sure they were all making the same assumptions about who would be working on which subsystem, how they would handle critical interfaces, how they would handle critical choice points during the proposal period, and so on. Many of the principals went to the meeting with a great deal of skepticism, if not impatience. They wanted to "get on with the job," which to them meant writing the proposal. Spending a couple of days talking about "how we're going to do things" was not defined by them as productive work. After the meeting, and after the proposal had been written and delivered to the customer, a critique was held on the process used. Those involved in general reported very favorably on the effects of the meeting which took place at the beginning of the proposal-writing cycle. They reported things such as: "The effect of having spent a couple of days as we did meant that at that point when we then charged off and started actually writing the proposal, we were able to function as if we had already been working together for perhaps two months. We were much more effective with each other and much more efficient, so that in the final analysis, it was time well spent." By giving attention to their ways of getting work done, they clearly had facilitated their ability to function well as a team.

Away from a Primary Emphasis on Competition Toward a Much Greater

Emphasis on Collaboration. A pervasive value in the organizational milieu is competition. Competition is based on the assumption that desirable resources are limited in quantity and that individuals or groups can be effectively motivated through competing against one another for the possession of these resources. But competition can often set man against man and group against group in dysfunctional behavior, including a shift of objectives from obtaining the limited resource to blocking or destroying the competitor. Competition inevitably results in winners and losers, and at least some of the hidden costs of losing can be rather high in systemic terms.

Collaboration, on the other hand, is based on the assumption that the desirable limited resources can be shared among the participants in a mutually satisfactory manner and, even more important, that it is possible to increase the quantity of the resources themselves.

As organizational work becomes more highly specialized and complex, with its accomplishment depending more and more on the effective interaction of individuals and groups, and as the organic or systems views of organizational functioning become more widely understood, the viability of collaboration as an organizational mode becomes even clearer. Individuals and groups are often highly interdependent, and such interdependency needs to be facilitated through collaborative behavior rather than walled off through competition. At the same time, collaborative behavior must come to be viewed as reflecting strength rather than weakness.

In organizations which have a high degree of interdependency, one of the problems people run into regarding the handling of this interdependency is that they look for simple solutions to complex problems. Simple solutions do not produce very good results because they deal with the symptoms rather than with the real problems. A major reorganization recently took place within TRW Systems. The president of the organization sketched out the broad, general directions of the reorganization, specifying details only in one or two instances. He assigned to a large number of working committees the development of the details of the new organization. The initial reaction of some people was that these were things that the president himself should be deciding. The president, however, did not feel he had enough detailed understanding and knowledge to come up with many of the appropriate answers. He felt strongly that those who had the knowledge should develop the answers. This was an explicit, conscious recognition on his part of the fact that he did indeed need very important inputs from other people in order to effect the changes he was interested in making. The working committees turned out to be very effective. As a result of the president's approach, the reorganization proceeded with far less disruption and resistance than is typically the case in major reorganizations.

Another example involved a major staff function which was experiencing a great deal of difficulty with other parts of the organization. The unit having the trouble made the initial decision to conduct briefings throughout the organization to explain what they were really trying to accomplish, how they were organized, what requirements they had to meet for outside customers, and so on. They felt that their job would be easier if they could solicit better understanding. What actually took place was quite different. Instead of conducting briefings to convince the "heathen," the people in this unit revised their plan and met with some key people from other parts of the company who had to deal with them to ask what the unit was doing that was creating problems at the interface. After receiving a great deal of fairly specific data, the unit and the people with whom they consulted developed joint collaborative action items for

dealing with the problems. This way of approaching the problem quickly turned interfaces that had been very negative and very hostile into ones that were relatively cooperative. The change in attitude on both sides of the interface provided a positive base for working toward satisfactory solutions to the problems.

Some Implications of These Values in Transition

Many people would agree with the value trends stated in this paper and indeed claim that they use these guidelines in running their own organizations. However, there is often quite a gap between saying that you believe in these values and actually practicing them in meaningful, important ways. In many organizations, for example, there is a management-by-objectives process which has been installed and used for several years —an approach which can involve the implementation of some of the values stated earlier in this paper. If, however, one closely examines how this process takes place in many organizations, it is in fact a very mechanical one, which is used very defensively in some cases. What emerges is a statement of objectives which has obtained for the boss what he really wants, and, at the end of the year, protects the subordinate if he does not do everything that his boss thought he might do. It becomes a "Pearl Harbor file." The point that needs emphasis is that the payoff in implementing these values by techniques is not in the techniques themselves but in how they are applied and in what meaning their use has for the people involved.

To us, the implementation of these values clearly involves a bias regarding organizational development efforts. Believing that people have vast amounts of untapped potential and the capability and desire to grow, to engage in meaningful collaborative relationships, to be creative in organizational contexts, and to be more authentic, we feel that the most effective change interventions are therapeutic in nature. Such interventions focus directly on the hangups, both personal and organizational, that block a person from realizing his potential. We are referring to interventions which assist a person in breaking through the neurotic barriers in himself, in others around him, and in the ongoing culture.

We place a strong emphasis on increasing the sanity of the individuals in the organization and of the organization itself. By this we mean putting the individuals and the organization more in touch with the realities existing within themselves and around them. With respect to the individual, this involves his understanding the consequences of his behavior. How do people feel about him? How do they react to him? Do they trust him? With respect to the organization, it involves a critical examination of its culture and what that culture produces: the norms, the values, the decision-making processes, the general environment that it has created and maintained over a period of time.

There are obviously other biases and alternatives available to someone approaching organizational development work. One could concentrate on structural interventions: How should we organize? What kind of charters should people in various functional units have? The bias we are stating does not mean that structure, function, and charters are irrelevant, but that they are less important and have considerably less leverage in the early stages of organizational development efforts than working with the individuals and groups in a therapeutic manner. Furthermore, as an individual becomes more authentic and interpersonally competent, he becomes far more capable of creative problem-solving. He and his associates have within them more resources for dealing with questions of structure, charters, and operating procedures, in more relevant and creative ways, than

does someone from outside their system. Such therapeutic devices include the full range of laboratory methods usually identified with the National Training Laboratories: sensitivity training, team building, intergroup relationship building, etc. They also include individual and group counseling within the organization, and the voluntary involvement of individuals in various forms of psychotherapy outside the organization.

In order to achieve a movement towards authenticity, focus must be placed on developing the whole person and in doing this in an organic way. The program cannot be something you crank people through; it must be tailored in a variety of ways to individual needs as they are expressed and identified. In time, therapy and individual growth (becoming more in touch with your own realities) become values in and of themselves. And as people become less demotivated and move toward authenticity, they clearly demonstrate that they have the ability to be creative about organization matters, and this too becomes a value shared within the organization. Once these values are introduced and people move towards them, the movement in and of itself will contain many forces that make for change and open up new possibilities in an organization. For example, as relationships become more trustworthy, as people are given more responsibility, as competition gives way to collaboration, people experience a freeing up. They are more apt to challenge all the given surroundings, to test the limits, to try new solutions, and to rock the boat. This can be an exciting and productive change, but it can also be troublesome, and a variety of responses to it must be expected.

Therapeutic efforts are long-term efforts. Movement towards greater authenticity, which leads to an organization's culture becoming more positive, creative, and growthful, is something that takes a great deal of time and a great deal of energy. In this kind of approach to organizational development, there is more ambiguity and less stability than in other approaches that might be taken. Patience, persistence, and confidence are essential through time if significant change is to occur and be maintained.

For the organizational development effort to have some kind of permanency, it is very important that it becomes an integral part of the line organization and its mode of operating. Many of the people involved in introducing change in organizations are in staff positions, typically in personnel. If, over time, the effort continues to be mainly one carried out by staff people, it is that much more tenuous. Somehow the total organization must be involved, particularly those people with line responsibility for the organization's success and for its future. They must assimilate the effort and make it a part of their own behavior within the organization. In other words, those people who have the greatest direct impact on and responsibility for creating, maintaining, and changing the culture of an organization must assume direct ownership of the change effort.

In the transition and beyond it, these changes can produce problems for the organization in confronting the outside world with its traditional values. For example, do you tell the truth to your customers when you are experiencing problems building a product for them, or do you continue to tell them that everything is going along fine? For the individual, there can be problems in other relationships around him, such as within his family at home. We do not as yet have good methods developed for dealing with these conflicts, but we can certainly say that they will take place and will have to be worked out.

As previously stated, the Career De-

velopment program at TRW Systems, now in its fifth year of operation, is an effort in which both authors have been deeply involved. We feel it is one of the more promising examples of large-scale, long-term, systematic efforts to help people move toward the values we have outlined.[6]

One question that is constantly raised about efforts such as the Career Development program at TRW Systems relates to assessing their impact. How does one know there has been a real payoff for the organization and its members? Some behavioral scientists have devised rather elaborate, mechanical tools in order to answer this question. We feel that the values themselves suggest the most relevant kind of measurement. The people involved have the capacity to determine the relevance and significance to them and to their organizational units of what they are doing. Within TRW Systems, a very pragmatic approach is taken. Questions are asked such as: Do we feel this has been used? Are these kinds of problems easier to resolve? Are there less hidden agenda now? Do we deal more quickly and effectively with troublesome intergroup problems? The payoff is primarily discussed in qualitative terms, and we feel this is appropriate. It does not mean that quantitative judgments are not possible, but to insist on reducing the human condition to numbers, or to believe that it can be done, is madness.

The role of the person introducing change (whether he is staff or in the line) is a very tough, difficult, and, at times, lonely one.[7] He personally must be as congruent as he can with the values we have discussed. If people perceive him to be outside the system of change, they should and will reject him. He must be willing and able to become involved as a

---

[6] This program is described in detail in Davis (3).

[7] Each Winter Quarter, UCLA's Graduate School of Business Administration offers a residential program in Organizational Development for individuals instrumental in the change activities of their organizations.

person, not merely as the expert who will fix everybody else up. He, too, must be in process. This is rewarding, but also very difficult.

Introducing change into a social system almost always involves some level of resistance to that change. Accepting the values we have described means that one will not be fully satisfied with the here and now because the limits of man's potential have certainly not been reached. All we know for sure is that the potential is vast. Never accepting the status quo is a rather lonely position to take. In effect, as one of our colleagues has put it, you are constantly saying to yourself, "Fifty million Frenchmen are wrong!" From our own experience we know that this attitude can produce moments when one doubts one's sanity: "How come nobody else seems to feel the way I do, or to care about making things better, or to believe that it is possible to seek improvements?" Somehow, these moments must be worked through, courage must be drawn upon, and new actions must follow.

We are struck with and saddened by the large amounts of frustration, feelings of inadequacy, insecurity, and fear that seem to permeate groups of behavioral science practitioners when they meet for seminars or workshops. Belief in these values must lead to a bias towards optimism about the human condition. "Man does have the potential to create a better world, and I have the potential to contribute to that effort." But in addition to this bias towards optimism, there has to be a recognition of the fundamental fact that we will continuously have to deal with resistance to change, including resistance within ourselves. People are not standing in line outside our doors asking to be freed up, liberated, and upended. Cultures are not saying: "Change us, we can no longer cope, we are unstable." Commitment to trying to implement these values as well as we can is not commitment to an easy, safe existence. At times, we can be bone weary of confrontation, questioning, probing, and devil's-advocating. We can have delightful fantasies of copping out on the whole mess and living on some island. We can be fed up with and frightened by facing someone's anger when we are confronting him with what is going on around him. We can be worn out from the continuous effort to stretch ourselves as we try to move toward living these values to the fullest.

On the other hand, the rewards we experience can be precious, real, and profound. They can have important meaning to us individually, for those with whom we work, and for our organizations. Ultimately, what we stand for can make for a better world—and we deeply know that this is what keeps us going.

REFERENCES

1. Bennis, W. G. *Changing Organizations.* New York: McGraw-Hill, 1966.
2. Blake, R. R., and Mouton, J. S. *The Managerial Grid.* Houston: Gulf, 1964.
3. Davis, S. A. "An Organic Problem-Solving Method of Organizational Change." *Journal of Applied Behavioral Science*, Vol. 3, No. 1 (1967), pp. 3–21.
4. Likert, R. *The Human Organization.* New York: McGraw-Hill, 1967.
5. McGregor, D. M. *The Human Side of Enterprise.* New York: McGraw-Hill, 1960.
6. McGregor, D. M. *The Professional Manager.* New York: McGraw-Hill, 1967.

QUESTIONS

1. Discuss the implications of each of the following values that are given in the article:
   a. Away from a view of man as essentially bad toward a view of him as basically good.

    b. Away from walling off the expression of feelings toward making possible both appropriate expression and effective use.

    c. Away from maskmanship and game playing toward authentic behavior.

2. How are the existing values and customary modes of behavior of people in organizations derived?

3. For practicing managers what are the implications and likely consequences of their behaving according to the humanistic values expressed by the authors?

4. How do the values and actions advocated by the authors relate to reality as you have experienced it in work organizations?

PART VI

Financial Compensation

In designing and administering a comprehensive financial compensation program, personnel specialists must be able to identify the goals they wish the program to accomplish. Basically, four principal goals can be specified.

First, the wage and salary levels of the firm ought to be sufficiently competitive to attract the amount and quality of labor desired.

Second, the pay structure and increments ought to be equitable in order to retain people on the payroll and to minimize discontents and grievances.

Third, the pay system ought to induce and reward better performance. Pay can have a real incentive value if the system is designed for this purpose.*

Fourth, a carefully constructed compensation program—with job evaluation, pay scales, and employee-classification procedures—can enable management to control wages, salaries, and labor costs.

Direct wage incentive plans for production workers in industry are supposed to motivate high levels of output, increase employee earnings, and reduce unit labor costs. However, wage incentive installations that have been in operation for several years often deteriorate and lose some of the desired benefits. In "Restoring the Incentive to Wage Incentive Plans," Mitchell Fein analyzes the difficulties involved in incentive systems and offers a novel solution.

Dale S. Beach, in his article "Compensation Systems for Managers," shows how pay levels and pay structures for middle-

---

* See the article by David C. McClelland, "Money As a Motivator: Some Research Insights," in Part V-B, for a discussion of the meanings attached to pay in relation to motivation.

and top-level managers in industry are established. His article then focuses upon incentive compensation plans for executives such as bonuses, various types of stock options, performance shares, and deferred compensation. The special problems attendant to these incentive schemes are discussed.

Edward E. Lawler's article presents evidence to indicate that certain deeply held beliefs about management compensation are in fact fallacious. Whereas designers of executive pay systems tend to believe that their plans closely relate pay to performance and that pay thus motivates improved performance, research data give contrary conclusions. Although secrecy in pay matters is widely believed to be desirable, Lawler shows that such a policy often has negative effects.

35.

Restoring the Incentive to Wage Incentive Plans

MITCHELL FEIN

Increased productivity is now a top priority national goal, with general agreement that it is essential to revitalizing the economy. The Javits and Percy amendments to the Economic Stabilization Act passed in December 1971 were designed to raise employee salaries, Senator Percy's amendment authorizes ". . . wage and salary increases . . . paid in conjunction with existing or newly established employee incentives programs which are designed to reflect directly increases in employee productivity." Pay Board policy exempts individual incentive pay gains when a concomitant increase in productivity can be demonstrated. Payment for performance is encouraged.

In fact, however, the Bureau of Labor Statistics' latest study of wage incentive practices show that there has been a reduction in the use of wage incentives in industry—from 26% in 1963–1968[1] to 20% in 1968–1970.[2] Moreover, the BLS study concludes that: "It appears unlikely that there will be substantial shifts in the incidence of workers paid under incentive plans over the next few years. . . ." [3] This sharp decline is the more significant in view of the prevalence of incentives from 1948 to 1968 at a level of about 26%.

The low use of incentives for workers hardly seems to jibe with managements' attitudes toward incentives in general. Studies show that 86% of salesmen are on incentive[4] and 63% of the top three officers of manufacturing companies are

Reprinted from *The Conference Board Record*, Vol. IX, No. 11 (November 1972), pp. 17–21 by permission of The Conference Board.

Mitchell Fein, PE, is a consulting industrial engineer and adjunct associate professor of industrial engineering, New York University.

[1] George L. Stelluto, "Report of Incentive Pay in Manufacturing Industries," *Monthly Labor Review* (Bureau of Labor Statistics, U.S. Dept. of Labor), July 1969, Vol. 92, No. 7.

[2] John H. Cox, "Time and Incentive Pay Practices in Urban Areas," *Monthly Labor Review* (Bureau of Labor Statistics, U.S. Dept. of Labor), Dec. 1971.

[3] George L. Stelluto, op. cit.

[4] David A. Weeks, "Incentive Plans for Salesmen," *Studies in Personnel Policy* No. 217 (National Industrial Conference Board, 1970).

paid on an incentive basis.[5] Management is obviously not opposed to incentives, only to worker incentives.

Managers avoid incentives for blue— and white—collar workers because of apprehensions they will not be able to control the plans. Various techniques have been developed to control their operation, with varying success. Dedicated maangers can control and operate successful incentive plans, but it takes determination and expertise. Most managers, I think, are so fearful they will not be able to control incentives that they avoid them altogether.

After an examination of several hundred wage incentive plans, it is also my judgment that all are designed on principles which, over a period of time, must act to undermine the plans' basic objectives.[6] Three main reasons appear to underlie the problem:

• Gradual improvements are made in process and equipment over a period of time which are not detected by management nor reflected in new time standards; these might be called creeping changes.
• Errors in judgment are made by management and by industrial engineers in setting standards and designing incentive plans.
• The standards management does set are beat by employee ingenuity.

As incentives deteriorate, employees are reluctant to keep increasing output, fearful that management will find a reason to tighten the standards, which will force them to increase their output to maintain their past earnings. More often, the employees will hold production at a level they deem safe from management's scrutiny, which obviously holds down output. In capital intensive industries such restrictions on output are very costly.

When operations under incentive plans are examined closely, the root cause of incentive deterioration is apparant in a principle which lies behind most plans: *no ceiling on incentive earnings.*

The no-ceiling is management's guarantee that high earnings will not trigger a reduction in time standards, and this is offered as a promise of equity to employees. Yet it is just this that is the self-destruct mechanism causing the plans to fall apart in time. Despite this failure to operate in practice, the principle of no ceiling on earnings is still upheld as essential to the success of incentive plans. Indeed, it is so strongly established that the mere questioning of the efficacy of the principle causes wide consternation, particularly among industrial engineers and managers.

No Ceiling on Earnings!

The origin of the no-ceiling principle is understandable. When incentives gained popularity in the early 1900's it was quite common for managers to cut rates indiscriminately when employee earnings rose beyond levels management deemed warranted. Employees protected themselves with the only weapon they had, the withholding of production. Management's response to this was the open guarantee against rate cutting and the establishment of the principle of no ceiling on earnings.

The guarantee of no-ceiling means different things to employees and management. Managers believe that the lack of a ceiling will encourage an increased will to work. But workers who wish to increase their earnings see the guarantee as the legitimizing of all routes leading to increased output. However, in the work measurement sense, a standard for an operation represents not pieces per hour

[5] Harland Fox, "Top Executive Compensation," *Studies in Personnel Policy* No. 213 (National Industrial Conference Board, 1969).
[6] Mitchell Fein, "Wage Incentive Plans," in *Industrial Engineering Handbook,* 3rd edition, Harold B. Maynard, ed., (New York, McGraw-Hill, 1971).

but the work required to produce the pieces per hour. There is an important technical difference between the two concepts.

Workers clearly understand this difference. When management adds to the work requirements—for example, an extra operation, more frequent inspections, reduced machine speeds and feeds—there is an immediate demand by the employees that management allow extra time for the operation. This is an inviolate requirement in the maintenance of equitable time standards which workers never relinquish. But this principle must work both ways if a work measurement and incentive system is to operate equitably. When the operation is improved by the elimination or reduction of the requirements of the operation, the time must be proportionately reduced.

Employees on incentive are very serious and concerned about their earnings and anything that affects them. It takes only a short time for employees to see that incentives are a game in which they can often increase their earnings more by ingenuity than by their physical efforts. And since employees know that management will scrutinize the work of anyone who exceeds a "reasonable" level, they use all sorts of stratagems to avoid detection.

No ceiling on earnings is really a myth. There are real and effective ceilings in all incentive plants. The concept that an individual worker's ability to produce is limited only by his own desire and skill is not nearly as valid as it appears to be. When time standards are soundly set and conform to work measurement definitions and criteria, effective limits are established because the range of human work capacity has physiological limits. A few highly skilled workers will reach higher levels than others, but these are rare.

More important, there are powerful social forces operating on the plant floor which affect employees' motivation. If there is withholding of production because of employee differences with management, the individual will probably go along with the group. Conversely, where production is high because of high skills of the employees or because they want to maximize their earnings, this, too, will have an effect. An employee's desire to produce does not altogether rest on his own desires. He produces within limits which are unofficially established by his group and his work situation.

The Morality of the Incentive Game

Management's pronouncement of a no-ceiling on incentive earnings sanctifies practically all employee actions to increase their earnings except cheating. Though the official rules of the game provide that employees must perform the operations as specified by management, employees often use their own discretion. Supervisors who are anxious to raise overall productivity and maintain good relations conveniently look aside.

When employees use their ingenuity to increase their output beyond that possible with management's prescribed methods, they firmly believe the extra output belongs to them. Since they know that management would appropriate their ingenuity if it were discovered, they have no compunction about hiding their improvements. Withholding output does not bother their conscience since all productivity above standard is voluntary. Withheld production means lost earnings, but they see this as necessary to protect their productivity gains and to prevent management from learning that they have innovated changes. Each plant and even each department has a safe productivity level which, when exceeded, will trigger an investigation. Seasoned employees know how to hold their output from exceeding the safe level.

Employee ingenuity, even when it is the creation of a single employee, is considered as the collective property of all employees. When management uncovers employee methods' changes and attempts to revise the official operations sheet and the time standard, all the employees indignantly protest the change. They believe management is appropriating their creativity. No amount of discussion convinces employees that management has a right to their extra productivity.

Seasoned managers avoid such disputes by openly alerting employees to the dangers of defying the safe limit. Management knows that a sharp crackdown brings reciprocal actions from the employees, who then employ greater caution in the future to prevent a recurrence of management interference with their earnings. Unions similarly do not relish disputes over productivity increases through employee ingenuity and try to avoid such clashes.

The limits employees set on their productivity are visibly demonstrated day after day, but over a long period average productivity can be seen to rise steadily from one to one-and-a-half percentage points each year. In examining hundreds of plans I have rarely seen a situation where incentive earnings did not rise in this manner. Moreover, if the steady rise is interrupted, usually because of a business drop that year or major changes in product or manufacturing methods which caused substantial changes in standards, it invariably picks up again.

The first impulse is to attribute the steady productivity rise to increased skills of the workforce. But close examination reveals that the upward trend results from imperceptible increases during the year as employees control their output. I believe the increase would be even more rapid and sometimes dramatic were it not that employees fear that management would react to perceptible changes and attempt to limit or reduce incentive earnings which exceed a "safe" level.

The reason the minute upward rise is not detected in routine examinations by management is that 1% divided by 50 weeks is so insignificant. Even checking from one year to the next will not disclose the trend. Only when a comparison is made over a 10-year period does the trend stand out significantly.

Yet, an increase of 10 to 15 percentage points over a 10-year period erodes the incentive plan and the work measurement system. New standards can no longer be set by the original criteria because these would yield incentive earnings which are too low by comparison with earnings on the older standards. The employees then have to invent all sorts of ways to increase their earnings on the new standards. The incentive plan can only deteriorate under the total pressure for upward movement.

A Defense Against Deterioration

The factors that inhibit continued productivity increase can be removed, in my experience, if two changes are made in our current practice:

1. Establish a formal ceiling on incentive earnings.
2. Buy back the increased productivity which employees innovate above the ceiling.

As a first step, I propose that the unreal principle of no ceiling on incentive earnings be eliminated. It encourages practices which undermine incentive plans. It does not benefit employees nor does it protect them from management abuse. Instead, a formal limit should be established on incentive earnings by agreement between employees and management. This simple change establishes an entirely different set of rules under which employees have no incentive to violate the various conditions of the incentive plan to increase their earnings. Once a ceiling is set, increased output beyond the ceiling will only bring idle time during the day; it will not add to employee take-home pay. Since the ceiling is expressed in productivity per hour, the employees cannot produce eight hours of work in four hours and go home early, or sit around till the end of the day.

The major advantages of a ceiling are

• The incentive to beat the game is removed.
• The deterioration process that results from creeping changes is halted.
• Uneven earnings in departments and between various groups are eliminated. This is a major source of difficulty in industry when incentive earnings run away on relatively simple work, which then pays higher earnings than more skilled work.
• The rat-race of workers trying for higher and higher earnings is eliminated. Older workers, who cannot produce at the rate they could when they were younger, are not pressed by younger workers with greater stamina.
• A change in standards is less hotly contested by employees because it will not reduce their earnings although it will increase their output.

Ceilings have been successfully employed in numerous plants over the past 10 years, to my own knowledge. The stability obtained is remarkable. Surprisingly, the greatest opposition experienced has come from management, fearing unions might fight the ceiling. Actually, the ceiling has tended to relieve union leaders from the bickering on the plant floor because of inequitable earnings.

The ceiling is easy to establish in a plant which never had an incentive plan, since the increase in earnings is substantially higher than before and the ceiling represents no block. When incentives already exist, problems may be encountered in adopting a ceiling, depending upon the level of earnings. One approach is to pay cash settlements to employees earning over the ceiling, and then impose the ceiling. Another is to "red circle" the over-ceiling employees for the difference between their past earnings and the ceiling, which they continue to receive, but this is not extended to new employees.

As a second step, I propose that management should buy back the productivity above the ceiling which is attained through employee creativity. The buy-back is an extension of the suggestion plan principle, long established in industry. It already offers employees an opportunity to exchange their ingenuity for cash. How would buy-back work?

Consider a plant where an incentive plan with a 30% ceiling is in operation for a group of employees assembling a product. After some time, they develop techniques and improvements which enable them to increase their output to 140%. Since they cannot receive the extra 10% in pay, they produce to the ceiling and the 10% potential is lost. But with the buy-back in effect, the employees should request management to reduce the time standard!

In this case, if the time standard is reduced by 10%, employees who produce to the 140% level on the old standard will still earn the 30% maximum. But management now gets 10% extra production, and it would propose that the employees involved should receive a cash payment equal to the savings for a full year. Suppose the employees work all year on the operation and receive $7000 for a year's pay. Each would receive $700 in cash.

Management's costs for the next year have not changed, however, for if the standard had not been reduced, the employees would have been working under the old standard. After one year, management receives the full benefits from the reduced standard.

The buy-back principle thus permits continual improvement in productivity by the standing offer to employees to use their ingenuity to increase productivity and receive substantial rewards for their efforts. This removes the heart of the resistance under conventional incentive plans to changes in time standards, and it prevents incentive plans from deteriorating and retarding increased productivity.

Paying for Improved Productivity

Having established the basic principle that management will pay employees for improvements which they initiate, all employees should receive some share, even when they do not create the improvements, if plant-wide support for the improvement concept is going to be obtained. This could be secured under the following arrangement: (a) If no person or persons can claim credit for the improvement, all who work on the operation share the gains. (b) Where the innovators of the improvement are identifiable, they

receive the major share of the savings. Then, to suggest one approach to sharing the gains, the innovators receive 75%, the group or department receives 20%, and the entire plant receives 5%.[7]

In initiating a buy-back policy, management might wisely consider all looseness in time standards as due to employee ingenuity and not attempt to split hairs on whether management or the employees innovated change. The important objective is to get the ceiling and buy-back accepted by the employees and placed into operation.

There is agreement that when management innovates changes in an operation which reduce the time required, the time standard is reduced to match the change. But such changes are usually fought by

Case 1: *No one claims credit*

$7000/empl × 10 empl × 10% =	$7000 annual savings	
innovators are group; $7000 × 75% =	$5250	
each employee received $5250/10 =	520	
plus 20% × $7000 = $1400 to group/10 =	140	
Total to each employee	$ 665	
5% to plant-wide pool	$ 350	

Case 2: *Two employees are the improvement innovators*

to innovators:	75% × $7000 savings = $5250		
to group:	20% × $7000 savings = 1400		
to plant pool:	5% × $7000 savings = 350		
each innovator receives: $5250/2		= $2670	
plus $1400/10		= 140	
Total to each innovator		$2810	
each of the other eight in group receive		$ 140	
plant-wide pool receives		$ 350	

Case 3: *Individual production operation where one employee is the innovator*

to innovator: 75% of annual savings
to others in operation: share 20% of annual savings
to plant pool: 5% of annual savings

The unit value of the savings is the difference between the present and the new time standards. The total annual value of the savings can be calculated on the previous 12 months' production, or a projection of the next 12 months, adjusted at the end of the year. Payments can be divided into thirds: ⅓ when the standard is changed, ⅓ in 6 months, and ⅓ at the end of the year. The plant-wide and department pools can be paid out at the end of the year. With or without computers, calculations to keep track of annual savings present no appreciable problems.

[7] For example: Assume a production line of 10 employees who each earn $7000 per year; they innovate a productivity improvement of 10%.

employees because with no ceiling, they can use looseness in the standard to raise their earnings, if not in the present, possibly in the future. With the ceiling in effect, looseness will not add to earnings above the ceiling but only reduce the work load. If standards are set fairly, the fight for looseness for increased pay is far more intense than for a reduced work load.[8]

I also believe there is much to be gained by paying the involved employees a lump sum when the new time standard is instituted, equal, perhaps, to 5 to 10% of a year's savings, in recompense for the increased pieces they will produce. Such small payments should go a long way toward establishing a feeling of equity among the employees—they would be participating as improvements are made, even though these are instituted by management.

The buy-back, of course, is a one-time cost—part of the cost of establishing the improvement. When employees under conventional practices make improvements which they hide, the cost improvement is rarely recovered by management. But the buy-back permits an instant change in standard and a corresponding rise in productivity without the protracted delays and arguments that so frequently arise in standard changes.

Once they were generally accepted, the ceiling and the buy-back would create an entirely new set of rules for the operation of wage incentive plans. Many labor leaders have openly stated they are not opposed to productivity improvement, but to industry's steadfast refusal to share the gains. The buy-back principle, in my opinion, establishes an equitable way to provide employees with a fair share of the productivity improvement which they create. Moreover, the job enrichment which behaviorists counsel as beneficial to employees and to productivity will have greater attraction to more employees when they can enrich themselves with money by involvement in their work rather than with the psychic income now promised by job enrichment programs.

In Nonincentive Plants, Too

The buy-back approach described for wage incentive plans can similarly be used to encourage employees to raise productivity in measured day work plants. Since the ceiling already exists, all that is needed is the buy-back.

Managers in nonincentive plants know that high level productivity requires the establishment of time standards and production norms, not only as targets for the employees but to clearly establish management's concept of a fair day's work. Management and employees in these measured day work plants accept the norms as ceilings on production. No employee will try to exceed the standards. The social forces within the plant clamp a tight ceiling on productivity at management's norms.

Theoretically management can keep changing production standards as improvements are made. But in actual practice, changes in standards are as difficult to introduce as they are in incentive plans. Since employees have nothing to gain from increased productivity and, in fact, can be penalized in the process by reduced working hours or even layoffs, they resist increased output.

[8] There is an aspect of management-created changes, sometimes more psychological than actual, which employees resent. When an operation is improved so it takes less time, the employee must handle and be responsible for more pieces. In a physical sense the employee feels he is doing more work. But in a work measurement sense, since he has the time to perform the operation, he is required to absorb the extra work. What makes sense under work measurement rules does not go down easily with the employee, who complains that he is doing more work. There is no gainsaying this claim.

The cash buy-back, therefore, offers a solid reason for employees in all plants to accept increased output norms, and the creative ones will gain substantially.

QUESTIONS

1. It has been said that direct wage incentives for production employees are designed to reward increased physical effort but not increased mental effort and ingenuity. Is this true? Discuss.
2. Do you think management should have a right to appropriate the creativity of workers who figure out better work methods by cutting the time standard per unit?
3. Do you think the author's answer to the problem of restriction of output is a feasible solution?
4. Is there any difference between the "buy-back" of savings proposed by the author and a normal suggestion plan award based upon a percentage of the first year's savings? Explain.
5. Why do workers, on both incentive and daywork jobs, typically control their output well below the limits set by physical and mental endurance?

36.

Compensation Systems for Managers

DALE S. BEACH

There has been a pronounced trend in recent years towards the use of more formalized methods for determining pay, bonuses, and benefits for managers. In this sense, executive pay adminstration has followed the bureaucratic manifestations that have characterized pay administration for hourly and non-exempt office personnel since the 1940's.

In this analysis we shall concern ourselves with salary administration for middle and top management. We shall not deal with the issue of pay administration for front-line supervision.

For many years the American Management Association has been conducting surveys of executive compensation. These surveys have revealed a number of interesting relationships. First, large companies tend to pay their executives more than smaller ones. Second, the salary of

the chief executive is instrumental in regulating the pay of subordinate executives. Third, the level of compensation for comparable positions among industries varies widely. Fourth, the pay-level relationship among various management functions is reasonably constant from industry to industry.[1]

Arch Patton, who has written extensively on the subject of executive pay, claims that the great differences in salary levels among industries are directly related to the extent of competition in the product market and the nature of the decisions that influence profits (such as innovation and creativity). Surveys have indicated that executive pay in banking, life insurance, railroads, and public utilities is low compared to that in the automobile, chemical, petroleum, and electrical industries. Patton relates the lower

[1] Arch Patton, *Men, Money and Motivation* (New York: McGraw-Hill Book Company, 1961), p. vii. A *Fortune* magazine computer correlation analysis of the total compensation of the highest paid corporate officers of one hundred very large companies further substantiates Arch Patton's finding that the size of a company is a major determinant of top executive pay. *Fortune* correlated total compensation with five variables: sales, assets, net income, number of employees, and earnings-per-share growth rate (in 1957–1967). There turned out to be no meaningful correlation between growth rate (earnings-per-share) and pay. But the correlations of executive pay with measures of corporate size (assets, sales, net income, and employees) were very high. See "Performance Doesn't Pay," *Fortune* (June 15, 1968), p. 362.

pay in the former group to a more sheltered competitive life, government regulation, centralized decision making, and a lesser need for innovation.[2]

The broad outlines of salary systems for managers are similar in their elements to those for lower level groups. Job content information is obtained by interviewing the managers themselves. Job descriptions for management are commonly called position guides or responsibility guides. They do not contain detailed statements of duties and operating procedures. Rather, they cover areas of responsibility, scope of authority, and relationships with other positions and organizational functions.

Although it is probably true that executive jobs cannot be analyzed, described, and evaluated with the same degree of exactitude and precision as hourly jobs, many organizations have successfully applied job-evaluation techniques and created formal pay structures for executives. The techniques are different from those for hourly and office jobs, it is true. It is one thing to argue that executive salary determination is a complex problem and requires special methods. Most would agree with this. It is quite something else to argue that there is no need for a system or a procedure. Few would agree with this.

Where job-evaluation plans are used, they are almost always tailormade to the special requirements of the organization. Sometimes point plans are used, but most commonly combination point-and-factor-comparison plans are employed. One well-known plan is the guide chart-profile method developed by Hay Associates, a management consulting organization.[3] This method is used in over 700 companies, nonprofit organizations, and governmental jurisdictions in the United States, Canada, Mexico, the United Kingdom, and Australia.[4]

There are three main compensable factors in the Hay system. The first factor is "know-how," which is the sum total of the skills required for acceptable job performance. The second factor is "problem solving," which is the degree of original thinking required for analyzing, evaluating, creating, reasoning, and arriving at conclusions. The third factor is "accountability," which is answerability for an action and its consequences.

After all the management positions have been evaluated and points assigned, it is necessary to group these into grades. This process is guided somewhat by the hierarchy depicted in the organization chart. In a 25-grade-level system the chief executive officer would be at grade 25, the executive vice-president at grade 24, group vice-presidents at grade 23, and so on down to the lowest level of management. Of course the points assigned to the positions would determine in which grades particular positions would belong. An assistant plant manager might come two grades below the plant manager position and would not necessarily occupy the next grade in descending order.

After executive positions have been evaluated it is necessary to assign salary rates to these positions or to the grades into which these positions have been grouped. Three general approaches are used to price executive positions. These are the *top-down* approach, the *bottom-up* approach and the *budget* approach. In the top-down method the minimum salary for the chief executive officer is set first and the other top ranking positions

---

[2] Patton, op. cit., Ch. 3.

[3] Edward N. Hay and D. Purves, "The Profile Method of High Level Job Evaluation," *Personnel* (September 1951), pp. 162–170; also by the same authors, "A New Method of Job Evaluation: The Guide Chart-Profile Method," *Personnel* (July 1954), pp. 72–80.

[4] Herbert G. Zollitsch and Adolph Langsner, *Wage and Salary Administration*, Cincinnati: South-Western Publishing Company, 1970, p. 699.

are set in a definite percentage relationship to it. The bottom-up method uses either the pay of the front-line supervisor or that of the highest non-managerial position as a base reference point. It then works upward through the hierarchy to set grade level rates according to designated ratios of the reference point. The budget method prices positions by assigning a certain percentage of the total payroll to executives in, say, top management or in top or middle management. With this method the positions included in top and middle management must be precisely defined.[5]

Comparative salary data is important in pricing a job structure.[6] Well-known salary survey services provided by management and trade associations and by consulting firms classify managerial salaries by company size, by industry, and by functional responsibility (such as controller, industrial relations director, and marketing manager). Some surveys also indicate the relationships among different jobs within companies. Thus they may indicate that in a given industry the top operating executive gets 80 per cent of the chief executive's salary, on the average, and that the top financial executive gets about 60 per cent.

Salary survey data is useful as a guide in setting the pay rates for "bench-mark" positions within one's own company. A bench-mark position is one which is important in one's company and for which reliable survey data is available. The pay rates for other positions and for the salary grades can be set with reference to the rates for the bench-mark jobs. It should be clear that management does not merely mimic the prevailing rates in its particular industry in setting its salary policy. It considers other factors as well, such as financial strength of the company, supply and demand situation for executives, and geographical variations in salaries.

Salary ranges for executives typically provide a spread from minimum to maximum of from 30 to 70 per cent. There is usually considerable overlap of one grade with the next higher one.

In-grade raises in pay are almost always based upon performance of the individual. The total sums available for raises are usually tempered by the profitability of the firm from year to year. Formal performance appraisal plans are used in the process of determining pay raises for individuals.Usually raises are granted on the anniversary date of the manager's appointment. No one is guaranteed a raise, however. This depends upon performance and availability of funds.

Executive Incentives

For middle-level managers, salary and earned salary increases constitute the principal forms of financial compensation. For top executives, pay supplements in the form of year-end bonuses, stock options, performance stock shares, and various fringe benefits comprise a very large share of their total annual compensation. Middle-level managers often receive some of these kinds of pay supplements too, but these represent a smaller portion of their total pay.

Corporate compensation specialists design executive incentives to attract and retain highly qualified talent, to induce superior performance, and to generate greater profits for the firm. Because managers who receive high direct compensation must pay a large percentage of it to

[5] These three position pricing methods are explained in Zollitsch and Langsner, ibid., pp. 707–712.

[6] Salary survey information is available from cooperative company salary surveys, company proxy statements, trade associations, the American Management Association, periodic reports published in *Business Week* and *U.S. News & World Report*, and publications of the Dartnell Corporation and The Conference Board.

the government under our progressive income tax structure, companies have tended to devote considerable (and perhaps too much) attention to tax-saving features of stock options, deferred compensation arrangements, and fringe benefits.

Incentive Bonuses. Year-end bonuses in cash or company stock have been a common feature of executive compensation programs for many years. Alfred P. Sloan, Jr., president of General Motors in the 1920's and 1930's, credited GM's famous bonus plan with much of the success of the corporation in that era.[7]

When stock options came into vogue because of favored tax treatment conferred by Congress in amendments to the Internal Revenue Code in 1950, cash bonuses declined in relative popularity for several years. Until 1964, the top personal income tax rate was 91 per cent for those in very high income brackets. This made the cash bonus less attractive. In 1964 the top rate was reduced to 70 per cent and in 1972 it was cut to 50 per cent. Therefore, cash and stock bonuses (which are treated as cash income by the Internal Revenue Service) have come into renewed popularity.[8]

The fund of money from which bonuses are paid is usually a predetermined portion of the company's profits. Less often, the fund is discretionary on the part of the board of directors each year. The share of the fund distributed to each participant can be based upon the individual's performance, upon his salary level, or a combination of these. When the amount is determined by performance, a systematic performance-appraisal program must be utilized to judge fairly each executive. The judging is customarily done by a committee superior (in the hierarchy) to those being evaluated. Bonuses for the chief executive officer and vice presidents are usually handled by a committee of the board of directors.

Stock Options. A stock option is a right to buy a specified number of shares of stock from the corporation where one works at a stipulated price within a definite period of time. Stock options achieved great popularity as a result of the 1950 enactment of Section 130A of the Internal Revenue Code, which provided that gains in value between the option price and the selling price of the stock would be taxed at the capital gains tax rate, which was one-half the ordinary income tax rate and which went up only to a maximum of 25 per cent. Stock options are primarily offered only to the top executive group which is presumed to be in a position to affect the profits and growth of the firm. This is supposed to be reflected in increasing prices of the company's stock on the stock market.

During the 1960's there was growing public and Congressional criticism of stock options because they bestowed very favored tax advantages upon a special group. These same benefits were not available to regular stockholders. Also, it was felt that executives who exercised their option rights were evading their fair share of tax responsibilities for the operation of our government. The Revenue Act of 1964 made the conditions for the use of stock options more stringent. Congress further tightened the rules in the Tax Reform Act of 1969.

A *qualified stock option* is one which meets all of the conditions specified in the law in order to be eligible for favorable capital gains tax treatment. The main requirements specified in the law are that (1) the option period may not exceed

---

[7] Alfred P. Sloan, Jr., *My Years with General Motors*, New York: Doubleday & Company, 1964, pp. 425–428.

[8] A McKinsey & Company compensation survey of major companies in 1972 showed that 71 per cent had annual executive bonus plans, up from 63 per cent in 1970 and only 50 per cent in 1968. Source: *Wall Street Journal*, September 5, 1973.

five years from the time it is granted, (2) the option price must equal or exceed the fair market value of the stock at the time the option is granted, (3) the executive must hold his stock at least three years after time of actual purchase. The 1969 Act specifies that there shall be an added 10 per cent tax on certain tax preference income. Tax preference income is defined as the spread between market value on date of exercising the option and the option price. In addition, capital gains are now taxed at rates up to 35 per cent, compared to the former maximum of 25 per cent. Because of their less favorable tax treatment, qualified stock options are being issued and exercised much less frequently than in the 1950's and early 1960's.

Non-qualified stock options have come into prominence in recent years. Non-qualified options get no special tax treatment by the Internal Revenue Service but there is great flexibility in handling them. The option can be granted by the company at any price, it can be exercised any time within 10 years, and the stock can be sold by the executive after holding it only six months. The capital gains tax (maximum rate of 35 per cent) applies if the shares are held for longer than six months.

Restricted Stock Plans. A restricted stock plan is an arrangement in which an employer corporation transfers stock to a manager, subject to a restriction of some kind that limits the stock's value during the period of the restriction. Typical restrictions are that the individual is not allowed to sell his stock for a designated period, say five years or until retirement. Another restriction might be that he would forfeit the stock if he should resign his job. Under the rules of the Tax Reform Act of 1969 the individual who receives restricted stock for

services performed is required to pay tax on that stock in the first year in which his rights in the stock become transferable, or are not subject to a substantial risk of forfeiture, whichever occurs first. Thus, if his interest in the stock at the time he receives it is subject to a substantial risk of forfeiture, he does not, at the time of receipt, include the value of the stock in his income for tax purposes.[9]

Performance Shares. Since the early 1970's performance shares of stock have become a popular form of top-management incentive compensation. They are awarded to key executives, usually, every other year, in the form of phantom shares or bookkeeping units. They are paid out at the end of a performance period that could be from three to six years, but usually is four years. But the performance shares may never be paid at all if the executive fails to measure up to desired performance or if he leaves the company. Thus a performance share is a stock bonus but with the reward based upon *long-term goals* instead of traditional one-year objectives. A typical goal for a company president might be a cumulative 10 per cent growth in company earnings per share for a five-year period.

Unlike stock options, performance shares cost the manager nothing and there is no risk associated with a decline in the market value of the shares. If the executive performs up to expectations, the reward is assured.

DEFERRED COMPENSATION

Part of a manager's compensation can be paid in future years when his tax bracket will be lower (after retirement, for example). This can be accomplished by an individual employment contract or as part of a general employee benefit plan (pension and profit sharing). Under an individual employment con-

---

[9] "Restricted Stock and Stock Options Under Tax Reform Act," *Pension Plan Guide* Supplement, No. 194, Chicago: Commerce Clearing House, Inc., Feb. 12, 1970.

tract, a bonus of cash or stock can be paid out over a number of years—to keep the tax rate in a lower bracket, or paid after retirement.

Under Internal Revenue Service rules, a pension or profit-sharing plan cannot be limited to a small group of top executives —a broader coverage of employees is necessary. It would be proper to include all salaried employees. However, top executives can get higher benefits by tying them to their higher base salaries.

FRINGE BENEFITS

A way of rewarding executives with compensation on which they do not have to pay taxes is through the provision of benefits and services that are paid for entirely by the company. Examples are group life, medical and disability insurance, free medical service, payment of club membership dues, company automobiles, liberal vacations, free financial counseling, low-interest loans, payment of education costs at universities, and scholarships for their children. There is some question whether discriminatory granting of these benefits to a chosen elite of executives may not be destructive of morale among other employee groups in the organization.

QUESTIONS

1. Why are the pay ranges of managerial salary grades typically quite large?
2. Is it possible to be completely objective when assigning so-called merit or performance increases in salary to managers? Discuss.
3. Of the total pay of top executives, why is such a sizable portion typically allocated to bonuses, stock options, and similar "add-ons"?
4. Should middle-level managers be entitled to a full array of incentive "add-ons" and fringe benefits as are top executives? Discuss.

37.

The Mythology of Management Compensation

EDWARD E. LAWLER III

A host of decisions have to be made every day concerning compensation practices, decisions that are of critical importance in determining the success of any business organization. Unfortunately, relatively little is known about the psychological meaning of money and how it motivates people. Unanswered are such critical questions as:

• How often should a raise be given?
• What are the effects of secrecy about pay?
• How should benefit programs be packaged?

In the absence of systematic knowledge, executives have had to answer these kinds of questions for themselves. Many have drawn primarily from their own and others' experience in arriving at their answers. Unfortunately, common sense derived from experience can be loaded with implicit assumptions which may not be as valid as they seem. It is my purpose here to examine a number of commonly accepted assumptions about pay and to attempt to determine if they are valid.

What are the currently accepted principles and assumptions about how pay should be administered? In order to answer this question, a study was conducted among 500 managers from all levels of organizations. The managers were asked to indicate whether they agreed or disagreed with five statements that contained assumptions about the psychological aspects of management compensation— assumptions which have important implications for the administration of pay. The following are the five assumptions and the percentage of managers agreeing with each:

• At the higher-paid levels of management, pay is not one of the two or three most important job factors (61 per cent).
• Money is an ineffective motivator of outstanding job performance at the management level (55 per cent).

© 1966 by the Regents of The University of California. Reprinted from *California Management Review*, Vol. 9, No. 1 (Fall 1966), pp. 11–22, by permission of The Regents and the author.

Edward E. Lawler III is Professor of Psychology, The University of Michigan.

• Managers are likely to be dissatisfied with their pay even if they are highly paid (54 per cent).
• Information about management pay rates is best kept secret (77 per cent).
• Managers are not concerned with how their salary is divided between cash and fringe benefits; the important thing is the amount of salary they receive (45 per cent).

As can be seen, better than 50 per cent of managers participating in the study agreed with the first four assumptions and 45 per cent agreed with the last assumption.

Recently, research results have begun to accumulate which suggest that some of the assumptions may be partially invalid and some completely invalid. Let us, therefore, look at each of these assumptions and examine the evidence relevant to it.

What Is the Role of Pay?

The history of the study of pay shows that we have progressed from a model of man that viewed him as being primarily economically motivated to a view that stresses social needs and the need for self-actualization. Unfortunately, in trying to establish the legitimacy of social and self-actualization needs, the proponents of this view of motivation tended to overlook the importance of pay. In some cases, they failed to mention the role of pay in their systems at all, and in other cases they implied that, because workers and managers are better off financially than they used to be, pay is less important than it was previously.

Because of this failure to deal with the role of pay, many managers have come to the erroneous conclusion that the experts in "human relations" have shown

that pay is a relatively unimportant incentive and, as a result, have accepted the view that pay is a relatively unimportant job factor.[1] This is illustrated in the results of my study mentioned above. When the managers were asked to indicate how they thought the typical expert in human relations would respond to the statement that for higher-paid managers pay is not one of the most important job factors, 71 per cent of the managers thought that the majority of the experts would agree with it, while 61 per cent said they agreed with it themselves.

Undeniably, those writers who have stressed social and self-actualization needs have performed an important service by emphasizing the significance of nonfinancial incentives. It is now clear that people are motivated by needs for recognition and self-actualization as well as by security and physiological needs. But does this mean that pay must be dismissed as unimportant? I do not think the evidence justifies such a conclusion.

The belief that pay becomes unimportant as an individual accumulates more money has its roots in an inadequate interpretation of Maslow's theory of a hierarchy of needs. Briefly, Maslow's theory says that the needs which individuals seek to satisfy are arranged in a hierarchy. At the bottom of the hierarchy are needs for physical comfort. These lower-order needs are followed by such higher-order needs as social needs, esteem needs, and finally, needs for autonomy and self-actualization.

According to Maslow's theory, once the lower-order needs are relatively well satisfied, they become unimportant as motivators, and an individual tries to satisfy the higher-order needs. If it is then assumed, as it is by many, that pay satisfies only lower-level needs, then it be-

[1] This is not to imply that the leading figures in the "human relations" movement do not understand the importance of pay. But, by emphasizing other rewards and by not dealing explicitly with the role of pay, they have opened the door for others to interpret their writings as implying that pay is unimportant.

comes obvious that once a person's physical comforts are taken care of, his pay will be unimportant to him.[2] But this view is based upon the assumption that pay satisfies primarily lower-level needs, an assumption which I question.

Pay As Recognition

I would like to emphasize the neglected viewpoint that pay is a unique incentive —unique because it is able to satisfy both the lower-order physiological and security needs and the higher-order needs, such as esteem and recognition. Recent studies show that managers frequently think of their pay as a form of recognition for a job well done and as a mark of achievement.[3] The president of a large corporation has clearly pointed out why pay has become an important mark of achievement and recognition for managers.

Achievement in the managerial field is much less spectacular than comparable success in many of the professions . . . the scientist, for example, who wins the Nobel prize. . . . In fact, the more effective an executive, the more his own identity and personality blend into the background of his organization, and the greater is his relative anonymity outside his immediate circle.

There is, however, one form of recognition that managers do receive that is visible outside their immediate circle, and that is their pay. Pay has become an indicator of the value of a person to an organization and as such is an important

form of recognition. Thus, it is not surprising to find that one newly elected company president whose "other" income from securities approximated $125,000 demanded a salary of $100,000 from his company. When asked why he did not take a $50,000 salary and defer the other half of his salary until after retirement at a sizable tax saving, he replied, "I want my salary to be six figures when it appears in the proxy statement."[4]

It is precisely because pay satisfies higher-order needs as well as lower-order needs that it may remain important to managers, regardless of the amount of compensation they receive. For example, one recent study clearly showed (Figure 1) that although pay is slightly less important to upper-level managers (president and vice-president) than it is to lower-level managers, it is still more important than security, social, and esteem needs for upper-level managers.[5] At the lower management level, pay was rated as more important than all but self-actualization needs.

We can turn to motivation theory to help explain further why pay is important to many managers. Goals that are initially desired only as a means to an end can in time become goals in themselves. Because of this process, money may cease to be only a path to the satisfaction of needs and may become a goal in itself. Thus, for many managers, money and money making have become ends that are powerful incentives. As one manager put it when asked why his salary

[2] It should be pointed out that neither Maslow nor any of the leading figures in the "human relations" movement has stated that pay satisfies only lower-order needs. Others make the interpretation that it satisfies only lower-order needs (e.g., Robert B. McKersie, "Wage Payment Methods of the Future," *British Journal of Industrial Relations*, I [March 1963], 191–212).

[3] Edward E. Lawler and Lyman W. Porter, "Perceptions Regarding Management Compensation," *Industrial Relations*, III (Oct. 1963), 41–49; and M. Scott Myers, "Who Are Your Motivated Workers?" *Harvard Business Review*, XLII (Jan.–Feb., 1964), 72–88.

[4] Arch Patton, *Men, Money, and Motivation* (New York: McGraw-Hill Book Co., Inc., 1961), p. 34.

[5] Lyman W. Porter, "A Study of Perceived Need Satisfaction in Bottom and Middle Management Jobs," *Journal of Applied Psychology*, XLV (Feb. 1961), 1–10.

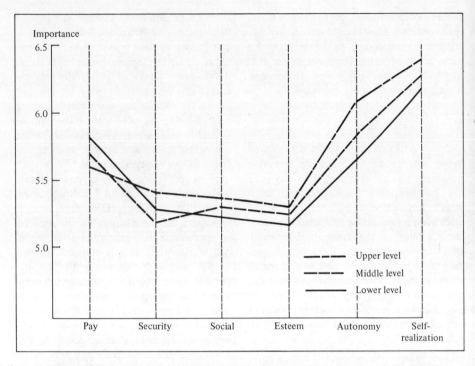

Importance

6.5

6.0

5.5

5.0

------ Upper level

——— Middle level

——— Lower level

Pay   Security   Social   Esteem   Autonomy   Self-
                                                    realization

FIGURE 1   Importance attached to six needs by managers at three levels.

was important to him, "It is just like bridge—it isn't any fun unless you keep score." In summary, the evidence shows that, although pay may be important to managers for different reasons as the amount of pay they receive increases, pay remains important to all levels of management.

The evidence that is usually given to support the belief that pay is ineffective as an incentive is the finding that a number of incentive plans have failed to produce expected increases in productivity. This view is expressed well by the following statement of a company president: "Wage systems are not, in themselves, an important determinant of pace of work, application to work, or output." [6] That this view is being more widely accepted by managers in industry is reflected in the decline of the use of incentive systems at the worker level. In 1935, 75 per cent of a sample of companies replied that they used wage incentive programs. By 1939 the number had fallen to 52 per cent and by 1958 to 27 per cent. The fact that managers have tended to stop using incentive plans for their workers points up the general disillusionment with the effectiveness of pay as an incentive among managers. This disillusionment is also reflected in my study which showed that 55 per cent of the managers sampled felt that pay is not a very effective incentive at the management level.

Managers' Pay

What experiences have these managers had that might cause them to be disillusioned? I believe that one cause of the disillusionment is in the misunderstanding

[6] Wilfred Brown, *Piecework Abandoned* (London: Heineman and Co., Ltd., 1962), p. 15.

of how pay functions as a motivator. In current practice, the logic is that if pay is tied to productivity, then productivity should increase. This logic seems to be supported by the law of effect which states that behavior (productivity in our case) which is seen as leading to a reward (pay) will tend to be repeated.[7] However, recent research shows that one problem is that, although incentive schemes are designed to relate pay to productivity, many managers do not see them as doing this. I have considerable evidence that many managers who work under systems which, as far as their organizations are concerned, tie productivity to pay simply do not feel that better job performance will lead to higher pay.

I recently distributed a questionnaire to over 60 middle- and lower-level managers in a variety of organizations. These managers were asked what factors determined their pay. The consensus of these managers was that the most important factor in determining their pay was their training and experience, and not how well they performed their jobs. A look at the relationship between how well they were performing their jobs as rated by their superiors and their pay showed that they were correct. There was virtually no relationship between their pay and their rated job performance. Under these conditions, there is no reason to believe that pay will function as an incentive for higher job performance, even though these organizations claimed to have incentive pay systems.

Some other data that I collected from the same managers shows one condition under which pay can be an effective incentive for high job performance. Of the managers studied, those who were most highly motivated to perform their jobs effectively were characterized by two attitudes:

• They said that their pay was important to them.
• They felt that good job performance would lead to higher pay for them.

To return to the law of effect, for these highly motivated managers, pay was a significant reward and they saw this reward as contingent upon their job performance. Thus, it would seem that one of the major limits on the effectiveness of pay as an incentive is the ability of management to design compensation programs that create the perception that pay is based upon performance.

It is not enough to have a pay plan that is called an incentive system. Not only the people who design the plan but the people who are subject to the plan must feel that it is an incentive plan. At the management level, one step in the direction of tying pay more closely to performance might be the elimination of some of the stock option and other deferred payment plans that exist now. Many of these pay plans are so designed that they destroy rather than encourage the perception that pay is based upon performance. They pay off years after the behavior that is supposed to be rewarded has taken place, and in many cases the size of the reward that is given is independent of the quality of the manager's job performance.

There are two other factors which suggest that cash payments may be particularly appropriate at this time. A recent study found that managers preferred cash payments to other forms of compensation.[8] Further, the new tax laws now

---

[7] There is evidence that the law of effect can work where a clearly perceived relationship between the behavior and the reward does not exist. However, the important point is that rewards are maximally effective when they are seen as being clearly tied to the behavior that they are intended to reward. (See, e.g., John A. McGeoch and Arthur L. Irion, *The Psychology of Human Learning* [New York: Longmans, Green and Co., 1952.])

[8] Thomas A. Mahoney, "Compensation Preferences of Managers," *Industrial Relations,* III (May 1964), 135–144.

make it possible to get almost as much money into the hands of the manager through salary as through stock option plans and other forms of deferred compensation.

In addition to failing to create the perception that pay is based upon performance, there are two other reasons why incentive plans may fail. Many pay plans fail to recognize the importance of other needs to individuals, and, as a result, plans are set up in such a way that earning more money must necessarily be done at the cost of satisfying other needs. This situation frequently occurs when managers are paid solely on the basis of the performance of their subordinate groups. Conflicts appear between their desire for more production in their own groups, no matter what the organizational costs, and their desire to cooperate with other managers in order to make the total organization more successful.

A second reason why incentive plans fail is that they are frequently introduced as a substitute for good leadership practices and trust between employees and the organization. As one manager so aptly put this fallacious view: "If you have poor managers you have to use wage incentives." Wage incentives must be a supplement to, and not a substitute for, good management practices.

The results of Herzberg's study of motivation have been frequently cited as evidence that pay cannot be an effective motivator of good job performance.[9] According to this view, pay operates only as a maintenance factor and, as such, has no power to motivate job performance beyond some neutral point. However, this interpretation is not in accord with the results of the study. The study, in fact, found that pay may or may not be a motivator, depending upon how it is administered. A careful reading of Herz-

berg shows that where pay was geared to achievement and seen as a form of recognition by the managers, it was a potent motivator of good job performance. It was only where organizations had abandoned pay as an incentive and where organizations were unsuccessful in fairly relating pay and performance that pay ceased to be a motivator and became a maintenance factor.

Incentive for Performance

In summary, I think the significant question about pay as an incentive is not whether it is effective or ineffective, but under what conditions is it an effective incentive. It appears that pay can be an effective incentive for good job performance under certain conditions:

• When pay is seen by individuals as being tied to effective job performance in such a way that it becomes a reward or form of recognition for effective job performance.
• When other needs are also satisfied by effective job performance.

The statement is frequently made that, no matter how much money an individual earns, he will want more. And indeed, as was pointed out earlier, the evidence does indicate that pay remains important, regardless of how much money an individual earns. But the assumption, accepted by 54 per cent of the managers in my study, that managers are likely to be dissatisfied with their pay even if they are highly paid does not follow from this point. There is an important difference between how much pay an individual wants to earn and the amount he feels represents a fair salary for the job he is doing. Individuals evaluate their pay in terms of the balance between what they put into their jobs (effort, skill, educa-

---

[9] Frederick Herzberg, Bernard Mausner, and Barbara Bloch Snyderman, *The Motivation to Work* (New York: John Wiley and Sons, 1959).

tion, etc.) and what they receive in return (money, status, etc.).[10]

Dissatisfaction with pay occurs when an individual feels that what he puts into his job exceeds what he receives in the form of pay for doing his job. Individuals evaluate the fairness of their inputs relative to their outcomes on the basis of the inputs and outcomes of other employees, usually their coworkers. Managers tend to compare their pay with that of managers who are at the same management level in their own and in other organizations. Thus, dissatisfaction with pay is likely to occur when an individual's pay is lower than the pay of someone whom he considers similar to himself in ability, job level, and job performance. But when an individual receives an amount of pay that compares favorably with the pay received by others who, he feels, have comparable inputs, he will be satisfied with his pay.

However, because an individual feels his pay is fair, it does not mean that an opportunity to make more money through a promotion or other change in inputs would be turned down, nor does it mean that more money is not desired. It simply means that at the moment the balance between inputs and outcomes is seen as equitable.

The results of a recent study of over 1,900 managers illustrates the point that managers can be, and in fact frequently are, satisfied with their pay.[11] The managers were first asked to rate on a 1 (low) to 7 (high) scale how much pay they received for their jobs. They were next asked to rate, on the same scale, how much pay should be associated with their jobs. As can be seen from Figure 2, which presents the results for the presidents who participated in the study, those

executives who were paid highly, relative to other presidents, were satisfied with their pay. For this group[12] (earning $50,000 and over), there was no difference between how much pay they said they received and how much pay they thought they should receive. However, those presidents whose pay compared unfavorably with the pay of other presidents said there was a substantial difference between what their pay should be and what it was.

The same results were obtained at each level of management down to and including the foreman level. The highly paid managers at each level were quite satisfied with their pay; it was the low-paid managers at each level who were dissatisfied. In fact, highly paid foremen ($12,000 and above) were better satisfied with their pay than were company presidents who earned less than $50,000.

There is some evidence that managers can, and do, feel that they receive too much pay for their management positions. Of the 1,900 managers studied, about 5 per cent reported that they received too much pay for their management positions. These managers apparently felt that their outcomes were too great in proportion to their inputs when compared with those of other managers. Although the number of managers who feel that their pay is too high is undoubtedly small, as indicated by the 5 per cent figure obtained in this study, the fact that this feeling exists at all is evidence that individuals do not always feel they deserve more and more pay.

The feeling of overcompensation by some managers is also evidence that some organizations are not doing the best possible job of distributing their compensation dollars. It may be wise for organizations

---

[10] J. Stacy Adams, "Wage Inequities, Productivity and Work Quality," *Industrial Relations*, III (Oct. 1963), 9–16.

[11] Edward E. Lawler and Lyman W. Porter, *op. cit.*

[12] The presidents in this sample tended to come from smaller companies and, hence, the relatively low level of their compensation.

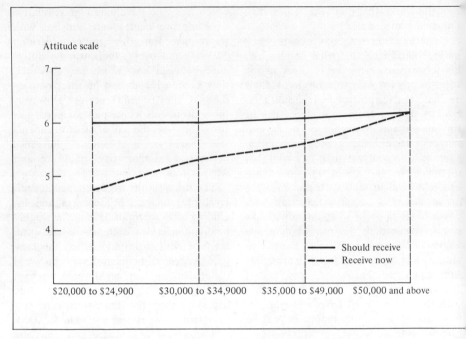

Attitude scale

Should receive
--- Receive now

$20,000 to $24,900 $30,000 to $34,9000 $35,000 to $49,000 $50,000 and above

FIGURE 2   Attitudes of corporation presidents toward their pay.

to give more weight to the value that subordinates and peers place on a manager's job performance when they are considering pay raises for a manager. Giving a high salary to a manager who is considered to be a poor performer by other employees can have several negative effects.

First, it can cause dissatisfaction with pay among other managers: dissatisfaction that comes about because managers who are good performers may come to see their own pay as suddenly inadequate relative to the pay of someone whom they regard as a poor performer, but who has received a raise. If such practices are followed, it is undoubtedly true that good performers will never be satisfied with their pay.

Second, and more important, giving a raise to a poor performer is a signal to other managers that pay is not necessarily based upon merit: an attitude that can destroy any motivational impetus that

might be created by an otherwise well-administered compensation program. As can be seen from the results of my study of managers' assumptions about pay administration, perhaps the most commonly accepted axiom of good personnel practice is that information about management compensation rates should be kept secret. Many organizations go to great lengths to maintain this secrecy. Information about management pay rates is frequently kept locked in the company safe and the pay checks of top management receive special handling so that the size of the check is not known even by the personnel manager.

The reason typically given to defend the policy of keeping pay information secret is that secrecy helps to reduce dissatisfaction with regard to pay. According to this view, managers who do not know how much others earn are not likely to feel their pay compares unfavorably with that of other managers. Thus, personnel managers are never faced with a situation where Joe thinks he is better than Jack but knows that Jack is making more than he.

Pay Rates Secret

However, such reasoning fallaciously assumes that secrecy policies eliminate pay comparisons. As was pointed out earlier, the evidence indicates that managers do evaluate their own pay in terms of what other managers earn. What is not clear is what effect the secrecy policies have on the accuracy with which managers estimate the pay of other managers and the effects of the secrecy on how satisfying and motivating these comparisons are.

In order to gather some evidence that might serve as a basis for evaluating the effects of secrecy, I recently conducted an attitude survey. Questionnaires were completed by 563 (response rate 88.7 per cent) middle and lower-level managers in seven organizations. Four of the organizations were private companies engaged in a wide variety of activities ranging from rocket manufacturing to supplying gas and electricity. The other three organizations were government agencies also engaged in a variety of activities. The four private companies all had strict secrecy policies with regard to management compensation rates, while the three government agencies did make some information public about their pay rates.

A two-part questionnaire was used. The managers were first asked to estimate the average yearly salary of managers in their organizations who were at their own level, one level above them, and one level below them. The organization provided actual average salaries in order that comparisons could be made. The managers were also asked to indicate how well satisfied they were with several aspects of their organizations' compensa-

tion systems. In addition to being asked to express their satisfaction with their own pay, they were asked to indicate whether there was too much or too little difference between their own pay and that of their superiors, and between their own pay and that of their subordinates.

The results of the study clearly showed that the managers did not have an accurate picture of what other managers in their organizations earned. Apparently, the secrecy policies were effective in keeping these managers from knowing what other managers earned. However, rather than committing random errors in estimating other managers' salaries, these managers consistently tended to overestimate and to underestimate. When the managers were asked to estimate the pay of their superiors, they consistently underestimated. When they viewed the pay of their subordinates, they consistently overestimated. One-third of the managers overestimated the pay of their subordinates by more than one thousand dollars. Similarly, they also tended to overestimate the pay of managers at their own level.

Interestingly, the managers in the government organizations were consistently more accurate in estimating the pay of other managers than were the managers in the private organizations. Because the government managers had more information about the compensation programs of their organizations, it was expected that they would be more accurate. However, this finding does serve to emphasize the point that the cause of the managers' misperceptions of other managers' pay was the secrecy policies of their organizations.

The question that now remains to be answered is what effects did these distorted pictures of what other managers earn have on the managers' job satisfaction and job performance. The effects on satisfaction with pay can be seen in the managers' answers to the three questions concerned with satisfaction with pay.

They stated that there was too small a difference between their own pay and that of their superiors and also too small a difference between their own pay and that of their subordinates. These attitudes are not surprising since the managers tended to see these differences as smaller than they actually are.

Effects of Secrecy

Secrecy policies are causing some of this dissatisfaction by giving the managers inaccurate pictures of what others earn. Since managers evaluate their own pay in terms of what others earn, it is not surprising that the data shows that those managers who feel their own pay is too close to that of their superiors and subordinates also feel that their own pay is too low. Undoubtedly, part of the managers' dissatisfaction with their own pay has its basis in unfavorable pay comparisons between what these managers know they make and what they think other managers make. On the basis of this evidence, it appears that *one effect of secrecy policies is to increase dissatisfaction with pay*.[13]

There is another way in which secrecy may contribute indirectly to both increased dissatisfaction with pay and lower motivation to perform a management job effectively. Secrecy allows a manager to avoid the responsibility of communicating to his subordinates his evaluation of their performance.

An example of what can and frequently does happen is that a manager who has to distribute raises capitalizes upon secrecy to avoid what he considers to be an unpleasant task. The manager does differentially distribute raises among his subordinates on the basis of their perfor-

mance. So far, so good! However, when he explains the raises to his subordinates, if he does this at all, he tells all of them that he has given them as large a raise as he could and that he is satisfied with their performance. The manager may reason that he has done the right thing. "After all," he thinks, "I did reward good performance with higher pay and I didn't cause any unhappiness as I would have if I had told the poor performers how dissatisfied I was with them."

However, the differential raises have no positive effect since they do nothing to encourage the perception that pay is based upon performance. The good performer is not sure he is getting a larger raise than the poor performer, and the poor performer may feel he is being rewarded for the type of performance he has been demonstrating. Eventually, of course, the word begins to get around about how much other people got in raises (undoubtedly slightly inflated), and this information is bound to make a number of managers unhappy with their pay, as well as distrustful of their superiors.

The secrecy policies of organizations and the consequent tendency for managers to estimate incorrectly the pay of other managers may also affect the managers' motivation to perform their jobs effectively in other ways. Several studies have shown that accurate feedback about task performance is a strong stimulus to good job performance.[14] People perform better when they receive accurate information about how well they are performing relative to some meaningful standard. For managers, pay is one of the most significant and meaningful pieces of feedback information they receive. High pay is considered a sign that the manager's

---

[13] Further support for this interpretation comes from the finding that there was a significant tendency for those managers who had an accurate picture of their subordinates' pay to be more satisfied with their own pay than were those managers who had an inaccurate picture of their subordinates' pay ($r = .35, p = .01$).

[14] Victor H. Vroom, *Work and Motivation* (New York: John Wiley and Sons, 1964).

job performance is good. Low pay is a signal that the manager is not performing his job well and that new behavior is needed.

The results of this study indicate that, because managers have misperceptions about what other managers earn, they are unable to evaluate correctly their own pay. Because of the tendency managers have to overestimate the pay of their subordinates and peers, the majority of the managers see their pay as low and in effect are receiving negative feedback. Moreover, although this feedback suggests that they should change their job behavior, it does not tell them what type of change they should make in their behavior. In cases where managers are not doing their jobs well, this negative feedback is undoubtedly the type of information that should be communicated; in other instances, it gives a false signal to change to those managers who are performing their jobs effectively.

Reduced Motivation?

Increased pay is one of the most significant rewards that an individual receives in return for taking on the responsibilities and work associated with higher-level management jobs and, therefore, is one of the important incentives in motivating managers to work toward obtaining higher-level jobs. However, as pointed out earlier, our data indicate that managers tend to underestimate the pay of managers at higher levels. This has the effect of making the attainment of higher-level jobs less desirable because it causes managers to underestimate the rewards that are attached to the positions. Thus, the secrecy policies of organizations may be indirectly reducing the motivation of managers to gain higher-level jobs.

If, as the evidence indicates, secrecy policies have significant costs in terms of job satisfaction, motivation for effective job performance, and motivation for pro-

motion, does it not seem logical that organizations should alter these policies? Perhaps organizations that now have secrecy policies could give out information on pay ranges and average salaries for all management levels. If they started by giving out only partial salary information, they could better prepare their employees for full disclosure, and eventually the salaries of all members of an organization could be made available to all other members of that organization. It may well be better to provide an individual with accurate information upon which to make pay comparisons than to have him make unfavorable comparisons based upon misinformation.

Role of Fringe Benefits

When any organization is asked to determine how much money it spends on compensation, it usually adds the money spent for salaries and fringe benefits. Similarly, an organization determines how much money an individual earns by adding his salary and the costs to them of his benefit package. Union contracts are typically spoken of as settlements involving an x cents per hour compensation package. Implicit in these measures of compensation cost is the assumption that a dollar spent on cash salary is equal to a dollar spent on life insurance or other fringe benefits. From an economic standpoint and in terms of costs to the organization, it seems reasonable that the value of a compensation package is equal to the simple sum of all its parts. It is probably the reason why 45 per cent of the managers sampled endorse the view that managers are not greatly concerned with how their pay is divided among various fringe benefits.

However, I would like to suggest that dollars spent on the different parts of the compensation package may not be equal in terms of what they earn in the recipient's perception of the value of his compensation package. Several studies have shown that individuals value some compensation benefits more than others, even though the cost to the company is the same.[15] For example, one study found that employees strongly preferred receiving hospital insurance to receiving additional pension money, even though the insurance and the pension plan cost the organization the same amount. In effect, a dollar spent on compensation can have a different value to the recipient, depending upon the type of benefit the organization chooses to buy with it.

The studies on compensation preferences among both workers and managers show that the preferences of individuals for different benefits vary greatly, depending upon such factors as their age, sex, number of children, and marital status. For example, older workers value pension plans much more highly than do younger workers, and unmarried men value a shorter work week more highly than do married men. These studies suggest that, at the very least, organizations may need different benefit packages in different locations, depending upon the personal characteristics of the workers in each installation.

A further step that organizations could take would be to design different packages for groups of individuals who have similar characteristics. Indeed, it may be that the optimum solution to this problem of different compensation preferences is for organizations to adopt a "cafeteria" compensation program. A "cafeteria" compensation plan would allow every employee to divide his compensation dollars among the benefits offered by his company. This would allow each employee to select the compensation options that he values most without adding to the compensation costs of the company. Pre-viously, such a program would have been impractical because of the high administrative costs that would be involved. However, with the advent of the computer, it is possible.

"Buffet" Benefits?

"Cafeteria" wage plans would appear to have a particularly bright future among managers where union negotiations and contracts are not likely to be a hindrance. "Cafeteria" wage plans have two additional benefits that strongly argue for their use.

First, they allow employees to participate in an important decision about their jobs. Even among managers, opportunities for actual participation as contrasted with pseudo-participation are rare enough so that in every situation where participation can be legitimately and reasonably employed, it should be.

Second, "cafeteria" wage plans help to make clear to the employees just how much money is involved in their total compensation package. There are many reports of situations where employees do not even know of the fringe benefits for which their organizations are paying. With "cafeteria" wage plans, this situation would be virtually eliminated.

Research Conclusions

What are the lessons to be learned from the recent research on the psychological aspects of compensation practices? I believe that the following conclusions are warranted.

• Even at the higher paid levels of management, pay is important enough to be a significant motivator of good job performance. However, it will be a motivator only when it is seen by the managers

[15] Stanley M. Nealey, "Pay and Benefit Preference," *Industrial Relations*, III (Oct. 1963), 17–28; Thomas A. Mahoney, *op. cit.*; and I R. Andrews and Mildred M. Henry, "Management Attitudes Toward Pay," *Industrial Relations*, III (Oct. 1963), 29–39.

themselves to be tied to their job performance.

• Managers can be, and in fact frequently are, satisfied with their pay when it compares favorably with the pay of other managers holding similar positions.

• Secrecy policies have significant hidden costs attached to them. The evidence indicates that secrecy may lead to lower satisfaction with pay and to a decreased motivation for promotion.

• In order to get the maximum value for money spent on compensation, organizations may have to institute "cafeteria" wage payment systems. Such a system would allow each manager to select the benefits that have the greatest value to him.

What the Future Holds

Will organizations be willing to innovate in the area of salary administration and to implement such programs as "cafeteria" wage plans and openness about salary levels? This question can finally be answered only five or ten years from now when we will know what the wage program of the future looks like. However, there are at least two reasons for believing that organizations will be slow to consider these new programs.

First, as one critic has put it, most organizations seem intent on keeping their compensation programs up with, but never ahead of, the Joneses in a sort of "me too" behavior.[16] It is unfortunate that many organizations got so badly "burned" when they tried to install incentive wage schemes that ignored needs other than that of money. Undoubtedly, this experience has led to the current air of conservatism that exists where innova-

tion with regard to salary administration is concerned.

Second, since none of the implications for practice that have been drawn from the results of this group of studies offers a miraculous cure for the present ills of any organization's compensation program, slow movement may be desirable. These studies imply that there may be better ways to do things, but they also imply that there may be costs and risks involved in trying these new policies.

For example, the idea of eliminating secrecy, no matter how well handled, will probably cause problems for some employees. In particular, openness will be difficult for the relatively low-paid managers to handle. But I believe that the gains would outweigh the costs and that there would be an over-all gain in motivation as a result of openness with regard to pay. I am led to this belief because, by making pay information public, pay can become an effective satisfier of such needs as esteem and recognition and thereby become optimally effective as a stimulant of effective performance. The same general point is true about "cafeteria" wage plans or tying pay more clearly to performance. There are certain costs that are associated with this type of innovative behavior, but there are also large potential gains possible where the practices are successfully installed.

I have found that the top management of organizations is always questioning and testing the value of their present compensation systems, and I hope that the ideas and research results presented here will be of aid in this process of inquiry and self-correction.

QUESTIONS

1. What meaning does pay have for managers? What kinds of needs does pay satisfy?
2. Why do management compensation systems often fail to serve as motivators of performance?

[16] Marvin D. Dunnette and Bernard M. Bass, "Behavioral Scientists and Personnel Management," *Industrial Relations*, III (May 1963), 115–130.

3. How can pay plans be designed so that pay does actually motivate improved performance?
4. Why is the prevailing practice of secrecy in pay matters often self-defeating?
5. What factors determine the preferences of employees and managers for different fringe benefits?

PART VII

Health and Safety

Neither the health of employees nor their safety on the job can be taken for granted. The physical and mental health of workers (these are really an integral whole) not only constitutes their state of well-being, it also exerts a large influence upon productivity. Likewise, accidental work injuries significantly affect labor costs, plant performance, and employee welfare. The attitudes of management are crucial in determining whether the establishment shall conduct progressive health and safety programs or whether the people shall suffer from neglect.

Until 1971 the responsibility for regulation of health and safety in industry was vested in the states. But this all changed with the enactment of the Occupational Safety and Health Act of 1970 (which became effective in 1971). This act was adopted because of mounting concern by workers, union leaders, the occupational safety profession, and governmental leaders about the rising toll of illnesses and injuries caused at the workplace. In 1961 the injury frequency rate in manufacturing (defined as disabling work injuries per million employee-hours worked) reached an all-time low of 11.8. However, it rose steadily all through the 1960's until it stood at 15.2 in 1970. Also, improved industrial medicine demonstrated that many chronic and serious illnesses were caused by various chemicals, gases, and dusts in industrial establishments.

John F. Burton, Jr., explains the background leading to the passage of The Occupational Safety and Health Act, its objectives and major provisions. He also discusses the plight of coal miners, which is handled by an entirely separate law and system of enforcement.

Alan A. McLean explains the concepts of mental health and mental illness and shows that there is a trend by both employers and unions toward acceptance of some responsibility for providing treatment for mental disorders of employees. He also discusses the role of Workmen's Compensation in the treatment of mental illness.

38.

The Occupational Safety and Health Act

JOHN F. BURTON, JR.

The Occupational Safety and Health Act was signed by President Richard M. Nixon on December 29, 1970, and became effective 120 days later. Thereby, the federal government became deeply involved for the first time in the area of safety. However, any state may share jurisdiction over safety if it develops an acceptable safety and health program. By April, 1971, federal planning grants totalling $6.8 million had been made to the states to enable them to develop such programs.

The Act in General

The Act permits the Secretary of Labor to promulgate occupational safety and health standards. Thereafter, the Secretary or his authorized representative may, "without delay," enter the premises of any employer who is covered by the Act, which includes virtually every private sector employer. A citation is then issued for any violation, either of a standard or of the employer's general obligation to provide a place of employment which is "free from recognized hazards that are causing or are likely to cause death or serious physical harm." In addition to the citation, the Secretary may assess penalties, which the employer may appeal to the independent Occupational Safety and Health Review Commission.

In the first nine months of fiscal year 1972, a total of 20,688 establishments were inspected. While 23 per cent of these establishments were found to be in compliance with the safety and health standards, 16,370 citations were issued and $1,444,686 in penalties were proposed. By the end of fiscal 1972, the Review Commission expects to have 45 full-time Judges (known as Hearing Examiners in other federal agencies) to hear appeals on these citations.

The Act, in its 34 sections, contains numerous other provisions relating to occupational safety and health. An entirely new position—the Assistant Secre-

Reprinted from the *Labor Law Journal*, Vol. 23, No. 8 (August 1972), pp. 501–504 by permission of the publisher and author.

John F. Burton, Jr. is Associate Professor of Industrial Relations and Public Policy, Graduate School of Business, University of Chicago.

tary of Labor for Occupational Safety and Health—has been created, in addition to a National Institute for Occupational Safety and Health with research and educational functions, within the Department of Health, Education, and Welfare. Further, the Act directs a Workmen's Compensation Commission to "undertake a comprehensive study and evaluation of state workmen's compensation laws" and requires all covered employees to keep extensive records of all work-related injuries, diseases, and deaths.

PUBLIC CONCERN

Passage of the Occupational Safety and Health Act manifests a substantial interest on the part of the public and Congress in industrial safety for the first time since probably the early decades of this century. What caught the public's fancy at this time was the emergence of a serious industrial injury problem. In 1907, for example, 7,000 workers were killed in two industries alone—railroading and bituminous coal mining. Further, this was also the muckraking era when journalists flourished on such facts (William Hard's classic, "Making Steel and Killing Men—Unnecessary Accidents in the Steel Mills," [1] indicated a variety of ways in which the south Chicago plant of U. S. Steel managed to average almost one fatality a week in 1906.)

One result of the public's concern with the lack of industrial safety was legislation. By 1920, for example, most states had enacted workmen's compensation laws. A justification for workmen's compensation was that by charging an employer for the benefits paid to his injured workers, the employer would be given a strong incentive to improve his safety record.

INJURY FREQUENCY RATE

The accident record for the decades following World War I suggested that the industrial safety problem was being resolved. In particular, the number of work-related deaths had dropped to 19,000 by 1930, and the decline has continued more or less unabated up to the present time. The National Safety Council now estimates that about 14,200 workers are killed annually in industrial accidents. Unfortunately, their data are of uncertain accuracy, as the estimates for recent years are based in part on extrapolations from 1964 estimates by the Bureau of Labor Statistics on the proportion of disabling work injuries which involve deaths.

While the record for deaths seems fairly favorable, the record for injuries is not so encouraging. Although the number of permanent disabilities declined from 102,600 in 1942 to about 76,700 by 1958, it has since increased so that now nearly 90,000 workers a year are permanently disabled. The same pattern emerges for temporary total disabilities. In 1942, about 2.1 million workers per year were disabled enough to lose some work time; by 1958, the number had been reduced to about 1.7 million annually. However, the number has again increased to the current rate of 2.1 million temporary total disabilities each year.

Of course, the labor force has expanded over the decades and one might therefore expect the number of injuries to increase. But the same pattern emerges with the injury frequency rate, which measures the number of disabling work injuries per one million man-hours. The injury frequency rate in manufacturing in 1930 was 23.1 injuries per million man-hours. By 1960 it had declined to 12.0, but by 1970, the rate was 15.2. Since 1961, there has been a steady increase in the injury frequency rate in manufacturing.

---

[1] Reprinted in Arthur and Lila Weinberg, *The Muckrakers*, (New York: Simon and Schuster, 1961), pp. 342–58.

What explains the apparent deterioration in the injury rates since the early 1950's? We don't really know. One suggestion is that during the 1960's, the labor force expanded rapidly, and the accident rate went up because younger workers are generally more accident prone. I don't know if this is an adequate explanation. One of the difficulties in sorting out the cause is the data problem. The Bureau of Labor Statistics' survey on which the injury frequency data are based comes from a voluntary schedule sent to employers, and fewer than 20 per cent of all manufacturing firms, employing less than half of all manufacturing employees, are surveyed. So what appears to have been a deterioration in the last decade may only be a statistical artifact. Fortunately, we are now on the verge of emerging from the dark ages of accident statistics, as one of the consequences of the Occupational Safety and Health Act is a very detailed reporting requirement. All work-related diseases, injuries, and deaths must be reported, beginning with the last six months of 1971. Thus, within the next year or two, greatly expanded and much more reliable data on industrial accidents will be available.

Whether due to the deteriorating injury rates or other factors, we have apparently entered a new era of general concern for industrial safety. It is even a "certified" problem, now that Ralph Nader has touched it with one of his studies— *Occupational Epidemic,* which in the paperback edition weighs three pounds. This study is a who's who of the bad guys in occupational safety; employers, government, trade unions—almost no one is spared from this attack. As there hasn't been much academic work in this area, the academic community escaped without extensive indictment.

Federal Legislation

The Occupational Safety and Health Act is the most obvious manifestation of the recent concern for industrial safety, but there has been a rush to legislation, patricularly at the federal level, and it is not clear that all of this legislation is desirable. One example of particular concern is the Federal Coal Mine Health and Safety Act of 1969, which provides Black Lung benefits to coal miners and their survivors. As a result of 1972 amendments, the benefit payments will increase substantially. One estimate is that payments will total almost 1 billion dollars a year, to be paid out of general revenues for the next 18 months. To put this figure in some perspective, annual payments for workmen's compensation benefits in all 50 states at the present time total about 3 billion dollars.

I recognize the serious plight of many miners. One problem is that many workmen's compensation acts did not adequately provide benefits for work-related pneumoconiosis. But why not cover byssinosis, the brown lung disease to which workers in the textile industry are subject? Why not cover heart disease, which can be work-related and yet is inadequately covered in many workmen's compensation statutes? Or why not include a whole series of other work-related diseases, which are excluded from the workmen's compensation coverage in some states? I don't think there is an adequate answer to these questions.

Conclusion

The emergence of interest in safety provides a chance for the Industrial Relations Research Association to make a major contribution. One commentator has suggested that health and safety will be the most critical collective bargaining issue of the 1970's. That may be an exaggeration, but I believe the 1970's will be comparable to that pre-World War I period in terms of a general concern for safety and health. Some laws are already on the books, but pressure is building for further legislation. I hope that members of this Association will provide some inputs to the process, which I suspect will set the pattern for safety and health legislation for the next several decades. We appear to be on a 60 to 70 year cycle of public interest in safety, and it may be during the decade of the 2030's before public concern with the issue again reaches a peak.

QUESTIONS

1. Prior to the enactment of the Occupational Safety and Health Act, the regulation of health and safety in the nation's work establishments had been almost the exclusive responsibility of the states. Why did it become necessary to enact a comprehensive Federal law in this field?
2. What should be the responsibility of the following for workplace health and safety: (a) the employer, (b) the employees, (c) the union, (d) government?
3. Who should bear primary responsibility for bearing the financial costs of such chronic occupational diseases as black lung (pneumoconiosis)?
4. Although the real causes for the increase in work injury frequency in the United States that occurred from 1960 to 1970 are not fully known, give as many possible causes as you can. How might one gather research evidence to get at the true causes?

39.

Mental Health in Industry— Who Pays the Bill?: A Clinical Perspective

ALAN A. McLEAN

Mental health in industry is a topic of enormous breadth and complexity. Whose responsibility is the mental health of the millions of working people in American industry? What is industry's role in supporting their mental health? As the only psychiatrist on this panel, I would like to try to help define our terms. The phrase "mental health" has become very popular, but it seems to mean many things to many people. For some, it means the illusive absence of frustration and a subjective feeling of well-being. For others, its meaning is the exact opposite. It is synonymous with mental illness in its most severe form.

These are two subjects—"mental health" and "mental illness"—they are not *necessarily* related. It is for this rea-son that we must distinguish between the concepts.

"Mental Health"

First, the pleasanter but more diffuse question of mental health. Is it the responsibility of industry to enhance employee satisfaction through a sense of performing purposeful, productive work?

This is a relatively new concept; that of an employer's responsibility to provide meaning, satisfaction, and stimulation, but no stress or anxiety, in a work situation. Regardless of one's definition of "mental health," no employer is really able to assume such a contractual commitment. This is an impossibility even for a company which has, high on its list of

Reprinted from *Journal of Occupational Medicine* (original title: "Who Pays the Bill?: A Clinical Perspective"), Vol. 9, No. 5 (May 1967), pp. 244–250, by permission of the publisher.

Alan A. McLean, M.D., is Psychiatric Consultant, International Business Machines Corporation and Program Director, Center for Occupational Mental Health, Cornell University Medical College.

corporate values, a belief that every worker should be placed in a job situation properly suited to his skills and interests. Products and processes are ever-changing. Industrial growth means change, and change disrupts the comfortable and satisfying routine of many jobs. Out of change itself come feelings of tension and anxiety. But out of some tension and some anxiety comes the stimulus for personal growth—the motivation for broadening levels of skill and ability. Industry must change to survive. Its fundamental role in life is not the fostering of mental health, but the creation of marketable products and services in a competitive world.

However, a concept of "mental health" may be examined, and factors which can support healthy behavior at work briefly reviewed.

The mental health of any single individual is the product of a unique, overwhelmingly complex personality interacting with a total life situation. By the time someone comes into the work force, his personality is well formed. His ability to cope with future life situations in a healthy way or a less healthy one has already been largely determined.

DEFINITION

The work of Solley and Munden,[1] at the Menninger Foundation in Topeka, produced a definition which says the individual who is mentally healthy is one who has a wide variety of sources of gratification. While he does not have irons in every fire, his pleasure comes in different ways and from many things. He is an individual who is flexible in situations which are stressful for him. He rolls with the punch. When faced with problems, he can see alternate solutions. He treats others as individuals. He recognizes they have different value systems and he does not attempt to inflict his own beliefs on them. He is not tied up in himself. Likewise, he has an understanding and an acceptance of his own limitations and assets. He sets his goals realistically and does not bite off more than he can chew. Finally, such an individual is one who is active and productive—appropriately and realistically participating in the world around him.

This is a definition of an ideal personality. It is also a definition of healthy behavior. While few employers have an overriding sense of obligation to stimulate healthy behavior among their employees, many would acknowledge that it would be pleasant, indeed, if their work force could be made up of people who at least approached the characteristics in this definition. And while one cannot alter basic personality, one *can* encourage such behavior.

A constricted, monotonous, and limited job can be made to provide additional sources of satisfaction by a thoughtful management. Through job enlargement, the encouragement of interests and participation beyond the narrow task at hand, the individual worker can be led to broaden his horizons. Additional sources of gratification can come in appropriate rewards from supervision, and from the work group.

The definition suggests allowing flexibility of individual reactions and behavior. If an organization defines narrow patterns of expected behavior and spells out rules for each possible action, it will probably get just what it asks for. No more, or less. Treating an employee as a child provokes child-like behavior. Allowing an individual freedom of expression and judgment tends to provoke more mature, responsible, and adult behavior, the stimulation of innovation and involvement with the ultimate advantage accru-

---

[1] C. M. Solley, and K. J. Munden, Behavior of the mentally healthy. *Bull Menninger Clin* 26: 178, 1962.

ing to both the individual and the organization.

If realistically handled, a job allows an individual to test his own beliefs about himself and his skills and abilities as well as his inadequacies. Through various job-appraisal systems, he has an opportunity to validate his own beliefs about his productive skills. Properly handled, these techniques can be harnessed to provide continuing feedback to the worker. Whether it be through wage increases based on performance, through promotion, or through assignment to more interesting jobs, reinforcement of perceptions of one's strengths and weaknesses becomes both a prop to mental health and a useful motivating force for the employer.

The stimulation of mental health may be far from the minds of most employers. It may be an elusive Utopian goal. No research study has yet proven a direct correlation with productivity. But there seems to be ample evidence that the mutual goals of industrial efficiency and productivity share a set of common concepts based on respect for the individual.

"Mental Illness"

Mental disorder has its roots in the same equation of an individual personality interacting with its total life situation. But such disorders are specific diagnostic entities. They are carefully and officially defined in the Diagnostic and Statistical Manual for Mental Disorders published by the American Psychiatric Association,[2] and included in the Standard Nomenclature of Diseases and Operations approved by the American Medical Association. They are determined by careful psychiatric and psychological evaluation of a single patient.

One could argue convincingly that industry should not be singled out for a particular responsibility for the mental disorders of its employees. After all, the employer receives an end product—an extraordinarily complex personality, well-formed and difficult to assess fully. The potential for development of a mental disorder comes with each worker, in varying degrees. The work situation which may trigger an overwhelming psychotic reaction in one employee may be the very situation which proves a stimulus to mental health in another. Should industry be held accountable for the provision of a stress-free environment when each individual's vulnerability is so unique? I am not convinced that such accountability is either fair or reasonable!

There is, however, a definite trend toward *some* acceptance by employers and by unions of reasonable responsibility for providing treatment for mental disorders of employees and members of their families. In-company medical programs of a great many larger employers are increasingly concerned with such illnesses. The occupational physician responsible for such programs is becoming much more sophisticated in the diagnosis and the management of these disorders. The doctor in industry is now concerned with early detection of such illness, recognizing as he does that most such disorders are far more amenable to treatment at their onset than later. He is concerned with appropriate referral of employee-patients for evaluation, and with treatment by a private physician or a community agency. He also has a goal of work assignments which consider the employees' psychiatric status. No physician in or out of industry wants to see his patient placed in a work situation which would make a known mental disorder worse.

Through increasing support of in-company medical programs, the management

---

[2] *Diagnostic and Statistical Manual, Mental Disorders.* American Psychiatric Association, Washington, D.C., 1952.

of our larger and more sophisticated companies increasingly express an appropriate responsibility for both physical and mental health at work. I do not suggest that all industrial medical programs are sophisticated or that all large employers have assumed a like responsibility for employee health. I speak of a trend.

There is also a trend toward the assumption of financial obligation for the treatment of mental disorder. American management and the American labor movement, separately and together, through in-company programs and insurance coverage, through clinics and the support of community mental-health agencies, have made vast strides in recent years toward the goal of providing realistic treatment programs for the psychiatrically disabled worker. Recent, widely publicized employment contracts—particularly in the automobile and agricultural equipment industries—will make available excellent programs of insurance coverage for large numbers of workers, but such an employee benefit is not new. Several insurance carriers have provided policies which have not differentiated between mental disorder and physical disorder. Basic hospitalization plans and major-medical coverage have provided psychiatric care for millions of employees and their dependents. While no two plans are exactly the same, most of those provided and financed by employees have been established as a result of a growing awareness of responsibility for the employee.

Mr. Greathouse will report more directly on union activities and concerns. These have also accelerated in recent years. For example, in 1946, the Labor Health Institute of Teamsters Local 688 in St. Louis included psychiatric service as part of its comprehensive health program. Since then a number of additional programs have appeared. There has generally been something innovative about each of them. An early one, for instance, was established by the United Mine Workers of America, which contracted with a private mental hospital in Virginia to serve its members and dependents through a program of travelling clinics. As the demand for service grew, these clinics became permanent establishments in several communities, partly supported by a retainer from the UMW and partly by fees from nonunion patients. In 1959, the Retail Clerks Local 770 in Los Angeles won its first contract which provided funds for psychiatric services. More recently, four union locals in Chicago have collaborated to establish a psychiatric clinic at the Union Health Center which includes two training programs in the recognition and handling of emotional disorders—one for union physicians and one for union leaders.[3] There are many more.

Despite the variation in union-sponsored programs, it is clear that a pattern of services has been initiated. The labor movement, in part feeling that management has been neglectful of its responsibilities in this area, and recognizing its own broader responsibilities to its members, is continuing to press for mental health services.

PREVENTION

Union and management have, therefore, *both* assumed a measure of responsibility. Meanwhile, from psychiatry itself has come developments not only of new treatment techniques but also of concepts and programs of prevention of mental disorder. And here are techniques increasingly available to industry. Many psychiatrists have broadened their perspective, no longer restricting their work to diagnosis and treatment. They provide con-

[3] A. A. McLean, Occupational mental health: Review of an emerging Art. *Amer J Psychiat,* *122*:961, 1966.

sultation to physicians and surgeons in the general hospital to help their patients adjust to the crisis of hospital life, and they train non-psychiatric physicians to be more sensitive to their patient's disturbed patterns of behavior. In industry, psychiatrists have developed programs of education for supervisors, executives, and occupational physicians. They have clearly demonstrated the success of early referral of employee-patients in time to effect treatment which has often prevented the development of incapacitating disorder. And they have become active in studies of stressful factors in the work environment.

From military psychiatry, we have learned more about the effect of the immediate environmental situation in the production of psychiatric disorder, and developed techniques to moderate these unhealthy influences. For instance, during the Korean conflict, experiences on the front line indicated that the incidence of "combat neurosis" was related more to the circumstances of the combat situation than to previously existing personality factors of the individual. The symptoms were significantly related to the degree of support given the individual by his buddies, by his group, and by his leaders. In 1957, Glass[4] showed that the defensive patterns adopted by individuals in the face of stress are molded in part by the social pressures in his group. In the same year, Bushard[5] described soldiers in noncombat conditions and described how a system of consultation with unit leaders helped to modify the social forces in order to prevent mental disorder.

Work from college mental-health clin-ics such as that of Farnsworth at Harvard, has clearly demonstrated that the psychiatrist can be effective not only with the emotionally disturbed student but with faculty and administrative people as well. "The more a psychiatrist can help the individual faculty member with his counseling problem, the better off the entire institution will be. Every time a professor or a dean works through a delicate situation with some professional help in the background the more capable he is of solving the next situation effectively." [6]

WORKMEN'S COMPENSATION

There is another development which I have been asked to deal with specifically. This is Workmen's Compensation coverage of those mental disorders which, in the legal phrase, appear to "arise out of and in the course of employment."

Workmen's Compensation is a system which exists by virtue of statutes in each state and in federal jurisdictions, to provide medical expenses and a weekly benefit for disabilities resulting from industrial accidents. Increasingly, we have seen mental illness held compensable. Increasingly, no actual physical injury has been required to meet the definition of accident. Held as compensable have been: (1) emotional disability caused by physical trauma, (2) physical disability resulting from emotional stress, and (3) disabling psychiatric disorder resulting from emotional stress.

The case which stimulated our recent interest in this subject was decided by the Supreme Court of the State of Michigan, Dec. 1, 1960. By a 5–3 decision, the Court sustained an order of the Work-

[4] A. J. Glass, Observations upon the epidemiology of mental illness in troops during warfare. *Symposium on Preventive and Social Psychiatry.* Walter Reed Army Medical Center, Washington, D. C., 1957.

[5] B. L. Bushard, The U. S. Army's mental hygiene consultation service. *Symposium on Preventive and Social Psychiatry*, Walter Reed Army Medical Center, Washington, D.C., 1957.

[6] D. L. Farnsworth, Potential problem areas of mutual interest to the dean and the psychiatrist. *Ment Hyg* 37:209, 1953.

men's Compensation Appeal Board awarding compensation to one James Carter for a psychosis resulting from emotional pressure encountered in his daily work as a machine operator. One of the most lucid commentaries on the Carter case appeared in the *Archives of Environmental Health,* by the Baltimore attorney, Theodore C. Waters:

His (Carter's) duties required him to work on an assembly line production. Medical evidence was offered that the claimant had a personality disorder and a predisposition to development of a schizophrenic process. The particular operation required him to take a hub assembly (consisting of a case and cover) from a nearby fellow employee's table to his own workbench, remove burrs with a file, grind out holes in the assembly with a drill, and place the assembly on a conveyor belt. Evidence indicated that he was unable to maintain the pace of the job unless he took 2 assemblies at a time to his workbench. He was instructed repeatedly by his foreman not to take 2 assemblies at a time because the assembly parts became mixed up on the conveyor belt when he did so. Thus, when he took only 1 hub assembly at a time, he fell behind and took 2 assemblies, and when he took 2 assemblies he got them mixed up and was criticized by his foreman. On October 24, 1956, he suffered an emotional collapse described in the evidence as paranoid schizophrenia and schizophrenic reaction residual type. The referee awarded compensation for a disability described as "traumatic neurosis, traumatic psychosis, functional disability and sequelae thereof." [7]

It was the appeal of this case which was largely sustained by the Supreme Court of Michigan.

In the Carter case, the ruling of the majority opinion was to the effect that it was not necessary to attribute the condition of the plaintiff to a single injury but that the series of events, the pressures of a job, and the pressure of his foreman had caused an injury or disability under the

law. In addition, as attorney Waters said, "No single incident was essential to provoke or sustain the claimant's rights to recovery, but the cumulative efforts resulting in his concern about his job and his violation of the instructions of his foreman caused the condition of which he complained."

Mr. Waters concludes, "It is indicative of the trend of judicial reasoning to make an employer responsible under the Workmen's Compensation laws for any and all human ills which may arise out of and in the course of employment."

CAUSE

Before citing additional examples of Workmen's Compensation awards for mental illness, I would like to suggest a point of sharp disagreement between psychiatry and the law, one not susceptible of ready resolution. It stems from two totally different points of view.

The legal profession and the psychiatric profession are worlds apart when it comes to defining a single word: The word is "cause." The doctor, of course, considers "cause" as those primary underlying factors which produce the pathology of an illness. Legally, the term "cause" includes *any* factor which contributes to producing disability, whether it triggers, or aggravates, or renders symptomatic an underlying condition. We are talking, then, about a "last straw" situation when we use the legal definition of "cause," not a more realistic medical concept which acknowledges all those factors contributing to the disability.

Here is the basis of the legal reasoning. It goes back to a 1910 case in the House of Lords (The Spanner Wrench Case). The words of the House of Lords were, "The employer takes the employee as he finds him." Despite that fact that the man in that case exerted very little more than customary effort in throwing his

[7] T. C. Waters, Mental illness: Is it compensable? *Arch Environ Health* 5:178, 1962.

weight behind a wrench as it tightened a nut, his widow was awarded the benefits of the compensation insurance. The yank on the tool caused an exertion which raised his blood pressure and ruptured an already strained blood vessel. The widow was granted benefits by the House of Lords on appeal and the finding was that it made no difference that an individual who would have been healthy, without a congenital aneurysm, would not have so responded to the stress. The fact is that the individual had an infirmity; his work stress was superimposed upon that infirmity; and it was that which produced his death. Accordingly, the employer takes the employee as he finds him, and since the work stress produced death in this case, compensation benefits must be granted and that widow was granted a weekly pension.

It doesn't make any difference whether this trauma is psychic or whether it is physical. And it doesn't make any difference whether, as in the Spanner Wrench case, it would not have produced a disability in an individual who was healthy and able to withstand it.

At a recent American Psychiatric Association annual meeting, Philip J. Lesser, a well-known compensation attorney in Washington, D.C., discussed the compensability of mental disorder. He provided several more examples suggesting the direction of Workmen's Compensation thinking. For example, emotional stimulus, not physical stimulus, can cause organic reaction and death. In one instance, a business agent for a union was working on an extremely difficult jurisdictional dispute and was not very successful in settling the dispute. He reported on the results of his negotiations to his union council and was subjected to ridicule and harassment during the meeting. The business agent became more and more heated in his responses to council members. He suddenly went white, keeled over, and died an hour later. The cause of death

was, as in the Spanner Wrench case, a ruptured aneurysm. Testimony was unanimous that the excitement during the union meeting precipitated the rupture of the aneurysm, and compensation was awarded to the widow. Here was a situation where the only trauma was of an emotional nature.

The more common and long-established awards for an emotional disability caused by physical trauma would be exemplified in the case of so-called "traumatic neurosis." An example would be the employee working alongside a truck who slipped and whose head fell alongside the rear wheel of the truck in very soft sand. He thought the truck had run over his head but was pulled out of the sand fully conscious. His only physical injury was a minor laceration. But his head continued to ache and he had dizziness and vertigo which was disabling and which continued for months. Here was a man who was disabled for a long period of time as a result of a serious, psychic trauma.

But the cases that cause the most difficulty, so far as clarity of medical cause is concerned, continue to be those, like the Carter case, where emotional stress causes a mental disorder. Again we may go back to the King's Bench in 1910 for the first such case. It was Yates against Fellows and Colliers, which is now classic. The fright and the shock of a coal miner reacting to the sight of the mangled remains of a deceased fellow worker who was trapped in the mine shaft "caused" him to develop such an incapacitating emotional reaction that he was never able to work in the mines again. This was held compensable. And there have been many cases since which suggest the increasing compensability of physical injury resulting from emotional stress, of emotional disability resulting from physical trauma, and of psychiatric disorder as the result of emotional stress. These are the statutory bases of financial responsibility for the development of mental illness, assumed by the employer through his Workmen's Compensation insurance coverage. I would be surprised indeed if increasingly liberal judgments were not rendered in the future, perpetuating a trend now apparently established.

There is a very real danger in liberalizing the legal concept of cause to the point where anyone may successfully claim that regularly expected performance on the job is responsible for his mental disorder. In psychiatry, cause is not that simple. That a man dislikes his foreman and becomes anxious when in his presence probably had its origins or cause in the man's relationship with an earlier authority figure in his life. The individual, of course, may firmly believe the fault is with the foreman, stay away from work pleading nervousness, and seek compensation. If the compensation courts sustain this type of judgment they will seriously impede the process of treating the individual, reinforcing his false beliefs as to the cause of his anxiety. How can a psychiatrist treating such a man bring him to the point of understanding the real reason for his difficulty if the courts say otherwise—and pay him for so believing?

But another digression: not so much an argument as a challenge. The challenge is that of seeing that individuals who need it are brought to psychiatric care as quickly as possible. I have been appalled at hearing the number of disabled individuals, supported by Workmen's Compensation Insurance, who supposedly have had an organic injury but who are obviously psychiatrically disabled. Many of these individuals have been organically overtreated for months. Very often such treatment has gone on so long that when they do get psychiatric care they don't respond.

This, I think, is a challenge not only to the medical profession, but also to the legal profession, since I am convinced that both astute attorneys and Workmen's Compensation Board members are better able to perceive these malignant situations than they might like to admit.

The main problem here is this: An individual who is physically disabled as a result of an element in his employment which triggers that disability, is entitled to benefits and entitled to a percentage of his wages to prevent him and his family from becoming a drag on society. But the very provision of these benefits for many of the emotionally disabled may unfortunately act as a deterrent to treatment, prevent or prolong his rehabilitation, and prevent him from giving up his symptoms and going back to work. Certainly this problem is not being successfully handled within the framework of existing legislation.

Summary

Business is assuming a responsibility through industrial medical programs which increasingly stress the appropriate placement of individuals in positions for which they are well suited. But medicine is not an exact science, nor is job placement. And in a dynamic, competitive American economy, the limited knowledge of both medical and personnel people is sorely taxed to do a sophisticated job. We are learning, but we have not yet the tools of totally effective, nonstressful placement. As we develop those tools, we may run head-on into the realities of the possible, as opposed to the ideal, for the individual. Surely one cannot expect American business to provide nonstressful positions for every man. On the other hand, for many, what was anticipated as stressful has often turned out to be stimulating. For others, it boils down to a difference between a stressful job and no job at all. At any rate, strides are being made in the direction of more successful placement and this is a role and a responsibility increasingly assumed by management.

Management has in many instances, without prodding, provided appropriate insurance coverage for employees and their dependents for the treatment of psychiatric disability.

Unions for their part, have come to the fore in recent years, both sponsoring clinics which include psychiatric care for their members and successfully bargaining for broader insurance coverage to include such treatment at community facilities and through private physicians. Together, unions and management have begun to attack the problem successfully.

Workmen's Compensation is contributing, but, as I see it, for the wrong reasons and in a less healthy way. Nonetheless, a significant facet of the impetus for providing industrial sponsorship (which is passed ultimately to the consumer) for the treatment of psychiatric disorders must be acknowledged through Workmen's Compensation court decisions.

Unions, management, and the Workmen's Compensation courts are together providing some of the answers to the question, "Who has the responsibility for the treatment of the employee with a mental illness?" Others also have a share of responsibility, *not the least of whom is the employee himself.*

It is well and good that management, labor, and the compensation courts are making provisions for the treatment of mental disorder. Most of us are enthusiastic about the broadened federal role in stimulating community mental-health centers for such treatment. We are, within the framework of limited resources, making it easier for people to obtain needed treatment. But the ultimate responsibility is with the individual and his family. You can lead a horse to water, but he must be thirsty. Not only must the individual feel a need for professional assistance, he must be willing to make the move, to reach out for help. For many, this is a painful decision, often postponed too long.

I submit that a final responsibility will be to develop the educational techniques to assist us in overcoming the continuing stigma associated with psychiatric care.

QUESTIONS

1. What is mental health? mental illness?
2. Do you feel that employers should accept some degree of responsibility for providing mental health services for their employees? Discuss.
3. How might one's job contribute toward mental illness?
4. How might greater progress in the treatment of industrial mental illness be achieved?

PART VIII

Collective Bargaining

Collective bargaining is a major institution in the United States. It exerts a great impact not only upon the lives of working men and women but also upon employers, the economy, and the customs and laws of the land. In the immediate employer–union–employee situation of the individual company, collective bargaining is an instrument for determining wage levels and wage structures, hours of work, health and welfare programs, working conditions, job-rights systems, and procedures for administrative justice. Labor settlements and labor–management conflicts have a material effect upon industrial output, costs, and efficiency. Managers in nonunion organizations must also be cognizant of collective bargaining patterns because their own labor standards and practices often are influenced by these "external" market pressures.

A major phenomenon that burst upon the scene in the 1960's was the very rapid spread of unionization and collective bargaining in government at all levels—federal, state, local, and public schools. Louis V. Imundo, Jr., presents a comprehensive comparison of collective bargaining in the public and private sectors of employment. Although there are many similarities, the traditional concept of sovereignty of government has placed impediments in the way of collective bargaining for public employees. With the advent of collective bargaining in the public sector the conventional role and functions of civil service commissions have undergone change.

In his article, "A Political System for a Political World—in Public Sector Labor Relations," Robert D. Helsby points out the distinct roles of the employer–executive (such as a mayor of a city or a superintendent of schools) and the legislature. There is a basic dilemma in public sector bargaining, he points out. What happens if a legislature supplements or supplants the bargain made with a union by the employer–executive? Dr. Helsby offers cogent views on the perennial question of whether public employees should be granted the right to strike, as has occurred under limited circumstances in a few states. The pervasive political implications of public sector collective bargaining make the situation distinctly different from its counterpart in the private sector.

In "Collective Bargaining and Industrial Peace," David L. Cole, a professional mediator and arbitrator, takes issue with those who claim that strikes and economic force are essential and integral parts of the institution of collective bargaining. He foresees a gradual attenuation of economic force as employers accept collective bargaining as a way of managing a work force and as unions become permanent parts of the labor–management structure.

40.

Some Comparisons Between Public Sector and Private Sector Collective Bargaining

LOUIS V. IMUNDO, JR.

In the complex field of public sector labor-management relations many authors have made the point that government labor-management relationships are unique when compared to the relationship between labor and management in the private sector.[1] Others have maintained that no real differences exist between labor-management relations in the public sector and labor-management relations in the private sector.

Examination of federal executive orders and state statutes show that in certain respects meaningful comparisons with the private sector can be developed. In other respects the relationships are unique to the point where meaningful comparisons cannot be developed. In the areas where comparisons can be developed, the present state of collective bargaining in the public sector is comparable to private sector collective bargaining during the 1930's and 40's. Many of the private sector collective bargaining relationship problems of the 1930's and 40's which precipitated bitter conflicts have been settled only to arise again to restrict public sector collective bargaining.

During the 1930's and 40's, bitter conflicts between private sector labor and management erupted over labor's right to organize and the scope of negotiable issues. Until the Wagner Act guaranteed labor the right to organize and collectively bargain with their employer, many managements refused to recognize or negotiate with unions. Once organized labor secured the right to organize and negotiate agreements, managements, in

Reprinted from the *Labor Law Journal*, Vol. 24, No. 12 (December 1973), pp. 810–817 by permission of the publisher and author.

Louis V. Imundo, Jr., is an Assistant Professor of Management at Wright State University.

[1] Glenn Stahl, *Public Personnel Administration* (New York: Harper and Row, 1971). Dr. Stahl is the foremost writer in the field of public administration holding this view.

the name of "managements' rights" attempted to limit the scope of negotiable issues. Changes in the law, NLRB and court interpretations of the law, increased union power and a maturing of management and labor were all factors that brought about an eventual broadening of the scope of negotiable issues. When the scope of negotiable issues in the private sector was compared with the scope of negotiable issues in the public sector, significant differences were found to exist. The scope of negotiable issues in the private sector is generally broader than the scope of negotiable issues in the public sector.

The Problem of Sovereignty

In the private sector the law is structured to make the bargaining parties equals. In the public sector, the sovereignty doctrine makes it impossible for labor and management to bargain as equals. Two states, Alabama and North Carolina, have statutes that forbid public employees to join unions for the purposes of collective bargaining. At the end of 1970, eight states had not accorded their employees legal protection for collective bargaining. A number of states that have enacted legislation have stipulated that management's only obligation is to "meet and confer" with public employee unions. There is no mention about "collective bargaining in good faith." [2] In effect, a number of states have labor-management relations policies comparable to conditions in the private sector during the 1930's.

The sovereignty doctrine, i.e., the rights of the state, is at the forefront of many of the problems in public sector labor-management relations. In certain respects the sovereignty doctrine is comparable to the issue of management's rights in the private sector. In other respects the doctrine is a broader concept and meaningful comparisons are difficult to develop. The concept of sovereignty is inherent in the supreme power of a political state. Any state that possesses and maintains supreme power can determine whether or not an individual or a group of individuals can initiate a claim against the state. Sovereignty may be exercised by an individual, as in the form of an absolute monarchy, or by a body politic as is the case in contemporary society.[3]

The concept of sovereignty is difficult to understand and over time this inherent difficulty has caused considerable misunderstanding in the area of government labor-management relations. The difficulty of the concept lies in the fact that sovereignty conveys two ideas: legal sovereignty and political sovereignty. In the legal sense, sovereignty means that a governmental source of law must exist which is final and definitive.[4]

With regard to government's relationship with its employees, the theoretical application of the sovereignty doctrine permits only the government employer to establish the terms and conditions of employment. Any system of collective bargaining under which unions and government jointly determine the terms and conditions of employment is incompatible with this doctrine.[5]

The theoretical interpretation of the sovereignty doctrine as applied to government employees has been advanced for nearly one hundred years by govern-

[2] Joseph P. Goldberg, "Public Employee Developments in 1971," *Monthly Labor Review*, Volume 95 (January, 1972), p. 63.

[3] Kenneth O. Warner and Mary L. Hennessey, *Public Management at the Bargaining Table* (Chicago: Public Personnel Association, 1967), p. 248.

[4] Willem B. Vosloo, *Collective Bargaining in the United States Civil Service* (Chicago: Public Personnel Association, 1966), p. 19.

[5] M. Moskow, J. Lowenberg, E. Koziaria, *Collective Bargaining in Public Employment* (New York: Random House, 1970), p. 17.

ment officials at all levels who believed that there could be no questioning of the decisions made by the state. Their logic was based upon the belief that: "Government service is public in character, belonging to and responsible to the people of our country." [6]

In the area of labor-management relations, state statutes and federal executive orders have been carefully shaped around preserving the sovereignty doctrine. Even the most recent change in the federal government's labor-management relations policies, Executive Order 11616, August 16, 1971, is carefully worded to protect federal government sovereignty. Section 12 of the order carefully delineates management's rights in unilateral decision making. In addition, federal government employees are denied the right to strike and the subject areas of wages, fringe benefits, and hours normally covered within the scope of collective bargaining in the private sector are still nonnegotiable because they are covered by statute and U. S. Civil Service Commission regulations. Section 13 of the order limits the use of the negotiable grievance procedure to the interpretation and application of the negotiated agreement. Many of the state and local laws reflect the tone of the federal executive order.[7]

The Political Faction

A paradox exists when we consider that the government employee lives in a democratic society. However, when he is in the employ of the same government which guarantees and maintains his democratic rights, he finds that his rights as an employee are severely limited. Aside from the argument that the government has a sovereign status, another rationale is used to justify this paradox. This other rationale is that the government employee's share in the control of his working life should be exercised through his capacity as a voting citizen of the state rather than as an employee of the state. The government employee through the use of his vote can exert political pressure upon the legislative and executive branches of government which establish the conditions of employment.[8] This argument is fallacious in that the political activities of government employees are often limited by statute.[9] In effect statutes make it illegal for government employees to be active in any real sense in political affairs.

Another problem arises when we examine labor-management relationships with regard to political sovereignty. Political sovereignty is the exercising of sovereignty in an independent government system. The operation of government is organized around a system of checks and balances that delimit the exercise of power by an individual or group. The check and balance system exists because of separation of powers, elections, and constitutions. Employment and personnel policies are shared by legislatures, governors, departments, independent agencies, commissions, and even political parties.[10]

[6] United States Civil Service Commission, *The Government Personnel System*, Personnel Management Series No. 4 (November, 1960).

[7] Joseph Goldberg, "Labor Management Relations Laws in Public Service," *Monthly Labor Review*, Volume 9 (June, 1968). Review of the laws enacted since 1968 show the same pattern, pp. 48–55. And Joseph P. Goldberg, "Public Employee Developments in 1971," *Monthly Labor Review*, Volume 95 (January, 1972), pp. 56–66.

[8] Civil Service Assembly, Committee on Employee Relations in the Public Service, Gordon R. Clapp, Chairman, *Employee Relations in the Public Service* (Chicago: C.S.A. of the U. S. and Canada, 1942), p. 47.

[9] Donald R. Harvey, *The Civil Service Commission* (New York: Praeger Publishers, 1970), p. 16.

[10] Kenneth O. Warner and Mary L. Hennessey, *Public Management at the Bargaining Table* (Chicago: Public Personnel Association, 1967), p. 249.

Decentralization of authority causes a limiting of the negotiable subjects because one branch of government cannot make decisions regarding public employees when another branch of government may hold the power of determination.[11] This viewpoint is supported by the fact that in the federal government the President may recommend pay increases for federal government employees but the Congress must grant the pay increases. Similar situations exist in many of the states.

In the same vein, decentralization of authority limits the bargaining authority of local management. Many subject areas covered under collective bargaining agreements in the private sector are also covered by statutes, executive orders, civil service regulations, and agency policies and regulations; thus, management representatives often find themselves in the position where they "cannot", rather than they "will not" negotiate with the unions.

Because a locus of authority to conclude an agreement often does not exist, public employee unions are all too often shunted around among the conflicting or overlapping authorities of particular agencies, public officials, and commissions.

Although this condition often presents a constraint on collective bargaining, unions have used it to their advantage. The unions will often circumvent managements and apply political pressure to elected officials to secure their needs. Continuance of this system of circumvention will not facilitate meaningful collective bargaining at the local levels where agreements must be implemented.

The lack of authority on the part of local management to conclude an agreement is analogous to private sector labor-management conditions in the 1930's. In the 30's the union negotiators often had great difficulty in locating the seat of corporate authority. Today this problem rarely exists in the private sector.

The government employee is again limited in his attempts to collectively bargain with his employer, considering the fact that in the final analysis government employees' salaries come from taxes. The Government's position is a function of the specific power and personnel relationships between individuals and groups at any one time. Many organized pressure groups outside of government have as their main objective the reduction of taxes. In effect the reduction of taxes means either a reduction in the number of government employees or the reduction of salary levels.[12] The organized government employee is but one of many interest groups attempting to exert pressure upon government. Governments are generally reluctant to raise taxes because of the political infeasibility. For this reason the wages and fringe benefits of government employees, especially at the state and local levels, have generally lagged behind their counterparts in the private sector.[13]

In the private sector the situation is different. While government must cover increased labor costs primarily by eventual increases in taxes, firms in the private sector can meet rising labor costs in a number of ways. One, they can raise prices, which is analogous to government's raising taxes. Two, they can increase efficiency. Generally, it is easier

---

[11] B. V. H. Schneider, "Collective Bargaining and the Federal Civil Service." *Industrial Relations*, Volume 3 (May, 1964), pp. 97–120.

[12] Civil Service Assembly, Committee on Employee Relations in the Public Service, Gordon R. Clapp, Chairman, *op. cit.*, p. 49.

[13] The objectives of the Federal Salary Reform Act of 1962, the Federal Pay Comparability Act of 1970, the Federal Coordinated Wage System of 1967, are to maintain federal government employees salaries at levels comparable to their counterparts in the private sector. The states have not enacted similar legislation.

for firms producing goods to increase efficiency than firms producing services. The product of government is service. Therefore it is often difficult for government to increase efficiency. Last, firms in the private sector can absorb increased costs by reducing profits. Government cannot absorb increased costs by reducing profits because government does not produce profit as defined by accountancy practices.

Civil service commissions or their counterparts have had the responsibility for administering and implementing government personnel policies and programs. These policies and programs are designed to protect the rights and benefits of government employees. In implementing and administering these policies and programs, the civil service commissions interpret their language, promulgate guidelines for personnel management, and, to varying degrees, the guidelines for labor-management relations. In addition, the civil service commissions are the guardians of the older merit system principles—open and equal competition and equal pay for equal work.[14]

Public employee unions do not view the civil service commissions as the protectors of the employees' rights but rather as an extension of management. Jerry Wurf, President of the American Federation of State, County, and Municipal Employees, and John Griner, past president of the American Federation of Government Employees, have both argued that in their experience Civil Service Commissions have been extensions of management.[15] Underlying their statements is the belief that administration of government personnel by Civil Service Commissions is incompatible with collective bargaining. This incompatibility is based on government sovereignty as reflected in management paternalism and the individualism of the merit system.[16] Merit systems at the federal and state levels have deep historical roots and have been slow to change.

This condition is analogous to labor-management relations in the private sector during the 1930's. In the past, management rights in developing and administering personnel policies and procedures were unquestioned. Today, largely due to changes in the law and union power, private sector managements are more careful, more responsible, and more responsive in personnel matters. As unions in the public sector develop more power and continue to bring about changes in the law, the merit system and role of the commissions will also change. Government management will also be more careful, more responsible, and more responsive in personnel matters.

The Use of the Strike

A major problem in public sector collective bargaining is the use of the strike. Although the use of the strike in the private sector as a means of compelling disputing parties to reach an agreement has in recent years become increasingly controversial, its use as a bargaining tactic is still widespread. In accord with the sovereignty doctrine, federal, state, and local governments have by statute

[14] Frederick Mosher, *Democracy in the Public Service* (London: Oxford University Press, 1968), p. 195.

[15] Robert T. Woodworth and Richard B. Peterson (editors) *Collective Negotiations for Public and Professional Employees* (Glenview, Illinois: Scott Foresman and Company, 1969), p. 26. Article by Everett M. Kassalow, "Prospective on the Upsurge of Public Employee Unionism," citing Jerry Wurf, p. 26.

"The Unions' View of Public Management's Responsibilities in Collective Bargaining," *Public Employees Relations Library*, No. 26, citing John Griner (Chicago: Public Personnel Association, 1970), p. 5.

[16] Frederick Mosher, *op. cit.*, p. 197.

and executive order denied employees and their unions the right to participate in a strike against the government.[17] The right to strike as a social and economic weapon in private sector labor-management relations has been legally accorded workers and their unions since 1935.[18] Without the right to strike, unions in the public sector are limited in their ability to effectively negotiate with management. In lieu of the right to strike, government unions have used political pressure to meet their objectives. The limitation of political pressure is that it does not bring about results as quickly as striking.

The logic underlying the government's position prohibiting use of the strike consists of two points:

1. Strikes against the government cannot be tolerated since the government is sovereign and cannot share its sovereign authority with its employees or their unions. Any strike against the government is an attack upon the state and a challenge to the government's authority.[19]

2. In the private sector, the use of the strike by labor and the lockout by management are economic and social weapons used for testing the strengths and weaknesses of the bargaining parties when impasses occur. Governments do not use the politically infeasible lockout because the government provides essential services to society. Any disruption of these essential services by a strike would repudiate the function of government. Therefore, the strike is not an appropriate means for settling collective bargaining impasses in the government. Even if some government services are not essential it is impossible or infeasible to attempt to differentiate between nonessential and essential services, permitting strikes in the former but not in the latter.[20]

In recent years, a number of writers have expressed the view that the sovereignty doctrine and the prohibition of the right to strike limits meaningful collective bargaining in the public sector. Although the government continues to assert its sovereignty by imposing severe penalties on individuals and groups who strike the government, there is some doubt as to whether the strike ban is enforceable. Statistics on strike data for the period 1958 through 1968 show that the number of government employee strikes per year rose from 15 to 254. The number of workers involved rose from 1700 to 202,000. Man-days lost increased from 7500 to 2.5 million.[21]

During this same period, strikes in the private sector increased, but at a lower rate than those in government. In 1958 government employee strikes constituted four-tenths of 1 per cent of all strikes, eight one-hundredths of a per cent of the workers involved, and three-one-hundredths of a per cent of total idleness. By 1968 these ratios had risen to 5.0 per cent, 7.6 per cent, and 5.2 per cent, respectively.[22]

Essentiality of service means that the consumers' demand for the service is inelastic. Except for some limited functions, such as the armed forces, there is no empirical evidence demonstrating differences in elasticity of demand between private

---

[17] Joseph Goldberg, *op. cit.* In the federal government Public Law 55-330 and Executive Order 11616 deny government employees the right to strike.

[18] The National Labor Relations Act legally accords workers in the private sector the right to strike.

[19] Ann M. Ross, "Public Employee Unions and the Right to Strike," *Monthly Labor Review*, Volume 92 (March, 1969), p. 15.

[20] John F. Burton, Jr., "Can Public Employees Be Given the Right to Strike?" *Labor Law Journal*, Volume 21 (August, 1970), pp. 469–70.

[21] Sheila C. White, "Work Stoppages of Government Employees," *Monthly Labor Review*, Volume 92 (December, 1969), pp. 29–30.

[22] *Ibid.*

sector services and government services.[23] Government services are expanding in scope and increasingly the services provided are similar to those available from private industry. As far as the public is concerned, a strike is the same whether it is in a privately operated hospital or a government operated hospital, in a transportation system privately operated or government operated.[24]

Government's denial of strike rights to any of its employees in any of its services makes no distinction between the essentiality or nonessentiality of the service. John F. Burton's analysis of Bureau of Labor Statistics' strike data for 1965-68 showed that some state and local governments differentiate between a strike in an essential service and a strike in an nonessential service by their use of countersanctions.[25] A few states now permit some, but not all, of their employees the right to strike. Pennsylvania permits its public employees (certain employee groups are specifically prohibited) to strike or refuse to cross a picket line after the statutory impasses have been exhausted. "This action will not be prohibited unless it creates 'a clear and present danger to the health, safety, or welfare of the public'." [26]

In an attempt to make collective bargaining more meaningful while maintaining its sovereignty, government at the federal and many state and local levels has established provisions for third-party fact-finding or arbitration to settle collective bargaining impasses. The pros and cons of third-party intervention in settling labor-management impasses have been debated both publicly and privately for a number of years. The use of fact-finding does not mean that the disputing parties are compelled to abide by the fact finders' recommendations. Agreement to the recommendations of fact finders implies that both parties have developed bargaining maturity or that other circumstances such as threats of illegal strikes or adverse publicity have compelled the parties to agree.

Some writers believe that compulsory arbitration in lieu of the right to strike spells an end to collective bargaining. Their logic is based on the belief that the negotiating parties will prepare for the arbitration procedure instead of for the give and take environment of private agreement. In arbitration proceedings the payoff is greatest to those willing to take extreme positions.[27]

Conclusion

Compared to labor-management relations in the private sector, labor-management relations in the public sector is a recent development. Some governments, notably the federal government and New York, Wisconsin, and Minnesota state governments, have enacted comprehensive legislation that covers the total environment of labor-management relations. However, most of the state and local governments have failed to follow suit. Many of the statutes initiated at the state and local levels have been oriented toward specific groups and are limited in scope. The failure to enact comprehensive legislation means that inconsistencies be-

---

[23] John F. Burton, Jr., *op. cit.*, p. 475.

[24] George W. Taylor, "Public Employment: Strikes or Procedures," *Industrial and Labor Relations Review*, Volume 20 (July, 1967), p. 625.

[25] John F. Burton, Jr., *op. cit.*, p. 474.

[26] Terrence N. Tice, ed., *Faculty Power: Collective Bargaining on Campus.* (Ann Arbor, Michigan: Institute of Continuing Legal Education, 1972), p. 181 citing Penna Stat. Ann Tit. 43, 1101.101—1101.2301, added by Act No. 195, effective July 23, 1970.

[27] Kenneth O. Warner, editor. *Collective Bargaining in the Public Service: Theory and Practice*, "When Bargaining Fails," Jacob Finkelman (Chicago: Public Personnel Association, 1967), pp. 126–26.

tween the various laws affecting certain groups are apt to develop. This fragmentation will increase the confusion that presently exists. As confusion increases, the frequency, intensity, and duration of disputes are likely to increase.

Government's tenacious grip on the sovereignty doctrine, the concept of "meet and confer" rather than "collectively bargaining in good faith," and limitations on union security clauses, limiting the scope of negotiable issues and the right to strike will not facilitate meaningful collective bargaining in government. Indications are that unions at all levels of government will attempt to equalize the bargaining relationships. Governments that continue to assert the traditional aspects of sovereignty and resist collective bargaining efforts can expect a repeat of the private sector experiences which occurred during the 1930's and 40's.

QUESTIONS

1. In what ways is collective bargaining in the public sector different from that in the private sector?
2. Show that raising salaries of government employees almost always causes higher taxes whereas the same action in the private sector may or may not result in higher prices.
3. Do you think that equality of bargaining power between governmental units and unions representing employees is possible or desirable? Discuss.
4. Should government employees be given the legal right to strike?
5. How should contract negotiation impasses be settled in the governmental sector?
6. What do you think the author means by the last sentence in the article, which says, "Governments that continue to assert the traditional aspects of sovereignty and resist collective bargaining efforts can expect a repeat of the private sector experiences which occurred during the 1930's and 40's."?

41.

A Political System for a Political World–in Public Sector Labor Relations

ROBERT D. HELSBY

During the past decade a substantial body of experience has evolved as public employees have sought and have obtained the right to organize and to bargain. It is not an overstatement to point out that some 38 separate experiments are underway in the various states with respect to public sector labor relations. Although the approach of each state law has some similarities, there are enough variations so that over time it may well be that experimentation will provide a means to evaluate and to choose the best of these various approaches.

However, a fundamental question raised at the beginning of the era of public sector labor relations remains unanswered. I suspect that perhaps the question has actually been answered in practice although not all participants will accept the answer which I think has emerged.

The answer also depends on how one phrases the question. The Taylor Committee, in its original report proposing the New York Law in 1966, phrased the question as follows: "How should collective negotiation in the public service be distinguished from collective bargaining in the private sector?" Others, including such distinguished practitioners as Theodore Kheel, have wondered whether or not collective bargaining as it has evolved in the private sector is possible or appropriate in the public sector. Certainly this, and the related questions which flow from it, are not as theoretical as was the case five or ten years ago.

In fact, I think that time and experience have provided a pretty clear answer. Whether you call it collective bargaining or collective negotiations, I submit that the process in the public sector is different.

Reprinted from the *Labor Law Journal*, Vol. 24, No. 8 (August 1973), pp. 504–511 by permission of the publisher and author.
Robert D. Helsby is Chairman, New York State Public Employment Relations Board.

429

Components of
Public Sector Negotiations

Dr. Seymour Scher, a one-time professor of political science and more recently a city manager in two of New York State's larger cities, outlines five basic components of public sector negotiations:

1. The mood, needs, and demands of the community constituency.
2. The mood, needs, and demands of the political establishment.
3. The limitations, restrictions, and requirements of constitutions, statutes, ordinances, civil service, education laws, municipal charters, etc.
4. The mood, needs, and demands of the employer.
5. The mood, needs, and demands of the employees.

Dr. Scher points out that the first three of the five elements he has listed do not exist in the private sector. Whether one agrees with his listing or not, there is certainly one major factor which differentiates the public from the private sector. The bargaining process in the public sector takes place in a political arena and the parties to the bargain—both the union and the executive—must seek political ratification of their product. The union, of course, also faces the problem of obtaining acceptance from the membership —the public employees affected. The political ratification to which I refer, however, means acceptance by the appropriate legislative body; in most situations at least the part of the agreement which costs money must have such ratification. In short, funds have to be appropriated to implement the agreement.

Let me be concrete. Two years ago in response to rising clamor about the cost of public employee pension systems in New York State, Governor Rockefeller and the Legislature appointed a pension commission. Two years later the commis-

sion made its report. The New York State Constitution precludes diminishing existing public employee pensions. Therefore, the commission recommended that public employee pensions be removed from the bargaining table and the various existing pension systems be closed and that a new system covering all State and local public employees in the State except police and firemen be created. While the details of the proposed new system are not pertinent here, I note that under the proposal the long-run cost to public employers would be reduced from 20 per cent of payroll to 10 per cent of payroll, that there would be a Social Security offset against the pension, that the system would be non-contributory, and that there would be a substantial reduction in benefits. At this point, I would not wish to venture a prediction as to the ultimate fate of these recommendations in the Legislature.

Review of Pension Commission

I think it is instructive to review for a moment the genesis of the pension commission. Council 37, AFSCME, negotiated a pension improvement for most New York City employees which would have provided retirement at half pay after twenty years' service at age 55. Changes of this type in the various pension systems applicable to New York City employees require approval in the State Legislature. It produced substantial public outcry. Legislation to approve the agreement at the State level never got out of committee the following year. Council 37 and the Teamsters Local considered this an affront and struck. This was the famous strike during which various drawbridges were left open and untreated sewage was poured into the waters around New York City. After a day or two, the City and the affected unions negotiated what the *New York Times* characterized as a "face-saving agreement" which provided, in effect, that if the Legislature failed to approve the pension improvement, the City would provide alternate and equivalent benefits. Two legislative sessions have now nearly passed, and in the current climate, the Legislature seems most unlikely to approve the pension agreement between New York City and Council 37.

In this situation the State Legislature was, of course, one level removed from that of the bargaining process. The resulting strike was clearly not against the employer involved but against the State Legislature. The strike was illegal. It caused substantial disruption and inconvenience to thousands of people.

In this particular situation, the rent in the social fabric was not irreparable. The situation may, in fact, have taught a valuable lesson to all concerned. The State Legislature can, and sometimes will, repudiate a bargain between, in this instance, a subsidiary government—New York City—and a union coalition. The Legislature could reject, but so far has not, an agreement between State employee unions and the Office of Employee Relations— the negotiating arm of the Governor. And it is at least a reasonable probability that the Legislature may modify nearly every existing agreement in the State by substantially modifying the pension system for new employees.

Thus one major key to the difference between bargaining in the public sector and in the private sector is the role of the legislative body. It is not the semantic difference between collective negotiations and collective bargaining. The dynamics of the bargaining process itself are essentially similar in both the public and the private sectors. The basic fact of public sector bargaining is that a substantial part of the bargain arrived at must be ratified, directly or indirectly, by the appropriate Legislature. Whatever else may be involved, the Legislature must appropriate the money to effectuate the bargain. The Legislature is composed of a group of elected people in a democracy, each with his or her own political constituency, accountability and needs for survival.

Right to Strike

At its meeting in May 1972, the Western Assembly in considering "collective bargaining in American government" concluded that public employees should have the right to strike. The Western Assembly also recognized that "in some instances, federal and state legislatures will be compelled to adopt legislation that supplants or supplements collective bargaining on some issues in the public sector."

At this point one has to recognize the potential of the collision course. The Western Assembly report also states "in government the basic policy-making decisions are primarily the responsibility of legislative bodies, while collective bargaining is engaged in by governmental agencies whose duty it is to effectuate these policies." Herein, it seems to me, is to be found a dilemma which so far defies solution. To phrase the question as dramatically as possible, what happens if a legislature "supplements or supplants" the bargain or, as the New York State Legislature did in the aforementioned episode, simply refuses to act? If the result is a strike, how does it get resolved?

Fortunately most situations are not this draconian. Normally the parties at the table have some realistic notion of the political parameters within which they are constrained to operate. Difficulties, of course, may arise if their respective assessments of the parameters differ. In fact, this is the normal situation encountered in public employee strikes. The parties at the table are unable or unwilling to reach a bargain. Occasionally such strikes may even be part of the political dynamics necessary to get the ultimate agreement ratified.

At this point, recognition needs to be given to the fact that the situation differs at various government levels. Somehow or other the situation is not exactly the same when a city manager or a mayor arrives at an agreement with a public employee union which a city council repudiates. If this does happen, the city manager is probably looking for other employment. The mayor is undoubtedly in political difficulty. The difference is even more significant in smaller governments and school districts where the employer-executive and the legislative body are essentially the same. But what if the State Legislature rejects an agreement negotiated by a Governor or his agent and unions representing state employees? Is the situation any different if Congress repudiates an agreement negotiated by presidential agents and the result is a strike?

The essential question thus becomes, what resort, if any, does a public employee union have if the applicable legislature repudiates all or part of a bargain arrived at between the executive and the union? Or, to state the question another way, if the joint political efforts of the employee union and the executive-employer fail to get the bargain implemented, what happens then?

In recent years the question of what happens when the political process yields an undesirable result from a point of view of the activists has been with us in a good many forms. Some forms of social action are obviously more tolerable than others. Rallies, peaceful demonstrations, informational picketing, vigils, etc., have been commonplace in recent years.

The question I am really asking is: After the development of a collectively negotiated agreement, why should the rights of a public employee be any greater or any less than those of any other citizen?

This is the issue, it seems to me, that those who advocate an unrestricted right for public employees to strike have simply not faced up to. What the bargaining process does in the public sector is to give public employees, through their bargaining agent, a meaningful voice in the determination of what the executive-employer proposes to the legislature with respect to terms and conditions of employment. The public sector bargain cannot be more than this. Hopefully it is not less.

Once the parties have balanced the needs of the union, the needs of the employees and the public, the resources which the executive-employer thinks he can commit, and agreed that their mutual understanding of the political parameters within which they are operating are essentially the same, both have an obligation to seek legislative approval of their joint product.

At this point the union, in seeking legislative approval of the agreement, has the same right as any other group of citizens to attempt to pressure the legislature to take desired action.

If, for some reason, the legislature fails to approve all or part of the bargain, it seems clear that giving public employees the right to strike at this point is giving them a right which no other citizen has. Should other groups adversely affected by legislative decisions be given the right to strike or its equivalent, whatever that is? One suspects that the answer is no in both cases.

In any event, such limited experience as we have suggests that strikes by public employees at this point would be largely futile, particularly at the state or federal level. The concept of the general strike is generally unknown and unaccepted in this country. Abroad, public employee strikes (excepting a few nationalized industries) are generally one- or two-day protest movements, usually announced in advance, rather than a fight to the finish as in the private sector in the United States.

If the economic strike against a legislature and therefore against the political process is in all probability liable to be ineffective on the one hand and intolerable on the other, and the concept of the general strike is both unknown and unacceptable, then the question arises can a strike against the executive-employer resulting from failure to reach agreement at the table be tolerated and institutionalized. This is really what those who advocate the right to strike for public employees seem to favor, at least within limits. Those public employee statutes which do provide a limited right to strike mandate impasse procedures which must be exhausted before the strike becomes legal. Even then the threat to public health and safety must be assessed.

In New York State, about 3,000 contracts are negotiated annually in the public sector. Third-party assistance is required in reaching about 30 per cent of these agreements—mediation, fact-finding, or both. Strikes—illegal ones—occur in about one per cent of these situations—about 30 per year—although not all are caused by bargaining. Some result from disputes over working conditions during the term of the contract and related questions.

About 90 per cent of public employees in New York State—900,000 of some 1,000,000—presently exercise their rights under the Taylor Law. The passage of a law applicable to all state and local public employees brought about almost instant unionization. Those public employees not organized are either management-confidential employees or are employed by very small employers—less than ten. I have the impression but cannot document the fact that there have been similar developments in those states which have adopted a law, or laws, applicable to all state and local public employees.

In contrast, in the private sector in New York State, only about 30 per cent of non-farm employment is organized. While there are many factors which limit the ability of *private* sector unions to organize or to penetrate more than they have, there seems to be general agreement that the ability to organize and to bargain effectively depends in large measure on the ability and the willingness of the employees involved to strike—thus the maxim that there cannot be real collective bargaining without the right to strike.

Is the Maxim Applicable to the Public Sector?

In 1966 and 1967 if one listened to the sound and fury of the debates in New York State, both in the Legislature and outside, out of which grew the Taylor Law, one would have to say that most of the labor leadership thought so. At that point in time, union leadership and their allies in the Legislature contended with vim, vigor and vitality that there could be no genuine collective bargaining in the public sector without the right to strike. Within a month after the Taylor Law was passed, some 15,000 unionists gathered in Madison Square Garden to denounce the Law and establish a fund for its repeal. It was characterized as anti-union. Public management was equally vehement—strikes were intolerable and should never take place under any circumstances.

Six years later the situation is somewhat different. This is not to say that the parties have officially reversed their 1966 and 1967 positions. Almost all union leaders still officially advocate the right to strike for public employees. I am not aware of any management representatives in New York State who have officially reversed their positions. However, I think it is fair to say that these positions have become more ritualistic than real. Certainly the noise and the din on the labor side are diminished. There has not been a repetition of the Madison

Square Garden rally. Nor has management conducted any celebrations on the anniversaries of its enactment. Government has learned not to panic at the threat of a strike, or indeed in an actual strike; employees have often learned to their sorrow that a strike has not been the great pressure for equity which they had formerly envisioned.

In private discussions with both sides, one can begin to perceive the development of a reversal of position. Public management would rather continue the present system than face up to some of the alternatives. And, more particularly, at least some representatives in public management would rather legalize the strike than be faced with compulsory arbitration. On the labor side there is some private recognition that most public employees might be in a weaker position with a law which permitted strikes than at present. Both sides will generally concede, even though there are particular aspects that one or the other would like to see changed, that the present system works.

This is another way of saying that in the past six years a workable labor relations system for the public sector has gradually evolved in New York State. This evolution is, of course, still in process. It is not the traditional collective bargaining of the private sector which utilizes the bargaining-strike syndrome. Rather it is a political process which utilizes a whole new array of techniques and processes in the negotiation of an agreement. One cannot predict the ultimate direction, but I think it can safely be said that no radical changes are in the offing for the immediate future.

The basics of the system, I think, can be briefly outlined as follows. The executive-employer and the public employee union go to the table and do their thing. Seventy per cent of the time they appear to be able to agree upon the applicable political and economic parameters and to

be able to reach a mutually satisfactory bargain. Where they cannot, mandated impasse procedures become applicable. At the mediation stage, settlement can generally be reached—historically in about half of the cases that go to impasse —if the parties are divided only by economic or technical issues, but not if the mix includes basic disagreement on both the economic and political parameters. Of the cases which go to fact-finding, a substantial number—historically about 40 per cent—are mediated by the fact-finder, e.g., the threat of what he might recommend is enough to bring the parties to agreement. In about a fourth of these cases, the report and recommendations become a politically and economically acceptable document which both parties can buy. In about 40 per cent of the cases which go to fact-finding, the report and recommendations provide a political and economic frame within which and upon which the parties generally manage to reach agreement. Additional third-party assistance is sometimes required. And, of course, as has already been indicated, there are occasional strikes. Approximately 20 of the 30 strikes a year result from failure of the bargaining process and impasse procedures—considerably less than one per cent of the agreements. There are about an equal number of valid strike threats. Taken together, some would say that these are necessary to lubricate the system.

Thus bargaining in the public sector has become, in New York State and I suspect in many other jurisdictions, a process for the mutual formulation of the public employee compensation package and related matters, before it is dropped into the legislative-political arena to compete with other claimants for the allocation of public resources. However imperfect, this is the only process which we have to legitimately resolve such questions. It is not a particularly neat and tidy process, but neither are the tugs and hauls of public opinion which constitute the democratic system.

If the only alternative is to give public employees the right to strike, the question needs to be asked not only what effect would this have upon the continuity of public service but what effect would it have upon public employees? Would their bargaining strength be increased or weakened? For some, particularly in the large unions, their position would quite clearly be strengthened. For many others, however, the opposite would be the case. My judgment is that in New York State, for example, 60 to 70 per cent are probably better served by the present system. Oftentimes the news media refer to our PERB-appointed and financed mediators, fact-finders, and conciliators as the "public employee rescue battalion." Unless employees have the will and ability to mount a cohesive strike, the right to strike by itself becomes meaningless. In short, their circumstances are such that a strike weapon is not a viable alternative.

As experience builds in the public sector, what we really need is less ideology and more research. We need to take a hard look at what is going on in the various "experiments" which have been under way in various states for some time. To be truly objective this effort should be made by others than those who have a vested interest—in other words, not by agencies administering programs or by representatives of the parties.

Someone recently said: "Arbitration is to collective bargaining what artificial insemination is to reproduction; it takes all the fun out of it." Sometimes I think those who advocate the right to strike for public employees are taking a somewhat similar position. Somehow, they feel that without the right to strike, the whole process is less fun.

It may be fun, however, which we neither need nor can afford. When I see communities literally torn apart from a strike of teachers for example; when I see the acrimony and divisiveness caused by youngsters on picket lines, teachers pitted against boards of education, neighbor against neighbor, parents and families divided in bitter battles which leave wounds and scars which are so hard to heal; then I believe that our quest must be to find a better way.

What is really emerging is a system of employee participation in the determination of conditions of employment—a bargaining process applicable to and more appropriate for the political process.

Conclusion

To summarize, I believe that

1. The political world in which public employees negotiate their conditions of employment calls for very different considerations than the predominantly economic world of the private sector.

2. Contrary to the characterization by some, this does not make a second-class citizen of the public employee. Rather, it calls for approaches which are different from, and more appropriate to, the public sector.

3. The requirement for ratification by appropriate legislative bodies is one basic element of the political equation which drastically influences every aspect of public sector bargaining.

4. Out of the vast array of experimentation taking place in the various states, many techniques and systems are developing to balance the needs of government, its employees and the public interest.

5. The tenet of collective bargaining in the private sector—namely, the need for the right to strike as an inherent requirement of the process—is being seriously questioned in the public sector. Both employers and employees are taking a long constructive look at the alternatives.

6. A whole new system of dispute settlement is emerging which uses the

widest possible variety of mechanisms— mediation, mediation-arbitration, fact-finding, arbitration, etc.—with the utmost of tailormade flexibility. In short, it is a political system which responds to the tug and haul of public opinion in a democratic society. The Taylor Law in New York is one such experiment. Its initial six years would indicate considerable promise for such systems.

7. The components of this exciting new field of human relations are as complex as human nature and as dynamic as democracy itself. And the stakes for success are high indeed.

QUESTIONS

1. Discuss the political and economic implications of collective bargaining agreements negotiated by one branch of government and ratified or rejected by another.
2. How can the public interest and the legitimate needs of public employees be balanced and reconciled?
3. What pressures, if any, should a public employee union be able to exert upon the executive and the legislative branches of government?
4. The author argues against granting public employees the legal right to strike. Evaluate his position and give your own views.
5. The author asserts that public employee collective bargaining "is a political system which responds to the tug and haul of public opinion in a democratic society." Explain.

42.

Collective Bargaining and Industrial Peace

DAVID L. COLE

People are emotional on the subject of strikes. To some, this is because of the feeling of injustice which gave rise to the modern era of labor organization and its traditional concomitant of the strike. To others it is due to the indignation over use of the strike as they see for other purposes—offensive rather than defensive. To still others, commonly falling into the designation of the public, the feeling is of resignation and "a plague on both your houses" attitude.

Even when we see people apparently agreeing, there is much confusion and heat. I propose, therefore, to go back to elementary considerations, so that we may better evaluate the question and apply a better and more rational perspective.

Any evaluation of the type of effort undertaken by the Industrial Peace Commission should start with comprehension of the nature and purpose of collective bargaining. Implicit in such a process is, first, the premise that the employees are free to organize and choose their representatives, and that the employer will treat with such representatives on behalf of the employees with regard to all features of the employer-employeees relationship. Acceptance of this premise and recognition by the employer were not easy to achieve, and this was the cause of some of the most bitter strikes in our industrial history.

But the purpose of collective bargaining must not be obscured. It is to reach accord as to the terms and conditions of employment for a specified period of time through negotiations by duly selected and accredited representatives. If they can reason with each other and persuade one another to come to agreement then the purpose is fulfilled. If they cannot and must resort to trial by economic battle, the purpose is also fulfilled, but by no means is it essential or desirable that settlements be reached through such means.

As a matter of fact, most of the champions of collective bargaining have proceeded in the belief that as employers accept the collective bargaining approach

Reprinted from the *AFL-CIO American Federationist*, Vol. 80, No. 8 (August 1973), pp. 22–24 by permission of the publisher.
David L. Cole is a professional arbitrator and mediator.

and as unions become permanent parts of the labor-management structure, reliance on the strike will be attenuated. The thought has been expressed over and over that as the collective relationship matures, the process of collective bargaining will become increasingly one of reasoning and persuasion, and less of economic force. The parties have a distinct interest in resolving their disputes, of course, but they also have an interest in doing so with as little pain or cost as possible and in a manner which will not impair their ability to work together in an amicable atmosphere.

Consistent with this thought is the proposition that if the parties are unable in negotiations to reconcile their differences, it is still part of the design of collective bargaining to devise or employ procedures by which these differences may be resolved without relying solely on the strike or other punitive measures. In doing so, the parties are truly engaging in collective bargaining. They are still proceeding through the mechanism of agreement, even though the agreement pertains only to procedures for arriving at a fair basis of settlement.

It has been proclaimed that without the strike it is not possible to have collective bargaining. This is like saying that in international affairs, if we renounce war we cannot have diplomacy. The precise opposite seems true. In such situations we need more effective bargaining, just as we need more effective diplomacy.

In any event, we know that we cannot eliminate either wars or strikes by the simple process of outlawing them. We can only endeavour to minimize reliance on them. All we can hope to accomplish is the encouragement of the disposition of those who have the responsibility of conducting collective bargaining to make it function as the means of reconciling conflicting positions—if they cannot quite do so directly, then to be willing to look with favor on procedures by which others can help them. The disposition is the vital quality; the form is only secondary.

Another virtue of collective bargaining as seen by its strongest supporters has been its ability to adapt to changing conditions. To insist now that it must remain in a rigid mold in which the moving force remains essentially only the threat of the strike is a disappointing distortion of what has been expected to be the design and purpose of collective bargaining.

There is nevertheless still a surprising amount of adherence to the thought that we cannot have collective bargaining without constant reliance on or use of the strike. Perhaps it would be helpful to review industrial history, and to analyze the transformation in our views on the strike. For some reason we tend to overlook the lengths to which we have gone from time to time to cut down reliance on the strike.

In this respect, the help of government through legislative and administrative action has been extensive. Many matters in which differences commonly led to active labor friction and strikes are now regulated by law. The right to organize and the duties to recognize and to engage in good faith bargaining are outstanding examples. Others are minimum wages, maximum hours, safety and protective conditions, workmen's compensation, unemployment and retirement programs.

We take for granted now that there should not be strikes over grievances. But this was at one time a rife cause of interferences with operations. The development of more effective grievance procedures with the last step of arbitration is an accomplishment of labor and management themselves, and I have never heard any serious regrets expressed over the elimination of this cause of strikes.

And surely we have not forgotten the frequency of strikes over jurisdictional and raiding disputes among unions. The labor movement has by its own initiative imposed restraints on itself through a variety of agreements or procedures, and the result has been a substantial amount of relief from strikes which have been demonstrated to be avoidable and unnecessary.

Nor is it a fact that the strike has consistently been regarded as essential to the process of collective bargaining, or to negotiations.

On the contrary, it takes very little research to demonstrate that historically this position has often been subject to question. It may surprise some of you to know that over a century ago, for more than a generation, major industries in Great Britain submitted their unsettled disputes over wages and working conditions to arbitration. Before then, moreover, a similar pattern was followed for years in France and Belgium.

If the argument is made that the experiences and conditions in our country are different, let me point out that we have also engaged in a good deal of arbitrating of contract-making disputes. We were familiar with this before the beginning of this century. The printing trades had such programs. Since 1896 the Amalgamated Street Railway Union in its constitution has required its locals to offer arbitration before calling a strike. The IBEW has followed a similar practice in the public utility industry.

Moreover, few realize how much arbitration of contract terms was going on in the 10 or 15 years following the end of World War II. I have reviewed my own arbitrator files. In that period I served as arbitrator in such cases more than 50 times. I do not recall that this was brought about by any general concerted program. Yet on an ad hoc basis there were probably hundreds of such disputes in which strikes were voluntarily bypassed by agreements to resort to binding arbitration instead.

This happened in a variety of industries and under varying circumstances.

Public utilities and their unions preferred to avoid shutdowns. Similar considerations applied in the milk processing and delivery. Retail establishments and newspapers went to arbitration rather than to a test of strength. In some instances, unions or employers who were fearful of strikes elected to arbitrate because of their economic weakness. Air transportation companies and the pilots' organization became strong advocates of third-party procedures of various kinds in their efforts to keep service going. In some instances relatively strong unions, like the Teamsters, were prevailed upon by other unions to forbear and resolve their differences through arbitration instead of shutting down their service on which others depended.

I emphasize this because it should be made clear that reliance on the strike as the vital or essential force in collective bargaining has not always been accepted as an immutable tenet. Certainly, there have been circumstances or times when this has been questioned.

It is sufficient to note the facts and observe that in the areas or segments where such doubts have been seen, it does not appear that the progress and effectiveness of collective bargaining as an institution has been impaired by any appreciable degree.

This may be a good point at which to say something about the classical criticism of contract-making or interest arbitration, which is that the lack of criteria or standards makes such a procedure unacceptable because the outcome is unpredictable. If arbitration is used to resolve the remaining issues separating the parties engaged in negotiations because they feel it necessary or desirable in the given circumstances to avoid a strike, this course must be recognized as having the higher priority. If predictability is the sine qua non, one may well ask what predictability is there when strike action is undertaken, particularly when equally strong and determined parties are opposed to one another. Furthermore, is it realistically so difficult for sophisticated negotiators to estimate fairly closely what an acceptable arbitrator is likely to determine in such a proceeding?

The urge to avoid strikes and the burdens imposed by strikes on management and workers requires both sides to be willing to forego something which they may regard as an immediate advantage in return for the benefits they will have. It will not do to insist that, if arbitration is resorted to, the function of the arbitrator will be solely to determine what the union could have achieved if it had proceeded with strike action.

A more desirable and realistic criterion is what would it have been reasonable for the parties to have agreed upon under the prevailing facts and conditions. This is the criterion I have applied in the many interest arbitrations I have conducted over the years.

I remember with a good deal of respect what CIO President Philip Murray once told me about matters of this kind. Explaining why he never seemed to have difficulty in getting the Steelworkers' wage policy committee to approve settlements he had tentatively reached, he said:

"Steel is a basic industry. When we are deadlocked the President may call Ben Fairless of U.S. Steel and me into the White House and warn us that the country cannot stand a shutdown of steel production and that he insists we work out some arrangement to prevent this. I would then see how much I could get from Mr. Fairless short of a strike. When I went back to my committee I told them that in my judgment the offer I had was as good as it could be without a strike and that I was satisfied we owed it to the country and the President not to strike. I added that probably if we struck we might get another five cents an hour. I then

told them that I wanted them to vote on whether they had confidence in my judgment, or whether they preferred to tie up the nation for 'the last lousy nickel.' There never was any serious doubt about their vote."

AFL-CIO President George Meany, in sponsoring in major industry programs of voluntary arbitration rather than the strike, has emphasized the costliness and the heavy burden of many of such strikes on the unions and their members. He also is of the view that it is possible to obtain fair results through such arbitration, and that in several situations the welfare of the industry is of direct and practical concern to those who work in it.

Although it is apparent that I favor a program which promotes voluntary alternatives to the strike in the private sector, this does not mean that the strike is to be outlawed or permanently discarded. It must be kept available for possible use. Examples would be if either side should take an unusually extreme and obstinate position, or if, as United Mine Workers President John L. Lewis used to put it, some employer should begin to dream of the good old golden days when there were no unions.

In a number of industries it has become evident that management and labor are learning that they have many basic common interests which are of far greater weight than the use of the strike.

I believe the Industrial Peace Commission should dedicate itself to a missionary and educational task. We should seek to induce in labor and management representatives an understanding of the purpose of collective bargaining and the disposition or desire to have it function effectively on a constructive, rather than destructive basis. Without such a disposition, there is little that government can do to improve collective bargaining or to safeguard the public interest.

I do not favor any form of legislative compulsion, because I am convinced you cannot compel people to work in harmony unless they have the urge to do so. We need good will, but we cannot obtain it by decree or by law.

QUESTIONS

1. The author states that "implicit in collective bargaining is the premise that the employees are free to organize and choose their representatives, and that the employer will treat with such representatives on behalf of the employees with regard to all features of the employer-employees relationship. Acceptance of this premise and recognition by the employer were not easy to achieve, and this was the cause of some of the most bitter strikes in our industrial history." Explain the meaning of these statements by referring to the history of American labor-management relationships.
2. Do you feel that the strike is a necessary concomitant of genuine collective bargaining? Explain.
3. Show how reliance upon strikes to settle differences is becoming less common. What other mechanisms are helping to reduce the use of strikes to resolve differences?
4. Distinguish between arbitration of contract-making disputes and arbitration of grievances. Explain similarities and differences.

PART IX

Building and Assessing Organizations

Conventional financial statements of both private enterprises and public organizations fail to record investments in, or depletion of, human resources. In fact, hard-driving, exploitive leadership can often show a short-term profit by using up and depleting the value of the human capital of that enterprise. In the longer run, the organization may suffer a serious decline in performance. Researchers, writers, and consultants are now working with corporate executives to show them how to build and value their human resources.

An innovator and pioneer in this field is Rensis Likert, who for many years was Director of the Institute for Social Research of The University of Michigan. In his article "Human Resource Accounting: Building and Assessing Productive Organizations," Dr. Likert identifies the key causal variables that control intervening variables and ultimately control organizational performance. The critical causal variables are managerial leadership and organizational climate. Dr. Likert shows how resultant performance can be predicted when one has a knowledge of the causal variables in a given organization.

43.

Human Resource Accounting: Building and Assessing Productive Organizations

RENSIS LIKERT

The major source of the present-day apathetic and hostile attitudes of not only blue-collar workers, but also white-collar employees and supervisors, is the kind of management that focuses on short-range results—the kind of management that commonly used accounting methods encourage and reward. But when current financial reports are accompanied by dollar estimates of the change in the value of the human organization for the same reporting period, the kind of management that builds more productive human organizations will be fostered, because such management creates the will to work and at the same time contributes to employee health and satisfaction.

The resources to make these dollar estimates and to build these more productive organizations have been created by a half-century of social science research. Tens of millions of dollars, provided largely by business, have been spent on this research. The resources it has developed are these:

- Knowledge of the key dimensions of a human organization.
- Instruments for measuring these dimensions.
- Knowledge of the interrelationships among the human organizational dimensions.
- Knowledge of the relationship of each of these dimensions to performance results, both current and one or two years later.
- Evidence that there are, for all types of industry, consistent and dependable relationships between the human organizational dimensions and the end-result performance data.
- Knowledge of the nature and operating characteristics of a system of managing the human organization that, in comparison with the management system used

Reprinted by permission of the publisher from *Personnel*, Vol. 50, No. 3 (May–June 1973), © 1973 by AMACOM, a division of American Management Associations.

Rensis Likert is former director of the Institute for Social Research, The University of Michigan, and is now board chairman of Rensis Likert Associates.

by most firms today, is 20 to 40 per cent more productive and yields better employee satisfaction and health.

To begin with the first point, the human organization of any enterprise (or segment of it) can be measured by a relatively small number of key dimensions, which fall into two classes—causal and intervening, or intermediate. Management can alter the causal variables, thereby producing changes in the intervening variables and, in turn, in the end-result performance data. These causal variables categories are organizational climate and managerial leadership. Policies and behavior at top managerial levels determine organizational climate variables, imposing constraints, either favorable or unfavorable, on what lower levels of managers can do. The elements used to measure the different dimensions of managerial leadership and organizational climate (causal variables) are shown in Figure 1.

The intervening, or intermediate, variables reflect the internal state and health of the organization, for example, the loyalties, attitudes, motivations, performance goals, and perceptions of all members and their collective capacity for effective interaction, communication, and decision making. These intervening dimensions are measured by the elements shown in Figure 2.

The end-result, dependent variables reflect the achievements of the organization, such as its productivity, costs, scrap loss, earnings, and market performance.

Performance—Determined by Quality of the Human Organization

Studies involving more than 200,000 employees and 20,000 managers or administrators in virtually all kinds of business and in governmental agencies, hospitals, schools, voluntary associations, and other organizations show that favorable

MANAGERIAL LEADERSHIP
• *Support:* Friendly; pays attention to what you are saying; listens to subordinates' problems.
• *Team building:* Encourages subordinates to work as a team; encourages exchange of opinions and ideas.
• *Goal emphasis:* Encourages best efforts; maintains high standards.
• *Help with work:* Shows ways to do a better job; helps subordinates plan, organize, and schedule; offers new ideas, solutions to problems.

ORGANIZATIONAL CLIMATE
• *Communication flow:* Subordinates know what's going on; superiors are receptive; subordinates are given information to do jobs well.
• *Decision-making practices:* Subordinates are involved in setting goals; decisions are made at levels of accurate information; persons affected by decisions are asked for their ideas; know-how of people of all levels is used.
• *Concern for persons:* The organization is interested in the individual's welfare; tries to improve working conditions; organizes work activities sensibly.
• *Influence on department:* From lower-level supervisors, employees who have no subordinates.
• *Technological adequacy:* Improved methods are quickly adopted; equipment and resources are well managed.
• *Motivation:* Differences and disagreements are accepted and worked through; people in organization work hard for money, promotions, job satisfaction, and to meet high expectations from others and are encouraged to do so by policies, working conditions, and people.

FIGURE 1   Elements used to measure human organizational causal variables.

scores on organizational climate and managerial leadership dimensions are associated quite consistently with favorable scores on the intervening variables and with high performance when trends

PEER LEADERSHIP

• *Support:* Friendly; pays attention to what others are saying; listens to others' problems.
• *Goal emphasis:* Encourages best efforts; maintains high standards.
• *Help with work:* Shows ways to do a better job; helps others plan, organize, and schedule; group shares with each other new ideas, solutions to problems.
• *Team building:* Encouragement from each other to work as a team; emphasis on team goal; exchange of opinions and ideas.

GROUP PROCESS

• Planning together, coordinating efforts.
• Making good decisions, solving problems.
• Knowing jobs and how to do them well.
• Sharing information.
• Wanting to meet objectives.
• Having confidence and trust in other members.
• Ability to meet unusual work demands.

SATISFACTION

• With fellow workers; superiors; jobs; this organization compared with others; pay; progress in the organization up to now; chances for getting ahead in the future.

FIGURE 2   Elements used to measure human organizational intervening variables.

over time are examined. Conversely, unfavorable climate and leadership scores are associated with unfavorable states of the intervening variables and poor performance results when the trends in performance over time are examined.

A smaller, but rapidly growing, number of studies demonstrate that these patterns of relationships exist also for changes in the causal variables—that is, improvement in the causal variables yields improvement in the intervening variables and, in turn, in performance results, whereas an unfavorable shift in the causal variables leads to a worsening in the intervening variables and in the end-result performance data over time, even

though short-run increases often intervene. Moreover, the magnitude of the change in the causal variables is reflected in the size of changes in the intervening and end-result variables—large changes in the causal produce sizable shifts in the other variables. In widely different kinds of work, it has been demonstrated that changes in the human organization variables can cause from 30 per cent to more than 70 per cent of the total fluctuations in performance data such as productivity and costs.

Figure 3 shows the magnitude of the relationships among the human organizational variables and the relationships of the variables to performance data.

The width of each arrow is meant to be roughly proportional to the relationship between the variables connected by the arrow. The overall direction of causality is in the direction the arrow points—that is, the width of each arrow reflects the magnitude of the square of the coefficient of correlation (r^2) between the variables. The value of r^2 for each relationship is shown at the side of each arrow. Thus, for example, the .27 next to the arrow between managerial leadership and group process means that 27 per cent of the variance in group process is accounted for by managerial leadership. Similarly, 67 per cent of the variance in the job satisfaction of subordinates is accounted for by variations in organizational climate.

The arrows in Figure 3 are all shown as unidirectional, flowing from managerial leadership to the other variables and from the intervening variables to total productive efficiency. This is, of course, an oversimplification of the relationships, since there are feedback loops and some circularity among the variables. For example, the organizational climate of a unit is determined by the behavior of managers above the manager of that unit. This organizational climate is a causal variable for that unit; it provides limits—

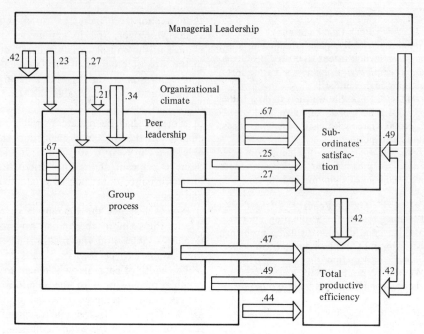

FIGURE 3 Relationships among human organizational dimensions and to performance.

favorable or unfavorable—within which the unit's manager is free to exercise his own style of leadership behavior. Nevertheless, the arrows in Figure 3 show the major flow of influence. Top managerial leadership determines organizational climate. These two variables are causal in character, determining the state of the other variables shown. These other dimensions are intervening variables, except for total productive efficiency, which, of course, is an end-result variable.

The magnitude of the relationships among the human organizational dimensions and end-result performance data is influenced greatly by the accuracy—that is, reliability and validity—with which the performance results are measured. Low correlations are often obtained because of inaccurate performance data. It is quite common for members of an operating unit, both supervisory and nonsupervisory, to protect themselves by deliberately reporting erroneous performance results. Their "adjustments" are known as the "fudge factor," and whenever the performance data, whether productivity costs, scrap, or other measurements, have been influenced by fudge factors or other alterations, they are correspondingly inaccurate.

These inaccuracies, or "noise," of course, lower the observed relationships —the coefficients of correlation—between the human organizational dimensions and the end-result performance variables, and are a common source of low correlations. Where the performance data are highly inaccurate because of fudge factors or other distortions, it is often useful to obtain an estimate of what the magnitude of the relationships between the human organizational dimensions and performance variables would be if the performance data were accurate. A statistical method called correcting for attenuation produces an estimate of what the coefficient of correlation would be if the performance data were highly reliable.

Any coefficients of correlation that have been corrected for attenuation should not, however, be used in computing changes in the value of the human organization. When evidence shows that computed correlations are substantially less than their true relationship because of errors and distortions in the performance data, management should take corective steps, but such steps should not be punitive in any respect. Punitive action will increase hostilities and lead to greater, not lessened, use of fudge factors and even greater errors in the performance data.

Changes in the key dimensions of the human organization appear to be dependable indicators for forecasting changes in the productivity and financial performance of an organizational unit that the human organization will be able to sustain over substantial periods of time (in contrast with levels that can be achieved for shorter periods in response to punitive threats). Moreover, when changes in the human organizational dimensions occur, predictions can be made of the magnitude of changes that will occur subsequently in the output performance of that human organization, whether it be an entire corporation, a division, or a single unit. The accuracy of these predictions will vary, of course, from situation to situation and depending on several factors, such as the kind of work being done, but in each situation the relative accuracy of the prediction can be assessed by computing the probable error of the estimate. The prediction then can be interpreted and used in the light of its probable error.

Estimating Changes in Value of Human Organizations in Dollars

To estimate in dollars changes in the value of the productive capability of any human organization it is necessary to measure the key dimensions of that human organization at each time period,

say, at one year ago (T1) and now (T2). Changes in scores on these dimensions from T1 to T2 can then be used to predict the change in the productive capability of that human organization. For example, if the causal dimensions of the human organization of a profit center showed a gain from T1 to T2 of one unit, the productive capability obviously increased. If, from statistical calculations, each unit of gain or loss in the causal scores is known to produce a corresponding shift in the productivity of the human organization that alters unit costs by $3.50, then improvement in the causal scores of one unit would yield a predicted improvement in total costs of $350,000 for a total production of 100,000 units. This estimate in dollars of the change in the productive capability of the profit center's human organization can be used to compute the change in the value of that human organization as an asset by capitalizing it at an appropriate rate. If 20 per cent is used, the $1,750,000 increase in value of the human organization can be treated as an increase in the asset value of the profit center's human organization.

If the human organization of the profit center in our example had worsened, the decrease in asset value of the human organization would be computed in essentially the same manner. If, for example, there had been a decrease in the causal variable scores of the one unit from T1 to T2, the computations would show a predicted increase in annual production costs of $350,000 for 100,000 units. This would mean an estimated decrease of $1,750,000 in the asset value of the profit center's human organization.

Figure 4 shows the computational steps used in arriving at the dollar estimates; it is based on the following data about the plant in the example:

• The plant is one of 20 comparable plants engaged in essentially the same operation and using the same technology.
• For these 20 plants, the correlation be-

tween the causal human organizational scores and unit production costs is −0.70. (The correlation is negative, since the better the causal scores are, the lower are the unit costs.)

• The standard deviation in the human organizational scores is 0.25.

• The standard deviation in the unit production costs is $5.00.

• The plant has an annual production of 100,000 units; it had at T1 a causal human organizational score of 3.6; and it had at T2 a causal human organizational score of 3.85. (The human organizational variables, shown in Figures 1 and 2, are measured on a scale of 1 to 5, with 5 being the most favorable.)

As the above data and Figure 4 show, the improvement in the causal human organizational scores is from 3.6 to 3.85, or +.25. This gain, when converted to standard scores by dividing the gain by the standard deviation in the human organizational scores, is +1.00 (+.25 ÷ .25 = +1.00). In turn, this gain of +1.00 is converted to an estimated gain in standard scores in the unit production costs by multiplying it by the coefficient of correlation (−0.70) between the human organizational scores and production costs (+1.00 × −0.70 = −0.70). Converting this reduction in unit production costs of −0.70, expressed in standard scores to dollars, yields an estimated reduction in unit costs of $3.50. This conversion to dollars requires multiplying the estimated reduction in standard scores by the standard deviation of the unit production costs (−0.70 × $5.00 = $3.50). The total annual reduction in costs is $350,000 (100,000 × $3.50), since annual production is 100,000 units.

The Most Profitable Way to Use Superior Managers

An important conclusion emerges from these human resource accounting computations: As a rule, it will prove more profitable for a firm to bring a below-average operation to average than to move an above-average operation to a very high level. This conclusion follows from two facts. First, an increase of one unit in human organization scores yields the same estimated improvement in cost savings and increased value of the human organization regardless of the original or final level of the human organization score at T1. (See Figure 4.) Second, an improvement in the human organization from below average to average can be maintained at this new level by a manager who has not yet become what I call a System 4 manager, but who is at least moderately skilled. (System 4 will be discussed in detail later on.) The increase in productive capability and asset value of the human organization is, consequently, retained.

On the other hand, when a human organization is built from above average to very good, it takes an excellent System 4 manager to hold it at this level. Under any less skilled manager, the human organization will regress toward its previous state, and the firm will lose this gain in productive capability and human asset value. There may be some circumstances, however, that would lead a firm to use a highly skilled System 4 manager to move an operation from an above-average level to a very high level. For example, the firm may wish to have a model of an excellent human organization to study its nature, operating characteristics, and potential.

Hidden Costs of the 1969–71 Recession

Changes in the productive capability of a firm's human organization cannot be assessed correctly unless periodic measurements of the causal and intervening dimensions of that organization are made regularly. Since most firms do not obtain these measurements, they are unable to detect the changes that are occurring in

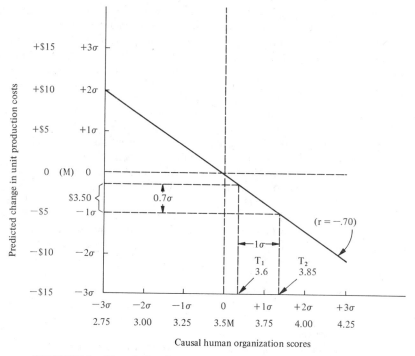

FIGURE 4 Translating human organizational values into dollars.

their human organizations, and even worse, current profit-and-loss reports often encourage them to believe that changes are occurring that are the exact opposite of the shifts that actually are taking place. When profits go up, it is often assumed that the human organization has become more productive, but steps taken to maintain earnings or prevent losses may actually result in a decrease in the productive capability of the human organization, even though a short-range increase in reported profits is attained.

This has happened in many firms during the past few years. They have experienced a sizable, but often unrecognized, drop in the productive capability of their human organizations, a decrease now showing up in the difficulties of achieving high-quality production and low costs as markets again become firm.

These unrecognized losses are a direct consequence of the cost-reduction moves that these firms made to meet the financial pressures caused by the recession. For example, a company manufacturing consumer durables had been growing rapidly and profitably as the market for its products expanded. The 1969-71 recession brought a pause in market expansion and exposed severe problems in inventory and production control, labor productivity, and a long accounts-receivable period. Overnight, profitability vanished, and the familiar action steps were ordered for the reduction of overhead personnel, for the reduction of inventory, and for a major effort to step up collections on overdue accounts; budgets were tightened, personnel were exhorted to reduce costs, and pressure was put on production workers to meet or exceed standards. The cost-reduction steps brought increases in reported earnings, but with a serious deterioration in the productive capability of the firm's human organization.

The Net Loss from Slashing Costs: A Case History

With these kinds of cost-reduction steps, the long-range costs typically exceed the short-range gains; it is clear that better cost-reduction strategies are needed, even in crises. The experience of one plant of several hundred employees is a case in point. A management consulting firm that was brought in to carry out a cost-reduction program analyzed the staffing of each department in the plant against standards the consultants themselves established and found about a third of the departments appreciably overstaffed. For each of these departments, teams made up of persons from other departments, corporate or division staff, and the consulting firm were assigned to study the department and recommend ways to achieve labor savings. The manager of each affected department served as liaison, but no one from the department was on the team. After a plan for the labor savings was developed and approved, the managers of the affected departments were ordered to introduce the specific changes and achieve the the designated savings, which totaled approximately $250,000 annually.

Measurements of the human organization of the plant were obtained before this cost-reduction program was started (T1) and again one year later (T2):

The overstaffed departments where intensive cost-reduction efforts were undertaken were those that at T1 had the poorest management in terms of their human organizational scores. These departments were especially poor in terms of the causal variables. (See Figure 5.)

The cost-reduction program treated the symptom of poor management by reducing overstaffing, but no effort was made to help the managers of the overstaffed departments learn how to manage their human organizations more effectively. After the overstaffing had been reduced, the repeat measurements at T2 revealed that the managerial behavior as shown by the scores on the causal variables was actually worse than it was at T1. (See Figure 6.) There also was a general deterioration in the human organization from T1 to T2. Only two indexes showed an improvement from T1 to T2—peer help with work and peer team building, but, ironically, the increases in these scores occurred among nonsupervisory employees and reflected better teamwork focused on *restricting* production, shown by the sizable drops in the motivation scores of the employees and unfavorable attitudes toward the company. Thus, treating the symptoms resulted in worsening the cause, poor management. In other words, a less productive organization emerged from the effects of the cost-reduction program.

Computations based on the unfavorable shifts in the causal and other human organizational dimensions from T1 to T2 revealed that there had been a loss in the productive capability of the plant's human organization that would increase costs at least $450,000 annually, so, by treating symptoms, the cost-reduction program had achieved an annual savings in labor costs of $250,000, but an estimated continuing annual cost of $450,000. The plant's actual experience over the past several years has confirmed the accuracy of the measurements of the human organization and of these predictions: The plant has sustained substantial costs of the kind that poor management produces—slowdowns, restriction of output, poor quality, excessive scrap, dissatisfied employees, and poor labor relations.

The conclusion should not be drawn from these findings that it is unsound to seek low costs or to take action when the

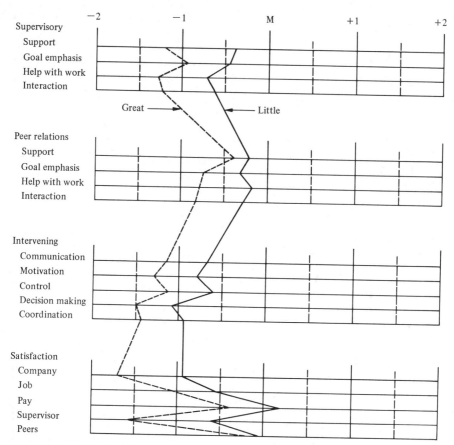

FIGURE 5 Relationship of human organizational variables to intensity of cost-reduction effort—major indexes profile.

economic survival of the firm is threatened. Quite the contrary. It is in the interests of all—management, consumers, employees, and shareholders—that efficient low-cost operating methods be used, but the question is how lower costs should be achieved.

Profitable Cost Reduction Through Highly Productive Human Organizations

Fortunately, there is a management system that achieves a much more productive human organization and has the capability of rapid action when it is necessary to reduce costs by methods that build, rather than worsen, the productive capabilities of the human organization—a system derived from the same research that has made possible dollar estimates of the changes in the productive capability of a human organization. This system is based on the principles and insights of the managers who are achieving the highest productivity and lowest costs and who have the most satisfied and healthy employees and the best labor relations. It is more complex than the usual management system and requires learning more effective leadership and problem-solving skills, but it produces human or-

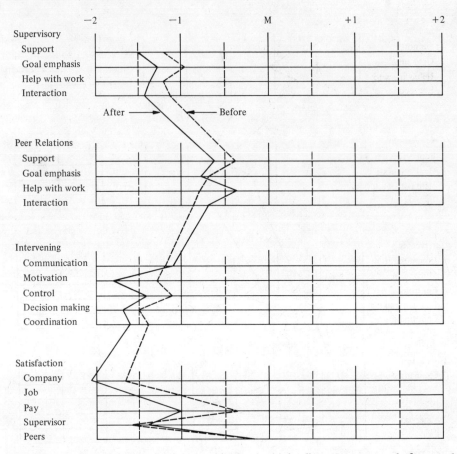

FIGURE 6 Human organizational variables in high-effort department before and after cost-reduction effort—major indexes profile.

ganizations that are about 20 to 40 per cent more productive than average. Called System 4, it can be described by using the limited number of human organizational dimensions, both causal and intervening, discussed at the beginning of this paper. System 4 scores at the high, or favorable, end of each of the variables. By way of explanation, System 1 is exploitative-authoritative, System 2 is benevolent-authoritative, and System 3 is consultative; System 4 we call participative group.

To give an idea of the System 4 climate, characteristically, these factors are present:

• A great deal of confidence and trust is shown in subordinates.
• Subordinates' ideas are frequently sought and used constructively.
• A great deal of cooperative teamwork exists.
• The usual direction of information flow is downward, upward, and sideways.
• Subordinates are fully involved in decisions related to their work.
• Organizational goals are established by group action (except in crisis).
• Review and control functions are widely shared.

An effective means of enabling any firm or department to build a System 4 human organization is the survey feed-back method. The human organization is measured and its scores on the causal and intervening dimensions are computed for each work group and for each of the larger units and then for the entire firm. Each manager, from the top executive down to and including first-level super-visors, is given the human organizational measurements of his work group and of the larger entities whose behavior and performance he is responsible for. Using System 4 as the desired model, each man-ager is encouraged and assisted to assess his own situation, to recognize his strengths and weaknesses, and, with the participation of his subordinate group, to plan and take the action needed to move his behavior and the human organization toward System 4. (For a description of this process and the coaching used, see *Improving Organizational Performance*, 1971, Rensis Likert Associates, Ann Arbor, Mich.)

In this process, not only are the human organizational dimensions used for analyses and problem solving, but the operating problems of the firm or depart-ment that are caused by inadequate human organization are also examined and solved by the relevant work groups. The focus is on task accomplishment, rather than on interpersonal process. When interpersonal obstacles develop, they are worked through directly, but only to the extent that they impede group effort to reach action on its central prob-lems. As task problems are solved and procedures are established to handle them, roles and role relationships are changed. These, in turn, lead to improve-ment in interpersonal relationships and a more effective human organization. This cycle should be repeated at regular intervals, usually annually.

If the discrepancies between where an enterprise is now and where it wants to be are large, the change toward System 4 should be a gradual one, taken step by step. One huge leap should not be at-tempted, since most persons cannot successfully make great changes in their values, skills, expectations, and relation-ships in a short period of time.

The Relation of System 4 to Performance-Improving Procedures

Many firms today are achieving appre-ciable improvement in performance by applying one or more procedures like management by objectives (MBO), pos-itive reinforcement, autonomous teams, and job enrichment or redesign. But the gains that these firms are experiencing from the use of these procedures would be very much greater if used with System 4 management.

When MBO is used by a System 4 com-pany, it becomes management by group objectives (MBGO). The objectives are set by the manager and his subordinates in group problem-solving meetings. Each subordinate knows both the team objec-tives and the objectives that he must attain. This team use of the MBO con-cept results in better understanding by team members of the responsibilities of each. Participation in setting the group's objectives heightens the motivation of each member to achieve the objectives and to help colleagues in attaining them. Each member expects each of the others, as well as himself, to do his best to reach the stated goals. Loyalty to other mem-bers is added to loyalty to the superior as a source of motivation. MBGO, con-sequently, is superior to MBO in achieving better understanding among members of the group of their inter-dependent objectives and relationships, mobilizing greater motivation among the manager's subordinates to reach the ob-jectives and establishing better teamwork and coordination.

Positive reinforcement as ordinarily used involves reinforcing behavior by the manager, for example, his giving recognition for a task well done. In a System 4 management, the positive reinforcement comes not only from the individual's manager but from all of the others in his work group. Reinforcement from one's teammates in a well-knit team adds substantially greater motivation and positive behavioral change than does reinforcement from the superior only. (Restriction of output, widespread in American industry, demonstrates the power of reinforcement by teammates.)

Job enrichment or the redesign of jobs is usually carried out with the involvement of the worker whose job is being changed, and often with the participation of other members of his work group. This involvement motivates the employee to do well on the new job, and if they have participated, those whose work is related to the changed job understand the changes and are able and willing to cooperate in coordinating their efforts. Job enrichment or redesign, when done well and with the full involvement of those persons whose work is affected, typically yields increased productivity and greater employee satisfaction, but it may boomerang in time, except in a System 4 atmosphere.

When job enrichment is carried out with the participation of those affected, they realize from their experience that their participation in decisions concerning this one part of their job has increased both productivity and their satisfaction. But if participation in matters affecting one aspect of their job yields such good results, most workers are likely to press to be involved in decisions dealing with all the other parts of their work life. Denying these requests of supervisory and nonsupervisory employees to be involved in decisions affecting them will make them dissatisfied and frustrated, so unless a firm is willing to shift to System 4, it should take a hard look before using any form of job enrichment that includes employee participation.

The reason that System 4 achieves substantially better results than other management systems from such procedures as MBO and positive reinforcement is its much greater capacity to mobilize high levels of cooperative motivation. For the same reason, it is capable of obtaining appreciably better results from the many other procedures that are useful in achieving improved performance, such as production teams and work simplification.

System 4 Improvements in Action

Moving the human organization of a department of about 200 employees in a large fabricating plant toward System 4 yielded substantial improvement in one year's time. Productivity increased 28 per cent, scrap losses dropped to 25 per cent of their previous level, and written grievances dropped from over 50 per month to an average of less than three per month. Other measures of performance and labor relations, too, showed comparable gains. This improvement effort was extended to the entire plant and within three years had yielded cost savings in excess of $5,000,000.

A sales region of a large consumer products firm was helped by means of the survey feedback method to move its human organization toward System 4. Over an eight-month period, the human organization scores were improved by about 20 per cent, and sales as a percentage of quota showed an even greater increase. This region continued to improve its performance, breaking all previous sales records and selling a larger volume than another region that had a sales potential about one-fifth greater.

Comparable improvements in both the human organization and in performance are being obtained in other situations involving widely different kinds of work, but not every attempt to build more productive human organizations and achieve better performance succeeds so well. For example, a particular department may be part of a larger organization whose top management does not want the management of the subordinate department to shift toward System 4. Or a manager may be so fearful of failing that he is unwilling to undertake the risk of trying to shift toward System 4.

To sum up, social science research has provided the resources to enable any firm or any manager to build a more productive human organization and achieve better performance. This research is also creating the methodology for estimating in dollars the value of the changes in the productive capability of any firm's human organization. As these dollar estimates become an integral part of the management information system of every well-managed organization, they will lead to sounder decisions based on more adequate information. Top managements and boards of directors will move much more rapidly than at present to the use of science-based management because of System 4's demonstrably greater capacity to achieve and maintain low costs accompanied by employee satisfaction and health.

QUESTIONS

1. Distinguish between causal, intervening, and end-result variables.
2. How can the causal variables be strengthened or improved in an actual enterprise?
3. Show how hard-driving, cost-reduction-oriented management may make a company's profit and loss statement and balance sheet look good in the short run of, say one to three years, at the risk of serious detriment over a longer time span.
4. Think of an organization in which you have worked (or in which you now work). How would you rate it on the causal and intervening factors or variables that Dr. Likert describes? To what extent does it exhibit System 4 characteristics? How effective is the organization in terms of end-result variables such as productivity or profits?
5. How do such specific programs as management by objectives and job enrichment relate to System 4 management?

PART X

Ethics in Management

There has been increased public concern about the quality of behavior exhibited by leaders in our society, both in the public and private sectors. It is difficult to say whether ethical and moral standards have been declining or improving. But for sure we can say that much more is being said about these issues, both in professional journals and in the popular news media, than was said in the past. For far too long undergraduate and graduate programs in business administration and management have skirted these issues. But this situation is rapidly changing. In a world where traditional values have been attacked and modified and where new values are emerging, there is real need to face these matters squarely.

Edgar H. Schein states that research on moral education in business is lacking. In his article Schein focuses on the concept of moral education from the perspective of teaching a value system as part of the general preparation of candidates for a particular occupational role. He argues that moral issues should be covered in training students for management careers. The multiplicity of clients of the manager makes it difficult to clarify the moral issues and solutions. Nevertheless, there is real need for vigorously pursuing empirical research in this complex area.

44.

The Problem of Moral Education for the Business Manager

EDGAR H. SCHEIN

When we refer to the moral[1] education of the business manager, we may have one of three different concepts in mind: (1) education for general character which would reflect itself in moral behavior in any occupation; (2) morality in the *process* of education itself—that is, an educational process that *exemplifies* the moral values to be taught; and (3) the teaching of a particular value system as part of the general preparation of a candidate for a particular occupational role. This paper will focus on the third of these concepts.

I have chosen this focus deliberately, in order to stimulate research on moral education in the business realm. Such research has been carried out in medicine, dentistry, and law, but is lacking in the business area. I suspect that one reason for this is the difficulty in elucidating what may be moral questions and moral solutions for business managers. My at-

tempt here will be to provide some clarifying categories drawn from a socio-psychological frame of reference which, I hope, will make it possible to select research questions and testable hypotheses that are relevant to the moral problem, whether we are talking about the behavior of practicing managers or the teaching of management.

Some Categories for Classifying Moral Values

Moral or ethical behavior and the values from which such behavior derives are often believed to be generalizable across all kinds of situations and all kinds of human relationships. Yet most research on such behavior consistently finds that people apply different standards to different situations. For example, killing is wrong, yet we may do it in wartime or in self-defense. Stealing is wrong, yet a

Reprinted from *Industrial Management Review*, Vol. 8, No. 1 (Fall 1966), pp. 3–14, by permission of the Industrial Management Review Association.

Edgar H. Schein is Professor of Organizational Psychology and Management, Sloan School of Management, Massachusetts Institute of Technology.

[1] For purpose of this discussion I will not distinguish between concepts of "ethical" and concepts of "moral." The two words will be used interchangeably.

prisoner of war may steal from his captor. Lying is wrong, yet we may and are supposed to lie if we must do so to protect someone's self-esteem. In the recent cases of price-fixing in the electrical industry, this point came out in the defense argument that the forces at work in the particular situation offered the executives no choice but to collude, just as the soldier has no choice but to try to kill the enemy.

If we accept the argument that one must analyze values and moral standards in reference to *particular* situations or relationships, we can next ask: What kinds of categories would help us to classify such situations?

My major classifying principle will be to consider who is involved in the relationship. I shall ask: With respect to whom is the behavior being judged as moral or immoral? Following a detailed discussion of this classification, I will discuss briefly some additional issues, such as who benefits vs. who gets hurt, the closeness of the behavior to the consequences thereof, the reversibility of the behavior, the problem of intentions vs. effects, and sins of commission vs. sins of omission.

WHO IS INVOLVED? THE MULTIPLE CLIENTS OF THE MANAGER

There are a number of ways of defining a profession. One of my favorites comes from the sociologist Everett Hughes,[2] who has stated the simple proposition that a professional is someone who knows better what is good for his client than the client himself does. This definition includes the more usual definition that the professional has had extensive training in a body of knowledge and skills which he exercises on behalf of his clients.

If we examine this definition in reference to the well-established professions of medicine and law, we find that the values

or moral issues of the profession tend to be defined around the relationship with the client. Both doctor and lawyer receive moral training in how to exercise responsibility in their relationship with clients, and in how to work for the client's welfare—even if this means the sacrifice of self-interest or the compromising of some other value. Doctors are expected to make economic sacrifices if the patient's welfare demands it, to ignore the welfare of their own family if midnight calls require their services, to lie to their patients about their conditions, and so on. Perhaps the best example comes from the prisoner of war camp where the doctor's oath required him to treat enemy officers in clear violation of the patriotic standards of the POWs who were witness to the behavior and who viewed it as traitorous.

If we accept this definition of professionalism—knowing better what is good for the client than the client himself—we may speculate that it is the *vulnerability of the client* which has necessitated the development of moral and ethical codes surrounding the relationship. The client must be protected from exploitation in a situation in which he is unable to protect himself because he lacks the relevant knowledge to do so.

In recent years we have tended to view the businessman and industrial manager as becoming increasingly professionalized. There is a broader base of technical knowledge and skills required to be a manager, a longer period of training for managerial responsibility, and a greater tendency for managers to be able to move from one type of organization to another, implying that managerial skills are quite general. If, then, the manager is becoming a professional, who is his client? With respect to whom is he exercising his expert knowledge and skills? Who needs protec-

[2] Hughes, E. C. (1).

tion against the possible misuse of these skills?

The Consumer As Client. Business generates products and services that are purchased by various types of consumers, thus raising the obvious possibility of exploitation of the consumer. Traditional economic theory minimized this problem by assuming that the marketplace was an automatic arbiter of prices and quality, hence the businessman enjoyed no special power relative to the consumer. *Caveat emptor,* let the buyer beware, was a not-so-gentle reminder to the consumer to exercise what power he had to prevent himself from being exploited. This assumption in turn legitimized any practice that any manager may have wished to engage in vis-à-vis the consumer, and thereby bypassed the moral issues altogether.

The point is well made by the story of the storekeeper whose son asked him what it meant to be in moral conflict. The father replied: "If a customer comes into the store and looks at some material, and asks how must it costs, and I tell him it is $1.00 per yard, and he asks for one yard, and pays me the dollar, and as he is leaving the store I discover that there are two one-dollar bills stuck together—then I face the moral conflict—do I tell my partner about it or just keep the extra dollar."

Many economists argue persuasively that the traditional economic assumptions have never been validated by experience; that the marketplace has not been able to curb the power of the businessman vis-à-vis the consumer; that the consumer has not been in a position to know what he was buying and hence was, in fact, in a relatively vulnerable position. Thus we have seen the development of formal codes, laws, and informal ethical standards pertaining to cleanliness in production processes, weights and measures in packaging, truthfulness in stating contents

of products and in making advertising claims, rights of consumers to sue businesses for the return of their money if they have been cheated, and so on.

Clearly then, one whole area of values deals with the relationship between the manager and consumers, and one area of moral training for the individual manager concerns the development in him of a sense of responsibility to his customers. Whether graduate schools of management actually attempt to inculcate a sense of responsibility to the consumer is an important question for empirical research. Our own school, if it touches the area at all, does so implicitly. Courses in marketing tend to focus heavily on the technical issues, not on the moral ones. I would hypothesize that most of our faculty would assume that the requisite set of responsible feelings and values are already "built into" our students, hence do not have to be a subject of concern in graduate courses.

The Stockholder As Client. The consumer is a client of the manager only in a very limited sense. Most managers do not deal directly with customers, and only a small percentage of their decisions have anything to do with the final consumer relationship. Instead, one often hears the assertion that the manager's only responsibility is to the stockholder.

According to this concept, the manager is a person who uses his expert knowledge and skills to bring to fruition some ideas about how to build or develop a product or service for profit, to implement these ideas, and actually to generate a reasonable rate of return on the investment of the stockholders. The client-professional relationship is here defined as primarily an economic one, and the vulnerability of the client lies in the possibility that the manager may misuse, misallocate, steal, or otherwise mishandle the economic resources entrusted to him.

Deriving from this concept is a second

area of potential moral training, having to do with embezzlement, misappropriation of funds, not taking advantage of inside financial information, nepotism, and a variety of other behaviors which have in common that they reduce the profitability of the enterprise and thus take advantage of the stockholders. The power of the stockholder to protect himself is greater than that of the consumer, however. He has a potential organization in the form of the annual meeting and his representative body, the Board of Directors. He can and often does demand more direct surveillance of the financial activities of the managers to supplement those of regulatory agencies such as the Securities and Exchange Commission.

The Community As Client. A third client of the manager is the community, viewed broadly as the individuals and other organizations who are in some way interdependent with the business enterprise. The individuals in the community who depend upon the company for jobs are vulnerable to discriminatory hiring policies, the suppliers are vulnerable to discrimination, exploitation, and bribery, and the community as a whole is highly vulnerable to economic loss if the business moves or conducts its affairs in such a way as to minimize the economic return to the community. The company can bring in its own labor force, refuse to buy supplies or raw materials from local vendors, fail to support community activities, and so on.

It is interesting to note that in this value area, as in the others, the legal sanctions tend to be applied where vulnerability is at a maximum, such as in the case of discriminatory hiring practices, or of minimum wages for employment.[3] The more difficult moral decisions occur, however, where ambiguity is greater, as in the pro-

cess of defining the economic responsibilities of a company if it is the sole employer in a community.

A special case of the community as client results when businesses have overseas subsidiaries and the managers become not only representatives of the particular organization vis-à-vis the local foreign community, but become representatives of the United States as a nation with a certain kind of value system. In this situation it is often not clear who is more vulnerable—the local community, the business enterprise, or the United States in having its image tarnished. Do we expect the overseas manager to uphold the values of service and community development, the values of efficiency and economic growth for the business, the values of democracy and free enterprise, or the values of nationalism, patriotism, and allegiance to the United States? These values can and often do come into conflict with each other. What is best for the local community, for the business, and for the United States are often not the same things.

We have had to face this issue in the Sloan School when we were selecting candidates for our Fellows in Africa and Fellows in South American programs. In each case our graduate was expected to become an employee of the local government and to convince it that he could be trusted. He had to have a value system that would permit him to work on behalf of his employer, even if this meant short-run disregard of United States interests, as in the case of planning a local development program that might draw most of its financial and technical resources from the Soviet Union if these were more accessible than their U. S. equivalent. In our selection we were clear about one thing: We could not afford to send super-patriots

---

[3] One might hypothesize that legal sanctions tend to develop when (a) vulnerability is at a maximum, (b) there is a specific identifiable target who is potentially vulnerable, (c) the manager's behavior is potentially observable and unambiguous, and (d) there are immediate or short-run consequences of the managerial behavior.

or individuals whose prime motivation was to export their own concept of American values to another culture. Whether our Fellows faced such conflicts, and how they handled them if they did, constitutes an important research question which we are currently trying to answer.

The Enterprise As Client. A fourth client is the enterprise itself—the organization that employs the manager.[4] With the increasing tendency to analyze business organizations as complex social systems comes an increasing tendency for the manager to view himself as being basically responsible to the system as a whole. He is responsible for its efficiency, maintenance, effectiveness, and growth. He is expected to make decisions on behalf of these values even if they run counter to the short-run interests of consumers, stockholders, and the community.

The important value referent becomes the organization as a whole, and the assumption is made that in the long run what is good for the organization will be good for the consumer, the stockholder, and the community. Considerations of profit, consumer benefits, and community involvement are subordinated to the ethic or values of efficiency and growth, based on criteria of the "health" of the organizational system. What is required of the manager is commitment and dedication to organizational goals.

Thus, whether the manager decides to hire only certain kinds of employees at certain very low wages is based not on moral considerations in the usual sense but on considerations of what is required to produce the product efficiently. I know of one industry that has solved this dilemma by moving to countries where labor was cheap and no legal sanctions existed concerning hiring practices.

Teaching the importance of commit-

ment and loyalty to the enterprise as values may be particularly important because the enterprise, being an abstraction, is not in a good position to control such behavior. It is highly vulnerable to low commitment, indifference, disloyalty, apathy, sabotage, and treason. Business organizations cannot apply legal sanctions against such behaviors as easily as nations can and do through their governments. Businesses can only fire the apathetic person, but if apathy is widely spread through managerial ranks there may be a tendency not only to condone such behavior but to develop practices of concealing it from top management, the Board of Directors, and the stockholders.

Most of the technical courses in a business school probably take the values of enterprise efficiency and growth for granted. Organizational goals are accepted as given; the only problem is how best to achieve them. If ethical or moral dilemmas are involved in the choice of means, they are either ignored or settled by considering whether the means are in fact illegal. If the survival of the organization depends upon it, even illegal means are sometimes condoned with the argument that the law is not fair in the first place.

The Subordinate As Client. A fifth type of client of the business manager is his subordinate-employee. Many kinds of managerial behaviors labeled as immoral or unethical deal with aspects of the superior-subordinate relationship—starvation wages, excessive working hours, unsafe working conditions, withholding a promotion or raise to enforce subordination, and arbitrary layoffs. Employees as clients have been so vulnerable to these kinds of behavior on the part of their managers that they have had to band together and, through unions and the pas-

---

[4] Since the organization is an abstraction, can one view it as a client? I believe we can treat it as an "object" in the same sense in which clubs, fraternal organizations, political parties, and countries exist as objects to which we give loyalty and attention and from which we obtain material and symbolic rewards.

sage of protective legislation, reinforce their own position.

Thus, much behavior formerly labeled immoral is now defined as illegal, but the issue remains unsettled in that a more subtle counterpart of each of the above kinds of behaviors is possible. Bosses can still threaten their employees with the withholding of rewards or with subtle punishments; they can still exercise arbitrary and unfair authority; they can play favorites, fail to give credit where credit is due, persecute someone until he quits, steal their subordinates' suggestions, or fail to recommend their best subordinates for promotion.[5]

As one story puts the issue, a company wanted to institute a new benefit program more favorable to employees. All employees signed up except one older clerk who held up the entire proceedings by refusing to sign. His boss told him of the great benefits, but to no avail. The boss asked the vice-president to try, but no amount of persuasion could get the old employee to sign. After several more futile attempts to get the man to understand the benefits, the president himself was told about the case. The president called the old man in, sat him down at the desk, put the paper in front of him, and said, "Listen you S.O.B. Sign that paper right now or you're fired." The old man signed. The president, somewhat puzzled, asked him why he signed so readily when others had had such difficulty getting him to sign. The old man said, "Well, sir, you were the first one who really explained the program to me."

The values implied by traditional management theory have always held that the boss is the boss and should only do that which is good for the enterprise. The argument has been that no special obligations or responsibilities accrue to workers and/or managerial subordinates beyond those specified by the contract or law. On the other hand, the human relations movement has usually been viewed as an attempt to reverse this trend and to argue that managers are responsible to their subordinates, should consider their needs, should treat them as human beings and not merely as interchangeable economic resources, and that they should do this because it is right in and of itself in a democratic society.

A third argument, which many human relationists/behavioral scientists claim for themselves, is that managers should consider the needs of their subordinates not because it is basically immoral not to do so but because it will in fact lead to greater economic and productive efficiency on the part of the enterprise. Since commitment, loyalty, and energy are desirable in employees for good organizational performance, it is argued that these qualities are most easily obtainable by treating people fairly, by considering their needs, and by attempting to enhance rather than weaken their sense of individuality and contribution to the organization.

We have here an area where values and science overlap to an unknown degree since the evidence is not yet clearcut whether in fact people will generally perform better if trusted and treated well, or whether this happens only under certain special conditions. If the latter is the more accurate statement of where our scientific knowledge lies, the manager is in the difficult position of having to be a diagnostician in an area where it is not at all clear whether the issues are scientific or moral ones.

What we then teach in a school of management may well be a function of whether the teacher is an economist who leans toward traditional assumptions about economic man or a behavioral sci-

---

[5] William Evan points out that in organizational life employees do not have the protection of due process of law and a system of appeals as they do in the larger society. (2)

entist who leans toward assumptions of a complex man capable of a variety of involvements in organizations.[6] In our school we teach both positions.

The Peer and/or Boss As Client. A sixth type of client for the manager is his peer and/or boss. I am assuming that the manager is by definition a part of an organized enterprise, and that any organized enterprise depends on the coordinated behavior of all its members. The nature of organized effort thus makes the members of the organization highly interdependent, and therefore highly vulnerable to certain kinds of behaviors vis-à-vis each other. For example, the boss is highly vulnerable to having his subordinates lie to him about what is going on in those portions of the organization which he cannot check on directly. Peers are very vulnerable to having negative information about themselves passed on to their boss, which is one aspect of the set of activities generally referred to as "playing politics."

Where departments of a single organization are arrayed competitively with each other, the manager of each may be motivated to exaggerate the virtues of his own group and devalue the other group, and may implement the motive by falsifying figures, by failing to pass on key information, by subtle distortions, and the like. All the pathology of intergroup conflict in society and community can play itself out inside the organization, with managers being tempted into various kinds of questionable behavior in regard to their peers and superiors.

Part of the value dilemma in this area is that we do not have clear ethical or moral standards pertaining to collaboration-competition. Not only is it unclear in our society how far one should go in defining the game as being a competitive one, but it is not clear how far one can go in bending or breaking rules in the process of trying to win. We say that free enterprise is by definition a competitive game and that competition is good for all the various enterprises engaging in it, yet we find that competition breeds behavior that is clearly harmful, and against which society must protect itself. For example, for a company to win over a competitor may mean reducing its costs by cutting its labor force, compromising on quality of product, making untrue advertising claims, or sabotaging the competitor, to the point where government intervention becomes necessary to redefine the rules of the game.

Most companies assume that the productivity of individuals as well as departments within their organization can be enhanced by having them compete with each other. Rarely do they observe until too late some of the costs of such competition—in the amount of distortion of information, hiding of failures, falsification of figures, empire building, and mutual mistrust among managers presumably working for the same enterprise. Are these managers immoral, or does competition stimulate certain kinds of behavior which are well within the rules of the *competitive* game? It is only in the context of persons attempting to work together that some of these behaviors look questionable.

I would state the hypothesis that most schools of management start with the values of individualism and competition, rarely examining the consequences of these values inside the enterprise. Group effort, collaboration, and cooperative coordination tend to be viewed as fuzzy inventions of the behavioral scientists, not as concepts to be taken seriously. The only group in our faculty that believes in the effectiveness of *group* incentives (which force cooperation among workers) is the labor-relations–organizational psychology group. The economists,

6 Schein, E. H. (3)

mathematicians, marketers, and others are clearly in favor of individual effort and individual incentives and, by implication, the ethic of competition.[7]

The Profession As Client. A final type of client can be thought of as the profession with which the person identifies and to which he belongs. To the extent that management has become a mature profession with clear standards, the individual manager can judge his own behavior against those standards, regardless of the requirements of the various other client systems. In a sense the manager then becomes his own client in that he protects his own self-esteem and his professional identity at the same time that he upholds the profession. However, the profession as client may not solve the problem of identifying moral standards in that the professional standard may merely be to try to serve the various other client systems as well as possible.

Summary and Implications. The various *clients* of the manager are represented in Figure 1. The manager as a professional has obligations and responsibilities to each of these clients. This very fact has a number of implications:

• The managerial role, in contrast to many other professional roles, tends to be defined in terms of a system of *multiple clients*. It is not yet clear in the profession which clients, if any, are to be considered the primary ones.

• Because the values which underlie the different manager-client relationships differ from each other, creating potential conflict situations, and, because we have not yet defined primary client responsibilities for the managerial role, *we cannot specify a single set of values and moral behaviors for the manager.* The search for such a single value system is doomed to failure until we define to whom we ulti-

mately want the manager to be responsible.

• The responsibilities with respect to one client system often require the compromising of responsibilities to another client system. Just as members of organizations have often been found to suffer from role conflict because of the multiple links they have to others, so they suffer from potential *value conflict* or *moral conflict* because of the conflicting responsibilities to different client systems.

• Because of the potential value conflicts which the manager faces, we cannot glibly label his behavior as moral or immoral in any particular situation. We must know the *frame of reference* within which the behavior occurred in order to judge it. In other words we must know which of several values the individual was trying to implement before we praise or condemn him.

• By classifying types of behavior in terms of the client relationship involved, we can study empirically the kinds of values managers hold, and how these vary as a function of other variables such as rank, type of job in the organization, age, prior experience, and so on. It would be extremely valuable to know, for example, whether managers are more likely to view as immoral behavior that hurts a consumer rather than behavior that hurts a subordinate. At present we have no value theory which would be able to make any predictions about this sort of question.

• The nearest thing to a superordinate value is the assertion that the manager is ultimately responsible to the enterprise. Much of the teaching in our school seems to be based on this premise, and most often when managers are under attack they seem to retreat to this as the ultimate defense: What is good for the company is ultimately good.

• If indeed we are moving toward an or-

---

[7] Schein, E. H. (4)

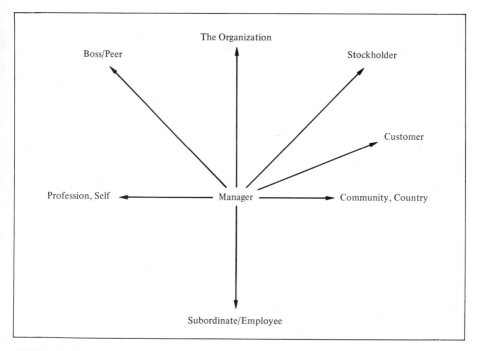

FIGURE 1 Various client systems toward which the manager has responsibilities. Each arrow defines one area of values and moral behavior.

ganizational ethic of the type implied above, it becomes essential to study carefully the implications of this "ultimate" value position. If managers are taught primarily to respond to the needs of the organization, will this undermine or subvert other important values, or are the needs of the organization indeed compatible with the needs of the consumer, the employee, and the community?

WHO GETS HURT AND WHO BENEFITS?

A second way of classifying moral value questions is according to the criterion of whether the immoral behavior involved is defined as immoral because it unfairly benefits the person doing it, or unfairly hurts one or more others who are affected by it. To exemplify the distinction, discriminatory hiring practices or personal prejudice leading to unfair treatment of an employee are immoral be-

cause they are unduly harmful to the recipient of the behavior. Embezzlement on a small scale, theft of company office supplies, financial gain due to inside information, accepting bribes or kickbacks from suppliers, etc., are immoral because they are unduly beneficial to the person committing the deed. The latter type of behavior may in fact be doing no one any visible harm in the short run. But it implies that there are certain categories of rewards to which people are not entitled or certain means of obtaining benefits which are not sanctioned regardless of whether anyone else is harmed or not.

A closely related issue concerns whether the potential harm from an immoral action is directed at a particular individual or small group, or whether it is widely distributed among an anonymous mass. I would conjecture that we tend to label behavior as immoral much more readily if the harm is directed at particular persons.[8] Thus, to cheat a customer in a face-to-face relationship is considered more immoral than to cheat an anonymous mass of customers by mislabeling a package. To fire twenty particular men from a hundred-man work force is considered more immoral than to order an arbitrary 20 per cent reduction in the labor force and draw names out of a hat. Stealing office supplies, tools, and materials from the "company" is not as immoral as stealing a single tool from a fellow worker which may make his job more difficult to perform.

The double standard we use in this regard is illustrated by the story of the man whose son came home from school complaining that a friend had taken his pencil. The father told his boy that it was probably accidental, not to worry about it, and gave him another pencil. The next day the boy reported that the friend had again taken his pencil. Once more the father played the issue down and gave his son another pencil. When the behavior was repeated a third and a fourth day, the father finally got mad, called the friend's father and said, "Look Fred, my boy tells me that your boy has been taking his pencils. I want you to see that this stops. It is the principle of the thing which is bothering me, not the pencils, I can get plenty of those at the office."

It is not clear whether the tendency to condone cheating or stealing with respect to a large anonymous mass like a company comes about because of the belief that the anonymous mass can somehow afford it, and that it is not really hurt, or whether it is simply easier to commit hurtful deeds when the hurt party is not there to reproach or induce guilt. The latter position would lead to the proposition that the greater the physical or psychological distance between the manager and the client, the easier it would be for him to commit irresponsible hurtful acts toward the client.

Some recent experiments by Milgram[9] support the idea that morality is easier to give up as psychological distance builds up between the person hurting and the person hurt. In Milgram's experiments, subjects are asked to give extremely painful electric shocks to a partner whenever he makes an incorrect response on a learning problem. In fact there is no partner, but the subject believes that there is one. Not only did Milgram find that a surprisingly high number of people will give extreme shocks to partners in this situation if ordered to do so by the experimenter, but that they are more likely to do so if they cannot see, hear, or feel the reactions of the partner. In other words, fewer subjects will obey the experimenter if they can hear moans whenever they give a shock, and still fewer will obey if the "partner" holds hands with the subject and clenches the hand strongly every time the presumed shock is delivered. Apparently we *do* find it easier to be cruel if we *don't* have to witness the effect of our cruelty.

If this phenomenon is general, one might suppose that the manager is most likely to be moral with his immediate subordinates, peers, and superiors, and least likely to be moral with customers (unless he is in sales), the community (unless he is in public relations), and stockholders (unless he is a large one himself or the treasurer who must report to them). It suggests also that one of the most effective means of curbing immoral behavior or training for morality is to maintain close contact between the man-

[8] Both "helping" and "hurting" are *interpersonal* concepts with limited meaning when applied merely as a trait like "helpful" or "mean." They become meaningful as we specify *who* is hurt or *who* is helped.

[9] Milgram, S. (5)

ager and those clients toward whom one wants him to be particularly responsible. In conflict situations, one might predict that the person will choose behavior which will be least hurtful to those clients (including the person himself) who are psychologically closest to him.[10, 11]

A further hypothesis would be that we tend to view either self-enhancement or hurting as more immoral if the person is viewed to be acting on his own behalf rather than as an agent or representative of some group. One of the commonest defenses against charges of immoral behavior is that the person was only carrying out orders (as in the Milgram experiment and the Nuremberg trials) or was only representing the best interests of some other client system with which he is identified.[12]

If the last hypothesis is supportable, it has implications for the way in which we train members of any profession. To the extent that we teach them to identify with groups, to allow themselves to become representatives, and to develop loyalties, to that extent we are encouraging them to abdicate more personal concepts of responsibility. Perhaps one of the functions of professional associations is to "drain off" the belongingness needs of the individual professional lest he join a group that will bias his moral judgments.

REVERSIBILITY, SINS OF OMISSION, AND INTENTIONS VS. CONSEQUENCES

When we consider society's judgments with respect to certain categories of immoral behavior, it appears clear that not only are the amount of harm and the fairness of the deed considered, but that irreversible harms are more severely judged than reversible ones. Thus, killing is most severely punished because it is most harmful and totally irreversible. Rape, maiming, and other physical insults fall under this same umbrella. Do they have a counterpart in the realm of managerial behavior?

Blacklisting a fired employee and thus depriving him of a livelihood, driving someone out of business by unfair means, ruining a colleague's career by a whispering campaign that destroys his reputation, and stealing a patent all have a certain quality of irreversibility, but the judgment is not too easy to make in many cases. It is easier to identify the clearly reversible cases such as those which involve cheating a customer (wherein the customer can recover his money), fraud (wherein the injured party can sue for damages), or accepting a bribe (which the person can be forced to return).

The most difficult judgments arise in situations where it is not easy to determine what harm was done. Suppose a supervisor deliberately gives low ratings to an employee whom he dislikes even though the employee's performance is excellent. If the low ratings cause the employee to be passed over for promotion, he has clearly been harmed, but neither he nor the boss may know whether this has actually occurred. As was noted previously, employees in organizations do not have the protection of anything comparable to due process of law. The manager, especially, is highly vulnerable with respect to higher levels

---

[10] One might speculate that the *motivation* to help or not hurt comes from the *feelings* of compassion, fear, or guilt, not from a *rational* assessment of need or vulnerability. We are more likely to give something to a beggar who confronts us than a starving country which may need our help more but which arouses no direct feeling in us. In any case this is an hypothesis worth testing.

[11] Robert Kahn has suggested the further implication of organizing our enterprise as small units, possibly federated into larger ones, to insure a maximum of close contacts among managers and their various clients. (6)

[12] I am indebted to John Thomas for this point.

of management, and has few channels of appeal in most organizations. Hence, even if immoral behavior were reversible in principle, it often would not be in practice.

In discussion with Robert Kahn another dimension was identified which poses difficult judgment problems. This dimension concerns essentially the distinction between sins of commission vs. sins of omission. Most of my discussion so far has taken its examples from sins of commission—some clear behavior which was irresponsible with respect to some client. Yet many kinds of situations become unduly hurtful or beneficial only if the manager does *not* do certain things.

For example, the manager may not transmit his positive evaluation of a subordinate and thus undermine the subordinate's chance for promotion. He may fail to report to the production manager information received from customers pertaining to defects in a product, and thus make the production department more vulnerable to criticism. He may allow slipshod practices in the organization to continue rather than correct them, thus weakening the competitive position of the company. He may fail to report a potential problem in a product to the customer, thus endangering the customer. Failing to inform car buyers of possible safety hazards in certain models or failing to notify NASA of weak spots in a missile system or booster would be extreme examples of this sort.[13]

How do we tend to judge this category of "sins of omission"? Two criteria that appear to be involved are (1) the amount of potential harm that can result from the omission, and (2) whether the manager knew that he was withholding behavior and knew of the potential consequences. In the case of commission we

generally hold the person responsible for the consequences whether or not he knew what he was doing. "Ignorance of the law is no excuse." But in the case of sins of omission, ignorance or good intentions appear to be sounder defenses. If this hypothesis is supportable, it suggests that specific training in thinking through the consequences both of acting and not acting becomes an important part of professional training, particularly for the manager.

It is my impression that such training is indeed heavily emphasized in graduate schools. Without stating specific value criteria for the student, we emphasize being able to think through various courses of action and accurately assessing consequences in order that the person should learn how to implement those values that he holds.

Concluding Remarks

I have tried to clarify the issue of moral education for the manager by pointing out the inherent difficulty of classifying for this emerging profession what is moral and what is not. Not only is it not clear to which client the manager is ultimately responsible, but it is difficult to judge the amount of benefit or harm, the effect of psychological distance from the client, intentions within a given frame of reference and the obligations of the manager to do more than avoid illegal or clearly immoral actions. All of these difficulties should make us cautious in glibly labeling particular managerial acts as moral or immoral.

On the other hand, the issue cannot be dismissed merely because it is difficult. We should vigorously pursue empirical research to clarify the conditions under which different kinds of behavior will in

---

[13] The obvious, more general case is the passive behavior of the witness to a crime, as in recent cases in New York City, i.e., failing to help where help is needed.

fact occur and how various groups in our society judge these behaviors. We should determine what kinds of value positions are held in our professional schools of management and how these jibe with values in business and in the larger community. And we should stimulate inquiry among students themselves to begin investigation of the educative process on the part of its recipients.

Until we have more data, we should attempt to discern what the trends are in our present educative process. I would like to conclude this paper by pulling together some of these trends, as I see them from the perspective of our own Sloan School.

• Most faculty members tend to avoid the value issues, concentrating instead on what they call "analytical approaches" to problem-solving. This means that goals are taken as given and the focus of the course is on how best to achieve the goals. The emphasis is on means and how to choose among competing means in terms of criteria of efficiency. A corollary emphasis is to "know the consequences of your own behavior" and choose means appropriately in terms of rationally assessed consequences.

• If the faculty member is pushed on the value issue or asked what are the ultimate goals toward which the means are to be used, he would most often choose the enterprise as the relevant client. The goals are to maximize the economic performance of the enterprise or to insure the survival and growth of the enterprise as a social system. The values are efficiency and effectiveness. I am not aware that any course seriously questions whether any given enterprise should in fact exist or not. Such questions are treated as being outside the realm of most of our courses.

• If asked about other clients such as consumers, employees, and community, the faculty member would tend to respond that "other courses" worry about these unless it happens to fall squarely within his own area. Thus, obligations to employees are the concern of psychology or labor relations courses, not economics or mathematics. Within the area, emphasis on the pragmatic means tends to be maintained. Speaking for my own area of organizational psychology, I would tend to justify moral behavior toward employees, colleagues, and superiors on the pragmatic basis that such behavior insures better organizational performance, thus seemingly removing the question from the moral realm.

• A recent survey of the beliefs and values of our faculty revealed that in a number of areas there were considerable differences, as a function of teaching area. If these findings are reliable, they suggest that even though, as individual teachers, we may try to de-emphasize the value questions, in fact we do feel differently about certain basic issues; and students probably are well aware of this. I have evidence also that students definitely are influenced by faculty beliefs and values. But, since we differ as a function of teaching area, we influence the student differentially as a function of the courses he takes.[14]

• If we have within the school a kind of pluralism with respect to values, the ultimate responsibility for value choice seems to fall to the student himself. Either we force him through a pattern of required courses exposing him to a variety of positions which he must then integrate, or we let him choose his own courses and thus force him to make value choices during the process of education itself, or some of both. In the Sloan School I believe we do both, but we do not provide a clear forum during the students' second

[14] See Schein, 1967, *op. cit.*

year of education for integrating the diverse points of view or forcing an examination of value issues. The fact that such integrative courses have been difficult to design and to teach may well reflect the difficult value questions with which they would have to deal.

REFERENCES

1. Hughes, E. C. *Men and Their Work*. Glencoe, Illinois: Free Press, 1958.
2. Evan, W. M. "Due Process of Law in Military and Industrial Organizations." *Administrative Science Quarterly*, 1962, 7, 187–207.
3. Schein, E. H. *Organizational Psychology*. Englewood Cliffs, New Jersey: Prentice-Hall, 1965.
4. Schein, E. H. "Attitude Changes During Management Education: A Study of Organizational Influences on Student Attitudes." *Administrative Science Quarterly*, 1967, in press.
5. Milgram, Stanley. "Some Conditions of Obedience and Disobedience to Authority," in *Current Studies in Social Psychology,* edited by I. D. Steiner and M. Fishbein. New York: Holt, Rinehart and Winston, Inc., 1965, 243–262.
6. Kahn, R. L. Personal communication.

QUESTIONS

1. Why have ethical codes of conduct been created for professions?
2. Identify the multiple clients of the manager. What are the principal moral issues involved in each relationship?
3. What do you think of the argument that no special obligations or responsibilities accrue to workers and/or managerial subordinates beyond those specified by the labor contract or the law?
4. Give examples of value conflicts that may confront the manager.
5. Evaluate the statement "What is good for the company is ultimately good."
6. Do you think that university faculty members in business management courses should directly discuss value and moral issues or should they adopt a neutral analytic approach?